ESSENTIAL PAPERS ON KABBALAH

ESSENTIAL PAPERS ON KABBALAH

Edited by Lawrence Fine

NEW YORK UNIVERSITY PRESS
New York and London

NEW YORK UNIVERSITY PRESS
New York and London

Library of Congress Cataloging-in Publication Data

Essential papers on kabbalah / edited by Lawrence Fine.
p.   cm. — (Essential papers on Jewish studies)
Includes bibliographical references and index.
ISBN 0-8147-2623-2 (cloth). — ISBN 0-8147-2629-1 (pbk.)
1. Cabala—History. 2. Mysticism—Judaism—History. I. Fine,
Lawrence. II. Series.
BM526.E83   1995
296.1'6—dc20   94-36161
                        CIP

10   9   8   7   6   5   4   3   2   1

For my sons, Jacob and Aaron, with love

Contents

Acknowledgments

It is my pleasure to express my thanks to Robert Seltzer and Arthur Green for their helpful suggestions concerning the Introduction to this volume. My gratitude as well to my brother Roger Fine and my wife, Deborah, for their useful stylistic comments on the Introduction. The article by Rachel Elior was translated from Hebrew by Jeffrey Green, while Yehudah Liebes's article was translated by Eli Lederhandler. My thanks to both of them. I am also grateful to Niko Pfund, editor at New York University Press, for his help in the preparation of this volume.

Several articles were abbreviated or edited for the purposes of this volume, including the omission of Hebrew. To preserve the spirit of every scholar who has contributed to the volume, I have kept the variety of transliteration or notation styles used by the contributing authors.

Introduction

Lawrence Fine

Gershom Scholem (1897–1982), the extraordinary German-born scholar of Jewish mysticism whose reputation has approached legendary proportions, was fond of recalling the obstacles he encountered as he developed an interest in Kabbalah as a young man:

From 1915 on I timourously began to read books about the Kabbala, and later I tried my hand at original texts of kabbalistic and Hasidic literature. This was fraught with great difficulties in Germany at that time, for though it was always possible to find Talmud scholars, there was nobody to guide one in this field. Once I tried to induce [my teacher] Dr. Bleichrode to read such a text with a few of us; it was a famous treatise on kabbalistic ethics from the sixteenth century. After a few hours he said: *"Kinderlach,* we have to give it up. I don't understand the quotations from the Zohar and can't explain things to you properly." Thus I had to try to become familiar with these sources by myself.[1]

Scholem's story vividly portrays the state of kabbalistic studies in Germany as he experienced it in the early part of the twentieth century. The problem, however, goes far deeper. Beginning in the nineteenth century, Germany had been the center of modern Judaic scholarship; but the relationship of these early scholars to Judaism's esoteric traditions was complicated. With some noteworthy exceptions (as I will show below), scholars of the Jewish Enlightenment *(Haskalah)* had either repudiated the study of Jewish mysticism and Kabbalah altogether, or treated it in highly derogatory and tendentious ways. Many of the scholars of what came to be known as the "Science of Judaism" *(Wissenschaft des Judentums)* were profoundly disconcerted by aspects of Jewish tradition which they regarded as irrational, foreign to Judaism, and bereft of authentic spirituality.[2] The most notorious representative of such an attitude was the important Jewish historian Heinrich Graetz (1817–1891). Writing, for example, about the Zohar, the seminal work of Spanish Kabbalah, Graetz expressed himself in the most contemptuous terms: "Thus the secret lore of Moses de Leon naturally has free play to pervert everything and anything, and give it the seal of sublimity, and in this manner to promulgate a false doctrine, not only absurd, sometimes even blasphemous and immoral."[3]

In the nineteenth century, a period when many European Jews, as is well known, were bent on demonstrating the humanistic, rational, and universal character of Judaism, historians such as Graetz had nothing but disdain for what they regarded as "blasphemous chimeras" and "primitive inspiration." Even more, many of the negative qualities with which they associated the mystical tradition were believed to be embodied in the masses of Hasidic Jews in Eastern Europe, a living source of embarrassment to "civilized" Jews seeking to gain acceptance in a Gentile culture.

Writing in 1941, Scholem leveled vigorous criticism at such apologetically motivated scholarship:

The exposition of Jewish mysticism ... abounds in misunderstandings and consequent misrepresentations of the subject-matter under discussion. The great Jewish scholars of the past century whose conception of Jewish history is still dominant in our days, men like Graetz, Zunz, Geiger, Luzzatto and Steinschneider, had little sympathy—to put it mildly—for the Kabbalah. At once strange and repellent, it epitomised everything that was opposed to their own ideas and to the outlook which they hoped to make predominant in modern Judaism. Darkly it stood in their path, the ally of forces and tendencies in whose rejection pride was taken by a Jewry which, in Steinschneider's words, regarded it as its chief task to make a decent exit from the world. . . . We are well aware that their attitude, far from being that of the pure scholar, is rather that of the combatant actively grappling with a dangerous foe who is still full of strength and vitality; the foe in question being the Hasidic movement.[4]

In an interview published in 1975, Scholem went so far as to assert that "in the nineteenth century not a single sensible thing was written on *kabbalah.*"[5] Scholem's uncompromising critique and sweeping dismissal of almost all earlier kabbalistic research has by now been subjected to a certain degree of reevaluation.[6] For while his views have been echoed many times by others, the picture of early kabbalistic scholarship (and nineteenth-century historiography as a whole) is more complex than that painted by Scholem.

Certain contemporary scholars[7] have pointed out there were in fact a number of important European authors whose appreciation of Jewish mystical tradition was sympathetic, and who often made meaningful contributions to its study. These included, among others, Eliakim ha-Milzahagi (c. 1780–1845), Adolphe Franck (1809–1893), Salomon Munk (1808–1867), Meyer Landauer (1808–1841), Adolph Jellinek (1820–1893), and Israel Zinberg (1873–1938). Sometimes the views of these individuals were wildly mistaken; more often than not they lacked the knowledge and training necessary to study the texts properly. But despite such significant shortcomings, many of them *sought* to approach their materials in an unbiased manner, and treated Kabbalah in a serious way. Thus we agree with Moshe Idel's assessment that "far from being negatively biased against Kabbalah, some of the pioneers in Jewish studies in the nineteenth and early twentieth centuries not only were interested in this lore but also made several original contributions that were to lay the foundation for the later study of Kabbalah."[8]

Even if there were others before him whose curiosity led them into the world of Kabbalah, however, it is still the case that Gershom Scholem's fateful realization that "I had to try and become familiar with these sources on my own" proved to have incalculable consequences. For when the history of the development of Judaic scholarship in the twentieth century is written, Gershom Scholem's name—along with such other luminaries as Salo Baron, S. D. Goitein, and Harry Wolfson—will have center stage.[9]

Scholem, scion of a highly assimilated German-Jewish family, decided against a doctorate in mathematics in order to pursue the implausible course of a Ph.D. in the study of Kabbalah. In light of the state of affairs described above, it is clear that his decision to do so must itself be regarded as a measure of the intellectual fearlessness and resolute independence that characterized Scholem's personality and career. These traits are apparent in Scholem's autobiographical recollections about his initial attraction to Jewish mysticism:

I could not say why, but it seemed improbable to me that the kabbalists could have been such charlatans, buffoons, and masters of tomfoolery as he [i.e. Graetz] made them out to be. Something seemed to me to be hidden there, and it was this that attracted me. The lasting impression which Buber's first two volumes on Hasidism made on me surely played a part as well. Still wholly written in the style of the Vienna School and of the *Jugendstil* [the German version of *art nouveau,* ca. 1895–1905], they drew attention to this area in romantic transfiguration and flowery metaphors.[10]

Following his studies, Scholem, a fervent Zionist, migrated to Palestine in 1923. There, he embarked on a career for the next sixty years which would result in a fundamental transformation of our understanding not only of the Jewish mystical tradition, but also of the history of Judaism as a whole. As has often been pointed out, one of the basic effects of Scholem's work was to demonstrate that far from being peripheral to Jewish history and thought, or "un-Jewish," mysticism has played a vital role in virtually every period of Judaism from late antiquity on. Combining immense talents—that of a brilliant linguist and philologist with extraordinary historical and phenomenological sensibilities—Scholem produced one scholarly masterpiece after another. His book *Major Trends in Jewish Mysticism,* based on lectures given in New York at the Jewish Institute of Religion in 1938, and published originally by Schocken books in Jerusalem in 1941, may be the single most influential title in all of twentieth-century Jewish scholarship.[11]

Scholem's legacy also embodies itself in generations of doctoral students who made the Hebrew University in Jerusalem the center of kabbalistic studies for decades. Beginning in the 1960s, another great scholar, Alexander Altmann (1906–1987), established Brandeis University as an academic locus for the study of Jewish mysticism.[12] Altmann, a Hungarian-born, German-trained rabbi and scholar of extraordinary breadth and erudition, came to Brandeis in 1958 by way of England. At Brandeis he became a doctoral mentor for students of Jewish philosophy and mysticism. The importance of the "Altmann School" endures as a new generation of scholars has come under the influence of Altmann's disciples. At the same time the study of Jewish mysticism also flourished in France under the tutelage of the distinguished medievalist Georges Vajda.

I provide this brief tour of the history of the field partly to convey a sense of how far we have come since the youthful Gershom Scholem searched in vain for someone who could teach him the Zohar. Even though it remains a relatively small scholarly field, the study of Jewish mysticism has ripened to the point that it now occupies a central place in the agenda of contemporary Judaic studies. A perusal of curricular

offerings in colleges and universities, of the programs of scholarly conferences, of the contents of academic journals, would supply plentiful
evidence of the significant role research in Jewish mysticism now plays,
and of how indebted scholarship is to Scholem's choice "to become
familiar with these sources by myself." The clearest measure of the
vitality of the field is the very fact that many of the assumptions held
by the pioneers mentioned here are themselves undergoing scrutiny,
challenge, and re-vision.

Let me say a few words about what I mean by the term "Kabbalah" in
order to identify the scope of this book. It can and has been used in a
variety of different ways. It is thus important to be precise concerning
how it is employed here. Kabbalah (which prekabbalistically signified
'tradition' in general or a teaching transmitted from one to another) is
sometimes used to refer in the broadest possible way to any and every
aspect of Jewish mysticism, from its beginnings in the rabbinic period to
Eastern European Hasidism in the eighteenth and nineteenth centuries.
This popular, noncritical use of the term is often favored by traditionalists for whom historical and scholarly distinctions concerning different
periods and types of Jewish mysticism are of little or no concern. The
word Kabbalah takes on an even wider scope for those who include all
of the non-Jewish esoteric and occult phenomena, past and present,
which have been regarded as kabbalistic.[13]

From a more narrowly construed scholarly point of view, however,
Kabbalah refers to a discrete body of literature that became clearly
identifiable beginning in Provence in the late twelfth century and northern Spain in the thirteenth.[14] Southern France was the provenance for
the appearance of the first extant kabbalistic book, *Sefer ha-Bahir,* or
The Book of Clarity. In distinctive and colorful mythic symbolism this
book describes ten *Sefirot,* attributes or "lights" that comprise the inner
life of God. As the reader of this volume will discover, the concept of the
ten *Sefirot,* the complex schema depicting the divine "persona," is the
basis for most of kabbalistic literature. Although the precise circumstances of the book's composition are still unclear, among the Spanish
kabbalists of the thirteenth century *Sefer ha-Bahir* was believed to be an
ancient and authoritative work, thought to have been "composed by the
mystic sages of the Talmud."

Owing to the *Bahir* and a small circle of prominent Kabbalists in

Provence, Kabbalah spread to Spain by the beginning of the thirteenth century. A number of important centers were established, initially in Catalonia, especially in the city of Gerona, after which it gradually spread to central Spain, Castile. This classical phase of Kabbalah, which produced a large number of kabbalistic treatises, reached its climax with the composition of the Zohar *(Book of Splendor)*, the seminal work of Spanish Jewish mysticism. An extraordinary work of the imagination, the Zohar was written largely if not exclusively by Moses de Leon, who began to circulate manuscripts of Zohar materials in the 1280s and 1290s.[15] The Zohar was, then, the culmination and crystallization of a century of kabbalistic literary creativity and, in turn, served as inspiration for centuries of Jewish mystical literature and life.

Beginning in the fourteenth and fifteenth centuries, the traditions of Spanish Kabbalah, especially the Zohar, were carried to many parts of the Jewish world, including the Franco-Ashkenazi provinces. It was in the sixteenth century, however, following the expulsion of Jewry from Spain and the forced mass conversion of the Jews of Portugal, that Kabbalah experienced its most powerful rejuvenation.[16] Weary, displaced Jews settled mostly in North Africa, Italy, and throughout the Ottoman Empire, bringing with them the literature of Kabbalah and knowledge of its practice. In Italy, even prior to the Spanish Expulsion, a distinctive orientation developed in which Kabbalah was interpreted in philosophical ways and was suffused with magical techniques.[17]

The most consequential resurgence of post-Expulsion Kabbalah took place, however, in the land of Israel, especially after it became part of the Ottoman Empire in 1517. The small Galilean village of Safed became the scene of an intense messianically oriented mystical community whose foundations were built on Spanish Kabbalah.[18] In the seventeenth century the most significant, not to mention turbulent, expression of kabbalistic life was the messianic movement known as Sabbatianism, which galvanized around the charismatic but troubled personality of the Turkish Jew Shabbatai Sevi (1626–1676).[19] Sevi became infamous for his dramatic mood swings, his practice of violating Jewish law, and his ultimate apostasy when he converted to Islam under duress.

Kabbalah survived the turmoil of Sabbatianism, but by the eighteenth century it had lost most of its potency as a living phenomenon. This was a result of various factors, not the least of which were the vast challenges to *all* types of traditional Judaism posed by the assimilationist and secularizing trajectory of modernity. At the same time, an altogether different development coopted the creative energy of Kabbalah, namely, Hasidism. While much in Hasidism owes its very existence to kabbalistic tradition, the fact is that the mass appeal and vibrant energy of Hasidism relegated the study and practice of Kabbalah to the periphery.[20] Given all this it is surely remarkable that kabbalism, as I will show below, resurfaced in the twentieth century, assuming an intriguing array of guises.

These several periods of Kabbalah's most creative existence—between the twelfth and seventeenth centuries—are united by a thickly woven literary and textual tradition. Despite striking innovations and differences from one phase to another, they are bound to one another by a distinctive constellation of ideas, images, and symbols, as well as by modes of religious experience.

All of the movements that I have described fall under an even more specific category which is typically referred to as *theosophical* or *theurgical* Kabbalah. These kabbalistic systems are theosophical in that they are built around the structure of the ten *sefirot* and speculation about the inner life of God; they are theurgical insofar as they are based upon the conviction that all human action reverberates in the world of the *sefirot*, and thus influences the life of divinity. Proper action helps to restore harmony and unity to the world of God, while improper action reinforces the breach within God brought about originally through human transgression.

In contrast to theosophical/theurgical Kabbalah there is another form of medieval Jewish mysticism which is also considered a type of Kabbalah. I refer to what is known as "prophetic Kabbalah" or "ecstatic" Kabbalah, associated with a Spanish Jew by the name of Abraham Abulafia (1240–1291). Abulafia was born in the city of Saragossa, in the province of Aaragon, but spent much of his life traveling, including journeys to the land of Israel, Greece, and Italy. Abulafia developed a highly distinctive contemplative system built on an eclectic array of techniques, including the reciting and combining of names of God, and various kinds of breathing exercises and body postures. Abulafia spurned traditional Kabbalah in favor of his own system, the goal of which was ecstatic union with God, described primarily in terms borrowed from Maimonidean philosophy. One of the effects of the work of

Moshe Idel has been to give Abulafian mysticism a far more prominent place in the study of Kabbalah than it has hitherto occupied, and, as importantly, to demonstrate ways in which the ecstatic tradition reverberates in later Judaism.[21]

The studies in *Essential Papers on Kabbalah* are largely concerned with the dominant trend, theosophical/theurgical Kabbalah. We have excluded altogether studies that focus primarily on nonkabbalistic forms of Jewish mysticism. These are the *Hekhalot* or *Merkavah* ('throne') mysticism of the rabbinic period, *Hasidut Ashkenaz*, the German Pietist movement of the twelfth and thirteenth centuries which developed along the Rhineland, and Eastern European Hasidism. Rather than attempt to cover the entire spectrum of Jewish mysticism, we felt that the kabbalistic traditions were sufficiently variegated and complex to justify a more focused volume. Another collection in the series of which this volume is a part, *Essential Papers on Hasidism,* is devoted entirely to this important movement. At the same time, the reader will find that certain of the papers in this book, while *concentrating* on theurgical Kabbalah, do in fact make substantial reference to other phases of Jewish mysticism, particularly German Pietism, Abulafian or ecstatic Kabbalah, and Hasidism. Indeed, some of the studies included here were chosen in part precisely because they demonstrate the *development* of a theme or problem across time, as is the case, for example, with Daniel Matt's study of *Ayin* or mystical Nothingness, Arthur Green's "The Zaddiq as *Axis Mundi* in Later Judaism," and Moshe Idel's "Mystical Techniques."

Aside from their focus on Kabbalah, and their uniformly superb quality, studies were chosen for inclusion in this volume on the basis of several other criteria. I have sought to provide the reader with a sense of the historical range of Kabbalah, yet without any pretense to historical completeness. I also wanted to offer examples of various *kinds* of approaches, including those of intellectual and social history, history and phenomenology of religions, motif studies, ritual studies, and women's studies. Furthermore, I hoped to do justice to certain aspects of the history of Kabbalah which have been relatively neglected, as the discussion below will make clear. Needless to say, any collection such as this one had to exclude the work of many fine scholars simply by dint of physical limitations.

This collection of papers is divided into three parts: "Mystical Motifs and Theological Ideas," "Mystical Leadership and Personalities," and "Devotional Practices and Mystical Experience." Part One, "Mystical Motifs and Theological Ideas," is introduced by Arthur Green's "The Zohar: Jewish Mysticism in Medieval Spain." This article provides a lucid, systematic presentation of the historical and literary development of early Provençal and Spanish Kabbalah, paying special attention to the symbolism, theology, and spiritual character of the Zohar. Such an overview of the classical phase of Kabbalah offers the reader an orientation with which to walk further into the garden of medieval Jewish mysticism.

One of the inescapable challenges in the study of mystical religion is to make sense of the complex relationship between mystical ideas and actual experience. What *scholars* examine as "ideas" are to *mystics* themselves less often conceptual realities than they are experiential ones. Nowhere is this more evident than in the phenomenon of *ayin,* or "Nothingness," in Kabbalah. For while *ayin* can be analyzed and dissected as an intellectual *notion,* ultimately it is more properly understood as identifying a state of *mystical consciousness.* A foundational and fundamental problem in Kabbalah, *ayin* connotes both the *idea* that in its deepest recesses God is no-thing, and the *experience* of a mystical void, a sort of bountiful "black hole" beyond which imagination and consciousness cannot penetrate. *"Ayin:* The Concept of Nothingness in Mystical Judaism" by Daniel Matt is distinguished by its comprehensive treatment of this phenomenon within the broad context of Western philosophical and religious thought, as well as by its sensitivity to the nature of "Nothingness" as contemplative experience.

In "The Doctrine of Man in the Zohar," Isaiah Tishby discusses a question that is absolutely central to Kabbalah, namely, its view of human nature, and the crucial significance of human action in the mystical scheme of things. In conventional rabbinic terms, the notion that human beings are created in God's image means essentially that they are capable of imitating God. Insofar as they are endowed with speech, the ability to reason and to distinguish right from wrong, individuals are in a position to choose moral life. Thus, while we can find passages in rabbinic literature in which the soul is said to *resemble* God in that it is invisible, or that the soul sustains the body much in the way that God sustains the world, the soul is never quite identified as being divine in nature. Kabbalah, however, takes a fundamentally different approach.

To the mystics the human personality represents the totality of the sefirotic structure and, even more, is imbued with the very essence of divine life. This is especially true of the highest part of the soul, the *neshamah*, which is considered to derive directly from God. Insofar as all individuals possess a spiritual essence that links them with the sefirotic world, each person has the inherent capacity to affect the life of God, as mentioned earlier in connection with the notion of theurgy. As a microcosm, a perfect paradigm of the upper world, and as one link in a cosmic chain of being, a person simultaneously reflects the world of deity and arouses it—only to be aroused and nourished in return. Tishby's systematic treatment of this important set of issues is the most thorough to be found.

Another essential problem with which Kabbalah is intensely concerned is taken up by Joseph Dan in "Samael, Lilith, and the Concept of Evil in Early Kabbalah." Medieval Jewish philosophy—in both its Neoplatonic and Aristotelian forms—tended to treat the problem of evil in highly intellectualized terms, thus ameliorating its radical character. As Alexander Altmann once wrote in distinguishing between the "divergence in existential attitude" in medieval philosophy and mysticism, "in Jewish mysticism, evil is experienced as having real existence." [22] Dan's study traces the development of kabbalistic notions of evil by focusing on the thirteenth-century Spanish kabbalist Isaac ha-Kohen. In Isaac's important book, *A Treatise on the Left Emanation,* composed in the generation before the Zohar, we discover a comprehensive, mythic account of evil. [23] The protagonists in the realm of evil are the satanic "husband" and "wife" Samael and Lilith, a pair who are locked in combat with the cosmic forces of good. Dan demonstrates that Isaac's theories of evil were adapted, in significant part, from the writings of German Pietism, and in turn exerted profound influence upon the Zohar and subsequent Kabbalah.

"The Meaning of Torah in Jewish Mysticism" by Gershom Scholem is a great classic of kabbalistic scholarship. In this highly influential study—based upon one of the many lectures given during his regular visits to the annual Eranos conferences in Ascona, Switzerland—Scholem analyzes a variety of esoteric conceptions about the nature of the Torah in Kabbalah. He organizes his study around three fundamental and interelated motifs: (1) the Torah as a complex set of symbolic "names" of God; (2) the Torah as constituting the structure of a divine organism; and (3) the principle of the infinite meanings of the divine word. The crucial feature common to these several conceptions is the notion that the words of Torah are not merely representative of God's *will*, but expressions of God's very being. The Torah ultimately must be read with the knowledge of a kabbalist who possesses the hermeneutical keys with which to unlock its esoteric and *inner* truths.

The articles by Matt, Dan, and Scholem treat specific aspects of kabbalistic symbol and myth. Yehuda Liebes, in an article entitled "Myth versus Symbol in the Zohar and Lurianic Kabbalah," raises fundamental questions concerning the ways in which the concepts of myth and symbol have been understood in kabbalistic scholarship. He then seeks new ways of distinguishing between these categories, and illustrates these distinctions by analyzing material from the two most important bodies of kabbalistic literature. Liebes contends that Kabbalah operates at both symbolic and mythic levels, and that these need to be distinguished carefully. In the case of symbolism, a person, for example, may represent or signify some aspect of the divine world; but Kabbalah is mythic where the signifier is commingled with the realm of the divine in some essential way. For example, at times individual figures from the Bible are understood as merely representing one of the *sefirot*, while at others the divine is actually invested in them, that is, they possess both human and "divine" status at the same time. Indeed, a figure in the Zohar such as Rav Hamnuna Saba is clearly mythic or supernatural when his self-disclosure to others is represented as the disclosure of "the face of God." Liebes goes on to argue that when it comes to Lurianic Kabbalah in the sixteenth century, the symbolic gives way altogether to mythic discourse.

This section concludes with two articles that are concerned, in very different ways, with kabbalistic notions having to do with the transmigration of souls, or metempsychosis. We learn from these two papers not only that medieval Judaism developed highly elaborate systems of transmigration, but also that they played a prominent part in mystical literature and community. In her paper, "The Doctrine of Transmigration in *Galya Raza*," Rachel Elior discusses this question through the study of an anonymous sixteenth-century text which occupies an important place in the development of kabbalistic theories of transmigration. As Elior shows, the author of this treatise focused his attention upon the relationship between the problem of evil and exile and metempsychosis. Evil is an essential ontological dimension of all reality, ruled over by the demonic figure of the *Sitra Ahra* (lit. the 'Other Side'). One of the basic goals of human activity is thus to help purge the realm of holiness of its evil aspects, a project that involves, among other things, the placating and appeasing of the *Sitra Ahra*. The processes of transmigration of souls stands at the epicenter of this cosmic struggle. Transmigration, an intrinsic part of the long process of exile, is regarded as crucial to achieving the redemption of the Jewish people. It is a means of purifying Israel, and all of its exiled souls, by purging it of whatever evil clings to it, and by wresting Israel from the grip of the *Sitra Ahra*.

Alexander Altmann's paper, "Eternality of Punishment: A Theological Controversy within the Amsterdam Rabbinate in the Thirties of the Seventeenth Century," discusses the role the question of transmigration played within the context of a lively communal and theological debate. Altmann describes in fascinating detail a lengthy debate which took place between Isaac Aboab, a devotee of Kabbalah, and Saul Morteira, Amsterdam's leading rabbi and a distinguished talmudist. The controversy centered around the question of whether every Jew, no matter what his or her sins may have been, has a place in the world-to-come. The philosophically inclined talmudist Morteira took a traditional, conservative stance, according to which those who sinned gravely could look forward to nothing less than eternal punishment. Aboab, however, seeking to ensure salvation for Amsterdam's large *converso* community, argued that "matters of this kind have been entrusted only to the Kabbalists, illumined as they are by the light of truth."[24] Aboab based his argument in favor of a radically more lenient view in large part upon kabbalistic traditions concerning the particular nature of Jewish souls. This study gives us an unusually fine opportunity to see how kabbalistic convictions—still potent in the early modern period—exerted a powerful impact on the life of a European Jewish community. It represents an example of Kabbalah studied simultaneously from the perspectives of intellectual and social history.

Part Two, "Mystical Leadership and Personalities," consists of two papers that approach the history of Kabbalah in a way which has not received the attention it deserves. Little effort has been devoted to trying to understand the role of individual personalities in the shaping of the mystical tradition, with the important exception of Hasidism.[25] Part of the reason for this has to do with the virtual absence of both autobiography and biography among the kabbalists themselves. Indeed, up until the sixteenth century we find no true hagiographical or biographical tradition in kabbalistic circles, no less an autobiographical one. As R. J. Z. Werblowsky aptly observed, the "literary attitude" which prevailed in rabbinic tradition mitigated against personal disclosure, ensuring that "the biographies of famous Jewish rabbis are rarely more than a thin cloth of hazardous combinations of guesses, wrapped round a meagre skeleton of assured fact." [26] Still, the history of Kabbalah can hardly be told fully without taking into account the role played by individual personalities, as well as by the various *conceptions* of religious leadership which kabbalists held.

In "The Zaddiq as *Axis Mundi*," Arthur Green takes up the second of these questions by tracing the development of the mythic notion that charismatic individuals play a pivotal role in sustaining the cosmos. He traces the evolution of this notion from its origins in rabbinic thinking, through medieval Kabbalah, to Hasidism. Green's article is a superb example of how an insight drawn from the history of religions can be meaningfully applied to kabbalistic materials. My own paper, "The Art of Metoposcopy: A Study in Isaac Luria's Charismatic Knowledge," serves to demonstrate how some of the kabbalistic conceptions that Green describes came to life in the midst of the mystical community of Safed. Luria, one of the several most influential figures in the history of the mystical tradition, was regarded by his disciples as an individual with the spiritual powers to bring about the redemption of the cosmos. My paper explores the nature of Luria's charismatic authority by focusing on his role as a diagnostician and physician of the soul.

Part Three, "Devotional Practices and Mystical Experiences," also confronts an immense field of inquiry which kabbalistic scholarship has largely neglected. Earlier scholarship overwhelmingly concentrated its efforts on study of the mythic and theological *ideas* of Kabbalah, at the expense of its devotional and experiential aspects. This has sometimes led to the wholly mistaken impression that Kabbalah is little more than a theoretical system, a speculative structure dressed up in symbolic and mythic garb. In a discussion of kabbalistic historiography, Moshe Idel demonstrates that from its beginnings in the period of the Renaissance, critical reflection on Kabbalah has been characterized by the tendency to view it in *philosophical* terms.[27] Jewish Renaissance scholars of both Platonic and Aristotelian persuasian debated the merits of kabbalistic literature in terms that measured its compatablity or lack of compatability with their own philosophical allegiances. Despite the fact that men such as Altmann and Scholem found the study of Kabbalah attractive precisely because of its distinctly mythic and transrational character— and because it held out the promise of providing a fuller perspective on the nature of Judaism than their rationalist predecessors had offered— they too (like all other mortals) were constrained by the intellectual cultures from which they had come. In their groundbreaking work far less attention was paid to the actual practices of Kabbalah than to its doctrines and ideas.[28] The studies in this section of *Essential Papers* attest to some of the gratifying developments that have taken place in this regard, mostly in the recent past. Still, this is a wide-open field of inquiry which remains to be mined.

In "Prayer and Devotion in the Zohar," Isaiah Tishby analyzes the role that mystical "intentionality" *(kavvanah)* plays in Spanish Kabbalah. He shows in detail how the kabbalists endowed traditional liturgical prayer with esoteric and theurgic significance, and in the process radically transformed the character and meaning of religious practice. Even if elements of theurgy can be traced back to late antiquity and rabbinic literature, as Moshe Idel has suggested in his work *Kabbalah—New Perspectives,* it was not until the rise of medieval Kabbalah that such impulses assumed systematic form on a wide scale.

Elliot Ginsburg's study, "Kabbalistic Rituals of Sabbath Preparation," explores these issues further by focusing on a specific set of ritual practices having to do with the Sabbath. He shows how certain ordinary customs and obligations connected to preparing for the Sabbath take on the most profound mythic significance in the context of a kabbalistic perspective. Drawing upon a wide array of kabbalistic sources, Ginsburg analyzes the ways in which such preparatory rites as nail-paring, bathing, and dressing signify complex processes within the sefirotic cosmos and transform the practitioner's awareness.

As with their counterparts in other mystical traditions, Jewish mystical devotees have been highly *innovative* when it comes to ritual practice. In addition to transforming existing halachic practice and ritual customs in the ways suggested above, kabbalists also fashioned altogether new devotional rites to meet their special needs. Moshe Idel

examines several important types of contemplative and devotional practices, including weeping, rituals of contemplative ascent, Abulafian let-
ter-combination, and the visualization of colors, in his "Mystical Techniques."

In "Circumcision, Vision of God, and Textual Interpretation: From
Midrashic Trope to Mystical Symbol," Elliot Wolfson demonstrates that
the experience of visualizing God is understood in the Zohar as a type
of sexual union between an individual and God. More specifically, he
explores thematic and phenomenological relationships between the
physical act of "opening" which circumcision entails, the interpretive
task of revealing the esoteric meaning of a text, and the disclosure of
God in a vision.

We end this section with a piece that bears both on the question of
religious experience and *women's* spirituality. Reading Gershom Scholem's remarks about this subject in *Major Trends* leaves the impression
that there have been no female mystics in Jewish tradition, and that
there is nothing further to be said about the question. In the past several
years, however, a small number of scholars have sought to reexamine
this problem, especially in connection with Hasidism.[29] In a pioneering
study, "Woman as High Priest: A Kabbalistic Prayer in Yiddish for
Lighting Sabbath Candles," Chava Weissler opens up the question of the
involvement of women in kabbalistic life and ritual. She examines
women's petitionary prayers *(techinnes)* developed in Eastern Europe in
which the influence of kabbalistic motifs and symbols upon women's
Sabbath practice can be shown. Weissler describes a textual passage in
which women assume the role of the ancient High Priest, who by lighting
the candles on Sabbath eve and concentrating kabbalistically arouses
love in the realm of the *Sefirot*. Here we find, then, unequivocal evidence
of women being called upon to perform a ritual with kabbalistic intentionality.

There is, in my view, enough evidence to suggest that women partici-
pated in the world of kabbalistic practice in certain limited ways. It
should hardly surprise us if women living in kabbalistic families or
communities appropriated kabbalistic practice and *weltanschauung*.
After all, we know that nonkabbalistic women shared the world of
rabbinic culture. It is hardly plausible that women living with men
whose lives were dominated by kabbalistic practice and study were
immune from its influence. The idiosyncrasies of living a kabbalistic life

must have been too great to be ignored even where women were not directly implicated. Even more, evidence suggests that they *were* implicated in a number of significant ways.

There are still other significant trends in kabbalistic scholarship which are not represented in this collection, but of which the reader ought to be aware. A number of important students of literature and literary theory have in recent years shown a strong interest in Kabbalah, especially its interpretive and hermeneutical aspects. Thus, for example, in his *Kabbalah and Criticism* the eminent critic Harold Bloom discovers in the stance of the kabbalists toward Jewish tradition "the classic paradigm upon which Western revisionism in all areas was to model itself."[30] The most important accomplishments in this arena of inquiry are those of Susan Handelman. Her work examines the uses to which kabbalistic notions of revelation and language, as well as interpretive strategies, have been put by certain contemporary theorists.[31]

The early investigators of the general phenomenon of "mysticism" in the nineteenth and twentieth centuries wrote almost exclusively out of Christian perspectives of one type or another. Even when they sought to take into account mystical traditions beyond Christianity, the thinking of individuals such as Evelyn Underhill, Rudolph Otto, and Rufus Jones was severely constrained by Christian categories and preconceptions. It certainly never occurred to any of them to include Jewish tradition in their analyses of world mysticism or their constructions of the nature of mystical religion. Fortunately, this situation has changed dramatically in the past several years as a result of the scholarly successes in the field of Jewish mysticism, as well as a far less myopic view of the study of religion on the part of Western scholars. If we look, for example, at entries such as "mystical union" and "mysticism" in *The Encyclopedia of Religion,* an international scholarly project published in 1987, we see the extent to which consideration of the Jewish mystical tradition has become integrated into historical and theoretical treatments of mysticism. Some of the most thoughtful and influential theoretical work in the recent past on the general phenomenon of comparative mysticism has been done by Steven T. Katz, a scholar steeped in the knowledge of Jewish traditions.[32]

We noted earlier that Altmann's article on "Eternality of Punishment" is an example of the study of Kabbalah from the viewpoint of social history. Several important full-length studies by cultural historians have recently appeared in which Kabbalah stands at the center. For example, David Ruderman has studied the career of Abraham Yagel, an Italian physician, kabbalist, and naturalist.[33] Ruderman examines the role played by Kabbalah in relationship to the complex nexus of religion, magic, and science in the sixteenth and seventeenth centuries. Elisheva Carlebach has explored the phenomenon of later Sabbatianism and the rabbinic responses to it within the context of eighteenth-century European Jewish life and community.[34] These books exemplify the ways in which kabbalistic scholarship has begun to penetrate the work of scholars in diverse areas.

While I have spoken of Kabbalah and literary theory, we also find an interest in the study of *narrative* materials found in traditional kabbalistic sources. Studies by Joseph Dan and Aryeh Wineman exemplify work in this area, although this subject remains a fruitful area of research.[35] In this connection it's worth mentioning that a wide range of *contemporary* authors have drawn upon Kabbalah and Hasidism for literary and fictive purposes, including writers as disparate as Shmuel Yosef Agnon, Isaac Bashevis Singer, Elie Wiesel, Cynthia Ozick, and Chaim Potok.

Kabbalistic imagery, language, and ideas, have also assumed an increasingly prominent role in modern and contemporary Jewish *theology*.[36] This is evident in the case of seminal thinkers such as Abraham Isaac Kook,[37] A. D. Gordon, Martin Buber, and Abraham Joshua Heschel, as well as a younger generation of theologians, most notably Arthur Green, Lawrence Kushner, Zalman Schachter, and Adin Steinsaltz.[38] Feminist thinkers such as Judith Plaskow, Lynn Gottlieb, and Rachel Adler have begun to ask about the value of kabbalistic imagery—especially in connection with the *Shekhinah*—for theological and liturgical purposes.[39] The most elaborate attempt to introduce kabbalistic imagery and language into contemporary Jewish liturgy is *Kol Haneshamah,* a prayerbook produced by the Reconstructionist movement.

From all this it is clear that in addition to vibrant scholarly discourse, and in no small part as a consequence of it, there is another kind of conversation taking place within certain contemporary circles, both in Israel and the United States. In these circles[40] the poetic tropes of the Zohar, the mystical fellowship and ritual celebration of the kabbalists of Safed, the images of cosmic mending associated with Isaac Luria, the portrait of a God who is both masculine and feminine, as well as the joyfulness, passion, and spontaneity characteristic of classical Hasidic tradition, appear to be nourishing the imagination and helping to shape religious consciousness.

A FINAL WORD ON FURTHER READING

The interested reader will find it possible to walk down endless paths to further reading by following the notes that accompany the articles in this volume. For further bibliographical information the reader may find it helpful to consult my own annotated suggestions at the end of my essay, "Kabbalistic Texts," in *Back to the Sources* (New York: Summit Books, 1984), edited by Barry Holtz. *Kabbalah* (New York: Keter Publishing, 1974) contains the entries which Gershom Scholem wrote for the *Encyclopedia Judaica*. These articles are accompanied by lengthy, if somewhat dated, bibliographies. An outstanding bibliographical essay which surveys the entire history of Jewish mystical tradition—while pondering the state-of-the-art—is Elliot Ginsburg's "Jewish Mysticism" found in *The Schocken Guide to Jewish Books* (New York: Schocken, 1992), edited by B. Holtz.

NOTES

1. G. Scholem, *From Berlin to Jerusalem—Memories of My Youth* (New York, 1980), p. 113. For further autobiographical reflections by Scholem on his early involvement with Kabbalah, see "With Gershom Scholem: An Interview," in his *On Jews and Judaism in Crisis* (New York, 1976). The great historian of Jewish philosophy and mysticism, Alexander Altmann, who studied in Germany in the late 1920s, corroborates Scholem's anecdote with the following observation: "It is a strange fact that German rabbis, except for very few, had no inkling of Hasidic, let alone cabbalistic texts. Even after Martin Buber had opened up the world of Hasidism to the West rabbis hardly read hasidic works in the original. They were blissfully unaware of the depth and boldness of Jewish mystical theology. Not until the impact of Scholem's superb studies had made itself felt in our generation did this area enter the scholar's field of vision, too late for the German rabbinate." See Altmann, "The German Rabbi: 1910–1939," *Leo Baeck Institute Year Book* 19 (1974): 49.
2. For Scholem's view of the biases that characterized nineteenth-century Ger-

man Jewish scholarship, see "The Science of Judaism—Then and Now," in idem, *The Messianic Idea in Judaism* (New York, 1971), pp. 304–313.

3. H. Graetz, *History of the Jews* (Philadelphia, 1894), vol. 4, p. 15. It is a matter of rich irony that *despite* Graetz's vigorous denunciation of Kabbalah, both he and Moritz Steinschneider, another opponent of Jewish mysticism, actually made valuable contributions to the study of its historical development. As M. Idel aptly observed: "These two giants of Jewish scholarship must be seen not only as critics of Kabbalah but also as two of the founders of its academic study. Graetz performed the first major historical survey of Kabbalistic literature, larger than that of Landauer, and Steinschneider's articles dealing with . . . Kabbalistic personalities . . . and with Kabbalistic works such as those of Abraham Abulafia are pioneering discussions, although they are colored with partiality." See *Kabbalah—New Perspectives* (New Haven, 1988), p. 10.

4. G. Scholem, *Major Trends in Jewish Mysticism* (New York, 1941), pp. 1–2.

5. *On Jews and Judaism in Crisis*, p. 17. At the same time Scholem, in preparing the "Kabbalah" entry for the *Encyclopedia Judaica* (Jerusalem, 1974, vol. 10), begrudgingly acknowledged that "even from this limited perspective, however, important contributions to the investigation of the Kabbalah were made by Samuel David Luzzatto, Adolphe Franck, H. D. Joel, Senior Sachs, Aaron Jellinek, Isaac Meises, Graetz, Ignatz Stern, and M. Steinschneider." Moreover, in more than a few places, Scholem actually refers to the work of one or another of these scholars in a way that makes it clear that he was able to build on their contributions.

6. Two attempts to revise Scholem's views on nineteenth-century historiography as a whole are G. Cohen, "German Jewry as Mirror of Modernity," *Leo Baeck Institute Year Book* 20 (1975): ix–xxxi, and I. Schorsch, "From Wolfenbuttel to Wissenschaft—The Divergent Paths of Isaak Markus Jost and Leopold Zunz," *Leo Baeck Institute Year Book* 22 (1977): 109–128. More recently M. Idel has subjected Scholem's reading of early historiography on Kabbalah, in particular, to a reevaluation in *Kabbalah*, pp. 7–10. For an important discussion of this whole problem, see D. Biale, *Gershom Scholem—Kabbalah and Counter-History* (Cambridge, Mass., 1979), pp. 1–51.

7. In addition to Biale and Idel, mentioned in the above note, see also I. Tishby, *The Wisdom of the Zohar*, vol. 1, pp. 43–50.

8. Idel, *Kabbalah*, p. 10.

9. For discussions of Scholem's scholarly contribution, see J. Dan, *Gershom Scholem and the Mystical Dimension in Judaism* (New York, 1987); A. Altmann, "Gershom Scholem (1897–1982)," *Proceedings of the American Academy for Jewish Research* 51 (1984): 1–14; Idel, *Kabbalah*, pp. 10–11; and a collection of essays edited by H. Bloom, *Gershom Scholem* (New York, 1987). See as well Biale, *Gershom Scholem—Kabbalah and Counter-History*.

10. *From Berlin to Jerusalem*, pp. 112–113. Alexander Altmann, in reflections

on *his* attraction to the study of Jewish mysticism in Germany, provides further information about this question. Aside from the influence of Scholem's earliest studies themselves upon him, Altmann's interest was aroused by recent writing about religion that was fashionable in the period with which we are concerned. Rudolph Otto's *Das Heilige,* one of the most influential books on religion in this century, was published in 1917. Influenced by Martin Luther's emphasis on the significance of religious intuition and the sense of the inward presence of God, as well as by Friedrich Schleiermacher's recovery of "feeling" in religious experience, Otto set out to elucidate what he construed to be the uniquely *religious* element in religious experience. He thus elaborated upon the nonrational character of religion, introducing his now classic notions of the *numinous, mysterium tremendum,* and *mysterium fascinans.* In considering the evolution of a new phase of Jewish studies following the First World War, Altmann drew attention to the influence of Otto's "phenomenology of the Holy." Altmann appears also to have been impressed with other important writings on the nature of religion of this period, including Max Weber's notions of charisma and Wilhelm Dilthey's emphasis on how sympathetic historical study can enable individuals to understand religious experiences of depth and intensity. The common thread in the thinking of all of these individuals was that they posed a challenge to earlier views of religion which had defined it primarily in ethical and rational terms—views which we have seen were a cornerstone of *Wissenschaft des Judentums.* As Altmann himself reflected, "In the study of religion a deeper understanding of the irrational and mystical element was gaining ground." For more on this question, see L. Fine, "Alexander Altmann's Contribution to the Study of Jewish Mysticism," in the *Leo Baeck Institute Year Book* 34 (1989): 421–431.

11. The third and last revision was published by Schocken in 1954; the book has been reprinted numerous times and has been translated into German, French, Spanish, and Japanese.

12. For an overview of Altmann's life and work, see D. Swetschinski, "Alexander Altmann: A Portrait," in *Mystics, Philosophers and Politicians: Essays in Jewish Intellectual History in Honor of Alexander Altmann,* ed. by J. Reinharz, D. Swetschinski, and K. Bland (Durham, N.C., 1982), pp. 3–14. For a treatment of Altmann's work in the field of Kabbalah, see my paper cited in note 10.

13. Walk into any bookstore that stocks books on popular esoterica and spirituality and you can find numerous books on such matters as theosophy, tarot, and astrology that purport to be teachings of Kabbalah. There is also, of course, an important, older scholarly tradition of Christian Kabbalah in which various individuals sought to harmonize Christian theology and kabbalistic symbols and doctrines. This development, which has its roots in the Italian Renaissance of the late fifteenth century, exerted considerable influence on theosophically and esoterically inclined European circles at least as late as the eighteenth century. On this subject, see G. Scholem, "Zur Gesch-

ichte der Anfänge der christlichen Kabbala," in *Essays Presented to Leo Baeck* (London, 1954); F. Secret, *Les Kabbalistes chrètiens de la Renaissance* (Paris, 1964); and C. Wirszubski, *Pico della Mirandola's Encounter with Jewish Mysticism* (Cambridge, 1989).

14. The question of the origins of Kabbalah is currently undergoing renewed scrutiny. Whereas Gershom Scholem tended to emphasize the *innovative* character of Kabbalah as it manifested itself in the Middle Ages (while at the same time seeking to identify some of its roots in Late Antiquity), Moshe Idel, in his influential book, *Kabbalah—New Perspectives,* advances the thesis that there is a far greater *continuity* between ancient Jewish conceptions and medieval kabbalistic ones. In chapters on theosophy and theurgy Idel raises the prospect of discovering the roots of these fundamental kabbalistic themes in normative rabbinic literature. The most elaborate presentation of Scholem's research on these issues is his *Origins of the Kabbalah* (New York, 1987), originally published in German under the title *Ursprung und Anfänge der Kabbala* (Berlin, 1962). Idel's views on this and other topics has generated lively debate within the field. See the review-essays by Elliot Wolfson and me in *Religious Studies Review* 17, no. 4 (1991): 313–321, and by Hava Tirosh-Rothschild, *AJS Review* 16 nos. 1–2 (1991): 161–192.

15. The critical question of the authorship of the Zohar has long preoccupied kabbalistic scholarship. This question appeared to have been settled with Scholem's extensive investigation of this problem, whose conclusion was that Moses de Leon, a thirteenth-century Spanish Jew, was the sole author of the bulk of the Zohar (excluding the portions known as *Raaya Mehemna* and *Tiqqunei Zohar).* Recently, however, Yehuda Liebes has proposed an intriguing and provocative alternative theory according to which the Zohar was authored by a group of individuals with Moses de Leon at the center. See Liebes, "How the Zohar Was Written," in idem, *Studies in the Zohar* (New York, 1993), pp. 85–138.

16. For an original exposition and analysis of the various trends in Kabbalah that emanated from Spain at the end of the fifteenth century, see M. Idel, "Particularism and Universalism in Kabbalah, 1480–1650," now anthologized in D. Ruderman, ed., *Essential Papers on Jewish Culture in Renaissance and Baroque Italy* (New York, 1992), chapter 11.

17. See M. Idel, "The Magical and Neoplatonic Interpretations of the Kabbalah in the Renaissance," and "Major Currents in Italian Kabbalah between 1560 and 1660," anthologized in Ruderman, *Essential Papers on Jewish Culture in Renaissance and Baroque Italy.*

18. On this subject see Scholem, *Major Trends,* lecture seven; L. Fine, *Safed Spirituality* (New York, 1984).

19. The unrivaled study of Sabbatianism is Scholem's magisterial *Sabbatai Sevi* (Princeton, N.J., 1973). See also his studies in his *The Messianic Idea in Judaism,* as well as the more recent contributions of Y. Liebes, *Studies in Jewish Myth and Jewish Messianism* (New York, 1993).

20. On Hasidism, see now G. Hundert, ed., *Essential Papers on Hasidism* (New York, 1991).

21. See the following works by Idel: *Kabbalah—New Perspectives*, especially chapters 3–5; *The Mystical Experience in Abraham Abulafia* (New York, 1988); *Studies in Ecstatic Kabbalah* (New York, 1988); and *Language, Torah, and Hermeneutics in Abraham Abulafia* (New York, 1989).

22. A. Altmann, "Maimonides' Attitude Toward Jewish Mysticism," *Studies in Jewish Thought*, ed. A. Jospe (Detroit, 1981), p. 210.

23. A somewhat abbreviated version of this work is translated in *The Early Kabbalah* (New York, 1986), tr. and ed. by Joseph Dan and Ronald C. Kiener, pp. 165–182.

24. See Altmann's article, p. 278.

25. A prominent exception to this observation is Scholem's study of Sabbatai Sevi, referred to in note 19.

26. R. J. Z. Werblowsky, *Joseph Karo, Lawyer and Mystic* (Oxford, 1962), p. 84.

27. Idel, *Kabbalah*, pp. 1–16.

28. I have discussed this historiographical problem in many places, including my "Approaching the Study of Jewish Mystical Experience," *Association for Jewish Studies Newsletter* 19 (1977): 10–11; "Popularizing the Esoteric: Recent Studies in Jewish Mysticism," *Judaism* 28 (1979): 494–496; "The Contemplative Practice of *Yihudim* in Lurianic Kabbalah," *Jewish Spirituality*, vol. 2, ed. Arthur Green (Crossorad, 1987), pp. 64–65. See as well the important treatment of this issue by Idel in *Kabbalah*, pp. 27–29, and by Yehudah Liebes, "New Directions in the Study of Kabbalah" [Hebrew], *Pe'amim* 50 (1992): 150–154. It ought to be pointed out that Scholem himself *did* pay some attention to these matters, as attested, for example, in his chapter on Abraham Abulafia in *Major Trends* (as well as other writing on the techniques of ecstatic Kabbalah), and "Tradition and New Creation in the Ritual of the Kabbalists," in his collection of essays *On the Kabbalah and Its Symbolism* (New York, 1965).

29. See, for example, A. Albert, "On Women in Hasidism, S. A. Horodecky and the Maid of Ludmir Tradition," in *Jewish History: Essays in Honour of Chimen Abramsky*, ed. Steven J. Zipperstein and Ada Rapoport-Albert (London, 1988), pp. 495–525, and N. Polen, "Miriam's Dance: Radical Egalitarianism in Hasidism," *Modern Judaism* 12 (1992): 1–21.

30. H. Bloom, *Kabbalah and Criticism* (New York, 1975).

31. S. Handelman, *The Slayers of Moses* (New York, 1982); *Fragments of Redemption* (Bloomington, Ind., 1991).

32. See the three books on this subject which he has edited, *Mysticism and Philosophical Analysis* (London and New York, 1978); *Mysticism and Religious Traditions* (New York, 1983); and *Mysticism and Language* (New York, 1992).

33. D. Ruderman, *Kabbalah, Magic, and Science* (Cambridge, Mass., 1988).

34. E. Carlebach, *The Pursuit of Heresy* (New York, 1990).

35. J. Dan, *The Hebrew Story in the Middle Ages* [Hebrew] (Jerusalem, 1974); A. Wineman, *Beyond Appearances* (Philadelphia, 1988).

36. On this subject see, for example, my article, "Tikkun: A Lurianic Motif in Contemporary Jewish Thought," in *From Ancient Israel to Modern Judaism: Essays in Honor of Marvin Fox,* vol. 4, ed. J. Neusner, E. Frerichs, and N. Sarna (Atlanta, 1989), pp. 35–53.

37. See my article, "Rav Abraham Isaac Kook and the Jewish Mystical Tradition," in *Rabbi Abraham Isaac Kook and Jewish Spirituality* ed. L. Kaplan and D. Shatz (New York, 1995), pp. 23–40.

38. A. Green, *Seek My Face, Speak My Name—A Contemporary Jewish Theology* (Northvale, N.J., and London, 1992); L. Kushner, *God Was in This Place and I, I Did Not Know* (Woodstock, Vt., 1991); Z. Schachter, *The First Step: A Guide for the New Jewish Spirit* (New York, 1983); A. Steinsaltz, *Thirteen-Petalled Rose* (New York, 1985).

39. J. Plaskow, *Standing Again at Sinai* (New York, 1990), chapter 4; L. Gottlieb, "Speaking into the Silence," *Response* 41–42 (Fall-Winter 1982): 23, 27; R. Adler, "Second Hymn to the Shekhinah," *Response* 41–42 (1982): 60.

40. The neo-Kabbalistic/neo-Hasidic spirituality which I have in mind here owes much of its *social existence* in the United States to the *Havurah* movement. In Israel, as well, a strong interest in Kabbalah has taken hold in certain study groups.

I

MYSTICAL MOTIFS AND THEOLOGICAL IDEAS

1.

The Zohar: Jewish Mysticism in Medieval Spain

Arthur Green

The Zohar, the central work of Spanish-Jewish mysticism in the Middle Ages, is the product of an entirely distinctive literary and esoteric tradition. While the writings of the Kabbalists, as the Jewish mystics are called, were often composed in temporal and geographical proximity to those of Christian and Muslim mystics, they are essentially a product of the unique and separate religious teachings that the Jews carried into medieval Europe. Both the Kabbalah's enemies among later Jews and its devotees among Renaissance Christians and later occultists tried to separate Kabbalah from Judaism, seeing it as essentially Christian rather than Jewish in spirit, or viewing it as an "alien growth" on the historic body of Judaism. Nothing, as we shall see, could be further from the truth.[1]

Before approaching the Zohar, we shall have to look briefly at the origins of the Kabbalah and the cultural setting in which it originated. From there we shall move to questions of authorship and structure in the Zohar, and finally to the esoteric content of the book itself.

It was in that area of southern France called Provence, culturally akin in the High Middle Ages to northern Spain, that the speculations which led to the Zohar, the culmination of a hundred-year development, first appeared. The Provençal Jewish community in the twelfth century was one of great cultural wealth, forming something of a bridge between the spiritual legacy of Jewish creativity in Spain in Muslim times and the rather separate world of Jewry in the Ashkenazic or Franco-Rheinish

Reprinted from *Introduction to Medieval Mystics of Europe*, edited by Paul Szarmach, by permission of the State University of New York Press, Albany, 1984.

area. Here were the great works of Jewish philosophy, including those of Maimonides, translated into Hebrew, so that a Jewry not conversant with the Arabic original could appreciate them. Provence was a great center of creativity in *halakhah*, religious law, and the ongoing legal discussion of the Talmud which is ever at the forefront of literary activity among medieval Jews. Traditional homiletics were also cultivated, and important works of Midrash, or homiletic commentary on the Bible, were edited in Provence. But other studies were encouraged as well in this rather "enlightened" atmosphere: biblical exegesis, theology, and poetry all flourished among Provençal Jewry.

In this cultural area there appears, toward the latter part of the twelfth century, a tradition of esoteric theosophical speculation, or speculation on the inner life of the Deity, known in later literature as Kabbalah. The origins of this literary movement are obscure and are still much debated. We do not yet know how much of the tradition was native to Provence and how much was imported from elsewhere (either from pietistic circles in the Rhineland or directly across the Mediterranean from the Near East.) Nor have scholars ceased debating whether there is some connection between the origins of Kabbalah and the Albigensian movement in Provence of the time.[2] For our purposes, however, we shall trace the beginning of Kabbalah to the appearance in Provence of a document that without a doubt can be called the first kabbalistic text, and is indeed one of the strangest and most fascinating documents in the long history of Hebrew literature. This slim volume is known as *Sefer ha-Bahir*, awkwardly renderable as *The Book of Clarity*. We first find reference to it in Provençal works of the late twelfth century, and from that time forward it has a continuous history as a major shaper of Jewish mystical ideas.[3] The Bahir takes the form of ancient rabbinic Midrash, expounding on biblical phrases, tying one verse of Scripture to another, and constructing units of its own thought around what it offers as Scriptural exegesis. Like the old Midrash, it makes frequent use of parables, showing special fondness for those that involve stories about kings and their courts, in which God is inevitably compared to "a king of flesh and blood." In form, then, the Bahir is quite traditional. But as soon as we open its pages to look at the content, we find ourselves confounded:

Whence do we know that Abraham had a daughter? From the verse: "The Lord blessed Abraham with all" (Gen. 24:1). And it is written: "All is called by My name: I created, formed, and made it for My glory" (Is. 43:7). Was this blessing his daughter or was it perhaps his mother? It was his daughter. To what may this be compared? To a king who had a faithful and perfect servant: he tested him in various ways, and the servant passed all the tests. Said the king: What shall I do for this servant, or what can I give him? I can only hand him over to my elder brother, who may advise him, guard him, and honor him. The servant went to the brother and learned his ways. The elder brother loved him greatly, and called him 'beloved': "The seed of Abraham my beloved" (Is. 41:8). He too said: What can I give him? What can I do for him? I have a beautiful vessel which I have fashioned, containing the most precious pearls, the treasures of kings. I shall give it to him, and he will attain his place. This is the meaning of "God blessed Abraham with all." [4]

What is the meaning of the verse: "From the west I shall gather you" (Is. 43:5)? From that attribute which leans ever toward the west. Why is it called 'west' (*Maarav*)? Because there are the seed is mixed (*mitarev*). To what may this be compared? To a king's son who had a beautiful and modest bride in his chamber. He continually would take the wealth of his father's house and bring it to her. She took everything and hid it, mixing it all together. After some time, he wanted to see what he had collected and gathered. This is the meaning of "From the west I shall gather you". And what is it? His father's house, as the verse earlier states: "I shall bring your seed from the east". This teaches that he brings from the east and sows in the west. Later he gathers in that which he has sown. [5]

The reader familiar with Midrash (as was the intended audience of the Bahir) will immediately notice something out of the ordinary here. The text simply does not work as Midrash. Questions are asked but not answered, or answered in such ways as only to call forth more questions. An image is proposed (that of the king), which always refers to God, and then suddenly that king turns out to have an older brother. Abraham's daughter, well known from earlier Midrash, here might be his mother. What sort of questions are these, and what sort of answers? The scholar is almost tempted to emend the text!

If one comes to the Bahir, on the other hand, with some familiarity with the methods of mystical teachers, particularly in the Orient, the text seems not quite so bizarre. Despite its title, the purpose of the book is precisely to mystify rather than to make anything "clear" in the ordinary sense. The reader is being taught to recognize how much there is that he does not know, how filled Scripture is with seemingly impenetrable mystery. "You think you know the meaning of this verse?" says the Bahir to its reader. "But here is an interpretation to throw you on your ear and to show you that you understand nothing of it at all." Everything in the Torah, be it a tale told of Abraham, a verse of prophecy, or an obscure point of law, hints at some reality beyond that which you can attain by the ordinary dialectic of Talmudic training.

As we read on in the Bahir, it becomes clear that the author (we speak of him in the singular only informally; the text is undoubtedly the product of several layers of compilation) is not merely advocating obscurantism for its own sake. He has in mind a notion, often expressed only in the vaguest terms, of what it is that lies beyond the many hints and mysteries of the Scriptural word. To say it briefly, the Bahir and all Kabbalists after it claim that the true subject of Scripture is God himself, that revelation is essentially an act of self-disclosure by God. Because the majority of people would not be able to bear the great light that comes with knowing God, however, divinity is revealed in the Torah in hidden form. Scripture is strewn with hints as to the true nature of "that which is above" and the mysterious process within divinity that led to the creation of this world. Only in the exoteric, public sense is revelation primarily a matter of divine *will,* teaching the commandments man is to follow in order to lead the good life. The inner, esoteric revelation is rather one of divine *truth,* a network of secrets about the innermost workings of God's universe.

A careful reading of the Bahir also shows it to document a religious vision not found anywhere in prior Jewish sources. Its language, to be sure, is good rabbinic/medieval Hebrew. It is written wholly from within the rabbinic world, showing complete familiarity with a wide range of earlier sources. Frequent reference is found in the Bahir to "the blessed Holy One," a standard rabbinic way of speaking about God. But it also becomes clear that this "Holy One" is not alone in the divine universe. There seem to be many potencies, all of them bearing some degree of divine description, and standing in relationship of some sort to another. Of course outright polytheism is out of the question here (though the Kabbalah has been accused of this too); what we seem to discover in the Bahir are various elements or stages of divine life, figures within the Godhead that interact with one another. No Neoplatonic flow from rung to rung is yet to be seen here; that will be added to Kabbalah only in the succeeding century. Here these entities seem to relate in a freer, more mythlike, and more complex manner. Most of the Bahir text leaves them quite undefined in order of relationship, and skips continually back from one to another. There is one passage, however, undoubtedly determinative for later Kabbalah, that enumerates the potencies as ten, setting them out as parallel to the ten utterances ("Let there be . . .") by which God supposedly created the world. We quote the first half of this passage:

What are the ten utterances? The first is the sublime crown, blessed are His name and His people. And who are His people? Israel, as Scripture says: "Know that the Lord is God; it is He who has made us and not [consonantally: *L*'] we ourselves" (Ps. 100:3). Read rather "We belong to Aleph *[L']*—to recognize and know the One of Ones, united in all His names.

The second: wisdom, as it is written: "The Lord acquired me at the beginning of His way, before His deeds of old" (Prov. 8:22). And there is no beginning but wisdom, as Scripture says: "The beginning of wisdom: the fear of the Lord" (Ps. 110:11).

The third: the quarry of the Torah, the treasury of wisdom, hewn out by the spirit of God. This teaches that God hewed out all the letters of the Torah, engraving them with the spirit, casting His forms within it. Thus it is written: "There is no rock *[zur]* our God" (I Sam. 2:2). Read rather: "There is no artisan *[zayyar]* like our God".

This is the third. What is the fourth? The fourth is the righteousness of God, His mercies and kindnesses with the entire world. This is the right hand of God.

What is the fifth? The fifth is the great fire of God, of which it is said: "Let me see no more of this great fire, lest I die" (Deut. 18:16). This is the left hand of God. What is it? They are the holy beasts and seraphim on left and right; they are the exalted and beautiful ones unto the heights, of which Scripture says: "the higher ones above them" (Ecc. 5:7) and "Their rings were high and dreadful; the rings of the four were full of eyes round about" (Ez. 1:18). Around it are angels, around them, bowing and prostrating before them, proclaiming: "The Lord, He is God! The Lord, He is God!" [6]

One gets the impression here—though not for certain—that "God himself" is to be identified with the first of these figures, and that the others belong to him in some secondary way. This impression is not consistent throughout the Bahir, however: the passage in which the king refers to his "elder brother," for example, seems to indicate something different.

The reader will also notice by now the strong attraction of the Bahir to *symbolic* speech. This remains true of the Zohar and throughout the Kabbalah: God is best to be approached by way of symbols. Here the mystics take their stand against the long and highly developed tradition of rational philosophy among medieval Jews, especially in Spain, claiming that discursive reasoning and the language that embraces it can never reach beyond those bonds of ordinary human intellect that keep us from true knowledge of the divine world. Knowledge of God requires a breaking out of our limited ways of thinking, a reaching beyond into a level of reality (and consciousness) where ordinary language cannot accompany us. Symbols, with their pictorial richness and seemingly endless depth, with their willingness to breach contradiction (e.g., "God's fire is water"; "true being is nothingness," etc.) and their ability to penetrate arcane levels of our individual minds and our collective human memory, can alone remain of language as we use it to express these divine mysteries which, in their essence, are ever beyond words. One may define the most basic spiritual endeavor of Kabbalah, from its very beginnings, as symbol making. The thought it produces, particularly in such a work as the Bahir, is a symbolic narration of events and processes that exist in a realm higher than and prior to ours, events that without these symbols would remain utterly beyond the grasp of language. To say it in a word, kabbalistic thought is essential mythic.[7]

For several generations in the late twelfth and early thirteenth centuries, these new mystic/mythic ways of thinking were preserved in closely guarded esoteric circles. One family, that of Rabbi Abraham ben David of Posquières, himself a major legal authority, had a leading role in the transmission of these "secrets," as they were called. Members of this group are depicted, however, not merely as transmitters of literary sources. Several members of the circle are said to have had "revelation of Elijah," meaning that Elijah the Prophet had come to them while in a supersensory state and had revealed some new portion of the secret lore. The student of medieval Judaism knows, moreover, that the reference to Elijah serves to legitimate a claim to divine revelation, one which formally was not supposed to occur since the canon was sealed and "prophecy was taken from the prophets and given to children and fools." The early Kabbalists in fact made a dual truth-claim for their esoteric readings of Scripture and their boldly new speculative ideas: they claimed both that they were ancient, the secret wisdom passed down by countless generations, only now given to public reading, and also that they were new, freshly revealed by heavenly voices to the sages of immediately preceding generations.[8]

The teachings of this circle, aside from the Bahir itself, were largely centered around the act of mystical prayer. We find among the Provence mystics detailed instructions for *kawwanah* or inner direction in prayer. Here *kawwanah* does not simply mean "intentionality," as in the earlier rabbinic sources, nor does it refer to a general air of serious intensity in worship; rather, it indicates a series of very specific steps in which the text of the liturgy is related to a series of meditations on those same ten potencies, or *sefirot,* that we have seen in the Bahir. The words of prayer, either individually or in phrases, becomes a series of guideposts by means of which the worshipper is to rise in contemplative ascent through the higher realms. Here we have the aspect of practice that was missing from the Bahir itself; what appeared as a gnostic tradition, offering esoteric *knowledge* about the inner divine world, is interpreted here as a contemplative tradition, one in which the devotee may *partici-pate* as he successively directs his prayers to ever higher realms within God.

Unlike the Bahir itself, some of these sources speak of a "cause of causes" or "root of roots," a hidden Godhead that lies beyond the active mythic world of divinity that is manifest in the *sefirot.* Here we see emerging for the first time a dichotomy that is to be universally accepted by later Kabbalists: the hidden God, beyond all knowing, address, and even naming, and the revealed God, the one-amid-ten of the sefirotic universe. From the viewpoint of the historian, what we also see here is the integration of the Bahir's radically different gnostic teaching into a theological mindset more familiar to medieval Jewry. The hidden God and his potencies are now *structurally* parallel (though surely not identical) either to the hidden Neoplatonic God and the intelligences emanating from him or the Aristotelian deity who is one with all his attributes.

We have yet to traverse, albeit briefly, two more steps before we are ready to speak of the Zohar itself. It was in the opening years of the thirteenth century that the doctrines of Kabbalah, still kept as closely guarded secrets, began to cross the Pyrenees and attract followers in Catalonia or northeastern Spain. This region, already long under Christian domination, contained a large and well-educated Jewish community that was linked by close ties, cultural as well as socio-economic, to the Jews of Provence. In the town of Gerona there developed a circle of kabbalistic devotees, including a number of writers who were most important for the later history of the movement. It is from this circle that the earliest major kabbalistic books, aside from the Bahir, have come down to us.[9] The range of their subject-matter and forms typifies the writings of Jewish mystics for many centuries to come: we have commentaries on the prayerbook, a commentary on the Song of Songs, explanations of the Talmudic legends, a polemical work against the writings of a philosopher, and a commentary on the Torah which, while by no means exclusively or even chiefly kabbalistic, contains frequent references to explanations of Scripture "according to the way of Truth." This last work, the Torah commentary of Moses Nahmanides, was an important departure in the history of Kabbalah. Nahmanides (1194–1270) was perhaps the best known and most widely revered Jewish intellectual of the thirteenth century. Respected as a conservative in theological matters (he sided with the opponents to Maimonides' philosophy), he was a widely accepted authority in Jewish legal circles, author of numerous *responsa* (legal opinions in response to queries) and commentaries on various tractates of the Talmud. The fact that a man of his stature had become a central figure in the Gerona mystical circle, and that he was willing to refer (albeit in a somewhat veiled manner) to kabbalistic secrets in a volume intended for popular distribution, clearly did much to pave the way for the acceptance of this new way of thinking.

In the Gerona school, the influence of religious philosophy has become more pronounced, and it is clear that Kabbalah has taken on a Neoplatonic hue. This first means that emanation, the flow of the *sefirot* out of the hidden self of God beyond, the infinite and unknowable, is now taken to be the most essential kabbalistic mystery. True, the identification of certain rites and terms with individual potencies in the supernal realm, the way of the Bahir in revealing secrets, continues in Gerona. This especially characterizes the Torah commentary of Nahmanides. But one has a sense in the longer works of this circle that a *system* has now developed out of the Bahir's more random symbolic identifications. The ordered flow of the *sefirot*, each from one another and ultimately all from the primal One, is now taken for granted. The relationship of these potencies, especially the uppermost ones, to their source in the hidden Godhead, remains perhaps intentionally vague in this literature, a point we shall discuss further when outlining the Zohar's version of this system.

Neoplatonism has also had a major impact on the *psychology* of the Kabbalah, its doctrine of the soul. The mystics of Gerona accepted the general medieval understanding of a sharp distinction between soul and body, the latter being merely the outer shell that contains the true person as manifest in the soul. They also learned from the philosophers the

tripartite division of the soul, a notion which they combined with ancient rabbinic speculations and adapted for their own purposes. The
essential point they sought to establish is that the soul has its origins in
God and that the human being, body as well as soul, bears the stamp of
its divine source. The ten *sefirot,* the essential building-blocks of all
reality, make up the structure of the soul as well; because of this it is by
turning inward, by self-knowledge at its most profound level, that a
person can come to know God. This turn inward, the necessary first step
in any contemplative system, also implies a rejection of things external
except insofar as they are a manifestation of God's glory. The inward
journey upon which one then embarks leads from the lower levels of self
into a discovery of the true soul *(neshamah),* its likeness to the divine
world and its endless longing to be returned to its source. "To use the
Neoplatonic formula, the process of creation involves the departure of
all from the One and its return to the One, and the crucial turning-point
in this cycle takes place within man, at the moment he begins to develop
an awareness of his true essence and yearns to retrace the path from the
multiplicity of his nature to the Oneness from which he originated." [10]

Paralleling the tendency toward a more philosophic Kabbalah in
Gerona, there emerged in the same or a slightly later period another
circle, the one with which the Zohar's author is most closely identified.
This group, sometimes referred to by modern scholars as the "gnostic"
circle, seems to have reacted, perhaps predictably, against the growing
philosophical influences on Kabbalah, and sought a more direct linkage
with the mythic world first so darkly hinted at in the Bahir. Their works,
rather than explaining or commenting in order to make a difficult text
more accessible, prefer to follow the Bahir tradition by expanding and
creating the myth. Here, in the works of such figures as Moses of Burgos
or Todros Abulafia of Toledo (the latter an important political leader of
the Castilian community), the fantastic elaboration of a mystical cosmos
is the center of kabbalistic activity. Angels, principalities, and especially
demons filled the imagination of these writers; it was this school that
first elaborated the notion of an "other side" opposing divinity, containing ten demonic *sefirot* of its own parallel to those in God, an idea
that was to have great importance in the later history of the Kabbalah.
The free-flowing mythic creativity of these Kabbalists clearly prepared
the way for the Zohar, a work of inspired mystical-mythic imagination
if ever there was one. [11]

The Zohar is a voluminous work, usually printed in three thick volumes along with various addenda. It is without question the apex of kabbalistic thought, a point agreed upon by traditional mystics and contemporary historians. For Jewish mystics the work attained a sort of canonical status, the only work after the Talmud of which this may be said. Pious Jews from the fifteenth century onward—including many, especially of Near Eastern origin, even today—would rank it alongside the Bible and the Talmud as a source of unimpeachable religious truth. The famous Hasidic master, Rabbi Pinhas of Korzec (1728–91) thanked God for having created him in the period when the Zohar was already known, "for the Zohar kept me a Jew." [12] Legend has it that Rabbi Pinhas' son, who owned a printing house in Slavuta, prepared for the publication of the Zohar edition by having the printing presses dipped in a ritual bath so that they, profane vessels that they are, might be fit to print so holy a text. The enchanting character of this work, whose title is perhaps best rendered as "The Book of Enlightenment," has fascinated readers Jewish and Christian, devotee and skeptic, for many hundreds of years.

The Zohar began to make its appearance in Castile during the closing decades of the thirteenth century. We speak of it in this indirect way, for it was precisely in that most appropriate manner that the work first came to be known, mere bits and fragments revealed while the rest was kept secret. A number of kabbalistic authors in that generation, including Joseph Gikatilla and Bahya ben Asher, the famous Bible commentator of Barcelona, seem to have been close to the source of these writings, but not to have betrayed their secret. As larger portions of the book became available, it was referred to not at all as one of the writings of contemporary Spanish Kabbalists, but rather as "the Midrash of Rabbi Simeon ben Yohai," the ancient and presumably long-hidden work of a famous second-century teacher. Rabbi Simeon lived in the Holy Land during the period of Roman persecution; according to later legend, surely treated as history in the Middle Ages, he and his son dwelt for thirteen years in a cave, where they lived a life of unblemished asceticism and conversed with one another on mystical matters. When in 1305 the travelling Kabbalist Isaac of Acre finally traced the Zohar manuscripts to their source and disseminator, Rabbi Moses De Leon, he was indeed told that they were copied from the works of that ancient sage. [13]

As though to buttress the claim of antiquity, the Zohar is composed not in Hebrew, the sole literary language of Jews in Christian Spain, but in Aramaic, the language spoken in the land of Israel during the early rabbinic period. In the Middle Ages this language was known only poorly, preserved insofar as was needed for comprehending the Talmud and other literary sources of late antiquity. To one who reads the original, the work is surely a linguistic marvel; its sonorous Aramaic tones lend to it a quality of arcane majesty, of a truth always veiled by being presented in a tongue just not quite fully comprehended, this all the more so because the Zohar is replete with words not to be found in any other Aramaic document, many of these forming the essential technical terms needed for a comprehension of the text's most basic meaning.[14]

Despite the relatively concise form in which it is published, it is difficult to think of the Zohar as a single book; it gives the appearance of a vast literary corpus, the complete reading of which would take years of careful study. There is no continuous narrative or single form that embraces the entirety of the work. A breakdown of the Zohar into its parts shows that it is comprised of some twenty-two literary units, each of these entirely unique as to length, content, and style. Perhaps half of the total Zohar corpus is contained in the main body of the work, the so-called Zohar on the Torah. As the name indicates, the text is organized (though rather loosely so) as a series of comments and homilies following the order of the Torah, divided in accord with the divisions of Scripture for weekly reading in the synagogue. Rather than offering real commentary, the Zohar will use the biblical verse as a point of departure, finding constant occasion in Scripture to expostulate upon its own theosophical system. We take as an example some passages from the Zohar's account of the birth of Moses and the tale of his discovery by Pharaoh's daughter.

A MAN WENT FORTH FROM THE HOUSE OF LEVI AND TOOK A DAUGHTER OF LEVI (Exodus 2:1). Rabbi Yose began: "My beloved has gone down into his garden, into the bed of spices" (Canticles 6:2). "His garden" is the Community of Israel, for she is the "bed of spices", wreathed from all sides, containing the fragrant aromas of the World-to-Come. In the hour when the blessed Holy One goes down into his garden, all the souls of the righteous are crowned and give off their aroma. Of this the Scripture says: "The aroma of your oils is of all the spices" (Canticles 4:10). These are the souls of the righteous and Rabbi Isaac has said that all such souls ever present and ever to be present in this world exist in the earthly Garden of Eden, in the very form and image that they have in this world. This secret has been transmitted to the wise. . . .

"A man went forth from the house of Levi"—this is Gabriel, of whom it is said: "The man Gabriel, whom I had seen in a vision" (Daniel 9:21). "From the house of Levi"—this is the Community of Israel, coming from the left side. He "took a daughter of Levi"—this is the soul, as it is taught: in the hour when the body of a righteous person is born in this world, the blessed Holy One calls upon Gabriel to take that soul from the garden and bring it down into the newborn body; he is then given the task of guarding that soul as well. But if you should say that the angel who guards the souls of the righteous is called "night" [following a tradition of the Talmud], and wonder why we have called him Gabriel, the answer is thus. He comes from the left side, and anyone who comes from that side will bear this name.

"A man went"—this refers to Amram. He "took a daughter of Levi"—this is Jochebed. A heavenly voice came forth and told him to join himself to her. The hour of Israel's redemption had drawn near, and it was to take place through the child born of them. The blessed Holy One helped him, for we have learned that the divine presence (shekhinah) hovered over their bed. Both of them desired to cleave as one to the shekhinah, and for that reason the shekhinah never departed from the son they were to bear. Thus Scripture says: "Sanctify yourselves and you shall be holy" (Leviticus 11:44). When a person sanctifies himself below, the blessed Holy One makes him holy from above. Just as their desire was to cleave to the shekhinah, so did the shekhinah attach itself to the one whom they brought forth by their act. . . .

HIS SISTER STOOD FROM AFAR (Exodus 2:4). Whose sister? The sister of the One who calls the Community of Israel "my sister", as in "Open for me, my sister, my beloved" (Canticles 5:2). "From afar", as it is said: "From afar the Lord appears to me" (Jeremiah 31:3). What does this mean? That the righteous, before they come down into this world, are known to all above. Surely this is true of Moses. It also means that the souls of the righteous are drawn from a high place, as we have learned. The soul has a father and a mother, just as the body has father and mother on earth. Everything both above and below comes about through male and female. This is the secret of "Let earth bring forth a living soul" (Genesis 1:24). "Earth" here is the Community of Israel: the "living soul" is that of Adam, as has been taught.[15]

A well-known event of the biblical narrative has been transformed here in several ways. First it is supplied with a poetic or romantic introduction, typically drawing upon the erotic imagery of the Song of Songs. But this introduction also serves to change the essential locus of the event itself. Rather than a bit of history, we have an event replete with symbolic mystery. Levi and Jochebed, Moses' parents, are here taken as symbols for the bridegroom and bride (or garden) of the Canticle, reminding the reader that the true mystery of conception takes place above, that the human soul is born of a union within the divine realm.

From the realm of the *sefirot,* the soul is handed over to the angel Gabriel for protection and safe conduct into the lower world. The angels represent an intermediary world for the Zohar, linking the mysterious universe of inner divinity to the human world below. Only after Gabriel has the soul readied for entry into the body may the narrative turn (beginning of the third paragraph, as we have divided it here) to the realm in which Moses' parents join together to conceive a child. Here the account is essentially moralistic, and serves to remind the reader of the great rewards to be obtained by those who keep their minds turned to holy thoughts during the time of intercourse.

The advent of Moses' sister in the narrative gives the Zohar one more chance to return the scene to the upper realms. "Sister," like "bride" is a favorite term for the *shekhinah,* the last and most essentially feminine of the *sefirot,* which is also called here "The Community of Israel."

The biblical story, then, has served as an occasion to reflect upon the inner divine universe, source of the human soul and the true locus of *all* events, from the birth of a child to the redemption of Israel, that befall mankind. The lower world and its history are but a reflection of that which goes on above in the hidden inner life of God. The narrative of Israel's sacred history has, in the truest sense, been reread as myth.

Interwoven with this mythical Midrash, as it may be called, is a series of narratives, intended to provide a "natural" setting in which the various discourses of Rabbi Simeon and his companions are offered. The rabbis will be walking along the road, staying at an inn, or meeting some mysterious stranger; the tale is one of mystical wanderers ever in search of someone who can offer them a new bit of illumination. The companions will chance upon a great tree or a wise child; their inspiration may come from either the natural order or the human world, but always it will lead them back to "the world of truth," the inner universe of divine contemplation. Some of these encounters blossom forth into longer narratives, containing all sorts of fantastic tales that somehow come to be interwoven with the esoteric subject at hand. In a passage shortly following on that we have just quoted, still concerned with the origins of the soul, the following encounter takes place:

Rabbi Eleazar and Rabbi Abba were going from Tiberias to Sepphoris. While they were on their way, a certain Jew met up with them and joined them. . . .

[The stranger told them the following tale:] One day I was walking in the wilderness, and I saw a rare and precious tree. Beneath it was a cave. As I approached it, aromas of all sorts wafted from the cave. I took courage and went in, going down some steps until I came to a place of tall trees that gave off fragrant spices and aromas, more than I could bear. There I saw a certain man with a sceptre in his hand. He was seated at another entrance, but when he saw me he stood up in astonishment. "What are you doing here, and who are you?" he asked me. I was very much afraid, but I said "Sir, I am one of the companions [Kabbalists]. Thus-and-so did I see in the wilderness, and I entered the cave and came down here." He said to me "Since you are one of the companions, take this bundle of writings and give it to those who know the secret of the souls of the righteous. He struck me with his sceptre and I fell asleep. In my sleep I saw great crowds of people following the path to that place. But that man struck them with his sceptre and said: "Take the path of the trees!" As they were walking they were lifted up into the air and began to fly, I know not where. I heard a sound of many people and did not know what it was. I awoke and saw nothing, and was quite afraid. Then I saw that man and he asked me if I had seen anything. I told him what I had seen in my sleep, and he said, "The spirits of the righteous pass by this path on their way to Eden. The sound you heard was of those who are in Eden, bedecked in the form they take in this world, rejoicing at those spirits of the righteous who have just arrived. Just as the body is composed of a mixture of the four elements and takes on form in this world, the spirit too is formed in the garden by the four winds that blow there; it is they who clothe it in its bodily form. Without these winds, which make up the air of the garden, the spirit would remain unadorned and would have no form at all. These four winds are tied together as one; it is from the wind [or spirit] that the spirit gets its form, just as the body is formed by the four elements below. That is why "From the four winds come, O spirit!" (Ezekiel 37:9): from the four winds of Eden by which the spirit is formed. Now take this bundle of writings and go on your way to deliver it to the companions."

Rabbi Eleazar and the companions came forward and kissed him on his head. Said Rabbi Eleazar: "Blessed is the merciful One who has sent you here. Surely this is the proper interpretation, and it was God Himself who put that verse into my mouth." [16]

He gave them the bundle of writings. Rabbi Eleazar took it and opened it, but a flame burst forth and surrounded him. He saw whatever he saw in it, and it flew out of his hands. Rabbi Eleazar wept and said "Who can stand in the treasure-house of the King! 'O Lord, who can reside in Your tent; who can dwell in Your holy mountain' (Ps. 15:1). Blessed is this path and this hour when I came upon you!" [17]

Other sections of the Zohar are composed in an entirely different, much more concise style. Here, in the so-called *matnitin* (Hebrew *mish-nayot*), or *tosefta* (addenda) we find a terseness that imitates the legal codex rather than the expansive manner of fanciful homiletic works. In a few carefully chosen words, replete with the boldest of images, some secret is let out, offered with no explanation, and left to puzzle the reader. In such passages we cannot but have recourse to one of the later commentaries on the Zohar, hoping that its author was able to make sense of a passage that, however fascinating and glorious, seems to remain quite beyond comprehension.

O sublime beloveds, masters of intellect, look, O renowned rulers! Who among you has eyes to see, come with the power of that sight and know this: In the hour when there arose in the mystery of mysteries the will to come forth, three colors were joined together as one: white, red, and green. These three colors were interwoven, coupling with one another. The spade below receives its color from these, and all of them are seen in it. This is a sight to behold, the wondrous appearance of bdellium. As she is stricken within, the three colors appear surrounding her from without. The color goes forth, rising and descending. Guardians fuming with smoke (?) are present within her. The colors, joined as one, carry her upward by day and come down at night. A burning candle is seen at night, but it is hidden during the day in two hundred and forty eight worlds, all of them coming down from above for her sake, hidden below within the three hundred and sixty-five limbs. He who goes forth to seek her will break these hidden "wings" and "shells"; then will he open the gates. The one who merits to see will see with mind and intellect, like one seeing from behind a wall, except for the sublime and faithful prophet Moses, who saw with his very eyes that which is above and remains unknown.[18]

Similar in style to these *matnitin* are the most esoteric portions of the Zohar, the *Book of Concealment* and the *Greater* and *Lesser Assemblies,* the sections of the work that have exercised the greatest fascination on the non-Jewish occultist traditions of the West ever since they were first "discovered" by believing humanist scholars in the Renaissance.

The question of the Zohar's true authorship has been debated almost since the work was first presented to the world. At first it was language, variety, and the sheer immensity of the work that pointed to ancient origin, at least for some part of the Zohar literature. The seemingly natural tales of the rabbis and their peregrinations around the Holy Land, the many parallels between zoharic and other midrashic sources, echoes of a spiritual allegory reminiscent of Philo's or of a Gnosticism that sounded like that of late antiquity, were all used at one time or another to support these claims. On the other side were those who suspected from the very beginning that the Zohar was the work of Moses De Leon's own hand, and that the ancient manuscript from which he was said to have copied was but another figment of his imagination. Some sought out base motives in this "forgery," while others considered it a legitimate case of pseudepigrapha, much like the attribution of the first-century apocalyptic works to Enoch, Abraham, or Moses. Such ascription allows the author to express his vision boldly, with limited fear of censorship or condemnation, since the text is to be offered to the public as the writings of an ancient and venerable sage, one whose teachings are surely beyond reproach, and must in fact occasion the reinterpretation of "later" works which do not agree with it.

In our own generation the question of authorship has finally been resolved by the painstaking historical and philological research of Gershom Scholem.[19] Scholem has argued on literary-historical grounds that the ideas of the Zohar are dependent upon the century of kabbalistic development that had preceded it, and not the other way around, as some defenders of the text's antiquity had argued. He has shown that the author was well-read in medieval Jewish philosophy, that the terminology of the book is much influenced by the literary Hebrew of the thirteenth century, and here and there, indeed, even by the Spanish that was the spoken language of Castilian Jewry. He has further shown that the author's supposed familiarity with Palestinian geography is a sham and, most convincingly, that the Aramaic in which the Zohar is written is a totally artificial language: that it corresponds to no dialect ever spoken, but is rather a hodgepodge of the Aramaic preserved in those literary sources that would have been most read by a medieval Jew in search of recovering that language. Finally, he has demonstrated a regular pattern of syntactical error in the usage of Aramaic verbs—a pattern that corresponds to the distinctive verb forms to be found in Moses De Leon's long-known Hebrew treatises. Scholem has shown that these literary and linguistic patterns are found diffused throughout the work, with the exception of two sections that he demonstrates to be slightly later imitations of the Zohar by another hand. Critical opinion is virtually unanimous in accepting Scholem's conclusions, excepting those within the Orthodox Jewish community who still consider such views to be heretical.

But the problem of the Zohar's authorship, and especially of the relationship between Moses De Leon and Simeon ben Yohai, is not yet fully solved. True, the entire Zohar was composed by one man, an individual of breathtaking imaginative scope who was surely one of the great religious authors of the Middle Ages. But *how* did he write the

Zohar, and what did *he* believe was the relationship between his writing and his claim that the book was authored by Rabbi Simeon? Many a passage in the Zohar is written with such an extra measure of spiritual intensity and transcendent enthusiasm that one could reasonably believe the author had felt himself possessed by a spirit other than his own as he was writing it. Could De Leon have felt that Rabbi Simeon was speaking *through* him, that he was the mere vessel the ancient sage had chosen for the revelation of his secrets? Here we will do well to remember that the Kabbalists were believers in reincarnation, an idea that plays a major role in the Zohar itself. Could the author have seen himself as Rabbi Simeon *redivivus?* Did he believe that the soul of that earlier teacher had been reborn in him and was now seeking to reveal ancient truths that had long been preserved in silence? It is to these questions that the current generation of scholars, with their keen interest in mystical psychology, will surely turn. Here the author of the Zohar will have to be studied not only in his own cultural context, but also in tandem with such figures as Jacob Boehme or William Blake, masters of a poetic imagination so extraordinary that any attempt to account for it, either by the author himself or by his readers, seems to lead beyond theories of poetics and towards some form of prophecy or revelation.

What then do we know of Rabbi Moses De Leon, surely the greatest figure in the history of Jewish mysticism until the sixteenth century? Given his prominence, we know surprisingly little. He was born around 1240, probably in the town of Leon, lived most of his adult life in Guadalajara, and in his last years moved to Avila, all of these being towns in north-central Spain, an area containing an ancient and highly cultured Jewish community. He was a man of very considerable erudition in rabbinic literature (particularly Midrash) as well as in the esoteric sources. On the other hand, he was no great master of *halakhic* (legal) literature. In contrast to Nahmanides, De Leon was a man wholly given to the kabbalistic enterprise; all of his writings that we possess are of a mystical nature. We also know that De Leon had at least dabbled in philosophical literature; there is extant a manuscript copy of Maimonides' *Guide for the Perplexed* written expressly for him in 1264. De Leon died in Arevalo in 1305.

It appears that the Zohar's author saw himself as belonging to a general movement of orthodox reaction to the rationalist rereading of Judaism that had been taking place under the influence of Aristotelian philosophy, particularly as typified by readers of the *Guide*. Philosophy had brought about a certain cynicism in matters of faith and was leading, so some claimed, even to a laxity in religious practice. Many were the voices raised in the thirteenth century against these evils, and De Leon counted himself among them; this partially accounts for his willingness to reveal so much of the "ancient" secret lore. In one of his Hebrew writings we hear him say:

Concerning this matter there are hidden mysteries and secret things which are unknown to men. You will now see that I am revealing deep and secret mysteries which the holy sages regarded as sacred and hidden, profound matters which properly speaking are not fit for revelation so that they may not become a target for the wit of every idle person. These holy men of old have pondered all their lives over these things and have hidden them, and did not reveal them to every one, and now I have come to reveal them. Therefore keep them to yourself, unless it be that you encounter one who fears God and keeps His Commandments and the Torah. . . . I looked at the ways of the children of the world and saw how in all that concerns these [theological] matters, they are enmeshed in foreign ideas and false, extraneous [or heretical] notions. One generation passes away and another generation comes, but the errors and falsehoods abide forever. And no one sees and no one hears and no one awakens, for they are all asleep, for a deep sleep from God has fallen upon them, so that they do not question and do not read and do not search out. And when I saw all this, I found myself constrained to write and to conceal and to ponder, in order to reveal it to all thinking men, and to make known all these things with which the holy sages of old concerned themselves all their lives.[20]

Such are the very bare essentials of Moses De Leon's life, including most of what is known to us. While it is fair to say that of his external life we know very little, there is available in his writings a tremendous wealth of material that would help us draw a picture of his inner life. This too is a task that stands before the scholar, but is one that can be appreciated only as we turn, finally, to the actual contents of the Book of Enlightenment.

The Zohar must be viewed as a great compendium of all the kabbalistic thought that had come before it, reworked and integrated into the author's own all-embracing poetic imagination. Ideas contained in bare hints or clumsy expressions in the generations before him now spring forth, full-blown as it were, as a part of the ancient wisdom. This is true of the Zohar's notion of God, especially of its views on the origin and power of evil, as well as its speculations on man, his soul, and the religious world of Judaism. It is to these that we shall now successively turn our attention.

It may be said that God is the essential subject of all the zoharic writings. Whether ostensibly searching out one of the commandments, commenting on a seemingly non-theological verse of Scripture, or taking note of the mere "ways of the world," the Zohar is ever seeking out that which it calls "the secret of faith," the inner life of God in the world of the *sefirot*. The pattern of the *sefirot*, their infinitely complex relations with one another and their influence on all that happens in the world are a source of boundless fascination to the author's mind. It is time now for us to examine these ten manifestations so that we may understand this most basic key to kabbalistic thinking.

Of God as *eyn sof*, the boundless, undefined and indescribable One existing before and beyond the *sefirot*, the Zohar has relatively little to say. This ultimate reality exists always and remains unperturbed and inaccessible, beyond prayer and seemingly even beyond contemplation; there are but occasional hints to the contrary. Certainly *eyn sof* is not to be thought of in *personal* terms; this hidden Godhead is the source of all being, but not Father, not King, not Lord of the universe. Within the mysterious depths of "the endless" there takes place an inner stirring, a movement toward the establishment of an Archimidean point, one that will stand to define the very beginning, the primal unit out of which are to evolve all of space and time. This inward process, the first awakening of direction or will within the infinite, is identified by the Kabbalist as the first *sefirah*. Surely not yet defined as a "thing," for it precedes even that point which is to come about through it, one may nevertheless say that this rippling in the ocean of infinity bears within it, at least as the impulse to create bears the creature, all that is ever to come about in the world. This manifestation of primal will within the hidden Godhead is referred to by Kabbalists, for reasons that will be clear later, as *keter*, the crown. Because it is the catalyst of all being, but not yet a thing in itself, it is also called, in the paradoxical language of which the Zohar is so fond, "Nothing," or sometimes "the primal Nothing." This "air that cannot be grasped," to use another favorite kabbalistic term for it, lies wholly within *eyn sof*. Since it exists before and beyond time, it might be argued that *keter* is eternally present as an aspect of *eyn sof*, that within the infinite which is potentially turned toward creation. Kabbalistic history is filled with ongoing debate as to the nature of *keter* and its relationship to *eyn sof,* a debate in some ways reminiscent of the arguments about the eternity of the Second Person in early Christianity. This seems to be the Zohar's position: *keter* is eternally present within *eyn sof,* but is not to be identified with it.[21]

The primal point brought about through this movement of will is called "beginning"; it is the starting point of both emanation and creation, of the divine world and the world below. Everything that is ever to be already exists in that infinitesimal point as it emerges within God; as the first defined Being, however vague that definition, it becomes the source of all further being. The most widespread name for this point is *ḥokhmah* (wisdom), a usage often tied to an old midrashic reading of Genesis 1:1 as "In wisdom God created the heaven and the earth." It is in speaking of these primal movements of the first *sefirot* that the Zohar's language is most obscure and mystifying. Typical is this famous passage, which opens the Zohar's rendition of the story of creation:

IN THE BEGINNING. As the will of the King began to come forth, He engraved signs in the uppermost pure light. Within the most hidden recesses a flame of darkness issued, from the mysterious *eyn sof,* a mist within formlessness, ringed about, neither white nor black nor red nor green, of no color at all. Only when measured did it bring forth light-giving colors. From deep within the flame there flowed a spring, out of which the colors were drawn below, hidden in the mysterious concealment of *eyn sof.*

It broke through and yet did not break through the ether surrounding it. It was not knowable at all until, by force of its breaking through, one hidden sublime point gave forth light. Beyond that point nothing is known. Therefore it is called "Beginning"—the first utterance of all.[22]

The imagery of this passage, particularly that of the "flame of darkness" and the "spring," sets the tone for much that is to follow in the volume. It is in images of light and water, flashing sparks, deep wells, springs, flowing rivers, and shining stars that the Zohar most likes to talk about its secrets. In fact the conventional names given by Kabbalists to the sefirot (*keter, ḥokhmah,* etc.) are used rather rarely by its author, who seems to have the poet's instinctive sense that symbols freeze when they become conventionalized. The language of paradox is also very much to the Zohar's liking; only in this, it seems, can ordinary human speech be sufficiently stretched and distressed that it might be applied to a realm so utterly beyond the domain of language. The "flame of darkness" (Is it shining against the background of brilliant divine light?) is the instrument by which the *sefirot* are to be formed; like the workman's torch as it hews them out of an airy quarry, giving to each some measure of distance from the others in such a way that all, while remaining within God, can form a unity of One-in-ten, but not be completely absorbed into one another or swallowed back into *eyn sof*.

The spring which emerges from the flame is the third *sefirah*. From it will bubble forth, in an unending creative stream, the seven remaining *sefirot* and all the "lower worlds." In the passage below this same *sefirah* is referred to as a "palace." As soon as the first point (*hokhmah*) is defined, it is surrounded by a great light; the light that rings the primal point, also depicted as the chamber or palace in which that light comes to dwell, is the next stage of emanation. It is the crucial moment in the emergence of the divine self; this third rung is most frequently described in terms that are *maternal,* as the womb out of which the seven children are to be born, and as the loving one to whom all will return and be set aright at the end of time.

In fact, as we examine the symbols of this next passage, we will see that the relationship between *hokhmah* and *binah* (literally: "understanding," as this third *sefirah* is often called) has been described here in erotic terms. The light of *hokhmah* is also its "seed," entering into *binah* in an explosion of light that certainly also bears the marks of sexual climax.

In the most hidden concealment a mark was made—unseen, not revealed. That mark was made and not made; neither persons of intellect nor those whose eyes are open can grasp it. Yet it is the existence of all. That mark is so tiny it cannot be seen or discovered; it exists through the will and gives life to all, taking what it does from that which has no marks or even will in it, from that which remains deeply hidden. The mark longed to cover itself, so it made a certain palace in which it might hide. It brought that palace out from within its own self, stretching it forth vastly in all directions. It decorated the palace in splendid draperies, and opened fifty gates which lead into it. Inside the palace that mark kept itself recondite and hidden. But once it was hidden there, as soon as it entered, the palace filled up with light. From that light are poured forth other lights, sparks flying through the gates and giving life to all.[23]

As *binah* is womb or mother, *hokhmah* turns out here to be father and progenitor, the indeed hidden source whence all birth is to come. This primal pair, existing in eternal and undisturbed union, are the first stations in the boundless flow of divine energy that emerges beyond them, first as the seven lower *sefirot,* aspects of the divine *persona,* and then as *shefa',* the flowing bounty of divine presence that brings life to all the worlds below.

The earliest Kabbalists were fascinated with questions of the divine name, and mystic lore assigned each of the names or terms for God in the Bible to one of the *sefirot.* This allowed for a rather easy key to kabbalistic exegesis, whereby the name of God employed in a verse would tell the reader which *sefirah* was its secret subject. In this context the name *elohim,* the generic term for "god" in Hebrew, was attached to *binah.* Since this is the word used in the opening verse of Genesis, the Zohar offers a radical new twist to that verse: "God" is now object rather than subject of the verse; Genesis 1:1 is here taken to mean: Through *hokhmah* He (or It, a hidden subject) created "God"! Such an understanding, utterly opposed of course to the plain meaning of Scripture, is precisely the sort of reading that would have been considered arch-heresy by the early rabbis, positing as it does a realm higher than that of "God." In the kabbalistic apologetic, of course, it is always emphasized that *eyn sof* and all the *sefirot* are one, and therefore that no such charge is appropriate. In fact, however, the personal God of rabbinic Judaism has been reduced by several notches, assigned in the Zohar to a combination of several *sefirot* below *binah,* as we shall see presently.

Here we must interrupt our outline of the *sefirot* to deal with a question that by now may be troubling the reader. What has all this to do with *mysticism?* If by that term we mean a religion that turns on inner experience, building on the heart's strivings toward unification with the One, the question is indeed legitimate, though we have not yet seen the end of the sefirotic system. The point is that we find very little in kabbalistic literature that speaks directly and *confessionally* of religious experience. "The Kabbalists, however, are no friends of mystical autobiography. They aim at describing the realm of divinity and the other objects of their contemplation in an impersonal way . . . they glory in objective description and are deeply adverse to letting their own personalities intrude into the picture."[24] In a larger sense, however, we may say that the Zohar is precisely mystical in origin. The descriptions offered are not the result of speculation in the casual sense, but rather a mirroring onto the cosmos of stages and states that the adept has known in his own inner life. The *language* of Kabbalah is cosmological. Hence, as our experiences are structured by the language system within which we work, the Kabbalist envisions his inner reality as the unfolding of universal life out of the Godhead; his chief preoccupation is the cosmos, not 'merely' his own soul. In our day, when mystical cosmology seems so distant and our shared language is rather that of psychology and inner experience, we might speak of these primal stages of emergence out of the depth in terms of the mystic himself rather than in terms of God or the cosmos. "Having been sunk completely into the unity of all things," we might say, "beyond all separation and self-consciousness, the mystic feels stirring within him that first impulse toward a reawakening of individual consciousness. That impulse, transforming him and not transforming him, taking him from the oneness of God and yet leaving him wholly within God, brings him in an eternal instant to utter silently the words: I am. This is his new birth, his first beginning."

Thus might a Kabbalist of our own period express what the Zohar says in the passages quoted. The difference between these two remains great, as vast as the difference between any two mystical texts composed in divergent religious contexts. But it is essential for the reader to understand that the choice of cosmological language does not mean that the Zohar is any less "truly mystical" for it. The task of the sensitive reader is in part (and cautiously!) to translate the Zohar's projected metaphysic back into those terms of inner enlightenment and successive states of transformed consciousness in which he can best comprehend it. The kabbalistic authors, cautious for their own reasons, do not do this for us.

Out of the womb of the Great Mother within God, or out of the spring that flows atop the deep well, if you prefer, there are born (issue forth), six children (streams), each of them having a particular function and character, and all of them uniting once again in the last of the ten *sefirot*, the bride (sea or garden). This last potency too is part of God, flowing from *hokhmah* as the end is the fulfillment of the beginning. But in relation to the six above her she occupies a passive role, that of bride receiving the affections of her beloved (the six combined as one), as sea taking into herself the multiple streams of water, or as moon receiving the reflected light of the sun, then giving it to her children, those who dwell in the lower worlds.

The six *sefirot* that intervene between mother and bride are often taken as a single figure, a "male" potency that stands between the female who is his origin and the one who is his mate. It is this figure with whom the rabbinic person-God is identified, Father of all the lower creatures, to be sure, but "son" when viewed from the perspective of that which stands above:

Rabbi Simeon lifted up his hands and rejoiced. He said: This is the time to reveal—a full revelation is now required! It is taught: In the hour when the holy Ancient One, the hidden of all hidden, sought to be established [i.e. revealed]. It arranged all as male and female. Having been joined together, male and female no longer exist except in further configurations of male/female. *Ḥokhmah*, containing all, came forth shining in male/female form as it emerged from the holy Ancient One: since *ḥokhmah*, as it spread forth, brought out *binah* from within itself, it is in male/female form. *Ḥokhmah* is father, *binah* is mother: *ḥokhmah* and *binah* are equally balanced, male and female. Because of them everything exists as male/female; otherwise none would exist.

This beginning is father of all, father of all the patriarchs; they are joined to one another and give light to one another. When they are joined they have offspring, and faith [the sefirotic world] spreads forth. In the narrative of Rav Yeva's school it is taught: What is *binah*? When *yod* and *heh* [the first two letters of God's name, *ḥokhmah* and *binah*] are joined together, she becomes pregnant and gives birth to *ben* [literally: "son"].[25]

Therefore is she called *binah*, the son of *yod heh*, the fulfillment of all. The two of them join together with the son between them in their form. Total fulfillment: father, mother, son, daughter. These words were given to be revealed only to the saints above, those who have come in and gone out, who know the ways of God and do not turn aside right or left. Of them it is said: "The ways of the Lord are straight. The righteous shall walk in them, but sinners shall stumble in them" (Hos. 14:10).[26]

These six figures taken as a unit are also identified with the six days of the week, flowing into the Sabbath, and the six directions of space (the four compass points, up and down). Taken individually they form two triads, the lower chiefly a reflection of the higher. This upper triad is often symbolized by the three patriarchs, Abraham personifying the love of God, Isaac the fear of God, and Jacob embodying peace, or the resolution of these two religious attitudes into one. Abraham, placed on the right side of the sefirotic diagrams (more on these below), signifies the right hand of God, the boundless and freely given love God has for his world. Isaac, the left side, stands for justice, the limitations God has to place on that love in order to be an effective ruler. This tension between the "aspect of mercy" and "aspect of justice" within God is part of the Kabbalists' legacy from older rabbinic Judaism. Here that tension is taken to an extreme, and the demonic is said to arise from the impulse within God to act as Judge. Only as these two forces are synthesized in Jacob, the sefirotic rung most often identified with "the blessed Holy One" or the God of rabbinic Judaism, is this tension resolved; the struggle between these two poles within God is a frequent theme of concern in the Zohar. The right and left sides of God, or *ḥesed* and *din* as they are conventionally called, each has a lower manifestation, bringing its particular power to bear in God's conduct of the universe. The lower form of "Jacob" (*tif'eret* or glory in the conventional terminology) is the ninth *sefirah*. This element is designated variously as Joseph, as the great "pillar," the "sign of the holy covenant," or simply "the righteous." All of these names may in one way or another be shown to refer to male potency; this *yesod* is seen as the "foundation" of the sefirotic universe. All the powers of the upper sefirot are concentrated together in it for their great flow into the tenth *sefirah*, bride or sea, moon or garden, to which we have referred above.

Rabbi Hiyya opened by saying: "A song of ascents, to Solomon. If the Lord build not a house, in vain have its builders worked on it; if the Lord guard not a city, in vain does the watchman stand" (Ps. 127:1). Come and see. At the time when it arose in God's will to create the world, He brought forth a mist from the darkened spark. It shone forth in the darkness, remained above and went below. That darkness was lighted with a hundred paths, lanes narrow but great, and the house of the world was made.[27]

That house is at the very center of all; it has many chambers and entrances all about it, holy sublime places. There the birds of heaven nest, each according to its kind. From the midst of the house there comes forth a great and mighty tree, having many branches and abundant fruit; there is food for all in it. That tree rises to the clouds of heaven and is hidden between three great mountains. It comes forth and rises from behind these mountains, goes upward and comes down. The house is watered by it, and it hides within itself sublime treasures which are not known. Thus is the house built and completed. That tree is revealed during the day but hidden at night; the house rules at night but is hidden in the daytime.[28]

Our understanding of the last sefirah will be enhanced if we look briefly at some of the names by which it is called in the kabbalistic sources. As *malkhut*, it is the *kingdom* of God, that over which the King has dominion and in which he takes pleasure, sustaining and protecting her as the true king takes responsibility for the sustenance of his kingdom. At the same time it is this potency that is charged with the rule of the lower worlds; the biblical personage with whom it is associated is David (surprising, given its usual femininity), the symbol of kingship. While *malkhut* receives the flow of all the upper *sefirot*, it is usually held that she has some special affinity for the left, the side of *din* or judgment. In this way she is called "the aspect of gentle judgment," though several Zohar passages paint her in portraits of seemingly ruthless vengeance in the punishment of the wicked. A most complicated picture of femininity appears in the Zohar, ranging from the most highly romanticized to the most bizarre and frighteningly demonic.

The last *sefirah* is also called by the term *shekhinah*, an ancient rabbinic term for speaking of the divine presence in the world. It appears that in later midrashic literature, well before the Zohar, this figure of speech has already become hypostatized as a winged angel-like being, though the attribution of feminine character to it is an innovation of the Kabbalah.[29] This symbol considerably alters our view of the Kabbalists' theology. Insofar as she is *malkhut*, ruler of the world, the system is quite theistic, i.e. God and his created universe remain quite distinct from one another. But *shekhinah* had always been a term for the in-dwelling presence, that which filled the Temple, which spoke to Moses, and so forth. If the *shekhinah* is in the world, however, (or the world in the *shekhinah?*) the Zohar seems to veer closer to pantheism, a religious tendency common to mystics throughout the world. In fact it is impossi-ble to define the Zohar as either theistic or pantheistic: though its God seems to relate to the world in an essentially theistic manner, we are never sure, either with regard to *eyn sof* or in connection with the *shekhinah*, quite what it means to say that the world is "outside" God. It is clear, however, that the *shekhinah* is to be found in this world, and that such was God's intent in creation: the *shekhinah* would continue the life-giving flow of emanation onward from the sefirotic world, down through realms of palaces and angels, countless realms of heavenly light, and into the natural and human orders. Originally centered in Eden, the *shekhinah* followed man into his life as a mortal, and took up residence amid the patriarchs and the people of Israel. When they went down into Egypt, the *shekhinah* was with them, and thus she accompanies Israel in all their exiles, the earthly state of the people bearing witness to the *shekhinah*'s own condition as a hapless wanderer through history, her fate subject to the vicissitudes of human virtue or misdeed. Only with the final redemption and the rebuilt Temple will she again take

up residence in Jerusalem, linking the world to God in joy and harmony as it was when the smoke of the holy altar rose and reached to
heaven. Nonetheless, something of the *shekhinah* still abides, however
mournfully, in her sacred home, for the rabbis long before the Zohar
had taught that "the *shekhinah* has never departed from the Western
Wall."

Another name given to this rung of divinity will again complicate our
picture of the relationship between God, *shekhinah,* and world. She is
called, very frequently in the Zohar, by the name *kenesset yisra'el,*
Community of Israel. That term, always reserved in rabbinic writings
for the Jewish people itself, is now chiefly applied to *malkhut,* and
the people Israel are *kenesset yisra'el* only as her beloved children.
Accompanying the redefinition of this term in the early Kabbalah is a
new reading of the Midrash on the Song of Songs, long a basic document
of Jewish devotional life as well as theological self-understanding. The
old midrashic sources had always read the Song as a dialogue of love
between God and the people Israel, his chosen bride whom he had
brought forth as a poor slave-girl from Egypt and wed as his beloved at
Mount Sinai. The liturgical poetry of earlier ages is replete with echoes
of this reading. While many sources had sought to "purify" this love
poem of its original erotic context, allowing in it only references to
matters of history and law, there existed also an ancient esoteric reading
of the Song, one highly anthropomorphic in its view of God and shock-
ing to many a later reader.[30] Now the Kabbalists, following certain
developments in medieval philosophical exegesis, elevate the Canticle to
an entirely new plane. The love of which King Solomon speaks in fact
takes place wholly within the divine world. Rather than God and his
people calling out in affection to one another, we now find male and
female, bridegroom and bride, *within* God as the subjects of the Song.
Israel the folk are now relegated, along with the angels, to the status of
"daughters of Jerusalem," those who witness the great romance, or even
facilitate it by their hymns and praises, but are not quite part of the
heavenly embrace. Using the full force of its mythic imagination, the
Zohar depicts the Canticle in cosmic terms, "heaven" calling to "earth"
or deep to deep, the words of the Song betokening the ultimate profundi-
ties of the love and eternal longing that exist within God, of which
human longing is but a pale shadow. Here the Zohar contrasts the Song
of Songs with the Song of Moses at the Sea and the Psalms of David:

Come and see. The song that Moses sang does refer to higher matters, not to things below. But he did not offer song like King Solomon; there was never a human being who rose so high in song as Solomon. Moses ascended in song and praise, giving thanks to the supreme King for having saved Israel, and for performing miracles and wonders for them in Egypt and at the sea. But King David and his son Solomon spoke another sort of song. David worked at preparing the maidens, adorning them for the Queen so that She and Her maidens might appear in beauty. It was this that he was striving for in his songs and praises, until finally he had prepared and adorned them all, Queen and maidens. When Solomon came he found the Queen fully adorned and her maidens beautifully arrayed. He sought to bring her to the Bridegroom, and brought the Bridegroom to the wedding canopy along with His Queen. He then spoke words of love between them so that they be joined as one, that both of them be as one whole, in love fulfilled. In this Solomon rose in sublime praise above all others. . . . There had been no man, since the creation of Adam, who had brought about love and affection through words of coupling above, until King Solomon. First he brought about their union above, then he invited the two of them together into the house that he had prepared for them.[31]

The Zohar's views on the question of evil and its origins are hardly less innovative than its view of God. Here too we are dealing with a mythic universe, a fantasy life richly nourished by the speculations of those Castilian Kabbalists who had preceded the author, and also more generally by the fascination that the forbidden demonic universe held for many a medieval mind.

Given the rather narrow range of possibilities open to Western theology in confronting the problem of evil and the sufferings of the righteous, the Zohar opts for a limited dualism. Content neither to deny the reality of evil, as Neoplatonism generally had, nor to ascribe evil to God himself, thus compromising his goodness and justice, the Kabbalists spoke of a real and active cosmic force of evil in the world, but one given vital support only by the moral and ritual defilement of human sin.

The cosmic powers of evil are not totally unknown to Jewish thought before the Kabbalah. Particularly in popular religion, demons and evil spirits are attested to in a great many sources, the formal theology of Judaism notwithstanding. The figure of Satan, known from but meager references in the Bible (the tale of Job and a single prophetic verse), lives on in rabbinic literature and already there is associated, as accuser, with the "evil urge" within each person that tempts humans into sin. The female aspect of the demonic world, headed by Lilith, also has roots that reach back into Babylonian antiquity. All these earlier sources are drawn upon by the Zohar, which both augments their ranks and systematizes them in a way that had never been done previously.

Since there is nothing in the world that does not ultimately have its roots in *eyn sof*, a myth of the origins of evil was essential to any explanation. Evil does not have its root in God, according to the Zohar, but is a negative by-product of the process of emanation. The dominant form this myth takes has to do with the necessary tension that exists as the fourth and fifth *sefirot*, *hesed* and *din*, emerge from *binah*. *Din*, the force of divine rigor or judgment, resents being tied to *hesed*, the unmitigated flow of love. In the very moment of its emanation it broke forth from the sefirotic system, saying, in the words of the Zohar "I shall rule!" The measuring rod of the *sefirot*, the flame of darkness, used the power of *eyn sof* to quickly force *din* back into line, but in that moment of escape some portion of its power was released that could not be retrieved. That portion of *din*, now turned against God, began its own sefirotic emanation in mocking imitation of the divine world. It too has ten emanated rungs, and in the union of Samāel and Lilith it represents the cosmic acting out of illicit sexuality.[32]

The moral lessons to be learned from this choice of myth are especially interesting. The Zohar sees evil as originating in justice itself, when that justice is not tempered with compassionate loving-kindness. The force of *din* within God has a legitimate role, punishing the wicked and setting out to limit the indiscriminate love-flow of *hesed*, which itself can be destructive if not held in proper balance. But once *din* has escaped the demands of love, it is no longer to be trusted. It then becomes a perversion of God's justice, one that would use his punishing powers to wreak destruction without cause. It is also interesting to note that images of the feminine and of sexual union are fully as prominent here as they are in discussions of the divine world. The Zohar represents an extreme case of the generally bipolar view of sexuality among medieval Jews: the same human drive represents the most sublime of mysteries and the most debased of sins.

The existence of an independent realm of evil was theologically problematic for the early Kabbalists. Even a demonic force somewhat lesser than the divine left them open to charges of dualism. Could God abolish the demonic powers, complete with the serpents, sea-monsters, and spirits that did their bidding? If not, he would be somehow less than God, and if he could, why had he not done so? The Zohar seems to answer apologetically that the forces of evil are a weapon God uses in the punishment of the wicked; in this sense *din* and the evil side are not clearly separate, it would seem, in the author's imagination. But the real answer to this question lies elsewhere: God has chosen to abdicate his responsibility for the destruction of evil so that man be tested, so that the righteous themselves be given the task of combatting evil in the name of God. In fact the existence of an independent realm of evil creates a much more serious theological dilemma than that we have mentioned. If evil comes from *sitra ahra,* the "other side," as it is often called, and not from man himself, how is the person to be held morally accountable? How can there be punishment for human sin, or reward for righteousness, for that matter, if evil is the result not of human choice but of the influence of outside forces?

The Zohar deals with this problem by positing a delicate balance between the forces of cosmic evil and those of moral evil stemming from within the human heart. *Sitra ahra* is allowed by God to exist, but is given no share in divine power. As it was cut off from the sefirotic world, it lost its access to the life that flows from *eyn sof,* the vital force that allows for existence. It therefore exists only as dead matter, and would have no power at all were not man to arouse it by his evil deeds. Thoughts and acts of sin give strength to the forces of evil, just as we shall see that good thought and deed energize the world of the *sefirot.* Once evil is aroused, it tempts man into further sin, requiring his sins for its own very sustenance. All it can do is tempt, however, for man is never released from the responsibility for his own actions. Of course the temptations offered by an old friend are more enticing, and the Zohar, a work that has significant moralistic intent, is filled with dire warnings to those who become too familiar with the forces of evil.

The question of evil has brought us to the threshhold of the more general question of man, his nature, and the meaning of human life. The myth of the Zohar is a highly anthropocentric one, and while the text seems much preoccupied with God and the upper realms, it can as well be read as a guide-book for the conduct of human life, and one that places squarely on man's shoulders full responsibility not only for his moral life but for the very survival of God's universe.

The notion that human beings are created in the image of God has a long and varied career in the history of Judaism. The Bible offers no explanation of the phrase (Genesis 1:27), but its original meaning was probably quite literal, and had as much to do with bodily form as it did with qualities of mind or spirit. The old Aramaic translation of the Bible preserves this meaning when it translates "image" *(zelem)* in that verse by the Greek loan-word *ikon.* Rabbinic sources seem divided on the question of the body's part in that likeness, a few remaining close to that literal meaning while most, possibly in fear of ascribing corporeality to God, veer toward the sense that the soul alone is in the divine form. Medieval Judaism outside the Kabbalah, with its general tendency to spiritualize the Bible far beyond what the rabbis had done, was quite unanimous in its view that soul alone was in God's image, the body serving as its temporary home, formed from dust and returning to dust. The belief in the bodily resurrection of the dead at the end of time does not seem to have mitigated this position.

Overlapping this discussion of the divine image was the question of the origin of the soul, particularly once its separateness from the body and its own inner three-part structure became the common understanding. Again, the dominant voice that emerged from rabbinic tradition, especially as refined in the Middle Ages, said that the soul was of divine origin, the body from earth. For the Zohar it was important to go beyond these claims. It insisted that the soul was not only divinely *bestowed,* but that its actual origin was in the upper world. The "home" for which it longed and which it, when unimpeded, sought to imitate, was the universe of the *sefirot.* It bears within it the stamp or "memory" of that primal union which formed it: kabbalistic learning is, in good Platonic fashion, an education to recall that which had been known to the soul eternally but forgotten in birth. The secret lore of the Kabbalist is thus seen not as alien and bizarre to the one who truly learns it, but as the hidden truth of his own soul. The highest portion of the soul is of the same "substance" as the *sefirot.* In a sort of "spiritual genetics," if you will, the Zohar therefore teaches that it too bears the sefirotic structure, that the hidden flow out of *keter,* the tensions of *hesed* and *din,* and the union of *tif'eret* and *malkhut* are all replicated in each person who bears a divine soul. This aspect of the mystical psychology of the Zohar becomes especially important for later Kabbalah and is of dominant interest to Hasidism in the eighteenth and nineteenth centuries.

Theories of exactly how the birth of the soul comes about, its life before it comes into the body, and the precise manner in which it is related to the *sefirot* all abound in early Kabbalah; quite a variety of these is found even within the Zohar. It is especially here that we sense the unsystematic character of the work and its role as compendium for the many views that its author had learned, and perhaps the varied visions of these matters he encountered in his own mystical life. In what is perhaps the dominant view, human souls (like the *sefirot* themselves) are conceived in *binah*, the highest possible source. Thence they are carried into *malkhut*, which serves as a treasure-house of souls, bestowing them to newborns as bodies are conceived in the lower world.

This emphasis on the divine nature of the soul should not give us the impression, however, that the Zohar sees the handiwork of God in soul and not in body. The Kabbalists are dramatically unusual in the medieval West in finding that body as well as soul reflects the inner structure of divinity. This was clearly one of the notions in the Zohar that later occultists most favored, and as a result it is among the best-known—and most often distorted—ideas of the Kabbalah.

Among the many images used for the ten *sefirot* and the patterns of relationship in which they stand to one another is that of the human body. The upper nine *sefirot*, as they are mother, father, and offspring, or as they are well, spring, and flowing streams, or roots, trunk and branches of a great inverted tree, are also depicted as limbs of a cosmic ideal "body." This is not to say that God is corporeal, or that man is wholly divine, but rather that the form of the human body is a copy in matter of the sublime and spiritual mystery of the *sefirot*. The charts that depict the *sefirot* in this way[33] see the first three *sefirot* as constituting a head, sometimes with *keter* as crown or forehead and *ḥokhmah/binah* as the two eyes. *Ḥesed* and *din*, as already indicated, are the two "arms" of God, their actions united in *tif'eret*, the trunk of the bodily form. *Neẓaḥ* and *hod* are then the two hips of the form, and as they receive the flow from above they pass it into *yesod*, the phallus and the final channel of divine energy. We should add here that this structuring in part accounts for the tremendous emphasis the Kabbalists placed upon purity and chastity in sexual matters: all sexual activity below aroused either divine or demonic energy above. From the "sign of the holy covenant" (i.e., circumcision) divinity flowed into *malkhut*, the female counterpart of this form, waiting to give the fruit of its seed to the lower world.

This view of the body and its limbs as created in the ideal holy form gives to the "image and likeness" of God a new lease on quasiliteral meaning. It also bespeaks the great ambivalence we see in the author's mind toward the human body and its passions. He was typical of his age in depicting the body as made of coarse matter, its drives and passions often at odds with the right goals of the pure soul, and as the element in man that kept him from the purity needed to unite with his Creator. But he also had a vision of the body that transcended all this, one that saw the whole person, body and soul, as capable of *imitatio Dei,* or even of *participation* in the divine process, in an utterly uncompromised manner. This is especially to be found in certain passages dealing with sexual union, in its proper setting:

Come and see: It is written "Six days shall you labor and do all your work", and the seventh day is a Sabbath to the Lord your God" (Exodus 20:9). "All your work"—those six days are devoted to human labors. Because of this the companions do not have intercourse except at that time when there is nothing to be found of human labor, but only the work of God. What is His work? Uniting with the Queen, so that holy souls will be brought forth into the world. Therefore on this night the companions are sanctified with the holiness of their Lord and direct their hearts. Good children come forth [from such a union], holy children who turn aside neither right nor left, children of King and Queen. Of these Scriptures says: "You are children of the Lord your God" (Deuteronomy 14:1); "the Lord your God" indeed [the two names indicate] these are His children, children of King and Queen. It is to this that the companions put their mind; those who know this secret cleave fast to it. That is why their children are called God's children, and it is for their sake that the world survives. When the world is being judged, God looks at these children and has mercy for their sake. Of this Scripture speaks in saying: "All with true seed" (Jeremiah 2:21)—"true seed" indeed, for "truth" is the holy and perfect seal, as it says: "Give truth unto Jacob" (Micah 7:20) and all is one. That, indeed, is the "true seed." [34]

Here the mortal union of the companion and his wife parallels the union of the blessed Holy One and *shekhinah* above, each a priest in his Temple serving the ultimate mystery of the Godhead, souls and bodies born at once in their sublime and co-ordinated rites.

Such a vision of body and soul united in God's service, the most human of acts performed with the most divine of intent, has a particular contextual meaning within Judaism. The general tendency toward spiritualization in mysticism encountered certain limits in the Kabbalah, given the very real commitment of Judaism and its all-embracing legal system to the realm of this-wordly action. A pious Jew lives within the domain of the Torah and its commandments. These require the action of the limbs as well as commitments of mind and heart. *Halakhah* serves as a constant reminder to the Jew that he lives bound by certain physical restraints: what he eats, what he wears, where he goes, how he speaks, and many more areas of daily life are governed by the Law. We will recall that the Zohar was much concerned with full and proper observance, and was written partly as a defense of tradition against rationalist incursions. It remains, then, for us to describe the link between the self, body and soul, and the God in whose image that self is so fully made. That link, for the Zohar, is the wondrous and infinitely mysterious world of the Torah. The inner structure held in common by the divine and human selves is also to be found in God's word, the Torah. Both the written Torah and its centuries-long accompanying tradition of oral commentary and expansion are the means God offers Israel for self-fulfillment and approach to divinity. The text itself is alive with mystery, and all the intellectual talents of the Kabbalist must be directed toward the penetration of its secrets.

Rabbi Simeon said: If a man looks upon the Torah as merely a book presenting narratives and everyday matters, alas for him! Such a torah, one treating with everyday concerns, and indeed a more excellent one, we too, even we, could compile. More than that, in the possession of the rulers of the world there are books of even greater merit, and these we could emulate if we wished to compile some such torah. But the Torah, in all of its words, holds supernal truths and sublime secrets.

See how precisely balanced are the upper and the lower worlds. Israel here below is balanced by the angels on high, concerning whom it stands written: "who makest thy angels into winds" (Ps. 104:4). For when the angels descend to earth they don earthly garments, else they could neither abide in the world, nor could it bear to have them. But if this is so with the angels, then how much more so it must be with the Torah: the Torah it was that created the angels and created all the worlds and through Torah are all sustained. The world could not endure the Torah if she had not garbed herself in garments of this world.

Thus the tales related in the Torah are simply her outer garments, and woe to the man who regards that outer garb as the Torah itself, for such a man will be deprived of portion in the next world. Thus David said: "Open Thou mine eyes, that I may behold wondrous things out of Thy law" (Ps. 119:18), that is to say, the things that are underneath. See now. The most visible part of a man are the clothes that he has on, and they who lack understanding, when they look at the man, are apt not to see more in him than these clothes. In reality, however, it is the body of the man that constitutes the pride of his clothes, and his soul constitutes the pride of his body.

So it is with the Torah. Its narrations which relate to things of the world constitute the garments which clothe the body of the Torah; and that body is composed of the Torah's precepts, *gufey-torah* [bodies, major principles]. People without understanding see only the narrations, the garment; those somewhat more penetrating see also the body. But the truly wise, those who serve the most high King and stood on mount Sinai, pierce all the way through to the soul, to the true Torah which is the root principle of all. These same will in the future be vouchsafed to penetrate to the very soul of the soul of the Torah.[35]

Like many of his medieval contemporaries (in Christianity and Islam as well as Judaism) the Zohar's author knows of a multileveled truth to be found in Scripture. It is essential to his exegesis that the literal level, including the legal meanings derived by the rabbis, remain in force, while the mystical truth of his own reading is added to the Torah's meaning. At the same time, this and other passages make no secret of the fact that it is this esoteric reading that he considers "most" true or significant; here is where the heart of the Torah lives. The Torah is the ultimate corpus of secrets, pointing in every way to the "world of truth," a well of profundity never to be fully fathomed. In addition to the ongoing commandment to constantly study that profundity, man may embody the Torah's mysteries by the kabbalistic fulfillment of the life of the commandments.

Rather little in the realm of ritual life is innovated by the Zohar. The commandments to be performed are those of the Torah, as understood by the Zohar in common with all of rabbinic Judaism; only occasionally is there a minor addition or change of custom. But the *meaning* of this life of religious action is entirely transformed. No longer are the commandments either the arbitrary will of the Creator, intended to show one's faithful discipline, or the wise and educating law of the noble Monarch. Rather they are the secrets of the universe itself, each mysteriously locked inside a particular act which the devotee is to per-form, and which he only partially fulfills until he fathoms its secret meanings.

We have already seen the imitation of God as a motif in the religious life, exemplified in the Kabbalist who directs his thoughts to heaven as he fulfills "be fruitful and multiply," the first commandment to be mentioned in the Bible. We have also seen that this is a particular kind of "imitation," one that reaches beyond the separateness of imitator and imitated and points toward the participation of man in the inner life of God, which is the fulfillment of his own inner life as well. As in this act he is able to bring forth holy souls by right deed and contemplation; so in other *mizwot* can he affect the condition of his own soul, defeat his own evil urge, cause encampments of angels to dwell about him and protect him, and in various ways save himself from those demonic powers that are all too ready to hold sway over him should he do wrong. The mythic mindset of the Zohar's author is at times also a superstitious one, if such a term can be used without pejorative intent. His universe is so peopled with flying demons and ill-intending spirits that the build-up of protection against them becomes a major motif in his religious life. At the same time, the accretion of merit for one's good deeds is not only a defense against evils; the more good the soul does, the higher the rungs of soul-life it is allowed to attain, and the closer it will come to that life of *zohar,* enlightenment, which the Zohar ever preaches: the life in which the soul adheres to God.

The goal of all religious life, for the Zohar as for other mystic works, is the return of the soul to God. The great mystery of existence is two-fold: how the world of multiplicity came out of the One, and how it may be returned there in a way of fulfillment that lies short of destruction. The Zohar has responded to (though hardly answered) the first question in speaking of *sefirot;* its response to the latter question comes in its understanding of *mizwot,* the *sefirot* as embodied in the commandments of the Torah. In giving the Torah to Israel, God has placed his own self within human access. Here, through the subtlety of symbolic language, divinity, human actions, and even the objects required for human action have become one. As the worshipper binds together the four species of plant used for the celebration of the *Sukkot* festival, he is actually drawing together, in his very hands, *hesed* and *din, tif'eret* and *malkhut.* As the householder lifts his two loaves of bread for the Sabbath blessing, he holds in his hands the union of Jacob and Rachel, sun and moon, heaven and earth. As he holds them, so is he held by them, and the soul that contemplates the mysteries of these moments and their deeds is transported into a realm where the *sefirot* acting upon him and his acting upon them are processes not separable from one another. At the same time, the objects he has used in such rites, palm-branch and citron, loaves of bread, or whatever, are transported with him to that higher realm. Not only his soul is uplifted and transmuted, but the lower material world as well, through those symbolic objects that have achieved the transcendence of sanctification. The essential religious task becomes one of *attachment* and *uplifting,* the soul seeking adhesion to God, but doing so through the commandments in order that the corporeal world be raised up and transmuted with it.

The emergence of the universe out of God has been a graduated, step-by-step, process. The *shekhinah*, standing at the lower end of the sefirotic world, is at the head of a myriad of palaces, throne-rooms, antechambers and angelic choruses. Beneath those lie the spheres with their varying degrees of corporeality, ending in this world of coarse matter and its temptations. On the other side of this world lie as many realms of evil, "shells," mythical beasts, and demons that reach down into the mouth of the great pit. The human being, and especially the Jew who has that Torah which allows for the presence and fulfillment of his divine soul, stands at the very center of this universe. Something of him reaches down into its depths, but the roots of his soul extend to the uppermost heights. With the life of Torah as his guide, his task stands before him. He is the one who can draw the entire universe upward, raising matter to the level of spirit, spirit to the level of soul, soul to the level of *shekhinah*, reaching ever higher until his inner concentration effects that great *yihud* or union that allows the *shekhinah* herself to transcend her exile, to be united fully, through him, with God beyond, allowing the flow of divine life to abound through all the worlds, the joy of divine light to shine with undimmed brilliance. Only man can do this, for the Torah was given to him alone; his and his alone is the ecstatic task and the staggering responsibility of restoring the world to God.

Happy is the man who goes in and out, who knows to contemplate the mysteries of his Lord and to cleave to Him. By these secrets a person is able to adhere to God, to attain full wisdom, the most sublime of mysteries. When he serves God in prayer, willingly and with a direction of heart he attaches his will to God like the flame to the coal. By this he unites the lower rungs in a holy manner, crowning them with a certain one of the lesser names. Thence he proceeds to unify the higher and innermost rungs, making them all one with that highest heaven that stands above them. Even while his mouth and lips are yet moving he should direct his heart and his will higher, higher, uniting all with that mystery of mysteries, the root of all thought and desire, the mystery that dwells within *eyn sof*. Every day he should have this intent in each of his prayers. In such worship will all his days be crowned with the mystery of those supernal days.[36]

NOTES

1. Nineteenth and early twentieth century scholarship treating the history of Judaism generally relegated Kabbalah to an obscure and somewhat shameful corner. Such treatment was motivated by apologetics, by a set of theological presuppositions about Judaism rendered difficult by the presence of

Kabbalah, and by a genuine distaste for the material. This attitude was epitomized by the treatment of Kabbalah in the works of the great Jewish historian Heinrich Graetz. The study of Kabbalah has been revolutionized by the career of Gershom Scholem, the leading historian of Judaism in this century, who has devoted his full energies to a study of Jewish mysticism and its restoration to its rightful place in the history of Judaism.

2. See the extended discussion by Scholem in *Ursprung und Anfänge der Kabbala* (Berlin, 1962) also appearing as *Les origines de la Kabbale* (Paris, 1966). An English translation of this volume was published under the title *Origins of the Kabbalah* (Philadelphia, 1987). Summaries of Scholem's views on the earliest Kabbalah can be found in his articles *Kabbalah* and *Bahir* in the *Encyclopedia Judaica*, re-issued in the volume *Kabbalah* (Jerusalem, 1974). See also the article by Shulamit Shahar in *Tarbiz*, 40 (1971), 483–507.

3. The Bahir was translated into German by Scholem, published in Berlin, 1923. An English translation by Aryeh Kaplan was published in New York, 1974. It is generally reliable as a translation, through the introduction that accompanies it is not historically grounded.

4. Bahir 78. References to the Bahir follow the standard edition of R. Margulies (Jerusalem, 1951).

5. Bahir 156. See Scholem, *Ursprung*, p. 155.

6. Bahir 141–45. See Scholem, *Ursprung*, pp. 111–14.

7. On the nature of myth and symbol in the Kabbalah see Scholem, "Kabbalah and Myth" in his collection *On the Kabbalah and Its Symbolism* (New York, 1965). A further study of kabbalistic symbols is that by Tishby in his *Netivey Emunah u-Minut* (Israel, 1964), pp. 11–22.

8. The seeming contradiction between claims of antiquity and assertions of new revelation was not a problem for the Kabbalists or the intended audience for such claims. Ancient secrets, hidden in documents unknown or whispered through the ages by an esoteric elite, have the same flavor as heavenly secrets, preserved above through the ages, and now freshly given by the angels or through a visit of Elijah.

9. On the Gerona period in Jewish mysticism, see Scholem, *Ursprung*, pp. 324–420. For those who read Hebrew but not French or German, Scholem's lecture notes from courses at the Hebrew University have been printed and are available from the university's Akademon Press. Among these is an entire volume of lectures on Kabbalah in Gerona. The English reader must meanwhile remain satisfied with the summaries to which we have referred in n. 2.

10. Scholem, *Encyclopedia Judaica* 10:607.

11. Rather little research has been done on this so-called "gnostic" school. Their basic texts have been edited and studied by Scholem in *Mada'ey ha-Yahadut* 2 (1927) and *Tarbiz* 2–5 (1931–35). Two new studies by Joseph Dan also treat of this circle: "Samael, Lilith, and the Concept of Evil in the Early Kabbalah," *AJS Review* 5, (1982) and "The Beginning of the Messi-

anic Myth in Thirteenth Century Kabbalah" (Hebrew), Hebrew University Institute of Jewish Studies (Jerusalem, 1981).

12. Quoted by Scholem in *Major Trends in Jewish Mysticism* (New York, 1954), p. 156ff.

13. The complicated tale of the search Isaac of Acre conducted for this manuscript, culminating in De Leon's widow's assertion that it never had existed at all, is told in full by Scholem in *Major Trends*, pp. 190–92. *Major Trends* contains two chapters devoted to the Zohar. These constitute the best summation of current scholarship regarding this work.

14. A number of these terms are discussed in the footnotes to *Major Trends*. The "dictionary" which Scholem promises in n.7, p. 385, is partially available now in the dissertation of his student Yehuda Liebes, *Sections of the Zohar Lexicon* (Jerusalem, 1976). This lexicon, concentrating on the most interesting and unusual of the Zohar's vocabulary, has become an indispensible aid to an understanding of the Zohar.

15. Zohar II 11a–12.

16. In the immediately preceding narrative Rabbi Eleazar himself is discoursing on Ezekiel 37:9.

17. Zohar II 13a–b.

18. Zohar I 232a–b. Color symbolism is quite extensive in the Zohar. Scholem has discussed this matter in *Eranos Jahrbuch*, 41 (1972), 1–49, now translated into English in *Diogenes* 108–09 (1979–80).

19. *Major Trends*, lecture five.

20. Quoted from ibid., p. 201ff. Scholem's translation.

21. This matter is discussed fully by Tishby in *Mishnat ha-Zohar*, v.1 (Jerusalem, 1957), pp. 107–11.

22. Zohar I 15a.

23. Zohar II 68b.

24. *Major Trends*, p. 15ff.

25. The four letters of *binah* in Hebrew, *bet, yod, nun, heh*, are thus accounted for: the two "parents" and their "son."

26. Zohar III 290a, Idra Zuta. The Zohar has a penchant for daring sorts of religious imagery that sound nearly christological. These certainly reflect not a christianizing tendency (as many a latter-day Christian Kabbalist has dreamed), but rather a search for a new anthropomorphism appropriate to kabbalistic thinking. "Son" goes with "daughter"; this same pair are "bridegroom" and "bride." Still, the extra measure of cautionary language surrounding this paragraph is easy to understand.

27. Here the author seems to have taken an earlier conventional phrase, *bet 'olam*, usually thought of as "eternal home," and allowed his imagination to give it pictorial content. Many examples of this intentional over-literalism can be found in the Zohar.

28. Zohar I 172a. Compare Bahir 156, quoted above. This passage may be better understood with a glance at the sefirotic chart printed below. We have intentionally avoided placing such a chart at the outset of our discussion of

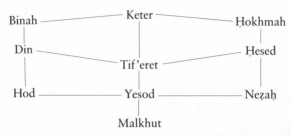

the *sefirot,* and here too we offer it with hesitancy. When the kabbalistic symbols are overly conventionalized, either in terms of name or position with respect to the others, they tend to lose their freshness and richness of meaning. Charts are especially susceptible to this danger, and none is included in the Zohar itself. But here the spatial relations will be helpful. The bottommost *sefirah, malkhut,* is the house, again in feminine symbol. She is at the center of all, being the lowest link in the sefirotic chain but the uppermost in the worlds below, as we shall see presently. The tree that rises within her is *yesod;* the "male" principle that links her with the worlds above fructifies her so that abundance for all will be provided. *Yesod* reaches upward to the three great mountains (or patriarchs), *hesed, din,* and *tif'eret,* is hidden behind them, and then rises on still higher, though now his ascent is hidden in clouds of obscurity. The entire sefirotic world, from *keter* to *malkhut,* is connected by a single "central pillar," though its upper reaches cannot be seen. The male principle *(yesod,* or *tif'eret)* rules during the day, while *malkhut,* moon, she who has no light of her own, rules at night.

29. On the *shekhinah* see Scholem, *Von der mystischen Gestalt der Gottheit* (Zürich, 1962), pp. 135–91; Hebrew version in *Pirqey Yesod be-Havanat ha-Qabbalah u-Semaleha* (Jerusalem, 1976), pp. 269–307.

30. The relationship between the Song of Songs, as midrashically understood, and the literature called *shi'ur qomah,* comprising mainly gigantic measurements of the limbs of a divine body, has yet to be fully clarified. There is a large literature on the *shi'ur qomah* in recent scholarship. Its relationship to the Song of Songs was first suggested by Saul Lieberman in an addendum (in Hebrew) to Scholem's *Jewish Gnosticism, Merkabah Mysticism, and Talmudic Tradition* (New York, 1960).

31. Zohar II 245a.

32. Zohar I 17a. See Tishby, *Mishnat ha-Zohar,* v. 1, p. 296ff. and the further sources quoted there.

33. The reader is referred to the chart in n. 28.

34. Zohar II 89a–b.

35. Zohar III 152a. Translation from Scholem's *Zohar* (New York, 1949), p. 121ff. On the Torah in Kabbalah see also his *On the Kabbalah and its Symbolism,* pp. 32–86.

36. Zohar II 213b.

2.

Ayin: The Concept of Nothingness in Jewish Mysticism

Daniel C. Matt

There is allure and terror in mystical portrayals of nothingness: Meister Eckhart's *niht,* John of the Cross's *nada,* the Taoist *wu,* the Buddhist *sunyata.* Despite appearances, these terms do not express an identical meaning, since each mystic names the nameless from within a discursive realm shaped by his own training, outlook, and language.[1] Here I wish to trace the development of the concept of *ayin* ("nothingness") in Jewish mysticism. In medieval Kabbalah *ayin* functions as a theosophical symbol, the beginning of the elaborate system of *sefirot,* the stages of divine manifestation. Everything emerges from the depths of *ayin* and eventually returns there. Proceeding from Kabbalah to Hasidism, the focus changes. Now the psychological significance of *ayin* dominates; it becomes a medium for self-transformation. The mystic experiences *ayin* directly and emerges anew.

The word *nothingness,* of course, connotes negativity and nonbeing, but what the mystic means by divine nothingness is that God is greater than any *thing* one can imagine, *no thing.* Since God's being is incomprehensible and ineffable, the least offensive and most accurate description one can offer is, paradoxically, *nothing.* David ben Abraham ha-Lavan, a fourteenth-century kabbalist, corrects any misapprehension: "Nothingness [*ayin*] is more existent than all the being of the world. But since it is simple, and all simple things are complex compared with its simplic-

Reprinted from *The Problem of Pure Consciousness,* edited by Robert K. C. Forman, by permission of Oxford University Press, New York, 1990.

ity, it is called *ayin.*" David's mystical Christian contemporaries concur. The Byzantine theologian Gregory Palamas writes, "He is not being, if that which is not God is being." Eckhart says, "God's *niht* fills the entire world; His something though is nowhere."[2]

I

Mystics contemplate the void, but not in a vacuum. The kabbalists were influenced not only by Jewish philosophers but also, directly or indirectly, by pagan and Christian Neoplatonic thinkers: Plotinus, Pseudo-Dionysius, and John Scotus Erigena. Philo, the mystical philosopher who straddled the first centuries BCE and CE, was unknown to the kabbalists, but it was he who introduced the concept of the unknowability and indescribability of God. Philo paved the way for negative theology, emphasizing the unlikeness of God to things in the world. "God alone has veritable being. . . . Things posterior to him have no real being but are believed to exist in imagination only."[3] The goal of religious life is to see through the apparent reality of the world and to shed the consciousness of a separate self. "This is the natural course: one who comprehends himself fully, lets go totally of the nothingness that he discovers in all creation, and one who lets go of himself comes to know the Existent."[4] One of the great mysteries is the contrast between the power "of the Uncreated and the exceeding nothingness of the created."[5]

Philo's nothingness *(oudeneia)* refers to the unreality of creation in the face of the only true reality, the divine. Here, nothingness has a purely negative quality; it describes a fundamental lack. In the overwhelming discovery that everything is an expression of the divine, creation as an independent entity collapses and is reduced to nothing. By contemplating this basic fact, one is transported into the presence of God. "For then is the time for the creature to encounter the Creator, when it has recognized its own nothingness." The ideal is "to learn to measure one's own nothingness."[6]

God is immeasurable, nameless, and ineffable. In this, Philo foreshadows the Gnostics, some of whom surpass him in applying negative language to God. The Gnostic God, as distinct from the creative demiurge, is totally different, the other, unknown. He is "the incomprehensible, inconceivable one who is superior to every thought," "ineffable, inexpressible, nameable by silence."[7] Trying to outdo his predecessors in negative theology, Basilides, the second-century Alexandrian Gnostic, opposes even the term "ineffable" as a predicate of God. His words are preserved by Hippolytus of Rome, who cites him in his attack against various prevalent heresies: "That which is named [ineffable] is not absolutely ineffable, since we call one thing ineffable and another not even ineffable. For that which is not even ineffable is not named ineffable, but is above every name that is named."[8]

God transcends the capacity of human language and the category of being. Basilides speaks of the "nameless nonexistent God." This negation is clarified in another Gnostic treatise, *Allogenes:* "Nor is he something that exists, that one could know. But he is something else . . . that is better, whom one cannot know. . . . He has nonbeing existence."[9]

Nonbeing best describes God's incomprehensible otherness. For Basilides a distinct but related nonbeing is also the source of creation.

The nonexistent God made the cosmos out of the nonexistent, casting down and planting a single seed containing within itself the whole seed-mass of the cosmos. . . . The nonexistent seed of the cosmos cast down by the nonexistent God contained a seed-mass at once multiform and the source of many beings. . . . The seed of the cosmos came into being from nonexistent things [and this seed is] the word that was spoken: "Let there be light!"[10]

Basilides thus offers an extreme formulation of creation *ex nihilo,* a theory whose mystical career entwines with negative theology. In the Hellenistic age it was widely held that the stuff of which the world is made is amorphous *hyle,* formless matter. Thales and Parmenides had taught that nothing can arise from what does not exist, and Aristotle writes: "That nothing comes to be out of that which is not, but everything out of that which is, is a doctrine common to nearly all the natural philosophers." Until the rise of Christianity there was apparently no Greek, Roman, or Jewish Hellenistic thinker who asserted creation from nothing.[11]

The theory of creation *ex nihilo* first appears in second-century Christian literature, evoked by the confrontation with Gnostic heresy and Greek philosophy. It represents a denial of the prevailing Platonic notion that creation was out of eternal primordial matter, a notion that compromises the sovereignty of God. As Augustine writes, "Nor had You any material in Your hand when you were making heaven and earth."

Theophilus, bishop of Antioch, points out that if God made the world from uncreated matter, He would be no greater than a human being who makes something out of existing materials.[12] The formula *creatio ex nihilo*, in fact, may have been coined in opposition to the philosophical principle that nothing is made from nothing, *nihil ex nihilo fit*. Christian thinkers also felt challenged to refute the Gnostics, who had set up other powers alongside God and asserted that one of these created the world. (Basilides' apparent attribution of creation to the hidden God is unusual for a Gnostic.) Creation *ex nihilo* provided a defense for the belief in one free and transcendent Creator not dependent on anything. It became the paradigm for God's miraculous powers and served as the chief underpinning for the supernatural conception of deity. Its denial was tantamount to the undermining of revealed religion. In the words of Moses Maimonides, "If the philosophers would succeed in demonstrating eternity as Aristotle understands it, the Law as a whole would become void." [13]

There is little if any evidence that the normative rabbinic view was of creation *ex nihilo*.[14] The passage from *Sefer Yetsirah* ("The Book of Creation") later exploited as an expression of *ex nihilo* is ambiguous: "He formed something actual out of chaos and made what is not *[eino]* into what is *[yeshno]*. He hewed enormous pillars out of the ether that cannot be grasped." [15] *Sefer Yetsirah* was composed sometime between the third and sixth centuries. Here is the first time in Hebrew literature that we find mention of creation from *ayin*, or rather, the adverbial *eino*. The noun *ayin* appears in an ontological sense only much later. "What is not" may refer to *hyle*, primordial matter, which the Platonists called "the nonexistent" *(to me on)*.[16] The intent would then be not absolute nothingness but rather that which is not yet formed or endowed with qualities.

Though the doctrine of *creatio ex nihilo* was not indigenously Jewish, under the influence of Christian and Moslem thinkers it penetrated Jewish philosophical and religious circles. The phrase *yesh me-ayin* ("something out of nothing") came to describe the process of Creation, though the theory was both less venerated and less theologically crucial than in Christian thought. Creation from nothing was accepted by Maimonides; yet he suggests that various obscure passages in the Torah seem to prove the validity of the Platonic theory. According to the philosopher Joseph Albo, the denial of *yesh me-ayin* is mistaken but does not render one liable to a charge of heresy.[17]

The theory of *ex nihilo* inevitably collided with the theory of emanation taught by Plotinus, a master of negative theology whose God creates without will. Plotinus denies the biblical story of creation by design. Everything that exists emerges from the One in a gradated yet eternal process of emanation, and everything aspires to return to the One.

Plotinus established negation as a type of divine attribute, which he included in a formal classification. He employs the technique of *aphairesis* ("removing, abstraction") to negate predicates of God, which means not that the opposite can be predicated but that God is excluded from that realm of discourse. The One is "something higher than what we call 'being.' " "Even being cannot be there." [18]

The mystic experiences the One not as some transcendent substance but in an objectless vision: "The vision floods the eyes with light, but it is not a light showing some other object; the light itself is the vision. . . . With this, one becomes identical with that radiance." [19] As the spiritual explorer discovers that the One is beyond images, his own image of a separate self also dissolves: "One formed by this mingling with the Supreme . . . becomes the Unity, nothing within him or without inducing any diversity. . . . Reasoning is in abeyance and all intellection and even, to dare the word, the very self: caught away, filled with God. . . . He is like one who, having penetrated the inner sanctuary, leaves the temple images behind him." [20]

Plotinus's conception of simplicity *(haplosis)* requires the abolition of all difference between oneself and the One. In the ultimate bliss of the "flight of the alone to the alone," the One is no longer other. "How can one describe as other than oneself that which, when one discerned it, seemed not other but one with oneself?" [21] The mystic shares the sublimity of nonexistence. "The essential person outgrows being, becomes identical with the transcendent of being."

Medieval Christian, Moslem, and Jewish philosophers were deeply influenced by Plotinus's negative theology and his theory of emanation. The contradiction between creation *ex nihilo* and the eternal emanation of the world from God was unmistakably clear. Augustine, defending the traditional Christian position, writes, "They were made from nothing by Thee, not of Thee." [22] Though *ex nihilo* was widely espoused, certain Christian thinkers more enamored of Neoplatonism attempted to resolve the contradiction between emanation and creation from nothing. They reinterpreted *ex nihilo* as implying the temporal generation of the world from the essence of God. The troublesome Plotinian element of eternity was eliminated, and "creation from nothing" was transformed into a mystical formula for emanation from the divine.

The apophatic theology of Dionysius the Areopagite contributed to this transformation. The fifth-century Syrian monophysite who wrote under this pseudonym calls God *hyperousion* ("beyond being"). God is the "cause of being for all, but is itself nonbeing, for it is beyond all being." [23] Ecstatic experience matches this theological insight. "By going out of yourself and everything, . . . you will raise yourself to the ray of divine darkness beyond being." [24]

From the ninth century on, both Islamic and Christian sources offer a Neoplatonized, mystical version of *ex nihilo*. The Irish theologian redundantly known as John Scotus Erigena was the first Christian to teach such a theory and the first Latin thinker to focus on negative theology. His thinking was deeply influenced by Dionysius, whom he translated from Greek into Latin, though John's pantheistic tendencies go far beyond his Dionysian sources. He applies the name *nihil* to God, intending by this not the privation but the transcendence of being. Because of "the ineffable, incomprehensible and inaccessible brilliance of the divine goodness . . . it is not improperly called 'nothing.' " It "is called 'nothing' on account of its excellence." [25]

John takes the expression *ex nihilo* to mean *ex Deo;* the nothing from which the world was created is God. In bold imagery he interprets the entire first chapter of Genesis according to this new sense of *ex nihilo*. Creation is the procession of the transcendent *nihil* into differentiated being, into the division of nature. In its essence, the divine is said not to be, but as it proceeds through the primordial causes, it becomes all that is. "Every visible creature can be called a theophany, that is, a divine appearance." "God is created in creation in a remarkable and ineffable way." [26] The *nihil* is the ground for this divine self-creation. God descends into His own depths, out of which all proceeds and to which all eventually returns. Unknowable in itself, the divine nature becomes knowable in its manifestations.

Medieval Christian mystics who speak of divine nothingness, for example, Meister Eckhart, the Franciscan Petrus Olivi, the anonymous author of *Theologica Deutsch,* and Jacob Boehme, are indebted to John Scotus and Dionysius. John's impact would have been even greater if the exploitation of his work by Albigensian heretics and philosophical pantheists had not resulted in its condemnation by Pope Honorius III in 1225.

Meanwhile, in the world of Islam, Neoplatonic emanation theory engendered a similar reinterpretation of *ex nihilo*. Plotinus's doctrine became widely known under the guise of *The Theology of Aristotle*, an Arabic synopsis of Neoplatonism based on the *Enneads* and the teachings of Porphyry, Plotinus's disciple. In the long version of the *Theology* the divine word *(kalima)* is said to transcend the conflict of the categories, to be beyond motion and rest. It is called "nothing" *(laysa)*—a nothing from which creation stems. A similar view is found among the Shiite Isma'iliya: God and the Nothing-with-him are one unity. This nothing is not outside of God but rather a manifestation of His hidden essence from which all proceeds.[27]

II

Maimonides did not endorse a mystical interpretation of "nothing," but his negative theology, inspired by the Moslem philosophers Alfarabi and Avicenna, was an important ingredient in the kabbalistic theory of *ayin*. All three thinkers claimed that existence is predicated of God and of other beings not in the same sense but ambiguously and equivocally. God has nothing in common with any other being. His existence is totally unlike anything we conceive: God "exists but not through existence."[28]

Avicenna made negative theology philosophically respectable; Maimonides extended and radicalized it, developing a system of negative attributes. He was the first to state explicitly that all positive terms affirmed of God are to be taken both negatively and equivocally. Thomas Aquinas cites and disputes Maimonides' view, as does the Jewish philosopher Gersonides.[29] For his part, Maimonides openly promotes the controversial method and encourages his reader to progress in discovering what God is not: "Know that the description of God . . . by means of negations is the correct description, a description that is not affected by an indulgence in facile language and does not imply any deficiency with respect to God. . . . You come nearer to the apprehension of Him, may He be exalted, with every increase in the negations regarding Him."

Even negation, though, cannot capture the infinite. Maimonides concludes that "apprehension of Him consists in the inability to attain the ultimate term in apprehending Him. . . . The most apt phrase concerning this subject is the dictum in the Psalms [65:2]: 'To You silence is praise,' which means: Silence with regard to You is praise."[30]

The medieval Jewish mystics adopted Maimonides' negative theology, at least as it pertains to the infinite nature of God. The thirteenth-century kabbalist Azriel of Gerona, who was deeply influenced by Neoplatonism, notes the similarity between the mystical and philosophical approaches: "The scholars of inquiry [philosophers] agree with the statement that our comprehension is solely by means of 'no.' "[31] Shem Tov ibn Gaon grants that "the words of the philosophers and the wise are correct . . . [in that] they have instructed us to negate from Him all negations. . . . Since the root of all is endless and incomprehensible, it is impossible to call Him by any name."[32]

Yet, paradoxically, the very strategy of negation provides a means of indicating the ineffable. Negative attributes carve away all that is false and culminate in a positive sense of nothingness. The mystics now claim to surpass the philosophers. "How hard they toiled and exerted themselves—those who intended to speak of negation; yet they did not know the site of negation!"[33] According to Moses de León, there is glory in nothingness. *Ayin* is revealed as the only name appropriate to the divine essence.

The new positive sense of *ayin* derives in part from the eleventh-century poet Solomon ibn Gabirol. In his masterpiece, *Keter Malkhut*, in a stanza dealing with divine wisdom, we read:

> To draw the flow of the *yesh* ["something"] from the *ayin*,
> as light emerging from the eye is drawn forth. . . .
> He called to the *ayin* and it was cleft,
> to the *yesh* and it was thrust.[34]

The abstract terms *ayin* and *yesh* are here animated mythically, but Gabirol was a philosopher as well as a poet, and *ayin* may allude to formless matter or to the realm of essence prior to existence. Shlomo Pines has suggested that Gabirol based his description of this primal ontological event on a passage from Avicenna: "Praise be to God, who cleaved the darkness of nothingness [or "privation"] with the light of existence." Gabirol's cryptic and pregnant words in *Keter Malkhut* seem to endow *ayin* with a new dimension of meaning: ontological essence.[35] Since we know that the kabbalists were indebted to Gabirol for a number of images and terms, it is not surprising that the mystical career of *ayin* is linked to his poetry.

Another poet, who lived some fifteen hundred years before Gabirol, provided the kabbalists with a precious prooftext for their reevaluation of nothingness. In order to bolster the new theory, the kabbalists were fond of intentionally misreading various scriptural verses in which the word *ayin* appears. In biblical Hebrew *ayin* can mean "where," as well as "nothing." The poet who composed the twenty-eighth chapter of the book of Job poses a rhetorical question (28:12): "Where [*me-ayin*] is wisdom to be found?" The kabbalists of the thirteenth century transform this question into a mystical formula: "Divine wisdom comes into being out of nothingness." Asher ben David writes, "The inner power is called *ayin* because neither thought nor reflection grasps it. Concerning this, Job said, 'Wisdom comes into being out of *ayin*.' " As Bahya ben Asher puts it, the verse should be understood "not as a question but as an announcement." [36] Refracted through a mystical lens, Job's question yields its own startling answer. In the words of Joseph Gikatilla, "The depth of primordial being . . . is called Boundless. It is also called *ayin* because of its concealment from all creatures above and below. . . . If one asks, 'What is it?,' the answer is, *Ayin,* that is, no one can understand anything about it. . . . It is negated of every conception." [37]

III

As we have noted, the kabbalists adopted Maimonides' negative approach to the description of the essence of God. They parted company with him, however, in their discussion of divine attributes. Maimonides, subjugating biblical thought to Greek thought, denied the existence of real, unequivocal attributes. The kabbalists sensed that the philosophical unmoved mover was incompatible with the traditional Jewish view of God as a living, responsive being. Despite their appropriation of theological negation, certain kabbalists criticize the philosophers on just this point: "Their wisdom is based solely on negation. . . . All their words are intended to negate the divine designations; they keep on negating and negating." The poet Meshullam Da Piera complains that "those who deny the proper attributes of God speak out until faith has been drained." [38]

The kabbalists insisted on an entire array of positive, vibrant attributes: the ten *sefirot.* The *sefirot* are stages of divine being, aspects of divine personality. Prior to their emanation, God is unmanifest, referred to simply as *Ein Sof,* Infinite (literally, "there is no end"). The *sefirot* reveal what can be conveyed of the divine nature. By advocating this system of mystical attributes, the kabbalists sought to counter extreme intellectualism and preserve the fabric of faith. It is insufficient, they claim, to believe in the denuded infinity of God. Such an abstract theology endangers the daily regimen of holiness. Isaac of Akko dreams that he sees a "curse against the rebels who believe only in *Ein Sof* . . . and neither pray nor bless, for they say, 'What need does He have for our prayers? What benefit can He derive from our blessings?' " Isaac castigates "the foolish philosophers, . . . ignorant of the ten *sefirot,* the name of the blessed holy One. Their faith is deficient and wrong, for they disdain prayer and blessings and are frivolous toward the *mitsvot.*"[39] The *sefirot* are like a body for the infinite divine soul; they provide a name for the nameless and an address for prayer. Certain philosophers had charged that kabbalistic descriptions of the *sefirot* were corporeal or heretical. Shem Tov ibn Gaon retorts: "This is the principle upon which all depends: what the philosophers think is the site of rebellion is really the site of faith."[40] The *sefirot* are referred to as *raza di-meheimanuta,* "the mystery of faith."

From above to below, the *sefirot* enact the drama of emanation, the transition from *Ein Sof* to creation. From below to above, they are a ladder of ascent back to the One. *Keter 'Elyon* ("highest crown") is the first *sefirah,* coeternal with *Ein Sof.* It is this *sefirah* that the kabbalists identify as *ayin.* The other *sefirot* portray God in personal, anthropomorphic terms; they represent, e.g., divine wisdom, understanding, love, judgment, compassion, and dominion. The highest *sefirah,* however, is characterized by undifferentiation and impersonality. It verges on *Ein Sof,* and some kabbalists do not distinguish between them.

The designation of the first *sefirah* as *ayin* may date from the twelfth century, though it does not appear in the earliest kabbalistic text, *Sefer ha-Bahir.* It was conveyed by the Gerona kabbalists in the thirteenth century and accepted on their authority and the authority of their teacher, Isaac the Blind, "the father of Kabbalah."[41] Moses de León offers an explanation of the symbolism and then draws an analogy between divine and human ineffability.

Keter 'Elyon . . . is called the pure ether that cannot be grasped.[42] It is the totality of all existence, and all have wearied in their search for it. . . . The belt of every wise person is burst by it, for it is the secret of the Cause of Causes and brings all into being. . . . God, may He be blessed, is the annihilation of all thoughts; no thought can contain Him. Since no one can contain Him [with] anything in the world, He is called *ayin.* This is the secret of what is said: "Wisdom comes into being out of *ayin.*"

Anything sealed and concealed, totally unknown to anyone, is called *ayin,* meaning that no one knows anything about it. Similarly, . . . no one knows anything at all about the human soul; she stands in the status of nothingness, as it is said [Ecclesiastes 3:19]: "The advantage of the human over the beast is *ayin.*" By means of this soul, the human being obtains an advantage over all other creatures and the glory of that which is called *ayin.*[43]

Certain kabbalists maintained that the first *sefirah* is symbolized by *alef,* the first letter of the Hebrew alphabet, but de León objects: *ayin* cannot be represented by even a single letter.[44] Gikatilla, de León's friend and colleague, suggests that among the letters of the divine name *YHVH* only the tip of the *yod,* the smallest letter of the alphabet, alludes to *Keter.* The highest *sefirah* "has no specific letter of its own, for there is no one who can estimate, imagine, or draw it, even by the shape indicating a letter." The name that God gives himself, "I am" (*Eheyeh,* Exodus 3:14), signifies that "His existence is not conceived by anyone other than Him. . . . 'I alone know my existence.'"[45] Keter is so transcendent that, according to one view, it does not stoop to know the other layers of divinity, the nine lower *sefirot.* "Because of the nature of His concealment, *Keter 'Elyon* does not recognize the other levels."[46] On their part, the *sefirot* cannot comprehend *Ein Sof,* the infinite nature of God. Even *ayin,* which is coeternal with *Ein Sof,* has only a vague knowledge of It. In the words of the Zohar, "*Ein Sof* does not abide being known. . . . All these lights and sparks [*sefirot*] are dependent on It but cannot comprehend. The only one who knows, yet without knowing, is the highest desire, concealed of all concealed, *ayin.* And when the highest point and the world-that-is-coming [the second and third *sefirot*] ascend, they know only the aroma, as one inhaling an aroma is sweetened."[47]

IV

The deepest mystery of the *sefirotic* process and of the entire chain of being lies in the transition from *ayin* to *yesh,* from "nothing" to "something." Like the Christian and Islamic Neoplatonists, the kabbalists too reinterpreted *ex nihilo* as emanation from the hidden essence of

God. Ezra of Gerona, paraphrasing Maimonides, cites Plato against the literal meaning of *ex nihilo:*

Plato . . . says that it is absurd to think that the Creator should produce something out of nothing; rather there is preexistent matter, which is like clay to the potter or iron to the blacksmith, who form it as they please. So the Creator, may He be blessed, forms from matter heaven and earth and sometimes something different. The fact that He does not create something out of nothing does not indicate any deficiency on His part, just as it does not indicate any deficiency that He does not produce what is logically absurd, e.g., creating a square the diagonal of which is equal to its length or combining two contraries at the same instant. Just as this does not imply any deficiency in His power, so there is no deficiency if He does not emanate something from nothing, but rather from something.[48]

Unlike Maimonides, who rejected Plato's theory of primordial matter, Ezra manages to harmonize this too with emanation. He insists that the roots of the revealed *sefirot* are preexistent; in the process of emanation they simply emerge from their primordiality. "The essences were in existence; the emanation was innovated."[49] For the kabbalists there *is* a "something" that emerges from "nothing," but the nothing is brimming with overwhelming divine reality; it is *mahut,* the "whatness," the quiddity of God.[50] The something is not a physical object but rather the first ray of divine wisdom, which, as Job indicates, emerges from *ayin.* It is the primordial point that marks the beginning of the unfolding of God. In the lyrical words of the Zohar: "The flow broke through and did not break through its aura. It was not known at all until, under the impact of breaking through, one high and hidden point shone. Beyond that point, nothing is known. So it is called Beginning."[51]

The opening words of Genesis, "In the beginning," allude to this first point, which is the second *sefirah, Hokhmah,* divine wisdom. Though second, it "appears to be the first" and is called "beginning" because the first *sefirah—ayin—* is unknowable and uncountable. In the words of Moses de León, the point is "the beginning of existence."

The beginning of existence is the secret of the concealed point and is called . . . primordial wisdom. It is the mystery of the conceptual point . . . the beginning of all the hidden things [the *sefirot*]. From there they spread out and emanate according to their species. . . . From a single point you can draw forth the emanation of all things. You should understand that when that which is hidden and concealed arouses itself to existence, it produces at first something the size of the point of a needle; afterwards, it produces everything from there. . . .

Contemplate this: When the emanation was emanated out of *ayin* . . . all the levels [the *sefirot*] were dependent on thought. . . . That which . . . rests in thought is called *Hokhmah* ["wisdom"]. It has been said, "What is *Hokhmah? Hakkeh mah.*" This means that since . . . you will never attain it, *hakkeh,* "wait," for *mah,* "what" will come and be. This is the primordial wisdom emerging out of *ayin.*[52]

Whereas *ayin* cannot be symbolized by any letter, the primordial point of wisdom is identified with *yod,* "the letter that is smallest among all the letters." *Ayin* is "the ether that cannot be grasped," while this conceptual point is "the ether that can be grasped." It is "the beginning of all beginnings," the potentiality of all things.[53] The transition from nothingness to something, from *ayin* to *yesh,* is the decisive act of creation, the real context of Genesis. Azriel of Gerona, the first kabbalist to speak at length about *ayin,* describes the relatedness of these two opposite states:

If one asks you, "How did He bring forth something from nothing? Is there not a great difference between something and nothing?" Answer him, . . . "The something is in the nothing in the mode of nothing, and the nothing is in the something in the mode of something."[54] Therefore they have said [*Sefer Yetsirah* 2:6]: "He made His nothing into His something" and not "He made something from nothing," to indicate that the *ayin* is the *yesh* and the *yesh* is the *ayin.* . . . The node of *yesh* as it begins to emerge from *ayin* into existence is called faith. . . . For the term "faith" applies neither to the visible, comprehensible *yesh,* nor to *ayin,* invisible and incomprehensible, but rather to the nexus of *ayin* and *yesh.*[55]

The wording of *Sefer Yetsirah* could mean: "He made [relative] non-being [i.e., prime matter] into being" or "He made nothing into something," but Azriel insists that the transformation takes place within God: divine wisdom emerges out of divine nothingness.[56] Creation originates in this nothingness, which is the medium of every transformation.

At times, Azriel employs another Hebrew term for "nothing," *efes,* as when he speaks of the three principles of being: matter, form and *efes.*[57] In Hebrew philosophical terminology *efes* represents the Aristotelian concept of *steresis* (privation).[58] For Aristotle no thing comes into being simply from nonbeing. Change involves a substrate (matter) acquiring a form that it did not previously possess. Each succeeding form realizes part of what matter can become. To have one form is *ipso facto* to be deprived of the opposite form. The substrate neither comes into being nor passes away; it is always in existence and is free of nonbeing.

Privation refers to nonbeing in the sense of the absence of a particular form.[59] One may say that a thing comes into being from its privation, but not from naked privation, only from privation in a substrate. A new thing comes into being from that which it is potentially but not actually.

Azriel transforms privation into a mystical category. A hundred years earlier, the philosopher Abraham bar Hiyya had written: "When it arose in the pure [divine] thought to actualize [form and matter], He removed *efes* from them and attached form to matter."[60] Here it is already difficult to recognize Aristotelian privation. For Azriel *efes* represents the entirety of potential forms that can inhere in matter, each one "invisible until its moment of innovation." New forms emerge as a pool spreads out from a spring.[61] Reading his sources through the eyes of a Neoplatonic mystic, Azriel misunderstood them creatively. On the one hand, as in the actual Aristotelian theory, the transformation of matter is traced back to the privation of the particular new form. On the other hand, change is linked with the concept of mystical nothingness, out of which all creation emerges. As matter adopts new forms, it passes through the divine nothing; thus the world is constantly renewed. An explicit formulation appears in the teaching of Joseph ben Shalom Ashkenazi (early fourteenth century), who speaks of the "stripping away of form and its privation, resulting from the power of *ayin*." "Being constructs, while *ayin*, which is privation, destroys."[62] In every change of form—in each gap of existence—the abyss of nothingness is crossed and becomes visible for a fleeting moment.

V

Contemplation enables one to uncover this depth of being by retracing the individual words of prayer. Azriel counsels: "You should know that one who prays must push aside every hindrance and obstruction and restore each word to its nothingness *[afisato]*. This is the meaning of *efes*." A true prayer is one in which "we have directed the words to the nothingness of the word *[efes davar]*."[63] Though humans "walk in the multiplicity" of the material world, "one who ascends from the form of forms to the root of roots must gather the multiplicity, . . . for the root extends through every form that arises from it at any time. When the forms are destroyed, the root is not destroyed."[64]

At the deepest levels of divinity, all opposites and distinctions vanish, overwhelmed by oneness. Azriel describes this undifferentiated state in language influenced by John Scotus or other Neoplatonists who speak of *indistinctio* and *indifferentia*. Scotus had written that God "is the circuit of all things that have or do not have being . . . and that seem contrary or opposite to Him. . . . He gathers and composes them all with an ineffably beautiful harmony into a single concord." [65] Azriel speaks of "the complete undifferentiation *[hashva'ah gemurah]* in the perfect changeless oneness." *Ein Sof* "is undifferentiated by anything *[shaveh la-kol]*, and everything unites in its undifferentiation *[hashva'ato]*, . . . for all is undifferentiated *[shaveh]* in it." [66] Paraphrasing another Neoplatonic formula, Azriel insists that it is not enough to believe "that God is more than all and that there is nothing outside of Him." If one does not also believe "that He is *shaveh la-kol,* . . . one detracts from God's power . . . by not acknowledging this essential point: that He is both openly and secretly undifferentiated by *ayin* or *yesh* without distinction. He is in a state of simplicity and total undifferentiation, that is, oneness." [67] The Infinite is neither this nor that, "neither *yesh* nor *ayin.*" [68]

The mystic must assimilate to the divine undifferentiation *(hashva'ah)* and manifest complete equanimity *(hishtavvut).* According to a tradition cited by Isaac of Akko, indifference to praise or blame is a prerequisite for "linking your thought" with God. Here the kabbalists drew upon Bahya ibn Paquda and Sufi teaching, transforming the Cynic and Stoic moral ideals of *ataraxia* and *apatheia* into mystical goals. [69]

While God's undifferentiation is reflected in human equanimity, the divine incomprehensibility is mirrored by a contemplative "unknowing." David ben Judah he-Hasid describes this as "forgetting":

The Cause of Causes . . . is a place to which forgetting and oblivion pertain. . . . Why? Because concerning all the levels and sources [the *sefirot],* one can search out their reality from the depth of supernal wisdom. From there it is possible to understand one thing from another. However, concerning the Cause of Causes, there is no aspect anywhere to search or probe; nothing can be known of It, for It is hidden and concealed in the mystery of absolute nothingness *[ha-ayin ve-ha-efes].* Therefore forgetting pertains to the comprehension of this place. So open your eyes and see this great, awesome secret. Happy is one whose eyes shine from this secret, in this world and the world that is coming! [70]

The *sefirot* are stages of contemplative ascent; each one serves as an object and focus of mystical search. In tracing the reality of each *sefirah,* the mystic uncovers layers of being within himself and throughout the cosmos. This is the knowledge that the kabbalist strives for, supernal wisdom. However, there is a higher level, a deeper realm, beyond this step-by-step approach. At the ultimate stage the kabbalist no longer differentiates one thing from another. Conceptual thought, with all its distinctions and connections, dissolves. Ezra and Azriel of Gerona call the highest *sefirah* "the annihilation of thought" *(afisat ha-mahashavah):* "The ancient *hasidim* elevated their thought to its source. They would recite the *mitsvot* and the *devarim*,[71] and through this recitation and the cleaving of [their] thought [to the divine], the *devarim* were blessed and increased, receiving an influx of emanation from the annihilation of thought. This can be compared to one who opens a pool of water, which then spreads in all directions."

"Thought . . . rises to contemplate its own innerness until its power of comprehension is annihilated."[72] Here the mystic cannot grasp for knowledge; rather, he imbibes from the source to which he is joined. In the words of Isaac the Blind, "The inner, subtle essences can be contemplated only by sucking, . . . not by knowing."[73]

Ayin cannot be known. If one searches too eagerly and pursues it, he will be overtaken by it, sucked in by the vortex of nothingness. Ezra of Gerona warns: "Thought cannot ascend higher than its source [the *sefirah* of Wisdom]. Whoever dares to contemplate that to which thought cannot extend or ascend will suffer one of two consequences: either he will confuse his mind and destroy his body or, because of his mental obsession to grasp what he cannot, his soul will ascend and be severed [from the body] and return to her root."[74]

Here the return to the source is viewed as a danger and a negative experience, though Ezra's colleague, Azriel, is aware of a positive return, characteristic of Neoplatonic mysticism. He explains that when the priest offers a sacrifice, his soul ascends "and returns to her root, whence she was taken."[75] Similarly, Isaac of Akko notes that *"Ein Sof . . .* surrounds everything, and this [rational] soul will cleave to *Ein Sof,* becoming total and universal. Having been individual, imprisoned in her palace, she will become universal, in accord with her original nature."[76]

Devequt ("cleaving" to God) was the primary goal in early Kabbalah. Isaac the Blind is reported to have said, "The essence of the service of the enlightened and of those who contemplate His name is 'Cleave to Him' [Deuteronomy 13:5]."[77] Isaac of Akko balances the positive and negative aspects of the experience of return. He describes *devequt* as "pouring a jug of water into a flowing spring, so that all becomes one";

yet he warns his reader not to sink in the ocean of the highest *sefirah:* "The endeavor should be to contemplate but to escape drowning. . . . Your soul shall indeed see the divine light and cleave to it while dwelling in her palace." [78] A Hasidic mystic combines the motifs of the root and the ocean: "The branch returns to its root and is unified with it. The root is *Ein Sof;* thus the branch too is *Ein Sof,* for its [independent] existence is annihilated, like a single drop that falls into the ocean. . . . It is impossible to recognize it as a separate entity." [79]

In Kabbalah the theme of returning pertains not only to the individual mystic but to the entire realm of the *sefirot,* in accord with the Neoplatonic principle that spiritual entities tend to ascend to their source. The essences of the *sefirot* exist primordially,[80] and many kabbalists would agree with Moses de León: "From her *[Keter]* they [the *sefirot*] emerged; to her they will return." [81] At the culmination of cosmic history, all things return to God. Moses Nahmanides describes the great Jubilee, "when the Will reverses itself, restoring all things to their original essence, as someone drawing in his breath, . . . [upon which they] will return to . . . absolute nothingness *[ha-afisah ha-muhletet]*." [82] David ben Judah he-Hasid concurs: *Keter* "absorbs and swallows all the levels *[sefirot]* and everything that exists in the year of . . . the great Jubilee." [83]

For various thirteenth-century kabbalists the return is an immediate goal of prayer and meditation. In a text that appears to stem from Gerona, we hear about "those who contemplate and unify the great Name, stirring the fire on the altar of their hearts. By means of [the mystic's] pure thought, all the *sefirot* are unified and linked to one another until they are drawn to the source of the endlessly sublime flame." [84] In a commentary on the *Shema* we read: "One should intend, as it were, to cause all of them [the lower nine *sefirot*] to enter *Keter,* whence they emanated." [85]

Ezra of Gerona teaches that the *sefirot* were uprooted from their hidden preexistence and transplanted into the present pattern of emanation.[86] They strive to return, but the human task, according to him, is to counteract this upward tendency so as to ensure the continued flow of blessing toward the lower worlds. "Their desire and intention is to ascend and cleave to the place from which they suck. Therefore our sages established the [prayers of] blessing, sanctification and union in order to emanate and draw forth the source of life to the other *sefirot*." [87]

Contemplative prayer aligns the *sefirot* and orients them toward the world. So does righteous action, whereas human evil threatens to force their return and removal. In this context Ezra cites Isaiah 57:1: "Because of evil, the *tsaddiq* is taken away [*ne'esaf,* literally: "gathered"]." [88] The *tsaddiq* ("righteous one") is understood as referring to the ninth *sefirah*, which includes the emanation of all the preceding *sefirot,* from *Keter* to *Malkhut.*

The vital mythical role played by human beings in the functioning of the divine world is characteristic of Kabbalah. Joseph Gikatilla is one of many who promote such mystical activism:

The attribute [*middah*] of *Tsaddiq* stands gazing out at humanity. When he sees human beings engaged in Torah and *mitsvot*—humans who want to purify themselves, to conduct themselves in purity, then the measure [*middah*] of *Tsaddiq* expands and broadens, filling itself with all kinds of flowing emanation from above, to pour out on *Adonai* [*Malkhut,* the last *sefirah*], in order to give a good reward to those holding fast to Torah and *mitsvot* and purifying themselves. Thus the entire world is blessed by means of those *tsaddiqim* [righteous ones]. The *middah* of *Adonai* is likewise blessed through them. . . . If, God forbid, humans defile themselves by moving far away from Torah and *mitsvot,* by perpetrating evil, injustice and violence, then *Tsaddiq* stands to gaze at what they have done. And when he sees . . . he gathers and contracts himself and ascends higher and higher. Then all the channels and flows are interrupted, and *Adonai* is left as a dry and empty land, lacking all good. This is the secret meaning of "Because of evil, *Tsaddiq* is gathered." . . . One who understands this secret will understand the great power a human has to build and to destroy. Now come and see the great power of the righteous who hold fast to Torah and *mitsvot:* they have the power to join all the *sefirot.*[89]

The continuity of emanation is dependent on human righteousness. Several kabbalists advance a precise theory of correspondence between individual *mitsvot,* which perfect the human body, and the *sefirot,* the divine "limbs." Joseph of Hamadan speaks of "limb strengthening limb" (*ever mahaziq ever*), "which means that when one's limbs are complete, and one maintains all the limbs of the Torah, namely, the 613 *mitsvot,* one thereby maintains all the limbs of the chariot [the *sefirot*] and strengthens them." [90] In *Sefer ha-Yihud,* written toward the end of the thirteenth century in Joseph's circle, the limb imagery appears in the context of the return to nothingness.

When a human being below blemishes one of his limbs [by not performing a specific *mitsvah*], . . . it is as if he cuts the corresponding limb [*sefirah*] above. The meaning of this cutting is that the supernal limb is cut, contracted and gathered into the depths of being, called *ayin*. It is as if that limb is missing above. When the form of a human being is perfect below, it causes perfection above. In the same manner, the impurity of a limb below causes its paradigm above to be gathered into the depths of nothingness *['imqei ha-ayin]*, thereby blemishing the supernal form, as it is written: "Because of evil, the *Tsaddiq* is taken away," literally![91]

The correlation between human sin and the negative aspect of the return is formulated concisely by David ben Abraham ha-Lavan: "One who sins returns the attributes to *ayin,* to the primordial world, to their original state of being, and they no longer emanate goodness down to the lower world."[92] For this kabbalist the depths of nothingness are a danger lurking behind the return. "If, God forbid, she [the universal soul] were to return to the depths of nothingness, to her original world, the powers [of all human souls] would be rendered void."[93] In the aftermath of the cosmic return, the infinite nature of God would be all that is, as it originally was. "The cause that has no cause actualizes *yesh* from *ayin* and acts through the word. If all the powers were to return to *ayin,* then the Primordial One, the Cause of all, would stand in Its unity in the depths of nothingness, in undifferentiated oneness, blessed be He and blessed be His name."[94]

Typically, the Jewish mystic cannot resist appending a personal formula to the divine—even when the object of his contemplation is undifferentiated oneness concealed in the depths of *ayin*. Lest the divine personality dissolve in mystification, the kabbalist implores God to emerge and manifest. "Out of the depths I call you, *YHVH.*" Mystically understood, this verse from Psalms (130:1) describes a human cry not from one's own state of despair but to the divine depths in which God lies hiding, from which the mystic calls God forth.[95] The mystical invocation of the depths is eminently practical. People desperately need the resources of *ayin;* so by reaching for it, one can alleviate suffering. "Human beings must quickly grasp this *sefirah* to secure healing for every trouble and malady, as it is written: 'I lift my eyes to the mountains; my help comes from *ayin.*' "[96]

VI

In eighteenth-century Hasidism the kabbalistic material is recast and psychologized; now the experiential aspect of *ayin* becomes prominent.

The emphasis is no longer on the *sefirot,* the inner workings of divinity, but on how to perceive the world mystically and how to transform the ego. Dov Baer, the *Maggid* ("preacher") of Mezritch, encourages his followers to permute *aniy* ("I") into *ayin,* to dissolve the separate ego in nothingness.[97] The dissolution is ultimately not a destructive but a dialectical and creative process.

The kabbalists refer occasionally to "the annihilation of thought" and a state of "forgetting" that overwhelm the mystic as he approaches *ayin.* The *Maggid* elaborates, describing how one arrives at the gate of *ayin* and enters.[98] The conceptual dimension of *ayin* recedes, as theosophical processes are translated into psychological reality.

One must think of oneself as *ayin* and forget oneself totally. . . . Then one can transcend time, rising to the world of thought, where all is equal: life and death, ocean and dry land. . . . Such is not the case when one is attached to the material nature of this world. . . . If one thinks of oneself as something *[yesh],* . . . then God cannot clothe Himself in him, for God is infinite. No vessel can contain God, unless one thinks of oneself as *ayin.*[99]

One must shed the illusion of being separate from God. There is of course a danger that the breakthrough to *ayin* will generate megalomania. Perhaps that is why the *Maggid* emphasizes the link between *ayin* and humility. Nothingness has an ethical and interpersonal dimension: it is a prerequisite for intimacy. "One cannot bind himself to his fellow human being unless he makes himself small and considers himself as *ayin* compared to his fellow."[100] The *Maggid* charts a progression from awe to humility and finally to *ayin.* To defend an independent sense of self is a sign of false pride; the most profound humility is the consciousness of *ayin.*

The essence of the worship of God and of all the *mitsvot* is to attain the state of humility, namely, . . . to understand that all one's physical and mental powers and one's essential being are dependent on the divine elements within. One is simply a channel for the divine attributes. One attains such humility through the awe of God's vastness, through realizing that "there is no place empty of Him" [*Tiqqunei Zohar* 57]. Then one comes to the state of *ayin,* which is the state of humility. . . . One has no independent self and is contained, as it were, in the Creator, blessed be He. . . . This is the meaning of the verse [Exodus 3:6]: "Moses hid his face, for he was in awe. . . ." Through his experience of awe, Moses attained the hiding of his face, that is, he perceived no independent self. Everything was part of divinity![101]

Moses surpassed Abraham, who, in saying "I am dust and ashes" (Genesis 18:27), still claimed a certain degree of existence. By posing the question: "What are we?" (Exodus 16:7), Moses demonstrated that "he did not consider himself to be even dust!" [102]

The kabbalists had taught that *ayin* is the only name appropriate for God. For the *Maggid, ayin* is the only state of mind appropriate for one who seeks to become a divine vessel. In "the annihilation of the intellect" distinctions vanish: "All is equal." [103] Emptying himself, the mystic makes room for an infusion of divine wisdom from beyond the normal borders of consciousness. "One must leave intellect and mind to reach the fence of nothingness. Afterwards, 'wisdom comes into being out of nothingness.' " [104]

The historical exodus from Egypt is interpreted as a paradigm of the liberation of consciousness from narrowness. "This is the meaning of the redemption from Egypt *[mitsrayim]*. As long as our intellect is concerned with our selves, situated within the gate of being, it is contracted and narrow *[metsarim]*, but when we come to the root it expands." [105] Normally, God is contracted in human thought, which thinks divine thought but in a constricted mode. The annihilation of thought, of the thinking subject, liberates the divine element that thinks within and leads it back to its source. New letters from the divine mind then flow into the human mind, where they are defined by human intellect. The immersion in nothingness does not induce a blank stare; it engenders new mental life through a rhythm of annihilation and thinking. "One [should] turn away from that [prior] object [of thought] totally to the place called nothingness, and then a new topic comes to mind. Thus transformation comes about only by passing through nothingness." In the words of the *Maggid*'s disciple, Levi Yitshaq of Berditchev, "When one attains the level of . . . gazing at *ayin,* one's intellect is annihilated. . . . Afterwards, when one returns to the intellect, it is filled with emanation." [106]

The creative pool of nothingness is described as the "preconscious" *(qadmut ha-sekhel),* that which precedes, surpasses and inspires both language and thought. "Thought requires the preconscious, which rouses thought to think. This preconscious cannot be grasped. . . . Thought is contained in letters, which are vessels, while the preconscious is beyond the letters, beyond the capacity of the vessels. This is the meaning of: 'Wisdom comes into being out of nothingness.' " [107]

The goal of contemplation is to pass beyond discursive thought, and this goal was bound to conflict with the traditional Jewish value of Torah study. The relative neglect of book learning in early Hasidism may be due, in part, to just such a conflict, though social factors contributed a great deal. The annihilation of self would seem to be incompatible also with teaching Torah, but here the *Maggid* offers advice: "I will teach you the best way to say Torah: not sensing oneself at all, only as an ear listening to how the world of speech *[Shekhinah]* speaks through him. One is not himself the speaker. As soon as one begins to hear his own words, he should stop." The student of the *Maggid* who cites this teaching adds a reminiscence:

Several times when he opened his mouth to speak words of Torah, it seemed to everyone as if he were not in this world at all. The *Shekhinah* was speaking out of his throat! I saw this with my own eyes. Sometimes, even in the middle of a subject or the middle of a word, he would pause and linger for a while. This all shows that one who is enlightened has to wait for knowledge; then speech comes forth conveying that knowledge.[108]

Here we encounter the phenomenon of automatic speech—the mystic serving as a mouthpiece for *Shekhinah,* the divine presence. Another witness reports: "I have seen great *tsaddiqim* who were joining themselves to the higher worlds and were stripped of bodily garments—and the *Shekhinah* rested upon them and spoke out of their throats. Their mouths spoke prophecies and told of the future. Afterwards those *tsaddiqim* themselves did not know what they had said because they had been joined to the higher worlds and the *Shekhinah* had been speaking out of their throats." [109]

Such a theory has social consequences; the preacher should not fear criticism because, like a prophet, he is transmitting God's word.

"Proclaim with full throat, do not hold back; like a *shofar* [ram's horn] raise your voice!" [Isaiah 58:1]. . . . One who preaches for the sake of heaven must consider that the intellect and the sermon are not his; rather he is as dead as a trampled corpse, and all is from God, may His name be blessed. Therefore one should not hold back the moral message nor fear anyone, for one is really like a *shofar* that lets the sound in and lets it out. . . . God is putting into his mind the words and the moral message that he is delivering to the congregation; so each word should feel like burning fire and he should feel compelled to let them all out. Otherwise, he is like a prophet who suppresses his prophecy.[110]

By dissolving the separate sense of self, *ayin* reveals the divine source of both speech and thought. "Arriving at the gate of *ayin,* one forgets his existence altogether. . . . All his speech is a vessel for the supernal word, as it were, namely, for the combinations of the supernal letters. The word emanates from the higher worlds and [words] are cast into his mouth."[111] "When one is *ayin,* his thought is the world of thought [the *sefirah* of *Binah*] and his speech is the world of speech *[Shekhinah]*. . . . When one arrives at *ayin,* he comprehends that 'wisdom comes into being out of *ayin*' and that the worlds of thought and speech speak through him." "One is simply like a *shofar,* emitting whatever sound is blown into it. If the blower were to remove himself, the *shofar* would produce no sound; so, when God is absent, one cannot speak or think."[112]

Hasidic prayer provides a context for such an experience. The mystic's only active role is the decision to pray and the effort to maintain the clarity essential for conveying divine energy.

The one in awe merely activates the will, for he wills to pray, but the praise is not his. . . . One who merits this level is nothing but a channel through whom are conducted words from on high. This person merely opens his mouth. . . . The essential condition for prayer is that one be clean from all dross, so that the voice from above not be corporealized in his voice. Everyone can merit this level. . . . Their voice is the voice of *Shekhinah,* as it were; they are simply vessels.[113]

In such a state the subject and the object of prayer are one and the same. One "worships God with God." God becomes like a high priest, serving Himself through human prayer.[114] In proclaiming the oneness of God ("Hear O Israel, *YHVH* our God, *YHVH* is one" [Deuteronomy 6:4]), the *hasid* "should intend that there is nothing in the world but the blessed holy One. . . . You should consider yourself to be absolute nothingness. Your essence is only the soul within, part of God above. Thus only God is! This is the meaning of 'one.' "[115]

Self-consciousness during prayer, even the thought of one's own devotion, dilutes the experience. "The body should be God's house, for one should pray with all his strength until he is stripped of corporeality and forgets his self; everything is the vitality of God. All of one's thoughts should be focused on God, and one should not be the least bit aware of the intense devotion of his prayer, for if one is, he is aware of his self."[116]

The contemplative union attained by the mystic is fragile and could be shattered even by the multiplicity of letters on the page of the prayer book. Initially the sight of the letters may enhance the experience of prayer, "but when one is cleaving to the upper world, it is better to close one's eyes, so that the sight will not undo his communion." According to one student of the *Maggid,* at the climax of contemplation, one sees all the words of prayer merging into a single point.[117]

Ideally such unitive consciousness extends beyond prayer. For the mystic who is aware of the pervasive immanence of God, all activity is divine activity. "Whatever one does, God is doing it."[118] Such selfless action reunites the physical world with its divine source. "When the *tsaddiq* has the attribute of surrender, then the divine portion within him performs the action. Thus everything is from God: decree and revocation. The *tsaddiq* is simply the throne and the palace for God's name. Since God clothes His presence and portion in the *tsaddiq,* the *tsaddiq* can act and bind the worlds to their root."[119]

In the mystic's gaze the world no longer appears as essentially distinct from God. "If we perceive the world as existing [independently], that is merely an illusion." In the Habad school of Hasidism, acosmism becomes a fundamental teaching: "This is the foundation of the entire Torah: that *yesh* [the apparent "somethingness" of the world] be annihilated into *ayin.*"[120] "The purpose of the creation of the worlds from *ayin* to *yesh* was that they be transformed from *yesh* to *ayin.*"[121] This transformation is realized through contemplative action.

It is stated in the *Gemara [Ketubbot* 5a]: "The deeds of the righteous are greater than the creation of heaven and earth." This means that the creation of heaven and earth was *yesh me-ayin* ["something from nothing"], while the righteous transform *yesh* back into *ayin.* In everything they do, even physical acts such as eating, they raise the holy sparks, from the food or any other object. They thus transform *yesh* into *ayin.* As our rabbis have said *[Ta'anit* 25a]: "The latter miracle is greater than the former!"[122]

The mystical perspective is neither nihilistic nor anarchic. Matter is neither destroyed nor negated but rather enlivened and revitalized. The awareness that divine energy underlies material existence increases the flow from the source *(ayin)* to its manifestation *(yesh).*

When one gazes at an object, one brings blessing to it. For contemplating that object, one knows that it is . . . really absolutely nothing without divinity permeating it. . . . By means of this contemplation, one draws greater vitality to that object from divinity, from the source of life, since one binds that thing to absolute *ayin,* from which all beings have been hewn from *ayin* to *yesh.* . . . On the other hand, . . . if one looks at that object . . . and makes it into a separate thing, . . . by his look that thing is cut off from its divine root and vitality.

Underneath it all, God is the only "thing," the only existent. "Apart from Him, all are considered nothing and chaos." The world, though, is allowed to enjoy the illusion of separate existence, so that it not lie utterly passive in the pool of *ayin.*

If the material world were constantly attached to the Creator without any forgetting, the creatures' existence would be nullified, [since] they would be attached to the root, to *ayin.* Thus they would do nothing, considering themselves to be *ayin.* So there had to be a breaking [of the vessels], which brought about forgetting the root. Everyone could then lift his hand and act. Afterwards, through Torah and prayer, they attach themselves to the root, to *ayin* . . . and thereby raise the sparks of the material world, . . . bringing pleasure to God. Such pleasure is greater than constant pleasure—as when a father who has not seen his son for a long time is reunited with him: the father is more overjoyed than if the son had been with him always. The son too, having not seen his father for such a long time, has greater desire and yearns all the more to be together with him.[123]

In Lurianic Kabbalah the image of the breaking of the vessels *[shevirat ha-kelim]* pertains to a flaw in the flow of emanation in the upper worlds; here the *Maggid* psychologizes it to explain the gap that allows for the human sense of self. This interpretive strategy is typical of the *Maggid:* "I teach the world to understand that all the things described in the book *Ets Hayyim* pertain also to this world and to the human being."[124] According to Luria, *shevirat ha-kelim* is preceded by *tsimtsum,* the divine "contraction" that enables the world to occupy space and time. "Without *tsimtsum,*" writes the *Maggid,* "all would be the simple oneness of the Infinite": "It is a great act of grace . . . that God contracts His *Shekhinah* and radiates His light to the worlds according to the power of the recipients. . . . Otherwise, the existence of the worlds would be nullified by the brilliance of the light and they would turn into *ayin.*"[125]

The mystic is acutely aware of the gap that allows for separate existence. She knows that attachment to self, to one's own will, prevents a bridging of that gap and blocks the path of return. The mere assertion of human will is incompatible with *ayin,* which "does not desire anything."[126] Only by following the lead of the soul, says the *Maggid,* can one enter the gate of nothingness. "How can a human being be in the state of *ayin?* If one does only that which pertains to the soul, one is in *ayin,* for the soul is something no one comprehends." The soul shares in the incomprehensibility of *ayin,* "that which thought cannot grasp." In the words of Moses de León, the soul "stands in the status of nothing-ness."[127]

World, mind, and self dissolve momentarily in *ayin* and then ree-merge. Every object, every thought is revealed as *ayin*'s epiphany. *Ayin* is not the goal in itself; it is the moment of transformation from being through nonbeing to new being. The *Maggid* conveys this thought with the image of a seed that disintegrates before sprouting. Annihilation is a natural process engendering new life. "When one sows a single seed, it cannot sprout and produce many seeds until its existence is nullified. Then it is raised to its root and can receive more than a single dimension of its existence. There in its root the seed itself becomes the source of many seeds."[128]

Ayin is the root of all things, and "when one brings anything to its root, one can transform it." "First [each thing] must arrive at the level of *ayin*; only then can it become something else." Nothingness embraces all potentiality. The *Maggid* identifies *ayin* with divine wisdom, which is also *hyle* (primordial matter)—capable of assuming any form. *Ayin* "strips off one form and puts on another." "Transformation is possible only through . . . *ayin*."[129]

Every birth must navigate the depths of *ayin*, as when a chick emerges from an egg: for a moment "it is neither chick nor egg."[130] Human rebirth is also engendered in *ayin*. "When one brings oneself to one's root, namely to *ayin* . . . one's attributes, such as love and awe, can be transformed and focused solely on the divine." As long as the ego refuses to acknowledge its source, to participate in the divine, it is mistaking its part for the all and laying false claim to that which cannot be grasped. In the words of Menahem Mendel of Kotsk, "The I is a thief in hid-ing."[131] When this apparently separate self is *ayin*ized, the effect is not total extinction but the emergence of a new form, a more perfectly human image of the divine. Only when "one's existence is nullified . . . is one called 'human.' "[132]

Ayin is a window on the oneness that underlies and undermines the manifold appearance of the world. The ten thousand things are not as independent or fragmented as they seem. There is an invisible matrix, a swirl that generates and recycles being. One who ventures into this depth must be prepared to surrender what he knows and is, what he knew and was. The ego cannot abide *ayin*; you cannot wallow in nothingness. In *ayin*, for an eternal moment, boundaries disappear. *Ayin*'s "no" clears everything away, making room for a new "yes," a new *yesh*.

Negative theology culminates in *ayin,* dissolving familiar and confining images of God. *Ayin* succeeds in "laying bare the white" of God.[133] This *"Nichts* of the Jews,*"* writes the metaphysical poet Henry Vaughan, exposes "the naked divinity without a cover."[134] One can extend the *via negationis* further and strip even nothingness of its conceptual abstractness. David ben Judah he-Hasid reduces the abstract noun to the simplest negation possible, calling God "No."[135] But *ayin* conveys more than a curt no. It implies the God beyond God, the power that is closer and further than what we call "God." *Ayin* symbolizes the fullness of being that transcends being itself, "the mysterious palace of *ayin,* in which everything dwells."[136] The appearance of things belies their origin, when all was "undifferentiated in the depths of *ayin* . . . like ink concealed in the inkwell, which becomes visible only through the power of the writer who draws it forth with his pen and draws the writing as he wishes."[137] The reality that animates and surpasses all things cannot be captured or named, but by invoking *ayin* the mystic is able to allude to the infinite, to *alef* the ineffable.

NOTES

1. See Steven T. Katz, "Language, Epistemology, and Mysticism," in *Mysticism and Philosophical Analysis,* ed. by Steven T. Katz (New York: Oxford, 1978), 51–54.
2. See David ben Abraham's *Masoret ha-Berit,* ed. by Gershom Scholem, *Qovets 'al yad* n.s. 1 (1936): 31. On Gregory and Eckhart, see Vladimir Lossky, *The Mystical Theology of the Eastern Church* (London: Clarke, 1957), 37; and Scholem, "Schöpfung aus Nichts und Selbstverschränkung Gottes," in *Über einige Grundbegriffe des Judentums* (Frankfurt: Suhrkamp Verlag, 1970), 74.
3. Philo, *Deterius* 160; cf. David Winston, *Philo of Alexandria* (Ramsey, N.J.: Paulist Press, 1981), 132–33.
4. Philo, *Somniis* 1:60.
5. See Winston, "Philo's Doctrine of Free Will," in *Two Treatises of Philo of Alexandria,* ed. by Winston and John Dillon (Chico, Calif.: Scholars Press, 1983), 186–89.
6. Philo, *Heres* 24–30.
7. "The Gospel of Truth," in *The Nag Hammadi Library in English,* ed. by James M. Robinson (San Francisco: Harper and Row, 1981), 38; and Hans Jonas, *The Gnostic Religion* (Boston: Beacon Press, 1963), 287.
8. Hippolytus, *Refutatio Omnium Haeresium* 7:20; see John Whittaker, "Basilides on the Ineffability of God," *Harvard Theological Review* 62 (1969):

367–71. Cf. Augustine, *Christian Doctrine* 1:6: "God should not be said to be ineffable, for when this is said something is said. . . . That which can be called ineffable is not ineffable."

9. Hippolytus, *Refutatio Omnium Haeresium* 7:26; Allogenes, in *The Nag Hammadi Library*, 450–51.

10. Hippolytus, *Refutatio Omnium Haeresium* 7:21–22; see Harry A. Wolfson, *The Philosophy of the Church Fathers* (Cambridge, Mass.: Harvard University Press, 1956), 1:551.

11. See Aristotle, *Metaphysics* 11:6:1062b; Winston, "The Book of Wisdom's Theory of Cosmogony," *History of Religion* 11 (1971): 185–202; Jonathan A. Goldstein, "The Origins of the Doctrine of Creation *ex nihilo*," *Journal of Jewish Studies* 35 (1984): 127–35; and the exchange between Winston and Goldstein in *JJS* 37 (1986): 88–91; 38 (1987): 187–94; Gerhard May, *Schöpfung aus dem Nichts* (Berlin: Walter de Gruyter, 1978).

12. Augustine, *Confessions* 11:7; Theophilus, *To Autolycus* 2:4. See Robert M. Grant, *Miracle and Natural Law in Graeco-Roman and Early Christian Thought* (Amsterdam: North Holland Publishing Company, 1952), 135–52.

13. Maimonides, *The Guide of the Perplexed* 2:25.

14. See *Bereshit Rabba* 1:9; and Samuel Yafeh Ashkenazi, *Yefeh To'ar* ad loc. Jonathan Goldstein claims that in this midrash Rabban Gamaliel II is attacking the theory of creation from primordial matter and defending creation *ex nihilo;* see his article and the exchange with Winston referred to above, n. 11. Cf. Alexander Altmann, *Studies in Religious Philosophy and Mysticism* (Ithaca, N.Y.: Cornell University Press, 1969), 128–29.

15. *Sefer Yetsirah* 2:6. See Yehuda Liebes, "Sefer Yetsirah etsel R. Shelomoh ibn Gabirol u-Ferush ha-Shir Ahavtikh," in *Re'shit ha-Mistiqah ha-Yehudit be-Eiropa,* ed. by Joseph Dan, *Mehqerei Yerushalayim be-Mahashevet Yisra'el* 6:3–4 (1987): 80–82.

16. Aristotle, *Physics* 1:9:192a.

17. Maimonides, *Guide of the Perplexed* 2:25; Joseph Albo, *Sefer ha-'Iqqarim* 1:2. The phrase *yesh me-ayin* appears for the first time at the end of the eleventh century in the anonymous Hebrew paraphrase of Saadia Gaon's *Kitab al-Amanat wa'l-I'tiqadat;* see Ronald C. Kiener in *AJS Review* 11 (1986): 10–12.

18. See Plotinus, *Enneads* 5:3:14; 5:5:13; 6:7:41; 6:9:3–4.

19. See Plotinus, *Enneads* 4:8:1; 6:7:36; 6:9:4.

20. Plotinus, *Enneads* 6:9:11. Gregory of Nyssa writes (*Life of Moses* 2:165): "Every concept that comes from some comprehensible image by an approximate understanding and by guessing at the divine nature constitutes an idol of God and does not proclaim God." Cf. Eckhart, "On Detachment": "Detach yourselves from the image, and unite yourselves to the formless being." In the *Rinzairoku* the ninth-century Zen patriarch I-Hsüan offers this advice: "If you meet the Buddha, kill him!"

21. Plotinus, *Enneads* 6:9:10–11; cf. 6:8:11: "To see the divine as something

external is to be outside of it; to become it is to be most truly in beauty." Cf. Eckhart's report of his mystical journey (cited by C. F. Kelley, *Meister Eckhart on Divine Knowledge* [New Haven: Yale University Press, 1977], vii): "There God-as-other disappears."

22. *Confessions* 13:33.
23. Pseudo-Dionysius, *The Divine Names* 1:1; cf. 4:3.
24. Pseudo-Dionysius, *Mystical Theology* 1:1.
25. John Scotus, *Periphyseon* 634d, 680d–681a; see Donald F. Duclow, "Divine Nothingness and Self-Creation in John Scotus Eriugena," *Journal of Religion* 57 (1977): 110.
26. John Scotus, *Periphyseon* 678c–d, 681a.
27. Scholem, "Schöpfung aus Nichts," 70–71.
28. Maimonides, *Guide of the Perplexed* 1:57. This sense of ambiguity originates in Alexander of Aphrodisias's commentaries on Aristotle; see Wolfson, *Studies in the History of Philosophy and Religion,* ed. by Isadore Twersky and George H. Williams (Cambridge, Mass.: Harvard University Press, 1973), 1:143–69, 455–77.
29. Aquinas, *Summa Theologiae* 1:13:2; cf. *Contra Gentiles* 1:33; Gersonides, *Milhamot Adonai* 3:3; see Wolfson, *Studies* 1:142; 2:195–246.
30. Maimonides, *Guide of the Perplexed* 1:58–59. On silence, cf. the Hermetic prayer quoted earlier, at n. 7, where God is called "ineffable, inexpressible, nameable by silence." Eckhart writes (Josef Quint, ed., *Meister Eckhart: Deutsche Predigten und Traktate* [Munich: Carl Hanser, 1965], 353): "The most beautiful thing that one can express about God is found in the fact that, out of the wisdom of inner treasures, one is able to keep silent about God."
31. Azriel of Gerona, *Perush 'Eser Sefirot,* in Meir ibn Gabbai, *Derekh Emunah* (Warsaw, 1890), 2b: *Ein hassagateinu ki im 'al derekh lo;* cf. Joseph Dan and Ronald C. Kiener, ed. and tr., *The Early Kabbalah* (Mahwah, N.J.: Paulist Press, 1986), 90. In another text Azriel writes similarly: *Yada'ti ki ein hassagato ki im 'al derekh lo, ke-lomar ayin va-afisah, she-ein lo heqer* (ed. Scholem, *Madda'ei ha-Yahadut* 2 [1927]: 231). The divine incomprehensibility leads one kabbalist to call God simply "No" *(lo);* see David ben Judah he-Hasid, *The Book of Mirrors: Sefer Mar'ot ha-Tsove'ot,* ed. by Daniel C. Matt (Chico, Calif.: Scholars Press, 1982), 261.
32. Shem Tov ibn Gaon, "Treatise on the Ten *Sefirot,*" ed. by Scholem, in *Qiryat Sefer* 8 (1931–32): 400–401.
33. Joseph Gikatilla, *Sha'arei Tsedeq* (ed. by Efraim Gottlieb, *Mehqarim be-Sifrut ha-Qabbalah,* ed. by Joseph Hacker [Tel Aviv: Tel Aviv University, 1976]), 140.
34. Solomon ibn Gabirol, *Keter Malkhut* 9:97–101. See Scholem, " 'Iqvotav shel Gevirol be-Qabbalah," in *Me'assef Soferei Erets Yisra'el,* ed. by Aaron Kabak (Tel Aviv: Keren ha-Tarbut, 1940), 167–68; Shlomo Pines, "Ve-Qara el ha-Ayin ve-Nivqa'," *Tarbits* 50 (1981): 339–47; Liebes, "Sefer Yetsirah etsel R. Shelomoh ibn Gabirol," 80–86. The notion that light

emerges from the eye and illuminates the objects of vision was common in medieval science.

35. Liebes, "Sefer Yetsirah etsel R. Shelomoh ibn Gabirol," 82. One cannot rule out the possibility that Gabirol is simply giving poetic expression to the literal sense of *yesh me-ayin;* see Pines, "Ve-Qara el ha-Ayin ve-Nivqa'," 347, n. 32. If so, the kabbalists easily read a more positive, substantive meaning into Gabirol's depiction of *ayin.*

36. Bahya ben Asher on Genesis 1:2; cf. his comment on Deuteronomy 10:20; and Jacob ben Sheshet, *Meshiv Devarim Nekhohim,* ed. by Georges Vajda (Jerusalem: Israel Academy Sciences and Humanities, 1968), 153. For Asher ben David's statement, see Gottlieb, *Ha-Qabbalah be-Khitevei Rabbenu Bahya ben Asher* (Jerusalem: Kiryath Sepher, 1970), 84. For other early versions of the mystical interpretation of Job 28:12, see Ezra of Gerona's letter edited by Scholem in *Sefer Bialik,* ed. by Jacob Fichman (Tel Aviv: Omanut, 1934), 156, where Ezra cites the authority of Isaac the Blind; Ezra's *Commentary on the Song of Songs,* in *Kitevei Ramban,* ed. by Hayyim D. Chavel (Jerusalem: Mosad ha-Rav Kook, 1964), 2:483; Nahmanides, toward the end of his commentary on Job 28. Nahmanides cites both the literal and mystical interpretations of the verse but expresses a reservation concerning the latter: "This is their way [of interpreting] those verses. While the words themselves are most praiseworthy, we do not know whether the context bears such an interpretation. If it is an authentic tradition, we shall accept it *[ve-im qabbalah hi' neqabbel]."* Nahmanides had learned this interpretation from his colleagues but did not receive it from his teacher, Judah ben Yaqar. Isaac the Blind's letter to Nahmanides, in which he accuses his former student Ezra of disclosing kabbalistic traditions, might be one reason for Nahmanides' hesitation; see Scholem in *Sefer Bialik,* 143–46; Moshe Idel, "We Have No Kabbalistic Tradition on This," in *Rabbi Moses Nahmanides (Ramban): Explorations in His Religious and Literary Virtuosity,* ed. by Isadore Twersky (Cambridge, Mass.: Harvard University Press, 1983), 52–73, esp. 57–58. In his commentary on the first verse of Genesis, Nahmanides mingles the exoteric and esoteric meanings of *ex nihilo.*

37. Joseph Gikatilla, *Sha'arei Orah* (Warsaw: Orgelbrand, 1883), 44a–b. In *Sha'arei Tsedeq* (ed. by Gottlieb, *Mehqarim,* 140), Gikatilla says simply: "All its answers are *ayin."* Azriel of Gerona in his *Perush ha-Aggadot* (ed. by Isaiah Tishby, 2d ed. [Jerusalem: Magnes, 1983], 103) writes: "There, questioner and questioned stand still." Cf. Moses de León, *Sheqel ha-Qodesh,* ed. by A. W. Greenup (London, 1911), 7; idem, *Sod 'Eser Sefirot Belimah,* ed. by Scholem, *Qovets 'al Yad,* n.s. 8 (1975), 374; and Shim'on Labi, *Ketem Paz* (Jerusalem: Ahavat Shalom, 1981), 1:91a: "Concerning everything that cannot be grasped, its question is its answer."

38. See Daniel Matt, "The Mystic and the *Mitsvot,*" in *Jewish Spirituality: From the Bible through the Middle Ages,* ed. by Arthur Green (New York: Crossroad, 1986), 396.

39. Isaac of Akko, *Otsar Hayyim,* cited by Amos Goldreich in his edition of

Isaac's *Me'irat Einayim* (Jerusalem: Hebrew University, 1981), 411, 414; see Matt, "The Mystic and the *Mitsvot,*" 374; cf. *Tiqqunei Zohar* 70, 131b; Scholem, *Kabbalah* (Jerusalem: *Keter,* 1974), 90.

40. Shem Tov ibn Gaon, "Treatise on the Ten *Sefirot,*" *Qiryat Sefer* 8 (1931– 32): 401. On the juxtaposition of rebellion and faith, cf. the Hebrew translation of Judah Halevi, *Kuzari* 1:77; Azriel of Gerona, *Perush 'Eser Sefirot,* 2b; Dan and Kiener, *The Early Kabbalah,* 90; Azriel, *Derekh ha-Emunah ve-Derekh ha-Kefirah,* ed. by Scholem, "Seridim Hadashim mi-Kitevei R. Azri'el mi-Gerona," in *Sefer Zikkaron le-Asher Gulak ve-li-Shemu'el Klein,* ed. by Simhah Assaf and Scholem (Jerusalem: Hebrew University, 1942), 207, 211; Ezra of Gerona, in Azriel, *Perush ha-Aggadot,* 41, variants to lines 9–11.

41. A cryptic remark on *ayin* is attributed to Abraham ben Isaac of Narbonne (1110–1179), who was the teacher and then father-in-law of Abraham ben David of Posquieres and the grandfather of Isaac the Blind. This remark is cited by Shem Tov ibn Gaon in his *Baddei ha-Aron;* see Scholem, *Ursprung und Anfänge der Kabbala* (Berlin: Walter de Gruyter, 1962), 178. Isaac the Blind is called *avi ha-qabbalah* by Bahya ben Asher in his commentary to Genesis 32:10.

42. Cf. *Sefer Yetsirah* 2:6; above, at n. 15; Azriel of Gerona, *Perush ha-Aggadot,* 107; Zohar 3:2a; David ben Judah he-Hasid, *The Book of Mirrors: Sefer Mar'ot ha-Tsove'ot,* introduction, 25, n. 183.

43. Moses de León, *Sheqel ha-Qodesh,* 23–24; cf. idem, *Sod 'Eser Sefirot Belimah,* 374. Azriel of Gerona, in *Perush ha-Aggadot,* 107, also cites the verse from Ecclesiastes but does not mention the human soul; cf. Asher ben David, cited by Idel, in *Mehqerei Yerushalayim be-Mahashevet Yisra'el* 3:1– 2 (1984): 27, n. 98; Jacob ben Sheshet, *Ha-Emunah ve-ha-Bittahon,* chapter 12, in *Kitevei Ramban* 2:385; Hanokh Zundel, *'Anaf Yosef* on *Tanhuma, Emor,* 15. (For this last reference I thank Dr. Ze'ev Gries.) John Scotus taught that the human intellect, "while it bursts out into various forms comprehensible to the senses, does not abandon the always incomprehensible condition of its nature" (*Periphyseon* 633c). Human self-ignorance is a sign of the *imago Dei:* "If in any way it could understand what it is, it would necessarily deviate from the likeness of its Creator" (*Periphyseon* 585b–c).

44. Moses de León, *Sheqel ha-Qodesh,* 111.

45. Gikatilla, *Sha'arei Orah,* 44a–b; cf. Zohar 3:65a–b. On the tip of the *yod,* cf. Talmud, *Menahot* 29a, 34a in a halakhic context.

46. David ben Judah he-Hasid, *The Book of Mirrors: Sefer Mar'ot ha-Tsove'ot,* 279.

47. Zohar 3:26b; see Matt, *Zohar: The Book of Enlightenment* (Ramsey, N.J.: Paulist Press, 1983), 147, 267–68. The Gnostics taught that the aeons (except for *nous*) are ignorant of the hidden God; see *The Gospel of Truth,* in *The Nag Hammadi Library,* 40. On knowledge as aroma, cf. *Shir ha-Shirim Rabbah* 1:20.

48. Ezra of Gerona, *Commentary on the Song of Songs,* in *Kitevei Ramban*

2:494; cf. Ezra's letter in *Sefer Bialik,* 157–58; Azriel of Gerona, *Perush ha-Aggadot,* 110–11; Altmann, *Studies,* 136–39; Gottlieb, *Mehqarim,* 82–83. Ezra draws on Maimonides, *Guide of the Perplexed* 2:13, 26.

49. Ezra's letter in *Sefer Bialik,* 158; cf. his *Commentary on the Song of Songs,* in *Kitevei Ramban* 2:494 (to be corrected according to Gottlieb, *Mehqarim,* 531); Azriel of Gerona, *Perush 'Eser Sefirot,* 3a–b; Dan and Kiener, *The Early Kabbalah,* 94; Shem Tov ibn Gaon, "Treatise on the Ten *Sefirot,*" *Qiryat Sefer* 8 (1931–32): 538; *Qiryat Sefer* 9 (1932–33): 126; Joseph ben Shalom Ashkenazi, *Perush Qabbali li-Vere'shit Rabbah,* ed. by Moshe Hallamish (Jerusalem: Magnes Press, 1985), 77, 209 n.5; Idel, "Ha-Sefirot she-me-'al ha-Sefirot," *Tarbits* 51 (1982): 241–43. "Essences" *(havayot)* is modeled on Arabic *huwiyyah,* Greek *ousia* or Latin *essentiae.*

50. On *Keter* as *mahut,* see Azriel of Gerona's treatise, ed. by Scholem, *Madda'ei ha-Yahadut* 2 (1927): 231. In *Sha'arei Tsedeq* (ed. by Gottlieb, *Mehqarim*), 140–42, Gikatilla contrasts the mystical and literal interpretations of *yesh me-ayin.*

51. *Zohar* 1:15a; see the full passage and commentary in Matt, *Zohar: The Book of Enlightenment,* 49–50, 207–10. Cf. Gabirol's image of the cleaving of *ayin,* above, at n. 34. The same image was applied by thirteenth-century mystics of the *'Iyyun* circle to the primordial ether *(avir qadmon).* In this Zohar passage the aura (or ether, *avira*), symbolizing *ayin,* is broken through. Cf. above, at nn. 15, 42; see Scholem, *Ursprung und Anfänge der Kabbala,* 292–93, 301–33.

52. Moses de León, *Sheqel ha-Qodesh,* 25–26. On the primordial point, see Scholem, *Major Trends in Jewish Mysticism* (New York: Schocken, 1961), 173, 218; idem, in *Tarbits* 2 (1931): 195, 206–7. The Pythagorean Philolaus of Croton (fifth century BCE) suggested that the point is the "first principle leading to magnitude." On *hakkeh mah,* see Asher ben David's wording cited by Tishby in Azriel of Gerona, *Perush ha-Aggadot,* 84, n. 4; cf. Moses de León, *Sod 'Eser Sefirot Belimah,* 375. Asher ben David is also the source for the statement that wisdom "appears to be the first *sefirah*"; see Gottlieb, *Ha-Qabbalah be-Khitevei Rabbenu Bahya ben Asher,* 83; cf. Joseph ben Shalom Ashkenazi, *Commentary on Sefer Yetsirah* (printed under the name of the Rabad), *Sefer Yetsirah* (Jerusalem: Lewin-Epstein, 1965), 1:5.

53. See Moses de León, *Sheqel ha-Qodesh,* 110–11; Jacob ben Sheshet, *Meshiv Devarim Nekhohim,* 113; cf. Azriel of Gerona, *Perush ha-Aggadot,* 84: *koah mah she-efshar li-heyot,* and Tishby's n. 4 on the kabbalistic reinterpretation of *hyle.* On the ether, cf. above, n. 51.

54. Cf. the anonymous Neoplatonic *Liber de Causis,* chapter 11: "The effect is in the cause after the mode of the cause, and the cause is in the effect after the mode of the effect" (*The Book of Causes [Liber de Causis],* tr. Dennis J. Brand [Milwaukee, Wisconsin: Marquette University Press, 1984], 30). This thesis concerning the "first things" is applied by Azriel to being and nothingness. On Azriel's probable knowledge of *Liber de Causis* see Scholem, *Ursprung und Anfänge der Kabbala,* 375.

55. Azriel of Gerona, *Derekh ha-Emunah ve-Derekh ha-Kefirah,* ed. by Scholem, "Seridim Hadashim," 207. Cf. Liebes, "Sefer Yetsirah etsel R. Shelomoh ibn Gabirol," 83.

56. Cf. Eckhart's experiential description of nothingness as the source of God
(cited by Bernard McGinn, "The God beyond God: Theology and Mysticism in the Thought of Meister Eckhart," *Journal of Religion* 61 [1981]:
10): "When the soul comes into the One, entering into pure loss of self, it
finds God as in nothingness. It seemed to a man that he had a dream, a
waking dream, that he became pregnant with nothingness as a woman with
child. In this nothingness God was born. He was the fruit of nothingness;
God was born in nothingness."

57. Azriel of Gerona, *Sod ha-Tefillah,* ed. by Scholem, "Seridim Hadashim,"
215.

58. See, e.g., Judah al-Harizi's Hebrew translation of Maimonides' *Guide of the
Perplexed* 1:17: *ha-efes ha-mugbal.* Samuel ibn Tibbon renders Maimonides' Arabic *'adam ("steresis")* with the Hebrew *he'der.*

59. See Aristotle, *Physics* 1:9, 192a: "Matter accidentally is not, while privation
in its own nature is not; . . . matter is nearly, in a sense, is substance,
while privation in no sense is." On *steresis,* see W. D. Ross, *Aristotle*
(London: Methuen, 1964), 63–66; W. K. C. Guthrie, *A History of Greek
Philosophy,* vol. 6 (Cambridge, U.K.: Cambridge University Press, 1981),
119–24.

60. Abraham bar Hiyya, *Megillat ha-Megalleh,* ed. by Adolf Posnanski (Berlin:
Mekize Nirdamim, 1924), 5; see Scholem, *Ursprung und Anfänge der Kabbala,* 372, n. 120.

61. Azriel of Gerona, *Sod ha-Tefillah,* ed. by Scholem, "Seridim Hadashim,"
215.

62. Joseph ben Shalom Ashkenazi, *Commentary on Sefer Yetsirah,* introduction,
3a; idem, *Perush Qabbali li-Vere'shit Rabbah,* 32; cf. Scholem, *Major
Trends in Jewish Mysticism,* 217.

63. Azriel of Gerona, *Sod ha-Tefillah,* ed. by Scholem, "Seridim Hadashim,"
215; idem, *Commentary on the Prayers,* in Scholem, "The Concept of
Kavvanah in the Early Kabbalah," in *Studies in Jewish Thought,* ed. by
Alfred Jospe (Detroit: Wayne State University Press, 1981), 167.

64. Azriel of Gerona, *Sod ha-Tefillah,* ed. by Scholem, "Seridim Hadashim,"
216; cf. idem, *Perush ha-Aggadot,* 82–83, where Azriel cites the identical
teaching in the name of Plato. Plotinus (*Enneads* 4:3:32) notes that "the
higher soul . . . gathers multiplicity into one. . . . In this way it will not be
[clogged] with multiplicity but light and alone by itself."

65. John Scotus, *Periphyseon* 517b–c. Cf. Meister Eckhart (cited in McGinn,
"The God beyond God," 7): "God is something indistinct, distinguished by
His indistinction."

66. Azriel of Gerona, *Perush 'Eser Sefirot,* 2b; Dan and Kiener, *The Early
Kabbalah,* 90; Azriel, *Commentary on Sefer Yetsirah* (printed under the
name of Nahmanides) 1:7; see the list of passages assembled by Tishby,
Hiqrei Qabbalah u-Sheluhoteha (Jerusalem: Magnes, 1982), 18, 22–23.

John Scotus is apparently the source for both Azriel and Nicholas of Cusa (1401–64), who developed the notion of *coincidentia oppositorum*. Johannes Reuchlin, in *De Arte Cabalistica*, connects Azriel's and Nicholas's terminologies; see Scholem, *Ursprung und Anfänge der Kabbala*, 389. Amos Goldreich has raised the possibility of an Isma'ili source for Azriel's terminology; see his "*Mi-Mishnat Hug ha-'Iyyun: 'Od 'al ha-Meqorot ha-Efshariyyim shel 'Ha-Ahdut ha-Shavah,' "* in *Re'shit ha-Mistiqah ha-Yehudit be-Eiropa*, ed. by Dan, 141–56. Cf. the wording of Shem Tov ibn Gaon, "Treatise on the Ten *Sefirot* (ed. by Scholem, *Qiryat Sefer* 8 [1931–32]: 541): "the undifferentiated oneness that has neither front nor back and in which no opposites can be imagined."

67. Azriel of Gerona, *Derekh ha-Emunah ve-Derekh ha-Kefirah*, ed. by Scholem, "Seridim Hadashim," 208–9. Azriel's wording, "more than all" *(yater 'al ha-kol)*, reflects Scotus' Latin *superesse* and the earlier Greek *hyperousia;* cf. above, at nn. 18, 23. In *Sefer ha-'Iyyun*, whose author(s) were apparently influenced by Azriel, we hear of "the unfathomable and infinite light that is concealed in the excess *[tosefet]* of the hidden darkness." *Tosefet* may be another Hebrew version of *superesse;* see Scholem, "Colours and Their Symbolism in Jewish Tradition and Mysticism," *Diogenes* 108 (1979): 103. For other parallels between Scotus and Azriel, see Gabrielle Sed-Rajna, "L'influence de Jean Scot sur la doctrine du kabbaliste Azriel de Gérone," in *Jean Scot Érigène et l'histoire de la philosophie* (Paris: Editions du Centre National, 1977), 453–63. For evidence that certain early kabbalists knew Latin, see "Seridim Hadashim," 218, where Asher ben David recounts a dream in which he heard a Latin interpretation of a divine name.

68. On this phrase, see Gottlieb, *Ha-Qabbalah be-Khitevei Rabbenu Bahya ben Asher*, 229. Cf. Pseudo-Dionysius, *The Mystical Theology*, 5: "It is . . . not something among what is not, not something among what is." Cf. ibid., 1:1: "In the earnest exercise of mystical contemplation, abandon . . . all nonbeings and all beings; thus you will unknowingly be elevated, as far as possible, to the unity of that beyond being and knowledge." Cf. idem, *The Divine Names* 5:8: "For it is not this but not that." The *Brhadaranyaka Upanishad* (4:5:15) states that the only suitable description of the Absolute is *neti neti* ("not this, not this").

69. See Isaac of Akko, *Me'irat Einayim*, 218; Idel, "*Hitbodedut* as Concentration in Ecstatic Kabbalah," in *Jewish Spirituality*, ed. by Green, 414–15; idem, in *Da'at* 14 (1985): 47–49, 76; Scholem, *Major Trends in Jewish Mysticism*, 96–97; R. J. Zwi Werblowsky, *Joseph Karo: Lawyer and Mystic* (Philadelphia: Jewish Publication Society, 1977), 161–62; Obadyah Maimonides, *The Treatise of the Pool*, ed. by Paul Fenton (London: Octagon Press, 1981), introduction, 63–64.

70. David ben Judah he-Hasid, *The Book of Mirrors: Sefer Mar'ot ha-Tsove'ot*, 227; see my introduction, 21–22. Various mystics describe an experience of forgetting. Plotinus states (*Enneads* 4:3:32): "The higher soul ought to be happy to forget what is has received from the worse soul. . . . The more it

presses on toward the heights, the more it will forget." The ninth-century Sufi Abu Yazid al-Bistami, who develops the notion of *fana* ("passing away") reports: "When He brought me to the brink of divine unity, I divorced myself and betook myself to my Lord, calling upon Him to help me. 'Master,' I cried, 'I beseech Thee as one to whom nothing else remains.' When He recognized the sincerity of my prayer and how I had despaired of myself, the first token that came to me proving that He had answered this prayer was that He caused me to forget myself utterly and to forget all creatures and dominions" (cited by Arthur J. Arberry, *Revelation and Reason in Islam* [London: Allen & Unwin, 1957], 96). The anonymous author of *The Cloud of Unknowing* writes (chapter 5): "You must fashion a cloud of forgetting beneath you, between you and every created thing. . . . Abandon them all beneath the cloud of forgetting." St. John of the Cross counsels (*Collected Works,* tr. Kieran Kavanaugh and Otilio Rodriguez [Washington, D.C.: Institute of Carmelite Studies, 1973], 675): "Forgetful of all, abide in recollection with your Spouse." In a Hasidic text edited in the circle of the *Maggid* of Mezritch (*Shemu'ah Tovah* [Warsaw, 1938], 71b, cited by Rivka Schatz-Uffenheimer, *Ha-Hasidut ke-Mistiqah* [Jerusalem: Magnes Press, 1968], 99), we read: "Arriving at the gate of *ayin,* one forgets his existence altogether."

71. Here *devarim* may refer to the words of prayer or the *sefirot;* see Scholem, *Ursprung und Anfänge der Kabbala,* 268; Tishby, *Perush ha-Aggadot,* 40, n. 11. The word may also be vocalized *dibberim,* referring to the Ten Commandments; see Idel, *Kabbalah: New Perspectives* (New Haven: Yale University Press, 1988), 46.

72. Azriel of Gerona, *Perush ha-Aggadot,* 40, 116. Cf. Ezra of Gerona, *Commentary on the Song of Songs,* in *Kitevei Ramban* 2:494, 526; Ezra's letter, ed. by Scholem, *Sefer Bialik,* 160; Moses de León, *Shushan 'Edut,* ed. by Scholem, *Qovets 'al Yad,* n.s. 8 (1975), 334; Menahem Recanati, *Perush 'al ha-Torah* (Jerusalem: Monzon, 1961), 51b; idem, *Sefer Ta'amei ha-Mitsvot,* ed. by Simhah Lieberman (London: Lieberman, 1962), 13c; and above, at n. 43: "the annihilation of all thoughts." On the *hasidim,* cf. Mishnah, *Berakhot* 5: 1.

73. Isaac the Blind, *Commentary on Sefer Yetsirah,* ed. by Scholem, *Ha-Qabbalah be-Provans* (Jerusalem: Akademon, 1970), appendix, 1, and cf. 9, 13; Scholem, *Ursprung und Anfänge der Kabbala,* 246–47. On the image of sucking, cf. *Sefer ha-Bahir,* ed. by Reuven Margaliot (Jerusalem: Mosad ha-Rav Kook, 1978), par. 177; Ezra of Gerona, *Commentary on the Song of Songs,* in *Kitevei Ramban* 2:485–86, 504–5; Azriel of Gerona, *Perush ha-Aggadot,* 82 (and Tishby's n. 7), 110; Jacob ben Sheshet, *Meshiv Devarim Nekhohim,* 113; Zohar 1:35a, 84b, 183a; 3:166b. Cf. the comment of Isaac of Akko, *Commentary on Sefer Yetsirah* (ed. Scholem, *Qiryat Sefer* 31 [1956]: 383): "No creature can understand them [the hidden paths of wisdom] except through contemplative thought, not through knowing, through the effort of study, but rather through contemplation."

74. Ezra of Gerona, in Azriel of Gerona, *Perush ha-Aggadot,* 39, and variants. Cf. Azriel's note of caution on 104: "One should not probe that which thought cannot grasp *[mah she-ein ha-mahashavah masseget]."* This last phrase is a designation for *Keter,* though it is applied to *Ein Sof* by Isaac the Blind; see his *Commentary on Sefer Yetsirah,* 1; Scholem, *Ursprung und Anfänge der Kabbala,* 238–39; and the passages cited by Tishby, *Perush ha-Aggadot,* 104, n. 6; cf. above, at nn. 15, 36, 42; Moses de León, *Shushan 'Edut,* 347; idem, *Sod 'Eser Sefirot Belimah,* 371; idem, *Sheqel ha-Qodesh,* 4; Recanati, *Perush 'al ha-Torah,* 37d–38a.

75. Azriel of Gerona, *The Mystery of the Sacrifice,* MS Oxford, Christ Church, 198, fol. 12b; see Idel, *Kabbalah: New Perspectives,* 52.

76. Isaac of Akko, *Otsar Hayyim,* MS Moscow-Günzberg 775, fol. 112a; see Gottlieb, *Mehqarim,* 237–38; Idel, *Kabbalah: New Perspectives,* 47–48.

77. Isaac the Blind is cited by Ezra of Gerona, *Commentary on the Song of Songs,* in *Kitevei Ramban* 2:522; cf. Azriel of Gerona, *Perush ha-Aggadot,* 16; Matt, "The Mystic and the *Mitsvot,"* 399–400; Idel, *Kabbalah: New Perspectives,* 35–58.

78. Isaac of Akko, *Otsar Hayyim,* MS Moscow-Günzberg 775, fols. 111a, 161b; see Gottlieb, *Mehqarim,* 237; Idel, *Kabbalah: New Perspectives,* 67; cf. idem, in *Da'at* 14 (1985): 50.

79. Yehiel Mikhel of Zlotshov, *Mayim Rabbim* (Warsaw: A. Schriftgiessen, 1899), 15a. Cf. *Katha Upanishad* 4:15: "As pure water poured into pure becomes like unto it, so does the soul of the discerning sage become [like unto Brahman]." As Idel notes (*Kabbalah: New Perspectives,* 67–70), Sufi and Christian mystics employ the image as well.

80. See above, at n. 49.

81. Moses de León, *Sheqel ha-Qodesh,* 6.

82. Moses Nahmanides, *Commentary on Sefer Yetsirah,* ed. by Scholem, *Qiryat Sefer* 6 (1929–30): 401–2, and n. 5; cf. Scholem, *Ursprung und Anfänge der Kabbala,* 397. This represents a kabbalistic version of the Christian doctrine of *apokatastasis;* cf. the Neoplatonic formula: *restitutio omnium rerum ad integrum;* and John Scotus, *Periphyseon* 696b.

83. David ben Judah he-Hasid, *The Book of Mirrors: Sefer Mar'ot ha-Tsove'ot,* 224; introduction, 33. The image of being swallowed is also applied, both positively and negatively, to mystical experience; see David's interpretation of Numbers 4:20 in *The Book of Mirrors,* 119; and Isaac of Akko's interpretation of the same verse, cited by Gottlieb, *Mehqarim,* 237; cf. Isaac's *Me'irat Einayim,* 189; Moses de León, *Sheqel ha-Qodesh,* 4; Idel, *Kabbalah: New Perspectives,* 70–73; Jonas, *The Gnostic Religion,* 182. St. John of the Cross, in *The Dark Night* 2:6, alludes to Jonah's terrible experience in the belly of the great fish. Shneur Zalman of Lyady writes (*Seder ha-Tefillah* [Warsaw, 1866], 1:26a): "This is the true *devequt:* becoming one substance with God, in whom one is swallowed."

84. See Scholem, "The Concept of *Kavvanah* in the Early Kabbalah," 168; 178, n. 38; Idel, *Kabbalah: New Perspectives,* 53–54; Meir ibn Gabbai, *'Avodat ha-Qodesh,* 2:6, 29a; cf. Isaac the Blind, *Commentary on Sefer Yetsirah,* 6.

85. See Idel, "Ha-Sefirot she-me-'al ha-Sefirot," *Tarbits* 51 (1982): 280.
86. Ezra of Gerona, *Commentary on the Song of Songs,* in *Kitevei Ramban* 2:504. Ezra offers a mystical interpretation of a passage in *Bereshit Rabba* 15:1 concerning the trees of the Garden of Eden: "The Holy One, blessed be He, uprooted them and transplanted them in the Garden of Eden." Nahmanides objects to this midrash in his commentary on Genesis 2:8; cf. Zohar 1:35b, 37a; 2:177a; Moses de León, *Maskiyyot Kesef,* cited by Scholem, in *Tarbits* 3 (1931): 54; Joseph ben Shalom Ashkenazi, *Perush Qabbali li-Vere'shit Rabbah,* 208–9; Recanati, *Perush 'al ha-Torah,* 9d; Idel, *Kabbalah: New Perspectives,* 181–82; Shim'on Labi, *Ketem Paz,* 3a, 76d, 87a, 109a–b, 111a. For the references to *Ketem Paz,* I am grateful to Dr. Boaz Huss.
87. Ezra of Gerona, *Commentary on the Song of Songs,* in *Kitevei Ramban* 2:486; see Idel, *Kabbalah: New Perspectives,* 182. Cf., though, Ezra's description of prayer in 2:494: "The entire structure [of the seven lower *sefirot]* will cleave to, unite with, and ascend to *Ein Sof.*"
88. Ezra of Gerona, *Commentary on the Song of Songs,* in *Kitevei Ramban* 2:504.
89. Joseph Gikatilla, *Sha'arei Orah,* 19a–b.
90. See Matt, "The Mystic and the *Mitsvot,*" 392; 402, n. 56; Idel, *Kabbalah: New Perspectives,* 185.
91. *Sefer ha-Yihud,* MS Milano-Ambrosiana 62, fol. 112b; cf. Recanati, *Commentary on the Torah,* 51b; Idel, "Perush 'Eser Sefirot u-Seridim mi-Ketavim shel R. Yosef ha-Ba mi-Shushan ha-Birah," *'Alei Sefer* 6–7 (1979): 82–84; idem, *Kabbalah: New Perspectives,* 184–85.
92. David ben Abraham ha-Lavan, *Masoret ha-Berit,* 39; cf. David's comment on *ayin* and *yesh,* above, at n. 2.
93. Ibid., 38.
94. Ibid., 31. Cf. Meir ibn Gabbai, *Derekh Emunah,* 16c: "Everything was hidden and concealed in the depths of nothingness." Shim'on Labi refers to *'imqe ha-ayin* frequently in his *Ketem Paz,* often in connection with the mystical interpretation of *Bereshit Rabba* 15:1 or the notion of "undifferentiated oneness"; see above, n. 86; and *Ketem Paz* 1:4a, 27c, 45d, 49b, 72c, 86b, 91b, 92c–d, 138d, 261b, 262c. In kabbalistic literature *Keter* is often referred to as "depth" *('omeq).*
95. See Zohar 2:63b; 3:69b–70a; Gikatilla, *Sha'arei Orah,* 37b–38a, 95a–b. On the conflict between the biblical conception of a personal God and the impersonal Neoplatonic conception, see Scholem, "Das Ringen zwischen dem biblischen Gott und dem Gott Plotins in der alten Kabbala," in *Über einige Grundbegriffe des Judentums,* 9–52. The Zohar (1:72b; 3:288b) enjoys confusing the Jewish Father in Heaven with the Aristotelian Prime Mover: it plays with the divine names *Sibbeta de-Sibbatin* ("The Cause of Causes") and *Saba de-Sabin* ("The Old Man of Old Men").
96. Gikatilla, *Sha'arei Orah,* 103a, citing Psalm 121:1: *Me-ayin yavo 'ezri.* Here again the literal meaning of *ayin,* "where," is exchanged for mystical nothingness; cf. above, at n. 36, concerning Job 28:12: "Wisdom comes

into being out of *ayin*." Cf. the teaching of the disciple of the *Maggid* of Mezritch, Hayyim Haika of Amdur (*Hayyim va-Hesed* [Jerusalem, 1953], 47): "God cannot come to my help unless I bind myself to *ayin*. This is the meaning of 'My help comes from *ayin*.'" Cf. Rumi, *Mathnawi* 6:822: "The whole world has taken the wrong way, for they fear nonexistence, while it is their refuge."

97. See Scholem, *The Messianic Idea in Judaism* (New York: Schocken, 1971), 214. On the kabbalistic roots of this play on words, see Gikatilla, *Sha'arei Orah*, 103a; *Sefer ha-Peli'ah* (Jerusalem, 1976), 14b–c, where *aniy* is a symbol of *Shekhinah*. I am focusing here on the circle of the *Maggid*; on further developments of *ayin* in Hasidism, see Rachel Elior, *The Paradoxical Ascent to God: The Kabbalistic Theosophy of Habad Hasidism* (Albany: SUNY Press, 1993), index, s.v. *ayin, ayin* and *yesh;* idem, *Torat ha-Elohut ba-Dor ha-Sheni shel Hasidut Habad* (Jerusalem: Magnes, 1982), index, s.v. *ayin;* idem, "Between *Yesh* and *Ayin:* The Doctrine of the Zaddik in the Works of Jacob Isaac, the Seer of Lublin," in *Jewish History: Essays in Honour of Chimen Abramsky*, ed. by Ada Rapoport-Albert and Steven Zipperstein (London: Peter Halban, 1988), 393–455; idem, "Yesh ve-Ayin: Defusei Yesod ba-Mahashavah ha-Hasidit," in *Sefer ha-Zikkaron le-Efrayim Gottlieb*, ed. by Amos Goldreich and Michal Oron (Tel Aviv: Tel Aviv University, 1994).

98. Dov Baer, *Maggid Devarav le-Ya'aqov*, ed. by Rivka Schatz-Uffenheimer (Jerusalem: Magnes Press, 1976), 91, 94. Cf. Schatz-Uffenheimer, *Ha-Hasidut ke-Mistiqah*, 99, 101; and above, end of n. 70.

99. Dov Baer, *Maggid Devarav le-Ya'aqov*, 186.

100. Ibid., 230; see Ze'ev Gries, "Mi-Mitos le-Etos," in *Ummah ve-Toledoteha*, ed. by Menachem Stern and Shmuel Ettinger (Jerusalem: Merkaz Zalman Shazar, 1983–84), 2:139–41; cf. Joseph Weiss, "Rabbi Abraham Kalisker's Concept of Communion with God and Men," *Journal of Jewish Studies* 6 (1955): 88–90.

101. Issachar Ber of Zlotshov, *Mevasser Tsedeq* (Berditchev, 1817), 9a–b; see Schatz-Uffenheimer, *Hasidut*, 114; cf. Dov Baer, *Maggid Devarav le-Ya'aqov*, 197–98. Cf. John of the Cross, *The Ascent of Mount Carmel* 2:7: "When one is brought to nothing *[nada]*—the highest degree of humility—the spiritual union between one's soul and God will be effected." Cf. Abraham Abulafia (cited by Idel, *Daat* 14 [1985]: 48): "One who knows the truth of reality will be more humble and lowly in spirit than his fellow." *Keter* is called *'anavah* ("humility") in an early kabbalistic text; see Scholem, in *Qiryat Sefer* 10 (1933–34): 507. Cf. Talmud, *Sotah* 21b: Rabbi Yohanan said, "The words of Torah become real only for one who makes himself as one who is not, as it is written: 'Wisdom comes into being out of *ayin*.'"

102. Hayyim Haika, *Hayyim va-Hesed* (Warsaw, 1891), 17b–c; cf. Dov Baer, *Maggid Devarav le-Ya'aqov*, 229; Philo, *Heres* 24–29.

103. Hayyim Haika of Amdur describes the attachment to divine will as *afisat*

ha-sekhel (the annihilation of the intellect); see *Hayyim va-Hesed,* 26c; cf. Schatz-Uffenheimer, *Hasidut,* 24; Joseph Weiss, *Studies in Eastern European Jewish Mysticism,* ed. by David Goldstein (Oxford: Oxford University Press, 1985), 152–53.

104. *Shemu'ah Tovah,* 49b; see Schatz-Uffenheimer, *Hasidut,* 101; idem, "Contemplative Prayer in Hasidism," in *Studies in Mysticism and Religion Presented to Gershom G. Scholem,* ed. by Ephraim E. Urbach et al. (Jerusalem: Magnes Press, 1967), 217.

105. *Shemu'ah Tovah,* 70b; see Schatz-Uffenheimer, *Hasidut,* 101; idem, "Contemplative Prayer," 216–17.

106. Dov Baer, *Maggid Devarav le-Ya'aqov,* 224; Levi Yitshaq, *Qedushat Levi* (Jerusalem, 1972), 71d; see Schatz-Uffenheimer, *Hasidut,* 122–23.

107. Dov Baer, *Or ha-Emet,* ed. by Levi Yitshaq of Berditchev (Bnei Brak: Yahadut, 1967), 15a. On *qadmut ha-sekhel,* see Scholem, *Devarim be-Go* (Tel Aviv: Am Oved, 1976), 2:351–60; Siegmund Hurwitz, "Psychological Aspects in Early Hasidic Literature," in *Timeless Documents of the Soul,* ed. by James Hillman (Evanston, Ill.: Northwestern University Press, 1968), 151–239.

108. Ze'ev Wolf of Zhitomir, *Or ha-Me'ir* (New York, 1954), 95c; see Schatz-Uffenheimer, *Hasidut,* 120. On the *Shekhinah* speaking out of one's throat, cf. Zohar 1:267a (and *Nitsotsei Zohar ad loc.*); 3:219a, 306b (all in *Ra'aya Meheimna*); Abraham Joshua Heschel, *Torah min ha-ftShamayim ba-Aspaqlareyah shel ha-Dorot* (London and New York: Soncino Press, 1965), 2:215–16.

109. Kalonymous Kalman, *Ma'or va-Shemesh* (New York, 1958), 51a; see Schatz-Uffenheimer, *Hasidut,* 118–19.

110. Benjamin ben Aaron of Zalozce, *Torei Zahav* (Mohilev, 1816), 56d; see Schatz-Uffenheimer, *Hasidut,* 117–18; cf. Weiss, "*Via Passiva* in Early Hasidism," *Journal of Jewish Studies* 11 (1960): 140–45. According to Mishnah, *Sanhedrin* 11:5, a prophet is forbidden to suppress his prophecy. The liberating effects of self-annihilation can be compared to the freedom experienced by Moses de León, the composer of the Zohar, who surrenders his identity and adopts the various pseudonyms and personalities of Shim'on bar Yohai and his circle; cf. Matt, *Zohar: The Book of Enlightenment,* 27–30. As I point out there, automatic writing may have contributed to the Zohar's composition.

111. *Shemu'ah Tovah,* 71b; see Schatz-Uffenheimer, *Hasidut,* 99; idem, "Contemplative Prayer," 214.

112. Dov Baer, *Maggid Devarav le-Ya'aqov,* 273; idem, *Or ha-Emet,* 3c; see Schatz-Uffenheimer, *Hasidut,* 111–12.

113. Uziel Meizlish, *Tif'eret 'Uzzi'el* (Tel Aviv, 1962), 53b–c; see Schatz-Uffenheimer, *Hasidut,* 119–20.

114. Avraham Hayyim of Zlotshov, *Orah la-Hayyim* (Jerusalem, 1960), 280a; see Schatz-Uffenheimer, *Hasidut,* 119. The Sufi mystic Ibn al-Farid writes in his *Ta'iyya,* verse 153 (cited by Schimmel, *Mystical Dimen-*

sions of Islam, 154): "Both of us are a single worshiper, who, in respect to the united state, bows himself to his own essence in every act of bowing."

115. *Liqqutei Yeqarim* (Lemberg, 1865), 12b; see Schatz-Uffenheimer, *Hasidut,* 27–28.

116. Dov Baer, *Or ha-Emet,* 4c; see Schatz-Uffenheimer, *Hasidut,* 103; idem, "Contemplative Prayer," 218.

117. *Liqqutei Yeqarim,* 1c; Asher Tsevi, *Ma'ayan ha-Hokhmah* (Korets, 1816), 43d; see Schatz-Uffenheimer, *Hasidut,* 97, 108; idem, "Contemplative Prayer," 211, 224.

118. Dov Baer, *Maggid Devarav le-Ya'aqov,* 12.

119. Reuven ha-Levi Horowitz, *Duda'im ba-Sadeh* (Israel, 1944), 9b; see Schatz-Uffenheimer, *Hasidut,* 121.

120. *Boneh Yerushalayim* (Jerusalem, 1926), 54; Shneur Zalman of Lyady, *Torah Or* (Vilna, 1899), 11a. On the Hasidic concept of *bittul ha-yesh* ("the nullification of *yesh"*), see Elior, *The Paradoxical Ascent to God,* 143–51; idem, " 'Iyyunim be-Mahashevet Habad," *Daat* 16 (1986): 157–66; idem, *Torat ha-Elohut ba-Dor ha-Sheni shel Hasidut Habad,* 178–243; idem, "Habad: The Contemplative Ascent to God," in *Jewish Spirituality: From the Sixteenth-Century Revival to the Present,* ed. by Green (New York: Crossroad, 1987), 181–98; Yoram Yakovson, "Torat ha-Beri'ah shel R. Shne'ur Zalman mi-Ladi," *Eshel Beer-Sheva* 1 (1976): 345–50. Cf. Eckhart's view (cited by McGinn, "The God beyond God," 11): "Let us eternally sink down into this Unity from something to nothing."

121. Shneur Zalman, *Torah Or,* 22b.

122. Dov Baer, *Maggid Devarav le-Ya'aqov,* 24.

123. Ibid., 124–27; see Schatz-Uffenheimer, *Hasidut,* 61; cf. Hayyim Haika, *Hayyim va-Hesed,* 58d.

124. Dov Baer, *Or ha-Emet,* 36c–d. *Sefer Ets Hayyim* ("The Book of The Tree of Life"), compiled by Hayyim Vital, is the most widely disseminated version of Lurianic Kabbalah.

125. Dov Baer, *Maggid Devarav le-Ya'aqov,* 196, 296; cf. 138, 144, 196, 227. On Hasidic interpretations of the kabbalistic concept of *tsimtsum,* see Yakovson, "Torat ha-Beri'ah shel R. Shne'ur Zalman mi-Ladi," 314–31; Elior, *The Paradoxical Ascent to God,* 79–91; idem, *Torat ha-Elohut ba-Dor ha-Sheni shel Hasidut Habad,* 61–77; cf. Scholem, "Schöpfung aus Nichts," 84–88.

126. Dov Baer, *Maggid Devarav le-Ya'aqov,* 94, 230. Cf. 125: "The breaking [of the vessels] came about because everyone said, 'I will reign.' " Plotinus *(Enneads* 5:1:1) sees self-assertion and the wish to belong to oneself as causing the soul's ignorance of its divine source. Azriel identifies Adam's sin as his assertion of will, which split him off from the divine; see Tishby, *Mishnat ha-Zohar* 2:291; Bezalel Safran, "Rabbi Azriel and Nahmanides: Two Views of the Fall of Man," in *Rabbi Moses Nahmanides (Ramban),*

ed. by Twersky, 76–77. Cf. Weiss, *Studies in Eastern European Jewish Mysticism,* 142–54; and Mishnah, *Avot* 2:4: "Nullify your will in the face of His will."

127. The *Maggid*'s statement is recorded in *Or ha-Emet* (Brooklyn, 1960); 45b; see Schatz-Uffenheimer, *Hasidut,* 101–102. For Moses de León's remark and the similar view of John Scotus, see above, at n. 43. On the phrase "that which thought cannot grasp," see above, n. 74.

128. Dov Baer, *Maggid Devarav le-Ya'aqov,* 209; cf. 134, 199, 210. This image is widespread. Cf. John 12:24: "Unless a grain of wheat falls into the earth and dies, it remains alone; but if it dies, it bears much fruit." Cf. 1 Corinthians 15:36: "What you sow does not come to life unless it dies." Cf. Plotinus, *Enneads* 4:8:6; and Koran 6:95: "God is the one who splits the grain of corn and the date-stone. He brings forth the living from the dead." Cf. Judah Halevi, *Kuzari* 4:23; and the Sabbatian tract cited by Scholem, *Mehqarim u-Meqorot le-Toledot ha-Shabbeta'ut ve-Gilguleha* (Jerusalem: Mosad Bialik, 1982), 43: "Belonging to these sects are those who believe that [with the advent of the Messiah] the Torah has been nullified and that in the future it will exist without *mitsvot.* They claim that the nullification of the Torah is its fulfillment, and they illustrate this by the image of a grain of wheat that rots in the earth." Abraham Isaac Kook writes (*Orot ha-Qodesh* 1:152): "This rotting of the seed is analogous to what the divine light does in planting anew the vineyard in Israel, in which the old values are forced to be renewed by the insolence that comes in the footsteps of the Messiah." See Dov Sadan, "Hittah she-Niqberah," *Divrei ha-Aqademiyah ha-Le'umit ha-Yisre'elit le-Madda'im* 1:9 (1966): 1–21; Gries, "Mi-Mitos le-Etos," 140.

129. Dov Baer, *Maggid Devarav le-Ya'aqov,* 49, 91, 134. On *hyle,* cf. above, n. 53. Joseph ben Shalom Ashkenazi (cited above, at n. 62) speaks of the "stripping away of form and its privation, resulting from the power of *ayin.*"

130. Dov Baer, *Maggid Devarav le-Ya'aqov,* 83–84; see Schatz-Uffenheimer, *Hasidut,* 100; idem, "Contemplative Prayer," 215.

131. See P. Z. Gliksman, *Der Kotsker Rebbe* (Warsaw, 1938), 32; Schatz-Uffenheimer, *Hasidut,* 67.

132. Dov Baer, *Maggid Devarav le-Ya'aqov,* 39, 134; cf. 253–54; Scholem, *The Messianic Idea in Judaism,* 226–27. Cf. the explanation of *fana* by the tenth-century Sufi Abu Nasr al-Sarraj in *Kitab al-Luma* (cited by Reynold A. Nicholson, "The Goal of Muhammadan Mysticism," *Journal of the Royal Asiatic Society* [1913]: 60): "Humanity does not depart from the human being any more than blackness departs from that which is black or whiteness from that which is white, but the inborn qualities of humanity are changed and transmuted by the all-powerful radiance that is shed upon them from the divine realities."

133. The phrase appears in Genesis 30:37 and is applied to *Keter* in early Kabbalah; see the passages cited by Scholem in *Qiryat Sefer* 10 (1933–

34): 505–8, passim; cf. Shem Tov ibn Gaon, *Migdal 'Oz* on Maimonides, *Mishneh Torah, Hilkhot Teshuvah* 5:5.
134. Scholem, "Schöpfung aus Nichts," 84.
135. Hebrew, *lo;* see above, n. 31.
136. Joseph Taitazak, cited by Scholem, *Sefunot* 11 (1967–78): 82.
137. Shim'on Labi, *Ketem Paz,* 92d–93a.

3.

The Doctrine of Man in the Zohar

Isaiah Tishby

A. THE NATURE AND STATUS OF MAN

I

The Zohar's view of man's position in the world is unmistakably anthropocentric. Man is regarded as both the acme and the final culmination of the creative process, the pillar that supports the world. "Rabbi Isaac said to Rabbi Judah: We have learned that when the Holy One, blessed be He, created the world He constructed the lower world on the pattern of the upper world. . . . Rabbi Judah said: This is indeed true, and He created man over everything . . . for he sustains the world, so that everything might be in a single perfection." From the very moment that he was created, man was destined to occupy the highest position in the lower world, to match God's unique position in the upper world. "Rabbi Isaac said: The Holy One, blessed be He, wished to make man superior to all His creatures, so that he might be as unique in this world as He was unique in the realms above." [1] Supreme authority was part of man's nature, and it could be perceived even in his outward appearance, in the holy image that was impressed upon him. Therefore, wherever he turned the world's creatures stood in awe of him. Man's exalted character was blemished by Adam's sin, but even so every person is assured of a superior place in the world provided that he does not do additional damage through sins of his own. [2] Here, for example, is just one of the

Reprinted from *The Wisdom of the Zohar* by Isaiah Tishby, by permission of Oxford University Press, Oxford, and the Littman Library of Jewish Civilization, Oxford, 1989.

luxuriant descriptions of human eminence and perfection. "Come and see. Everything in the world came into being only for the sake of man, and all [created things] continue to exist only for his sake. They did not appear in the world, they all waited, until he came who is called 'man' . . . for he is the perfection of all, and the summation of all. . . . When man was created, everything was put right, everything above and below, and everything was comprised in man."[3]

This anthropocentric view of the world, which we encounter time after time in the Zohar, can be paralleled in earlier Jewish sources. We can find many passages in the Talmud and the *midrashim* that are almost literally matched in the Zohar, and that were clearly the original source of inspiration: for example, "The whole world was created only for the sake of [the man who fears God]";[4] Adam was "unique in the world";[5] and "as long as man lives the creatures of the world stand in awe of him."[6] In this sense Joel[7] was justified in opposing Franck's view that the Zohar's elevation of man ran contrary to the previously established rabbinic attitude.[8]

However, Joel made a big mistake when he tried to demonstrate that, because there is some similarity between the approach of the Zohar and that of the aggadic literature to the place of man in the world, the whole of the Zohar's theory of man coincides with the traditional rabbinic view, without any originality or deviation whatsoever. He arrived at this apologetic conclusion by completely ignoring the basic principles of Zoharic anthropology. The passages in the Zohar that deal with the nature of man are not concerned primarily with establishing the relationship between man and the other objects of creation, but with showing the contacts that exist between man and the divine *sefirot* on the one hand, and between man and *sitra aḥra* on the other. This very complex subject, an integral part of which is the idea of man as the crown of creation, involves some very daring original ideas that find expression in the Zohar, but that cannot easily be paralleled in earlier aggadic literature.

Actually, Joel's view was shared by the kabbalists themselves, when they tried to explain the Zohar's idea of man. They thought of the kabbalah as a very ancient tradition that preserved the Jewish faith in all its purity. Naturally enough, therefore, they considered it to be perfectly in line with the beliefs and ideas found in earlier sources. What they tried to do was to demonstrate that the Zohar's view of man was strictly faithful to the original Jewish concept, in contrast to the alien and false idea of man propounded by the Jewish philosophers. Now since the pre-Lurianic kabbalists took the Zohar quite literally, and, unlike the modern apologists, attempted to substantiate the views they found there, their writings are a real help to us in our endeavor to discover the true meaning of the Zohar's idea of man. Of particular interest in this respect is the polemic of Rabbi Meir ibn Gabbai, a kabbalist from the beginning of the sixteenth century, against the views of the philosophers, particularly Maimonides, on the nature and function of man.[9] It is worth analyzing and explaining this polemic, since it is a key to a systematic interpretation of the Zohar's view of man.

Rabbi Meir ibn Gabbai embarked on a severe critique of Maimonides' anthropological views, and accused him of holding heretical opinions. The main points that seemed to him to be false and subversive were as follows: (a) The refutation of the arguments concerning the independent power of evil by the proposition that evil acts independently "only in some individual instances of mankind," and that, furthermore, man forms "an infinitesimal portion of the permanent universe";[10] (b) Maimonides' opposition to the view that the world was created for the sake of man, whose task it is to serve God, since "even if the Universe existed for man's sake and man existed for the purpose of serving God, as has been mentioned, the question remains, What is the end of serving God? He does not become more perfect if all His creatures serve Him and comprehend Him as far as possible." We must therefore give up our enquiry as to the end of creation and content ourselves with the answer that "it was the Will of God, or His Wisdom decreed it."[11] Rabbi Meir ibn Gabbai writes[12] in rebuttal of these ideas: "If [Maimonides] had known that there was a higher purpose in the creation and service of man, and that through perfecting himself he would perfect Him who had need of his perfection, the Rabbi would have had to concede that the question concerning the end of creation was a vital one and that it could not be resolved simply by saying that it was the Will of God or that His Wisdom decreed it, and he would have agreed that the end of all existence, of both the upper and the lower worlds, was man himself . . . [Maimonides] by this view of his breaches the wall of the Torah, despises the image of God, and belittles the likeness, namely, man, who is made according to a supernal pattern, constructed and perfected in the likeness of the parts of the celestial Chariot, and this is to cast a blemish on the sacred things of Heaven."

This controversy shows that the kabbalists were not content merely to assign man a supreme place in this world, which Maimonides also, with some reservations, was prepared to do.[13] They went further and maintained that man's eminence consisted in the fact that he was made "in the likeness of the parts of the celestial Chariot," that is to say, in the likeness of the divine *sefirot;* and that he had both the task and the ability "to perfect Him who had need of his perfection"; in other words, to perfect the powers in the Godhead through the process of perfecting himself. This second point involves also the ability of man to harm the divine powers by committing transgressions and thereby diminishing his own chances of perfection. This ability on the part of man to influence God both for good and ill is bound up with the existence of *sitra aḥra* ("the other side"), and its relationship to both God and man.

To this kabbalistic view of the supreme eminence of man must be added the belief that man's soul originates from the Godhead itself, in the world of the *sefirot.* This distinction is not clearly enunciated by ibn Gabbai in the passage quoted, but it is referred to later on in the same work:[14] "The truth, traditionally upheld in our nation, is that the source and level of the soul is higher than that of the ministering angels, and that it therefore has dominion over everything that is below it." Elsewhere in the same book,[15] and in other works of kabbalah, the divine origin of the soul is treated at greater length.

From Rabbi Meir ibn Gabbai's polemic against Maimonides we can therefore deduce three basic strands in the kabbalah's theory of man: (a) the divine origin of the soul; (b) the creation of man in the likeness of the *sefirot;* (c) the influence that man has on the realm of the Godhead. We must now investigate the way in which these strands are presented in the Zohar, and see how they are connected with the views propounded by earlier rabbis in the Talmud and the *midrashim.* Here I shall discuss the matter in only a general way. In the sections that follow, however, I shall be able to go into more detail.

II

The doctrine of the Zohar concerning the origin of the soul is bound up with the idea that the soul has a number of parts. Consequently, I cannot really begin a detailed examination of the doctrine without first clarifying what these parts of the soul really signify.[16] For our purpose here, we may content ourselves with remarking that, at the very least, the highest part of the soul, called *"neshamah,"* is regarded by the Zohar, without a doubt, as having a divine origin.

A number of symbols are used by the Zohar in its description of the dependent relationship of the souls to the Godhead. One symbol is that of the flood of souls in the divine river. "Rabbi Isaac said: It is all above, for from there souls *(neshamot)* go forth to this earth, which brings them out and gives [them] to all; for the river that stretches out continuously provides souls and brings them into this earth, which receives them and gives [them] to all". The "river" is *Binah* or *Yesod,* the souls' origin or the channel by which they are transmitted, and the "earth" is *Malkhut,* the *Shekhinah,* which receives the souls from above and transmits them downward. "The soul [of a member] of the house of Israel emerges from the trunk of the tree, and thence the souls fly into this earth, into the recesses of her womb." [17] The "tree" is *Tiferet* or *Yesod,* [18] from which the souls fly to the *Shekhinah* where they are received like semen into her womb. There is a connection here with the next and last description to be discussed, the symbol of childbirth. "We have learned the mystery of the matter. It signifies that the soul has a father and mother just as the body on earth has a father and mother, and it signifies also that in all realms, whether above or below, everything derives from male and female." [19] "Father and mother" in the upper realms are *Tiferet* and *Malkhut;* so the souls are the products of male and female in the world of the *sefirot.*

These and similar accounts show that the Zohar regards the soul as a spark of the divine essence, an entity that has a real and substantial propinquity to God, unlike other beings, including even the halls and the most exalted angels, who are no more than a nondivine extension, an emanatory projection from the last *sefirah.* The divine nature of the soul, even after it has assumed its human dimension, is central to a subtle argument of Rabbi Moses de Leon's: [20] "If the soul *(neshamah)* is in the image of God and is derived from Him, how can He possibly judge Himself, His own essential being, since it is actually He Himself?" Rabbi Moses de Leon sees the punishment of the soul as a kind of self-inflicted punishment on the part of God, since the soul is God's "own essential being."

The Zohar stresses the fact that the divine soul is the essence of man, and that his body is but an outer garment that has no relevance at all to his fundamental human nature. "How does Scripture describe the creation of man? 'You have clothed me with skin and flesh' (Job 10:11). What then is man? If you say that he is nothing but skin and flesh, and bones and sinews, you are wrong; for, in actual truth, man is nothing but soul. Clothes belong to man, but they are not man, and when man departs he is stripped of the clothes that he has put on."[21] In the Hebrew version of this passage in the writings of Rabbi Moses de Leon, the spirituality of man is even more strongly emphasized: "If skin and flesh are a garment, examine what man really is, for he is inside the garment. . . Man, indeed, in this world is man only when there are three things joined together in a single bond so that he might be the pattern of man, to wit, *nefesh, ruah* and *neshamah*. . . . And when man dies he does so only after stripping off the garment."[22] In other words, the root of man's essential being is embedded within God.[23]

We shall look in vain for a similar view in aggadic literature. The sages in the *aggadah* certainly stressed the exalted status of the soul, but they traced its source only as far as the Throne of Glory,[24] which is outside the realm of divinity. The utter exclusion of the body from a consideration of the true essence of man, and the concentration on the soul alone, does not exist in the early sources. There man is depicted as a creature composed, as to his essential nature, of both body and soul,[25] although, as we shall see, the early rabbis did posit the independent preexistence of souls before they entered the terrestrial world.

III

The view of man as an image of the *sefirot* is bound up with an idea central to kabbalistic teaching—the pattern or image relationship between the *sefirot* and everything that exists in the world. I have already dealt with the significance and the importance of this idea in volume I, and I also explained in some detail the symbolist view that is integral to it, according to which everything in the world is a reflection of the divine powers. I also pointed out the special position occupied by the image of man in this context, and I outlined the characteristics of the pattern relationship between the *sefirot* and *Binah*.

The object of these discussions was to explain the physical images that occur in descriptions of the *sefirot*, and I concentrated specifically on the reflection of God seen in the structure of the body as a whole and also in the individual parts of the body. Elsewhere, in connection with the *Raya Mehemna*'s concept of God, I dealt with the parallels drawn between man and God by using the organic structure of body and soul. But in the pattern relationship too, the body is seen as subordinate to the soul, which alone represents to the author of the Zohar a precise and supreme image of the array of the *sefirot*. "For the Holy One, blessed be He, takes pleasure only in the soul *(neshamah)*, whereas the body has no right to a place in the upper realm, even though the image of the body is part of a supernal mystery." The same idea is expressed more categorically in Hebrew by Rabbi Moses de Leon: "The body is not an image of the Creator, for a spiritual substance divorced from all physical accidents cannot be imaged in a body. What then is His image and His counterpart? The soul, without a doubt." [26]

The parallelism between the soul and the *sefirot* is connected with the Zohar's view of the different parts of the soul, and so I must defer a detailed examination of that until we come to that particular section. Let me confine myself here simply to the basic statement that the human soul with all its parts is a mirror in which the *sefirot* are reflected.

As to the idea that "the image of God" refers to a parallel between the human body and God—the source for this is not to be found in aggadic literature. We can see from a number of passages that the rabbis were worried by the theological difficulties raised by the narrative in the Torah concerning the creation of man "in the image of God," and this subsequently set the medieval philosophers a number of problems. They tried in their interpretations to remove the basic difficulty by denying the similarity of man to God, by stating, for example, that man was created in the image of the angels. [27]

The description of God as the unification of body and soul is also not to be found in the earlier sources, although sometimes body and soul are discussed in connection with God. The most important passage from this point of view is the rabbinic idea that it is right for the soul to praise and glorify God because it is like Him in five respects. " 'Bless the Lord, O my soul' occurs five times (Psalms 103–104). What prompted David to say them? He said them in respect of the Holy One, blessed be he, and in respect of the soul. Just as the Holy One, blessed be he, sees but cannot be seen, so the soul sees but cannot be seen; just as the Holy One, blessed be He, sustains the whole world, so the soul sustains the whole body; just as the Holy One, blessed be He, is pure, so the soul is pure; just as the Holy One, blessed be He, dwells in the innermost place, so the soul dwells in the innermost place. Let that which has these five qualities come and praise Him who has these five qualities." [28] This passage is often quoted by the kabbalists in support of their ideas.

However, its meaning in the *aggadah* is quite different from its meaning in kabbalah. In the *aggadah* the Holy One, blessed be He, is compared to the soul, but the counterpart of the body is not a divine force at all, but the world, which is under the suzerainty and control of God. This is not the case in the Zohar. According to the account there, that which is symbolized by the body exists within the realm of the divine. Let me quote as examples two passages where the interrelationship of soul and body in the upper world is described in different ways. In the first passage the comparison is made in order to explain concealment and revelation in the Godhead. "Come and see. Man's soul can be known only through the organs of the body, which are the levels that perform the work of the soul. Consequently, it is both known and unknown. In the same way, the Holy One, blessed be He, is both known and unknown, because He is the soul's soul, the spirit's spirit, hidden and concealed from all. But through these gates (i.e., the *sefirot*), which are the doors of the soul, the Holy One, blessed be He, may be known." [29] In this passage the Holy One, blessed be He, who is compared to the soul, is not, as is usually designated by this title, the *sefirah Tiferet,* but *En-Sof;* and the body symbolizes the whole sefirotic order. In the second passage the body is simply the *sefirah Malkhut,* while the soul is *Tiferet,* and above it is *Keter,* the soul's soul. "Come and see. So also above there is a garment, and a body, and a soul, and a soul's soul. The heavens with their hosts are the garment, and the Assembly of Israel (i.e., *Malkhut*) is the body that receives the soul, which is the glory *(Tiferet)* of Israel, and therefore is the body for the soul. The soul we have mentioned is the *Tiferet* of Israel, the actual Torah, and the soul's soul is *Atika Kadisha,* and the whole is interdependent." [30] In this account the world of the heavens is merely a garment, and the terrestrial world is not mentioned at all.

Obviously, the idea of the soul as the image of God still remains common to both. Even here, however, we can perceive a basic difference between the kabbalah and the *aggadah*. The rabbis of the *aggadah* were simply trying to draw an analogy between the soul and God by highlighting the similar characteristics or activities that they both had. They did not posit an integral and continuous connection between them.

That is to say, they did not think that the soul's likeness to God was essential to its character or its survival. With the kabbalists, however, the life of the soul, from the moment it was created and throughout its existence, was an image of the *sefirot*. It came into being and continued to exist as a kind of transfer or reflection of the original divine pattern. The relationship between the soul and the *sefirot* is similar to the connection between individual things and Ideas in Platonic philosophy. Plato describes things as "imitating" Ideas. On the one hand, the things "participate" in the Ideas, and, on the other, the Ideas "are present" in the things. Similarly, we can say of the soul that, in kabbalistic doctrine, its being an image of the *sefirot* implies being connected to them, both through its "participation" in the life of God, and also through the "presence" of God in the life of the soul. One cannot possibly maintain that the rabbis of the *aggadah* had any such idea. We have, therefore, to say that on this point also the kabbalah shows considerable originality.[31]

IV

From the idea of man as a spark of the divine and an image of the sefirotic order, a number of important conclusions follow concerning the status and role of mankind, and particularly the relationship between man and God. One of these conclusions leads the Zohar to a new height of originality in its philosophy of man.

The first conclusion, bound up specifically with the pattern relationship, is that man has the ability to perceive the mystery of the divine by contemplating his own human form, particularly his soul. After the Zohar has explained the system of the different parts of the soul it goes on to say: "So we see that there is [in the parts of the soul] a throne for a throne, and a throne for the most supreme above them, and when you examine the levels you will find the mystery of wisdom in this matter, and everything is wisdom, so that you might perceive in this way matters that are sealed." Here the "matters that are sealed" are the *sefirot*, as is evident from the writings of Rabbi Moses de Leon: "Since the man who intends to penetrate the royal palace needs first to know his own soul . . . [which] is modeled on its Creator who created it. . . . Therefore, when man knows the eminence and nature of the soul, his thoughts and understanding will spread from there to the secrets of royal matters."[32]

The second conclusion, derived primarily from the idea of the soul as a divine spark, is that the soul is alienated in this world and in the body, and that it yearns to escape upward and return to its source in God. "The soul has only one longing: for the place from which it was taken. And everything that [the Holy One, blessed be He,] made yearns after its kind."[33] The duality of soul and body, as two elements hostile to one another, is frequently mentioned in the Zohar, and the soul is therefore depicted as an exile or fugitive in this world. In the writings of Rabbi Moses de Leon we find a clear expression of the well-known Platonic idea that the soul "has been placed in the prison of the body."[34] Since everything is attracted to its own kind and longs to return to its source, the soul yearns to free itself from the shackles of the body and to go back to the place from which it was hewn. This desire can be realized temporarily in this life during moments of religious awakening and enthusiasm, when the soul is given the opportunity to enjoy the splendor of the *Shekhinah* in an experience of communion. But complete freedom and everlasting exaltation are possible only after the death of the body. Therefore the righteous, who are skilled in the mystery of the soul, rejoice when the end of their earthly existence approaches, as I shall explain in the introduction to the section on Death.

These ideas are not really original. They are rooted in the philosophy of Plato and Plotinus, and they had penetrated Jewish consciousness at least a century before the birth of kabbalah. They made their mark particularly in the writings of Neoplatonic philosophical circles.[35] In contrast to this we see in the third conclusion that is derived from the close relationship between the soul and God an original idea that was destined to have great influence on succeeding generations. According to this, the relationship between man and God is not confined to man's dependence upon God's mercy or his receipt of benign influence from above, but is one of mutual influence. They afford one another reciprocal aid. Man lives and has his being because of the flow of influence that originates from a stimulus in the upper world, but he in his turn can use his power to influence that world and give life and strength to the divine *sefirot*. The preservation of harmony in the life of the Godhead depends upon human actions. Man's influence upon the upper worlds, and their dependence on his actions are expressed most clearly through the relationship between man and the *Shekhinah*. Man is both able and obliged to sustain the *Shekhinah,* to strengthen her position, and to unite her with the other *sefirot,* and particularly with her consort, the *sefirah*

Tiferet, in the mystery of intercourse. The *Shekhinah* cannot sustain her position or act as she is supposed to in the upper and the lower worlds without man's active help. Furthermore, man is unique in that he is able to tarnish the *Shekhinah* and destroy her status. This reciprocal relationship between man and the *Shekhinah* is therefore absolutely crucial: the very existence of good and evil depends upon it.

The kabbalists were able to find some support for this idea in a few aggadic passages. "Rabbi Johanan said: The wicked depend upon their gods, but the righteous—their God depends on them, as it is said (Genesis 28:13), 'Behold, the Lord stood by him.' "[36] "When Israel perform the will of God they add power and strength, as it is said (Numbers 14:17), 'Let the power of the Lord be great.' But when they anger Him, it is as if 'You forgot the Rock that bore you' (Deuteronomy 32:18)."[37] However, passages like these, which are rare and uncharacteristic, are just insignificant jottings compared with the wide currency that this idea enjoyed in the kabbalah.

The basis of this belief in the kabbalah was, as I have said, the idea of the soul's relationship to God. Being a divine spark, the soul acts upon the upper world, and particularly on the *Shekhinah,* the soul's mother, like a son who supports his parents. Because, however, it is also an image of the *sefirot,* the influential power that the soul wields derives from its similarity to the Godhead. From this angle one might regard the stimulus that it provides from below as a kind of sympathetic magic. There is, however, a fundamental difference in the two ways in which man can influence the upper world. The purpose of magical activity is to coerce the superior powers into obeying man's will and thus to satisfy his own needs, while the theurgic activity described in the Zohar is intended to assist the upper worlds themselves.[38]

B. THE TRIPARTITE SOUL

I

For the sake of simplicity in dealing with the Zohar's basic philosophy of man, I treated the soul in the previous section as a single unit, and I only briefly touched upon the different parts of the soul. The Zohar, however, speaks frequently about the various faculties or parts of the soul, and my first task, therefore, must be to explain this in some detail.

In the main body of the Zohar, namely, the midrash to the Torah and most of the sections connected with it, we find generally speaking a consistent viewpoint and a regular terminology on the subject of the soul and its parts. In a few sections, however, and especially in the *Midrash ha-Ne'elam*, we have a very different view, together with a confused terminology. I shall therefore devote the last part of this introduction to the view of the soul in these particular sections.

The prevailing view in the Zohar is that the soul consists of three parts, called '*nefesh*,' '*ruaḥ*,' and '*neshamah*.'[39] They are joined to one another like the links of a chain, and they work together. The *nefesh*, the lowest part, receives illumination and sustenance from the *ruaḥ*; the *ruaḥ* is illumined and sustained by the *neshamah*, which receives light and influence from the upper worlds.

The *nefesh* is attached to the body, preserving it and satisfying its needs. "The *nefesh* is the lowest stimulus. It is close to the body, and nourishes it. The body depends upon it, and it depends upon the body." "The *nefesh* has no light of its own at all, [but it receives light from the *ruaḥ*], and it is this that shares in the mystery of the one body, nourishing it with all that it needs."[40] From these statements it would appear that the *nefesh* is the instinctive power of feeling and action needed to sustain the body.

The functions of the *neshamah* are described by the Zohar in a more varied manner, and in much more detail. It is the power of the *neshamah* that enables man to study Torah and observe the commandments. "And above all [the other parts of the soul] is the *neshamah*, for it is the supernal power by which one may know and observe the commandments of the Holy One, blessed be He." "[The Holy One, blessed be He] has put a holy *neshamah* [in man] in order to teach him how to walk in the ways of the Torah, and to keep His commandments, so that man might be suitably improved."[41] Beside and beyond the practical religious life the *neshamah* is active in the perception of the divine mystery. "Come and see. The Holy One, blessed be He, created man with the mystery of wisdom, and made him with great skill, and He breathed into his nostrils the breath *(neshamah)* of life, so that he might know and contemplate the mysteries of wisdom and gain a knowledge of his Maker's glory." Once man has arrived at a perception of the divine mystery through knowledge of the secrets of the Torah he is able, indeed he is obliged, to activate his soul into unifying the *sefirot* and supporting the *Shekhinah*. In other words, he is in a position to carry out those theurgic tasks which constitute the supreme and final human goal. "This is the meaning of 'I have created him for My glory' (Isaiah 43:7): for the sake of My glory, so that he might restore it with powerful pillars, and beautify it with improvement and adornment from below, so that My glory might be exalted through the merit of the righteous in the earth."[42] The common factor in all these functions is the idea of the *neshamah* as a spiritual-religious force that draws man near to God and preserves the bonds between them.

I have passed over *ruaḥ,* because I have not been able to find in the main body of the Zohar any specific function assigned to it. Generally speaking the *ruaḥ* is depicted simply as an intermediate power, whose task it is to illumine the *nefesh* and to sustain it with the light and influence that flow down upon it from the *neshamah.* To match this bridging and intermediary role, it is often described as the throne of the *neshamah,* or the luminary of the *nefesh.*[43]

Actually, some Zohar scholars speak with complete confidence about the part that the *ruaḥ* plays in the life of the soul. Franck[44] says that the *ruaḥ* is the home of the sensual desires, and that it controls both good and evil moral conduct. Müller,[45] on the other hand, speaks of the *ruaḥ* as if it were the seat of the emotions and intellectual thought. These ideas, however, are not supported by any reference to the text.[46]

I have come across just one passage in the Zohar that seems to deal with the specific role of the *ruaḥ:* "When man has gained *nefesh* they bestow upon him a certain crown called '*ruaḥ*'. . . . Then man is aroused by another exalted stimulus to contemplate the laws of the holy King. When man has gained *ruaḥ* they bestow upon him the supernal sacred diadem that comprises all, called '*neshamah.*' "[47] If the stimulus "to contemplate the laws of the holy King" is attributed to *ruaḥ,* an important area of the functions that are assigned to *neshamah* in other passages is here transferred to *ruaḥ,* namely, contemplation of the secrets of the Torah and the commandments or of the mystery of the Godhead. It would seem to me, however, that the text of the passage is not clear, and the meaning really is that by receiving the *ruaḥ* man becomes susceptible to mystical arousal, and for the purpose of this arousal, "they bestow upon him the sacred diadem" of *neshamah.* If this interpretation is correct, the *ruaḥ* here too plays the role of a mere intermediary, and religious-mystical activity remains the preserve of the *neshamah.*

In contrast to this, however, there is a passage in the *Sitrei Torah* in the Zohar that deals quite clearly with the role of the *ruah*. "Concerning this they have said that the *neshamah* of the *neshamah* arouses man with awe *(yirah)* and wisdom *(hokhmah)*; the *neshamah* arouses man with understanding *(binah)*. . . . The *neshamah* is aroused by repentance *(teshuvah)* called '*binah*' and 'Sarah.' And *ruah* is the voice and is called '*da'at*,' and it arouses man to raise his voice in the [study of the] Torah, and it is called 'the oral Torah,' and as for the intellectual *nefesh*—good deeds are aroused by it."[48] According to this it is the *ruah* that stimulates man to study the Torah. But this passage is most exceptional in the Zohar, not only in the way in which it assigns roles to the different parts of the soul, but also in the enumeration of those parts. It introduces a *neshamah* for the *neshamah*, above the *neshamah*; it differentiates between a holy *ruah* and an animal *ruah*, which latter is the evil inclination; and the *nefesh* also is divided into two—the holy *nefesh*, which is the intellectual *nefesh*, and the animal *nefesh*, which is on the side of the evil inclination. Consequently, this passage does not help us to form an opinion about the view of the Zohar as a whole.

The main attitudes of the Zohar toward the various functions of the *neshamah*, the *ruah*, and the *nefesh* are clearly enunciated in the writings of Rabbi Moses de Leon. "You ought to know and think upon the mystery of the *nefesh*, the *ruah*, and the *neshamah*. The *nefesh* is the power that is associated with the sensations of the body in all matters that are connected with the blood, and in all the factors that sustain the body throughout its life, through perception of this world with respect to everything that the body needs. This preserves the body. . . . The *ruah* is the power that enables the *nefesh* to maintain itself in the body, for the *nefesh* survives only because of the power of the *ruah*, which acts like the breeze that blows. It is because of the *ruah* that man is sustained by the power of the *nefesh*, for if the *ruah* were withheld from the *nefesh*, this would bring death in its train for the *nefesh* would not be able to maintain itself in the body. The *neshamah* is a matter of true intellect. It is hewn from the source of life, and from the well-spring of intelligence and wisdom. Glory comes to dwell in the body in order to sustain everything for the service of the Creator, in order to provide him with substance."[49] Here we have a clear division of roles. The *nefesh* sustains the body; that is to say, it provides man with all his physical needs in this world. The *neshamah* is the bridge between man and God and is the main force that sustains "everything for the service of the Creator" and brings man into the life of the world to come (it provides him "with substance"). The *ruaḥ*, however, has no independent role. Its activity merely helps the *nefesh* to preserve the body.

II

The tripartite soul, as I have already mentioned, is considered to be an image of the *sefirot*. The model-image relationship between the *sefirot* on the one hand, and the *neshamah, ruaḥ,* and *nefesh* on the other, is depicted in the Zohar in two ways.

According to one idea, which occurs in only a very few passages and even then in a rather obscure form, the three parts of the soul parallel *Ḥesed, Gevurah,* and *Tiferet.* In order to explain this idea I quote one passage, which, however, needs detailed explanation and analysis on the basis of a similar account in the writings of Rabbi Moses de Leon.

In this passage, which is included in our anthology, the Zohar discusses the connection between the various powers in the soul and the *sefirot* from the point of view of man's role as an instigator of activity and harmonious restoration in the upper realms. "Therefore 'I have created him (i.e., man)' on the model of the upper glory in which there are the following dispositions: creation on the left side, formation on the right, and it is said 'forming light and creating darkness,' and making in the middle, as it is said 'I am the Lord, Maker of all,' and it is written 'making peace and creating evil,' and it is also written 'making peace in His high places.' Therefore, 'I have created him, I have formed him; indeed, I have made him,' like the disposition on high. Consequently, since man is upon the earth and it is his obligation to restore 'My glory,' I have placed in him the dispositions of the upper glory . . . so that he might be like a model of the upper glory, restoring and blessing the lower glory. . . . In this fashion He created man upon the earth, who is like a model of the upper glory, in order to restore this glory and to complete it on all sides. The upper glory has these three; man below has these three, in order to complete the lower glory from above and from below so that it might be perfect on all sides."

This passage appears to be totally obscure, and first of all, therefore, I must explain the meaning of certain specific terms and symbols, which in this particular passage and in the Zohar as a whole are not sufficiently clear. We must pay special attention to the terms "creation," "formation," and "making." "The upper glory" and "the lower glory" are the *sefirot Binah* and *Malkhut,* which are called at several points in the Zohar "the upper *Shekhinah*" and "the lower *Shekhinah.*" *Binah,* the upper glory, bestows influence upon *Malkhut,* the lower glory, by means of the three dispositions that it has, that is, the three agents of activity, called "creation," "formation," and "making," which are situated respectively on the left, on the right, and in the middle. The terms "creation" *(beriyah),* "formation" *(yezirah)* and "making" *(asiyah)* are common in kabbalistic literature, being used to denote the three worlds that are below the world of the *sefirot,* which is called "the world of emanation" *(azilut).* But this usage is not found in the main body of the Zohar. It is clear, therefore, from the context that here the author has in mind the three *sefirot* between *Binah* and *Malkhut.* These *sefirot* are *Hesed, Gevurah,* and *Tiferet,* which are always represented by the right, the left, and the middle. They are also denoted by "light," "darkness," and "peace," which are included in the scriptural verses quoted. Man, who possesses a soul, was created "like a model of the upper glory," that is, with three powers in the soul, namely, *neshamah, ruah,* and *nefesh,* parallel to *Hesed, Gevurah,* and *Tiferet,* because his function in the lower world is to restore and bless through his actions the lower glory, *Malkhut,* in the same way as *Binah* restores and blesses her in the upper world by means of the *sefirot* in between. Consequently, in this passage, *neshamah, ruah,* and *nefesh* are the image of *Hesed, Gevurah,* and *Tiferet.*

This interpretation is further justified by a similar passage in the writings of Rabbi Moses de Leon, even though on this particular point, in the Hebrew version also, there is more darkness than light. "We must first say a few words, on the subject we have broached concerning the mystery of *nefesh, ruah,* and *neshamah,* about the actual way in which man originated from the mystery of the divine being. For the essence of his origin from the power of the Creator consists in those things that are separate when they are apart but unified in their united state, and they are the mystery of *beriyah, yezirah,* and *asiyah,* three stages within one whole, without any division between them. . . . Therefore, man was chosen to serve his Maker, and He created them for His glory, as is shown by the verse, 'Everyone that is called by My name—for My glory I have created him, I have formed him; indeed, I have made him' (Isaiah

43:7). Here we have the mystery of *beriyah, yezirah, asiyah*. . . . And concerning the mystery of the various stages of these things it is said, 'forming light, and creating darkness, making peace' (Isaiah 45:7). Here we have *beriyah, yezirah, asiyah,* which are on a higher plane than man. And in accordance with the root-principle of the inner wisdom, these things ascend and enter the innermost hall of the King, and they come to rest above the Throne of Glory and are secure there. Because of them the Throne stands in its rightful place above the Throne of David and his kingdom, and when light, darkness, and peace are united as one, then you will find that God is one, unified with His stages, with the association of none other. . . . To be sure the mystery of *beriyah, yezirah,* and *asiyah* is that the three of them are united in a single mystery, but they are divided as follows: *beriyah* is less than the mystery of *yezirah,* for *yezirah* is superior to *beriyah,* and *asiyah* includes them all, and they are all comprised within it. These things are necessarily so since they are parallel to *nefesh, ruah,* and *neshamah,* one being superior to the other. *Nefesh* is less than the mystery of *ruah,* for *ruah* is superior to the mystery of *nefesh. Neshamah* is superior to all of them, and includes them all." [50] Here it is clearly stated that *nefesh, ruah,* and *neshamah* are parallel to *beriyah, yezirah,* and *asiyah,* and that the three latter are *sefirot* that dwell in "the innermost hall of the King." The mystery of unification in the Godhead depends on the maintenance of the attributes of Love, Judgment, and Mercy, which are the *sefirot Hesed, Gevurah,* and *Tiferet,* in a state of balance and harmony. That is why it says "when light, darkness, and peace are united as one, then you will find that God is one, unified with His stages, with the association of none other." These *sefirot* are above *Malkhut,* symbolized by the Throne of Glory, and the Throne of David, which is sustained by the influence that they bestow upon it.

The second idea is that the *neshamah* represents *Binah,* the *ruah* represents *Tiferet,* and the *nefesh* represents *Malkhut.* This idea occurs in many passages, and is expressed much more clearly than the first, although even here it is veiled by hints and allusions.[51] The parallel between *neshamah, ruah,* and *nefesh* and the *sefirot* mentioned above is outlined most clearly in the passage that is meant to show that the tripartite soul forms one single whole. In this passage the paradox of unity in the midst of diversity is explained by describing the various kinds of light in a single flame. "Come and see. The *nefesh* is the lower stimulus that is attached to the body, like the light of a lamp. The lower light which is black is attached to the wick, and is never separated from it, but is sustained by it alone. Once it has been sustained by the wick, it becomes a throne for the upper white light, which rests upon the black light. After they have been both sustained, the white light becomes a throne for a hidden light, which cannot be seen and is not known, and which rests upon the white light, and then the light is perfect. . . . It is similar with the upper mystery." In this account the Zohar paints a picture of the mystery of unity in the world of the *sefirot,* alluded to here by the sentence "It is similar with the upper mystery." And it is perfectly clear that the three lights, the hidden light, the white light, and the blue-black light, symbolize *Binah, Tiferet,* and *Malkhut.*[52]

Even with regard to the concept of God Himself, the Zohar has great difficulty in maintaining the idea of perfect unity, and can do so only through the use of complex paradoxes. One can imagine, therefore, how much more fragmented and doubtful is its concept of the unity of the soul, whose nature and activity involve, according to most of the discussions in the Zohar, a separation of its various parts. These parts, as we shall see later,[53] have different points of origin, and survive after death in different areas.[54] And that is not all. The three parts do not enter the human body all at the same time, but only stage by stage, according to age and merit. Sometimes they never do exist together at one and the same time, and it is possible, as a result of man's sin, for the highest part, the *neshamah,* to leave the other parts.[55] We have here, therefore, a very shaky and uncertain type of unity. In other words, the Zohar's doctrine of the soul reveals most clearly the tension between monistic and pluralistic attitudes.

This tension is apparent even where the attempt is made to grade the various levels of the soul. The premise of unity means that the three parts of the soul must all be thought of as powers of holiness, and, in actual fact, even the *nefesh,* the lowest part, is described as "a holy restorer." Throughout the Zohar, however, great emphasis is placed on the hierarchy of the different parts of the soul. The superior status of the *neshamah* is stressed especially. It is called "the highest of all, the most concealed of all the concealed," and "the holy of holies,"[56] and whoever is deserving enough to receive the *neshamah* is called "holy" (4) or "one who loves the Holy One, blessed be He." Those who have reached this stage are regarded as if they had become "like holy angels."[57]

Now these differentiations can be seen merely as indications of differences in level, without any infringement of their total basic unity. This
cannot be said, however, of the passages that represent the lowest part,
the *nefesh*, as having an independent and close relationship to *sitra aḥra*
("the other side"), which is the very opposite of the holy. "We have
learned: There are those who merit possession of the *neshamah*, and
those who merit the stimulus of the *ruaḥ*, and those who merit possession of nothing but the *nefesh*. He who merits nothing but the *nefesh*,
and ascends no higher, is associated with the side of uncleanness. . . .
Woe to the wicked who do not deserve to be attached to their Master,
and have not gained merit through the Torah, for whoever has not
gained merit through the Torah does not deserve to possess the *ruaḥ*, or
the *neshamah*, but their attachment will be to the party of the evil kinds.
Such a man has no portion in the holy King. He has no share of
holiness."[58] This passage, which makes a real distinction between the
parts of the soul, is essentially similar to the comparison of *neshamah*,
ruaḥ, and *nefesh* to the righteous, middling, and wicked man respectively.[59] In other words, the *nefesh* on its own is seen as a concomitant
of evil.

One may assume that passages like these were written on the premise
that the *nefesh* did indeed have a holy origin, but that left to itself in the
human body without the help of its more exalted companions, it tended
to subject itself to the power of evil and to afford it positive help. But
even this idea, that a tendency to evil was a natural characteristic of the
nefesh, runs contrary to the idea of unity, and we can see here the
struggle that the author of the Zohar had with this particular problem.
It is possible that his indecision is connected with conflicts that the
author found in the sources that influenced him when he came to deal
with this subject. We shall examine this in the next section.

III

The terms *"nefesh," "ruaḥ,"* and *"neshamah,"* occur in the Bible without any clear differentiation of meaning between them. In the midrash
they are given explicit significance. "Five names are given to [the soul]:
'*nefesh*,' '*neshamah*,' '*ḥayyah*' (living), '*ruaḥ*,' and '*yeḥidah*' (unique).
Nefesh is the blood . . . *ruaḥ* ascends and descends . . . *neshamah* is the
disposition . . . *ḥayyah*, because all the organs die, but it lives on in the

body; *yeḥidah* because the organs are twofold, but it is unique in the body."[60] The kabbalists relied a great deal on this passage, and it is doubtless due to its influence that we find in kabbalistic teaching a five-part division of the soul: *nefesh, ruaḥ, neshamah, ḥayyah* and *yeḥidah.* Nevertheless it is obvious that the midrash is not the source of the division of the soul that occurs in the Zohar. The midrash actually is not concerned with divisions but only with the different names, each of which indicates a specific characteristic of the soul that in itself is "unique in the body." In an adjoining passage the midrash speaks explicitly of *nefesh, ruaḥ,* and *neshamah* as if they were merely synonyms. "Here [Scripture] uses *nefesh, ruaḥ,* and *neshamah,* and there it uses *ruaḥ* instead of *neshamah.* Why interchange the words like this? Scripture wants to draw an analogy between the use of *ḥayyim* (life) in one verse, and the use of *ḥayyim* in the other."[61] We can, however, find a few passages in aggadic literature that do allude to a differentiation between the powers or parts of the soul; for example, "When man sleeps, the body speaks to the *neshamah,* and the *neshamah* to the *nefesh,* and the *nefesh* to an angel. . . ."[62] or "*Aravot* (heaven) where are righteousness, justice, charity, treasuries of life, treasuries of peace, treasuries of blessing, the souls *(neshamot)* of the righteous, and the *ruḥot* and the *neshamot,* which are to be created in the future."[63] These slight allusions, however, do not provide any substantial grounding for the tripartite view of the soul that we have in the Zohar.[64]

The tripartite theory has its origins in Greek philosophy, in the writings of Plato and Aristotle. Plato described the soul as having three parts: intellect, power or anger, and desire. Aristotle supported the tripartite idea but changed the nature of the different parts or powers of the soul. He speaks of an intellectual faculty, an animal faculty, and a vegetative faculty. The Platonic division makes a strong connection between the parts of the soul and ethical qualities, whereas in the Aristotelian system the emphasis is on basic, primary functions. Both these types of division are found in Jewish philosophy, sometimes separately and at others mixed together,[65] and even some of the biblical accounts of the soul seem to be in accord with Greek ideas. A judaised version of Platonic terminology appears at the very beginning of Jewish philosophy in the work of Sa'adia Gaon: "When, now, the soul is united with the body, three faculties belonging to it make their appearance; namely, the power of reasoning, the power of appetition, and that of anger. That is why our language applied to them three distinct appellations, to wit: *nefesh, ruaḥ,* and *neshamah.* By the appellative *nefesh* it alludes to the soul's possession of an appetitive faculty. . . . By the appellative *ruaḥ* . . . it alludes to the soul's possession of the power to become bold and angry. . . . By means of the appellative *neshamah* it refers to the soul's possession of the faculty of cognition."[66] The author of the Zohar therefore already had in front of him, in the works of the Jewish philosophers, the attribution of the terms *neshamah, ruaḥ,* and *nefesh* to the three parts of the soul, *nefesh* being used for the lowest part, *ruaḥ* for the middle part, and *neshamah* for the highest part. The philosophers preceded him also in emphasizing the essential unity of these parts, for even Sa'adia, while accepting the Platonic division, contested the view that there were three completely separate parts and maintained, against Plato, that "the three were one soul."[67] This was stressed even more by Maimonides,[68] who in his theory of the soul followed Aristotle, both in his method of division and in his affirmation of the soul's unity. From another point of view, however, the tripartite division of the soul in the Zohar, bound up as it is with mystical ideas, is completely different from the philosophical one. We must investigate, therefore, whether the transfer of this tripartite principle from philosophy to kabbalah and its reformulation there took place originally in the Zohar and in the Hebrew writings of Rabbi Moses de Leon at the end of the thirteenth century, or whether certain steps had already been taken in this direction in the kabbalistic works that preceded the Zohar.

The *Sefer ha-Bahir,* the earliest literary document of kabbalah, does not mention the tripartite division of the soul.[69] This holds true also, generally speaking, of most of the writings of kabbalists from the school of Rabbi Isaac the Blind, chief among whom was the school of Gerona. In these writings we do find frequent mention of the words *"nefesh," "ruaḥ,"* and *"neshamah,"* but they are nearly always used as synonyms for the holy soul, which is seen as a single, indivisible entity.[70] There are, to be sure, occasional references to the powers or parts of the soul, but only in philosophical terms,[71] without any mention of a mystical tripartite system like the one in the Zohar.[72] In the works of Rabbi Ezra and Rabbi Azriel, however, we do find a clearly mystical division of the soul and an association of the different parts with the *sefirot.* For example, Rabbi Ezra writes,[73] "Everything derives its form from what is above, and then becomes form. Consequently, because of the delicate nature of the spirit and the change it undergoes, its name also changes, and they therefore speak of 'ruḥot,' 'neshamot,' 'nefashot,' 'yeḥidah,' and 'ḥayyah.' " We cannot say, however, that the Zohar's division of the soul originated in passages of this kind. For one thing, they speak of a fivefold, not a threefold division, and, for another, the use of the terms *neshamah, ruaḥ,* and *nefesh* is not consistent. *Neshamah* does not indicate a higher stage than *nefesh* or *ruaḥ;* occasionally, indeed, it appears to indicate the lowest stage.[74] These kabbalists who were strongly influenced by Jewish philosophers did not follow them entirely in this particular area, but developed their own ideas on the parts of the soul on the basis of the midrashic interpretation of the different names.

In contrast to this, the terms *neshamah, ruaḥ,* and *nefesh* do occur, in the Zoharic gradations, in the writings of kabbalists from the second half of the thirteenth century, whom Scholem identifies as a group of Gnostic kabbalists and whose writings, as he demonstrates, had a strong bearing on the teachings of the Zohar.[75] In one book the three terms are used as symbolic titles for the three first *sefirot:* "Consequently, the first three, *Keter Elyon, Ḥokhmah,* and *Binah,* the intellectual and spiritual *sefirot,* are called *ruaḥ, neshamah,* and *nefesh,* and the Cause of causes is the soul of souls (*neshamah of neshamot*), that is to say, of the three *sefirot.*"[76] This sentence puts *ruaḥ* before *neshamah,* but an examination of the whole passage shows that the order adopted was *neshamah, ruaḥ, nefesh.*[77] The correct order occurs in another work from the same school where it is stated that "the *neshamot,* the *ruḥot,* and the *nefashot* were ordained in the treasury of crowns,"[78] which means that their original source lay among the *sefirot.* The *neshamot* are emanated from *Binah* to the angels, the *ruḥot* flow down from *Tiferet* and *Yesod* to the prophets, and the *nefashot* come down from *Malkhut* to the sages and the pious. Here we see that *neshamah, ruaḥ,* and *nefesh* have very close links with the sefirotic system, as in the Zohar, but they are not regarded as three parts of a single soul but rather as souls of different types: the *neshamah* is in the angels, the *ruaḥ* in the prophets, and the *nefesh* in the sages and the pious. So we have the identical Zoharic terminology but used in a different way.

In the kabbalistic literature of the thirteenth century I have not found a division of the soul that is wholly identical with the tripartite division in the Zohar, apart from the *Sefer Sha'arei Orah* by Rabbi Joseph Gikatilla. One excerpt from the book will suffice: "This *sefirah* (i.e.

Binah) is called 'Repentance,' the reason being that the *neshamot* are emanated from this place, and the *ruḥot* from *Tiferet*, and the *nefashot* from the *sefirah Malkhut*. And they are bound to one another so that they can all be unified in the *sefirah Binah*. How? The *nefesh* is linked to the *ruaḥ*, and the *ruaḥ* to the *neshamah*, and the *neshamah* is in the *sefirah Binah*."[79] The last sentence quite clearly shows that we are dealing here with the parts of a single soul. And it is not only the tripartite system that is identical with that of the Zohar. The relationship between the different parts is also the same.

We cannot, however, consider the writings of Rabbi Joseph Gikatilla, a contemporary of Rabbi Moses de Leon, as source material for the Zohar. There are many indications, in fact, that Gikatilla already knew some of the Zohar texts.[80] Therefore we must assume that the transition from the philosophical to the mystical tripartite division of the soul took place at the end of the thirteenth century in the circle of the author of the Zohar, who was influenced also by the writings of the Gnostic kabbalists. What happened was that the terminology and the mystical significance of *neshamah*, *ruaḥ*, and *nefesh*, which these kabbalists attributed to different grades of soul, were combined with the philosophical view that the three divisions formed one single human soul. This hypothesis, namely, that it was the author of the Zohar who first gave a kabbalistic meaning to the philosophical tripartite division, will be supported by my explanation, in the last part of this introduction, of the *Midrash ha-Ne'elam*'s theory of the soul.[81]

C. THE ORIGIN OF THE DIFFERENT PARTS OF THE SOUL

I

The passage that I quoted above from Rabbi Joseph Gikatilla's *Sefer Sha'arei Orah* already raises the question of the origin of the three parts of the soul. Gikatilla states explicitly that they come from the sefirotic world: the *neshamah* from *Binah*, the *ruaḥ* from *Tiferet*, and the *nefesh* from *Malkhut*. This idea is similar to that in the *Sod ha-Neshamot ha-Penimiyot* that the *neshamot* of the angels come from *Binah*, the *ruḥot* of the prophets from *Tiferet*, and the *nefashot* of the sages and the pious from *Malkhut*.

The commentators on the Zohar attributed this view to the Zohar as well. But I have not found a single passage in the main body of the Zohar that expresses a view like it, apart from two passages that were written by the author of *Tikkunei ha-Zohar*.[82] The Zohar itself does establish a connection between *neshamah, ruah,* and *nefesh* and *Binah, Tiferet,* and *Malkhut,* but only an image connection, not a cause-and-effect connection.[83] On the question of origin the Zohar displays considerable confusion and inconsistency. A proper understanding of these passages in the Zohar requires first of all an examination of the basic ideas in the kabbalistic literature that preceded it.

Rabbi Azriel of Gerona, who maintained that the soul had five parts, as we have already seen, thought that they originated from the first five *sefirot.* "The power of the human soul derived from them and from their power, as follows: the highest stage *(Keter)* is in the power of the soul called '*yehidah*'; *Hokhmah* is in the power of the soul, *hayyah; Binah* is in the power of *ruah; Hesed* is in the power of *nefesh;* and *Pahad* ('fear,' i.e., *Gevurah*) is in the power called '*neshamah.*' "[84] This idea is based on the division of the *sefirot* into two sections of five, the five upper ones being the "spiritual" *sefirot,* and the five lower ones being the "physical" *sefirot.*[85] There is no mention of this view in the Zohar.

In the other works of the early kabbalists, most of which deal with just the single soul, we come across a number of different accounts of how the soul originated and developed from its divine source. The *Sefer ha-Bahir*[86] speaks of souls flying from the tree or the fount, referring, apparently, to the *sefirah Binah* or *Yesod.* The pupils of Rabbi Isaac the Blind transmitted a tradition in their master's name that the souls originated in *Binah,* and that they flowed down to this world by way of *Malkhut.* "I heard, in my master's name, that the place of the souls was in Repentance, which is the *sefirah* named '*Binah.*' They originate there and then move down to the Cause *(Malkhut),* and then they go forth and attach themselves to the human body."[87] This idea also occurs in Nachmanides, where *Tiferet* appears to be a stage in the journey of the soul from *Binah* to *Malkhut.*[88]

Rabbi Moses de Leon's *Sefer ha-Nefesh ha-Hakhamah* shows traces of being influenced by the *Sefer ha-Bahir* in the way in which it develops the image of the souls flying from the tree or the river, which it calls "the shining mirror" and "the Tree of Life," symbols of *Tiferet,* used also sometimes for *Yesod.* He also describes the souls as "the fruit of the deeds of the Holy One, blessed be He," or "the fruit of the Holy One, blessed be He."[89] But whenever he comes to the question of the origin of the three parts of the soul he becomes very obscure. "You might say with regard to the mystery of the three stages that we have mentioned, namely, *nefesh, ruah,* and *neshamah,* that it all comes from the one place; but one ought to know that the mystery of the uppermost souls *(neshamot)* alone is that they derive from the place of Truth, and from the stock of the root of the Tree of Truth."[90] There is a clear reference here to the fact that *ruah* and *nefesh* originate below the level of *Tiferet,* which he calls "Truth" and the "stock of the Tree," but it is not clear whether their source is among the lower *sefirot,* such as *Yesod* or *Malkhut,* or outside the divine domain altogether. And even with regard to the *neshamah,* the highest part, it is uncertain whether *Tiferet* is meant to be its actual point of origin; the author could mean that the *neshamah* was formed above the level of *Tiferet,* in the *sefirah Binah,* and that *Tiferet* was simply a stage on its journey. One or two expressions incline one to accept the second possibility: "And He placed in us the mystery of the holy *neshamah,* hewn from the holy place,[91] and from the mount of intellect He established its doors, the source of life";[92] "for the mystery of the highest *neshamah* is in the mystery of the true intellect, intellect from within intellect, through the power of the river whose waters never fail."[93] The term "intellect" fits *Binah* rather than *Tiferet,* and the last sentence states that the *neshamah* comes from the divine intellect "through the power of the river," that is, by means of *Tiferet* or *Yesod.*[94] If this interpretation is right, Rabbi Moses de Leon agrees with Rabbi Isaac the Blind and Nachmanides on the question of the origin of the *neshamah,* but he says nothing about the source of the *ruah* or the *nefesh.*

In another book Rabbi Moses de Leon deals explicitly with the origin of all three parts, and here he differs completely from Gikatilla's view—a view that is also attributed to the Zohar. "They say that the *nefesh* is a power that derives from the father's soul *(nefesh),* which enters the semen by way of the formative power, and therefore the *nefesh* is always associated with the body, and the philosophers call it 'the vegetative soul,' because it grows with the body and never departs from it. They also say that this *nefesh* receives aid from another place above, and because of this aid it is called 'vital,' and this aid comes from above by way of the *Ishim* (men), who are the angels nearest to human beings, and that is why they are called '*Ishim*' . . . The *ruah* comes from a different place, more exalted than the *Ishim*, and it is the mystery of the level called 'the lesser wisdom'. . . . The *neshamah* comes from the mystery of the male in the realms above, for the *neshamot* fly out from the river that flows out of Eden." [95] This passage means that the *neshamah* originates in *Tiferet* or *Yesod,* which are "the mystery of the male in the realms above"; the *ruaḥ* derives from *Malkhut,* "the lesser wisdom"; while the *nefesh* has its origin outside the divine realm altogether. The *nefesh* is a product of the father's soul, with additional help on the part of the angels called *"Ishim."*

However, as far as the origin of *neshamah* is concerned, Rabbi Moses de Leon tried to make his view conform with that of the earlier kabbalists who thought that the *neshamah* was rooted in *Binah*. And so he writes elsewhere in the same book: [96] "At all events, the mystery of *neshamah* is founded upon this name *[Eloah,* assigned here to *Binah],* as it is said 'By the *neshamah* of *Eloah*' (Job 4:9), for the power of the mystery of *neshamah* is there; even though the *neshamot* fly out from the river that flows out of Eden, the root and origin are nonetheless in the highest realms." By comparing these two passages one can see that the author hesitated between *Binah* and *Tiferet* in his choice of origin for the *neshamah,* and he tried to substantiate both, but as far as the *ruaḥ* and the *nefesh* are concerned his view is that consistently upheld in the *Sefer Shekel ha-Kodesh.* [97]

This view, that the *nefesh* has a nondivine origin, is introduced by "they say" and "they also say." This may be a purely artificial quotation, like most of the quotations of this kind in the writings of Rabbi Moses de Leon, where the reference is generally speaking to something that he had written or intended to write in the Zohar. And we do in fact find this idea in the Zohar, in the section entitled *Sitrei Torah,* [98] as we shall see below. There is reason to believe, however, that in this instance there is a clear indication of the original source of the idea: Maimonides' *Mishneh Torah,* where we find, [99] "God provides every physical body with a form suited to it by means of the tenth angel, who is the form called 'Ishim.' " He goes on to say that the "form" of man is knowledge, the intellectual soul. By *Ishim* Maimonides means the Active Intellect, which is tenth in the order of separated intellects. [100] On this point the dependence of Rabbi Moses de Leon and of the *Sitrei Torah* in the Zohar on Maimonides is beyond doubt. But an interesting change took place when the idea was transferred from one field to the other. Whereas

Maimonides holds that *Ishim* is the source of the intellect, the highest part of man's soul, kabbalistic literature sees it as the origin of the lowest part.[101] Changes of this type also occur with other ideas as they find their way from philosophy to kabbalah.

II

The descriptions in the *Sefer ha-Bahir* of the *neshamot* emerging from the world of the *sefirot*, as if they flew out of "the tree," or flowed down with "the river"—descriptions that we also find in the writings of Rabbi Moses de Leon—occur very frequently in many passages in the Zohar.[102] From the tree or the river, which symbolize *Tiferet* or *Yesod*, the *neshamot* find their way to *Malkhut*, depicted in these passages as garden, earth, sea, hall, or ark, and from there they descend to the world below. In passages like this nothing is said of the original source of the *neshamah*, and the accounts of flying or flowing, in themselves, do not give us any definite information on this subject, as I have already said.

There are, however, a few passages that do deal explicitly with the source of the *neshamah*, and assign to it a much more exalted origin. In one such, if I have understood the symbols correctly, there is a clear indication that the *neshamah* originated in the *sefirah* Ḥokhmah. "Rabbi Judah began by quoting 'Let every soul *(neshamah)* praise Yah' (Psalm 150:6). It has been taught: All the *neshamot* come from this holy body, and bestir themselves in human beings. From which place? From the place called 'Yah.' What is this place? Rabbi Judah said: It is written 'How numerous are Your works, O Lord, You have made them all with Ḥokhmah (Wisdom)' (Psalm 104:24). It has been taught: It is from Ḥokhmah, whose fountains flow out in thirty-two directions, that everything is perfected, everything both above and below, and it is called 'holy spirit,' for all the spirits are perfected by it." [103] There seems to be a clear distinction here between the original source of the *neshamot* and the place from which they actually emerge. They come into the lower world from "the holy body," but their original source is in "the holy spirit." "The holy body" sometimes denotes *Tiferet*, as in the descriptions of the trunk of the human body, or the trunk of the sefirotic tree, but in general, corporeality is attributed to the *sefirah Malkhut*, and such is the case here. "The holy spirit" is also a title given to *Malkhut*, but here there is no doubt that it indicates the upper Ḥokhmah, the proof being the name *Yah*, and the reference to the thirty-two directions. We may deduce from this passage, therefore, that the *neshamot* emerge from *Malkhut*, but their actual point of origin is *Ḥokhmah*.

In other passages also there are obscure references to the exalted origin of the *neshamah*, but it would appear that in most of them either *Binah* or *Ḥokhmah* is intended. In one[104] it is stated that the holy *neshamah* comes "from above," and emerges from the river, but it is nowhere explained what the realm "above" the river really is. The discussion of the *neshamah*'s origin in the *Sava de-Mishpatim*[105] is slightly clearer. " 'A priest's daughter married to a foreign man' (Leviticus 22:12)—this is the holy soul *(neshamah)*, drawn from a celestial place, and put into a secret place in the Tree of Life, and when the breath of the celestial priest blows, and puts souls into this tree, they fly from there and enter a treasury." The nature of the "celestial place," which is the original source, is not clear here either, but since it says that the *neshamot* enter the Tree of Life, that is, *Tiferet* or *Yesod*, when the breath of the celestial priest (that is, *Ḥesed*) blows, we may deduce that the celestial place is *Binah*, which adjoins *Ḥesed* in the sefirotic order.[106] Also the reference to the fact that the source of the *neshamah* is in "the life above"[107] seems to indicate *Binah*. In the Gerona school "life *(ḥayyim)*" was a symbol of either *Ḥokhmah* or *Binah*,[108] whereas in the Zohar it usually indicates the influence that flows from *Binah*.

In the Zohar to the Torah I have found only one passage that deals with the origin of the three parts of the soul, *neshamah*, *ruaḥ*, and *nefesh*, and even this is not in the main body of the Zohar but in the *Sitrei Torah*.[109] In this passage the source of the *nefesh* is stated to be in the realm of the angels called "Ishim," the origin of the *ruaḥ* is in the female, *Malkhut*, and the source of the *neshamah* is in the male, *Tiferet*. As far as the origins of the *neshamah* and the *ruaḥ* are concerned, this idea occurs in several passages in the main body of the Zohar, and we may deduce from them *in toto* that the source of the *nefesh* was thought to be outside the sefirotic system. "Now we may reveal that all the *neshamot* emerge from a tall and mighty tree, and from the river that flows out of Eden; and all the *ruḥot* from another, small tree. The *neshamah* is above and the *ruaḥ* below and they are joined together on the pattern of male and female, and when they are united they shine with a supernal radiance, and in this joint union they are together called 'ner' (lamp); 'the *ner* of the Lord is the soul of man' (Proverbs 20:27).

What is *ner?*—*neshamah ruaḥ.*"[110] The two trees from which *neshamah* and *ruaḥ* emanate are the Tree of Life and the Tree of Knowledge, that is, *Tiferet* and *Malkhut.*[111] It goes on to say that only in the lower Garden of Eden is *nefesh* joined to *neshamah* and *ruaḥ.* It is clear, therefore, that *nefesh* has its source below the world of the *sefirot.*

Finally, I should like to quote another passage, which says, apparently, that even the *ruaḥ* does not have a divine origin. "Come and see. The *neshamah* emerges, and enters the mountains of separation, and the *ruaḥ* becomes united with the *neshamah*. It descends farther, and the *nefesh* becomes united with the *ruaḥ*, and they all move and become united with one another."[112] One may deduce from the fact that the *ruaḥ* becomes united with the *neshamah* among "the mountains of separation" that the *ruaḥ* originates in a nondivine area, in the Chariot, or in the world of the angels, for "the mountains of separation" *(turei di-peruda)* is a term that denotes the worlds that are below the level of the *sefirot*, separated from God. "From [the *sefirot*] downward is called 'the mountains of Beter (lit., separation),' for it is written 'And from there it was separated and became four heads' (Genesis 2:10)—the mountains of separation."[113] "The mountains of separation" is a synonym for "the world of separation," which in the cosmological system of Jewish philosophy is the sphere of the separated Intellects. And so we cannot identify this passage with the view that the *ruaḥ* had its source in *Malkhut,* unless we assume that the unification of the *ruaḥ* with the *neshamah* took place at a level lower than the source of the *ruaḥ.*

To sum up: In the Zohar we find a number of inconsistencies and contradictions with regard to the source of the *neshamah,* the highest part of the soul. In some passages the *neshamah* is located in one of the higher *sefirot, Ḥokhmah* or *Binah.* In others its source is said to be *Tiferet.* In the first the author seems to ignore the problem of the origin of the *ruaḥ* and the *nefesh,* while in the second we find the idea that the *ruaḥ* comes from *Malkhut* and the *nefesh* from a nondivine source. The passages of the first type are similar to the views expressed by Rabbi Moses de Leon in his *Sefer ha-Nefesh ha-Ḥakhamah,* except that there is no mention there of *Ḥokhmah* as the source of the *neshamah.* The passages of the second type, however, are absolutely identical with the view of Rabbi Moses de Leon in his *Sefer Shekel ha-Kodesh,* and it is possible therefore that even here the original source of the *neshamah* is thought to be *Binah.* At all events there is no basis whatsoever for the traditional view that the Zohar as a whole maintains that the *neshamah* comes from *Binah,* the *ruaḥ* from *Tiferet,* and the *nefesh* from *Malkhut.* This view arose in two ways: first, because such an arrangement does exist in certain strata of the Zohar and in Rabbi Joseph Gikatilla's *Sefer Sha'arei Orah;* and second, because the Zohar sometimes describes *neshamah, ruaḥ,* and *nefesh* as images of the *sefirot Binah, Tiferet,* and *Malkhut.*

III

With regard to the source of the *neshamah* there is one particular view that occurs quite frequently in a number of passages in the Zohar and that seems to run counter to both the ideas outlined above. According to this the *neshamah* is the fruit of divine intercourse between *Tiferet* and *Malkhut.* "We have learned the meaning of the mystery of the matter, that the *neshamah* has a father and mother, just as the body on earth has a father and mother. It signifies that in all realms, whether above or below, everything proceeds from, and is sustained by, male and female." [114] A few passages depict the origin of the *neshamah* in terms of the pregnancy of the *Shekhinah* by her "husband," *Tiferet,* and of the formation of the embryo in its mother's womb. [115] The description of the *neshamot* as the products of the Holy One, blessed be He, which occurs frequently in the Zohar, assumes here a distinctly sexual symbolic flavor. "Rabbi Isaac said: It is written 'A river goes out from Eden to water the garden' (Genesis 2:10). This is the pillar upon which the world stands, and it waters the garden, and the garden is made fertile by it, and through it it produces fruit, and all the fruits fly into the world, and they sustain the world, and sustain the Torah. And what are they? The souls *(neshamot)* of the righteous, which are the fruit of the deeds of the Holy One, blessed be He." [116] The river is *Yesod,* the Righteous One, foundation of the world, the transmitter of seed in the intercourse between *Tiferet* and *Malkhut,* which is the garden; and from the seed that the garden receives the *neshamot* are formed, the fruits, as it were, of the garden.

All these passages speak of the soul in general without differentiating the three parts of the soul, just like those which ascribe the origin of the *neshamah* to *Binah,* but here there is no reference to *Binah* at all, the soul being depicted as a joint product of *Tiferet* and *Malkhut.* By connecting the *neshamah* with intercourse between male and female, this idea also conflicts with that in other passages which relate the *neshamah* to the male and the *ruaḥ* to the female. So we must conclude apparently that we have here a third view.

However, it would seem to me that the creation of souls through intercourse is just another way of expressing Nachmanides' view that the souls originate from *Binah* and proceed downward by way of *Tiferet* and *Malkhut.* The Zohar, generally speaking, sees divine intercourse not as a specific act of procreation, but as a continuous process by which influence is transmitted from the upper *sefirot,* particularly from *Binah.* From this point of view, the appearance of the soul in its original source, *Binah,* is like the tiniest drop of semen when it first appears in the brain,[117] and the formation of souls at intercourse is due to the transmission of semen from the brain. The new aspect in these passages is that the view of the early kabbalists concerning the movement of the *neshamot* from one level to another, from *Binah* to *Malkhut,* is expressed in sexual terms.

Rabbi Moses Cordovero faced the problem of the apparent contradiction between the ascription of the *neshamah* to *Binah* and the view that it was the result of intercourse, and I have followed his solution. He writes,[118] "It is known that the process of transmission of the soul *(neshamah)* from *Binah* to *Tiferet* and *Malkhut* is hidden and subtle, like the way in which semen moves from the brain of the male to the male organ, and from the brain of the female to the female organ." So we see that the passages that maintain that the *neshamah* was formed by intercourse are consistent with the view, expressed in other passages in the Zohar, that the *neshamah* originated in *Binah.*

D. THE PREEXISTENCE OF THE SOUL

I

One of the most important aspects of the theory of the soul, much debated by the medieval rabbis, was the question of the actual time of the soul's formation. Did the soul exist in a spiritual form in the upper world before it entered the body, or did its existence begin at the moment of union with the body? A number of other crucial problems are connected with the solution of this question: the nature of the soul, for example; is it an independent entity or not? And also the survival of the soul: does it have a separate existence once it has left the body at death?

The debate on this problem goes back to the schools of Plato and Aristotle. The dialogues of Plato, who posited the preexistence of the soul, are full of mythical accounts of the life of the soul in its preterrestrial existence, and his theory of knowledge too is based on the soul's recollection of the knowledge that it had acquired in the celestial world. Aristotle, in contrast, saw the soul as the form of the body, and so there was no room in his philosophy for the preexistence of the individual soul, because forms have independent existence only when they are joined to matter.

In aggadic literature the soul's preexistence is discussed as if it were part of traditional Jewish belief, but it does not go back as far as the Judaism of ancient times. It seems to have been picked up from Platonic philosophy. A few quotations will illustrate this. "*Aravot* (heaven) where are . . . the souls of the righteous and the *ruḥot* and the *neshamot* which are to be created in the future" [119] "With the supreme King of Kings, the Holy One, blessed be He, dwell the souls of the righteous, with whom He took counsel before creating the world." [120] There is a much more straightforward and precise statement in a later midrash: "You must know that all the souls from Adam to the end of time were created during the six days of Creation. They were all in the Garden of Eden, and they were all present at the Revelation of the Torah." [121] These statements, and there are many others like them, demonstrate conclusively that the rabbis of the *aggadah* believed in the preexistence of souls during the period of Creation, and that some of them believed they existed even before Creation. [122]

However, in the Middle Ages this was not accepted as a cardinal Jewish belief. The lines of debate were drawn as between the Platonists and the Aristotelians. Even Rav Sa'adia Gaon, who defined the soul as "a delicate substance, more pure, clear, and simple than the substance of the spheres," denied its preexistence and asserted that the Creator created it "simultaneously with the completion of the bodily form of the human being." [123] Maimonides, following Aristotle, is understandably of a similar opinion: "the soul that lives in man when he is born is a mere faculty." [124] They were opposed, however, by a group of Neoplatonists who either explicitly or implicitly maintained the preexistence of the soul. Here, for example, is a quotation from an anonymous author who holds that to deny the preexistence of the soul is heresy: "The view of the Torah and the God-fearing who possess the truth is that the soul is a spiritual substance, existing before the body and surviving after its destruction. . . . And I have come across a third view, namely, that the soul originates at the same time as the body, but does not perish with the body. This is the view of Avicenna, but it is not consistent with the Torah or with the view of the God-fearing who possess the truth, for the soul precedes that to which it is attached, just as sense precedes sensible things, and intellect precedes intelligible things." [125]

II

The actual belief in the preexistence of the soul is not questioned at all in the Zohar. The author describes in some detail the life and enjoyment of the soul in the Garden of Eden before it descends to the terrestrial world, as I shall explain below in the introduction to the section *Body and Soul*. But when one comes to analyze the belief, one finds certain difficulties, particularly with regard to the actual time of the soul's creation, and its nature immediately after it was created.

As we have seen, the rabbis of the *aggadah* maintained that the souls existed before the creation of the world, or at the very latest during the six days of Creation. There are similar statements, no doubt influenced by the *aggadah*, in the Zohar. At first glance, this view cannot be consistent with the idea that the souls were formed by divine intercourse, because the latter involves a continuous process that goes on even after the creation of the world. Rabbi Moses Cordovero posed the problem with absolute clarity: "What we must now investigate is this. It would appear from all these statements that the souls originate from a union between *Tiferet* and *Malkhut*, as we have already demonstrated. But this is an impossibility, because Rabbi Simeon ben Yohai has explicitly stated that the souls had all been created, at the very latest, by the time of the creation of the world." [126] Rabbi Moses Cordovero was particularly perplexed by the statement that the Holy One, blessed be He, had shown Adam all the souls that were to enter the world. The Zohar makes it quite clear that what Adam saw was not a vision of the future, nor an inspired view of souls that existed only within the divine thought, but souls that actually existed at that particular time, and were going to continue to exist. "You might say that [Adam] saw by means of the holy spirit that they were to enter the world, like someone who in his wisdom can see the future. But it was not so. He saw them all with his own eyes. In the form in which they were later to exist in the world he saw them all with his own eyes. . . . You might say that once he had seen them they did not continue to exist. Come and see. All the manifestations of the Holy One, blessed be He, actually exist, and are present before Him, until they come down into the world."[127]

Rabbi Moses Cordovero's solution was that six hundred thousand souls, corresponding to the number of those who came out of Egypt— in other words, the "root" souls of Israel—came into being and emanated from *Malkhut* with the soul of Adam, and it was these that Adam saw. But the remaining souls destined to enter the world are formed by a continuous process of divine intercourse. By adopting this forced solution to the problem, Rabbi Moses Cordovero wanted to forestall another possible solution, namely, that the souls had an independent existence at their first source within the Godhead before they emerged from the world of the *sefirot* by the process of intercourse. We can see this attempt to deny the preexistence of souls within the Godhead in another part of the same book: "It is a fact that when the *neshamah*, the *nefesh*, and the *ruah* were attached to their root before their emanation, they were not revealed in the state of their actual existence, but they were formed by being spread and poured into the female. . . . This means that [the soul] had no existence except like that of the semen formed by the subtle power that spreads from the brain. . . . So it is with the *neshamah*. In *Binah* it is like a light, and similarly with the influence in *Tiferet*, which is suited to the *ruah*, and the influence in *Malkhut*, which is suited to the *nefesh*. And by the process of unification (i.e., intercourse) this flow of influence becomes the form of *neshamah, ruah*, and *nefesh*."[128]

Indeed, the continuation of the passage in the Zohar about Adam supports Cordovero's view that it refers to a preexistence outside the realm of the *sefirot*. It says there[129] that when Adam saw the souls "they were all in the Garden of Eden." But the restriction of the number to six hundred thousand conflicts with the beginning of the passage, where it speaks of "all the souls that were to exist in the future within mankind." Consequently, we must conclude from the text of this passage that at the creation of the world all the souls were emanated and placed in the Garden of Eden,[130] and the contradiction between this passage and the others, which maintain that the souls were formed by a process of intercourse after Creation, remains unresolved.

Moreover, even with regard to preexistence itself there are a number of passages in the Zohar that conflict with the view expressed in the passage about Adam. Mention is made several times of the souls having an independent, individual existence before the creation of the world. "When the Holy One, blessed be He, sought to create the world, it was His wish that He should fashion all the souls subsequently to be given to mankind. And all of them were formed in His presence in the exact image that they were later to have in the world of men." [131] It would appear that the act of "fashioning" the souls described here took place within the divine realm. But this gives rise to a number of problems. In which *sefirah* were the souls formed before the creation of the world? Was this act of formation identical with the formation through intercourse, or were there two separate processes? Did some alteration take place in the life of the soul after the creation of the world?

It would seem to me that the key to the solution of these problems lies in one particular passage, which speaks of a number of stages in the birth of souls. "From the moment that it occurred in the [divine] thought to create the world, but before the world was created, all the spirits *(ruḥot)* of the righteous were stored up in thought before Him, each one in its own particular image. When He fashioned the world they were all revealed and they stood in their own image before Him, in the most exalted height. Afterward, He placed them in a single storehouse in the Garden of Eden, and this storehouse never becomes full. . . . This storehouse has only one desire, and that is to receive souls continuously." [132] Here we have three temporal stages in the souls' origin: before Creation, during Creation, and after Creation. These stages also denote different points in the development of the souls' nature and mode of life. However, the character of these differences is not clear and needs investigation. In the first stage, before Creation, the souls "were stored up in the [divine] thought." "Thought" when used in its narrowest sense in the Zohar denotes the *sefirah* Ḥokhmah, but one can at a pinch attribute it also to *Binah*. I have already established that according to a whole group of passages in the Zohar the soul has its original and highest source in *Binah* or *Ḥokhmah*. Therefore this first stage is the very root source of the souls, where they are described as being "stored up," but with "each one in its own particular image." This means, I think, that they possessed individuated forms in the divine thought, but no ontological existence. This latter is depicted in the second stage, at the creation of the world, and the change that takes place in the life of the soul is indicated by the words "revealed" and "stood" as against being "stored up" in the first stage. The place where the souls existed at the second stage is described rather vaguely as "the most exalted height," but the reference must be to one of the *sefirot* below the level of *Ḥokhmah,* and also apparently below the level of *Binah.* At the third stage, after Creation, the souls are placed in "a storehouse,"[133] but in contrast to the previous two places the storehouse never contains all the souls at one and the same time. They enter and leave it in a continuous process, and consequently "this storehouse never becomes full."

This passage does not explain how the souls get to the storehouse, which yearns to receive them, but it would appear from the context that the souls are produced by the *Shekhinah* after she has become impregnated with them in intercourse. Therefore we must take this passage, where intercourse is not mentioned at all, in conjunction with another. "Rabbi Simeon said: This verse is difficult. If it had said simply 'Who formed the spirit *(ruaḥ)* of man' (Zechariah 12:1), it would have been straightforward. But what does 'within him' mean? There is a mystery here from two points of view. From the river that flows forth continuously from there, the souls fly away and assemble in one place, and this level is [where] 'He formed the spirit of man within him.' It is like the woman who is impregnated by the male, and the child is a form in her womb, until its formation is completed in her womb. So here: 'He formed the spirit of man within him.' It exists 'within him' until man is created in the world, and then she (i.e., the *Shekhinah*) gives him *[ruaḥ].*"[134] The river is *Yesod,* which transmits the souls from *Tiferet* to *Malkhut* in the process of intercourse, and forms the souls within *Malkhut.* They assume their form within *Malkhut* like a child in its mother's womb. And when the time comes for them to descend into men's bodies, she produces them from within herself. It would seem from this passage that once the soul has left the realm of the *Shekhinah* it immediately enters the human body, but from the previous and other passages we know that the souls do not descend immediately and directly into the world below, but wait in a storehouse in the Garden of Eden, which is also termed "the body of the souls." We may assume, therefore, that we need to add the intercourse process and the birth of the souls as an intermediate stage between their life "in the most exalted height" and their entry into the storehouse.[135]

At this stage, the lowest stage in the divine realm, the souls become more crystallized as independent entities, for each soul's "formation is completed" within the *Shekhinah*. But the final touch to the individual shape of each soul is added in the storehouse in the Garden of Eden. "When the Holy One, blessed be He, resolved to create man, he was present before Him in his form and stature just as he is in this world. The whole of mankind, even before they entered this world, were all present in their own stature and shape, just as they are in this world, in a single storehouse, where all the souls in the world are clothed with their forms." In the storehouse the souls are clothed in a celestial garment of light, in which the individual lineaments of their corporeal garments in this world can already be discerned.

We see, therefore, that the preexistent life of the soul has four successive stages, becoming more and more individualistic. It is at first hidden within the divine thought, in *Hokhmah* or *Binah*. It is then revealed, and exists in its own particular image in "the most exalted height," which appears to be *Tiferet*. After this, it reaches its full form within the *Shekhinah,* and, finally, it is clothed in its own individual shape in the storehouse in the Garden of Eden. This view, which maintains that each soul has its own individual preexistent life even among the divine *sefirot*, is without doubt the dominant one in the main body of the Zohar, and Rabbi Moses Cordovero's interpretation is mistaken.[136]

III

Belief in the preexistence of the soul also finds expression in the writings of the kabbalists of the Gerona school, and it would appear that they too thought that the soul had an individualistic identity in the world of the *sefirot*. Nachmanides writes:[137] "The souls were all created before, as they said in *Bereshit Rabbah:*[138] 'He took counsel with the souls of the righteous'; and also in the Talmud:[139] '*Aravot* (heaven) where are treasuries of life, treasuries of peace, the souls of the righteous, and the *ruḥot* and the *neshamot* that are to be created in the future.' And Rabbi Judah ha-Levi said:[140] 'He prepared souls together with the primal light, the beginning of the word of the Lord.' This is why God asked Job whether he knew the way to the dwelling of light, and if he understood the paths by which it could be reached, and whether he realized that he was born at the same time as the light. . . . The misguided think that the souls are created separately every day, when men are born, but this is not the case, for God does not now make things *ex nihilo.* The upper worlds were created long ago, and lower substances which are subject to generation and decay are made from other substances, in a continuous process of shedding and assuming forms." Since Nachmanides supports his argument from the midrash that the Holy One, blessed be He, took counsel with the souls of the righteous about the creation of the world, he must have believed that the souls preceded the world in time. Consequently, the primal light that existed when the souls were born cannot be the physical light that was created on the first day of Creation, but *Ḥesed,* the first of the seven lower *sefirot,* which was emanated from *Binah,* and this is the origin of the souls. According to this passage, therefore, the souls came into being before the world of emanation was completed, and they originated within the sefirotic system.[141]

Rabbi Azriel of Gerona also refers to the souls' preexistence among the *sefirot.* He writes:[142] "All these (i.e., the things that existed before the creation of the world) were stored up in Thought, and when they arose in Thought light was made to suit their characteristics, and it was stored. Some of them were above the Torah, some in the Torah, some in the Throne of Glory, some below, some in the place of the Temple, each one was stored in a place that accorded with the characteristic that it was later to have. All the souls were created, and when the right time came they were placed in the body that was suited to them." The meaning here appears to be that the souls first existed in the divine thought without any individual identity. During the emanatory process they acquired a spiritual existence when their light was formed, this light being stored at and below the level of the divine attributes. The lights of the souls then descended by a continuous process from the place where they were stored, and entered the bodies that were designated for them.

It would seem then that Nachmanides and Rabbi Azriel both influenced the author of the Zohar when he came to crystallize his views on the preexistence of the soul. This influence can be seen even in the terminology. The phrase "stored up in Thought," for example, in the Zohar is derived from the passage in Rabbi Azriel.[143]

NOTES

1. See also *Zohar Ḥadash, Bereshit,* 5a *(Midrash ha-Ne'elam).*
2. See Zohar I, 71a.

3. Zohar III, 48a.
4. B.T. *Berakhot*, 6b.
5. *Bereshit Rabbah*, 21:5.
6. B.T. *Shabbat*, 151b.
7. D. H. Joel, *Midrash ha-Zohar, Die Religionsphilosophie des Sohar und ihr Verhältniss zur allgemeinen jüdischen Theologie* (Leipzig, 1849), pp. 95–103.
8. See A. Franck, *Die Kabbala oder die Religions-Philosophie der Hebräer* (Leipzig, 1844), pp. 165–66.
9. See I. Tishby, "Ha-Semel ve-ha-Dat ba-Kabbalah" in *Erkhei ha-Yahadut* (1943), pp. 62–66.
10. *The Guide for the Perplexed*, III, 12 (trans. Friedlander).
11. Ibid., 13.
12. *Sefer Avodat ha-Kodesh*, III, 1.
13. *The Guide for the Perplexed*, III, 12 and 13.
14. *Sefer Avodat ha-Kodesh*, III, 5.
15. See ibid., I, 17–18.
16. There are problems of terminology in dealing with the parts of the soul. There is no specific term for the psychic power representing the totality of the parts. We must perforce use *"nefesh"* or *"neshamah,"* but this can lead to misunderstanding because these terms are also used respectively for the lowest and the highest parts of the soul.
17. Zohar I, 13a.
18. It is possible that in this passage the tree symbolizes the whole sefirotic system and its trunk symbolizes *Tiferet*.
19. Zohar III, 174b.
20. *Sefer ha-Nefesh ha-Ḥakhamah* (Basle, 1608), II, sig. 3, fol. 4a. See G. Scholem, *Major Trends in Jewish Mysticism* (New York, 1946), p. 241.
21. Zohar II, 75b–76a. See also I, 20b.
22. *Sefer Shekel ha-Kodesh* (London, 1911), pp. 33–34. See also *Sefer ha-Nefesh ha-Ḥakhamah*, end of sec. 21, sig. 14, fol. 2a.
23. See R. M. Jones, *Studies in Mystical Religion* (London, 1919), pp. 229–34, on the soul as divine spark, in the teaching of Meister Eckhart. The author of the Zohar did not stress the divinity of the soul in the same way as the Christian mystic, but the two views do have a certain similarity.
24. See B.T. *Shabbat*, 152b; B.T. *Ḥagigah*, 12b.
25. See W. Hirsch, *Rabbinic Psychology* (London, 1947), pp. 152–63.
26. *Sefer ha-Nefesh ha-Ḥakhamah*, I, sig. 3, fol. 2a. See also end of sec. 21, sig. 14, fol. 2a. The variants here from the printed text are taken from Oxford MS 1630.
27. See *Bereshit Rabbah*, 8: 11; *Shemot Rabbah*, 30: 16.
28. B.T. *Berakhot*, 10a. An expanded version occurs in *Vayikra Rabbah*, ed. M. Margaliot (Jerusalem, 1953), 4: 8; and see the parallels mentioned in the notes. See also Rabbi Shabbetai Donnolo's *Ḥakhmoni (Sefer Yeẓirah)* (Warsaw, 1884), fols. 65a–65b.
29. Zohar I, 103b.

30. See Zohar I, 19b–20a; II, 156b–157a.
31. The nearest view to that of the kabbalists, on the soul's connection with the upper worlds in respect to both its origin and its character, is to be found in German hasidism. Here, for example, is a passage from the *Sefer Ḥokhmat ha-Nefesh* by Rabbi Eleazar of Worms (Lemberg, 1870), fol. 1a: "The soul is obliged to bless Him who created it, for it is like Him in respect to the appearance of His presence, and in respect to His being, for it was exhaled from Him, spirit from spirit." Similar passages occur elsewhere in the book, and they could possibly have had some influence on the author of the Zohar.
32. *Sefer ha-Nefesh ha-Ḥakhamah,* preface. One can trace close parallels to this idea in sources that the author of the Zohar may have used. In Al-Ghazali's *Sefer Moznei Ẓedek* (Leipzig, 1839) it says (p. 28): "Son of man, know yourself and you will know your God," and in a different version in the *Sefer Ḥokhmat ha-Nefesh* by Rabbi Eleazar of Worms, fol. 1d: "Whoever knows the mystery of the soul knows the mystery of the Unity." See A. Jellinek, *Moses ben Schem-Tob de Leon* (Leipzig, 1851), p. 10.
33. *Zohar Ḥadash, Bereshit,* 18b *(Midrash ha-Ne'elam).*
34. *Sefer Shekel ha-Kodesh,* p. 5.
35. On the soul existing in this world like an exile or prisoner, see Rabbi Baḥya ibn Pakuda, *Sefer Ḥovot ha-Levavot* III, 2; VI, 5; VII, 3 (end); IX, 3 [trans. Mansoor, *The Book of Direction to the Duties of the Heart* (London, 1973) pp. 181, 311, 396, 409]; Rabbi Abraham bar Ḥayya, *Sefer Hegyon ha-Nefesh* (Leipzig, 1860), 11b, 16a [trans. Wigoder, *The Meditation of the Sad Soul* (London, 1969), pp. 64, 74]. On the liberation of the soul from its physical bonds, see Rabbi Solomon ibn Gabirol, *Sefer Mekor Ḥayyim,* ed. Bluwstein-Zifroni (Tel-Aviv, 1926), 1:2; 5:43; *Ḥovot ha-Levavot,* X: 1 and 7 [Mansoor, pp. 427–28, 441–45]; Maimonides, *Moreh Nevukhim,* III: 8 and 51 [trans. Friedlander, *The Guide for the Perplexed* (London, 1904), 261ff., 390–91.]
36. *Bereshit Rabbah,* 69:3.
37. *Yalkut Shimoni,* I, no. 945.
38. For a similar differentiation between magic and mysticism, see E. Underhill, *Mysticism* (London, 1930), pp. 70–71.
39. [These are three words found in biblical Hebrew, each of which has the meaning "soul."]
40. Zohar II, 142a. This passage admittedly deals with the three parts of the soul in the *sefirot,* but it is modeled on the situation within man.
41. Zohar I, 186b. See also II, 182a.
42. See also Zohar II, 259a.
43. See Zohar II, 142a.
44. A. Franck, *Die Kabbala,* p. 168. See also C. D. Ginsburg, *The Kabbalah* (London, 1865), p. 114.
45. E. Müller, *Der Sohar und seine Lehre* (Vienna, Berlin, 1920), p. 32. See also H. Zeitlin, "Mafteaḥ le-Sefer ha-Zohar,' *Ha-Tekufah* 9:293.
46. However, in Rabbi Moses de Leon's *Sefer Mishkan ha-Edut* I did find a

definition of *ruaḥ*'s role that approximates to the view attributed to the Zohar in Franck's book. Oxford MS 1271, fol. 37b, reads "[the *ruaḥ]* rests (thus Oxford MS 1608) upon the soul in order to sustain it and support it with intellect and understanding and knowledge, so that it might know how to choose between good and evil, for the *ruaḥ* brings knowledge of good and evil since it is part of the mystery of the Tree of Knowledge of Good and Evil, and comes from there."

47. Zohar III, 70b.
48. Zohar I, 79b *(Sitrei Torah)*.
49. *Sefer ha-Nefesh ha-Ḥakhamah*, I, sig. 3, fol. 1a–1b. The errors have been corrected on the basis of Oxford MS 1630.
50. *Sefer ha-Nefesh ha-Ḥakahmah*, I. sig. 2, fol. 4b–sig. 3, fol. 1a. The text has been corrected on the basis of Oxford MS 1630. Compare *Sefer Shekel ha-Kodesh*, pp. 33–34; *Sefer Or Zarua* (Oxford MS 1278) fols. 200a–200b.
51. See Zohar I, 206a; II, 142a.
52. See also Zohar I, 50b–51b.
53. In the third section of this introduction, concerning the origin of the parts of the soul.
54. See Zohar II, 141b–142a; III, 70b.
55. See Zohar I, 62a.
56. Zohar III, 70b.
57. Zohar I, 12b.
58. Zohar III, 25a–25b.
59. See Zohar I, 62a.
60. *Bereshit Rabbah*, 14:9. And see the variant readings in Theodor-Albeck's edition.
61. *Bereshit Rabbah*, 14:10. The two verses under discussion are Genesis 2:7: "And He breathed into his nostrils the breath of life *(nishmat ḥayyim)*, and man became a living soul *(nefesh ḥayyah)*" and Genesis 7:22: "all in whose nostrils was the breath of the spirit of life *(ruaḥ ḥayyim)*."
62. *Vayikra Rabbah*, 32:2.
63. B.T. *Ḥagigah*, 12b.
64. See W. Hirsch, *Rabbinic Psychology*, pp. 151–52.
65. See S. Horovitz, *Die Psychologie bei den jüdischen Religionsphilosophen des Mittelalters von Saadia bis Maimuni* (1900), 2: 115; 3 (1906): 174; 4 (1912): 224–25.
66. *Sefer Emunot ve-Deot*, VI, 3 [trans. Rosenblatt, *The Book of Beliefs and Opinions* (New Haven, 1948), pp. 243–44]. See also Rabbi Abraham ibn Ezra's commentary to Exodus 23:25, where he has borrowed, with certain changes and enlargements, from the *Sefer Ḥokhmat ha-Nefesh* by Rabbi Eleazar of Worms, 5d. Maimonides used the terms *neshamah, ruaḥ,* and *nefesh* in a different sense. See his *Mishneh Torah, Hilkhot Yesodei ha-Torah*, IV, 8–9.
67. *Sefer Emunot ve-Deot*, VI, 3.
68. See his *Shemoneh Perakim*, I.

69. On the soul in *Sefer ha-Bahir*, see Scholem, *Reshit ha-Kabbalah* (Jerusalem, 1948), pp. 34–36, 43–45.

70. Even in the *Sefer Ma'arekhet ha-Elohut*, whose author was a pupil of Rabbi Solomon ben Adret, *nefesh* and *neshamah* are used as synonyms, and there is no mention of the tripartite division. See chap. 10 of the work.

71. These terms are also used in the writings of Rabbi Jacob ben Sheshet Gerondi, in the *Sefer ha-Emunah ve-ha-Bitaḥon*, attributed to Nachmanides, and in the *Sefer Meshiv Devarim Nekhoḥim*, which is extant in manuscript.

72. In a passage that exists in one version of Rabbi Ezra's *Perush ha-Aggadot* (Vatican MS 294, fol. 36a), in connection with a statement by Rabbi Jacob ha-Nazir concerning the two souls that man enjoys on the Sabbath, it is said that "man has three souls." The souls enumerated there are: the wise soul, the vital soul, and the animal soul. However, the whole of this passage, which is quoted verbatim in Rabbi Moses de Leon's *Sefer ha-Nefesh ha-Ḥakhamah* (sig. 8, fol. 1d), does not belong to Rabbi Ezra's *Perush*, as I have shown elsewhere (see *Perush ha-Aggadot le-Rabbi Azriel*, introduction, p. 13). The passage dealing with the three souls is textually very close to Rabbi Abraham ibn Ezra's commentary to Exodus 23:25, and it has no bearing whatsoever on the question of the tripartite nature of the soul in kabbalah.

73. *Perush ha-Aggadot le-Rabbi Ezra*, Vatican MS 441, fol. 34a.

74. See *Perush ha-Aggadot le-Rabbi Azriel*, p. 19, n. 5.

75. See G. Scholem, "Kabbalot R. Ya'akov ve-R. Yiẓḥak benei R. Ya'akov ha-Kohen," *Mad'ei ha-Yahadut* 2 (1927): 194–95; "Le-ḥeker Kabbalat R. Yiẓḥak ha-Kohen," *Tarbiẓ* II, p. 192; III, pp. 280–81; IV, p. 70; *Major Trends in Jewish Mysticism*, pp. 175, 177. See also above, pp. 462; 472, nn. 55, 57; 532, n. 3.

76. G. Scholem, "Kabbalot R. Ya'akov," p. 228. The version here follows text B, the clearer of the two, but as far as the present subject is concerned, and the terminology, there is no difference between the two. One ought to note, however, that the attribution of this passage, including text A, to the Gnostic school, is not absolutely certain. See op. cit., pp. 174–75.

77. Also the phrase "soul of souls" *(neshamah le-neshamot)* as a term for the Cause of causes, i.e., *En-Sof,* shows that the *neshamah* occupies the highest position.

78. Op. cit., p. 285, from the piece entitled *Sod ha-Neshamot ha-Penimiyot ve-ha-Ruḥot ve-ha-Nefashot*.

79. Rabbi Joseph Gikatilla, *Sefer Sha'arei Orah*, chap. 8.

80. See G. Scholem, *Major Trends in Jewish Mysticism*, pp. 194–96.

81. It must be said in qualification, however, that because of the present state of research into thirteenth-century kabbalah, where a large portion of the literature is still in manuscript, and where even the printed books have not been adequately studied, one cannot really express authoritative or definitive views on this subject.

82. See Zohar II, 94b, preface to *Sava de-Mishpatim; Zohar Ḥadash, Yitro,* 33b–34c.

83. Zeitlin attributes the above ideas to the Zohar on the basis of a passage that taken literally deals with an image relationship. See H. Zeitlin, "Mafteah le-Sefer ha-Zohar," *Ha-Tekufah* 9:288. In the references to the parts of the soul in *Midrash Ruth*, especially the sentence, "and they are from father, mother, son and daughter" (3), one might possibly see an identification of the image connection with the cause-and-effect connection, but the passages from the main body of the Zohar quoted below seem to rule out such an identification.

84. *Perush Eser Sefirot le-Rabbi Azriel* (Berlin, 1850), p. 3b. This commentary is printed at the beginning of Rabbi Meir ibn Gabbai's *Sefer Derekh Emunah.*

85. See *Perush ha-Aggadot le-Rabbi Azriel* p. 19, nn. 3 and 4.

86. See secs. 15, 29, 48.

87. *Perush ha-Aggadot le-Rabbi Ezra,* Vatican MS 294, fol. 48b.

88. Nachmanides on Genesis 2:7: "For [the soul] comes from the element *Binah* by way of Truth and Faith." Truth *(Emet)* and Faith *(Emunah)* here indicate *Tiferet* and *Malkhut.*

89. *Sefer ha-Nefesh ha-Ḥakhamah,* II, sig. 3, fol. 3b. This metaphor is also found in Rabbi Ezra's commentary to the Song of Songs, printed under the name of Nachmanides (Altona, 1764), fols. 3c, 23b.

90. *Sefer ha-Nefesh ha-Ḥakhamah,* loc. cit. The text has been corrected on the basis of Oxford MS 1630.

91. The MS reads "and hewn from the place of holiness." If this is correct, the reference is to *Ḥokhmah,* which is called "Holiness' *(Kodesh).*

92. Here the MS text is corrupt and fragmentary.

93. *Sefer ha-Nefesh ha-Ḥakhamah,* loc. cit.

94. See what he says in his *Sefer Shekel ha-Kodesh,* explained in the following section.

95. *Sefer Shekel ha-Kodesh,* pp. 34–36.

96. Ibid., p. 127.

97. At one point, p. 117, *Binah* is described as "the place from which the *ruah* comes." But it is clear that the text here is not terminologically precise and the *neshamah* is really meant. Rabbi Moses de Leon stresses frequently that he is not always particular about the use of the terms *nefesh, ruah,* and *neshamah.* See *Sefer ha-Nefesh ha-Ḥakhamah,* II, sig. 4, fol. 4a; *Sefer Shekel ha-Kodesh,* p. 75.

98. Zohar I, 81a.

99. *Hilkhot Yesodei ha-Torah,* IV, 6.

100. In Alfarabi's *Book of First Principles* (ed. S. Filipowski as *Sefer Hathalot* in *Sefer ha-Asif* [Leipzig, 1849], p. 2), and in Hebrew sources after Maimonides, the term *"Ishim"* is explicitly taken to mean the Active Intellect. See I. Klatzkin, *Ozar ha-Munahim ha-Filosofiyyim* 1:43–44.

101. From the point of view of terminology the change is not really noticeable

because Maimonides uses *nefesh* precisely for the intellectual soul. See *Hilkhot Yesodei ha-Torah*, IV, 8–9.

102. See Zohar I, 13a–13b, 76b *(Sitrei Torah)*, 205b; II, 246a, 259a, etc.
103. Zohar II, 174a.
104. Zohar I, 186b.
105. Zohar II, 95b.
106. Against this argument one could say that the reference is to Hokhmah, which is above Hesed on the right-hand side, but the explanation given seems to be the more correct.
107. Zohar III, 46b.
108. See *Perush ha-Aggadot le-Rabbi Azriel*, indexes, p. 130.
109. Zohar I, 81a–81b.
110. Zohar II, 99b *(Sava de-Mishpatim)*. [*Ner* is seen here as a combination of the first letters respectively of *neshamah* and *ruah*.]
111. See Zohar III, 170a.
112. Zohar I, 62a.
113. Ibid., 158a.
114. Zohar II, 12a; III, 174b.
115. See Zohar I, 13a, 197a, 209a.
116. Zohar I, 82b.
117. See K. Preis, "Die Medizin im Sohar," *MGWJ* (1928), pp. 181–82.
118. *Sefer Pardes Rimmonim*, VIII, 22.
119. B.T. *Hagigah*, 12b.
120. *Bereshit Rabbah*, 8:7.
121. *Midrash Tanhuma, Pikudei*, 3.
122. See W. Hirsch, *Rabbinic Psychology*, pp. 175–76. The author tries to prove that the rabbinic belief in the preexistence of the soul was an internal Jewish development, without any Platonic influence, but his arguments are not convincing.
123. *Sefer Emunot ve-Deot*, VI, 3 (Rosenblatt, p. 241).
124. *Moreh Nevukhim*, I, 70 (Friedlander, p. 106).
125. *Sefer Torat ha-Nefesh*, attributed to Rabbi Bahya ibn Pakuda (Paris, 1896), p. 5.
126. *Pardes Rimmonim*, VIII, 22.
127. This passage also derives from the *aggadah*. See B.T. *Avodah Zarah*, 5a.
128. *Pardes Rimmonim*, XXXI, 5.
129. Zohar I, 91b.
130. This interpretation of the passage means that it is identical with the view in the *Midrash ha-Ne'elam*.
131. Zohar II, 96b. See also I, 227b.
132. Zohar III, 303b *(Hashmatot)*. This passage also occurs, with some minor variations, in the *Zohar Hadash, Balak*.
133. The reference seems to be to the fifth hall in the supernal Garden of Eden.
134. Zohar I, 197a.
135. This explanation leads one to think that "the most exalted height" is *Tiferet*, from which the souls descend to *Malkhut* through intercourse.

136. See Scholem, *Major Trends in Jewish Mysticism*, pp. 241–42.

137. Commentary to Job 38: 21. See also his *Torat Adonai Temimah*, ed. Jellinek (Vienna, 1873), pp. 19–20.

138. 8:7.

139. B.T. *Ḥagigah*, 12b.

140. At the end of his poem *Barekhi azulah me-ruaḥ ha-kodesh*.

141. The origin of the soul by a process of divine emanation is described in one of Nachmanides' poems, *Me-rosh mi-kadmei olamim*, printed in M. Sachs, *Die religiöse Poesie der Juden in Spanien* (Berlin, 1901), Hebrew sec., pp. 50–51. See also now H. Schirmann, *Ha-Shirah ha-Ivrit bi-Sefarad u-vi-Provence*, 2:322. And see G. Scholem, *Major Trends in Jewish Mysticism*, p. 240.

142. *Perush ha-Aggadot le-Rabbi Azriel*, p. 98.

143. Rabbi Azriel earlier (p. 96) speaks of seven lights that were created before the creation of the world, and his words are quoted in the Zohar (III, 34b) in the form of a dialogue between Rabbi Hezekiah and Rabbi Eleazar.

4.

Samael, Lilith, and the Concept of Evil in Early Kabbalah

Joseph Dan

I

One of the major problems in the study of early kabbalah is the difficulty in distinguishing between old traditions used by kabbalists and new ideas presented in their writings for the first time. Early kabbalists often pretended to be using books and treatises by ancient authorities, a pretense which is usually characterized as pseudepigraphy; however, there can be little doubt that some kabbalists in the Middle Ages did have access to old traditions, transmitted orally or in writing, which they used to mould their own mystical attitudes, and the attempt to distinguish between the old and the new is, in most cases, very difficult, if not outright impossible. The main problem is that scholarly study can never prove a negative; one can do one's best to prove that a certain writer had such and such a source before him, but one can never conclusively prove that a writer did not know a certain text or idea. Still, it is the duty of scholarship to try to follow the development of ideas, themes and symbols, and to suggest, with the help of close textual analysis, to what extent a certain writer followed ideas and texts, and to surmise carefully what his original contribution was.

In this paper an attempt is made to clarify both the sources and the original contribution to the mythological concept of evil as developed by Rabbi Isaac ben Jacob ha-Kohen in Spain in the second half of the thirteenth century. The major text to be considered is Rabbi Isaac's

Reprinted by permission of the Association for Jewish Studies from *AJS Review* 5 (1980).

treatise on evil, entitled "A Treatise on the Left Emanation," published by Gershom Scholem in 1927.[1] In this text a kabbalist, for the first time after three generations of the development of the kabbalah, presented a comprehensive concept of evil, based on extreme dualistic attitudes, characterized by Scholem as "gnostic," which indeed bears close phenomenological resemblance to the ancient systems of the Marcionites, the Ophites and even the Manichaean gnostics. A significant detail in this system is that here, for the first time in a dated Jewish work, Samael and Lilith are described as husband and wife in the realm of the Satanic power, a concept which was later incorporated into the Zohar and became one of the most popular and well-known chapters in Jewish myths concerning evil.

The following analysis is divided into two parts: the first is an attempt to discover two types of sources which were used by Rabbi Isaac— mythological sources and theological sources; the second part is an attempt to point out the reasons for Rabbi Isaac's mythological attitude and his relationship to other kabbalists, both earlier and later. In this fashion, a conclusion might be reached concerning the role of mythological elements in the development of early kabbalah.

II

The sixth chapter in Rabbi Isaac's "Treatise on the Emanations on the Left"[2] is opened by a list of the "princes of jealousy and hatred," that is, the active powers of evil influencing the world, the first of which is Samael. After describing seven such "princes," Rabbi Isaac states: "Truly I shall give you a hint, that the reason for all the jealousies which exist between the princes mentioned above, and the [other, good] princes which belong to seven classes, the classes of the holy angels which are called 'the guardians of the walls,' the reason which evokes hatred and jealousy between the heavenly powers and the powers of the supreme host, is one form[3] which is destined for Samael, and it is Lilith, and it has the image of a feminine form, and Samael is in the form of Adam and Lilith in the form of Eve. Both of them were born in a spiritual birth as one,[4] similar to the form of Adam and Eve, like two pairs of twins, one above and one below. Samael and the Eve the Elder, which is called the Northern one,[5] they are emanated from below the Throne of Glory, and this was caused by the Sin."[6]

The author goes on to explain the disaster caused by the sin of Adam and Eve in the Garden of Eden, which, according to his description, caused sexual awakening among the two pairs of "twins," an awakening in which the snake, called here Nahasiel or Gamliel,[7] took part. The result was that the snakes became "biting snakes," that is, Evil came into its own, and began to express itself.

Several elements in this myth are new, unknown from any previous Jewish source, especially if other motifs, found in parallel passages in this treatise are used to explain this description.[8] But it seems that the first one to be considered should be the joining of Samael and Lilith as a pair, analogous to Adam and Eve. It is a fact that both Samael and Lilith are major figures in earlier Jewish traditions, but nowhere are they mentioned as a pair in a dated work before this passage in the second half of the thirteenth century.[9] Since talmudic times Samael was regarded as the archangel in charge of Rome, and therefore a satanic figure—especially in the mystical literature known as the Heikhalot and Merkabah literature[10]—though originally he was one of the fallen angels mentioned in the Book of Enoch.[11] The concept of Samael developed in the early Middle Ages. In the late midrash, Pirqei de-Rabbi 'Eli'ezer, he is one of the participants in the drama of the Garden of Eden, as he is also in the first kabbalistic work known to us—the Book Bahir.[12] But nowhere in these detailed descriptions is there a hint that he has a wife or a feminine counterpart, and Lilith is not to be found.

The history of Lilith is even more complex. She seems to have been an ancient Near Eastern goddess, mentioned in the Bible[13] and she is characterized several times in talmudic literature as a danger to infants.[14] A very unclear tradition in the midrash seems to hint that Lilith was Adam's first wife before the creation of Eve, and that from this union demons were born.[15] In all these sources, however, Samael is never mentioned. How, then, did Samael and Lilith become man and wife in the treatise by Rabbi Isaac ha-Kohen?

Part of the answer to this question may be found in the famous source of most of the legends concerning Lilith—the Alpha Betha of Ben Sira, which should properly be called "Pseudo-Ben Sira," a narrative work in Hebrew written late in the gaonic period. This book was recently studied in detail by Eli Yassif, who prepared a critical edition of the text, using dozens of manuscripts.[16] One of the most important conclusions reached by Yassif is that two versions of the work exist, one closer to the original and another, known in Europe since the eleventh century,[17] which was edited and enlarged by a later compilator. This distinction between the two versions, proved conclusively by Yassif, can shed some light on the history of Lilith and how she became Samael's spouse.

The early version of Pseudo-Ben Sira tells the following story:

When God created His world and created Adam, He saw that Adam was alone, and He immediately created a woman from earth, like him, for him, and named her Lilith. He brought her to Adam, and they immediately began to fight: Adam said, "You shall lie below" and Lilith said, "You shall lie below, for we are equal and both of us were [created] from earth." They did not listen to each other. When Lilith saw the state of things, she uttered the Holy Name and flew into the air and fled. Adam immediately stood in prayer before God and said: "Master of the universe, see that the woman you gave me has already fled away." God immediately sent three angels and told them: "Go and fetch Lilith; if she agrees to come, bring her, and if she does not, bring her by force." The three angels went immediately and caught up with her in the [Red] Sea, in the place that the Egyptians were destined to die. They seized her and told her: "If you agree to come with us, come, and if not, we shall drown you in the sea." She answered: "Darlings, I know myself that God created me only to afflict babies with fatal disease when they are eight days old; I shall have permission to harm them from their birth to the eighth day and no longer; when it is a male baby; but when it is a female baby, I shall have permission for twelve days." The angels would not leave her alone, until she swore by God's name that wherever she would see them or their names in an amulet,[18] she would not possess the baby [bearing it]. They then left her immediately. This is [the story of] Lilith who afflicts babies with disease.[19]

It seems that every reader of this story in the Middle Ages was puzzled by one question: Why did the angels leave Lilith alone? They were ordered by God to bring her back to Adam, and for an unstated reason they were convinced by her speech not to do so. But it is not just an unclear narrative point: in the story as stated in this version one might easily come to the conclusion that these three exalted angels were bribed by Lilith by the promise that she would never harm babies protected by them or by their names on amulets—and this might very well have been the author's point.[20] It is not surprising, therefore, to find that the editor of the later version, the one which became known in Europe, changed this part of the story. When describing the encounter between Lilith and the angels in the Red Sea, he wrote: "They tried to take her back, but she refused. They asked her: 'Why don't you want to go back?' She told them: 'I know that I was created for the sole purpose of making babies ill from their day of birth until the eighth day, when I have permission, and after eight days I have no permission. And if it is a female, [this is so] for twelve days!' They said to her: 'If you do not come back we shall drown you in the sea.' She answered: 'I cannot return because of what is said in the Torah—"Her former husband who sent her away, may not take her again to be his wife, after that she is defiled,"[21] that is, when he was the last to sleep with her. And the Great Demon has already slept with me.' "[22] The author goes on to describe the agreement between Lilith and the angels.

It is quite obvious that the editor of this version was confronted with the difficulty concerning the behavior of the angels, and supplied a halakhic reason for why Lilith could not return to her former husband. For this reason he added a new hero to the story, the Great Demon *(ha-Shed ha-Gadol)*, whose sole function is to serve as a pretext for Lilith's being unable to return to Adam, since she was defiled by somebody else. The "Great Demon" is a new term, unknown in previous Hebrew sources, but it is quite natural that he could not remain unnamed for long. Jewish tradition usually named the archdemons, as it did the archangels. There was only one possible name for this "Great Demon" added to the text of Pseudo-Ben Sira by the later editor, and that name was Samael. This was the only demonic name associated with the drama of the Garden of Eden, as described in the Pirqei de-Rabbi 'Eli'ezer and strengthened, in the eyes of the early kabbalists, by the inclusion of that description in the text of the Book Bahir.[23] It is impossible to decide exactly when and where Samael was identified with the "Great Demon," and whether Rabbi Isaac ha-Kohen had any part in that process. But there can be no doubt that it was Rabbi Isaac who gave the story of Samael and Lilith a new mythological dimension, uplifting it from the level of narrative gossip, as it was in the edited version of Pseudo-Ben Sira, and made it a part of cosmic, and even divine, history. The following passage is one example of his treatment of this subject:

And now we shall speak about that third Air.[24] The masters of tradition[25] said that a tradition was transmitted to their fathers that this Air is divided into three parts, an upper one, a middle one, and a lower one. The upper one was given to Asmodeus,[26] the great king of the demons, and he does not have permission to accuse or cause harm except on Mondays, as the masters of the tradition had mentioned. And we, with the help of our Creator, shall expand in this treatise [on this subject] to the extent that we can. Now Asmodeus, even though he is called "the great king," is subservient to Samael, and he is called "the great prince," when compared with the emanations above him, and "king of kings" when compared with the emanated powers below him. And Asmodeus is governed by him and serves him. The Grand Old Lilith[27] is the mate of Samael, the great prince and the great king of all demons. Asmodeus, the king of the demons, has as a mate Younger Lilith. The masters of this tradition discuss and point out many wonderful details concerning the form of Samael and the form of Asmodeus and the image of Lilith, the bride of Samael and of Lilith, the bride of Asmodeus. Happy is he who merits this knowledge.[28]

The author goes on to describe a lower pair of a demon and his mate, and associates these couples with some of the most cruel afflictions of this world, including leprosy and hydrophobia, in a very detailed description.

The way this myth was constructed is clearer in another chapter of that treatise:

In answer to your question concerning Lilith, I shall explain to you that most important part. There is a tradition received from the early sages who made use[29] of the *Use of the Lesser Palaces*[30] which is the *Use of Demons*[31] which is like a ladder by which one can transcend to the various degrees of prophecy and their powers.[32] In these sources it is explained that Samael and Lilith were born as a hermaphrodite,[33] just like Adam and Eve, who were also born in this manner, reflecting what is above.[34] This is the account of Lilith which was received by the sages in the *Use of the Palaces*. The Elder Lilith[35] is the wife of Samael. Both of them were born at the same hour, in the image of Adam and Eve, intertwined in each other. And Asmodeus, the great king of the demons, has as a wife the Younger Lilith, the daughter of the king, whose name is Kafzefoni,[36] and the name of his wife is Mehetabel daughter of Matred,[37] and their daughter is Lilith. This is the exact text of what is written in the chapters of the *Lesser Heikhalot*[38] as we have received it, word for word and letter for letter. And the scholars in this science have a very esoteric tradition from the ancient sages who found it stated in those chapters that Samael, the greatest prince of them all, is very jealous of Asmodeus the king of the demons because of this Lilith who is called Lilith the Maiden,[39] who is in the form of a beautiful woman from her head to her waist, and from the waist down she is burning fire; like mother like daughter.[40]

This paragraph clearly states Rabbi Isaac's sources, connected with the Aramaic mystical text describing Rabbi Akiba's ascent to the Heavenly Palaces, the Heikhalot Zutartei.[41] Since this text is known to us in several versions, it is easy to discover that Rabbi Isaac's reliance on it is completely apocryphal. Even if one may suggest that portions of this early mystical work were lost, it is still inconceivable that such a fascinating story was included in it (or anywhere else, for that matter), and no other source bothered to mention it until Rabbi Isaac cited it. There can be little doubt that the language of this paragraph is intended to enhance Rabbi Isaac's credibility concerning the previous descriptions of the Liliths, the mother and the daughter, and their relationships with their husbands, the kings of the demons. A mythological narrative was created here, most probably by Rabbi Isaac himself, who made use of various materials which were before him but changed their character completely. The ancient story concerning Lilith being Adam's first wife was not suitable to Rabbi Isaac's purposes because Samael did not take any significant part in it. He used the later edition of the Pseudo-Ben Sira to introduce Samael into the story, not as Lilith's second husband but as her original mate, creating a kind of parallelism between Adam and Eve and Lilith and Samael. This principle of parallel pairs was carried both forward and backward—reflecting the bisexual nature of the divine world (God and the Shekhinah) as well as the lower demonic pairs, like Lilith and Asmodeus or Kafzefoni and Mehetabel.

As Rabbi Isaac's concept of the divine world is mythical and dynamic, so are his views concerning the demonic world; an element of strife is introduced by the fight of Samael and Asmodeus over the Younger Lilith. This myth is carried on in a subsequent description until Rabbi Isaac's main concern—the final battle between good and evil—is reached.[42]

The possibility that further sources of Rabbi Isaac's myth concerning the demons will be discovered has to be taken into account, but even so it is quite clear that it was Rabbi Isaac who moulded previous traditions into a new narrative myth, expressing his vision of the world and contributing to his theology.

III

An attempt to clarify Rabbi Isaac's mysterious reference to the "third air," and the "air of the use of the demons"[43] leads us to another group of sources which helped Rabbi Isaac create his mythology of the evil powers—the theological works of the Ashkenazi Hasidim. Rabbi Isaac mentioned in his treatise at least twice that he had connections with the Jewish sages in Germany,[44] and it seems that in the second half of the thirteenth century several kabbalists emphasized such a connection as a source of their teachings.[45] This is not surprising, since the masters of this pietistic movement were respected throughout the Jewish world because of their ethical teachings, their interpretations of the prayers, their pronouncements on Jewish law, and their direct connection with early traditions received from the east.[46] These traditions had an element of magical knowledge and the performance of miracles, associated with several of the ancestors of Ashkenazi Hasidism,[47] and reflected in Rabbi Isaac's treatise in the story about the magical flight of Rabbi Eleazar of Worms riding a cloud.[48] It is no wonder, therefore, that the Ashkenazi Hasidim, especially Rabbi Judah the Pious (d. 1217), and his disciple, Rabbi Eleazar of Worms (d. ca. 1230),[49] were regarded by Rabbi Isaac and by some other kabbalists as an authoritative source for esoteric knowledge, with some emphasis on magical and demonological aspects of that tradition.

While it is quite clear that the concepts of the various "airs" between the earth and the divine world reflect the influence of terms from the Book of Creation (Sefer Yeṣirah) and the commentaries on that book, especially that of Rav Saadia Gaon,[50] upon Rabbi Isaac ha-Kohen, the connection between the "third air" and both prophecy and demonology poses a serious problem. In Rabbi Isaac's work, the demons represent cosmic and divine elements of evil, while in the sizable literature of the Ashkenazi Hasidim on this subject one cannot find any dualistic element: the demons represent a natural power which is an integral part of the created world, and their actions conform to the decrees of God exactly as do those of angels.[51] Still, there is a connection between Rabbi Isaac's myth and the Ashkenazi hasidic speculations, for it was the pietists in the late twelfth century and the early thirteenth who stressed the link between visions of demons and the phenomenon of prophecy.

Several discussions of problems concerning prophecy in Ashkenazi hasidic esoteric literature deal with a phenomenon traditionally called in Hebrew *sarei kos ve-sarei bohen*,[52] "the princes of the glass and the princes of the thumb." The term refers to a universal practice of divination, using a thin layer of oil spread upon a bright surface, which may be a piece of glass, a sword, a mirror or even a fingernail—all materials often mentioned in this connection in Hebrew descriptions. The belief was that demons can be compelled to reveal themselves on such surfaces, and when they are asked questions by a professional sorcerer (usually a non-Jew) they must reveal secrets. This practice was used to solve many everyday problems, most often to find lost articles or to catch a thief (generally to reveal where stolen goods were hidden).[53] The sorcerer or the witch would receive a request, the owner of the lost goods would usually participate in the ceremony, and when the right demon, who was responsible for that area was brought by the force of incantations, an answer would be revealed.

This common practice seems to have been very well known in medieval Germany,[54] probably after it had been brought from the east to Europe by the Arabs. The Ashkenazi Hasidim refer to it as a commonplace occurrence which does not have to be described and discussed in detail; no doubt the readers were familiar with it. The problem, however, is that of the relationship between this elementary form of magic and prophecy. It seems that here the Ashkenazi Hasidim found an unnoticed element in this practice which conformed easily to their theology.

The key detail in this magical practice was that neither the sorcerer nor the person requesting the practice could see the demons in the thin layer of oil. The demon could be seen only by a child, a small boy or a virgin girl. The adults surrounding the bright surface did not see anything, but the child would describe in great detail what he saw in the oil—a demon dressed in a certain manner having a certain identifying mark. Often the sorcerer would instruct the child to send that demon back and ask another one to come, until the right demon appeared. The ability of the child to perceive things hidden even from professional magicians was the key to the success of the whole practice.

This detail was the cause for the intensive interest of the Ashkenazi Hasidim in this practice, because it seemed to illustrate the central problem in their concept of prophecy. The pietists relied upon the famous dictum of Rav Saadia Gaon, who stated that what the prophets had seen was a created angel, called the divine Glory *(kavod).*[55] But only one faction among the medieval esotericists accepted Saadia's view; others held different opinions. Some claimed that the whole process of prophecy is an internal, psychological one, and no element of external revelation is involved; the prophets described their dreams and their inner thoughts when they described divine revelation. Others—and these include the main teachers of the Ashkenazi Hasidic school, like Rabbi Judah the Pious and Rabbi Eleazar of Worms—held, following Rabbi Abraham Ibn Ezra's interpretation of prophecy,[56] that the prophets did indeed see a divine revelation, and the revealed power is called the divine Glory. But this Glory is not a created angel, but a divine power, emanated from God, a spiritual being which is not bound by the laws of creation.

This controversy, which holds a central place in the esoteric theology of the Ashkenazi hasidic movement,[57] brought into discussion as a central theme the magical practice of *sarei kos* and *sarei bohen,* because at least two views could be supported by the procedure of this divinatory practice. Those who believed prophecy to be an internal, psychological process claimed that the demons invoked in this way have no real existence, they are nothing but dreams and imaginary visions, even though many people believe in their material existence. Others, like Rabbi Judah and Rabbi Eleazar claimed that this practice proves conclusively that prophecy is a real phenomenon, but that the revealed power is divine and not created. In biblical descriptions of prophetic visions there are some occurrences in which one person—the prophet himself—did see something—while other people standing beside him did not see anything, as in the case of Elisha and his servant when the city was surrounded by chariots of fire.[58] This proves, according to them, that the vision could not be natural, because natural phenomena can be seen either by all or by no one, being subservient to natural law; divine powers can have supernatural revelation of a selective kind, revealing themselves to a certain person while remaining hidden from others. Thus Rabbi Judah and Rabbi Eleazar proved that Rav Saadia's concept of created Glory was insufficient in explaining the process of prophecy, and only Ibn Ezra's description of the divine, emanated Glory can explain the facts. To this they added the fact that God implanted a miracle within the created world which can serve as a proof of this concept,[59] namely, the fact that only a child can see the demons when divination is practiced, while all others standing around see nothing; what can be done by every common witch can also be performed by the divine Glory, and therefore neither those who claim that prophecy is an imaginary process nor those who claim that a created angel is revealed can be right.

When Rabbi Eleazar explained the creation of the throne of Glory, he wrote:[60] "Another reason for its creation is for visions, for it is seen by the prophets in visions which include a divine message . . . and the Creator changes the visions according to His will.[61] I shall give you an example, as they evoke *sarei bohen* with a child and he sees in them what his master wishes. The Creator created visions, to teach the prophets the content of His decrees . . . And among the philosophers[62] there was a controversy about *sarei bohen* and *sarei kos*. Some of them said that the supervising angel[63] enters into the heart and creates thoughts in a person's heart and the child's, and changes his thoughts and gives him knowledge[64] which takes form in his mind like a thief and the stolen goods, and he sees everything, but he really does not see anything."

After reviewing this attitude, Rabbi Eleazar goes on to compare other interpretations, as does Rabbi Judah the Pious several times in his theological works.[65] In one place Rabbi Judah brings this practice as one example of the principle of *zekher 'asah le-nifle'otav*, the principle that states that every miraculous power of God has a "sign" or "remnant" in the world to prove God's powers[66] and concludes: "Do not be surprised because God's voice enters the prophet's ears and is not heard by others around him, for it is like a person talking into a tube, the other end of which is in someone else's ear, and, when he talks into it, one hears and the others do not hear. In the same way one sees divine visions and others do not. Is it not true that some people see in the fingernail and in the *sarei kos* and others do not see? In the same way do not be surprised about the visions of the prophets. For it is like a mirror, one can look into one and see everything that is in the opposite direction; so it is with *sarei kos* and *sarei bohen*—everything they see they see like a person looking into a mirror seeing a reverse image." [67]

The Ashkenazi Hasidim used the analogy of this magical practice concerning several theological problems, but the comparison to prophecy is the most frequent and insistent one. It is quite clear in the writings of these pietists that they never imagined an actual connection existing between the realms of demons and magic and the prophetic phenomenon; all their efforts were directed at analyzing the analogy between this practice and prophecy, based upon their monistic concept that the world of demons is an integral part of the world created by God, refuting any possibility of a dualistic attitude.

When seeking a source for Rabbi Isaac ha-Kohen's description of the "demonic air" which is described as the "air of prophecy" one cannot neglect the possibility that the Ashkenazi Hasidim's analogy somehow turned into fact in Spain, two generations after Rabbi Judah's and Rabbi Eleazar's works were written. It is quite clear from Rabbi Isaac's references to the Ashkenazi Hasidim that he was not a direct disciple of their school, and those ideas of theirs which did reach him did so through intermediaries, about whom we have no definite knowledge whether they really knew this esoteric doctrine from a first-hand source. It seems probable, therefore, that the information that reached the Spanish kabbalist was far from accurate, and Rabbi Isaac could interpret it to mean that there is an actual connection between the process of prophecy and magical divination by the revelation of demons. If this was so, it was possible to conclude that the prophetic vision and the "use" *(shimmusha)* of demons originate from the same cosmic source, the "third air" in his mythical description.

It should be noted that the difference between *sarei bohen* and *shimmusha de-shedei* could be much smaller than it seems if we take into account the possibility that Rabbi Judah the Pious and his disciples did not speak about *sarei bohen* but about *shedei bohen,* that is, not "Princes of the Thumb" but "Demons of the Thumb." The Hebrew letters can easily be confused, and in one homiletical discussion by Rabbi Judah of the talmudic section referring to these powers it is evident that he read "demons" and not "princes." [68]

It is probable, therefore, that Rabbi Isaac used inaccurate traditions originating in the schools of the Ashkenazi Hasidim to describe his concept of the world and the place of demons in it. It is possible, therefore, that he used the same sources, in a similar creative way, to devise his myth of the "destroyed worlds," which, unlike the "air of the use of demons" has a crucial place in his concept of evil and the creation of a mythological demonology.

IV

Rabbi Isaac ha-Kohen began his story of the origins of evil by describing a detailed myth concerning the "destroyed worlds," worlds which were created before our world but could not exist. The importance which he attributes to this myth is clear from the long opening statement, telling how this tradition had reached him: "Now we shall turn to speak about the system of the evil powers which are in heaven, of those which were created and then annihilated suddenly. When I was in the great city of Arles, masters of this tradition showed me a booklet, a very old one, the writing in it being rough and different from our writing. It was transmitted in the name of a great rabbi and a gaon called Rabbi Maṣliaḥ, for the old gaon, our Rabbi Pelatiah, was from the holy city of Jerusalem, and it was brought by a great scholar and Hasid called Rabbi Gershom of Damascus. He was from the city of Damascus and lived in Arles about two years, and people there told stories about his great wisdom and wealth. He showed that booklet to the great sages of that age, and I copied some things from it—things which the sages of that generation had understood, for they were not familiar with that particular writing like those earlier sages who learned it from that scholar and Hasid." [69]

After this story, which does not include even one name or fact that can be verified by any other source, Rabbi Isaac describes the emanation of the first evil powers from a curtain below the third sefirah in the kabbalistic system, which he calls, like many early kabbalists before him, Teshuvah (repentance). The first three evil worlds to be emanated were destroyed, and Rabbi Isaac's discussion of this is based on the talmudic and midrashic traditions about the earlier worlds—the one in the midrash stating that before God created this world he used to create other worlds and destroy them [70] and the talmudic tradition about the generations which were annihilated, 974 in number. [71] Rabbi Isaac even goes further in homiletical treatment of the subject, by ascribing names to the princes ruling these lost worlds—Qamtiel, Beliel and 'Ittiel, names derived from the verse in Job which served as a basis for the talmudic homily. [72]

The basic elements of this myth were taken, therefore, from well-known Hebrew homilies in popular sources. The major new twist given to the myth by Rabbi Isaac is centered on one element, which is completely new here; those previous worlds or generations were evil, and they were destroyed (nimhu, qummetu—the terms used by the midrash, which seem to be used by Rabbi Isaac in the sense of "inverse emanation." Their emanation was reversed)[73] because they were much too evil. It is impossible to state that they were destroyed because they contained a satanic element, for Rabbi Isaac's description of our world stresses the existence and the power of the satanic element in it; the destruction was caused by their being totally evil, whereas when our world was created some angelic and good powers were emanated as well.

When seeking Rabbi Isaac's sources for this myth we must concentrate on these two motifs: the identification of the destroyed worlds and generations as evil, and this evil as the cause of their destruction, while the existing world contains some good beside the evil element. Such a homily, containing exactly these motifs, is contained in Rabbi Eleazar of Worms' *Hokhmat ha-nefesh*.[74]

The subject discussed by Rabbi Eleazar is the purpose of the creation of the world:

Why did He create the world, for the Creator does not need the created and has no benefit from them, so why did He create the world? Before anything was created there were only He and His name alone, and He existed without any created being, so why did He need His creatures? Before the creation He did not need them [and he does not need them now]?

The truth is that God did not create the world for His own sake, for He has no benefit from a worthless world, but He said: "If I should create a world without the Evil Yeṣer[75] there will be no wonder if the creatures will be as good as the Ministering Angels[76] and if I put into them a strong Evil Yeṣer, they might be unable to overcome this Yeṣer. Still, I might find two righteous people among them, like David." He thus created worlds and destroyed them, for He did not find righteous people like David . . . and when He saw that there were no such righteous as David, He destroyed them.

He said: "The fact that there is not even one good person among all these is because I created the Evil Yeṣer too strong in them . . ." and the Creator said: "The reason why I created such a strong Yeṣer in them is, that if two [righteous] are found, He would be ungrateful if he did not create them. But he said: I created it too strong, therefore there is no good in them; I shall now create human beings with another Yeṣer, the Good Yeṣer.

Rabbi Eleazar's extensive homily includes references to many verses which he interprets as describing the destroyed worlds, and he goes on to analyze the destroyed generations, and the evildoers of the period of the deluge. His main argument is quite clear, relying to a certain extent on the midrashic treatment of the subject, but expressing some of the most important theological concepts of the Ashkenazi hasidic movement. Righteousness, according to these pietists, can be measured only by means of the opposition which one has to overcome; there can be no righteousness where the only drive is a good one. For this reason, the angels are not regarded as righteous. If so, ideal righteousness, the highest possible religious achievement, is one which is demonstrated against impossible odds, without any divine help, like a created person who has only an Evil Yeṣer in him and still succeeds, to some extent, to overcome it and be righteous (this might be the reason why the example of righteousness given is David; it cannot be doubted that he had a very strong evil inclination). The fact is that creation by Evil Yeṣer alone did not produce even one such person; still, God had to create these unsuccessful worlds, for he could not damn them into nonexistence before the evil was performed. If even two righteous persons were to overcome all the obstacles and do some good in those evil worlds, God would have been ungrateful if he did not create them.[77]

The creation of our world is therefore described as a compromise, a reluctant one, by God. He decided to add a Good Yeṣer to help human beings become righteous. This, of course, degrades their righteousness, for it is now achieved with divine help, and not by overcoming maximum difficulties. Still, this compromise is the only way to create a world that could exist, after the repeated failures of the previous period. Obviously, according to Rabbi Eleazar a world cannot exist unless there are in it at least two righteous persons. (It is possible to surmise that such existence is dependent also on the extent of their righteousness, which is smaller in our world than it could have been in the Evil Yeṣer worlds; it means, paradoxically enough, that the powers of existence of this world are lesser than in the ancient destroyed ones; if one of those could exist, it would have been much more valid than our own.)

Rabbi Eleazar's interpretation of the myth of the destroyed worlds is one according to which God tried at first to create "ideal" worlds which would be completely evil, and thus would be able to produce ideal, complete righteousness. Failing in that, he created a mixed world, in which good and evil are combined, and which successfully produces from time to time righteous persons which justify its existence. It is quite clear that there is no trace of a dualistic attitude in Rabbi Eleazar's theology. Evil comes from God directly, and it fulfills a divine function. The extent of evil in every phase of the creation is decided by God, according to his divine plan, which is a perfectly good one—to produce righteousness. Evil is a necessary means to bring righteousness forward, to test it in the most difficult circumstances,[78] and to justify the existence of the world by it. Rabbi Eleazar's achievement in this formulation includes an explanation of the evil character of this world: it is necessary for the sake of the righteous, who could not otherwise show their true nature. But this explanation of the meaning of evil does not include any dualistic or gnostic inclination.

This theology includes the basic elements of Rabbi Isaac ha-Kohen's myth of the destroyed worlds: The previous worlds were completely evil—they were destroyed because of their completely evil nature. The theology is radically different from Rabbi Eleazar's, for Rabbi Isaac does not offer an explanation as to why these worlds should have been evil according to the divine plan, but it seems that one can safely surmise that Rabbi Isaac's myth was produced under the impact of Rabbi Eleazar's radical theology, which was given a completely new twist in the framework of Rabbi Isaac's mythological concept of evil, which is so different from Rabbi Eleazar's instrumental one.

Rabbi Eleazar's system does not include an element of strife, except the struggle within the soul of the Hasid who is trying to become righteous. Rabbi Isaac's myth is based to a very large extent on descriptions of mythical struggle:

These souls,[79] which are angelic emanations, existed potentially within the depth of the Emanator, hidden from everything, but before they could come out of their potential existence into reality, another world was emanated, from strange forms and destructive appearances. The name of the ruler of this emanation, a prince over all its forces, is Qamṭiel. These are the Cruel Ones, who began to rebuke and to disrupt the emanation. Immediately there exuded a decree from the Prince of Repentance, who is called Karoziel,[80] who is also called the Echo of Repentance, and said: "Masokhiel, Masokhiel,[81] destroy what you have created and collect your emanations back to you, for it is not the wish of the King of Kings, blessed be He, that these emanations will exist in the worlds. They returned and were annihilated; in the same way that they were emanated they atrophied. Scholars explained this process by an example—like a string saturated in oil which is burning by the oil it constantly absorbs; when you wish to turn it off, you sink it into the oil which makes it burn; the same oil which makes it give light turns it back to nothing.

After this, another world was emanated, from strange forms and foreign appearances, the name of the ruler of their emanation and the prince of their forces is Beliel. These were worse than the first ones in rebuking and disrupting all kinds of emanation, until a decree came forth from the King of Kings, and they were annulled in a moment like the first ones. After that a third world was emanated from strange forms, stranger than the first and the second; the name of its ruler and prince of their forces is 'Ittiel. These are worst of all. It is their wish and ambition to be on top of the divine, to distort and cut the divine tree with all its branches, until there came a decree from the divine Will that it will be annihilated like the first and second ones, and it was decreed and decided that such an emanation will never again come to the world's air, will never be remembered or mentioned. These are the worlds about which the ancient sages said that God was creating worlds and destroying them.[82]

The difference between this mythical description and Rabbi Eleazar's homily is as clear as the similarities. Rabbi Eleazar's monism is replaced by a stark dualism in this realm, and the relatively systematic inquiry into the problems of the creation and divine providence is replaced by an unexplained myth, visionary rather than explanatory. Still, the idea that the destroyed worlds were ones of unmitigated evil, which caused their destruction, to be replaced by a world in which good and evil are combined, is based on Rabbi Eleazar's speculation.

V

The comparison between Rabbi Isaac ha-Kohen's treatise on the "Left Emanations" and those sources which we can identify with some extent of certainty does not diminish the impact of Rabbi Isaac's original concepts, but rather enhances it. These sources do not constitute basic elements of his mythological worldview, but only materials used when building the innovative kabbalistic system which was destined to have a major impact upon later kabbalists, especially the author of the Zohar. Though one can never be certain that most of the relevant sources have been found and properly analyzed, the three clear examples described above can at least offer the major outlines of the structure of Rabbi Isaac's use of previous sources. These outlines seem to suggest that Rabbi Isaac did rely on previous material in secondary motifs, whereas his basic attitudes cannot be found to date in any known Hebrew work.

If this is the situation at the present stage of the study of Rabbi Isaac's theology, the main questions remain: What drove Rabbi Isaac to create this novel attitude toward the world, creation, Satan, Samael, Lilith, demons, divination, and the destroyed worlds? What is the underlying mythical or mystical vision which brought forth this new combination of older material, painted in daring, new colors? In other words: What is the basic difference between Rabbi Isaac's concept of evil and that of all other Jewish writers before him?

In chapter nineteen of his treatise, after the detailed description of Samael and Lilith and the fight between Asmodeus and Samael over the "Younger Lilith," Rabbi Isaac states:

It is said that from Asmodeus and his wife Lilith a great prince was born in heaven, the ruler of eighty thousand destructive demons, and he is called Ḥarba de-'Ashmedai Malka ("The Sword of the King Asmodeus"), and his name is Alpafonias,[83] and his face burns like fire. He is also called Gorigor,[84] [for] he antagonizes and fights the princes[85] of Judah, who is called Gur Aryeh Yehudah. And from the same form from which that destroyer was born, another prince was born in heaven,[86] from the source of Malkhut,[87] who is called Ḥarba di-Meshiḥa ("The Sword of the Messiah"), and he too has two names, Meshiḥiel and Kokhviel.[88] When the time comes, and God wishes it, this sword will come out of its sheath, and the prophecies will come true: "For My Sword hath drunk its fill in heaven; behold, it shall come down upon Edom."[89] "There shall step forth a star out of Jacob,"[90] amen. Soon in our time we shall have the privilege of seeing the face of the righteous messiah, we and all our people.[91]

In the last paragraph where the myth of Samael and Lilith is developed, Rabbi Isaac states:

I shall now teach you a wonderful, unknown thing. You already know that Evil Samael and Wicked Lilith are like a sexual pair, who by means of an intermediary[92] receive an emanation of evil and wickedness, one from the other, and emanate it onwards. I shall explain this relying on the esoteric meaning of the verse: "In that day the Lord with His sore and great and strong sword will punish leviathan the slant serpent and leviathan the tortuous serpent" — meaning Lilith — "and He will slay the dragon that is in the sea."[93] As there is a pure leviathan in the sea and he is called a serpent, so there is a great impure serpent in the sea, in the usual sense of the term. And it is the same above [in the divine world], in a secret way. And the heavenly serpent is a blind prince,[94] who is like an intermediary between Samael and Lilith and his name is Tanin'iver (Blind Serpent) . . . and he is the one who brings about the union between Samael and Lilith. If he were created in the fullness of his emanation he would have destroyed the whole world in one moment . . . When there is a divine wish, and the emanation of Samael and Lilith diminishes somewhat the emanation achieved by the Blind Prince, they will be completely annihilated by Gabriel, the prince of power, who invokes war against them with the help of the prince of mercy, then the esoteric meaning of the verse we have quoted will come true.[95]

The concluding paragraphs of the treatise deal exclusively with this same subject. The final destruction of the powers of evil, Samael, Lilith and the serpent, by messianic powers, and a glowing description of messianic times, after evil has been overcome, conclude the treatise.

If we try now to answer the questions posed at the beginning of this section, we have to take into account the full scope of the myth told by Rabbi Isaac. In this way it will become evident that Rabbi Isaac did not combine the motifs he borrowed from earlier sources to produce a new description of the creation, or even to explain the existence of evil in the world in the past and in the present. The myth he presented in this treatise is a coherent one, starting with the powers of evil which preceded the creation and concluding with the description of the messianic victory over evil.

One of the basic characteristics of this myth is the consistent attempt to produce parallelisms, to describe all existence in terms of two similar antagonistic powers. This is evident both within the realm of evil— Asmodeus and Samael, the Older Lilith and the Younger Lilith—as well as in the relations between the evil powers and the good. The Sword of Asmodeus is reflected in the Sword of the Messiah; the pure leviathan is reflected in the evil leviathan, and so forth. Even the creation of Samael and Lilith is a parallel to the creation of Adam and Eve. Rabbi Isaac did not hesitate to depart radically from the content of his sources in order to achieve this, as he did in this last detail, forsaking the myth of Lilith as Adam's first wife in order to be able to present a complete parallel between the two pairs.

This basic attitude brings into focus the meaning of the title of the treatise, a meaning easily neglected because this idea became after Rabbi Isaac one of the most famous characteristics of kabbalistic thought— "Left Emanation," called by the Zohar *siṭra 'aḥra* (= "The Other Side," meaning Evil).[96] Rabbi Isaac's concept of two systems of divine emanations, similar in many details but one of good and one of evil, was not an idea standing alone, but an integral part of a mythological worldview which felt that all existence is governed by the antagonism between pairs of similar structure and conflicting content. This attitude can be found in almost every paragraph of this treatise.

As the examples translated above show, these pairs are in continuous conflict, both within the realm of evil and between the evil system and the good one. It seems that in this mythology the parallel pairs should by nature fight each other, and that this struggle will not cease until one side is completely annihilated and true unity will reign in the divine and earthly worlds. Thus, it is not just a dualistic mythology, but one which is marked by an internal structure which necessitates continuous struggle.

It seems that the outcome of this struggle might be the key to the main drive behind the creation of this myth, namely, the messianic victory and the annihilation of evil. It should be stressed that this treatise by Rabbi Isaac can be regarded as the first Hebrew apocalypse to be written in medieval Europe, and certainly it is the first treatment by a kabbalist of the messianic motif in any detail. The dualistic character of the work, its gnostic undertones and its stark demonological mythology are means to express the basic apocalyptic theme: the struggle between good and evil will come to its conclusion when the messianic sword is raised and destroys the powers of evil. The history of these powers is told in detail in order to lay the foundations of the story of the final victory over those powers.

Messianism was not the main subject, nor the main concern, of kabbalistic writers in the first hundred years of the kabbalah, nor even in the writings of nonkabbalistic authors of that period. The original vision of Rabbi Isaac should be seen against this background, and his main innovation should be seen as a whole: a mythology of evil expressing a messianic apocalypse.[97]

NOTES

1. The text was published by Gershom Scholem, "Qabbalot R. Ya'aqov ve-R. Yiṣḥaq benei R. Ya'aqov ha-Kohen," *Madda'ei ha-Yahadut* 2 (1927):244–64, as a part of the first study of the kabbalah of Rabbi Jacob and Rabbi Isaac ha-Kohen. (The study was also published as a separate book [Jerusalem, 1927], from which it is quoted here; the treatise on the Left Emanations appears on pp. 82–102.)

2. Scholem, *Qabbalot*, pp. 89–90 (pp. 251–52 in *Madda'ei ha-Yahadut*).

3. Hebrew: *ṣurah*, here probably meaning "a spiritual being," form as opposed to matter.

4. Hebrew: *toladah ruḥanit du-parṣufim,* a creature which is at first male and female together (see Genesis Rabbah, 8:1), and then divided into separate beings.

5. See Scholem's note (*Qabbalot*, p. 89, n. 4). Samael is identified with the north not only because of the biblical tradition that evil comes from the north, but also because of the possible reading of his name as "left," which is identical with north (if facing east). His spouse, therefore, receives the feminine form of "north."

6. My translation was prepared with the assistance of Mr. E. Hanker of Berkeley, California.

7. These names are in fact identical, because the snake *(naḥash)* had the form of a camel *(gamal)* before he was cursed; this midrashic tradition was included in the Book Bahir, sec. 200, based on Pirqei de-Rabbi 'Eli'ezer, chap. 13—both serving as the basic source for Rabbi Isaac's description of the story of the Garden of Eden.

8. Some further descriptions of Lilith are translated below.

9. A serious problem concerning the development of this idea is related to a medieval text of magic, *Sidrei de-Shimmusha Rabbah,* published by G. Scholem in *Tarbiz* 16 (1945): 196–209. It is quite clear that the author of that text knew that Samael and Lilith were related, and there are several other points which suggest a close relationship between it and Rabbi Isaac's

treatise. However, the chronological problem has not yet been solved, and it is impossible to decide with any amount of certainty whether Rabbi Isaac used ideas which were known some time before him and reflected in the *"Shimmusha,"* or that the author of the *"Shimmusha"* made use of some motifs he found in Rabbi Isaac's treatise.

10. Samael's role as a power of Evil is especially prominent in the section of Heikhalot Rabbati (Adolf Jellinek, *Beth ha-Midrash,* 6 vols. [Leipzig, 1853–77], 3:87) which describes the martyrdom of ten of the mishnaic sages, as well as in the separate descriptions of this martyrdom in the treatise on the Ten Martyrs (see my *The Hebrew Story in the Middle Ages* [Hebrew] [Jerusalem, 1974], pp. 62–69).

11. The development of the image of Samael is described in detail by G. Scholem in his *Kabbalah* (Jerusalem, 1974), pp. 385–89 (and see the detailed bibliography there).

12. Sec. 200 (the last section; in Scholem's edition—sec. 140).

13. See Isa. 34:14.

14. See Reuben Margulies's collection of the talmudic and midrashic traditions in his *Malakhei 'Elyon* (Jerusalem, 1945), pp. 235–37.

15. This tradition was preserved in Midrash Avkir and elsewhere; see G. Scholem, *Kabbalah,* p. 357 (and the detailed bibliography there concerning Lilith, pp. 360–61).

16. Eli Yassif, "Pseudo Ben Sira, The Text, Its Literary Character and Status in the History of the Hebrew Story in the Middle Ages" [Hebrew], 2 vols., Ph.D. diss., Hebrew University, 1977.

17. The later version is the one found in Bereshit Rabbati by Rabbi Moses ha-Darshan.

18. These three angels are Sanoi, Sansanoi and Samanglof, mentioned in the text of Pseudo-Ben Sira. Many attempts have been made to explain these names by the use of several oriental languages. It seems to me that they could have been created by the author of this work as a parody on the angelology of the Heikhalot literature (which often used names like Sansaniel, etc.).

19. Yassif, "Pseudo-Ben Sira," pp. 64–65. This version is close to the one published by David Friedman and S. D. Loewinger in *Ve-zot li-Yehudah* (Budapest, 1926), pp. 259–60.

20. The question of the meaning of this story depends on one's attitude toward the character of the Pseudo-Ben Sira. I still maintain that this is a satirical, and somewhat heretical, collection of stories by a religious anarchist (see my *Hebrew Story,* pp. 69–78), although Yassif regards them as usual folktales. (Compare also S. T. Lachs, "The Alphabet of Ben Sira: A Study in Folk-Literature," *Gratz College Annual of Jewish Studies* 2[1973]:9–28.) It is my intention to analyze the problem in detail elsewhere; but it is necessary to point out here that the whole story does not make sense if it is not understood as an expression of Lilith's bitterness toward God for the role assigned to her (in talmudic literature) of a baby-killer.

21. Deut. 24:4. Naturally, this whole "halakhic" discussion does not have any basis in actual Jewish law.

22. Yassif, "Pseudo-Ben Sira," pp. 23–24. This version is similar to (but not identical; the "great demon" is missing) the one published by Moritz Steinschneider in his edition, *Alphabetum Siracidis* (Berlin, 1858), p. 23.

23. Bahir, sec. 200 (and Pirqei de-Rabbi 'Eli'ezer, chap. 13).

24. Concerning these "airs," see below.

25. The author here constantly uses the term "qabbalah," which I did not translate as "mystical" but, in the sense that the author seems to try to convey, ancient tradition.

26. Concerning Ashmedai, see Margulies, *Malakhei 'Elyon*, pp. 215–21; G. Scholem, "Yedi'ot ḥadashot 'al 'Ashmedai ve-Lilit," *Tarbiz* 19 (1948): 165–75.

27. *Lilit sabbeta rabbeta.*

28. Scholem, *Qabbalot*, p. 93 (*Madda'ei ha-Yahadut*, p. 255).

29. *Shimmusha,* meaning: magical use.

30. *Shimmusha de-heikhalei zuṭartei.*

31. *Shimmusha de-shedei.*

32. Meaning that the "magical use" of the "air of demons" is connected with the process of attaining prophecy; see below.

33. See above, n. 5.

34. Meaning that the creation in this way reflects the bisexuality in the structure of the spiritual, or even divine, worlds.

35. It should be noted that in this section, as in several others in the treatise, the author turns to the Aramaic language to express the great, ancient traditions. He relies here on the ancient mystical text, *Heikhalot Zuṭartei,* which was really written mostly in Aramaic, but of course it does not contain any hint of the material referred to by Rabbi Isaac.

36. The element *"ṣefoni"* seems to be the meaningful part of this name (i.e., from the north—evil).

37. See Genesis 36:39. The kings of Edom mentioned in this chapter were interpreted as evil powers in later kabbalah, especially in the Zohar.

38. See above, n. 35, and below, n. 41.

39. *Lilit 'ulemta.*

40. Scholem, *Qabbalot*, pp. 98–99 (*Madda'ei ha-Yahadut*, pp. 260–61).

41. This work is found in several manuscripts, and was partly published in Solomon Musajoff's *Merkavah Shelemah* (Jerusalem, 1926), pp. 6a–8b. Several sections were translated by G. Scholem in his *Jewish Gnosticism, Merkabah Mysticism and Talmudic Tradition* (New York, 1960).

42. See below.

43. See above.

44. Rabbi Isaac stated that he and his brother met in Narbonne with a disciple of Rabbi Eleazar of Worms (see Scholem's introduction to the texts, *Gnosticism,* p. 8), and among other things he tells a hagiographic story about Rabbi Eleazar (chap. 10, p. 92). This story is told immediately after the

statement concerning the use of the "demon's air" for the purpose of prophecy.

45. A clear example of such an attitude toward the Ashkenazi Hasidim is to be found in the "Epistle of Worms," included by Rabbi Shem Tov Ibn Gaon in his kabbalistic treatise "Baddei ha-'Aron" (written in Palestine early in the fourteenth century), MS Paris 840. These examples attest to the fact that kabbalists in Spain used the reputation of the Ashkenazi Hasidim as great mystics and recipients of ancient traditions to enhance their own credibility.

46. Especially via Southern Italy; the arrival of Rabbi Aaron ben Samuel of Baghdad in Italy in the eighth century is regarded as the source of Ashkenazi hasidic prayer mysticism. See my *The Esoteric Theology of the Ashkenazi Hasidim* [Hebrew] (Jerusalem, 1968), pp. 13–20.

47. Rabbi Aaron of Baghdad is presented in the Megillat 'Aḥima'as as a magician as well as a mystic. A summary of these traditions is to be found in my paper: "The Beginnings of Jewish Mysticism in Europe," *The World History of the Jewish People: The Dark Ages*, ed. Cecil Roth (Tel Aviv, 1969), pp. 282–90.

48. Scholem, *Qabbalot*, p. 92. It should be noted that this story not only praises Rabbi Eleazar for his piety and his supernatural knowledge, but also states that he failed once in reciting the right formula, fell off the cloud, suffered injury, and remained crippled until his last day.

49. Concerning the date of his death see my *Studies in Ashkenazi Hasidic Literature* [Hebrew] (Tel Aviv–Ramat Gan, 1975), p. 69.

50. This stratification of "airs" or "winds" is based on *Sefer Yeṣirah*, chap. 1, secs. 9–10. Following Rav Saadia, Rabbi Eleazar of Worms in his commentary (Przemysl, 1883) described this hierarchy in detail (see especially p. 3c).

51. See my *Esoteric Theology*, pp. 184–90.

52. See Samuel Daiches, *Babylonian Oil Magic in the Talmud and Later Jewish Literature* (London, 1913); Joshua Trachtenberg, *Jewish Magic and Superstition* (New York, 1939), pp. 219–22, 307–8; and my study, "Sarei kos ve-sarei bohen," *Tarbiz* 32 (1963): 359–69 (reprinted in *Studies in Ashkenazi Hasidic Literature*, pp. 34–43).

53. The Ashkenazi Hasidim also used some more "prophetic" means to achieve this; compare the story told by Rabbi Judah the Pious concerning the discovery of a thief in *Studies in Ashkenazi Hasidic Literature*, pp. 10–12.

54. Lynn Thorndike, *History of Magic and Experimental Science*, 8 vols. (New York, 1923), 2:161, 168, 320, 354, 364–65, and 1:774. Compare Rashi to Sanhedrin 67b and 101a.

55. Dan, *Esoteric Theology*, pp. 104–18.

56. In the twelfth chapter of his *Yesod mora*, as well as in his commentary to Exod. 33; see Dan, *Esoteric Theology*, pp. 113–16.

57. Dan, *Esoteric Theology*, pp. 129–43, based on the detailed discussion in the first part of Bodl. MS Opp. 540, part of which was published in Dan, *Studies in Ashkenazi Hasidic Literature*, pp. 148–87.

58. Dan, *Studies in Ashkenazi Hasidic Literature*, pp. 165–66; 2 Kings 6:15–17.

59. This is one example for the use of a basic Ashkenazi hasidic theological idea, that God's miracles were implanted in the world to teach the righteous God's ways; see Dan, *Esoteric Theology*, pp. 88–93.

60. *Hokhmat ha-nefesh* (Lemberg, 1876), p. 18c–d (the pagination in this edition is completely arbitrary and wrong; this page is marked as p. 20. In the Safed edition, reprinted exactly word for word and line for line, the pagination has been corrected, and this is the pagination used here). See Dan, *Studies in Ashkenazi Hasidic Literature*, pp. 39–41.

61. According to the author, the changes in the visions are supernatural and therefore reflect divine characteristics.

62. "Philosophers" in this text means "sages," including Jews, and has nothing to do with Greek, Arabic or even Jewish philosophy, to which the Ashkenazi Hasidim were in fierce opposition. See Dan, *Studies in Ashkenazi Hasidic Literature*, pp. 31–33.

63. According to their concept of divine providence, there is a supervising angel *(memunneh)*, who directs the fate of each person; see Dan, *Esoteric Theology*, pp. 235–40.

64. The reading of this sentence in the manuscript is doubtful.

65. See Dan, *Studies in Ashkenazi Hasidic Literature*, pp. 41–43.

66. Dan, *Esoteric Theology*, pp. 88–93.

67. Dan, *Studies in Ashkenazi Hasidic Literature*, pp. 171–72.

68. A homily by Rabbi Judah the Pious (Bodl. MS Opp. 540, fol. 84*v*) explains the *leshad ha-shemen* ("a cake baked in oil") in Num. 11:8 as referring to these "princes," so that it is clear that he called them *"shedim"* and not *"sarim."* Prof. E. E. Urbach kindly informed me that in the commentaries in medieval halakhic literature concerning the relevant passages in Sanhedrin (above, n. 54), the halakhists often refer to *"shedim."*

69. Scholem, *Qabbalot*, pp. 86–87.

70. Genesis Rabbah 9:2, ed. Julius Theodor and Chanoch Albeck (Berlin-Jerusalem, 1903), p. 68, and compare Ecclesiastes Rabbah 3:11.

71. Hagigah 13b–14a.

72. Job 22:16.

73. According to Rabbi Isaac (Scholem, *Qabbalot*, p. 88), they were emanated as spiritual worlds, and their end came in a spiritual manner, like the burning tip in an oil lamp which is plunged into the oil in order to stop its burning.

74. *Hokhmat ha-nefesh*, p. 10c–d.

75. That is, in a perfect way.

76. This is based on the text in Genesis Rabbah, chap. 3, sec. 9.

77. Similar ideas were expressed elsewhere in the thirteenth century, as in the mystical *"Sefer Ha-hayyim"* (MSS Brit. Lib. Or. 1055, Munich 209). See Dan, *Esoteric Theology*, pp. 230–35, and compare *Sefer ha-yashar* (Venice, 1544), chap. 1.

78. See my discussion of their ethical attitude in *Hebrew Ethical and Homiletical Literature* [Hebrew] (Jerusalem, 1975), pp. 121–45.

79. Meaning: spiritual emanations.

80. From the Hebrew *karoz*, crier.
81. From the Hebrew *masakh*, curtain.
82. Scholem, *Qabbalot*, pp. 87–88.
83. The form of this name is quite mysterious, but it seems that it might contain the Hebrew element, *penei 'esh* ("fiery face"), which is included in the description of this power.
84. The Hebrew element *gur* ("cub") is evident here as a scion of Judah.
85. It should be "prince" in the singular.
86. The author follows the same structure of parallel births, as he had stated concerning Adam and Eve and Samael and Lilith.
87. "Malkhut," Kingdom, has here a double meaning, both as the tenth sefirah in the kabbalistic system and as a symbol of the Kingdom of Judah.
88. Based on the verse in Numbers 24:17 which was interpreted as referring to the messiah.
89. Isaiah 34:5.
90. Numbers 24:17.
91. Scholem, *Qabbalot*, p. 99.
92. This term is used here in a derogatory sense—an intermediary who leads one to sin.
93. Isaiah 27:1, and compare Bava Batra 74b. See Scholem's note, *Qabbalot*, p. 100, n. 5.
94. Samael's name is obviously interpreted here by Rabbi Isaac as derived from *suma* = blind.
95. Scholem, *Qabbalot*, pp. 101–2.
96. "Other" in the Zoharic terminology concerning evil means both "left" and "evil," while *sitra*, "side," refers to the system of emanations. See G. Scholem, *Kabbalah*, pp. 122–27, and Isaiah Tishby, *Mishnat ha-Zohar*, 2 vols. (Jerusalem, 1949), 1: 288–92.
97. It is possible to compare this process to a somewhat similar one which occurred several centuries before Rabbi Isaac, namely, the description of the evil power, Armilos, in the Book of Zerubbabel (see Yehudah Even-Shmuel, *Midreshei ge'ulah*, [Jerusalem–Tel Aviv, 1954], pp. 56–88, and compare my discussion in *The Hebrew Story in the Middle Ages*, pp. 33–46). In this case too we have a mythical description of an evil power, the son of Satan and a beautiful stone statue in Rome, who became the spiritual as well as political leader of the world and threatened to destroy the people of Israel. The original mythology of the power of evil is closely connected with the emergence of a new mythology of the messiah and a detailed description of messianic victories.

5.

The Meaning of the Torah in Jewish Mysticism

Gershom Scholem

I

Jewish mysticism is the sum of the attempts made to put a mystical interpretation on the content of Rabbinical Judaism as it crystallized in the period of the Second Temple and later. Obviously the process of crystallization had to be fairly far advanced before such a development could set in. This is equally true of the type of Judaism which centered round the law and which Philo of Alexandria undertook to interpret, and of the more highly developed Talmudic Judaism on which the endeavors of the medieval Kabbalists were based. Here it is not my intention to discuss the historical problems involved in the development of Jewish mysticism and specifically of the Kabbalah; I have done so elsewhere, particularly in my *Major Trends in Jewish Mysticism*. Suffice it to say that the subject I wish to discuss occupies a central position in Jewish mysticism.

In a religious system based on divine revelation and the acceptance of sacred books that define its content, questions concerning the nature of such revelation as set forth in the sacred books are unquestionably of the utmost importance. In times of crisis, moreover—and mysticism as a historical phenomenon is a product of crises—these questions become particularly urgent. Mystics are men who by their own inner experience and their speculation concerning this experience discover new layers of

From *On The Kabbalah and Its Symbolism* by Gershom G. Scholem. English translation © 1965 by Schocken Books, Inc. Reprinted by permission of Schocken Books, published by Pantheon Books, a division of Random House, Inc.

meaning in their traditional religion. When their experience and speculation did not lead them to break with the traditional institutions of their
religion, it was inevitable that they should come to grips with two
questions: how were they to find their own experience reflected and
anticipated in the sacred texts? And: how could their view of the world
be brought into harmony with the view accepted by their own tradition?[1] It is generally known that allegorical interpretations arise sponta-
neously whenever a conflict between new ideas and those expressed in a
sacred book necessitates some form of compromise. What is true of
allegorical interpretation is still more applicable to the specifically mystical interpretation of such texts.

Here it is not my intention to discuss mystical exegesis in its concrete
application to the Bible. Vast numbers of books have been written by
Jewish mystics attempting to find their own ideas in, or read them into,
the Biblical texts. A large part of the enormous Kabbalistic literature
consists of commentaries on Books of the Bible, especially the Pentateuch, the Five Scrolls, the Psalms, the Song of Songs, the Book of Ruth,
and Ecclesiastes. Many productive minds among the Kabbalists found
this a congenial way of expressing their own ideas, while making them
seem to flow from the words of the Bible. It is not always easy, in a
given case, to determine whether the Biblical text inspired the exegesis
or whether the exegesis was a deliberate device, calculated to bridge the
gap between the old and the new vision by reading completely new ideas
into the text. But this perhaps is to take too rationalistic a view of what
goes on in the mind of a mystic. Actually the thought processes of
mystics are largely unconscious, and they may be quite unaware of the
clash between old and new which is of such passionate interest to the
historian. They are thoroughly steeped in the religious tradition in which
they have grown up, and many notions which strike a modern reader as
fantastic distortions of a text spring from a conception of Scripture
which to the mystic seems perfectly natural. For one thing that can be
said with certainty about Kabbalists is this: they are, and do their best
to remain, traditionalists, as is indicated by the very word Kabbalah,
which is one of the Hebrew words for 'tradition.'

Thus it is important for us to understand the basic assumptions
underlying the concrete exegesis of the mystics. This is the problem we
shall now discuss. In our pursuit of it we are not dependent on conjec-
tures or inferences drawn from the exegeses, for the mystics have left us

extremely precise and illuminating formulations of their ideas. Mystical speculation on the nature of the Torah goes hand in hand with the development of certain general principles. Some of the mystics' ideas have a very peculiar history and are not common to all Kabbalists but characteristic only of certain trends. It is not uninteresting to observe the relationship between these different ideas and the basic principles from which they developed.

A great deal has been written about the allegorical exegesis of Philo of Alexandria and the assumptions on which it is based. At this point there is no need to say more. In discussing the specific conceptions of the Kabbalists with regard to the meaning of the Torah, we inevitably come across certain striking parallels to passages in Philo. Only recently so outstanding a scholar as Y. F. Baer attempted to demonstrate a profound structural kinship and even identity between the conceptions of Philo and those of the Kabbalists, and to interpret both as perfectly legitimate developments of the strictly Rabbinical conception underlying the *Halakhah*.[2] But this parallelism, as far as I can see, does not spring from any historical influence of Philo upon the medieval Kabbalists, although there have been numerous attempts—to my mind all unsuccessful—to demonstrate such a line of filiation.[3] Insofar as such parallels actually exist, they are based on similarity of purpose. As we shall see, the Kabbalists formulated their purpose with incomparable clarity and penetration, and one can easily be misled by reading Philo in the light of their sharp formulations. Similarity of purpose and hence in the fundamental structure of the mystical ideas about the nature of the Holy Scriptures accounts also for the parallels between certain Kabbalistic statements about the Torah and those of Islamic mystics about the Koran or of Christian mystics about their Biblical canon. Only a study of the historical conditions under which specific Kabbalistic ideas developed can tell us whether there was any historical connection between the speculation of the Jewish Kabbalists and that of non-Jews on the nature of the Holy Scriptures. I believe that I can demonstrate such an influence in at least one case, in connection with the doctrine of the fourfold meaning of Scripture.

But before I turn to our central problem, one more preliminary remark is in order. Most if not all Kabbalistic speculation and doctrine is concerned with the realm of the divine emanations or *sefiroth*, in which God's creative power unfolds. Over a long period of years, Kabbalists devised many ways of describing this realm. But throughout their history it remained the principal content of their vision, and always they spoke of it in the language of symbols, since it is not accessible to the direct perception of the human mind. Insofar as God reveals himself, He does so through the creative power of the *sefiroth*. The God of whom religion speaks is always conceived under one or more of these aspects of His Being, which the Kabbalists identified with stages in the process of divine emanation. This Kabbalistic world of the *sefiroth* encompasses what philosophers and theologians called the world of the divine attributes. But to the mystics it was divine life itself, insofar as it moves toward Creation. The hidden dynamic of this life fascinated the Kabbalists, who found it reflected in every realm of Creation. But this life as such is not separate from, or subordinate to, the Godhead, rather, it is the revelation of the hidden root, concerning which, since it is never manifested, not even in symbols, nothing can be said, and which the Kabbalists called *en-sof*, the infinite. But this hidden root and the divine emanations are one.

Here I need not go into the paradoxes and mysteries of Kabbalistic theology concerned with the *sefiroth* and their nature. But one important point must be made. The process which the Kabbalists described as the emanation of divine energy and divine light was also characterized as the unfolding of the divine *language*. This gives rise to a deep-seated parallelism between the two most important kinds of symbolism used by the Kabbalists to communicate their ideas. They speak of attributes and of spheres of light; but in the same context they speak also of divine names and the letters of which they are composed. From the very beginnings of Kabbalistic doctrine these two manners of speaking appear side by side. The secret world of the godhead is a world of language, a world of divine names that unfold in accordance with a law of their own. The elements of the divine language appear as the letters of the Holy Scriptures. Letters and names are not only conventional means of communication. They are far more. Each one of them represents a concentration of energy and expresses a wealth of meaning which cannot be translated, or not fully at least, into human language. There is, of course, an obvious discrepancy between the two symbolisms. When the Kabbalists speak of divine attributes and *sefiroth*, they are describing the hidden world under ten aspects; when, on the other hand, they speak of divine names and letters, they necessarily operate with the twenty-two consonants of the Hebrew alphabet, in which the Torah is written, or as they would have said, in which its secret essence was made communicable. Several ways of resolving this glaring contradiction were put forward. One explanation was that since letters and *sefiroth* are different configurations of the divine power, they cannot be reduced to a mechanical identity. What is significant for our present purposes is the analogy between Creation and Revelation, which results from the parallel between the *sefiroth* and the divine language. The process of Creation, which proceeds from stage to stage and is reflected in extra-divine worlds and of course in nature as well, is not necessarily different from the process that finds its expression in divine words and in the documents of Revelation, in which the divine language is thought to have been reflected.

These considerations take us to the very heart of our subject. There is a necessary relationship between the mystical meaning of the Torah and the assumptions concerning its divine essence. The Kabbalists do not start from the idea of communicable meaning. Of course the Torah means something to us. It communicates something in human language. But this, as we shall see, is only the most superficial of the various aspects under which it can be considered. In the following we shall see what these aspects are.

The Kabbalistic conceptions of the true nature of the Torah are based on three fundamental principles. They are not necessarily connected, although in our texts they often appear together, but it is not difficult to see how a relation can be established between them. These principles may be identified as

1. The principle of God's name;
2. The principle of the Torah as an organism;
3. The principle of the infinite meaning of the divine word.

Historically and presumably also psychologically, they do not all have the same origin.

II

The conception of God's name as the highest concentration of divine power forms a connecting link between two sets of ideas, the one originally associated with magic, the other pertaining to mystical speculation as such. The idea of the magic structure and nature of the Torah may be found long before the Kabbalah, in a relatively early midrash, for example, where in commenting on Job 28: 13: 'No man knoweth its order,' Rabbi Eleazar declares: 'The various sections of the Torah were not given in their correct order. For if they had been given in their correct order, anyone who read them would be able to wake the dead and perform miracles. For this reason the correct order and arrangement of the Torah were hidden and are known only to the Holy One, blessed be He, of whom it is said (Isa. 44: 7): "And who, as I, shall call, and shall declare it, and set it in order for me." '[4]

Obviously this statement carries a strong magical accent and implies a magical view of the Torah. It is well known that in the Hellenistic period and later the Torah was put to magical use both by Jews and non-Jews: divine names gleaned from the Torah were used for purposes of incantation. Often the methods of combination by which such magical names were derived from the Torah are unintelligible to us. Certain Hebrew and Aramaic texts of the late Talmudic and post-Talmudic periods indicate the specific use to which such magical names, allegedly taken from the Torah and the Book of Psalms, were put. The introduction to one of these works—*Shimmushe torah,* literally, the Theurgic Uses of the Torah—relates how Moses went up to heaven to receive the Torah, how he conversed with the angels, and how finally God gave him not only the text of the Torah as we know it, but also the secret combinations of letters which represent another, esoteric aspect of the Torah.[5] This book came to the knowledge of the first Kabbalists in Provence and in Spain about the year 1200. Moses ben Nahman (Nahmanides), one of the most prominent among the early Kabbalists, refers to it in the preface to his famous commentary on the Torah. 'We possess,' he writes,

an authentic tradition showing that the entire Torah consists of the names of God and that the words we read can be divided in a very different way, so as to form [esoteric] names. . . . The statement in the Aggadah to the effect that the Torah was originally written with black fire on white fire[6] obviously confirms our opinion that the writing was continuous, without division into words, which made it possible to read it either as a sequence of [esoteric] names *['al derekh ha-shemoth]* or in the traditional way as history and commandments. Thus the Torah as given to Moses was divided into words in such a way as to be read as divine commandments. But at the same time he received the oral tradition, according to which it was to be read as a sequence of names.

In view of this esoteric structure of the Torah, says Nahmanides, the
Masoretic tradition concerning the writing of the Bible and especially
the scrolls of the Torah must be observed with the utmost care. Every
single letter counts, and a scroll of the Torah must be rejected for use in
the synagogue if there is so much as a single letter too few or too many.
This conception is very old. As early as the second century, Rabbi Meir,
one of the most important teachers of the Mishnah, relates:

When I was studying with Rabbi Akiba, I used to put vitriol in the ink and he
said nothing. But when I went to Rabbi Ishmael, he asked me: My son, what is
your occupation? I answered: I am a scribe [of the Torah]. And he said to me:
My son, be careful in your work, for it is the work of God; if you omit a single
letter, or write a letter too many, you will destroy the whole world.[7]

The passage from Nahmanides clearly indicates the influence of the
magical tradition, which was of course far older than the Kabbalah.
From here it was only a short step to the still more radical view that the
Torah is not only made up of the names of God but is as a whole the
one great Name of God. This thesis is no longer magical, but purely
mystical. It makes its first appearance among the Spanish Kabbalists,
and the development from the old to the new view seems to have taken
place among the teachers of Nahmanides. Commenting on a passage in
the *Midrash Genesis Rabbah* to the effect that the word 'light' occurs
five times in the story of the first day of Creation, corresponding to the
five books of the Torah, Ezra ben Solomon, an older contemporary of
Nahmanides, who frequented the same Kabbalistic circle in the Cata-
lonian city of Gerona, writes: 'How far-reaching are the words of this
sage; his words are true indeed, for the five books of the Torah are *the
Name* of the Holy One, blessed be He.'[8] The mystical light that shines
in these books is thus the one great Name of God. The same thesis is to
be found in the writings of several members of the Gerona group of
Kabbalists, and was finally taken over by the author of the *Zohar*, the
classical book of Spanish Kabbalism.[9]

I believe that Nahmanides himself was perfectly familiar with this
new idea, but that he was reluctant to express so radically mystical a
thesis in a book intended for a general public unschooled in Kabbalistic
doctrine. To say that the Torah was in essence nothing but the great
Name of God was assuredly a daring statement that calls for an explanation. Here the Torah is interpreted as a mystical unity, whose primary

purpose is not to convey a specific meaning, but rather to express the immensity of God's power, which is concentrated in His 'Name.' To say that the Torah is a name does not mean that it is a name which might be pronounced as such, nor has it anything to do with any rational conception of the social function of a name. The meaning is, rather, that in the Torah God has expressed His transcendent Being, or at least that part or aspect of His Being which can be revealed to Creation and through Creation. Moreover, since even in the ancient Aggadah the Torah was regarded as an instrument of Creation, through which the world came into existence,[10] this new conception of the Torah must be regarded as an extension and mystical reinterpretation of the older conception. For the instrument which brought the world into being is far more than a mere instrument, since, as we have seen above, the Torah is the concentrated power of God Himself, as expressed in His Name. But this idea has a further implication. Another early Midrash says that God 'looked into the Torah and created the world.'[11] The author of these words must have thought that the law which governs Creation as such, hence the cosmos and all nature, was already prefigured in the Torah, so that God, looking into the Torah, could see it, although to us this aspect of the Torah remains concealed. This conception is actually formulated by Philo, who explains the fact that the Mosaic Law begins with a record of the Creation of the world by saying that 'Moses wished to set forth the genesis of the great world state *[megalopolis]*, since his own laws were the best possible copy of the structure of all nature.'[12] In the minds of the Kabbalists these ancient notions handed down in the Aggadic tradition fused into a single idea. The Name contains power, but at the same time embraces the secret laws and harmonious order which pervade and govern all existence. In addition the Kabbalists were able to read in the esoteric and apocalyptic books of the Talmudic period that heaven and earth were created by the Name of God.[13] It was only natural to combine statements of this kind with the notion of the Torah as the instrument of Creation, that is, the Great Name of God.

This basic idea of the Torah as the Name of God was the source of certain other Kabbalistic developments. It goes without saying that such an assertion about the Torah does not refer to the document written in ink on a scroll of parchment, but to the Torah as a pre-existential being, which preceded everything else in the world. This follows, for example, from the Aggadah according to which the Torah was created two thousand years before the Creation of the world.[14] For the Kabbalists this

'Creation of the Torah' was the process by which the divine Name or the divine *sefiroth* of which we have spoken above emanated from God's hidden essence. The Torah, as the Kabbalists conceived it, is consequently not separate from the divine essence, not created in the strict sense of the word; rather, it is something that represents the secret life of God, which the Kabbalistic emanation theory was an attempt to describe. In other words, the secret life of God is projected into the Torah; its order is the order of the Creation. This most secret aspect of the Torah, or one might say, the Torah in its occult form, is sometimes referred to in the Kabbalistic literature of the thirteenth century as *torah kedumah,* the primordial Torah, and is sometimes identified with God's *hokhmah (sophia),* His 'wisdom,' the second emanation and manifestation of the divine power, which sprang from the hidden 'nothingness.'[15] We shall see in the course of our discussion how certain Kabbalists conceived the state of the Torah when it was still contained in the mystical unity of God's wisdom. There were Kabbalists for whom this conception of the Torah as the Name of God meant simply that it was identical with God's wisdom or that it was a partial aspect of this same wisdom. But there were also other opinions.[16]

One of the most important variants of this theory occurs in Joseph Gikatila, a leading Spanish Kabbalist who wrote at the end of the thirteenth century and was no doubt familiar with parts of the *Zohar.* In his view, the Torah is not itself the name of God but the explication of the Name of God. To him the Name meant exactly what it had meant for the Jewish tradition, namely the tetragrammaton, which is the one and only true name of God. He writes: 'Know that the entire Torah is, as it were, an explication of, and commentary on, the tetragrammaton YHWH. And this is the true meaning of the Biblical term "God's Torah" *[torath YHWH'].*[17] In other words, the phrase *torath YHWH* does not mean the Torah which God gave but the Torah which explains YHWH, the name of God. Here Torah is understood as *hora'a,* a didactic exposition. But Gikatila's idea goes still further. In what sense is the Torah an 'explication' of the name of God? In the sense, he replies in several passages,[18] that the Torah was woven from the name of God. Gikatila seems to have been the first to employ this notion of a fabric, *'ariga,* to illustrate the recurrence of the Name in the text of the Torah. He writes for example: 'Behold the miraculous way in which the Torah was woven from God's wisdom.' And in another passage:

The whole Torah is a fabric of appellatives, *kinnuyim*—the generic term for the epithets of God, such as compassionate, great, merciful, venerable—and these epithets in turn are woven from the various names of God [such as *El, Elohim, Shaddai*]. But all these holy names are connected with the tetragrammaton YHWH and dependent upon it. Thus the entire Torah is ultimately woven from the tetragrammaton.[19]

These words, it seems to me, throw considerable light on Gikatila's thesis. The Torah is the Name of God, because it is a living texture, a *'textus'* in the literal sense of the word, into which the one true name, the tetragrammaton, is woven in a secret, indirect way, but also directly as a kind of leitmotiv. The nucleus in any case is the tetragrammaton. If Gikatila had been asked exactly how this weaving was done, he would doubtless have answered with his teacher Abraham Abulafia that the basic elements, the name YHWH, the other names of God, and the appellatives, or *kinnuyim*, or rather, their consonants, went through several sets of permutations and combinations in accordance with the formulas set forth by the Talmudists, until at length they took the form of the Hebrew sentences of the Torah, as we read them now. The initiates, who know and understand these principles of permutation and combination, can proceed backward from the text and reconstruct the original texture of names. All these metamorphoses of names have a twofold function. They serve on the one hand to give the Torah its aspect as a communication, a message of God to man, accessible to human understanding. On the other hand, they point to the secret operation of the divine power, recognizable only by the garment woven from the Holy Names when they serve certain specific purposes in the work of Creation.

In conclusion it should be said that this conception of the Torah as a fabric woven of names provided no contribution to concrete exegesis. It was, rather, a purely mystical principle and tended to remove the Torah from all human insight into its specific meanings, which are, after all, the sole concern of exegesis. But this did not trouble the Kabbalists. To them the fact that God expressed Himself, even if His utterance is far beyond human insight, is far more important than any specific 'meaning' that might be conveyed. So considered, the Torah is an absolute and has primacy over all human interpretations, which, however deep they may penetrate, can only approximate the absolute 'meaninglessness' of the divine revelation.

Certain Kabbalists, such as Menahem Recanati (c. 1300), went still further. Starting from an old saying: 'Before the world was created, only God and His Name existed,'[20] they taught that the name here referred to was not only the tetragrammaton YHWH, but the totality of the manifestations of the divine power—this, they said, was the mystical meaning of the true name of God. From here it was only one more step to saying that God Himself is the Torah, 'for the Torah is not something outside Him, and He is not outside the Torah.'[21] Recanati ascribes this quotation to the Kabbalists, and indeed a similar statement occurs in Gikatila's work on the mystical foundations of the Commandments: 'His Torah is in Him, and that is what the Kabbalists say, namely, that the Holy One, blessed be He, is in His Name and His Name is in Him, and that His Name is His Torah.'[22] Elsewhere in the same book he elucidates this statement, drawing upon an old formula from the hymns of the *merkabah* mystics: 'It is an important principle that the ancients expressed in the words: "Thy Name is in Thee and in Thee is Thy Name." For the letters of His Name are He Himself. Even though they move away from Him, they remain firmly rooted [literally: fly away and remain with him].'[23] He explains this by saying that the letters are the mystical body of God, while God, in a manner of speaking, is the soul of the letters. This comparison between God and His Torah on the one hand and soul and body on the other leads us to the second principle, which will be discussed in the following.

III

The principle that the Torah is a living organism falls in with several lines of Kabbalistic thought. The reference to body and soul in the passage we have just quoted from Gikatila suggests such a conception, and the notion that the Torah is woven of holy names is merely a metaphoric way of saying that it is a living fabric. But the idea of the Torah as a living organism is older than Gikatila. It has been formulated with penetrating clarity by the earliest Spanish Kabbalists. In his commentary on the Song of Songs, Ezra ben Solomon of Gerona writes that the Torah contains not so much as one superfluous letter or point, 'because in its divine totality it is an edifice hewn from the Name of the Holy One, blessed be He.'[24] The nature of this divine edifice, *binyan elohi*, may be gathered from a long discussion of this point by Ezra's younger contemporary, Azriel of Gerona, in his Kabbalistic commentary on the Talmudic Aggadah. He too starts from the assumption that the Torah is the Name of God and that it is a living body with a soul. The peculiarities in the Masoretic writing of the Torah, the different types of sections, paragraphs, etc., suggest to him a comparison with a complete, self-contained organism.

Just as in the body of a man there are limbs and joints, just as some organs of the body are more, others less, vital, so it seems to be with the Torah. To one who does not understand their hidden meaning, certain sections and verses of the Torah seem fit to be thrown into the fire; but to one who has gained insight into their true meaning they seem essential components of the Torah. Consequently, to omit so much as one letter or point from the Torah is like removing some part of a perfect edifice.[25] Thence it also follows that in respect of its divine character no essential distinction can be drawn between the section of Genesis 36, setting forth the generations of Esau [a seemingly superfluous passage], and the Ten Commandments, for it is all *one* whole and *one* edifice.[26]

Here we have a clear combination of the two principles. The Torah is a name, but this name is constructed like a living organism. Not only is the Name that is the root of all things an absolute, but, as manifested in the Torah, it breaks down into the different parts of an organic being. The only difference is that a common organism includes vital organs and others that are not vital, while in the Torah any such distinction is only apparent, for an authentic mystic discovers secret meanings even in the parts that seem quite unimportant; indeed, it is precisely from such passages that he may glean key words or symbols for profound insights or doctrines, as, for example, the *Zohar* and the Lurianic Kabbalah did from the thirty-sixth chapter of Genesis.

This conception of the Torah as a mystical organism is already attested in Philo's account of the Jewish sect of the Therapeutae in Egypt: 'For the entire Torah *(nomothesia)* seems to these people something akin to a living being; the literal sense is the body, while the soul is the secret sense underlying the written word.'[27] And on several occasions Philo bases his own developments on a similar conception.[28] A direct line of influence from the Therapeutae of Egypt or from Philo to the Kabbalists strikes me as very unlikely. Quite independently of one another, mystics took similar attitudes toward the Holy Scriptures and expressed them in related images.

This conception of the Torah as an organism is also fundamental to the *Zohar,* which appeared fifty years after Azriel's work. Here we read for example:

He who labors in the Torah upholds the world and enables each part to perform its function. For there is not a member in the human body that does not have its counterpart in the world as a whole. For as man's body consists of members and parts of varying rank, all acting and reacting upon one another so as to form one organism, so is it with the world at large: it consists of a hierarchy of created things, which, when they properly act and react upon each other, together form one organic body.[29]

Another metaphor for the same idea, this time based on the image of the tree, occurs elsewhere in the *Zohar*[30] and is expressed still more strikingly in one of the Hebrew works of Moses de Leon, whom I regard as the author of the main part of the *Zohar.* 'For the Torah,' he writes,

is called the Tree of Life. . . . Just as a tree consists of branches and leaves, bark, sap and roots, each one of which components can be termed tree, there being no substantial difference between them, you will also find that the Torah contains many inner and outward things, and all form a single Torah and a tree, without difference between them. . . . And although among the sages of the Talmud one forbids what the other allows, one declares a thing to be ritually clean which another terms impermissible, one says this and another that, nevertheless it is necessary to know that the whole is one unity.[31]

The author of the *Tikkune Zohar,* who wrote only a few years after the completion of the main body of the *Zohar,* also declares: 'The Torah has a head, a body, a heart, a mouth and other organs, in the same way as Israel.'[32] Here we have a parallel between the two mystical organisms: the Torah and Israel. The *Zohar* itself speaks of each of these organisms in different passages, and they are not brought into direct relation. A parallel between them seems first to have been drawn by the author of the *Tikkunim.* The mystical organism of the Torah, which embodies the name of God, is thus correlated with the mystical body of the Community of Israel, which the Kabbalists regarded not only as the historical organism of the Jewish people, but also as an esoteric symbol for the *Shekhinah,* its members being, as it were, the 'members of the *Shekhinah.*'[33] Later Kabbalists, as we shall see, draw still more explicit conclusions from this correlation.

But there is still another symbolism in which the idea of an organism is expressed, and in which certain particularly daring views about the nature of the revelation contained in the Torah first made their appearance. In order to understand these ideas, we must bear in mind the very old traditional distinction between the 'written Torah' and the 'oral Torah.' According to the exoteric usage of the Talmudic sources, the written Torah is the text of the Pentateuch. The oral Torah is the sum total of everything that has been said by scholars or sages in explanation of this written corpus, by the Talmudic commentators on the Law and all others who have interpreted the text. The oral Torah is the tradition of the Congregation of Israel, it performs the necessary role of completing the written Torah and making it more concrete. According to Rabbinical tradition, Moses received both Torahs at once on Mount Sinai, and everything that any subsequent scholar finds in the Torah or legitimately derives from it, was already included in this oral tradition given to Moses. Thus in Rabbinical Judaism the two Torahs are one.[34] The oral tradition and the written word complete one another, neither is conceivable without the other. From the outset these two conceptions played a significant part in the thinking of the Kabbalists, who connected them with the mystical symbolism of the *sefiroth*. The written Torah was looked upon chiefly as a symbol of the giving sphere of the Godhead, identified primarily with the *sefirah Tif'ereth,* while the oral Torah was seen as a symbol of the receptive sphere, which is at once that of the *Shekhinah* and of the 'Congregation of Israel.' In their active association, these two *sefiroth* manifest the action of God, and similarly the whole revelation of the Torah is given only in this unity of the written and the oral Torah. The forms in which the written and the oral Torah are given here on earth—e.g., the scroll of the Torah and the collections of Talmudic traditions—point back to those deeper spheres from which essentially they arose. In the above-cited passage from the *Tikkune Zohar,* the author goes on to identify the heart of the organism with the written Torah, the mouth with the oral Torah.

Speculations concerning these two aspects of the Torah are contained in the earliest books of the Kabbalists, the *Book Bahir,* for example.[35] But the most interesting discussion of the relationship between them occurs in a fragment which may be attributable to one of the very first Provençal Kabbalists, namely, Isaac the Blind. This fragment, which has come down to us only in manuscript, provides a mystical commentary on the beginning of the *Midrash Konen,* dealing with cosmogony.[36] This midrash repeats the above-mentioned conception that the pre-existent Torah was written in black fire on white fire, which, as we have seen above, Nahmanides already took as an indication of the mystical status of the Torah. Here the Torah seems to burn before God in black fiery letters on white fire, and it is this conception which inspired Rabbi Isaac, probably before Nahmanides, to write the following:

In God's right hand were engraved all the engravings [innermost forms] that were destined some day to rise from potency to act. From the emanation of all [higher] *sefiroth* they were graven, scratched, and molded into the *sefirah* of Grace *(hesed),* which is also called God's right hand, and this was done in an inward, inconceivably subtle way. This formation is called the concentrated, not yet unfolded Torah, and also the Torah of Grace. Along with all the other engravings [principally] two engravings were made in it. The one has the form of the written Torah, the other the form of the oral Torah. The form of the written Torah is that of the colors of white fire, and the form of the oral Torah has colored forms as of black fire. And all these engravings and the not yet unfolded Torah existed potentially, perceptible neither to a spiritual nor to a sensory eye, until the will [of God] inspired the idea of activating them by means of primordial wisdom and hidden knowledge. Thus at the beginning of all acts there was pre-existentially the not yet unfolded Torah *[torah kelulah],* which is in God's right hand with all the primordial forms [literally: inscriptions and engravings] that are hidden in it, and this is what the Midrash implies when it says that God took the primordial Torah *(torah kedumah),* which stems from the quarry of 'repentance' and the source of original wisdom,[37] and in one spiritual act emanated the not yet unfolded Torah in order to give permanence to the foundations of all the worlds.

The author goes on to relate how from the not yet unfolded Torah, which corresponds to the *sefirah* of Grace, there sprang the written Torah, which corresponds to the *sefirah* of Divine Compassion, which is *tif'ereth,* and the oral Torah, corresponding to the power of divine judgment in *malkhuth,* the last *sefirah.* He interprets the fiery organism of the Torah, which burned before God in black fire on white fire, as follows: the white fire is the written Torah, in which the form of the letters is not yet explicit, for the form of the consonants and vowel points was first conferred by the power of the black fire, which is the oral Torah. This black fire is like the ink on the parchment. 'And so the written Torah can take on corporeal form only through the power of the oral Torah, that is to say: without the oral Torah, it cannot be truly understood.' Essentially only Moses, master of all the Prophets, pene-trated in unbroken contemplation to that mystical written Torah, which in reality is still hidden in the invisible form of white light. Even the other Prophets gained only a fleeting glimpse of it in momentary intuitions.[38]

The mystical symbolism of this profoundly meaningful passage conceals the view that, strictly speaking, there is no written Torah here on
earth. A far-reaching idea! What we call the written Torah has itself
passed through the medium of the oral Torah, it is no longer a form
concealed in white light; rather, it has emerged from the black light,
which determines and limits and so denotes the attribute of divine
severity and judgment. Everything that we perceive in the fixed forms of
the Torah, written in ink on parchment, consists, in the last analysis, of
interpretations or definitions of what is hidden. *There is only an oral
Torah:* that is the esoteric meaning of these words, and the written
Torah is a purely mystical concept. It is embodied in a sphere that is
accessible to prophets alone. It was, to be sure, revealed to Moses, but
what he gave to the world as the written Torah has acquired its present
form by passing through the medium of the oral Torah. The mystical
white of the letters on the parchment is the written Torah, but not the
black of the letters inscribed in ink.[39] In the mystical organism of the
Torah the two spheres overlap, and there is no written Torah, free from
the oral element, that can be known or conceived of by creatures who
are not prophets.

IV

This principle of the Torah as an organism is closely connected with the
third principle, which we can now proceed to discuss. This is the principle of the manifold, not to say infinite, meanings of the Torah. Often the
different members of the Torah, seen as an organism, were not regarded
as organs of equal rank and importance, but as different levels of meaning within the Torah. They guide the mystical student of the holy texts
from the outward meanings to increasingly deeper layers of understanding. Thus the idea of the organism becomes identified with the conception of a living hierarchy of meanings and levels of meaning.

In this connection the Kabbalists adopted a line of thought which
they found in the Jewish philosophers of the Middle Ages, who in turn
had taken it from the philosophical tradition of the Arabs. I am referring
to the idea of the two levels of meaning—inward and outward—in the
sacred texts. This dualism was equally welcome on the one hand to the
esoteric rationalism of the philosophers and reformers, to which in our
generation Leo Strauss has devoted several significant works,[40] and, on

the other, to the religious interests of the mystics, who undertook to rediscover their own world in the depths of the Holy Scriptures. Here I need not go into detail about the Islamic groups, notably such esoteric sects as the Ismaili, which stressed the inner, allegorical, or mystical meaning of the Koran in contrast to the outward or literal sense, which in the higher stages of initiation lost all meaning. The Arabic authors refer to the adherents of these trends as *batiniyya,* or advocates of the inner meaning, that is to say, esoterics or spiritualists. It is interesting to note that the terms used by many Jewish philosophers to denote these two levels of meaning (*hitson* and *penimi,* outward and inward) never occur in this context in the older Jewish sources, but are literal translations of the corresponding Arabic terms. Thus it is evident that this terminology originated in Islam, whence it was taken over by the Jewish philosophers, who proceeded to identify the inner meaning with the philosophical interpretation of the text, which was not strictly speaking mystical. A mystical interpretation arose only when this terminology was taken over by the Spanish Kabbalists and finally by the author of the *Zohar,* who translated it into Aramaic. In many passages of the *Zohar* the principle is developed that the Torah is at once hidden and manifest, esoteric and exoteric, *'oraitha sethim ve-galya.*[41] The author finds this dualism not only in the Torah, but in every conceivable sphere of existence, beginning with God and embracing every realm and aspect of Creation.

On the other hand, it should not be forgotten that in the Spanish Kabbalistic period the climate was such as to favor an easy flow of ideas between the Christian and the Jewish communities. Two different branches stemming from the same root meet in the doctrine of the Torah as it finally took shape in the *Zohar.* The ancient root is undoubtedly Philo of Alexandria, to whom we may ultimately attribute all these distinctions between literal meaning and spiritual meaning, which were taken over by the Church Fathers and the Christian Middle Ages, and also by Islam (which derived them from Oriental Christian sources). Though it is perfectly possible that such ideas had also been preserved by Jewish groups which we have thus far been unable to identify, their historically visible expression is undoubtedly attributable to Christian and Islamic influence.

The question arises: was there a historical link between the Zoharic doctrine of different levels of meaning and the similar, but older, theory of the fourfold meaning of Scripture that had been developed by the Christian authors of the early Middle Ages?[42] Some seventy years ago Wilhelm Bacher tried, in a valuable article on the Biblical exegesis of the *Zohar*, to demonstrate a line of historical filiation.[43] But since he had no clear idea of the various literary strata of which the *Zohar* consists, he could not formulate his findings with the precision which in my opinion present-day scholarship has made possible.

But before we look into the conceptions underlying the *Zohar*, one more remark is in order. As we have said above, many Jewish philosophers identified the inner meaning of the Torah with philosophical allegory. And indeed many of their allegorical explanations smack strongly of Philo. Philosophical ideas are rediscovered in the Bible. But allegory in this sense was by no means the cornerstone of Kabbalistic exegesis, which was strictly symbolic. What Kabbalistic exegesis discovers behind the literal meaning of the Bible or of the Talmudic interpretations of the Bible was something very different.

What the Kabbalists looked for in the Bible was not primarily philosophical ideas, but a symbolic description of the hidden process of divine life, as it unfolds in the manifestations and emanations of the *sefiroth*. Their primary interest in the Bible may be termed theosophical. As for allegory proper, we find very different attitudes among the Kabbalists. So outstanding an authority as Nahmanides deliberately avoided the allegorical interpretations of the philosophers in his commentary on the Torah. He was well aware of the danger that might accrue to the observance of Jewish ritual from a pure spiritualization of the Torah such as a consistent application of the allegorical method would imply. He expressly warned against this danger in a passage in his commentary on Deuteronomy 29:29, which for some reason is lacking in our editions.[44] The danger, in his opinion, was not present in the mystical interpretation of the Biblical text, where the symbol became meaningful only through the actual enactment of the commandment. But not all the Kabbalists were so reserved toward allegory. Many regarded it as a legitimate instrument. The author of the *Zohar*, though interested primarily in a mystical and symbolic description of the hidden world of the Godhead, did not refrain from interpreting certain Bible passages allegorically. Thus the Book of Jonah and also the stories of the Patriarchs in Genesis become allegorical accounts of the destiny of the human soul—though this does not prevent the author from giving a purely mystical (and more far-reaching) interpretation of these same stories of the Patriarchs. Once the esoteric interpretation of Scripture had assumed two different aspects—the one allegorical, the other mystical—the way lay open to the doctrine of the four levels of meaning. While, for example, Joseph ibn Aqnin, contemporary of Maimonides, speaks, throughout his commentary on the Song of Songs, of three such levels of interpretation—literal, Aggadic, and philosophico-allegorical—the Kabbalists added a fourth, that of the theosophical mystery in the sense defined above. This level the *Zohar* terms *raza de-mehemanutha*—understanding according to the 'mystery of faith.'

This conception of the essentially fourfold meaning of the Torah made its appearance at roughly the same time, toward the end of the thirteenth century, in the work of three Kabbalistic authors who probably belonged to the same group or were at least in contact with one another. They are Moses de Leon, who was also the author of the main part of the *Zohar*, Bahya ben Asher, and Joseph Gikatila. Their definitions of the four levels of meaning differ in some degree. But the conception found its most significant development in the Zoharic literature; and it was this trend which also exerted the most lasting influence on later Jewish mysticism.

The earliest reference to the four levels is to be found in the *Midrash ha-Neᶜelam* to the Book of Ruth, one of the earliest works of the author of the *Zohar*. In it he writes: 'The words of the Torah are likened to a nut. How is this to be understood? Just as a nut has an outer shell and a kernel, each word of the Torah contains outward fact *(maᶜaseh)*, midrash, haggadah, and mystery *(sod)*, each of which is deeper in meaning than the preceding.'[45] This passage is remarkable in several ways. It makes use of no specific term or formula such as was later used to designate the four levels. *Haggadah* seems to refer to some allegorical or tropic form of interpretation, while by *midrash* is meant the hermeneutic method by which the halakhists, or legalists, of the Talmud derived their definitions from the Biblical text. The comparison of the Torah with a nut is not new in Jewish literature. It was already employed by the German and French Hasidim of the early thirteenth century, especially in connection with the *merkabah* (chariot) described in Chapter I of Ezekiel. The metaphor was particularly apt, because the nut was said to possess not only a hard outward shell, but also two finer inward coverings which protected the kernel. The same figure, it is interesting to note, was used in the twelfth century by Joachim of Floris, the famous Calabrian monk, in his *Enchiridion in Apocalypsim.*[46]

Essentially the same set of meanings, though formulated more explicitly, are set forth in a famous passage of the *Zohar,* which became a *locus classicus* for the Kabbalists.

Verily the Torah lets out a word and emerges a little from her sheath, and then hides herself again. But she does this only for those who know and obey her. For the Torah resembles a beautiful and stately damsel, who is hidden in a secluded chamber of her palace and who has a secret lover, unknown to all others. For love of her he keeps passing the gate of her house, looking this way and that in search of her. She knows that her lover haunts the gate of her house. What does she do? She opens the door of her hidden chamber ever so little, and for a moment reveals her face to her lover, but hides it again forthwith. Were anyone with her lover, he would see nothing and perceive nothing. He alone sees it and he is drawn to her with his heart and soul and his whole being, and he knows that for love of him she disclosed herself to him for one moment, aflame with love for him. So is it with the word of the Torah, which reveals herself only to those who love her. The Torah knows that the mystic [*hakim libba,* literally, the wise of heart] haunts the gate of her house. What does she do? From within her hidden palace she discloses her face and beckons to him and returns forthwith to her place and hides. Those who are there see nothing and know nothing, only he alone, and he is drawn to her with his heart and soul and his whole being. Thus the Torah reveals herself and hides, and goes out in love to her lover and arouses love in him. Come and see: this is the way of the Torah. At first, when she wishes to reveal herself to a man, she gives him a momentary sign. If he understands, well and good; if not, she sends to him and calls him a simpleton. To the messenger she sends to him the Torah says: tell the simpleton to come here that I may speak to him. As it is written [Prov. 9 : 47]: 'Whoso is simple, let him turn in hither, she saith to him that wanteth understanding.' When he comes to her, she begins from behind a curtain to speak words in keeping with his understanding, until very slowly insight comes to him, and this is called *derashah.*[47] Then through a light veil she speaks allegorical words [*millin de hida*] and that is what is meant by *haggadah.*[48] Only then, when he has become familiar with her, does she reveal herself to him face to face and speak to him of all her hidden secrets and all her hidden ways, which have been in her heart from the beginning. Such a man is then termed perfect, a 'master,' that is to say, a 'bridegroom of the Torah' in the strictest sense, the master of the house, to whom she discloses all her secrets, concealing nothing. She says to him: do you see now how many mysteries were contained in that sign I gave you on the first day, and what its true meaning is? Then he understands that to those words indeed nothing may be added and nothing taken away. And then for the first time he understands the true meaning of the words of the Torah, as they stand there, those words to which not a syllable or a letter may be added and from which none may be taken away. And therefore men should take care to pursue the Torah [that is, study it with great precision], in order to become her lovers as has been related.[49]

This fine simile, shot through with figures from the chivalric tradition of the Middle Ages, offers an excellent development on the short sentence, from the midrash to Ruth, referring to the Torah as a nut. It makes use of the same terminology, except that here the *ma'aseh*, the outward fact, is replaced by the more customary term *peshat*, designating the literal or simple meaning, which is preserved even in the mystical transfiguration, though it has been made transparent by the mystical light shining through it. A further step is taken in another Zoharic passage (III, 202a), where the different levels of meaning are expressly represented as parts of the organism of the Torah, which is the Tree of Life. Here, however, the old term *haggadah* is replaced by the new term *remez,* which in medieval Hebrew had come (under Arabic influence) to designate allegory. Here, in addition to the above-mentioned four levels of meaning, a fifth is mentioned, namely *gematria,* or interpretation through the numerical value of the Hebrew letters, which elsewhere is not regarded as an independent level of meaning.

At this stage the author of the *Zohar* had not yet conceived of a concise formula in which to sum up the whole conception. The above-cited passages were written between 1280 and 1286. But after completing the main part of the *Zohar* in pseudoepigraphical form as a collection of the dialogues and lectures of Rabbi Simeon ben Yohai and his pupils in the second century, Moses de Leon wrote a number of Kabbalistic works in Hebrew under his own name. In these he develops a number of ideas that were first set forth in the *Zohar.* We know that before 1290 he wrote a lost work entitled *Pardes,* which literally means 'paradise.' This title is based on a pun, which became widely known and was much used in subsequent Hebrew literature. This pun is based on the famous story in the Talmud about four great rabbis who engaged in esoteric studies in the second century. These four were said to have 'entered Paradise.' They were the Rabbis Akiba, Ben Zoma, Ben Azzai, and Aher. 'One saw and died, the second saw and lost his reason, the third laid waste the young plants [that is, became an apostate and seduced the young]. Only Rabbi Akiba entered in peace and came out in peace.'[50] The exact meaning of *pardes* in this passage has long been an object of speculation. I have discussed the matter elsewhere[51] and there is no need to go into it here. In any event, Moses de Leon employed this highly suggestive term, so rich in shades of meaning, as a cipher for the four levels of interpretation. Each consonant of the word PaRDeS denotes one of the levels: P stands for *peshat,* the literal meaning, R for *remez,* the allegorical meaning, D for *derasha,* the Talmudic and Aggadic interpretation, S for *sod,* the mystical meaning. The *pardes* into which the four ancient scholars entered thus came to denote speculations concerning the true meaning of the Torah on all four levels. In a work written not much later, Moses de Leon took up this image once again and combined it with the above-mentioned notion of the Torah as a nut composed of shell and kernel. A few years later, roughly between 1295 and 1305, an anonymous author, probably a student of Moses de Leon or a member of his circle, wrote the latest of the Zoharic books, namely, *Ra῾ya Mehemna,* 'The True Shepherd,' and *Tikkune Zohar,* a work containing seventy interpretations of the first section of the Torah (Gen. 1–5). This author took over the term *pardes,* denoting the four levels of meaning, and it is from this source that all subsequent writers derived it.

In his commentary on Genesis 2:10 ff., dealing with the four rivers that flow from the garden of Eden, or Paradise, the anonymous author gives a new turn to the old Talmudic anecdote about the four rabbis. In this version one went into the river Pishon, which name is here interpreted as *pi shone halakhoth,* that is to say, 'a mouth that learns the exact meaning of the *Halakhah.*' Here Pishon stands for the literal meaning. The second went into the river Gihon, which name is taken as a reference to allegory. The third went into the river Hiddekel, which name is interpreted as a combination of the two words *had* and *kal,* 'sharp' and 'deft,' hence a reference to the sharpness and deftness of the Talmudic interpretation, *derashah.* The fourth went into the Euphrates, which is related to the innermost kernel, the marrow whence flows the seed of life, which, in other words, discovers and develops ever new mysteries. Ben Zoma and Ben Azzai arrived only at the shell and inner coverings of the Torah; there they remained and incurred harm in these realms. Only Rabbi Akiba penetrated to the marrow of the Torah; he alone entered and emerged safe and sound.[52] The author of the *Ra῾ya Mehemna* has still another variant. In several passages he employs the catchword *pardes,* but he replaces *remez,* allegory, by *re'iyoth,* insights.[53]

The author of the *Tikkunim* identifies the *Shekhinah,* God's presence, conceived as the last of the ten emanations, or *sefiroth*, with the Torah in its total manifestations, embracing all its meanings and levels of meaning. Thus he calls the *Shekhinah*, 'the paradise of the Torah,' *pardes ha-Torah*.[54] Like Moses de Leon, he combines this conception with the motif of the nut: 'The *Shekhinah* in exile is called *pardes* [because it is clothed as it were in the four levels of meaning], but itself is the innermost kernel. Accordingly, we also call it nut, and King Solomon said when he entered this Paradise [of mystical speculation]: "I went down into the garden of nuts" (Song of Songs 6:11).'[55] The exact meaning of the '*Shekhinah* in exile' in this connection will be made clear later on in our investigation. In his *Book of the Rational Soul*, written in 1290, Moses de Leon himself connected the idea of the *pardes* with the first principle discussed above, namely, the principle of the Torah as the name of God. He says:

Under the title *Pardes* I have written a book about the mystery of the four ways, which the title in itself denotes, insofar as it refers to the four who entered the *pardes*, which is nothing other than *peshat, remez, derashah,* and *sod*. In this book I have commented at length on these matters in connection with the mystery of the stories and facts related in the Torah, in order to show that they all refer in a mystical sense to eternal life and that there is nothing in the Torah that is not contained in the mystery of His Name.[56]

The same fundamental principle of the fourfold interpretation of Scripture is used by Bahya ben Asher throughout his compendious commentary on the Torah, written about 1291 in Saragossa. Bahya does not use the term *remez*, but calls this allegorical method of interpretation, which for him is identical with an interpretation according to the principles of medieval philosophy, 'the rational way,' *derekh ha-sekhel*. The word *pardes*, however, was not yet known to him, for though he was familiar with certain sections of the main part of the *Zohar*, the later parts, in which the term occurs, had not yet been written when he began his commentary.

Still another way of defining four such levels of meaning is to be found in the fragmentary Kabbalistic commentary on Maimonides' *Guide to the Perplexed*. This text has been attributed to Joseph Gikatila and seems at all events to have been written toward the end of the thirteenth century.[57] The author says: 'The Torah can be interpreted in three or even more ways.' He calls these ways or methods *perush, be'ur, pesher,* and *derash*. *Perush* is for him the strict grammatical meaning, analogous to what was termed *peshat* above. *Pesher,* 'interpretation,' signifies a deeper penetration into the literal sense. *Derash* embraces both allegory and the Talmudic method of deducing the *Halakhah* from the words of Scripture and allegory. He calls the mystical meaning *be'ur.* Literally this means simply explanation, but by a mystical play on words in the Kabbalistic manner it is related to the Hebrew word *be'er,* or well, for the Torah is likened to a well of fresh water, whence spring ever new levels of hidden meaning. A very similar idea occurs in the *Ra'ya Mehemna,* whose author had read at least some of Gikatila's earlier writings. Here again the Torah is an inexhaustible well, which no pitcher *(kad)* can ever empty. The Hebrew word *kad* has the numerical value 24; to the author this means that even the twenty-four books of the traditional Biblical canon cannot exhaust the mystical depth of the Torah, the depth and fulness of the hidden essence of the Godhead, which is manifested through the books of the Bible.[58]

It is significant in this connection that in its attitude toward allegory the *Zohar* preserved all the aristocratic esotericism of the rationalist philosophers, The *Midrash ha-Ne'elam* shows a particular leaning toward allegorical interpretations. A highly remarkable passage is devoted to the interpretation of the well-known Aggadah about the Messianic banquet at which Israel will feast on leviathan.[59] The author is fully in agreement with Maimonides' philosophical interpretation of this banquet,[60] and uses it verbatim. Quite in the spirit of the philosophers, he justifies the crude figurative mode of expression employed by the rabbis, on the ground that the hope of this banquet and similar rewards helps the simple-minded populace to bear the miseries of exile. One of the speakers is made to say expressly that the popular faith should not be destroyed, but should on the contrary be reinforced.[61]

This fourfold aspect of the Torah bears a marked similarity to the conceptions of certain Christian authors of the early Middle Ages, such as Bede (eighth century). These ideas became widespread among the Christian authors of the late Middle Ages. They speak in this connection of history, allegory, tropology (which with them means moral homiletics), and anagogy (which usually meant the eschatological interpretation of Scripture). But here again the classifications vary. The strictly mystical interpretation is sometimes identified with *anagogia,* and sometimes, on the other hand, *allegoria* and *anagogia* become one.[62] Famous in this connection are the pedagogic verses of unknown origin, quoted by Nicholas of Lyra in the fourteenth century:

Littera gesta docet, quid credas allegoria,
Moralis quid agas, quo tendas anagogia.

Did the Kabbalists derive this conception from the Christians? This question has been answered in various ways. In his above-mentioned article, Wilhelm Bacher assumed the existence of such a historical connection, while recently Perez Sandler has tried to prove that the Kabbalistic doctrine of the *pardes* developed independently.[63] Though of course it is possible that the Kabbalists arrived at their theory of the four levels of meaning without outside influence, by simply dividing the allegorical interpretation into its two aspects, the one philosophical, the other theosophico-mystical, I am inclined to agree with Bacher. The simultaneous appearance of the idea in three Kabbalistic authors, all living in Christian Spain and all working with the same theory of the four levels though their classifications differed, suggests that they had somewhere come across this idea of four meanings and adopted it. One is almost forced to conclude that they were influenced by Christian hermeneutics. The *Zohar*'s account of the four levels shows a striking resemblance to the Christian conception. On the other hand, Gikatila (or Pseudo-Gikatila) would have had no good reason for distinguishing two varieties of literal meaning if he had not been interested a priori in bringing out a fourfold meaning of the Torah.[64]

The crystallization of this idea of the four levels in the hierarchical organism of the Torah was not the only contribution of the *Zohar* to the question that concerns us here. Another important thesis put forward in it is that every word, indeed, every letter, has seventy aspects, or literally, 'faces.' This notion did not originate with the Kabbalists. It is found in the late midrash *Numbers Rabbah* and was cited as early as the twelfth century by Abraham ibn Ezra, the famous Bible commentator, in the introduction to his commentary on the Pentateuch.[65] It does not occur in the Talmud but was developed from a Talmudic theme. Seventy is the traditional number of the nations inhabiting the earth. The Talmud states that every commandment that issued from God's mouth in the Revelation on Mount Sinai was divided and could be heard in all seventy languages.[66] A link between this and the later notion of the seventy aspects appears clearly in a passage of the *Alphabet of Rabbi Akiba*, a semi-mystical treatise of the early post-Talmudic period, which has never before been considered in this connection. In it we read: 'All the treasures of wisdom were given over to the angelic prince of wisdom Seganzagael, and all were disclosed to Moses on Mount Sinai, so that during the forty days that he spent there he was instructed in the Torah in all seventy aspects of the seventy languages.' [67] Later the seventy languages were dropped and the new formula was born. The *Zohar* makes liberal use of it. The different aspects are the secrets that can be discovered in every word. 'In every word shine many lights.' [68] This thesis was indeed advanced by an early twelfth-century author, held in high esteem by the Kabbalists of Spain. Abraham bar Hiyya writes: 'Every letter and every word in every section of the Torah have a deep root in wisdom and contain a mystery from among the mysteries of [divine] understanding, the depths of which we cannot penetrate. God grant that we may know some little of this abundance.' [69] The meaning of the holy text cannot be exhausted in any finite number of lights and interpretations, and the number seventy stands here of course for the inexhaustible totality of the divine word. Moreover, the light and the mystery of the Torah are one, for the Hebrew word *'or*, light, and the Hebrew word *raz*, mystery, have the same numerical value, 207. When God said, 'Let there be light,' he meant, as the author of the *Midrash ha-Ne'elam* puts it, [70] the mystery that shines in the Torah. And it was this hidden primordial light of Creation, which was so noble that it could not be abased to the use of creatures, that God enclosed in the Torah. In his mystical meditations on Scripture the Kabbalist catches a ray, 'light of the inexhaustible light.' A striking application of this notion to the *Zohar* itself is to be found in the work of the famous Kabbalist Hayim Vital (d. 1620). The word *zohar* means literally radiance. According to him, the radiance of the Torah's divine light is reflected in the mysteries of this book. But when these mysteries are shrouded in the literal meaning, their light is darkened. The literal meaning is darkness, but the Kabbalistic meaning, the mystery, is the *zohar* that shines in every line of Scripture. [71]

This devaluation of the simple literal meaning is no invention of the later Kabbalists. It is clearly stressed in certain passages of the *Zohar* itself.

Rabbi Simeon said: Alas for the man who regards the Torah as a book of mere tales and profane matters. If this were so, we might even today write a Torah dealing in such matters and still more excellent. In regard to earthly things, the kings and princes of the world [in their chronicles?] possess more valuable materials. We could use them as a model for composing a Torah of this kind. But in reality the words of the Torah are higher words and higher mysteries. When even the angels come down into the world [to fulfil a mission] they don the garment of this world, and if they did not, they could not survive in this world and the world could not endure them. And if this is true even of the angels, how much truer it is of the Torah, with which He created them and all the worlds and through which they all subsist. When she descends into the world, how could the world endure it if she did not don earthly garments? The tales of the Torah are only her outward garments. If anyone should suppose that the Torah herself is this garment and nothing else, let him give up the ghost. Such a man will have no share in the world to come. That is why David [Ps. 119:18] said: 'Open thou mine eyes, that I may behold wondrous things out of they Torah,' namely, that which is beneath the garment of the Torah. Come and behold: there are garments that everyone sees, and when fools see a man in a garment that seems beautiful to them, they do not look more closely. But more important than the garment is the body, and more important than the body is the soul. So likewise the Torah has a body, which consists of the commandments and ordinances of the Torah, which are called *gufe torah*, 'bodies of the Torah.' [72] This body is cloaked in garments, which consist of worldly stories. Fools see only the garment, which is the narrative part of the Torah; they know no more and fail to see what is under the garment. Those who know more see not only the garment but also the body that is under the garment. But the truly wise, the servants of the Supreme King, those who stood at the foot of Mount Sinai, look only upon the soul, which is the true foundation of the entire Torah, and one day indeed it will be given them to behold the innermost soul of the Torah.

The Torah, the author adds, needs an outward garment of narratives, just as wine, if it is to keep, needs a jar. But it is always necessary to penetrate to the secret that lies beneath them. [73]

The last and most radical step in the development of this principle of the infinite meaning of the Torah was taken by the Palestinian school of Kabbalists who flourished in the sixteenth century in Safed. They started from the old conception that the souls of Israel who went out of Egypt and received the Torah at Mount Sinai numbered 600,000. According to the laws of transmigration and the distribution of the sparks into which the soul disintegrates, these 600,000 primordial souls are present in every generation of Israel.

Consequently, there are 600,000 aspects and meanings in the Torah. According to each one of these ways of explaining the Torah, the root of a soul has been fashioned in Israel. In the Messianic age, every single man in Israel will read the Torah in accordance with the meaning peculiar to his root. And thus also is the Torah understood in Paradise.[74]

This mystical idea that each individual soul has its own peculiar way of understanding the Torah was stressed by Moses Cordovero of Safed (d. 1570). He said that each of these 600,000 holy souls has its own special portion of the Torah, 'and to none other than he, whose soul springs from thence, will it be given to understand it in this special and individual way that is reserved to him.'[75] With the help of the *Zohar*, the Safed Kabbalists developed the further idea that the Torah, which in its visible form contains only some 340,000 letters, is, in some mysterious way, made up of 600,000. Each individual in Israel possesses a letter in this mystical Torah, to which his soul is attached, and he reads the Torah in the particular way predetermined by this upper root of his in the Torah. Menahem Azariah of Fano, one of the great Italian Kabbalists (c. 1600), says in his treatise on the soul that the Torah as originally engraved on the first tablets (those that were broken) contained these 600,000 letters and that only on the second tablets did it assume its shorter form, which, however, thanks to a secret way of combining letters, still indicates the original number of 600,000 letters which form the mystical body of the Torah.[76]

NOTES

1. Cf. Chapter I, in which this question is discussed in detail.
2. Cf. Y. F. Baer's Hebrew article in *Zion*, XXIII-XXIV (1959), pp. 143 ff., especially up to p. 154, where reference is made to the first version of the present chapter, published in *Diogenes*, Nos. 14–15 (1956). Baer, who attempts to prove that logos and Torah are identical in Philo, goes still further than Erwin Goodenough (*By Light, Light: The Mystic Gospel of Hellenistic Judaism*, New Haven, 1935), who speaks of no such identification in his chapter on the Torah in Philo, pp. 72–94. Cf. also Harry A. Wolfson, *Philo*, I, pp. 115–43; Edmund Stein, *Die allegorische Exegese des Philo aus Alexandreia*, 1929.
3. Recently such an attempt has been made by Samuel Belkin in his Hebrew work, *The Midrash ha-Nec̀elam and its Sources in the Old Alexandrian Midrashim*, Jerusalem, 1958 (special edition from the Yearbook *Sura*, III, pp. 25–92). Belkin tries to prove that this important part of the *Zohar* is a midrash based on Alexandrian sources closely related to Philo. His undertaking does not stand up to criticism; cf. the penetrating critique of his work by R. Zwi Werblowsky in *Journal of Jewish Studies*, X, p. 276, note 3 (1959–60), pp. 25–44, 112–35. The rejoinder by Joshua Finkel, 'The Alexandrian Tradition and the Midrash ha-Nec̀elam,' in *The Leo Jung Jubilee*, New York, 1962, pp. 77–103, is wide of the mark.
4. *Midrash Tehillim*, ed. Buber, p. 33. The author of this statement is Eleazar ben Pedath, a teacher of the third century, whose interest in esoteric ideas is

also apparent in other utterances; cf. W. Bacher, *Die Agada der palästinensischen Amoräer,* II, Strassburg, 1896, p. 31. Bacher already refused 'to doubt the authenticity of this statement, which sounds like an early anticipation of the later so-called "practical Kabbalah".'

5. This preface has been published several times separately under the title 'The Source of Wisdom.' The text of the book itself has been preserved only in manuscript. A German translation in August Wünsche, *Aus Israels Lehrhallen, kleine Midraschim,* I, Leipzig, 1907, pp. 127–33, especially p. 132.

6. Likewise an utterance of Simeon ben Lakish, a Palestinian teacher very much inclined to esoteric mysticism. It has come down to us in several versions, first in the Palestinian Talmud, Shekalim, VI, end of *Halakhah* I. I shall deal further on with the mystical interpretation of this statement by one of the earliest Kabbalists.

7. Erubin 13a. Baer has stressed the implications of this passage for a mystical interpretation of the Torah, *loc. cit.,* p. 145.

8. Ezra ben Solomon, Commentary on the Talmudic Aggadoth, in Vatican MS Cod. Hebr. 294, Fol. 34a.

9. Cf. Azriel, *Perush Aggadoth,* ed. Tishby, p. 76; Pseudo-Nahmanides, *Sefer ha-'emunah vehabittahon,* XIX; *Zohar,* II, 87b; III, 80b, 176a. In III, 36a, we read: 'The entire Torah is a single holy mystical Name.'

10. *Mishnah Aboth,* III, 14; *Sifre* to Deut. 48, ed. Finkelstein, p. 142.

11. *Genesis Rabbah,* I, I. The antecedents or parallels to this passage in Plato and Philo have often been discussed.

12. Philo, *Vita Mosis,* II, 51.

13. Hekhalot Rabbathi, IX. Cf. my book, *Jewish Gnosticism, Merkabah Mysticism, and Talmudic Tradition,* New York, 1960.

14. *Genesis Rabbah,* VIII, 2, ed. Theodor, p. 57.

15. *Sophia* as the primordial Torah in the letter of Ezra ben Solomon, published by me in *Sefer Bialik,* 1934, p. 159; other interpretations in Azriel, *Perush Aggadoth,* p. 77, and the passages there cited by Tishby, the editor. Also in the commentary of Pseudo-Abraham ben David on *Yetsirah,* I, 2, we read: 'The primordial Torah is the name of God.'

16. Azriel's own interpretation, *loc. cit.,* is unclear. He also says here that 'each single one of God's *sefiroth* is named Torah,' because as an attribute of God it also gives instruction concerning the ideal conduct of man, which represents a striving to imitate the attributes of God, which are manifested precisely in the *sefiroth.*

17. Gikatila, *Sha'are 'Orah,* Offenbach, 1715, 51a.

18. Also in his three books *Sha'are 'Orah, Sha'are Tsedek,* and *Ta'ame Mitsvoth,* the latter preserved only in manuscript. This thesis does not yet appear in Gikatila's earlier *Ginnath 'Egoz.*

19. *Sha'are 'Orah,* 2b.

20. *Pirke Rabbi Eliezer,* III.

21. Recanati, *Ta'ame ha-Mitsvoth,* Basel, 1581, 3a. The statement God Himself is called Torah occurs also in the *Zohar,* II, 60a.

22. MS Jerusalem, 8° 597, Fol. 21b. This manuscript contains Gikatila's work under the (plagiaristic?) authorship of Isaac ben Farhi or Perahia. We possess many manuscripts of Gikatila's important work under this name.

23. *Ibid.*, Fol. 228b: *ki 'othiyoth porhoth ve-ʿomdoth bo.*

24. MS Leiden, Warner 32, Fol. 23a.

25. Cf. above the statement by Rabbi Ishmael and Note I, p. 39.

26. Azriel, *Perush Aggadoth,* p. 37.

27. Philo, *De vita còntemplativa,* ed. Conybeare, p. 119.

28. Cf. E. Goodenough, *By Light, Light,* pp. 83–84. Baer presumes that in Philo this conception of the Torah as an organism may go back to the similar metaphor of the logos as a *zoön* in Plato's *Phaedrus* (264 C), and that Philo no longer, like Plato, interpreted this logos as 'discourse', but as God's word. From Philo this idea of the organism was then taken over by Origen, whose words (*De principiis,* IV, 2, 4, ed. Kötschau, p. 312) to some extent anticipate the position of the *Zohar:* 'Scripture is like a man and has flesh [according to the literal meaning], soul [according to the allegorical interpretation] and spirit [in accordance with the mystery].'

29. *Zohar,* I, 134b.

30. *Zohar,* III, 202a.

31. Moses de Leon, *Sefer ha-Rimmon,* MS British Museum, Margoliouth No. 759, Fol. 100b.

32. *Tikkune Zohar,* Tikkun 21, Fol. 52b.

33. Cf. Chapter 3, pp. 103–9.

34. On these two concepts, cf. W. Bacher, *Die älteste Terminologie der jüdischen Schriftauslegung,* I, Leipzig, 1899, pp. 89 and 197; H. L. Strack, *Einleitung in den Talmud,* 5th ed., München, 1921, pp. 4ff. On their position in the theology of orthodox Judaism, cf. the highly interesting monograph of S. Kaatz, *Die mündliche Lehre und ihr Dogma,* Leipzig, 1922.

35. In the *Book Bahir,* 97 and 137, the last *sefirah* is called 'the treasury of the oral Torah', in which all commandments are contained. Cf. also 99 (according to the amended text): 'The written Torah [which is called "light"] needs the oral Torah, which is a lamp [that bears the "light"], in order to resolve the difficulties and to explain its secrets.'

36. In Jellinek, *Beth ha-Midrash,* II, Leipzig, 1853, pp. 23–34.

37. Primordial wisdom is the second *sefirah.* 'Repentance' (literally 'return' in Hebrew) is a name for the third, because all things 'return' to its womb in the end.

38. In the preceding I have followed the difficult text of 'Rabbi Isaac the Old' in MS 584/699 of the Enelow Memorial Collection in the Jewish Theological Seminary of New York. The manuscript forms a single codex, which a bookseller has arbitrarily broken into two parts.

39. The theory formulated in this early fragment must already have provided the foundation of the Kabbalistic treatise of Jacob ben Jacob Kohen of Soria concerning the forms of the letters, which is based on this distinction—

which first derives meaning from the context we have been discussing—
between an 'esoteric white form' and an 'exoteric black form'; cf. my edition
of this treatise in *Madda*c*e ha-Yahaduth*, II (1927), pp. 203–4.

40. Cf. in particular the subtle investigations of Leo Strauss in *Persecution and
the Art of Writing*, Glencoe, Ill., 1952.

41. Cf. *Zohar*, II, 230b (the exact same formulation already occurs in Gikatila,
Ginnath 'Egoz, Hanau, 1615, 3b), III, 75a and 159a. The same formula
occurs in the shift from the philosophical to the Kabbalistic use of the terms
'exoteric' and 'esoteric' in Isaac ben Latif, *Ginze ha-Melekh*, ed. Jellinek,
XXV, printed in Stern's *Kokhbe Yitzhak*, XXXII, Vienna, 1865, p. 9.

42. Ernst von Dobschütz, 'Vom vierfachen Schriftsinn. Die Geschichte einer
Theorie,' *Harnack-Ehrung, Beiträge zur Kirchengeschichte . . . Adolf von
Harnack . . . dargebracht*, Leipzig, 1921, pp. 1–13.

43. W. Bacher, 'L'Exégèse biblique dans le Zohar,' *Revue des Etudes Juives*,
XXII (1891), pp. 33–46.

44. Philo already referred at length to the dangers of radical spiritualization of
the Torah in a much discussed passage, *De migratione Abrahami*, 89–
94. Cf. also the long passage attacking such pure allegorization of the
Commandments in Moses de Leon's *Sefer ha-Rimmon*, which I have quoted
in *Major Trends in Jewish Mysticism*, New York, 1954, pp. 397–98.

45. *Zohar Hadash*, Jerusalem, 1953, 83a. Bacher failed to take note of this
earliest work of the *Zohar* complex.

46. Ch. J. Huck, *Joachim von Floris und die joachitische Literatur*, 1938, p.
291: *si ad nucis dulcedinem pervenire volumus, primo necesse est, ut amo-
veatur exteria cortex, secunda testa, et ita tercio loco perveniatur ad
nucleam*. Cf. also p. 148 of the same work. Moses de Leon uses the metaphor in diverse contexts: for the meaning of the Torah, for the meaning of
the *merkabah* and the dangerous demonic realms surrounding it; cf. his
Ha-Nefesh ha-Hakhamah, Basel, 1608, 21, quire O, Fol. I c–d. Even the
community of mystics is solemnly apostrophized in *Zohar*, I, 154b, as those
who have 'penetrated to the kernel.' In I, 19b, II, 15b, and other passages of
the *Zohar* the nut is the symbol of the *merkabah*, which here means Kabbalistic knowledge of the world.

47. *Derashah* means here the mode of interpretation practiced by the Talmudists, by which they derived the exoteric oral doctrine from the words of
Scripture in accordance with certain fixed norms.

48. The same use of *hida* for allegory, usual in medieval Hebrew, occurs also in
Moses de Leon at the end of his *Mishkan ha-*c*Eduth*, MS Cambridge, 54a:
'In the words of the wise men there are *Haggadoth*, some of which are
allegories *[hida]*, while others should be understood literally, without any allegory.'

49. *Zohar*, II, 99a-b. An excellent investigation of the history of this important
parable in late Kabbalistic literature is to be found in F. Lachover's essay,
'The Gate to the Tower' in c*Al gevul ha-yashan ve-he-hadash*, Jerusalem,
1951, pp. 29–78.

50. Hagigah 14b; cf. *Major Trends*, p. 52.
51. In Section II of my book *Jewish Gnosticism, Merkabah Mysticism, and Talmudic Tradition*, New York, 1960.
52. *Zohar*, I, 26b. The passage is not from the main part, but from the *Tikkune Zohar*.
53. The word must be read *re'iyyoth* and not *re'ayoth*, 'proofs,' which does not fit into the context. Bacher's assumption that *re'ayoth*, as he read, is in our editions a corruption of the correct term *remez* is refuted by the fact that the same interpretation of the word *pardes* occurs in two other passages which escaped him, *Zohar Hadash*, 102d and 107c. These passages also belong to the *Tikkune Zohar*.
54. *Zohar Hadash* (*Tikkunim* section), 102d.
55. *Tikkun*, No. 24, Fol. 68a–b. Here the shells, *kellippin*, are already related directly to the demonic forces and their power, from which the *Shekhinah* is freed only on the Sabbath, when she puts on sefirothic garments.
56. Moses de Leon, at the end of his *Sefer ha-Nefesh ha-Hakhamah*, Basel, 1608.
57. Georges Vajda, who has devoted a penetrating investigation to some parts of this text, doubts the justification of the traditional attribution of this text to Gikatila; cf. *Mélanges offerts à Etienne Gilson*, Paris, 1959, p. 656. Undoubtedly the question is deserving of further investigation. Not only are the printed pieces attributed to Gikatila, but also the largely unpublished fragments preserved in the Oxford MS, Neubauer, 1911.
58. *Zohar*, II, 114b, and Gikatila's commentary on Maimonides, in the second part of Saul Kohen's 'Questions Addressed to Abarbanel,' Venice, 1574, 21a.
59. Baba Bathra, 74b–75a; cf. L. Ginzberg, *The Legends of the Jews*, V, pp. 43–46.
60. *Hilkhoth Teshuvah*, VIII, 4.
61. *Zohar*, I, 135b–136a. It is interesting and not without a certain ironical significance that for popular faith the author uses the term *mehemanutha dekola*, which in many other passages of the *Zohar* is employed in a mystical sense, to mean not 'what all believe,' but the world-permeating power of faith, the system of the *sefiroth*.
62. Cf. for details the article of E. von Dobschütz, cited above.
63. P. Sandler, 'Le-ba'yath Pardes,' in the Jubilee Volume for Elias Auerbach, Jerusalem, 1955, pp. 222–35.
64. Here it seems worth pointing out that this relationship between Kabbalistic theory and the similar Christian conception was already noticed by Pico della Mirandola, the first Christian humanist to take a deep interest in the Kabbalah. In his *Apologia*, written in 1487, he writes: 'Just as with us there is a fourfold method of Biblical exegesis, the literal, the mystical or allegorical, the tropic and the anagogic, so also among the Hebrews. They call the literal meaning *peshat*, the allegorical *midrash*, the tropic *sekhel*, and the anagogic, the most sublime and divine of all, *kabbalah*.' Cf. *Opera*, Basel,

1557, pp. 178–9. The Hebrew terms are exactly the same as those employed by Bahya ben Asher, whose work must consequently have been used by Pico. The erroneous identification of *midrash* with allegory and of *sekhel,* which in Bahya actually means allegory, with tropology, shows that Pico's knowledge of these sources was very limited. The same mistake is repeated, in a more pronounced form, in the Apology for Pico, written by the Franciscan monk Archangelus of Borgo Novo. He cites the literature of the Midrash under the head of allegory, but such works as those of Maimonides and Gersonides are classified as tropology; cf. *Apologia fratris Archangeli de Burgonovo . . . pro defensione doctrinae Cabalae,* Bologna, 1564, 8b.

65. *Numbers Rahhah,* XIII, 15.
66. Shabbath 88b.
67. *'Othiyoth de-Rabbi Akiba,* ed. Wertheimer, Jerusalem, 1914, p. 12.
68. *Zohar,* III, 202a.
69. Abraham bar Hiyya, *Megillath ha-Megalle,* Berlin, 1924, p. 75.
70. *Zohar,* I, 140a; *Zohar Hadash,* 8b.
71. Vital, *Ets ha-Daʿath,* Zolkiev, 1871, 46–47.
72. This is a pun: the literal meaning of *gufe torah* is indeed 'bodies of the Torah,' but in the Talmud the words mean 'important doctrines of the Torah.'
73. *Zohar,* III, 152a.
74. Isaac Luria, *Sefer ha-Kavvanoth,* Venice, 1620, 53b. More on the subject in Vital, *Shaʿar Gilgulim,* XVII, Jerusalem, 1912, 17b; in Nathan Shapira, *Megalle ʿAmukoth,* Cracow, 1637, IX, and in Naphtali Bacharach, *ʿEmek ha-Melekh,* Amsterdam, 1648, 42a.
75. Cordovero, *Derisha be-ʿinyane Mal'akhim,* ed. Ruben Margolioth, Jerusalem, 1945, p. 70.
76. M. A. Fano, *Ma'amar ha-Nefesh,* Pyotrkow, 1903, III, 6, Fol. 17a.

6.

Myth vs. Symbol in the Zohar and in Lurianic Kabbalah

Yehuda Liebes

INTRODUCTION

There have been (and still are) many who believe that what characterizes Judaism as a religion is the strict separation that it interposes between the Creator and his creatures—unlike mythic religions, such as paganism or even Christianity, in which the two realms are intermixed. This belief has stemmed, at times, from an absolute negation of Judaism's mythic aspect. It has also been asserted that Judaism, as a monotheistic religion, is *ipso facto* antimythic and that its rejection of idolatry is a function of its negation of myth as such. In my opinion, such views of Judaism are erroneous and should be discarded. The God of Israel is a mythic god, and as such maintains relationships of love and hate with his creatures. But I shall not dwell on this overall proposition, which I have treated elsewhere at length.[1]

Even those, however, who recognize that in Judaism, too, there exists a mythic connection between God and his creatures, still posit a fundamental dichotomy between the realm of the divine and the human world. The contention that even this distinction is open to question, at certain important levels in the central core of traditional Judaism, has to overcome considerable psychological barriers in order to be given a proper hearing. That is what I aim to do in this essay.

Permission to translate and publish in English from the original Hebrew edition of *Myth in Jewish Thought*, ed. by Haviva Pedaya, granted by Ben-Gurion University of the Negev, Beʿer Sheva, 1994.

Most of us, I assume, recognize that the God of Israel is portrayed in human terms in the biblical text and in the Talmud, and especially in the Kabbala (where even "Adam" appears as one of the appelations of God himself).[2] Man is said to have been created in God's image and is considered God's representative on earth, in the lower sphere. Yet, even granting that much, the human and the divine are still seen as separate and distinct realms: ultimate reality above and "image" — or symbol — below. That is held to be the case both for the biblical text and the Talmud, as well as for kabbalistic literature. But is this really so?

In the Kabbala, as we know, the realm of the divine is portrayed as a system of ten aspects or *sefirot* (sing., *sefira*), each of which also bears the name of a human character. Thus, the *sefira* of *Hesed* (Grace) is known as Abraham. You may well explain this as a "symbol," and with some justification, as scholars of Jewish mysticism before me have done. It is also a convenient explanation, for it permits one to have one's cake and eat it, too: both to assert the mythic character of the Kabbala and to deny it in the same breath, thus preserving Judaism's "pristine" absence of myth. Everything can be turned, in this way, into a "symbol," a term that serves academic scholars the same way the qualifier "as-it-were" once served the kabbalists. The entity being symbolized is like the Kantian *Ding an sich,* of which we can know nothing except via its symbol, or, to put it another way (quoting Isaiah Tishby): "The symbol is the representation of an unseen thing or process which, in and of itself, is never revealed and cannot be directly expressed." [3]

Symbolic language of this sort, ascribed to the Kabbala by various scholars, is quite different from what I shall refer to as "mythic" language: that is, the direct reference to the divine entity itself, which is available on the same plane of awareness and meaning as are all other observable phenomena. I have chosen this definition of myth, though it may not be universally accepted among students of religion, because it seems to me that it is that direct relationship to the divine, to which I refer, that characterizes primitive religions, including the ancient Greeks (before they reinterpreted their religion in philosophical terms), from whose language we get the word "myth."

MOSES AND JACOB IN THE ZOHAR

Undoubtedly, many passages in the Zohar are consciously symbolic in nature, but there are exceptions, and we may begin by citing those already noted as such by other scholars, particularly G. Scholem and I. Tishby.

According to the Zohar, when a man studies Torah while away from home (and is thus separated from his earthly wife), he is engaged in "intercourse" with the Divine Presence *(Shekhina)*. Here, then, is a true intermingling of the human and the divine realms. But this symbolic coupling in turn depends upon its "real" counterpart: the *Shekhina* unites only with such a man for whom a "symbolic *Shekhina*"—his wife—awaits at journey's end. The single man is utterly condemned by the Zohar as a figure who can never attain communion with the *Shekhina*.[4] There is an exception, however, to this general principle: Moses, who abandons his wife in order to find his true "mate," the *Shekhina*.[5] Here, the Zohar demonstrates its awareness of the distinction between symbolic and mythic conjugal unions; hence, we may conclude that this distinction is not merely a modern scholarly invention.

The Zohar compares two men, Moses and Jacob. Both are considered to stand on a par with the *sefira* of *Tiferet* (Majesty) as "husbands" of the *Shekhina;* yet, they hold different ranks. Jacob's union with the *Shekhina* is said to be a union "in form" or "in spirit"—that is, symbolic—while his *actual* coupling takes place with his wives. Moses, on the other hand, is said to have actually and corporeally—that is, mythically—united with the *Shekhina*.[6]

This distinction between "body" and "spirit" holds yet another significance. Moses' union with the *Shekhina* was "in body," meaning during his own lifetime; while that of Jacob was "in spirit," referring to the time after his death. Here we also encounter an instance of inverted terminology, assigning physical union to Jacob's relationship with the *Shekhina*. Jacob did not unite with the *Shekhina* during his lifetime, but his body was brought for burial in the Land of Israel, which symbolizes the *Shekhina*. Moses, on the other hand, is not buried in the Land, for Jacob was already there, and the *Shekhina* could not be "married" to them both: she had to leave Moses and return to her original "husband," Jacob.[7]

This example affords even greater scope to the mythic element. If we were dealing only with symbols here, there would be nothing wrong with using multiple symbols for a single purpose; yet the Zohar insists that the *Shekhina* can have only one "husband" at a time. If Jacob is her first husband, and because of him Moses is prevented from entering the

Land, it might appear that Jacob stands higher than Moses. But the Zohar quickly denies such a conclusion, elaborating a new terminology. Jacob's union with the *Shekhina* is "in body" *only*, while that of Moses is "in spirit." Moses had no corporeal union at all, whether during or after his lifetime: whether with the wife whom he left once God was revealed to him, or with the *Shekhina* with whom he achieved a union "in spirit." The spirit of Moses, thus, was united during his lifetime with the essence of pure spirit: the *Shekhina*. Moses, we know, also died a "spiritual" death—his soul was taken by a kiss—and his body was never found ("his burying place is unknown").[8] As for his soul, it did not suffice for it to unite with the *Shekhina:* it returned to its even more sublime origin in the *sefira* of Understanding *(Bina).*

Jacob, on the other hand, was sexually united with his wives during his lifetime, and after death his union with the *Shekhina* had, similarly, to be corporeal. It was necessary to bring his embalmed body to the Land of Israel, which is the physical and symbolic (rather than spiritual and mythic) manifestation of the *Shekhina.* (In this regard, it should be remembered that Jacob represents the "body of the king," and that he is the "bodily [essence of] the Patriarchs").[9] The generation of Joshua, subordinate in spirit to the generation of Moses, stands on a par with the body of Jacob. Joshua's contemporaries, the children of those who had direct knowledge of God, are likened in status to the moon, in relation to the sun.

We may say, in restating this idea, that the distinction is one between the symbolic and the mythic. In developing this train of thought, the Zohar's initial statement that Jacob's union with the *Shekhina* was merely symbolic ("in form") loses its original formulation. True, Jacob's mythic union with the *Shekhina* takes place here only after his death, but in other passages the Zohar attributes mythic status to Jacob even during his lifetime.[10] It posits a distinction between Jacob outside the Land of Israel, where his consort is Rachel, and Jacob in the Land— the immanent qualities of the Land enabling a mythic union. It is not coincidental, the Zohar argues, that Rachel died once Jacob had entered the Land: her place was taken by the *Shekhina.* Hence, we are referred back to the biblical verse (Gen. 31:3) in which God commands Jacob, "Return to the Land of your fathers," adding "and I will be with you."

We find the same notion in the writings of Rabbi Itshak of 'Akko (Rida). This kabbalist was in direct touch with Rabbi Moshe de Leon

(Ramdal), the reputed author of the Zohar, as we know from his famous letter regarding the composition of the text.[11] Although the letter has served as a basis for research into the Zohar, it has somehow never spurred scholars to look into the nature of Rabbi Itshak's role vis-à-vis the Zohar, which emerges from his marvelous book, *Otsar hahayim:*[12] "It should be pointed out that our father Jacob, may he rest in peace, when still with the corporeal Rachel outside the Land, had not yet been united with the spiritual Rachel, whose presence dwells in the Holy Land. But as soon as he came to the Holy Land, the earthly Rachel died and his soul cleaved unto the heavenly Rachel."[13]

In light of this passage, I might add, it is worth correcting some scholars' assertions about Rabbi Itshak of 'Akko, namely, that this Palestinian-born sage assigned no special status to the Land of Israel and that he spiritualized the concept of the Land, robbing it of any empirical significance.[14] One might infer from this passage, in fact, that his purpose in leaving the country was to marry a flesh-and-blood wife.

Perhaps it is possible, in this regard, to identify a divergence of opinion among the members of the group around the Zohar, for we can see that the view of Rida (and its Zoharic parallel) contradicts that of Ramdal, one of whose Hebrew works contains Responsa bearing on the Kabbala.[15] The work in question deals largely, in fact, with the issue that is before us: the mystical significance of the patriarchal figures and their burial in the Land of Israel. Ramdal explains the death of Rachel, following Jacob's return to the Land, as follows: "So that he might not be married to two sisters on the soil of Israel."

Here, then, is an entirely different line of thought, looking at the issue entirely from within the *halakha* of incest. A violation of the incest code could not be countenanced, even prior to the giving of the Law, given the sacred status of the Land.[16]

It is possible that the divergent opinions among the group associated with the Zohar lie behind the passage discussed earlier, whose initial part implies Jacob's spiritual primacy vis-à-vis Moses: Jacob was the first and ultimate husband of the *Shekhina*, and was therefore buried in the Land of Israel, thus barring Moses' presence. Then, the argument is reversed: Moses was not buried in the Land because, spiritually, he was on a higher plane and ascended to the *sefira* of Bina.

To support this thesis of a clash of opinions, we may cite evidence from Ramdal's Responsa, mentioned earlier. There (on p. 33) we find a

Hebrew parallel to the text in the Zohar, regarding Jacob as the *Shekhina*'s first husband. But there is no mention of the subsequent demurral and explanation of Moses' superiority. It is likely that Ramdal objected to such a view, on the grounds that it appears to slight the status of the Land. The argument seems to imply that Moses and his generation were "above" entering the Land.[17] Alternatively, it may be that Ramdal objected to any human agency being involved in the *sefira* of *Bina*—human presence being restricted, in his view, to the lower *sefirot*. Indeed, there is a famous inconsistency between passages in the Zohar regarding the relationship between the *sefira* of Wisdom *(Hokhma)* and the *sefira* of *Bina*. Is theirs a union that is eternal, fixed, and automatic ("like two mated partners who are never to be parted")[18] or may they be parted,[19] providing an opportunity for human intervention? The inconsistency inspired much fruitful exploration in later kabbalistic thought, particularly in the thought of Rabbi Itshak Luria (the Ari).[20]

Moses is not the only figure associated in the Zohar with the *sefira* of *Bina*. In some other passages, this is also the case for Jacob. Before examining these instances, we should note that here, again, Ramdal voices a dissenting opinion. Perhaps an additional reason for his opposition in this regard is the suggestion of incest between "son" and "mother": that is, between Jacob, symbolizing *Tiferet*, and Leah, symbolizing the supreme "mother," *Bina*. In his Hebrew work, Ramdal is quite adamant that the sexual union involving Leah *(Bina)* is not with Jacob *(Tiferet)*, but rather with *Hokhma;* or, as he puts it: "This thing is not for our father Jacob, but rather, [his union is] with *sod hanekuda* [the hidden point, i.e., *Hokhma*]." Hence the verse (Gen. 30:16) referring to the union of Jacob and Leah—*"vayishkav 'imma balaila hu,"* and not *"balaila hahu"* (i.e., "and *that one* lay with her at night" rather than "and he lay with her that night")—is interpreted to mean that the subject of the verb was not Jacob-he but a different "he": the uppermost *sefira* known as He.[21] This view has its parallel in the Zohar, where the language is strongly polemical: "Was Jacob her mate? Not at all!"[22]

If this is a polemic, then it is an internal one, directed against a view expressed elsewhere in the text of the Zohar. Such is the case, too, with the contradictory formulations of Jacob's mythic status in the Land of Israel following the death of Rachel. There, Ramdal took one view, whereas Rida took the opposing view. This is quite possible, given the theory concerning the composition of the Zohar that I have advanced elsewhere, based similarly on internal contradictions and polemics in the text.[23] For example, there is a polemic in *Idra Rabba* between a monistic and a dualistic view, a clash that I have documented in other writings from the same Zoharic circle.[24] This is only one of several debates reflected in the Zohar.[25]

The extreme mythic tendency, then, was a matter that provoked dispute among the group that produced the Zohar, with Rabbi Moshe de Leon apparently taking a much more moderate position. Further evidence of Ramdal's caution in this regard is the absence of teachings from the *Idra* in his own Hebrew writings. Moreover, to the extent that mythic elements are present in his Responsa, in reference to Moses and Joseph, these are presented in summary form only and are preceded by a lengthy exposition of an ethical and symbolic nature.[26]

Let us turn, now, to the view expressed in the Zohar on the union of Jacob with *Bina*. Here we will have an opportunity to examine, as well, the realm of symbolic significance, for Jacob's coupling with the *sefira* of *Bina* is understood symbolically. Moreover, the meaning of the symbol is not without some ambiguity. It is not necessarily the case that what the symbol represents is hidden or unavailable for direct reference, as previous scholars would have it.

We go, then, to Part One of the Zohar, folios 153–154, where we see the figure of the pious patriarch standing between two female figures: his mother above him and his wife below. What is symbolized here is the *sefira* of *Tiferet*, situated between *Bina* (the mother)—"for Understanding is called mother"—and Kingdom *(Malkhut)*, *Tiferet*'s consort. The symbol is Jacob and his two wives, Leah and Rachel, with Leah corresponding to *Bina* and Rachel to *Malkhut*. Evidently, the way the symbol is used here was determined by the nature of what required symbolization, for nowhere else is there the slightest hint of a mother-son relationship between Leah and Jacob. The symbolic usage comes very close, in form and in content, to the Freudian-oedipal paradigm. Leah is Jacob's true wife, for a man truly longs for physical union with his mother ("all delight is linked to her"); but, at the same time, man abhors incestuous unions, which are taboo (cf. Gen. 29:31, and in the Zohar: "Hence, man naturally abhors an incestuous union with his mother"). Therefore, Jacob acts subconsciously ("his deeds were hidden from him") and while lying with Leah believes that it is actually Rachel, as per the text in Genesis. But it would appear that Jacob was not so much duped as he was willing to be duped. The matter is also interpreted mystically, in accordance with the symbolism of the *sefirot:* Jacob could not know in advance that it was Leah, for *Bina* is hidden wisdom, unattainable save through the revealed *sefira, Malkhut.*

This mingling of the mythic and the symbolic is wonderfully expressed in a complementary part of the foregoing description. Just as Jacob is situated between two female figures, so, too, is the "female"—the *Shekhina*—located between two "righteous" males: the supreme Righteous One, the *sefira* of Foundation *(Yesod),* whose seed permeates her; and the righteous male of the lower, human realm, whose devotion and desire for communion pour into her the "female waters" *("mayin nukvin")* that rise up to meet the seed and create the conditions for communion. I have discussed this subject, and its mythic character, elsewhere.[27] Here, I wish to comment on a somewhat different aspect: since the pious figure of the lower realm is human, it should not follow that this is a case of symbolism, since (according to previous scholars) symbolism is required only where the imperceptible and otherwise inaccessible is being symbolized. Yet here, in the same text in which Rachel "symbolizes" the *Shekhina,* two pious figures—the lower one and the supreme one—are "symbolized" by her two sons, Joseph and Benjamin! (It is worth noting, too, that Joseph's role as husband of the *Shekhina/ Rachel*—his mother—touches once again on the Freudian aspect already alluded to.)

THE YOUNG CHILD AND THE OLD MAN

The unequivocally mythic passages that we have thus far discussed revolve around figures from the biblical text, and it might therefore be argued that we are dealing with theoretical myth, and that the mingling of the human with the divine does not represent an actual religious experience of the authors of the Zohar. On the other hand, one could cite the general concept, already mentioned, that every righteous man stands between two feminine figures, so that whenever he is separated from his wife (either during weekday periods of abstinence or when on a journey), he is coupled with the *Shekhina.*

We need not rest there, however. In addition to biblical characters, the Zohar is also populated by mythic figures belonging to what scholars have called the "frame narrative" of the text. I have explained my objections to this term and proposed the thesis that these figures express the religious consciousness of the authors of the Zohar themselves, and that therefore the content of such passages is integrally related to the rest of the text—not simply an added "frame."[28]

The first of such figures is that of Rabbi Shimeon bar Yohai. As I have written elsewhere,[29] this character possesses mythic qualities. The departure of his soul is depicted as a union with the *Shekhina*, with messianic implications. When I first wrote about this matter, I believed that I had found yet another mythic "exception" (in addition to Moses); that, in fact, what we have with Rabbi Shimeon bar Yohai is an elaboration of the Moses myth, a returned or reincarnated Moses.[30]

Further examination reveals, however, that other figures from the "frame narrative" also exhibit a dual nature, with a status between the mortal and the divine. We have, for example, the Young Child *(Yanoka)*, the marvelous infant whom the companions encounter in a famous story in the Zohar,[31] which is full of hints that the child is in some way superhuman.[32] The companions express their view that this is no ordinary child, but an angel—perhaps as a figure of speech, and without undue ontological import attached. But then the child begins to speak, expounding upon the meaning of the word "angel," and proving that the word is sometimes used as an alternative appellation for the *Shekhina*.[33] Nevertheless, one ought to bear in mind that the child-figure is not necessarily "good," as might appear at first glance. The myth stands above good and evil.[34] The Yanoka displays arrogance and impudence (it would appear that, in this way, too, the visitors express the view that the child is "inhuman"), and he consistently violates one of the gravest prohibitions in the Zohar, deliberately provoking the "evil eye," believing that his status permits him to do so with impunity.[35] Such is not the opinion of the Yanoka's mother (who is more clearly a figure of goodness),[36] nor is it the opinion of Rabbi Shimeon bar Yohai. Indeed, as the Yanoka does not endure, it would seem that theirs is the correct view.[37]

One cannot speak of the Yanoka without referring as well to his father, Rav Hamnuna the Ancient One *(Sabba)*. The two are linked, as Rabbi Shimeon bar Yohai states: "The father's nobility of spirit shines upon his son."[38] Indeed, we see a certain merging of father and son. In the Introduction to the Zohar, the companions encounter a figure who mystically identifies himself as the son of Rav Hamnuna,[39] but afterwards they discover that he is Rav Hamnuna himself.[40] The character of Rav Hamnuna is supernatural,[41] possessing a clearly divine component. Thus, at the beginning of *Idra Zuta*,[42] he is called "the holy Ancient One, the unknown of all mysteries," a description that is also used in the same context for the face of God. Also, during the encounter between him and the companions, he is called "the Ancient One,"[43] perhaps also "the holy Ancient One," and "he who is most hidden of all."[44] From this we are able to relate the figure to the frequent appearance in the *Ra'aya Meheimana* and *Tikkunei Zohar* of a supernatural being called "the most Ancient One" *("sabba desavin")*, a phrase that is perhaps suggestive as well of the philosophers' god, the "cause of all causes" *("sibbat hasibbot")*, or the Original Man or Supreme Man. On the one hand, this figure is a venerable and ancient wise man who descends to Earth to instruct the sages in Torah; on the other hand, he is a kind of incarnation of the mythical Most Sublime Countenance.[45]

According to the Zohar's sacred history, Rav Hamnuna the Ancient One is no longer among the living. He is a sage of the generation that preceded Rabbi Shimeon bar Yohai (having made the ascent from Babylon to Jerusalem at that time),[46] and it is his spirit alone that is revealed to sages in bar Yohai's time. (On the last point the Zohar is not entirely consistent.)[47] Furthermore, according to the Yanoka, the significance of the father image transcends the historical dimension and possesses cosmic meaning. In every age and any place, whenever and wherever sages gather to study Torah while abroad on a journey, Rav Hamnuna himself must reveal himself and participate in their endeavor.[48]

It appears to me that this particular facet of the father image is connected with the notion (introduced earlier) that the *Shekhina* communes and couples with sages while they are away from home. Rav Hamnuna Sabba fulfills, therefore, the function of the *Shekhina*. Thus, after the sages behold the figure of Rav Hamnuna, they say, "We surely must die, for we have beheld God, and God has explicitly said, 'No man may behold me and yet live' (Ex. 33:20)." Rabbi Shimeon bar Yohai must then restore their souls to them, and calls them Peniel—for they have "seen God face to face and [were] saved" (Gen. 32:30).[49] Bar Yohai had the power to do so because a strong spiritual bond exists between him and Rav Hamnuna—the two mythic figures of the Zohar. They are revealed to one another in dreams, or else in a waking state when they close their eyes. They often depend on one another.[50] On one occasion, Rav Hamnuna is even referred to by bar Yohai's title, *Botsina Kadisha*. No one else is ever referred to as such, to my knowledge.[51]

This link is found also in the story of the "old man" in the section *Mishpatim,* where, once again, we find the same figure as before, though he is called Rav Yeiva Sabba, rather than Rav Hamnuna. It seems to me that the "old man's" presence in this passage, a narrative about a snowy day on which he and Rabbi Shimeon together sow multicolored beans (the number of the colors, 52, corresponds to the numerological value of the word *ben,* son), is meant as an allusion to Rav Hamnuna's speech in the Introduction to the Zohar regarding Benayahu ben Yehoyada, which mentions a "son" and a snowy day.[52] It should be noted that the two related mythic images—the old father and the young child—are depicted as polar opposites. As against the impudence of the child, the "old father" begins his self-revelation with a humility that is subtly and even humorously transformed to reveal his absolute supremacy over the companions. Perhaps this polarity should also be compared with the difference between the two Sublime Countenances in the *Idra* books: the greater, All-Merciful One, and the lesser, Quick-Tempered, Angry One.

The cosmic and mythic status of Rav Hamnuna has other expressions. When the companions ask (in the Introduction to the Zohar)[53] why he is dressed poorly, he answers that the letters *kaf-yod-samekh* could not unite in him. This, of course, is a play on the word *kis,* or purse, indicating that he lacks the financial wherewithal. But another level of meaning is brought forward here. The letter *kaf* could not descend on him for it is needed to hold up the *kissei hakavod*—the Throne of Glory. If it should leave its post, the throne would fall. Here, Rav Hamnuna alludes to the myth of the Creation, as he himself relates it in the Zohar a few pages earlier.[54] Now here, when asked whence he had come, he explains something about a tower hovering in midair, in which God and a certain poor man are to be found. Again, there is a simple level of meaning, relating to the letters *lamed-vav-dalet,* that form the name of the city Lud;[55] but there is also a hidden meaning, alluding to the divine status of Rav Hamnuna himself, in the guise of the *Shekhina* (that is called "poor") and that is positioned together with *Tiferet,* below *Bina.*

But most unexpected of all—and the most significant, from our perspective—is the content of Rav Hamnuna's speech and its relation to Moses, hitherto considered to be the most mythic character in the Zohar. At this point we should mention that the most far-reaching statements, in terms of Moses' mythic status, are assigned to Rav Hamnuna[56] and the Yanoka.[57] Here, the tie between content and "frame" is also extremely significant.

What the Ancient One and the Yanoka have to relate about Moses is said in order to demonstrate their own superior status. Rav Hamnuna enters upon his discussion concerning Moses in response to the companions, who inquire about his name. Instead of answering simply and directly, he embarks on a discourse about Benayahu ben Yehoyada. I shall not enter into the details of the speech and its precise kabbalistic import, but it is clear from the context that Rav Hamnuna identifies himself with the figure of Benayahu. Now, among the major missions undertaken by Benayahu (apart from the destruction of the First and Second Temples) is to bring about the death of Moses. Moses is the "Egyptian" whom Benayahu kills with his spear (II Sam. 23:21)—that is, with God's staff that he had stolen from him. Why did Benayahu/Hamnuna wish to slay Moses? *Cherchez la femme!* He objected to the manner in which Moses treated the *Shekhina* in striking her with the staff, rather than speaking softly and cajolingly (in the scene at Meribah: the striking of the rock).[58]

We must, then, conclude: viewing Moses as a mythic exception to the symbolic rule does not satisfactorily fit the outlook of the Zohar. Even in the circle that produced the Zohar, we find a mythic figure whose status surpasses that of Moses.

RABBI ISAAC LURIA (THE ARI) AND THE ZOHAR

It is difficult to define precisely the relation between the symbolic layer and the mythic layer in the Zohar. Even within the realm of the mythic, it is extremely difficult to describe the exact nature of the relationship between the human and the divine. These difficulties are rooted in the nature of the Zohar, a text that defies clear conceptual categories, whose unique character derives, in fact, from the intermingling of these elements. That is not the case, however, for later generations of kabbalists. They were divided according to their stance vis-à-vis the question of myth and symbol, and hence, in their respective interpretations of the Zohar.

Thus, I believe, the greater part of the kabbalists in the generation of the Spanish Expulsion tended toward a symbolic reading of the text, avoiding any blurring of the line between the human and the divine. The relationship between the two realms is of a theurgic nature: man stands below and acts so as to draw down God's beneficence from above, according to the tenets of Hermetic and Neoplatonic magic, in its popular, Renaissance-era mode.[59]

A change in that situation occurred in mid-sixteenth-century Safed, during the greatest efflorescence of mysticism in the history of the Kabbala. The circle of Safed mystics, out of their great empathy for the Zohar's kabbalists, endeavored to relive the atmosphere of that earlier period. That undoubtedly accounts for the fact that this great awakening took place, as it were, *in situ,* in the Galilee: the place where (so they believed) the Zohar had originated, in the vicinity of Rabbi Shimeon bar Yohai's tomb. Indeed, we find these kabbalists turning back to reconsider questions related to the souls of the heroic characters, both of Mishnaic and biblical provenance, who figure in the Zohar. And we find profound discussions over the Zohar's passages relating to Moses and Jacob, their relative status, and their burial in (or absence from) the Land of Israel.

We know of a query on this matter, posed by Rabbi Joseph Karo (author of the *Bet Yosef*) and responded to by his master, Rabbi Shlomo Alkabets.[60] Rabbi Moshe Cordovero also treated this issue at length.[61] Still, these men clearly distinguished between the human and the divine realms. To them, the cited texts from the Zohar were to be read in relation to the derivation of the soul, its origins among the *sefirot,* and the interrelationships among the souls themselves. (Moses's soul, in that context, is derived from *Bina* in terms of its inherent qualities, but not in terms of its cosmic function: his soul belongs to a previous cosmic cycle, or *shmitta;* Moses is buried outside the Land in order to allow him to aid those of his own generation—the desert generation—at the time of the resurrection.) But it seems apparent that these kabbalists did not turn the souls they thus characterized into elements of a myth about the divine realm itself. In the Zohar, on the other hand, we found a different tendency altogether, for there the subject was part of the sexual history of the *Shekhina!* Furthermore, the later kabbalists' interpretations bear a clearly symbolic stamp.

Not so with the Ari, leader of the Safed kabbalists of his day and a foremost figure in the history of the Kabbala. He grasped the matter in precisely the reverse sense. With him, all is myth, nothing is merely symbolic, as far as I can tell from his writings.[62] All of existence, in the Ari's system, constitutes one huge organism of many parts, with no inherent distinction among them. Therefore, one cannot speak of a mythic as opposed to a symbolic level, as the cognitive differentiation does not exist.

The nature of Lurianic myth also dictates the mode of expression and interpretation of the Zohar, as presented in the Ari's Kabbala. Since the mode of discourse is not symbolic, it leaves no room for the ambiguity of multiple meanings, which is possible in symbolic speech, where one entity may be symbolized by more than one symbol—even contradictory ones—at one and the same time. The Ari speaks of the divine realm directly, not via symbols; he therefore aspires (whether consciously or not) to an unequivocal, direct correspondence between his discourse and the reality he describes. The problem of the distinction between the word and what it represents (the thing-in-itself) presents no more difficulty here, and is not theoretically different, than in the general sense that applies to all human speech. I trust that it is clear to the reader that I do not use the word "myth" in its popular sense, either as "imaginary" and insignificant tales or else the rhetoric of high ideals. The opposite is the case here: "myth," in our context, signifies plain and direct speech, without rhetorical self-consciousness, describing a higher objective reality.

That is why the Ari's understanding of the Zohar robs it of its multidimensional character, flattening its textured richness and diminishing its literary aesthetic. On the other hand, Lurianic Kabbala succeeds in defining more sharply and in elucidating barely formulated concepts and connections implicit in the Zohar, erecting from them a comprehensive edifice. Thus, the Ari's Kabbala brings to the surface much that was latent or potential in the earlier teaching. In my view, and in the view of the kabbalists (and contrary to the opinions of modern scholars), the Ari stands out as the greatest interpreter of the Zohar of all time. Through a judicious reading of Lurianic Kabbala, one may penetrate to the most fundamental strata of ideas contained in the Zohar.

The Ari's procedure is to juxtapose myths that are to be found scattered throughout the Zohar and to combine them into a complete and complex system. (It is true that the Ari changed his mind on occasion, and his teachings were transmitted by various disciples, so that contradictions may often be discerned.) The Ari does not attempt to resolve the inconsistencies in the Zohar, nor does he impose an identity between disparate elements even where a link of some sort is implied in the original; rather, he incorporates all of them in one overarching structure, through a multiplicity of fine detail and a succession of stages. Here, I believe, lies the secret of the distinction between the Zohar and Lurianic Kabbala—not in the content of the myth, as has been claimed.

MAN IN THE LURIANIC MYTH

And now to our main subject: the world of man as depicted in the Lurianic model of reality. The human realm, too, is part of the vast system that is described by that model, and in principle it is not any different from any other component part. To the Ari, souls are "the inner essence" of the higher worlds.[63] Hence, the belief in the transmigration of souls that he developed—in particular, the well-known aspects of this belief, such as the method of recognizing the "root" of someone's soul by the appearance of their brow[64]—is an important feature of the ontological myth that is seemingly devoted to the heavenly *sefirot*.

Moreover, during the critical phase of the development of his system, the Ari's interest was focused on precisely this part of the myth, the part that touches on the soul. The rest of his ontological teaching served as a mere "introduction" to this matter, which has not been properly recognized by previous scholars. The reason why they did not, I believe, is because they did not stop to ask themselves what might have been the *religious* interest that is reflected in the Ari's writings. Instead, they looked for answers for abstract issues in Lurianic Kabbala, issues defined a priori as those presumed to be the most important. (This critique could equally well apply to other aspects of Kabbala scholarship.)[65] This method has led research in the field to conclusions diametrically opposed to the thesis that I am proposing regarding the issues of God and man. According to Scholem, Lurianic Kabbala lays a great emphasis upon the *distance* between the Creator and his creatures.[66] It is my opinion that Scholem attributed undue weight to the Lurianic theory of *tsimtsum* (the self-limitation or retraction of the divine to create room for the cosmos), while removing the theory from its plain meaning and making it conform conceptually to a model rather inconsistent with the Ari's mode of thinking.[67] The Ari's descriptions of *tsimtsum* bear this out. The space vacated through *tsimtsum* was not an absolute vacuum at all, for in it could be found the "roots" of Justice *(Din)* that were grounded in the Infinite *(Einsof)*, as well as traces of the light that had been retracted. While it is true that this idea may be found only in parts of the Lurianic source material, remaining only implicit elsewhere,[68] the descriptions all agree that immediately following the *tsimtsum* the light of the Infinite returned to fill the empty space, and that out of this light came the created worlds, which are not qualitatively different from the essence of the Infinite itself, except in intensity and in clarity.

The Ari was not the first to assert the unity of the divine and the human. He derived this from the Zohar and many other sources in kabbalistic literature, where man's soul is portrayed as a part of God. The Ari merely gave the idea full expression through his rigorous and detailed interpretation. Thus, for example, the famous myth of the shattered vessels is closely tied in with the story of the Ten Sages martyred by the Romans, the subject of a lengthy discussion, and of much greater importance than the shattered vessels.[69] Furthermore, the Martyrdom is not a one-time historical event: through the doctrine of transmigration of souls, it is linked to the ten brothers of Joseph and to the ten drops of Joseph's semen that seeped through his fingers, and from thence to Rabbi Shimeon bar Yohai and on to the Ari and his coterie.[70] It would appear that the myth of the shattered vessels and their ultimate restoration *(tikkun)* was for the Ari not merely a theory about distant times and transcendent worlds, but something very much alive, revealed in the faces of those around him.

But the examination of brows and communion with the dead through lying prostrate on their graves (one of the most important mystical techniques for the Ari)[71] are not the exclusive sources of the Lurianic myth. To these we must add the precise investigation of ancient texts, especially the Zohar. The Zohar itself implies a linkage between the Martyrdom and the destroyed primeval worlds.[72] Even earlier still, among the "gnostic kabbalists," the concept of the destroyed worlds was linked to the mystery of the bonding of souls through transmigration, known by them as *sod Ha'ibbur*.[73]

Now we can go back to the sources we have cited from the Zohar and briefly examine their interpretation by the Ari. To do that, however, we must note that Lurianic Kabbala may be divided into two main stages, in terms of its development. The first stage includes the Ari's interpretations of various Zoharic passages that he himself wrote in Egypt. The second stage involves his teachings during the last two years of his life, after his arrival in Safed and the crystallization around him of the famous coterie.

The first stage already reveals the method that I have outlined: the conflation of myths contained in the Zohar through an elaboration of detail. But at this stage, the developing ontological system is still relatively static—highly detailed in spatial, not in temporal, terms. At that point, the Ari had not yet emphasized the various phases of the divine manifestations ("Countenances")—such as their growth and ultimate restoration, ascent and descent, or the creation of these Countenances and their joining together—as he would do later on. This sort of idea is to be found only minimally in the earlier strata of his thought, and only when there is direct authority for it in the Zohar.

Similarly, in the Ari's first stage, we do not find extensive treatment of the human realm, regarding such matters as the transmigration of souls, the theories of *yihud* (human agency in the conjoining of male and female aspects of the divine) and of *kavvanot* (focusing of religious acts toward mystical ends). Certainly we do not find discussion of such topics as they might pertain to immediate reality (i.e., himself and his friends). Thus, we find little attention being paid to concepts related to the messianic, or to the theory of restoration/salvation *(tikkun)*. This first stage, in contrast to the second, is characterized also by a certain tentative, experimental quality, by repeated attempts to interpret the same passages from the Zohar, as if the author was dissatisfied with his initial interpretation.[74]

We find, for example, three variants of an interpretation to the opening passage of the Zohar, which is devoted to the verse: "Like a lily among the thorns, so is my beloved among the maidens."[75] All of the variants share one common element: they seek to understand the sense of the Zohar through further elaboration of detail and the discovery of new aspects of the *sefirot* of *Tiferet* and *Malkhut* (i.e., the "lily"). To do this, the Ari utilized the qualities of Jacob and Moses as described in the Zoharic material, reviewed here earlier. Again, what we have is not a finished, orderly exposition, but several experiments, all of which tend to follow the same pattern or direction. This gives us an opportunity to follow the Ari's method step by step, but as this would involve a long digression, I will simply summarize the interpretations and compare them, as a group, to the later thought of the Ari in the Safed period.

The Zohar's first statement (according to the Ari's reading) deals with two aspects of the last *"sefira"*: [76] the nether aspect, called *Malkhut,* which is contained within the *kelippot* (outer shells), and hence is like "a lily among the thorns"; and the higher aspect—"my beloved among the maidens." This higher aspect is the inner or essential nature of *Malkhut,* and is called *keneset yisrael* (the "Assembly of Israel"). The term is not an original invention: it is the name assigned to the entire *sefira* of *Malkhut* ever since the earliest kabbalistic texts, because of the connection between this lowest *sefira* and the people of Israel. But here it is given a novel explanation: *keneset yisrael* is the point at which "Israel" enters, as the higher or inner aspect of *Tiferet,* as opposed to the lower aspect, "Jacob." [77] Jacob's inner aspect is also called Moses, as we have seen in the Zohar,[78] and hence *keneset yisrael* is "the bride of Moses" *(kallat Moshe).*[79] Only the inner or essential nature of *Malkhut* is a worthy object of the true mystic's endeavor.

Through this distinction, the Ari explains the sin of Moses in striking the rock (instead of speaking to it), with the "rock" *(sela')* representing the lower aspect of *Malkhut,* while the "bride of Moses" is *tsela'* or "rib"—Adam's rib, or in other words, the female. The higher aspect, *tsela',* or "the bride," is linked to the mystery of speech, and when Moses was instructed to speak to the rock, and instead used brute force, he sinned. The link between the "rib" and oral speech expresses its sublime quality. Though *sela'* and *tsela'* may be pronounced almost exactly alike (in Sephardi Hebrew), the numerological value of the word *tsela'* is greater by thirty (the letter "ts" equals 90, and "s" is 60). In turn, the number 30 is a reference to the three higher *sefirot* which are responsible for speech and are not contained in *sela'.* The higher *sefirot* are "marrows," here meaning specifically the brain, the power of intelligence—for Moses was graced, as we know, with forty-nine "gateways" to understanding,[80] interpreted here in terms of "the bride of Moses." There may not be a direct correspondence between the "bride" and *Bina* (Understanding), since the "bride" is still conceived as the higher aspect of the lowest *sefira,* but she is positioned "in her mother's lap" (i.e., *Bina*). Hence, the higher divine Presence *(Shekhina)* may be referred to in the verse as "my beloved," for *Bina* is "my beloved" [81] while the lower Presence, the "lily," may be referred to as *sela'*. Numerologically, the *sela'* is equivalent to Cain: an allusion to Balaam's blessing to Cain (Num. 24:21): "Secure in your abode, and your nests set among the *rocks.*"

It may be demonstrated that all these motifs are drawn from the Zohar, especially from the *Ra'aya Meheimana* and *Tikkunei Zohar,* as taught by Rabbi Moshe Cordovero. The *Tikkunei Zohar,* for example, identifies *tsela'* with "the bride of Moses"[82] and the *Ra'aya Meheimana*[83] distinguishes between two "rocks," only the nether of the two deserving to be struck, but Moses confusing the two. While the *Ra'aya Meheimana,* taken in its simple sense, understands the nether rock as the "evil principle" *(sitra ahra),* Rabbi Moshe Cordovero interpreted this in a fashion that approaches that of the Ari.[84] Elsewhere,[85] Cordovero even identifies the higher *sela'* with *tsela',* which is the "bride of Moses."[86] Essentially, the Ari's endeavor at this stage does not go beyond a refinement of existing material, generally static in character, without entering into an investigation of the identity between biblical figures and their corresponding aspects of *sefirot* in the divine realm.

This picture changes during the Safed period. Again, the Ari finds two aspects of *Malkhut,* and once more the higher one is linked to *Bina,* but the link now possesses a different character. It expresses the dynamic myth of the vessels, their shattering, and their ultimate restoration. The *Shekhina* above is no longer the higher manifestation of *Malkhut* rising up toward its "mother's lap," but the opposite: the *lower* manifestation of *Bina,* having descended at the time of the shattering of vessels, turned into a manifestation of the *Shekhina*'s Countenance. This new description is supported by the discrepancy in the Zohar, raised earlier, about Jacob's wives. Here, however, instead of the "Freudian" analysis proferred by the Zohar, we have a mythic solution. Jacob, the "lesser" element, couples with that aspect of his mother that has descended to the status or level of a wife.[87] The terminology shifts, too: no longer do we have *Malkhut/sela'* as distinct from *knesset yisrael/kalat Moshe/tsela',* but rather "Leah's Countenance" as opposed to "Rachel's Countenance."[88]

But the most interesting change of all lies in the precise definition of the role of man in the system. Now people are part and parcel of the sublime manifestations of God—indeed, an essential part. They are the "seed" of the male and female aspects, consummating the sexual union between them. And thus, the Zohar's depiction of Joseph and Benjamin as "higher" and "lower" righteous male figures receives new significance. The Ari eliminates the Zohar's veiled ambiguity in which only the "higher" figure had symbolic meaning. Now the whole has become myth, and the lower figure also has significance in the divine universe: he is the source of the "female seed." [89]

Real people are involved here, incorporated as actual and quite central actors in the divine realm, without any shred of symbolism. That is why we find no more than one figure taking on any one function at the same time or on the same ontological plane. Benjamin, for example, who is the secondary or lower male figure, is the causal source of the "female waters"; if the same function is performed as well by Benayahu ben Yehoyada, that takes place on a different level and in a different way. Rav Hamnuna is, of course, Benayahu himself, but at a lower spiritual level. That is why he is always revealed to the sages as they travel and endeavor to consummate the joining of male and female aspects of the divine—their words of Torah function as female seed, and no intercourse (with *Malkhut*) is possible without this sexual instrument. [90] The statement of Rav Hamnuna, cited earlier, that the letter *"kaf"* cannot "descend" upon him, as it is needed to hold up the divine throne *(Kissei hakavod),* here acquires a more precise interpretation: the higher part of Rav Hamnuna's soul—namely, Benayahu—is an essential part of the sexual physiology of the *Shekhina.* [91]

Every sage in our own world who applies himself to Torah while away from home is joined to the spirit of a "lower" righteous figure (i.e., not those alone whose souls are "genetically" linked with that of Benayahu, but each sage with his own spiritual ancestor-soul or essential spirit), and are thus united to the spirit of Benayahu. Thus, he forms a part of the sexual organ of the *Shekhina,* or part of the soul of Benjamin. The figures of Benayahu or Rav Hamnuna form part of the living bridge between the level of the scholar-sage and the essence of that organ, located within the *Shekhina.* Thus, we also frequently find statements by Rabbi Hayim Vital that the soul of Benayahu or Rav Hamnuna entered or accompanied him. [92]

The connection between Rav Hamnuna and Moses is also explained in the Lurianic system through the principle of transmigrating souls. [93] That principle, according to which the soul is supported by other souls, representing elements of the divine *sefirot,* that have become incarnate within it, so that the soul is enabled to return to its earlier incarnations, has roots in the text of the Zohar. At times, the principle is used in the Zohar to link biblical figures to those of the "frame narrative." The Ari simply refined the doctrine and took it to its extreme conclusion, adding a layer relating to the souls of himself and his companions.[94]

The highly significant teachings of the Zohar that turn on the issue of the relative positions of Moses and Jacob (discussed earlier) receive here, in the Lurianic doctrine, a more specific meaning. Jacob's union with the Shekhina is "in body" because he achieves the "lesser" figure's union with the "female waters" in an actual, physical sense. Moses' union is on a higher plane, however: a joining of spirit to spirit, a union of the "kiss,"[95] and we are referred to the phrase, "mouth to mouth"[96]—the "bride of Moses" is called "mouth."

We recall that in the Zohar we also found the view that it was Moses, not Jacob, whose union with the Shekhina was corporeal. In Lurianic Kabbala, such contradictions merely serve as opportunities for new twists in the overall scheme. In the Ari's teaching, Moses' physical union with the Shekhina is assigned to a higher plane in the sefirot, so that both couplings are integrated into the complex ontological-anatomical structure: the "kiss" between the two lower Countenances is the true consummation of the father-mother union! But if each couple has a pair of unions, what of the higher one (the "kiss") of the father and the mother themselves? For this, the Ari introduces an additional figure, superior to Moses: Rabbi 'Akiba. His supremacy is a concept we find in much earlier sources, going back to the Talmud,[97] and here it is fleshed out in detail (as is true, as well, of the account of 'Akiba's death as a martyr upon pronouncing the last word of the Shema', in a death-agony of love for God that surpasses the kiss of death that takes Moses' life). Rabbi 'Akiba, of course, is the central figure in the Oral Law, all of which is "according to Rabbi 'Akiba."[98] The Oral Law is here related to the "mouth" of the divine, which achieves by a kiss the coupling of father and mother. Oral Law stands higher than the Written Law, which has a physical dimension. This idea, of the supremacy of Oral over Written Law, is, I believe, an innovation of the Ari's, for, in ordinary kabbalistic symbolism, the Oral Law represents the Shekhina, while the source of Written Law is Tiferet.

This matter possesses yet another level of significance, one that is central to our understanding of the relationship between God and man in Lurianic Kabbala. At this stage in the development of his doctrine, the Ari's personal identification with Moses reached the point of overwhelming conviction. He believed that Moses, who revealed the Written Law, was in turn a reincarnation of Abel and that, in a subsequent reincarnation as Rabbi Shimeon bar Yohai, he revealed the Zohar as well.[99] Now, in his newest guise, he was again the source of a new teaching, his interpretation of Kabbala.[100]

But this figure had its counterpart, one that might seem inferior at first, but in fact was potentially superior: namely, the figure of Rabbi 'Akiba, whose spirit goes back to that of Cain,[101] and who found his reincarnation in Rabbi Hayim Vital.[102]

We cannot be certain whether the above description of the relationship of Rabbi 'Akiba to Moses—penned by the Ari himself[103]—was written out of this sort of personalized approach; but even if, at that early stage, such an awareness had not yet reached its fully developed form, the subsequent evolution of the Ari's Kabbala was entirely directed in that personal vein. The Ari's words during the final days of his life to Rabbi Hayim Vital[104]—that he himself had come into the world for only one purpose, to fulfill the restoration/salvation of Hayim Vital's soul—are to be connected, I believe, to the development of this concept of the salvation/restoration of the soul of Cain-'Akiba-Hayim Vital, and—in overall terms—the concept of the function of the soul in the divine *sefirot*.

NOTES

1. " 'De Natura Dei'," in my book, *Studies in Jewish Myth and Jewish Messianism* (Albany, 1993).
2. See Yehuda Liebes, *Perakim bemilon sefer hazohar*, Ph.D. dissertation, The Hebrew University of Jerusalem, 1977, 2d printing, 1982, pp. 28–92 ("Adam").
3. Isaiah Tishby, "Hasemel vehadat bakabala," in his book *Netivei emuna uminut* (Ramat-Gan, 1964), p. 13.
4. See Isaiah Tishby, *The Wisdom of the Zohar* (Oxford, 1989), vol. 3, pp. 1357–1379.
5. See Gershom Scholem, *Major Trends in Jewish Mysticism* (New York, 1961), pp. 199–200, 226. Scholem explicitly states that Moses is the only mortal about whose relationship with God the Zohar speaks in terms of "sexual symbolism." On Moses, cf. Liebes (n. 2), pp. 182–183.

6. Zohar, Part One, 21b–22a; Part Three, 187a.

7. Zohar, Part One, 21a, cites the legal opinion that a woman who has been married twice will, at the time of the resurrection, return to her first husband. This contrasts with the view of Jesus, who was also called upon to answer such a question, and who claimed that after the resurrection marriage will not exist (Mark 12: 18–27). This difference is a good reflection of the contrast between the Zohar and Christianity in their appraisal of marriage. Compare the surprise expressed in the Zohar, by the figure of the Young Child, at the theoretical possibility that, had Adam not sinned, men might never have taken wives (Part Three, 189a).

8. Deut. 34: 5–6; Bava Batra 17a.

9. Zohar Part One, 251a. "Body of the king" refers in the Zohar to the *sefira* of *Tiferet*. See Liebes (n. 2), pp. 177, 220, 226–228, 265. In the *Tikkunei Zohar*, this distinction was developed still further, so that Jacob becomes the body of Moses, for Jacob is the outer form *(klippa)* of *Tiferet*, and Moses is its inner spirit; in addition, Moses' soul entered into Jacob when he wrestled with the angel. *Tikkunei Zohar, tikkun* 69, p. 101b (in the Mossad Harav Kook edition).

10. Part One, 160b, for example.

11. See Isaiah Tishby, *Mishnat hazohar*, Part One (Jerusalem, 1957), pp. 28–33.

12. See E. Gottlieb, "He'arot devekut unevua basefer 'otsar hahayim' lerab Itshak demin 'akko," in his book, *Mehkarim besifrut hakabbala* (Tel-Aviv, 1976), pp. 231–247. The essay represents only an initial examination of this important work, and does not deal with the relationship between R. Itshak's book and the Zohar. I will note here, for example, that the passage in the Zohar on Ruth (printed in *Zohar Hadash*, Mossad Harav Kook edition, 90a) also appears in *Otsar hahayyim*, but in quite different form. Ginzburg ms. 775 (photostat in the Scholem Collection at the Jewish National and University Library, Jerusalem, cat. no. 218), pp. 61ff. Likewise, attention ought to be paid to such expressions in the text as: "and this is the view of the 'great lion' Rabbi Shimeon bar Yohai, of blessed memory. . . . The lion has roared: who will not tremble for fear?" (ibid., p. 65a).

13. Ibid., p. 73b. Cited by Moshe Idel, *"Hitbodedut kerikkuz bakabbala haekstatit vegilguleha,"* Da'at 14 (1985), p. 56, n. 117. Compare: Y. Alaskar, *Tsofnat pa'aneah* (Jerusalem, 1991, facsimile edition of the ms.), p. 19a–b.

14. E. Gottlieb (n. 12), p. 242; M. Idel, "Ecstatic Kabbalah and the Land of Israel," in his book *Studies in Ecstatic Kabbalah* (Albany, 1988), pp. 96, 100.

15. I. Tishby (ed.), "Sheelot utshuvot lerabbi Moshe de leon be'inyenei kabbala," in his book *Hikrei kabbala ushluhoteha* (Jerusalem, 1982), pp. 36–75.

16. Ibid., p. 45. A similar view is taken by Nahmanides, in his Commentary to the Torah (Gen. 48: 7). But Tishby, in annotating the Responsa of Ramdal, added an interpretive note suggesting that the sentence be understood in terms of the myth of the Zohar (as outlined above). This assertion, I believe,

is incorrect, and is based on the axiomatic assumption that the entire Zohar reflects the views of Ramdal. This is the assumption of the scholars who have annotated the writings of Ramdal, beginning with Scholem and Tishby, who pointed out the parallels between Ramdal's writings and the Zohar. But they overlooked the differences and individual tendencies.

17. There is, in fact, a polemic in the Zohar over the honor and status of the Land. See Part Three, 189a.
18. See, for example, Zohar, Part Three, 4a, 120a, 290b *(Idra Zuta)*.
19. See, for example, Zohar, Part Three, 15b, 74b.
20. See Y. Liebes, "How the Zohar was Written," in my book, *Studies in the Zohar* (Albany, 1993), p. 222, n. 276.
21. *"Sheelot utshuvot"* (n. 15), p. 18.
22. Zohar, Part One, 156b. For the interpretation of Rabbi Luria, see below, n. 87.
23. See my essay, n. 20.
24. Ibid., pp. 34–35.
25. For example, in *Idra Rabba* there is sharp condemnation of he who "enters but does not exit" (Zohar, Part Three, 141a). But in the very same *idra* we find a description of the death of the companions while in an ecstatic state, and yet receive praise, albeit after a certain hesitation (144a–b). On this, see Liebes, "The Messiah of the Zohar," in the book cited in n. 20. True, at the time I first wrote that article (1982), I had not yet understood the nature of the circle associated with the Zohar and did not realize that I was dealing with an internal polemic. The problem of evaluating death that occurs through the force of communion with God *(devekut)* is one that goes back to the earliest phases of Judaism. See Y. Liebes, *Het'o shel Elisha', arba'a shenikhnesu lapardes, vetiva' shel hamistika hatalmudit* (Jerusalem, 1990), pp. 93–100.

I can cite another instance of internal polemic in the Zohar. The figure of the Young Child argues, with some vehemence and in polemical tones, that when Ruth the Moabite married Mahlon, she did not convert her religion, but simply practiced the customs of Judaism (Part Three, 190a). In the *Zohar Hadash* we find the opposite contention (Mossad Harav Kook edition, 79, col. A): "Heaven forbid that she would marry Mahlon while she was still a gentile; rather, she married once she had become a convert." I believe that this disagreement is tied to the well-known debate in Ramdal's circle over Jews who took a very lenient approach to relations with their female Moslem servants. Ramdal himself attacked this practice quite strongly in his Hebrew writings, citing and then refuting the arguments of his opponents. Parallels to Ramdal's view appear in the Zohar. (See Moshe de Leon, *Shekel hakodesh* [London, 1911], pp. 65–67. Cf. Itshak Baer, "Todros ben yehuda halevi uzemano," *Ziyon* 2 [1937], pp. 36–44.) This was a clear ideological and halakhic polemic, and it cannot be supposed that Ramdal altered his view on such a matter of principle. The words of the Young Child reflect the view of a different member of his circle.

26. "Sheelot utshuvot" (n. 15), pp. 50–55. The traditional interpretation of Joseph is that his presence in Egypt was for the purpose of undergoing a greater test. Ethical explanations regarding the burial of Joseph, Jacob, and Moses in the Land of Israel were added later by Avraham Azulai in the name of Rabbi Kalonymus. See Moshe Idel, " 'Al erets yisrael bamahashava hamistit shel yemei habeinayim," in M. Halamish and A. Ravitsky (eds.), *Erets yisrael bahagut hayehudit bimei habeinayim* (Jerusalem, 1991), p. 199. I would add that the teaching of R. Kalonymus is also cited by R. Itshak Luria himself, who developed the theme in other directions. See Hayim Vital, *Sha'ar hapesukim* (Jerusalem, 1912), 73a ("Beha'alotkha"). The symbolic quality of Ramdal's work is reflected in the recurring use of the phrase, "a mystery of resemblance of heaven" *("sod dugma shel ma'ala"),* as on p. 40. Thus, in order to explain why Moses did not enter the Land together with Joshua, Ramdal offers an analogy with the sun that does not shine upon the moon before the sun itself has set (in accord with the kabbalistic symbolism of sun and moon, and their connection with Moses and Joshua, and Bava Batra 75a). Moses' failure to enter the Land is thus explained symbolically (or allegorically) in terms of the necessity of his passing away in order to allow for the ascendance of Joshua, and in order to support him from on high. This explanation, though, also appears in the Zohar (Part Three, 156b–157a), and is cited by Tishby.

27. See above, n. 25, and cf. Y. Liebes, "Sefer tsaddik yesod 'olam—mitos shabta'i," *Da'at* 1 (1978), p. 107, n. 171.

28. See above, nn. 20, 25.

29. See above, n. 25.

30. Ibid., pp. 105–107.

31. The story of the Yanoka appears in the regular published editions of the Zohar (following the Mantua edition), in the section for "Balak," in Part Three, 186a–192a.

32. There are not a few points of resemblance between this figure and that of Jesus, or even Rabbi Gadiel the Boy. On the connections between R. Gadiel, the angel Metatron, and Jesus, see Y. Liebes, "Mal'akhei kol hashofar veYeshua' sar hapanim," in Y. Dan (ed.), *Hamistika hayehudit hakeduma* (Jerusalem, 1987), p. 182.

33. Zohar, Part Three, 187a.

34. I believe the Yanoka himself alludes to this in one of his speeches on the subject of the *Shekhina,* stating that the *Shekhina* does not sin, except as a daughter who plays or pampers herself *(mithattet)* with her father (Zohar, Part Three, 188b). This is a paraphrase of the well-known words of Shimeon ben Shetah about Honi Hame'agel, in which he recognizes Honi's exceptional charismatic status, which put him beyond ordinary halakhic norms (Ta'anit 23a). Regarding this text, which is an integral part of the Yanoka story, one finds in addition a similarity to the style of the *Ra'aya Meheimana.* It stands somewhere in between the Zohar and the *Ra'aya Meheimana.* The content of the text reappears in the *Ra'aya Meheimana*

itself, this time in its own full-blown and characteristic style (Zohar, Part Three, 272a).

35. According to a parallel description in the Zohar, Part One, 240a–b, it is his father's merit that protects the Yanoka from the evil eye.

36. The description here is very similar to the figure of Ben-Sira in the book *Alfa-beta deven-sira.* See A. Yasif (ed. and annotator), *Sippurei ben-sira bimei habeinayim* (Jerusalem, 1985), pp. 197–203. Ben-Sira is also a *Wunderkind* who instructs the sages and expresses condescension toward them. His mother, too, fears for him because of the evil eye, and he belittles that fear. The spiritual relationship between him and his father is reminiscent of the bond between the Yanoka and Rav-hamnuna the Ancient One (see further in the discussion). His virgin birth would appear to be a parody on the story of Jesus. Our Yanoka is also similar to the child figure in Hagiga 13a.

37. This fate was predicted by Rabbi Shimeon bar Yohai in Part One, 240a. It is fulfilled in Part Three, 192a.

38. Part Three, 188a. The version in which the word "messiah" *(meshihu)* appears (rather than *meshikhu,* emanation) seems to be an error. Rabbi Moshe Cordovero's commentary refers to an example he knew of in which the spirit of the father influenced that of the son: M. Cordovero, *Zohar 'im perush or yakar,* vol. 14 (Jerusalem, 1986), p. 139. It should be noted that in *Zohar Hadash,* 86, col. 4–87, col. 4 ("Ruth"), there is a passage that partly parallels the Yanoka story, dealing also with the esoteric significance of the blessings recited after a meal. We find there numerous references to words spoken by Rav Hamnuna the Ancient One, who to a certain extent takes the place of the Yanoka and of his teacher, Rabbi Shema'aya Hasida.

39. In responding to a query as to his father's name, he answers, a fish *(had nuna)* and the companions understand this as meaning "he is the son of Rav Hamnuna the Ancient One"—Part One, 6a.

40. Part One, 7a.

41. To my knowledge, this figure has not yet been studied, except for a seminar paper written by Boaz Huss.

42. Zohar, Part Three, 288a.

43. Part One, 6a.

44. Part One, 9a.

45. See my book (n. 2), pp. 37, 40.

46. Part Three, 72b; Part One, 225a. Elsewhere we find several other versions: "Rav Yeiva-sabba" rather than "Rav Hamnuna-sabba," but the two are probably both the same, as we shall see. One may find a literary source for Rav Hamnuna-sabba's ascent from Babylon, the epithet "sabba," his book, his relationship with the Yanoka, and his special relation to God in the following Talmudic passage: "The bodies of Rava bar Huna and Rav Hamnuna were brought from Babylon to [the Land of Israel] . . . and the Yanoka commented upon it [it is not clear whether only one sage or both are intended here], 'A scion of ancient stock from Babylon came/ With

records of prowess in combat and fame/ . . . When God views His world with displeasure,/ He seizes [great] souls in exacting measure,/ Awaiting their coming as new brides, with delight,/ And, riding on high heavens/ He welcomes the souls of the pure and the right' " (Mo'ed Katan 25a–b).

47. See the end of *Idra Rabba* (Part Three, 144b), where Elijah the Prophet apologizes for not having been present, because he had been preoccupied with rescuing Rav Hamnuna and his friends from the authorities.

48. Part Three, 186b. According to the *Tikkunei Zohar,* the soul of Rav Hamnuna descends to clothe itself in the "aura of Torah" (*Zohar Hadash,* 97, cols. 2–3). Compare the appearance of the soul of Rabbi Pinhas ben Yair (who is considered in the Zohar to be the father-in-law of Rabbi Shimeon bar Yohai) as a shadow, Part Three, 217a–220a. But R. Pinhas descends to this world because the sages were occupied with discussing something pertaining to him, while Rav Hamnuna descends whenever they are engaged in Torah. At the beginning of *Idra Zuta,* in addition to Rav Hamnuna-saba, R. Pinhas ben Yair's soul also appears, and there it is clear that his status is far lower. See Part Three, 288a. On a further visitation by R. Pinhas, parallel to the Zohar text, see M. Benayahu (ed. and annotator), *Sefer toledot haAri* (Jerusalem, 1967), pp. 176–177.

49. Part One, 7a–b. On the revival of the sages, see my critique of Moshe Idel's book, *Golem,* in *Kiryat Sefer* 63 (1991).

50. See Part Three, 187a–188b. The phrase, "the good master of all peace" (*shlama;* an alternate reading is *'alma:* i.e., "good master of all the world"; the former is preferable), which normally refers to God, refers here to Rabbi Shimeon bar Yohai. See also Part One, 7a–b, 9a.

51. Part One, 6a. See my book (n. 2), pp. 139–140. Only the Sabbateans began to call their prophet, Nathan of Gaza, by that name. Afterwards, the practice was extended to later hasidic *tsaddikim.*

52. Cf. nn. 46, 92.

53. Part One, 6a.

54. Part One, 2b–3a.

55. The point was brought home for me upon reading the commentary on the Zohar by Rabbi Shimeon Lavi. See S. Lavi, *Ketem paz* (Djerba, 1939), Part One, 17 col. a.

56. Part One, 6b. See also Rabbi Shimeon bar Yohai's addition to this statement, in Part One, 9a.

57. Part Three, 187b.

58. Compare this interpretation to that of Nachman of Bratslav, in *Likutei maharan,* Part One, 20. Cf. Y. Liebes, "*Ha-Tikkun ha-Klali* of R. Nachman of Bratslav and Its Sabbatean Links," in the book cited above (n. 1), p. 125.

59. See Moshe Idel, "Haperush hamagi vehaneoplatoni shel hakabbala bitkufat harenesans," *Mehkarei yerushalayim bemahshevet yisrael* 4 (1982), pp. 60–112.

60. S. Alkabets, *Brit haLevi* (Lemberg, 1863), 39, col. a–43, col. d.

61. His remarks have been noted recently by B. Zak, "Erets yisrael bemishnat R.

Moshe Kordovero," in Halamish and Ravitsky (eds.), *Erets yisrael bahagut hayehudit bimei habeinayim* (Jerusalem, 1991), pp. 332–341.

62. This is not Scholem's view, of course. He states that, concerning the core concepts of Lurianic Kabbala such as *tsimtsum* and the shattering of the vessels, "in truth these may be understood only in the symbolic sense." See Gershom Scholem, "Kabala umitos," in his book, *Pirkei yesod behavanat hakabbala usemaleha* (Jerusalem, 1976), p. 94. Other opinions, it is true, have been heard earlier, rejecting the idea of the symbolic character of Lurianic Kabbala. See Moshe Idel, *Kabbalah: New Perspectives* (New Haven, 1988), pp. 217–218. Idel characterizes the Ari's thought in a way similar to my own, but he still uses the term "symbolism." In his view, the transition to the Ari's way of thinking had its origins in the teachings of Rabbi David ben Yehuda Hehasid and Rabbi Yosef ben Shalom Ashkenazi. For a contention similar to mine about the nonsymbolic character of Luria's Kabbala, see R. Elior, "Hazikka hametaforit bein haadam la'el . . .," in Elior and Liebes (eds.), *Kabbalat haAri* (Jerusalem, 1992). I have pressed this argument for years, beginning with a debate on the matter with Professor Yosef Ben-Shlomo at the Conference of Departments of Jewish Thought, held at Tel-Aviv University.

63. He states this explicitly on several occasions. See, e.g., Hayim Vital, *Sha'ar hakavvanot* (Jerusalem, 1912), 23, col. a, regarding the reciting of the *"Shema',"* article 6.

64. See *Toledot haAri* (above, n. 48), pp. 156–157, and numerous parallels.

65. See my article, "Kivvunim hadashim beheker hakabbala," *Pe'amim* 50 (1992), pp. 130–170.

66. See Scholem (n. 5), p. 262.

67. I have detailed this contention in my article (n. 65), pp. 134–136, 161–166.

68. See I. Tishby, *Torat hara' vehaklippa bekabbalat haAri* (Jerusalem, 1963), pp. 42–59.

69. The concept of the shattered vessels appears only at a late stage in the Ari's Kabbala, whereas the martyred Ten Sages and their connection to the ten destroyed primeval worlds was already part of the system before Luria settled in Safed. See Hayim Vital, *Sha'ar maamarei Rashbi* (Jerusalem, 1959), 65, col. a–67, col. b.

70. See Hayim Vital, *Sefer hagilgulim* (Przemyslan, 1875; photo-reprint, Jerusalem, 1982), in *Sefer torat hagilgul*, Part One, 41, col. c–51, col. b, chaps. 39–43. The opening is taken from the cited work by Vital *Sha'ar maamarei Rashbi* (n. 69), but removed from the rest of its original context, which deals with the death of the kings.

71. See above, n. 67.

72. Part Two, 254b–255a. Cf. M. Idel, *"Hamahshava hara'a shel ha'el,"* Tarbits 49 (1980), pp. 360–364.

73. See my article (n. 20), pp. 134–135.

74. This hesitancy is described in the biographical material about him. See, e.g., Hayim Vital, *Eileh toledot Itshak,* in *Toledot haAri* (n. 48, above), pp. 247–

248. This characterization is definitely corroborated by the Ari's exegetical writings, as we will see in the course of the discussion.

75. Song of Songs 2:2. *Sha'ar maamarei Rashbi* (n. 67 above), 3, col. b–4, col. c.

76. This formulation may have originated from an error in the copy of the Zohar that was before him at the time. The line, "This is a lily, and that, too, is a lily," does not appear in most versions of the text. Even if we grant that the sentence is genuine, it is most likely to have referred simply to the dualism of the real and the symbolic lily, not to two of them, both within the divine realm, as the Ari read it.

77. See Yosef Angelet (published in a book attributed erroneously to R. David ben Yehuda Hehasid), *Livnat hasappir* (Jerusalem, 1913), 30, col. b: "And he called her *keneset* [i.e., Gathering of] Israel, for she brings together, lays up and receives the plenitude of the Glory *[Tiferet]* of Israel." The Ari read *Livnat sappir*, as is explicitly noted in *Sha'ar maamarei Rashbi* (n. 69), 32, col. d.

78. Cf. *Tikkunei Zohar*, cited above, n. 9.

79. On this expression, used in the Zohar and rabbinic literature, see Scholem (n. 5), p. 199, and n. 142.

80. See, e.g., Rosh Hashana 21b.

81. *Hokhma* and *Bina* are "two loving friends" (see above, n. 18).

82. *Tikkunei Zohar*, 12 (Mossad Harav Kook edition, p. 27a).

83. Zohar, Part Two, 279b.

84. *Or Yakar* 15, p. 91; first published by B. Zak, "Keta' miperusho shel R. Moshe Kordovero la-ra'aya meheimana'," *Kovets 'al yad* 10 (1982), p. 280.

85. M. Cordovero, *Pardes Rimonim* (Munkacz, 1906), Part Two, 37, cols. b–c. "Sha'ar erkei hakinnuyim," under *"tsela' "*: "Tsela' is *Malkhut* in its unseen dimension."

86. Ibid., 32, col. 4, under *"sela'."*

87. With respect to other passages in the Zohar that touch on this issue, the Ari resolves the question with the same method but in an opposite sense: the higher aspect of Jacob (Israel, or sometimes Israel-*sabba*, a surprising use of this epithet, in terms of the sources in midrash and the Zohar) rises up and couples with the lower part of the *sefira* of Bina, called *Tevuna* (Intelligence). See Hayim Vital, *Sha'ar hahakdamot* (Jerusalem, 1909), 45, col. d–46, col. b, which is an interpretation of the Zohar, Part One, 156b, according to which Jacob was not Leah's consort (see above, n. 22). As we saw, this reading conflicts with other texts in the Zohar. The Lurianic solution: *Jacob* did not have a consort, but *Israel* did. If Israel has this high status, Moses retains one still greater, for Israel couples with *Tevuna*, whereas Moses is joined with *Bina*.

88. See, e.g., *Sha'ar hahakdamot* (n. 87, above), 58, col. a–60, col. a. We know of an exegetical piece from the same period that continues the earlier version and uses the terminology of *sela'* vs. *tsela'* and "the bride of Moses," but develops them in a new direction, identifying *sela'* with the Countenance of

Rachel, and *tsela'*/"bride" with the Countenance of Leah. See *Likkutei tora* (n. 26 above), 83b.

89. True, even this "lower" pious figure is, in origin, male. He is the spirit left by the male inside the female during the first copulation, according to the theory in The Ancient One of *Mishpatim* (Zohar, Part Two, 99b–100a). I think that in the Ari's system, this, too, becomes part of the divine realm.

90. See *Sha'ar hakavvanot* (n. 63), 23, cols. a–c, on the *kavvana* of the *Shema'*, article 6. Cf. Hayim Vital, *Sha'ar hayihudim* (Lemberg, 1855; photo-reprint, Jerusalem, 1970?), 3, col. c, chap. 3.

91. *Sha'ar maamarei Rashbi* (n. 69), 13, col. b. This interpretation belongs to the earlier stratum of the Ari's thought, and the description does not change later; but it acquires a mystical purpose in the second stage. For a fascinating discussion on the subject of Rav Hamnuna, the Yanoka, Benay-ahu, etc., see Naftali ben Ya'akov Elhanan Bachrach, *'Emek hamelekh* (Amsterdam, 1648; reprint, Benei Berak, 1973), pp. 77–78.

92. Hayim Vital, *Sefer hahezyonot* (in the Eshkoli edition, Jerusalem, 1954), pp. 171–172. Here it is Rav Yeiva-saba who is mentioned, but the connec-tion with Rav Hamnuna was discussed earlier (see above, n. 52). Rabbi Hayim Vital apparently distinguished between the two, for elsewhere in the book (p. 69) he leaves open the question whether he received a vis-itation from Rav Hamnuna or Rav Yeiva. Vital considered Rav Yeiva-saba "the righteous one who is always with me" (ibid., pp. 16–17, and elsewhere). It should be stressed, however, that this figure was also consid-ered to be an earlier incarnation of Hayim Vital (ibid., p. 143, and else-where).

93. *Sha'ar maamarei Rashbi* (n. 69), 13, cols. b–c. Hayim Vital, *Sha'ar hagil-gulim* (Jerusalem, 1903), 47b, Introduction, 36. True, the Zohar's state-ment (as cited earlier) on the killing of Moses by Benayahu, who is identi-fied with Rav Hamnuna, makes it difficult to understand the connection between their souls.

94. See my article, "Terein orzilin deilta: derashato hasodit shel haAri lifnei moto," in R. Elior and Y. Liebes (eds.), *Kabbalat haAri* (Jerusalem, 1992).

95. In the Zohar, the kiss is considered "the cleaving of soul to soul." See, e.g., *Zohar Hadash*, 60, col. c, at the beginning of the commentary to Song of Songs. For more on Moses and Jacob, see *'Emek hamelekh* (n. 91), p. 79.

96. Num. 12:8.

97. E.g., Menahot 29b, where Moses asks the Almighty about Rabbi 'Akiba: "You have someone like that, yet you choose me to give the Torah?" On these *aggadot* and their meaning, and on the relationship of Moses to 'Akiba, see my article (n. 1).

98. See Sanhedrin 86a.

99. On the Ari's sense of kinship with R. Shimeon bar Yohai, see my article (n. 65). This link also had instrumental mystical significance, lending motivation to the Ari's activities and prompting him, apparently, to immi-grate to the Land of Israel.

100. See, e.g., *Sefer hahezyonot* (n. 92), p. 153, and also p. 213, which parallels with the passage cited above in n. 70.

101. On the souls of Cain and Abel, see, e.g., *Sefer hagilgulim* (n. 70), 20, col. c–31, col. d, chaps. 19–29. On R. 'Akiba and his comrades, see above, n. 70.

102. *Sefer hahezyonot* (n. 92), p. 140, p. 161. Elsewhere, though (ibid., p. 135), Rabbi Hayim Vital states that it was only in the year 1571 that the spirit of Rabbi 'Akiba entered into him. That is to say, the souls were not merged from the very first. This is important documentation of the process by which Vital reached the idea of the link between himself and Rabbi 'Akiba. The entire fourth section of the book, pp. 134–229, is devoted to the matter of Hayim Vital's spiritual source and its reincarnations.

103. *Sha'ar hakavvanot* (n. 63), 48, cols. a–c, on the subject of prostrating oneself, article 5.

104. *Sefer hahezyonot* (n. 92), pp. 134–190. Elsewhere, though, other views are expressed regarding the dissemination of the Ari's teachings to others. See, e.g., *Sefer hahezyonot*, p. 221. There, however, Vital instructs others not for the sake of their benefit, but precisely in order to "restore" those parts of his soul that had found their way into theirs, and to return those parts to himself. On the other hand, Vital's words in introducing *Sha'ar hahakdamot* (n. 87), pp. 1–4, are entirely for the purpose of propagating the Ari's teachings. In another instance, the Ari's young son was doomed to die because of a mystery that he (the Ari) had revealed to his companions, yet he states: "Even if all my sons and I myself are to die, I will not desist from instructing you in the mysteries and secrets of the Torah" (*Toledot haAri*, n. 48 above, p. 198). We find a similar ambivalence over the dissemination of the Ari's teachings in *Shtar hahitkashrut*. See G. Scholem, "Shtar hahitkashrut shel talmidei haAri," *Ziyon* 5 (1940), pp. 133–160; cf. my article (n. 94).

7.

The Doctrine of Transmigration in *Galya Raza*
Rachel Elior

The doctrine of metempsychosis, or the transmigration of souls, became widely recognized at the end of the sixteenth century[1] as Lurianic Kabbalah and the writings of Rabbi Hayyim Vital on reincarnation were circulated in various editions,[2] and the concept was associated with Safed. In fact, however, a generation before Lurianic Kabbalah, in the first half of the sixteenth century, this doctrine had already been discussed profoundly and developed with originality in *Galya Raza,* the work of an anonymous Kabbalist.[3] Since the doctrine of metempsychosis is extensively discussed there, and because the work was mistakenly attributed to Rabbi Abraham, a disciple of the Ari (Isaac Luria),[4] it was commonly assumed that the work was composed in Safed. However it does not seem that this hypothesis can be supported by the book itself,[5] either directly or by implication. The book was written between 1543 and 1553[6] in a place free from Christian censorship, by an author who knew some Arabic and Greek. There may be reason to assume that he wrote in Greece or Turkey,[7] that is to say, prior to Lurianic Kabbalah and isolated from its influence.

Before discussing the doctrine of metempsychosis as taught by the author of *Galya Raza* and noting its distinctiveness, let us clarify the source of his inspiration and examine the character and circumstances of his writing. His doctrine is outstanding in its originality and daring. It

Permisison to translate and publish in English from the original Hebrew edition of *Mehkarim be-Kabbalah be-Philosophia Yehudit u-Besifrut ha-Musar ve-Hahagut* granted by the Magnes Press, Jerusalem, 1981.

drew to some degree on earlier Kabbalistic sources, but its authority was not grounded in this heritage, and its validity did not derive from a tradition transmitted by sacred writings or teachers. Rather, it was written under the inspiration of dreams, visions, and illuminations possessing the power of celestial revelation, by a writer who believed he possessed a superior degree of spiritual perception: "Blessed be the Lord, God of Israel, who revealed to me exalted secrets which were never before revealed to a human being in this generation, from the time that the Lamp of Brightness [i.e., R. Shimon Bar Yohai, the author of the Zohar] departed from this world until this very day." [8]

The name of the book also indicates its nature, and the meaning to which it alludes is clarified in the context of the words of the Zohar [9] relating to dreams and their meaning: "For Gabriel is in charge of dreams, and his name is *Raza Galei* [Revealed Secret], which is the numerical value of "Gabriel," plus the number of the letters. [10] Therefore I have called my book, "Revealed Secret," for by the power of dreams in my visions at night, [11] and sometimes when awake, I built all the structures which I have made." [12]

The author of *Galya Raza* adopted the attitude of the Zohar, according to which a dream is a revelation granted to the soul sojourning in the world of angels. Gabriel is responsible for those dreams granted to the souls of the righteous, which are described as visions approaching prophecy in their essence. [13] In contrast to the tradition of most Kabbalists, who sought to preserve the esoteric nature of their work and refrained from speaking at length about their manner of conception, this Kabbalist, because of his special inspiration, was driven to write about himself at length and to describe his revelations:

And since I saw every day that innovations were revealed to me, as well as hidden and concealed secrets, I resolved to write them down. [14] Moreover I have another interpretation in the manner of secrets that stir in my bowels, and I will not be quiet until I have revealed it, because it has been aroused in my heart by heaven. [15]

And all that I have written, my heart was aroused to write and publish, since I was inspired by heaven while I was in my bed, in visions at night, half asleep. It has been put in my mouth insistently to speak the expression of our lips, and in the morning after returning from synagogue I sat and wrote that which was summoned to place in my heart, and with my small understanding I wrote all that I comprehended, within the limitations of my mind. [16]

The author of *Galya Raza* saw himself as an emissary who felt compelled to proclaim what he had heard and seen, and disseminate what was revealed to him and placed in his mouth. The promulgation of his visions was strongly influenced by the criticism leveled against the esoteric doctrine of the Kabbalah in the area where he lived;[17] the revelation of secrets from heaven was interpreted by the author as assisting in the struggle for the sanctity of the Zohar and the status of Kabbalah, which were controversial in his time and place. Here are his words on this subject:

Since I heard that certain men seem wise to themselves and mock those secrets of the Torah and precious stones which were expressed by the mouth of the Lamp of Brightness [R. Shimon Bar Yohai], . . . and I felt within myself that the merit of the elevated spheres helps me every time that I seclude myself with their words. Such awesome secrets are revealed as I have never heard and we have not seen . . . and seeing clearly that the help of heaven was with me, and I was granted understanding to know and comprehend things, and also the power to deduce one thing from another, I resolved to bring them forth from the potential to the actual and to write for everyone that which was revealed to me from heaven, so that these secrets might not be shut away and enclosed in thought, but that they should be revealed and written for everyone's eyes. Perhaps there would be people who desired them.[18]

The decision to commit his visions to writing derived to a large degree from his belief that the end of days was near, because of which the members of his generation merited the revelations of the Zohar. His words have a conspicuously apocalyptic tone:

How fortunate are we and how happy is our lot that we have merited the Book of the Zohar, which our forebears did not merit, the least of whom is thicker than our hips, such as Rabbi Hai Gaon, Rabbi Eliezer of Worms, Rabbi Sheshet Gaon, Nachmanides and the Rashba, and the Raavad, of blessed memory, who were wise in this wisdom. But they did not taste of the honey of Rabbi Shimon, the Lamp of Brightness, may he rest in peace, for in their time it was not revealed. Only now in the final generation, in which we are today, [is this wisdom revealed]. And in proof of this claim is a passage from *Tikkunei Zohar*, 'Elijah of blessed memory said to Rabbi Shimon, may he rest in peace, how privileged are you in that from this book of yours some elevated people will be sustained, until the book is revealed to those below in the end of days, and because of it each man shall return to his dwelling and every man shall return to his family' (Lev. 25), and therefore it is explained from here that by virtue of those who study the Zohar, our redeemer shall come quickly and in our time.[19]

These words, written in 1552, regarding the discovery of the Zohar in his generation, are surprising. In fact, they are copied without any indication of their source from the writing of Rabbi Judah Chayat, the author of *Minhat Yehudah*.[20] The conclusion which he drew from *Tikkunei Ha-Zohar* regarding permission to reveal secrets, and the obligation to publicize them because of the impending end of days, was one he shared with other Kabbalists.[21] The importance of the quotation from the *Tikkunim*, its influence on the spread of Kabbalah during the sixteenth century, and its place in the controversy over the printing of the Zohar has already been studied.[22] Here is additional testimony of the influence of this promise on the belief that by virtue of historical circumstances the time had come for revealing the secrets of the Zohar, secrets that had been hidden during the period of exile. Thus, promulgation of visions and dreams anchored in interpretations of the Zohar received legitimation and came to be regarded as another way of bringing redemption nearer.[23] The combination of intimations of the end of days,[24] enormous admiration for the Book of the Zohar and defense of its study, along with an original kabbalistic outlook based on the authority of dreams, revelations, and visions, led the author of *Galya Raza* to propose a new historiosophical interpretation of the meaning of the end of days. This interpretation entailed two interconnected angles of vision: the doctrine of evil and the doctrine of metempsychosis.

EVIL AND THE DOCTRINE OF METEMPSYCHOSIS

These two doctrines were bound up with each other ever since the beginning of Kabbalah. Both of them are based on the verse, "How they were withered before their time, and their foundation poured out like a river" (Job 22:16), which was interpreted as referring both to souls and to the element of evil, as well as to destruction in the various dimensions of time. In Talmudic commentary on this verse, it is said, " 'How they were withered before their time. . . .' This is the 974 generations which were withered in order to be created before the world was created, but were not created. The Holy One, blessed be He, stood and planted them in every single generation, and they are the impudent members of the generation.' "[25]

The Talmudic number of 974 generations derives from interpretation of the verse, "The promise He gave for a thousand generations" (Psalms

105:8), according to which the "promise" is the Torah itself, which was commanded a thousand generations before the creation of the world. However, according to the biblical chronology, only twenty-six generations passed from the time of creation to the giving of the Torah. Hence 974 generations are lacking to complete the thousand. These generations acted evilly, and therefore they were 'withered' and not created.[26]

The conception of the generations withered in untimely fashion is connected in kabbalistic exegesis to a well-known Midrash from *Bereshit Rabba:* "The Holy One, blessed be He, was creating worlds and destroying them."[27] At the very beginning of Kabbalah, when Rabbi Isaac Ha-Cohen[28] interpreted the Midrash about creating and destroying worlds as referring to the doctrine of evil and the emanation of the *qelipot* [the evil forces of impurity], he based his words on an alternative reading of the verse, "How they were withered before their time," and he presented the names of the three worlds that were eradicated in the arcana of creating and destroying worlds—Kamtiel, Bliel, and Etiel, names that were inferred from the Hebrew words of this verse. The Zohar, too, derived the doctrine of the destruction of the worlds known as the "death of the kings" from this Midrash, for they were the source of evil in the worlds that were destroyed or withered.[29] However, even before that, once the twelfth-century *Sefer Ha-Bahir* had related its doctrine of metempsychosis to the verse, "The promise He gave for a thousand generations," with the Midrashic interpretation of the 974 generations, the connection was forged between existence prior to the Creation, which is interpreted as the source of evil, and the doctrine of the pre-existence and post-existence of the soul.[30] The concept of "a thousand generations"—either prior to the Creation as a source of the existence of *evil,* or else as following Creation and determining the fate of the *souls* and the timing of their reincarnations—was connected with the doctrines of metempsychosis and evil throughout kabbalistic literature.[31]

The implied connection between the conception of evil and the notion of metempsychosis became, in the thought of the author of *Galya Raza,* a detailed doctrine that sought to clarify the nature of evil, to explain its rule over the fate of Israel, and to establish its relationship to the destiny of the soul and its reincarnations. In order to illuminate the interconnections between all of these from a broad historical perspective, the author presents a dualistic worldview.

The doctrine of evil that is delineated in this book is based on the assumption that the nature of evil dictates the character of history to a decisive degree, and that penetrating investigation of this topic will shed new light on the meaning of the destiny of the Jewish people. The ontological status of evil in the world, both in its celestial and terrestrial aspects, may be compared to the status of the firstborn, preferred for its essential priority. Evil preceded good just as darkness preceded light and absence preceded existence: " 'And these are the kings who reigned in the Land of Edom before the reign of the king of the Israelites' (Gen. 36:31). It should be known that absence is prior to being in the act of Creation. Absence is the darkness and being is the light, and the light which is the brain had its dwelling within darkness like the meat of a nut within its four shells [qelipot]." [32]

The general origin of existences, then, was within darkness, in the *Sitra Ahra,* which ruled alone before the Creation. The light was hidden within the darkness, "like water in a sponge," and henceforth this primal state of affairs determined the connection between sanctity and impurity. The connection between evil and good is the dialectical basis of reality, because all of existence comes from the *Sitra de-Smola* [the Sinister Side]. Existences that belong essentially to sanctity cannot exist without the "arousal" of darkness and the sinister, on the one hand, while the *Sitra de-Smola* has no existence without the light of sanctity, on the other hand:

'And darkness was upon the abyss' (Gen. 1)—here you have it that the light and the darkness were a single entity, 'and God said, Let there be light,' meaning let the light be visible—and He did not say, 'Let it be created'. Hence we see that the light and the darkness were as though with the one God, and the light was buried and hidden within the darkness like water within a sponge, and it was not visible. And when the light, which had been scattered within the darkness, was gathered together in a single place, the Holy One, blessed be He, separated it from the darkness, as it is written, 'And God divided between the light and the darkness' (Genesis I,4)—and then the light was visible.... And darkness remained on the *Sitra de-Smola.* . . . The *Sitra de-Smola* is Judgment, and it cannot exist without the help of the Right Side. . . . You must know that the world is founded upon the Side of the Feminine and that heaven is revealed on the Side of Darkness, and the lower firmament, and its descendants, and the earth and its external descendants, which is to say, its material ones. . . . And they are ruled by that side which has no shame, which does not fear Sabbath . . . and that is the prince of Esau, and therefore the Holy One, blessed be He, established this world on the Side of the Female. . . . And you should know that in order for things to have existence and success and blessing within them, arousal must come from the Side of the Feminine, and this is the *Sitra de-Smola*. . . . And the reason is that the light was hidden within the darkness, and before the world was created the darkness reigned. As it is written, 'And the earth was confusion and darkness was over the abyss' (Gen. 1:2). The spirits of all the polluted Sides, both the spiritual and the material, came from the Sides of Darkness, and from the Side of the Light which was hidden within the darkness came all of the Side of Purity and Sanctity.[33]

The distinction between the sides of darkness and light has a mythical-dualistic character, and the history of this idea, accompanied by a high degree of personification, receives extensive interpretation in the book; this interpretation is intended to decipher the secret of existence. According to this view, the priority of evil in relationship to good left its mark upon all of existence, the meaning of which required clarification from the standpoint of divine intention. The author, influenced by the Zohar,[34] describes in a precise way the primordial partnership between evil and good, stating that evil is like the outer shell *(qelipa)* of good: "The evil was the *qelipa* of the Side of Purity before the world was created . . . [and also] the light [emerged from] the darkness and all of the *qelipin* were enlarged with its marrow [from within] and the *qelipa* has no virtue except for the marrow within it which is enlarged with the *qelipa*."[35]

The relationship between impurity and purity, then, is like the relation between a shell and the nut. Just as the shell precedes the nut, so, too, evil precedes good. The reign of evil in the world is also based on this principle; evil rules over everything that is external or is a shell. The *Sitra Ahra* (the 'Other Side' or 'Evil One') strove to maintain this situation, both because sanctity is the source of its own being, and also because of its dominion over sanctity. However, the Holy One, blessed be He, did not take a favorable view of this connection between the *Sitra Ahra* and the *Sitra de-Kedusha*,[36] and so He separated them:

Therefore He parted and separated the Side of Darkness from the Side of Light, and 'One opposite the other did God make' (Eccl. 7:14)—and He placed names and epithets upon them, comparing them to the Side of Holiness, to flatter them, like "another god," "other gods," so that they would not be resentful of the Side of Purity, and He placed hostility between the Polluted Side and the Side of Purity to prevent a mating between them.[37]

However, the effort to separate holiness from impurity was unsuccessful because of the sin of the first man. The latter upset the equilibrium between good and evil, succumbed to the *Sitra Ahra* and increased

to a significant degree the dominion of evil over good.[38] Nor was the
Sitra Ahra reconciled with the decree of separation, and has sought since
then to restore the original state of affairs, both by accusation against
the *Sitra de-Kedusha,* with the intention of punishing it and thus restoring the *Sitra de-Kedusha* to the dominion of the *Sitra Ahra,* and also by
efforts to transfer the Side of Sanctity to its own control, by means of
ruses as well as by accepting its portion of the commandments:

> Therefore the *Sitra Ahra,* because he knows that all of the honor which he has
> in the upper realms is granted to him because of the purity which was removed
> from his Side, pursues the Side of Purity like an ape after human beings . . . and
> the *Sitra Ahra* has more desire for the [commandment concerning the] scapegoat,
> offered by the seed of Jacob on Yom Kippur, than for all the crowns and all the
> sacrifices which all the powers of Edom and Ishmael offer to him. And he derives
> more enjoyment from the [obligation of] "final washing" of the Children of
> Jacob [the ritual ablution before grace after meals] than from all the water in
> the world.[39]

THE STRUGGLE BETWEEN GOOD AND EVIL
AND THE JEWISH PEOPLE

The main arena of struggle between impurity and sanctity is the history
of the Jewish people. The entire discussion is set within the framework
of a historiosophical-mythical interpretation of the Bible, which turns
the whole biblical narrative into the story of the close affinity between
sanctity and impurity, on the one hand, and the myth of the ongoing
struggle between the forces of impurity and those of sanctity, on the
other. The guiding principle is "just as is done below in the nether
regions, so too is it done above in the upper regions."[40] The war of
Abraham against the four kings, the battle of the Red Sea, and the wars
of Moses against the Midianites are all interpreted as wars of sanctity
against impurity: "You should know that as war was aroused in the
netherland of corporeality by the four kings against the five, likewise it
was aroused between the *qelipot* of the Polluted Side and . . . the Side of
Holiness and Purity, which are higher spheres, and this is hinted in the
verse, as it is written, 'And these kings who ruled in the Land of Edom
before the kingship of the king of the Israelites' (Gen. 36:31). . . . Here
you clearly have before you that all of these wars were so that the Right
Side (i.e. Side of Holiness) might rule over the *Sitra de-Smola* and over
the Polluted Side."[41]

The author presented a dialectical system founded upon the tension between the two tendencies in the relations between good and evil—the initial divine decree to separate good and evil, which brought about the creation of a powerful dualism; and second, the strong attraction between the *Sitra Ahra* and the *Sitra de-Kedusha,* which led to the union of sanctity and impurity.

In forging a dualistic worldview, which sees existence as divided into two realms that are at war with each other, the author of *Galya Raza* was greatly influenced by the Zohar's conception of evil. The author of the Zohar viewed evil as a system of very powerful forces, precisely parallel to that of the forces of sanctity, and active both in the upper and nether realms.[42] The author of *Galya Raza* added a historical interpretation to the Zohar's conception. For example, he introduced the idea of "the Upper Tribunal," before which the powers of impurity and sanctity are judged, a concept intended to emphasize the subjection of evil to the divine dominion; it thus served to qualify the absolutely independent action of evil by creating an authority before which the conflict of the two adversaries for the fate of the Jewish people is decided.[43]

The dualistic conception that had crystallized in the Zohar became a central idea in *Galya Raza,* around which the author's historiosophical interpretation was built. However, unlike the Zohar, the crucial struggle does not take place in the world of the *Sefirot,* but rather on the stage of history. The struggle is between the Jewish people, who are called upon to separate good from evil, and the *Sitra Ahra,* which strives with all its might to return matters to their original state and to envelop sanctity within impurity: "And its desire and wish is always to bring itself near to the Side of Purity."[44]

The division is not unequivocal, nor can the tendencies be separated clearly, because man's sin has brought about the joining of impurity and sanctity and caused the *Sitra Ahra* to gain control over humanity, implicating himself in all of human affairs: "You should know that the sin of the first man caused all of this, that the serpent ruled over him and over all flesh."[45] Since then the dominion of evil has been expressed in prohibited union between Jewish men and foreign women, which is reflected in biblical narrative and in the chain of reincarnation, as I shall explain below.

THE SYMBIOTIC RELATIONSHIP BETWEEN EVIL AND HOLINESS

According to the view of the author of *Galya Raza*, the *qelipa* (evil shell) and *Kedusha* (sanctity) cling to one another throughout existence, from the foreskin that clings to the covenant of circumcision to the names of the impure animals that are found among the heavenly creatures in the heavenly chariot, or *Merkabah*. This close bond, which derives primarily from the need to preserve an equilibrium between the two forces in order to maintain the existence of the world, bears significant metaphysical meaning, for it expresses God's hidden intention: "And another clear proof that the Holy One, blessed be He, desired to give a place for the grip of the Evil Side and the Outer Ones, as it is said, 'And you shall see proof in the foreskin', which comes clinging to the covenant of circumcision that hints at the organ that is circumcised, known as the foundation." [46] The combination of impurity and sanctity is presented by the author of *Galya Raza* from two standpoints: that of the *qelipa*, which views an approach to the realm of sanctity as a *return* of existence to its correct state; and that of God, which explains the cleaving together of sanctity and impurity from a broad perspective, seeing in the various stages of history the possibility of contending against the *qelipa* by means of its own powers, [47] that is, with holy subterfuge.

The ethos demanded of individuals in view of this conception of the nature of evil and its affinity with sanctity is twofold—to assist in the struggle of sanctity to expunge impurity, on the one hand, and to appease and placate the *Sitra Ahra* and flatter it, on the other. The struggle is a subtle one, hinted at in the verse (Isaiah 49:17), "Your destroyers and they that made you waste will come out of you," which is applied to the *Sitra Ahra*. That is to say, victory over the *qelipa* and the overthrow of the *Sitra Ahra* is achieved by means of ruses and cunning and the use of their own forces against themselves: "And we find that the impure *qelipa* is annulled by its very own forces, and so must it be that truly its own forces will kick their master and nullify it and its impurity." [48] As part of the second aspect of the ethos of the battle against the *Sitra Ahra,* an individual is commanded to be scrupulous of its honor, for evil cannot possibly be altogether overcome before the redemption, "and also one must be cautious not to be contemptuous of the *qelipot* and their powers, for we have found that the Holy One, blessed be He, ordered Moses and Aaron to honor Pharaoh [the earthly symbol of the qelipa]," [49] and also to pretend and flatter and conceal man's intention of fighting against the *Sitra Ahra:* "And for this reason one must give some flattery to the *Sitra Ahra,* so that it does not see that we wish its nullification." [50]

The value of flattering, appeasing, and placating the *Sitra Ahra,* deriving from recognition of its might, and granting it some part of the worship of God in order to bribe it and silence it, was already known in kabbalistic thought.[51] The author of the Zohar, following Nachmanides,[52] interpreted the practice of certain commandments as a bribe to the *Sitra Ahra,* although the Zohar's justification of such appeasement arises from an argument opposite to that of our author. According to the Zohar, the dominion of the *Sitra Ahra* came from sanctity, and because its dominion is in accordance with the will of God, it too is entitled to its share of sanctity.[53]

The author of *Galya Raza* expanded the scope of the struggle between sanctity and the forces of evil and combined the tradition of the Zohar with his own original interpretation of it, thereby opening the way for mythical aspects of the conception of the commandments, as he proclaimed: "On this matter the entire Torah is founded"!

And the world [i.e., people] honors the *qelipa* for the fruit that dwells within it, as one honors a dog because of its master, and likewise the Torah commanded that honor and flattery be given to the *Sitra Ahra,* because of the purity which was hidden within it before the world was created.[54]

. . . Also, when He gives them the name of "god like other gods," "another god," and the like, all of this flatters the *Sitra Ahra* so that it will not accuse the children of Jacob. . . . Therefore it is proper to flatter them, and hence we see the reason why the Holy One, blessed be He, placed names of animals and beasts and fowl on His *Merkabah*[55] and a man to ride upon it, to show that all of them were created for man and to serve him; and just as we see that the Holy One, blessed be He, ordered us in the Torah regarding Azazel and the slaughter of sacrifices in the north, and the portions offered on the altar, and the fat which is burnt all night,[56] in order to flatter them, so it is all the more necessary that we be cautious not to do anything to divulge that we wish to nullify this power, as it is written, 'Thou shalt not muzzle an ox in its threshing' (Deut. 25:4). Therefore our Sages of blessed memory ordained in the blessing of thanksgiving that we bow down as we say "we thank" to show that we do not wish to vanquish them. . . . And in this way they will not accuse us, and blessed is He who gave us the Torah of truth and warned us to keep separate from them and from the shells of their shells and to purify ourselves and our foods and our clothing and our houses with the prohibition against mixing linen and wool and with the *mezuza,* so that no reason will be found for our impurity, and they will not rule over us. And on this matter the entire Torah, with its laws and judgments, is based.[57]

The author of *Galya Raza* did not confine himself to an exegetical generalization, but rather proposed a systematic explanation of the reasons for the commandments, which stated that for the most part they were given in order to flatter the *Sitra Ahra.* This flattery is meant to separate the forces of evil from holiness: "For the secrets of the sacrifices and the secret of meat and milk and the secret of impurity and purity and most of the negative and positive commandments fit into this order to flatter it to its own harm, and a word to the wise is sufficient;"[58] "and if you observe precisely you will find that in all of the commandments the Holy One, blessed be He, left a small corner portion to flatter him so that he shall not accuse the sons of Jacob."[59]

Galya Raza reveals a marked tendency to personify the forces of evil. Elsewhere in kabbalistic literature it would be difficult to find long dialogues in the first person between Samael and God concerning the struggle between the forces of evil and sanctity, such as those found in this work.[60] Intimations of a line of thought interpreting the biblical narrative as a war between the forces of good and evil can be found earlier in kabbalistic literature, and the clear tendency in the Zohar, under the influence of the circle of Rabbi Jacob Ha-Cohen and Rabbi Isaac Ha-Cohen, to personify the forces of evil and to interpret the biblical story as hinting at the battles between evil forces and sanctity, doubtless had a decisive influence on the author.[61] Nevertheless, it does not appear that this tendency had previously been accorded primary significance as part of a comprehensive interpretation intended to explain both the meaning of the commandments as well as the fundamental meaning of Jewish history.

This mode of thought reached its peak with the formation of the doctrine of metempsychosis in *Galya Raza,* which was influenced to some extent by earlier kabbalistic sources, but which based its essential contentions on visionary revelations, dreams, and illuminations, as described earlier.

Metempsychosis is presented here as a general axiom applying to all existence. But with respect to the Jewish people it is a law interpreted as a *temporary punishment* imposed for the sake of eternal grace. This punishment was imposed by the celestial tribunal and is carried out by the *Sitra Ahra,* while each of the two contending sides perceive a different aspect of it. In the war between the *Sitra Ahra,* represented by Samael, and the *Sitra de-Kedushah,* represented by the Jewish people, the two parties adopt various tactics: Samael attempts to compel Sanctity to approach it, and to that end he tries to entice the children of Jacob to sin so that he can punish them by reincarnating the sinners as animals subject to his dominion. At the end of the process they will be sacrificed, so that he will be able to enjoy their flesh.

The Side of Holiness, by contrast, wages a war of holy subterfuge and artifice, deceiving Samael by means of the union and marriage of great Jews with foreign women, the transposing of the souls of the reincarnated, and the allocation of portions of the commandments to appease and distract the accuser of Israel. The powers in struggle are not evenly matched, because after Adam's sin, Samael received dispensation from the heavenly tribunal to participate in the marital unions of the Side of Holiness, and so he received part of all its progeny on the feminine side, as the female element of existence derives from the *Sitra Ahra.*

The division into masculine and feminine elements is explained by the dualistic conception presented in the book. Existence is divided into right and left, which are parallel to male and female, light and darkness, *Hesed* and *Din.* The light is further divisible into inner and external light. On the left side, the side of the harsh mode of *Din* (Judgment), the female world stands within darkness, which is also divided into inner darkness and outer darkness. From the outer darkness were created the factions of impurity, vermin, crawling things, and evil spirits. From the inner darkness were created the nations of the world. In contrast, from the outer light were created the sons of Jacob, in cooperation with *"Sitra denukba dehoshekh penimi"* (the Female Side of Inner Darkness), "for He who decrees, the Holy One, blessed be He, has decreed that the inner darkness, which is the aspect of harsh Judgment, will enter a union with the aspect of mercy in the entire act of creating man." [62]

SITRA AHRA AND THE QUESTION OF PROHIBITED MARRIAGES

As against the tendency of sanctity to separate itself from impurity, the forces of the *Sitra Ahra,* as noted above, strive to unite with sanctity and pollute it by marital unions and progeny, which will tempt the Children of Israel to abandon their God. This line of thought is meant to explain why many of the heroes of the Bible illicitly married foreign women and became "sons-in-law of the *Sitra Ahra.*"[63]

The verse, "For Cain shall be raised seven-fold" (Gen. 4:24), is interpreted by the author of *Galya Raza* as "seven drops of impurity from the females of Samael,"[64] who are the seven daughters of Satan who were reincarnated as foreign women, and married to the Children of Israel to make them deviate from the right path. These include Rebecca, Laban's sister, who married Isaac; "Tamar who came to confound the kingdom of Judah by incest;" Zipporah the Midianite who married Moses; Ruth the Moabite who married Boaz; the Philistine women who married Samson; the two sisters, Laban's daughters, who married Jacob; the daughter of Putiel who married Elazar; the wife of Potiphar who wanted to seduce Joseph; and Rahab, who was matched with Joshua."[65]

Samael's intentions to make the Jewish leaders deviate from their God by means of marriages with his daughters, to subject the realm of holiness to his dominion, are frequently described in emotional language in the book:

And now I must reveal and proclaim the evil of Samael and the thoughts he thought to accuse Jacob of his doings, but the Holy One, blessed be He, repudiated his advice and in the cauldron where he planned to cook, there he was cooked. Samael thought that by the daughters of Laban, who belonged to his Side, he would vanquish Jacob. Samael thought that the daughters of Laban would seduce Jacob to follow the gods of their father, but they rebelled against their father and his gods. . . . And they and their children came to be needless thorns in his eyes, and if you look very carefully you will find that all the evil counsel which Samael took to accuse Jacob, everything worked out badly for him . . . and you shall see that what happened in Shechem and in Egypt ultimately did him no good, because the Lord watches over Israel.[66]

However, in actual fact, the *true* meaning of these marriages, which were exceedingly decisive for the fate of the Jewish people, was entirely different. The *secret* meaning of these forbidden marriages is inherent in the assumption that, for the sake of the battle against the powerful *Sitra Ahra,* one must *cooperate* with it to weaken its power from within by redirecting its own forces. Thus Satan's plan was his own undoing; the marriages that he planned in order to make the heroes of Israel change their faith became a weapon in the war against him precisely because he alone could unknowingly make the preparations for his downfall, according to the verse, "Your destroyers and they that made you waste will come out of you" (Isaiah 49:17): "Here you see why these marriages were made, to become thorns in the eyes of the *Sitra Ahra,* to use against him the verse, 'Your destroyers and they that made you waste will come out of you'—thus permission was given to him so that he himself could make the preparations for his own ill." [67]

On the historical level, the war against the *Sitra Ahra* and its minions, the nations of the world, necessitates finding an element of impurity in the warrior on the Side of Sanctity, to allow him to mediate between *Hesed* and *Din,* because everyone who battles against evil must have some affiliation with evil itself. Only thus can one vanquish Satan with his own arms:

For the Holy One, blessed be He, desired that when some king or hero arises to take revenge upon the nations, [that there should be] some bond or connection between the nations of the world and the king, who must be of the seed of Israel, in order to fulfill, "Your destroyers and they that made you waste will come out of you"—and you may see some proof in Joshua, who took Rahab the harlot as his wife, in order to overthrow the power of the thirty-one kings, and also Samson, who married foreign wives so as to overthrow the many Philistines, and also David, who is descended from Ruth the Moabite in order to overthrow the nations. And it is known to those who possess wisdom that everyone who was created to overthrow the adversaries of Israel must have some attachment to the *Sitra de-Smola.* [68]

The author of *Galya Raza* was not interested in the antinomian conclusions that could be drawn from this direction of thought, but rather in the mythical interpretation of the war between good and evil and in its historiosophical conclusions. In opposition to Samael's intention of uniting his own daughters with the sons of Israel, God transposed their souls, without the knowledge of the *Sitra Ahra,* and rather than the "seven spirits of pollution" he placed within those seven foreign women "seven pure souls to help their husbands [contend] against the Side of Pollution." [69] This substitution of souls took place by means of the reincarnation of sparks of the soul,[70] and it served as a weapon against Samael, because "the whole matter of the substitution of souls was not known to Samael, these are the secrets of metempsychosis . . . the secret of reincarnation was not known to Samael." [71]

The "holy subterfuge" was carried out by the exchange of souls, and therefore each one of the seven daughters of the *Sitra Ahra* was reincarnated in "other righteous women." Thus, by deceiving his forces from within and by foiling his plots by means of his own emissaries, the condition of "your destroyers and they that made you waste will come out of you" was fulfilled.

THE PURPOSE AND NATURE OF REINCARNATION

The crux of the war of sanctity against impurity centers around metempsychosis. The author of *Galya Raza* forged a new view regarding the meaning and purpose of reincarnation. He based his arguments on the assumption that reincarnation is not an individual punishment, but rather symbolic of the situation of the entire Jewish people, and that reincarnation is administered by the *Sitra Ahra*,[72] although, ironically, the secret of incarnation is not known to it.[73]

According to *Galya Raza*, metempsychosis applies to all existence, but regarding the Jewish people it is a means of repentance and of entry into the Garden of Eden. From an eschatological viewpoint it contains the dual aspect of *Hesed* and *Din:* "The Holy One, blessed be He, is merciful upon all things, and He effected the matter of reincarnation so that even against their wish they must repent, and so He did and does and shall do. . . . And by means of reincarnation they are refined and purified until they are cleansed of that taint, and thus merit life of the world to come."[74]

However, reincarnation has many aspects, and it varies according to its object. By decree of the *Sitra Ahra*'s tribunal, evildoers are reincarnated only three times, and if they have not become righteous, they will be returned to dust after severe punishments.[75] Those whose evil is not great, by contrast, may be reincarnated as many as a thousand times, until they repent for their sins by "refinement," "purification," and "distillation," and they complete their allotment of the six hundred and thirteen commandments,[76] which permits them to enter the Garden of Eden. With every reincarnation they rise from level to level, that is, the soul becomes elevated with Torah, good deeds, and the purging of sin:

You should know that the utter evil-doers have an allocation of reincarnations, which is only three times for a man (Job 33:29–30) and on the fourth time Israel shall not bring him back (Amos 1:3), it has no more allotment. But moderate sinners have an allotment of up to a thousand decrees of metempsychosis, as it is written, 'Punishing the iniquity of the fathers upon the children unto the third and fourth generation of those that hate me' (Ex. 20:5)—these are the utter evil-doers. 'And showing mercy to thousands of generations of those that love me and keep my commandments' (Ex. 20:6). But of the utter evil-doers it has been said, 'And there shall fall a thousand by your side' (Ps. 91:7), the quota of a thousand does not help them, meaning that the utter evil-doers are not worthy enough that the Holy One, Blessed be He, should take pains for them for up to a thousand generations, like the moderate ones, who rise in degree from reincarnation to reincarnation.[77]

This opinion, that reincarnation up to a thousand times is a general rule, is mentioned for the first time in the Kabbalah in *Sefer Ha-Bahir*, but it did not receive wide recognition or a central place in kabbalistic literature[78] until it was taken up by the author of *Galya Raza*. He added to this idea reincarnation into animals, as well as the transition from one seven-thousand-year cycle to another, making it into a system of purification by means of a multistaged punishment whose duration and rate are predetermined.

The reincarnation of souls in animals was already known in kabbalistic literature, but it was a doctrine that was received with reservations and presented allusively.[79] The author of *Galya Raza* was probably influenced by the daring doctrines of Rabbi Joseph of Shushan's *Sefer Taamei Ha-Mitsvot*,[80] either directly or by means of a summary of his ideas presented in Menachem Recanati's commentary on the Torah, or some other intermediary source.

Reincarnation in animals, which was taken by *Galya Raza* to a greater extreme with the inclusion of vermin and crawling things, is viewed as a dual process. On the one hand, it is a descent from the human level of existence to bestiality and a relative punishment for human transgressions, carried out both directly and indirectly by the *Sitra Ahra* following the decision of a "celestial tribunal." On the other hand, in the punishment of graded reincarnation there is a purification and gradual rise in degree from the world of animals to that of humans.

METEMPSYCHOSIS AND REDEMPTION

The historical issue of principle concern to the author of *Galya Raza* was that of exile. In an effort to clarify the true nature of exile and its underlying laws, he developed the question of metempsychosis, transforming the concept from individual punishment to the critical path for the redemption of the entire Jewish people. This entailed interpreting it as the exile of souls[81] and as a transition from history to metahistory. The author presented a comprehensive interpretation, perceiving exile as the purifying ritual bath of Jewish souls;[82] for they must be purified of the pollution of the *Sitra Ahra,* which is engraved upon their very existence. This purification takes place by means of purgative reincarnation, which is the secret of the spiritual and historical meaning of exile:

And know that the exile of Egypt and all the incidents and travails experienced by Israel, and those which they will undergo in the future, all of them are alluded to in our holy Torah. . . . The Holy One, blessed be He, told all of these secrets to Abraham when he divided the sacrificed animals (Gen. 15:10 ff.), and therefore Abraham was silent and did not make a prayer for the exile into Egypt. Nor did he say enough, for he knew that this exile was for the benefit of Israel and to save their soul from the *Sitra Ahra,* for they were delivered into its hand from time immemorial.

For all the souls that were born of Jacob until they stood at Mount Sinai were all former souls from the 974 generations that were withered in untimely fashion, and had to undergo reincarnation, and return to their original source. And thus they wandered for forty years in the desert until all of those who were born in Egypt perished, and those who went up to the Land of Israel, who were twenty years old, had the privilege of going up because they were new souls. And since the Holy One, blessed be He, did not want a single soul of Israel to be lost, it being the seed of our father Abraham, before all of these things, He wanted those who had been withered in untimely fashion to be purified and expunged of their sin, so that they would return to their origin. Thus their children would go up and inherit the land. Therefore the Holy One, blessed be He, separated the children of Israel from the nations, to be His chosen nation, and he ordered that their foreskin be circumcised.[83]

Exile was thus viewed as a complex and multiphased way to rescue the Jewish people from imprisonment by the *Sitra Ahra,* a notion based on the assumption that the Jewish people originated in the 974 generations that were seized by the *Sitra Ahra* at the dawn of time: the metahistorical transmigration of souls became a historical exile that was intended to extricate the Jewish people from the captivity of the *Sitra Ahra.*

The author of *Galya Raza* entirely condemned the common view that the 974 generations which were withered in untimely fashion, "were the souls of the wicked, and the thought occurred to the Holy One, blessed be He, to create them, and He saw that they were not worthy of being created, and they were withered in that they were wicked."[84] Instead he presented a concept based on the doctrine of the seven-thousand year cycle,[85] viewing the 974 generations as the souls of the Jewish people who passed from one seven-thousand-year cycle to another by means of reincarnation, because they had not yet managed to complete their extrication from the powers of evil.

On the basis of earlier kabbalistic ideas that regard metempsychosis as an individual punishment and explain the connection between reincarnation and levirate marriage, as well as the link between reincarnation and the fulfillment of the "garment of righteousness" of 248 commandments, the author of *Galya Raza* proposed a new interpretation of the doctrine of the seven-thousand-year cycle and the meaning of the 974 generations. In doing so he sought to invest metempsychosis with historical-national meaning, and, as we have seen, to interpret exile as a process of purification.

This original historiosophical point of view interpreted the struggle waged between the Jewish people and their oppressors as the rescue of the souls of the 974 generations from the dominion of the *Sitra Ahra*. It infused the experience of exile with new meaning by elevating all the trials and tribulations of exile from the status of arbitrary historical circumstances to a process invested with both religious and eschatological meaning. Exile was transformed into a stage in the struggle between the *Sitra Ahra* and the *Sitra de-Kedushah*.

Galya Raza was not content, however, with a historiosophical explanation of the biblical narrative as the story of the purification and reincarnation of the Jewish people in the past; he also pondered the realm of metahistory. He stated emphatically that "the Holy One, blessed be He, acted in this manner during every single seven-thousand-year cycle to benefit the Jews," meaning that the Jewish people experience reincarnation from one seven-thousand-year cycle to another. Metempsychosis is God's "weapon" to rescue the people from the hands of the *Sitra Ahra* and to bring them into the world to come upon the completion of their purification. Thus, the transmigration of souls is a transition from exile to eternity.

The obverse of the enigma of exile concerns the end of days and its timing within the context of metempsychosis, a subject with which *Galya Raza* dealt extensively. In order to clarify this issue, he delved deeply into the metaphysical meaning of the measurements, proportions, and numbers associated with the *mikveh,* or ritual bath. He concluded that all the earthly, physical quantities actually refer to *celestial* dimensions. Thus, for example, the 960 *logs* or measures of water needed for a ritual bath become the 960 limbs of *Shiur Koma,* the measurements of the Divine Structure according to ancient esoteric traditions. (The Hebrew word *mikveh* is composed of the same letters as *Koma.*) The extent of the process of reincarnation is deduced from the measurements of the ritual bath because metempsychosis is spiritual purification in the ritual bath of history, as a counterpart of physical purification in an earthly ritual bath.

From the measurements of the ritual bath the author of *Galya Raza* also derives a picture of the end of days based on the transition from history to metahistory. At the end of the process of metempsychosis, in the year 5760, after the fulfillment of six cycles of 960 years, 240 years before the end of the present six-thousand-year cycle, the order of creation will change. The world will be covered with water, and only the Land of Israel will remain, which will float upon the water and pass the seventh thousand years through the River Fire known as *Nahar Dinur.* The righteous individuals who have completed their "garment" of good deeds will rise to the rank of "Men" and enter the Garden of Eden, while those who have not managed to complete their celestial garments will continue to undergo the process of reincarnation and purification.

The end of the process of metempsychosis and the transformation of the purified into the people of Israel on high, who are called the hosts of the *Shekhina,* angels, or "Men," represent the end of history and the completion of the victory of holiness over the *Sitra Ahra.* This victory is expressed in the rescue of the Jewish people from the dominion of the *qelipa* and its transition from exile to eternity, or from the seven-thousand-year cycle of *Din* (Judgment) to that of *Hesed* (Mercy).

NOTES

1. See G. Scholem, "Ha-Gilgul," in *Pirkei Yesod Be-Havanat Ha-Kabbala U-Semaleha* (Hebrew, Jerusalem, 1976), pp. 337–349 (henceforth: Scholem, "Ha-Gilgul"); see also idem, *Major Trends in Jewish Mysticism* (New York, 1941), pp. 278–284.
2. Scholem, "Ha-Gilgul," p. 339; idem, "Shtar Ha-Hitkashrut Shel Talmidei Ha-Ari," *Zion* 5 (Hebrew, 1940), pp. 134–140.
3. On *Sefer Galya Raza* and its author, see G. Scholem, "Ha-Mekubal R. Avraham Ben Eliezer Ha-Levi," *Kiryat Sefer* II (Hebrew, 1935), pp. 119–124; idem, *Shabbetai Zvi* (Hebrew, Tel Aviv, 1957), pp. 47–49; idem, *Kabbala* (Jerusalem, 1975), pp. 73–74; idem, "Divrei Mavo Le-Maamar

Mishra Kitrin le-R. Avraham Ben Eliezer Ha-Levi" (Hebrew, Jerusalem, 1978, re-edited by M. Beit-Arieh), p. 19; I. Tishby, "Ha-Pulmus Al Sefer Ha-Zohar Ba-Meah Ha-Shesh-Esreh Be-Italia," *Perakim*, I, Yearbook of the Schocken Institute (Hebrew, Jerusalem, 1957–58), pp. 156–157; Rachel Elior, *Galya Raza*, critical edition, Research Projects of the Institute of Jewish Studies of the Hebrew University in Jerusalem, Publications Series I (Jerusalem, 1981). Henceforth Elior, *Galya Raza*.

4. See M. Steinschneider, "Maamar Al R. Avraham Ha-Levi," *Ozar Nehmad*, II (Hebrew, 1857), pp. 153–156; G. Scholem, *Maamar Mishra Kitrin*, p. 19; the introduction by R. Hayim Turar of Maahalov to *Galya Raza* (Mahalov, 1812).

5. Ten manuscripts of *Galya Raza* are known to us. The most complete of these is the Oxford MS, Bodleian, Oppenheim 104 (Neubauer Catalogue 1820), henceforth MS I. It contains 344 folios, and fols. 90–174 have no parallel in any other of the manuscripts. The other manuscripts are: Oxford, Bodleian, Oppenheim 526 (Neubauer Catalogue 1753, 6) (henceforth MS II); Oppenheim 551 (Neubauer Catalogue 1742, 2); Oxford Bodleian, Oppenheim 416 (Neubauer Catalogue 1819, 1); Oxford, Bodleian, Mich. 165 (Neubauer Catalogue 1792, 2); Jerusalem 8°2135; Amsterdam—Rosenthaliana Hs. Ros 5 (186, 2) (AI 1808), Fuks-Mansfeld Catalogue, par. 215; London Jews College 199, 4 (Neubauer Catalogue, Jews College, p. 34); Uppsala Heb. 28 (Zitterstein Catalogue 28); Zurich, National Library 180 (Heidrich Catalogue 92). The work called *Galya Raza* in the Paris manuscript, Bibliothèque Nationale, Heb. 869/1 (Zuttenberg Catalogue 869) is not the *Galya Raza* under discussion here. That work is Lurianic in character, and Scholem's remarks in *Kiryat Sefer*, II (1925–1926), p. 121, n. 1, must be corrected, for they are based on an error made by Zuttenberg.

There are significant differences in the comprehensiveness of the various manuscripts and in their editing because the book was written and circulated in fascicles, as the author states. See MS I, fols. 142a, 152a. Compilers copied the fascicles in varying order, leading to the differences among the manuscripts. For a detailed discussion of the manuscripts of *Galya Raza*, see Elior, *Galya Raza*, Introduction, pp. 17–20.

6. In MS I the dates of the writing of the book are mentioned often. See, for example, fols. 113a, 118b, 140b, 146r, 149b, 166b.

7. Elior, *Galya Raza*, Introduction, pp. vii–xiv.

8. MS II, fol. 7b.

9. Zohar, I, fols. 183a–184a.

10. The numerical value of the Hebrew letters in "Galya Raza" comes to 252, and that of "Gabriel" comes to 246. When one adds to this sum the number of Hebrew letters in Gabriel's name, six, one reaches 252. The correct name of the book is *Galya Raza*, which fits that number. All of the other variants, such as *Galei Razaya* are the errors of copyists and printers.

11. Regarding dreams, visions, and Gabriel, cf. Zohar I, fols. 183a–184a. See I. Tishby, *Mishnat Ha-Zohar*, II (Hebrew, Jerusalem, 1961), p. 128.

12. MS II, fol. 64b. Cf. the printed version, Mahalov, 1812, fol. 21a; MS I, fol. 52a.

13. For examples of his dreams see MS I, fol. 150a–b; MS II, fol. 110a.

14. MS II, fol. 102b.

15. MS I, fol. 141b; cf. MS II, fol. 104b.

16. MS I, fol. 146b; cf. ibid., fol. 44a.

17. See Rachel Elior, "Ha-Vikuah al Maamad Ha-Kabbala Ba-Meah Ha-16," *Jerusalem Studies in Jewish Thought* I (Hebrew, Jerusalem, 1981), pp. 177–190.

18. MS I, fols. 111a–112a.

19. Ibid., fol. 16a; regarding the messianic tone, cf. MS II, fol. 104b.

20. See the introduction of *Minhat Yehuda* by Judah Hayat, *Maarekhet Ha-Elohut*, Ferrara, 1558 (the introduction is not paginated), and the Mantua edition of 1558, 2b. There are significant differences between the two editions of the introduction of *Minhat Yehuda*. The Ferrara edition is the complete one, while the hand of a censor, either Jewish or Christian, is evident in the Mantua edition. See I. Tishby, "Ha-Pulmus Al Sefer Ha-Zohar" (above, n. 3), p. 156. Quotations from *Maarekhet Ha-Elohut* will be presented according to the Mantua edition of 1558, unless the Ferrara edition is explicitly mentioned.

21. Cf. the introduction of R. Abraham Azulay to *Or Ha-Hama*, Jerusalem, 1876: "And from the year 5300 [= 1540] of the creation it is the most select commandment, that both elderly and young should deal with it publicly, and by virtue [of the study of Kabbalah] the messianic king shall come, and by no other virtue."

22. See Tishby, "Ha-Pulmus al Sefer Ha-Zohar" (above, n. 3), pp. 154–158.

23. "And now that we have had the privilege of seeing the books of the great *Buzina De-Nehora*, Rabbi Shimon, may he rest in peace, its secrets have been revealed, for so said Elijah of blessed memory to Rabbi Shimon, may he rest in peace, in the end of days words and elevated secrets will be revealed to you . . . and thus I made my face as bold as flint and wrote what my limited intelligence has grasped, and I became a gossip and revealer of secrets," MS I, fol. 104b.

24. The work is replete with complex and detailed calculations of the end of days. The year 1560 was to be the year of redemption, but in addition the author of *Galya Raza* stipulated many dates dealing with the revival of the dead, the advent of the messiah, the war of Gog and Magog, and various processes connected with redemption. See MS I, fols. 123a, 140b, 144b, 145a, 146a, 113a, 114a–b, 117a, 151a–b, 155b, 118b, 165b–166a, 171b, et passim.

25. Hagiga 13a–14b.

26. See *Breshit Raba*, Theodor-Albeck, eds. (Jerusalem, 1965), sec. 28, p. 263; *Seder Eliahu Rabba*, M. Ish-Shalom, ed. (Vienna, 1904), p. 9, and see the editor's comments, pp. 61, 130; *Avot De-Rabi Nathan*, Sh. Z. Shachter, ed. (New York, 1945), chap. 31, fol. 46a.

27. *Breshit Raba,* sec. 9, p. 68, and see Albeck's comments there.

28. See G. Scholem, "Kabbalot R. Yaakov Ve-R. Yitzhak Bnei R. Yaakov Ha-Cohen," *Maddaei Ha-Yahadut,* II (Hebrew, 1927), pp. 183–195, 249–250.

29. Zohar I, 154b; 177a; 223b; II, 34a, 176b, 242b; III, 61a–b, 128a, 135a, et passim. On the connection found in the Zohar between the doctrine of *qelipot* and that of the worlds that were destroyed, see Scholem, *Kabbalot R. Yaakov* (above, n. 28), p. 195; I. Tishby, *Mishnat Ha-Zohar,* I (Hebrew, Jerusalem, 1957), pp. 138, 150, 296. Generally speaking, the terms *qelipa* or *qelipot, Sitra Ahra,* and *Sitra De-Smola* (the Sinister Side) are synonymous expressions for the forces of evil.

30. See *Sefer Ha-Bahir,* R. Margaliot, ed. (Jerusalem, 1978), paragraphs 57, 58, 195, which connect the doctrine of the soul and the matter of metempsychosis with the interpretation of the verse, "The promise He gave for a thousand generations," to the 974 generations, on the one hand, and to the idea of construction and destruction, on the other. See the interpretation of *Or Ha-Ganuz* ("The Hidden Light") to *Sefer Ha-Bahir* in paragraph 58, and see Scholem, *Pirkei Yesod,* pp. 311–312.

31. See *Maarekhet Ha-Elohut,* Mantua, 1558, fol. 89a–b: "And it is possible that when the thought of nobility, grace, and fear was raised, that is the worlds which He built and destroyed, that the generations which were to be and be created in them also rose up with them . . . and perhaps it was about these generations that they taught that they were withered in untimely fashion, these are the 974 generations." See also the exegesis of R. Yehuda Hayat, as well as *Sefer Ha-Temunah,* Lemberg, 1892, fol. 41a, in the words of the commentator and the comprehensive comments of R. Moses Ben Jacob of Kiev, *Shushan Sodot,* Koretz, 1784, fol. 57.

32. MS II, fol. 102b, and cf. *Minhat Yehuda, Maarekhet Ha-Elohut,* fol. 115b.

33. MS II, fols. 12b–13a, 16a–17a.

34. Zohar II, fol. 108b. Cf. I, 19b–20a; III, 227a–b, and see I. Tishby, *Mishnat Ha-Zohar,* I, pp. 292–293.

35. MS II, fol. 34b. The additions follow MS I, fol. 10b.

36. "Know that the Holy One, blessed be He, originally included the *Sitra Ahra* with the *Sitra De-Tahara* as when He made the light with darkness and afterward He separated them into two domains", MS I, fol. 126b.

37. MS II, fol. 17b.

38. Ibid., fol. 17b; and cf. ibid., fol. 27a: "All the pollution that comes into the world is from the side of the primeval serpent and from its powers, and the beginning of its expansion was with Eve, for she is the mother of all life, and from her it spread to Adam and to Cain, and to all the generations until today, and the dominion of the serpent is only upon the physical garment, which is the shell *(qelipa)* of the spiritual, since it itself is the *qelipa* which was created from darkness which was the *qelipa* of the light, and because of that it was made to rule over the external *qelipot* . . . and from then on Adam's sin caused its pollution to expand upon the sons of Adam and to rule over them."

39. MS II, fol. 31a. On the matter of the scapegoat and the *Sitra Ahra,* see *Pirkei Rabbi Eliezer,* chap. 46; Zohar I, 174b; III, 102a. Regarding the latter water and grace after meals, see Zohar II, 154b.

40. MS II, fol. 103a.

41. Ibid., fol. 102b.

42. For a detailed examination of the conception of evil in the Zohar, see I. Tishby, *Mishnat Ha-Zohar,* I, pp. 287–307.

43. Perhaps the distinction among the three domains—good, evil, and the celestial tribunal that decides between them—was influenced indirectly by *Sefer Yetzira,* which proposed an equal hierarchical status for good and evil beneath the divinity, which decides between them. See *Sefer Yetzira,* I, Mishnah 6: "Depth of good, depth of evil . . . One Lord, God the Faithful King, rules over them all." See also ibid. regarding the determination between opposing elements.

44. MS II, fol. 30b.

45. MS II, fol. 31b. The rule of the serpent over man is dual—it has hold over man's body, which was created from dust, "which is the bread of the serpent," and the sin of the first man caused the serpent to rule over him, because after the sin he wore "tunics of leather, which were from the serpent, which is the *qelipa.*" See MS II, fol. 27a.

46. MS II, fol. 35b.

47. Ibid., fols. 35b–37b.

48. Ibid., fol. 29b. On the attitude of the Zohar, see Y. Liebes, "Sefer Tzadik Yesod Olam—Mitos Shabbetai," *Daat* 1 (Hebrew, 1978), p. 87, n. 88.

49. MS II, fol. 36a.

50. *Galya Raza,* Mahalov, 1812, fol. 12b; cf. MS II, fols. 35b–36a.

51. See Todros Abulafia, *Shaar Ha-Razim,* MS Munich 209, fol. 89a: *Otzar Ha-Kavod,* Warsaw, 1879, fol. 19b.; MS Munich 103 of *Otzar Ha-Kavod,* fol. 90b—on the abolition of sacrifices in the future: "The deficiency above is the small quantity of emanation which comes from the source of the upper justice, and atonement must be in order to mollify the Emanator and to fill the deficiency." For a full expression of the matter, see G. Scholem, "Le-Heker Kabbalat R. Yitzhak Ben Yaakov Ha-Cohen," *Tarbiz* II (1931), p. 278, n. 3; Zohar I, 113b–114a; II, 237a; and also I, 64b, 65a. And see I. Tishby, *Mishnat Ha-Zohar* I, pp. 290–292. Also see R. Joseph from Shushan, *Taamei Ha-Mitzvot,* MS Cambridge Dd 4.2/6, Mitzvah 21 of the negative commandments: "Know that the kid alludes to the sects of impurity when the primeval serpent came to cast pollution upon the celestial Eve, and several sects of angels of destruction were created, the chief of which is called 'Kid,' and against him the Jews sent one scapegoat to Azazel on Yom Kippur . . . and therefore the Torah said regarding the blessing of Jacob . . . that his mother said to him, take me two goat kids from there . . . to bribe the celestial kid and the terrestrial kid, as the reason for the sacrifices, which is bribery to the sects of pollution." Cf. MS Paris, 850, 3, p. 190, the twenty-second of the negative commandments: MS Jerusalem 8°597, fol.

153a: positive commandment no. 44: "And the sheep is bribery to Samael and his hosts, so that he will not prosecute from the Holy One, blessed be He, to receive our offering." Ibid., commandment 47 (to make an additional sacrifice on the New Year): "And therefore we add a sacrifice in the commandment of our Father in heaven, as we were ordered, and to mollify powers in the world so that they do not come to intervene between Israel and their Father in heaven when the world is being judged, we add a sacrifice to mollify the powers in the world . . . and literally the Yom Kippur service is to mollify Samael and his hosts and powers in the world." See below in this source and cf. also *Sefer Ha-Temunah*, Lemberg 1892, fol. 49a; and *Shushan Sodot*, Koretz, 1784, fol. 19b: "The secret of the prohibition against waiting three hours"; fols. 18b, 47a: "The spilling of blood during circumcision appeases them and silences their tumult . . . and when they see that they have a part in the commandment, the jaw of every evil clenches," and see elsewhere in that work.

52. The idea that several commandments are to be seen as the struggle against demonic powers is found in the writings of Nachmanides. He proposes this explanation for the commandment of the scapegoat (Lev. 16:8), the red heifer (Num. 19:2), the broken-necked heifer (Deut. 21), and the purification of a leper (Lev. 16:53). See, for example, his commentary on the Torah, H. D. Shavel, ed. (Jerusalem, 1960), pp. 84, 88–91, 95–96, 267, 439–440. Cf. the remarks of Todros Abulafia, MS Munich 209, fol. 89a, who terms the commandments of the red heifer, the scapegoat, the leper's bird, and the broken-necked heifer "commandments whose worship is external." See also *Otzar Ha-Kavod*, Warsaw, 1879, fol. 19b. See also Zohar I, 113b–114a, 190a–b; II, 184b–185a, 237a.

53. "For even though this side is only that of pollution, it glows around it, and a person does not have to expel it. What is the reason? Because it glows around it. It has the side of holiness of faith, and one does not need to treat it as an infamy. And therefore it must be given a part in the side of the holiness of faith." Zohar II, 81b, quoted from the translation in I. Tishby, *Mishnat Ha-Zohar*, I, p. 301. Cf. Zohar II, 237b.

54. MS II, fol. 30b.

55. On the presence of the names of impure animals on the Merkabah, see question 16 of R. Judah Hayat and the answer of R. Joseph Alkashtil in G. Scholem, "Le-Yediat Ha-Kabbalah Bi-Sefarad Erev Ha-Gerush," *Tarbiz* 24 (1956), pp. 177, 203–204.

56. Regarding the connection between the offering of sacrifices and bribery and reconciliation, whether of the *Sitra Ahra* or of *Midat Ha-Din*, see Nachmanides' commentary on the Torah, Lev. 16:8, 17:7; Nachmanides, *Torat Ha-Temima* in *Kitvei Ramban*, H. D. Shavel, ed. (Jerusalem, 1963), pp. 165–166); *Sefer Ha-Temunah*, fol. 65a, of the book, fol. 68b of the commentator's remarks; Todros Abulafia, *Otzar Ha-Kavod*, Warsaw, 1879, Masekhet Shabbat, 19b; R. Joseph from Shushan, *Taamei Ha-Mitzvot*, MS Jerusalem 8°597, fol. 153a: Negative Commandments, no. 22 (Thou shalt

not cook a kid in its mother's milk); Joseph Gikatilia, *Shaarei Ora*, Jerusalem, 1960, fol. 74b–75a; and see the commentary there by Matitya Delacarte on "the stuffing of the mouth of the prosecutors." See also R. Z. J. Werblowsky, *Joseph Karo* (Philadelphia, 1965), p. 254.

57. MS II, fol. 35b–36a, and cf. *Shushan Sodot*, fol. 19b.
58. MS I, fol. 128a.
59. MS II, fol. 31a. And compare the words of Joseph Karo, *Maggid Meisharim*, Vilna, 1879, fol. 34a: "The entire endeavor is to drive away the polluted side from the holy side, and this is the secret of all the commandments."
60. See, for example, MS II, fol. 92a–b; ibid., fols. 17b–18a.
61. See G. Scholem, "Le-Heker Kabbalat R. Yitzhak Ben Yaakov Ha-Cohen," *Tarbiz* 2 (1931), p. 280.
62. Ibid., fol. 67b.
63. MS II, fol. 92a. On this question, see G. Scholem, *Shabbetai Zvi* (Tel-Aviv, 1957), pp. 48–49.
64. MS II, fol. 144a.
65. On the seven daughters of Satan and their reincarnations, see also MS II, fols. 68a–b, 70a, 96b–97b, 144b. MS I, fols. 89a, 105b–106a, 111a–b.
66. MS II, fol. 128b.
67. Ibid., fol. 68b.
68. Ibid., fol. 70a, and cf. Liebes (above, n. 48), p. 76, n. 21.
69. MS II, fol. 68b.
70. On the doctrine of the sparks of the soul, see Scholem, "Ha-Gilgul," p. 325.
71. MS II, fol. 68b; MS I, fol. 125b.
72. MS II, fol. 42b.
73. MS II, fol. 129b.
74. Ibid., fol. 6a; and cf. MS I, 133b: "The lovers of God, for of them it is said, 'And he does righteously to the thousands of those who love Him,' and those who observe His commandments are reincarnated until the thousandth generation . . . and in each and every reincarnation, when they come, they increase Torah and good deeds," and cf. Scholem, "Ha-Gilgul," p. 320. See *Sefer Ha-Temunah*, fol. 16a.
75. MS I, fol. 122b. Reincarnation just three times, based on the verse in Job 33:29–30, is viewed by most Kabbalists as a general reincarnation and not that of the wicked. See Scholem, "Ha-Gilgul," p. 321. The author of *Galya Raza* argued, by contrast, that the number of possible reincarnations for mediocre people is not limited, because it was God's intention to benefit His creatures and bring them to the world to come, whereas the triple reincarnation, which offers no possibility of purification and entry into the Garden of Eden, is the lot of the wicked.
76. See, on the garment of the 613 commandments, G. Scholem, "Levush Ha-Neshamot Ve-Haluka De-Rabanan," *Tarbiz* 24 (1955), pp. 290–306.
77. MS I, fol. 122b, and cf. ibid., 133b.
78. On the question of the application of reincarnation and its various durations, see Scholem, "Ha-Gilgul," pp. 320–321.

79. On reincarnation in animals, see R. Joseph from Shushan, *Taamei Ha-Mitzvot*, MS Cambridge, Dd. 4.2/6, Positive Commandment 40, fol. 307a; Commandment 51 (erroneously written 61), fol. 319b. Negative Commandment, Jerusalem MS 8°597, Commandment 16 (Not to muzzle an ox while it is threshing), fol. 145b; Commandment 17, fol 146b; Commandment 19 (Not to eat with blood), fol. 149b; Commandment 37, fol. 173a, et passim. See also, *Sefer Ha-Temunah*, fol. 39a–b, in the work and the commentary; fol. 41a–b, in the commentary; fols. 44a, 66b; R. Menachem Rekanati, *Perush Ha-Torah Al Derekh Ha-Emet*, Venice 1523, Parshat Noah, s.v. "And God saw the pleasant odor"; ibid., Parshat Shemini, s.v. "And some of the recent Kabbalists believe in the reincarnation of animals"; *Sefer Ha-Peliah*, Koretz, 1784, fol. 21, col. 4, and in the Pshemishl edition of 1884, fol. 31b. On the reservations of the Kabbalists regarding this doctrine, see R. Judah Hayat, *Maarekhet Ha-Elohut*, Ferrara, 1558, fol. 204b.
80. See A. Altmann, "Le-Sheelat Baaluto Shel Sefer Taamei Ha-Mitzvot Ha-Meyuhas le-R. Yitzhak ibn Farhi," *Kiryat Sefer* 40 (1965), pp. 256–276, 405–412.
81. See *Sefer Ha-Temunah*, fols. 56b–57a.
82. Cf. *Sefer Ha-Temunah*, ibid., and the words of the commentator: "And the exile was lengthened so that the souls would be purified and come purified before the Lord. . . . And the reincarnation of souls is to purify and cleanse them of all filth which comes from the side of the harsh measure from which comes some filth, and externality, and distance, which must be purified, and therefore the soul needs a purification that will purify it in pure water which comes from the side of eternity or in a ritual bath or in the river of fire. . . . And it must be immersed after its exile and reincarnation, because the soul needs great purity. And thus exile and immersions come to the souls, so that both body and soul will be purified, since the punishment and reincarnation are a purification for them."
83. MS II, fols. 60b–61b.
84. MS I, fol. 133a.
85. On *Torat Ha-Shemitot*, the seven-thousand-year cycles, see G. Scholem, *Reshit Ha-Kabbalah* (Hebrew, Jerusalem, 1948), chap. 7; G. Scholem, *Ursprung und Anfänge der Kabbala* (Berlin, 1962), pp. 407–419.

8.

Eternality of Punishment: A Theological Controversy within the Amsterdam Rabbinate in the Thirties of the Seventeenth Century

Alexander Altmann

Isaac Aboab de Fonseca (1605–1693), the distinguished Haham of Amsterdam Jewry,[1] has long been known to be the author of an unpublished treatise *Nishmat Hayyim* dealing with reward and punishment in the hereafter.[2] There is nothing extraordinary in the fact that Aboab's literary activity included a work of this kind. His colleague Menasseh ben Israel published a work of the same title, which became rather famous, in 1651, having brought out, in 1636, his tripartite treatise on the Resurrection of the Dead in both Latin and Spanish.[3] Saul Levi Morteira, Senior Haham in the Amsterdam Rabbinate,[4] wrote a tract on Immortality,[5] and another colleague, Moses Raphael d'Aguilar, likewise produced, in manuscript, a *Tratado da immortalidade*.[6] With Carl Gebhardt,[7] one may assume that the said works were meant to combat Uriel da Costa's denial of immortality and resurrection, following up Samuel da Silva's refutation of da Costa in his *Tratado da Immortalidade* (1623).[8] In 1633 da Costa had been placed under *herem* for the second time and the fresh publicity thereby given to the apostate's views during the last phase of his life—his suicide occurred in 1640—may have aroused a sense of obligation on the rabbis' part to fortify the community's belief in the traditional tenets of immortality and resurrection.

Reprinted by permission of the American Academy for Jewish Research from *Proceedings of the American Academy for Jewish Research* 40 (1972–1973).

Isaac Aboab's *Nishmat Ḥayyim,* though composed, as we shall see, in that very period, is the document of a controversy which had caused a rift within the Amsterdam Rabbinate itself. Those primarily involved in the dispute were Aboab and Morteira; but far from being a purely theological issue, the question at stake had created a great deal of ferment in the community. As our analysis will show, the conflict embraced two distinct, though closely related, levels, one theological and the other pragmatic, and the arguments advanced on the pragmatic level were clearly inspired by Marrano sentiment. The position taken by Aboab and the faction led by him reflected a basic concern to assert the inalienable Jewishness of all Marranos. Aboab himself was a former Marrano, born a Catholic in Castro d'Aire, Portugal. After a short stay in Saint-Jean de Luz in the southwest of France, his parents had brought him, at the age of seven, to Amsterdam, where he had studied with Haham Isaac 'Uzi'el of Fez and had become Haham of the congregation Beth Israel at the age of twenty-one. Another Marrano, Abraham Herrera, a disciple of Israel Sarug, had tutored him in Kabbala.[9] The mystical theology which he had adopted supplied the intellectual armor—and the stamina—with which he defended his viewpoint.

Saul Levi Morteira, on the other hand, was of Ashkenazi descent.[10] Born in Venice about the year 1596, he seems to have studied with Leone da Modena who, in a responsum,[11] referred to him as "one dear like a son" *(kebhen yakir li).* The fact that Morteira's name does not appear on da Modena's list of disciples "reared and brought up" by him [12] can be explained by his departure from Venice in 1616 at the age of twenty before he had matured as a scholar. In contrast to Aboab, the ardent devotee of Kabbala, Morteira seems to have caught his teacher's distrust of the mystical tradition. A Talmudist of no mean quality, he showed also some inclination toward Hebrew philosophical literature.[13] It could have been no matter of surprise to the Amsterdam community to find Aboab and Morteira on opposite sides of the fence in the conflict which erupted. Their radical difference in background and outlook must have been apparent for some time.

The documents testifying to the controversy are the following texts:

Text A (Ryl. Hebrew MS. 5, fols. 1r–4v), a Letter addressed to an unspecified rabbinic court, which gives a dramatic account of events at the early stage of the dispute, and makes a strong plea for support of the traditional doctrine of eternal punishment for certain grave offences. It cites an impressive array of authorities who upheld this doctrine in the past, and it implores the Beth Din to declare the contrary view an outright heresy *(kefirā)*. The document is undated and unsigned. The missing information can be easily inferred, however, from Text B, which leaves no doubt that Text A was written prior to January, 1636; that Haham Saul Levi Morteira was its author; and that his plea was directed to the Beth Din of Venice.

Text B (Ryl. Hebrew MS. 5, fols. *5r–6r*), a Letter written in Venice during the week of Parashat Shemot in the year 5396, which corresponds to one of the first few weeks in 1636. It is signed by two well-known Venetian rabbis, viz. Shemaʿya ben Moshe di Medina, grandson of the famous Samuel di Medina (MahaRaSHDaM),[14] and ʿAzarya ben Ephraim Figo, author of the homiletical work *Binā La-ʿIttim*.[15] The Letter sought to persuade Aboab to make a public declaration renouncing his view. It contains important information on the course of the conflict beyond the stage reflected in Morteira's Letter. The fact that this document bears a date enables us to place the outbreak of the controversy in the year 1635, if not somewhat earlier. The copyist's preamble reveals Morteira's role as Aboab's opponent, as has already been noted. Incidentally, the preamble also offers a clue to the year in which Texts A and B (which are by the same hand) were copied. For the scribe refers to Shemaʿya di Medina as one still alive and to ʿAzarya Figo as one already deceased. Since Figo is known to have died on Adar 4th in 1647, and since di Medina is known to have died on Siwan 13th in 1648, the copyist must have written these texts between the spring of 1647 and the summer of 1648.[16]

Text C, Aboab's elaborate treatise *Nishmat Ḥayyim*, is extant in three copies (C[1]; C[2]; C[3]), which enables us to present a critical edition of it. C[1] is Ryl. Hebrew MS. 5, fols. *9r–31v*. C[2] and C[3] are extant in the Library of the "Portugees Israëlietisch Seminarium Ets Haim," Amsterdam, bearing the shelf marks MS. 47 C 25 and MS. 47 C 3 respectively.[17] The title page of C[1] indicates that the *Sefer Nishmat Ḥayyim* was composed *(ḥibbero)* in Amsterdam in the year 5408 (1648) and copied *(nikhtabh)* by Isaac (ben Moshe Rafa'el) de Cordova. The same date of composition is given on the title page of C[2], which was likewise copied by Isaac de Cordova, as is attested by the colophon at the end of five more pieces in the same hand. C[3] bears the title *Maḥberet Nishmat Ḥayyim*. It was copied by David Franco Mendes in 1732.[18]

C[1] excels in beauty of workmanship. The title page is superbly illuminated. It shows a crown decorated with flowers and borne aloft by cherubs, and four biblical scenes (two on each side). They depict, over captions citing Scriptural verses,[19] the following events: David dancing before the ark; Samuel annointing David; Elijah bringing down fire from heaven upon the altar; and Solomon's judgment. A crown is hovering above each scene. The four crowns are inscribed as those of Tora, royalty, priesthood and *shem tobh*. The first word on the first page of the text is set within a garland, above which cherubs hold a crown with the inscription: ʿ*Ateret tifʿeret temagenkha* (Prov. 4:9).

C^2, though less ornamental, is written with equal skill. The title page shows beneath the vocalized (!) tetragrammaton, which is placed in an aureole on top, two cherubs floating and playing trumpets, with sheets of music in front of them, and down below King David playing the harp in a kneeling posture. He is flanked by two female figures standing on a platform in front of pillars under an arched roof with yet another cherub looking down. The title in the center forms a curtain held by the female figures. The title page of C^3 has a more elaborate wording than the other two MSS. It is decorated with an all-encompassing garland, and the initial sentence on page 1 is set within an oval mirror surrounded by flowers.

The fact that according to C^1 and C^2 the treatise was composed in the year 1648 is rather puzzling. Aboab could not have composed it in Amsterdam in that year because he left Holland for Brazil in 1642 and did not return until 1654. He had accepted an invitation to become the rabbi of the prosperous Jewish community of Recife, Brazil, which was under Dutch rule at the time, and had thus become the first American rabbi. When Portuguese rebel bands started a war of liberation in 1645, he remained with his flock and endured the terrible hardships of the siege of Recife in 1646. While many Calvinist preachers returned to Holland, he did not leave until after the final conquest of the city by the Portuguese troops in 1654, when all Jews were forced to emigrate. His epic poem *Zekher ʿastiti le-nefleʾot El* is considered by the historians an important document of the events of that time.[20] The terrors through which he and his congregants had passed are also referred to in the preface to his Hebrew version of Herrera's *Puerta del Cielo (Shaʿar ha-Shamayim,* Amsterdam, 1655). There he rendered thanks to God who had brought him out of the *kur ha-brazil* (the Brazilian furnace).[21] As recorded in the minute book of the United Congregation Talmud Torah

in Amsterdam on Elul 29th, 5414/September 1654,[22] Aboab was rein-
stated as Haham, a capacity in which he served until his death at the age
of eighty-nine in 1693.[23] Since there is incontestible evidence that he
stayed in Brazil from 1642 until 1654, the title page of C^1 has to be
understood in the following sense: *Sefer Nishmat Hayyim* composed by
Rabbi Isaac Aboab in Amsterdam (i.e., while still in Amsterdam). The
indication of the year 5408 (1648) in the next line refers to the year in
which de Cordova copied the text. As we have noted above, Texts A
and B were copied about the same time. It is not clear what prompted
the copying of the documents of the controversy just then, at a time
when Aboab was no longer in Holland.

Since the year 1642, in which Aboab left Amsterdam for Brazil,
represents the *terminus ad quem* for the composition of the treatise, we
still have to settle the question when precisely the work originated. In
our view this must have happened as early as 1636 or thereabouts.
Evidence to this effect is provided by such internal criteria as a degree of
emotional involvement that testifies to a desire to score points in an
ongoing debate; the explicit references to arguments brought forward by
Morteira; and, more especially, Aboab's angry rebuttal of the charge
that, compared with his opponent, he was a mere youngster. This charge
makes sense only on the assumption that it was put forward and answered at a time when Aboab was still comparatively young, which was
the case in 1635–36. He was then just thirty years of age and Morteira
forty. A few years later the difference in age would have been considered
quite irrelevant, and the rather brash manner of Aboab's retort[24] would
have been no longer excusable on grounds of youthful impetuosity.
Hence we may take it for granted that all three documents of the
controversy belong to the same period, i.e. 1635–36.

The course of events which emerges from the documents at our
disposal was as follows. As Morteira's Letter (Text A) described the
controversy at its initial stage, a new-fangled doctrine had taken hold of
many young people in the Amsterdam community. It assured every Jew,
no matter how grave his sins, of a share of bliss in the world-to-come.
The Mishnaic phrase "All Israelites have a portion in ʿolam ha-ba' "
(Sanh. 11:1) was being bandied about as a slogan in complete disregard
of the qualifications which had been applied to it in the Mishna itself
and in the classical rabbinic sources. In the words of the thesis (hasaʿā)
which it was Morteira's avowed purpose to refute: "Whosoever is called

by the name Israelite will not suffer eternal punishment, even though he may have committed the gravest possible sins." It was the Kabbalists, Morteira pointed out, who were responsible for the spreading of this false doctrine of salvation for all Jews. He more specifically character-ized those propounding the new theology as *"maskilim* who claimed to be proficient in the science of Kabbala," and he called the new heresy "a rock of offense and stone of stumbling[25] dressed up as Kabbala." To him the classical rabbinic sources were the only "trustworthy Kabbala."

The clash between him and the partisans of unconditional salvation of all Jewish souls is portrayed in the following account of a painful experience: In the course of a sermon[26] he had quoted the passage in *Rosh Ha-Shanā* 17a which affirms the eternality of punishment in hell for such grave offenders as *minim,* informers, *apiḳororosim,* etc. He had added a host of other quotations supporting this doctrine. The result was an outburst of indignation. Among the congregants "were some of those young men who were deficient *(bilti shelemim)* in this belief, and their party lodged such vigorous complaint against me that in my an-guish I was compelled to admit as controversial a perfect doctrine of our faith which we received from our Fathers, the Prophets, the *Tanna'im* and the *Amora'im,* and which, permitting no doubt, was upheld by the more recent authorities."

The rebels, on their part, had argued that a belief pronounced as normative *(halakhā)* must have been a subject of controversy. Another argument of theirs ran as follows: "By believing in the eternality of sin and punishment we support the religion of the Christians who say that Adam's sin was eternal and that, on this account, only God, who is eternal, could make atonement for it by his incarnation and death." The fear of lending support to the Christian dogma was so pronounced on the part of the young radicals that, in Morteira's words, "they demanded of the communal leaders *(parnassey ha-waʿad)* an injunction forbidding me to give further utterance to the truth that the wicked who commit grave sins and die without repentance do incur eternal punishment." It was with the object of impressing the community leaders with the seri-ousness of their demand that the representatives of the group formulated and signed the "thesis" quoted above. Morteira's report continues: "Since they realized that they would hardly find authoritative support for this doctrine, they formulated the following additional question: Is it heresy *(kefirā)* to believe that the wicked who committed grave sins are not subject to eternal punishment?" They were hopeful, Morteira explained, that a refusal to believe in eternal punishment would not be condemned as heresy, and were determined, he assumed, to adhere to their position so long as it was not branded as outright heretical. As Text B reveals, it was the Beth Din of Venice whose verdict was to settle the issue, and Morteira's account of the situation was intended to elicit an unequivocal condemnation of the anti-eternalist doctrine.

It will have been noted that Isaac Aboab's name is not mentioned in Morteira's Letter to the Venice authorities. The villains of the piece are the radical students referred to by him as "immature disciples" *(talmidim she-lo' shimeshu kol zorekam)*. To illustrate their immaturity and the excesses of which they were capable Morteira cites the case of one who publicly declared that he wished his soul were the soul of Jeroboam son of Nebhat which had been said to be sure of a portion in the world-to-come. Aboab was not altogether free from blame for statements of this kind since the young man in question may have heard him say that according to a kabbalistic view the soul of Jeroboam was to be reincarnated in Mashiaḥ ben Yosef. Aboab's *Nishmat Ḥayyim* quotes this opinion approvingly. It was, therefore, pardonable if his enthusiastic disciple entertained messianic aspirations.

The master was obviously unable to curb the zeal of his students but he himself seems to have kept in the background, at least at the initial stage of the conflict. Otherwise the two Venetian rabbis could not have expressed even feigned surprise when, somewhat later, he publicly championed the cause of the anti-eternalists. As their Letter indicates, the rift caused by the controversy made it imperative to the community leaders to submit the case to the Venice Beth Din. Both parties entered their respective pleas supported by elaborate arguments. Text A undoubtedly represents the plea submitted by Morteira. We do not possess the plea of the other party, unless we consider Aboab's *Nishmat Ḥayyim* to be it. This is most unlikely, however, for the following reasons. First, it neither addresses itself to any Beth Din, nor does it ask for a verdict. It constitutes a *pesak*, not a *she'elā* or a plea. Second, its length is that of a full-fledged polemical treatise. Third, it is so replete with personal references to himself—mentioning as it does his youthful age, his teacher Herrera, his attachment to Lurianic Kabbala—that the two Venetian rabbis, in their letter to him, could not have pretended to have been ignorant of his role in the conflict. We must therefore assume that the plea submitted by the radical group was a document now lost, in the drafting of which Aboab was involved but which was different in many respects from the treatise launched by him shortly afterwards, though not committed to print.

As Text B informs us, the Amsterdam lay leaders sent the documents of the case not direct to the Beth Din of Venice but to the old and venerable Abraham Aboab, one of the most highly respected members of the Venetian community,[27] requesting him to transmit the papers to the Court. Before acting upon this request Abraham Aboab took counsel, however, with rabbis Shemaʿya di Medina and ʿAzarya Figo, and they strongly advised against placing a matter of this kind before the Beth Din. The issuance of a *pesaḳ,* they argued, might be misinterpreted by the rank and file as evidence of some doubt in the matter, and this could have a morally damaging effect. Moreover, the Beth Din was sure to confirm Morteira's opinion. As a result, his opponent (whose identity was undoubtedly known to them) would find himself in an embarrassing position, and the strife would only become more heated. It was the delicacy of the situation, involving as it did two members of the Amsterdam Beth Din, which made it appear preferable to withhold the case from the Venice authorities. At di Medina's and Figo's suggestion Abraham Aboab returned the documents to Amsterdam, pleading at the same time with the community leaders to restore the peace by prevailing upon Isaac Aboab to renounce his view in public, and by his example to cause the rest of the dissenters to follow suit. It was the failure of this strategy which prompted the two rabbis to write directly to Aboab.

Their Letter (Text B) is a paradigm of ecclesiastic diplomacy. It opens with some flattering remarks about Aboab's high reputation as a Talmudist and thinker, which had awakened in them a desire to enjoy his friendship. God had willed to present him with an opportunity for evincing his full moral stature in public and thereby enhancing the glory of God, which they were sure was all he desired. Some time ago the aged Abraham Aboab had alerted them to the controversy that had arisen in Amsterdam and to the pleas that were to be submitted to the Venice Beth Din. After telling the story of the consultation and the advice they had given the Letter continues: "We were hoping for the day that would bring the message of peace . . . but our expectation has been frustrated. For we were again informed that the conflict persists and that the spokesman of those denying the belief in the eternality of punishment is none other than you, Sir *(hu' nihu mar)*, and that you preach thus openly and publicly." The two rabbis went on to say that they were not a little aggrieved to learn that the man whom they wished to honor and whose reputation they would hate to see tarnished in the least was in support of a view contrary to traditional doctrine. Their only consolation lay in the thought that it would have been far worse had the group been led by an irresponsible, self-willed person. The fact that its champion was a godfearing man gave grounds for hope since he could be trusted to live up to what was said in Proverbs 12:15: "He that is wise hearkeneth unto counsel."

The rest of the Letter is an eloquent appeal imploring Aboab to abandon a view which was opposed to the principles of the Talmud, and to refrain, above all, from preaching and publicizing it. What he ought to do was to announce at a public gathering that he had now seen the light and was firmly convinced that certain grave transgressions were indeed liable to be punished eternally. He would know best how to phrase his declaration and how to warn the group *(ha-kat ha-hamoni)* against venturing rash opinions on subjects of this kind. It was particularly appropriate to issue such warning to "those of our people who came from those places," i.e., Marranos, who "should seek only one thing, namely the way how to serve God in sincerity *(bitemimut)* and how to fulfil the *miṣwot* according to Halakha in all their minutiae."

Far from intimidating Aboab, the Letter of the two Venetian rabbis only served to stiffen his attitude. It seems that his *Nishmat Ḥayyim* was his answer, written in a spirit of anger and defiance. Had it been produced before, some reference to it in the Letter from Venice would have been inevitable. The fact that the rabbis only mentioned his preaching and urged him to refrain from preaching and publicizing his views appears to suggest that nothing was known about a treatise written, let alone in circulation. Aboab's *Nishmat Ḥayyim* presents itself as a *responsum (teshubhā)* to the question *(sha'al ha-sho'el)*: "Is there eternal punishment of souls or not? And what did our rabbis, of blessed memory, intend by saying, The following have no share in the world-to-come?" The answer opens with the ringing statement: "Truly speaking, matters of this kind have been entrusted only to the Kabbalists, illumined as they are by the light of truth." There follows a frontal attack upon the adepts of philosophy, who "lean upon a broken reed" and are unqualified to interpret the profound utterances of the rabbis.

By asserting the role of Kabbala as the only competent authority for the interpretation of rabbinic dicta Aboab clearly opposed Morteira's initial statement that the Talmudic tradition as such was the only "trustworthy Kabbala." Aboab's rejection of the philosophers' exegesis of rabbinic eschatology is likewise directed against Morteira who had quoted Maimonides and Albo. According to Aboab, "we have no dealings with Maimonides as far as this subject is concerned, for he discussed it from the aspect of philosophical inquiry, and not from the aspect of Kabbala." "Neither do we turn to the words of the philosopher R. Joseph Albo, for he has nothing to say *(al-bo)* in matters of kabbalistic science."

There is a note of bitterness in Aboab's complaint that his adversaries mocked at his zealous running after teachers of Kabbala: he did indeed belong to what his denigrators called *kat ha-shotim* (the party of fools) but the word had to be spelled with a *taw*. He was one of those who "drank" *(shotim)* the waters of Tora and sat at the feet of the wise. True, he was young in years but the true "elder" *(zaken)* was the one who had acquired wisdom, and in this respect he was older than his opponents who became more foolish as they advanced in years. Morteira had quoted some kabbalistic texts so as to take the wind out of the other party's sails, but his recourse to Kabbala had only incensed Aboab in whose view no one had the right of interpreting kabbalistic passages unless he had been initiated into the esoteric tradition by a qualified teacher who was himself a link in that tradition. Aboab proudly claimed to fulfil this requirement since his teacher Abraham Herrera had received Luria's teachings from Israel Sarug, who was a disciple of Luria's disciple Ḥayyim Vital.

Outwardly viewed, the conflict between Aboab and Morteira may seem to have been a mere rehash of the old rivalries between pure Talmudists, philosophizing rabbis and Kabbalists. This estimate would be justified had the controversy been purely academic. What makes it historically interesting are the non-academic, pragmatic arguments which were advanced on both sides and which evoked so much feeling on the part of Aboab's followers. The point pressed home by Aboab and his faction was the assurance of ultimate salvation for all Jewish souls. It was prompted, we suggest, by a sense of concern for those Marranos who had, as yet, not returned to the fold or, having returned, had either been remiss in their duties or had relapsed into their old ways. In other words, the issue at stake was the recognition of all Marranos as inseparably belonging to the people of Israel and sharing in its election and privileges. Underlying this claim was the mystical notion of the exalted nature of Jewish souls which had been increasingly stressed in the kabbalistic tradition.

The question of the status of the Marranos had been a matter of debate during the last phase of Spanish Jewry and among the generation of the expulsion,[28] and it had been rekindled in the early part of the seventeenth century.[29] There is ample evidence in the documents presented here that it was the Marrano question which loomed behind the discussion. In his plea to the Venice Beth Din, Morteira condemned the "crooked" and "corrupt" view of the anti-eternalists as one likely to embolden Marranos to return to the "impure land" and to their former "abominations" because any fear concerning the ultimate fate of their souls had been removed. Moreover, he asserted, the "disease" of this doctrine was bound to spread to would-be-emigrants and prevent their seeking refuge elsewhere. Finally, what was going to happen to the age-old readiness for martyrdom if salvation was in store for martyr and renegade alike? The two Venetian rabbis also pointed to the disastrous effect which the new doctrine was going to have on the Marranos.

Aboab's reply to the fears expressed was as follows: The doctrine of ultimate salvation for all Jewish souls did not promise a bed of roses to those who violated the commandments of God. It merely asserted that every Jewish soul would be purged of its sins in what might be a prolonged process of transmigrations entailing much suffering. It was therefore absurd to think that Marranos would be swayed by this doctrine to disregard the dire consequences of sin and prefer to remain in their present condition for the sake of material advantages. What is clearly implied in this answer is the recognition of all Marranos as actual or, at least, virtual Jews.[30] Aboab's treatise ends on this note: "This is what our rabbis, of blessed memory, meant when coining the phrase, 'Though he sinned, he is still an Israelite' (af 'al pi she-ḥaṭa' yisra'el hu').[31] They intended to convey the idea that though he sinned, he was not cut off thereby forever from the tree but remained a Jew; and even if he apostatized from the Lord (shehemir et Ha-Shem) and chose new gods, he will again be called a Jew as a result of transmigrations and punishments." For, in the words of David ibn Abi Zimra, quoted by Aboab in a previous passage, "All Israelites are a single body (guf *eḥad)* and their soul is hewn from the place of Unity *(mi-mekom ha-yiḥud neḥṣabha)."*

The radical students whom Morteira described as *"maskilim* claiming proficiency in Kabbala" were not only Aboab's disciples but, like him and the vast majority of Amsterdam Jews at the time, also of Marrano descent. Their argument that belief in the eternality of punishment reeked of Christian dogma must be evaluated against their personal background. What inspired it was more than mere theological quibbling. Behind it lies the question: Is it worthwhile for a Marrano to shed Christian beliefs if on arrival in Judaism he meets again the doctrine of eternal damnation? It must have been known in Amsterdam circles that Uriel da Costa had discarded Christianity because the dread of eternal damnation had tormented him in his youth, as he confessed in his autobiography.[32] True, his *Exemplar Humanae Vitae* was written as late as 1640 and was not published until 1687.[33] Yet his story was common knowledge among Amsterdam Marranos. His impassionate disavowal of both Christian and Jewish eschatological doctrines had occasioned some literary activity on the part of the Amsterdam rabbinate, as has been noted above.[34] The shadow of da Costa may be discerned behind the young intellectuals' argument that by affirming eternal punishment we were back in Christianity. This line of reasoning reflects at any rate a mentality typical of Marranos. What raised it to a pitch of emotional fervor was the mystical concept of the inalienable kinship between all Jewish souls and the concomitant notion of their ultimate *restitution in integrum* (which will be discussed further below).

There was, at the same time, an even larger setting to the controversy. The protest against the notion of a God who inflicts eternal punishment is indicative of an attitude which was just then gaining ground under the impact of the Enlightenment. From 1630 to 1638, in the very period with which we are dealing, at least ten Dutch translations of Socinian writings were printed in Holland, probably in Amsterdam, which, in the wake of the oppression of Socinianism in its native Poland, was rapidly becoming the center of the movement.[35] Though primarily concerned with the rejection of the trinitarian dogma, the Socinians, like the Arminians and Collegiants, represented a trend toward the liberalization of the rigorous Calvinist dogma of predeterminism and its corollary, the doctrine of eternal damnation. Foreshadowing deistic theology, these dissident groups sought to present religious ideas as consolatory rather than terrifying truths.[36] Ernst Soner (1572–1612), a crypto-Socinian,[37] wrote a little tract disproving the eternality of punishment on the grounds of its incompatibility with the justice of God.[38] This work was published in Holland in 1654. Its way of thinking could have been propagated much earlier. In the eighteenth century it became famous as a result of Leibniz's attempt to refute it and the controversy which ensued between Lessing, who defended, and Johann August Eberhard, who attacked, Leibniz.[39] Hugo Grotius, who had assailed Socinianism in 1617,[40] modified his opinions under the growing impact of the movement to such an extent that Socinian writers were inclined to claim him as a convert. His treatise *De veritate religionis Christianae,* which appeared in 1627, already testifies to his change of mind.

Grotius's contact with Menasseh ben Israel is well known,[41] and, in general, the lines of communication between the Amsterdam Jewish Ghetto and the intellectual world outside were wide open. Aboab's courage in taking so strong a stand against the eternalist position thus reflected the spiritual stirrings of his time. He motivated his unrelenting fight against the traditional view by pointing out that he could not bear to see God's mercies upon his creatures impugned, and more than once he used the phrase "God forbid" *(ḥas weḥalila)* when rejecting the doctrine of eternal punishment as irreconcilable with belief in a just and merciful God.

Notwithstanding his dislike of philosophical arguments, he made ample use of Albo's treatment of the theme: Isaiah (66:24) and Daniel (12:2) "did not mean to say that the punishment was eternal—'Far be it from God, that He should do wickedness; and from the Almighty, that He should commit iniquity' (Job 34:10)—to punish man, who is 'dust from the earth' (Gen. 2:7) and 'a wind that passeth away, and cometh not again' (Ps. 78:39), with an eternal punishment, while sin derives from his material part, which is corruptible and non-eternal. Thus David said, 'Also unto Thee, O Lord, belongeth mercy; for Thou renderest to every man according to his work' (Ps. 62:13), i.e., according to *his* work performed by *him* who is non-eternal, and dost not measure him, a mere creature, against Thee who art eternal, for Thou art not adversely affected by the evil deeds of men." Having outlined and substantiated his own view, Aboab concludes his treatise with the sentence: "All this is in accordance with God's righteous judgment *(ke-fi mishpaṭ ha-ṣedeḳ)."* His opponents, on the other hand, were afraid lest, apart from tranquilizing the moral fiber of the Marranos, the lenient new theology should create a bad impression among the non-Jews, i.e., the ruling Calvinist Church: "Why should the Gentiles say . . ., Surely, this is a nation trusting in its good fortune, the righteous and the wicked being alike, 'and now nothing will be withholden from them, which they purpose to do' (Gen. 11:6); for the fear of God is not before their eyes." One hears here an echo of the affirmation of the eternalist position in the regnant Dutch Church which sternly disapproved of the new liberal trends.

As a mystic and adept of the new Kabbala of Safed, Aboab could afford to be more liberal than the strict Talmudists and philosophizing rabbis. We meet a similar phenomenon in the seventeenth century Christian mystics of England and Germany who followed in the footsteps of Jacob Boehme. It was these mystics who ushered in a new eschatology by reviving the anathematized doctrine of *apokatastasis pantōn,* which goes back to Origen and proclaims the restoration of all things to their pristine harmony in God. They did so in open opposition to the orthodox theology of eternal damnation.[42] Aboab's treatise *Nishmat Ḥayyim* represents a seventeenth century Jewish attempt to break the spell of the traditional eschatology of hell by publicly embracing the Lurianic doctrine of *tikkun* (the Hebrew equivalent for *apokatastasis*) through the transmigration of souls. In so doing he reinforced a trend which had been in evidence ever since the notion of metempsychosis *(gilgul)* began to clash with the eschatological theory of hell,[43] and which had played a dominant role in the thinking of David ibn Abi Zimra, who was Isaac Luria's teacher.

Aboab was by no means an innovator. His merit lies in the boldness with which he not only affirmed the Lurianic stance but also attacked the time-honored eternalist position. The strenuous effort to dislodge the notion of eternal punishment made by Moses Mendelssohn in his time had been anticipated more than a century before by Isaac Aboab. Yet the radical difference in approach outweighs by far the resemblance. Mendelssohn argued from the purely deistic perspective of sweet reasonableness.[44] Aboab was not lacking this nuance but, primarily, he invoked the rich imagery of kabbalistic symbolism with which the Divine commandments *(miṣwot)* in particular had been invested. All laws of return and restoration found in the Tora are made to serve as symbols of ultimate salvation: The *miṣwā* of returning lost property *(hashabhat abhedā);* the laws of *shemiṭṭā* and the Jubilee year; of the healing of the leper; of the cleansing of the house upon which a plague had been pronounced; all these and other commandments assume the character of expressing in so many ways the great mystery of the eventual return of all things to God. Esotericism gives a new dimension to Halakha and, at the same time, permits the traditional eschatology of eternal punishment to be superseded by a new message. If Morteira felt to be on sure ground because he took his stand on the *terra firma* of the classical rabbinic sources, Aboab preferred to soar into the realms of kabbalistic lore which happened to resound also with echoes of kindred spirits in the contemporary world at large.

NOTES

1. See D. Henriques de Castro, *Keur van Grafsteenen op de Nederl.-Portug.-Israël. Begraafsplaats te Ouderkerk aan den Amstel*, I (Leiden, 1883), pp. 69–76; Cecil Roth, art. "Isaac Aboab de Fonseca," *Encyclopaedia Judaica* (1971), 2, pp. 95–96.

2. See de Castro, *op. cit.*, p. 73, No. g; M. Kayserling, *Biblioteca Española-Portugueza-Judaica* (Strasbourg, 1890), p. 5. The work is not listed in Johann Christoph Wolf's article on "R. Isaacus Aboab, junior" in *Bibliotheca Hebraea*, III (1727), pp. 537–539.

3. Cecil Roth, *A Life of Menasseh Ben Israel* (Philadelphia, 1945), pp. 93f., 97–99, *et passim*.

4. On Saul Levi Morteira (Morteyra; Mortera; Mortara; ca. 1596–1660) see Cecil Roth, *A Life of Menasseh Ben Israel*, p. 24ff, *et passim*; Kayserling, *Biblioteca*, p. 74f.; Shelomo Simonsohn (ed.), *Rabbi Yehuda Arye Mi-Modena, She'elot U-Teshubhot Zikney Yehuda* (Jerusalem, 5716/1956), Introduction, p. 47f.; Text, p. 75f.

5. It is part of his *Obras originaes* which are extant in manuscripts (420 pp.) at the Library of the "Portugees Israëlietisch Seminarium Ets Haim" in Amsterdam. See Carl Gebhardt, *Die Schriften des Uriel da Costa* (Amsterdam, 1922), p. 247.

6. Gebhardt, *loc. cit.*

7. Gebhardt, *op. cit.*, p. XXXII.

8. Gebhardt, *op. cit.*, pp. XXIX; 35–64 (65–101). Harry A. Wolfson has made it plausible that Spinoza too meant to oppose Uriel da Costa when he affirmed the immortality of the soul. See his *The Philosophy of Spinoza* (Cambridge, Mass., 1934; New York, 1969), II, p. 323ff.; 350; and *Religious Philosophy, A Group of Essays* (Cambridge, Mass., 1961; New York, 1965), p. 268.

9. For the biographical data see note 1 and the literature listed in Roth's article.

10. Wolf, *Bibliotheca Hebraea*, p. 1000 f., quotes from Daniel Levi (Miguel) de Barrios' *Arbol de la Vida* (Amsterdam, 1689) a reference to Morteira's German origin: "Fille Saul Levi Mortera de Alemania natural . . ."

11. *Zikney Yehuda* (see note 4), Nr. 54, p. 76.

12. See Yehuda (Ludwig) Blau (ed.), *Kitebhey Ha-Rabh Yehuda Arye Mi-Modena* (Budapest, 5666/1905), pp. 169–170.

13. His philosophical bent is manifested in his *Gibhe'at Sha'ul* (Amsterdam, 1645; Warsaw, 1912), a collection of homilies, and in the Letter (Text A) printed below, where he refers to Maimonides as "the leading spokesman" (*rosh ha-medabberim;* line 48) and quotes Isaac 'Arāma (lines 99–103), Joseph Albo (103–106), and Isaac Abrabanel's *Naḥalat Abhot* and *Rosh Amanā* (111–123). Like Abrabanel, he restricts transmigration of souls to a maximum of three times (Text A, 93–97; *Gibhe'at Sha'ul,* No. 48, pp. 297 and 299 in the Warsaw edition). Leone da Modena attacked the doctrine of *gilgul* altogether in a tract *Ben David* written during the winter of 1635–36, precisely at the time of the Amsterdam controversy, at the request of a certain David Finzi in Egypt, who had lost a young son. See Abraham Geiger, *Leon da Modena* (Breslau, 1856), p. 12.

14. A native of Salonica, Shema'ya di Medina was one of the rabbis of Venice, whose name appears under many decisions of the *yeshibha kelalit.* He wrote a commentary on *Proverbs* (unpublished) and edited his grandfather's sermons *(Sefer Ben Shemu'el)* with an introduction of his own, which contains many autobiographical references. See Mordecai Samuel Ghirondi and Hanan'el Neppi, *Toledot Gedoley Yisra'el U-Ge'oney Italia—Zekher Ṣaddiḳ Li-Bherakha* (Trieste, 1853), pp. 352, 323, 358; Shelomo Simonsohn, *op. cit.,* p. 48 (Introduction).

15. 'Azarya Figo (Pigo; Pichio), born in 1589, was a disciple of Leone da Modena's (1571–1648), whose list of favorite students he heads (see Blau, *op. cit.,* p. 168). A responsum addressed to him by his teacher vividly illustrates their happy relationship (see Blau, *loc. cit.,* No. 87, pp. 85–87). Figo published a commentary to the *Sefer Ha-Terumot* of Samuel ben Isaac Ha-Sardi under the title *Gidduley Terumā* (Venice, 1643). His *Binā La-'Ittim* followed in 1648. See Abba Apfelbaum, *Rabbi 'Azarya Figo* (Drohobitsch, 5667/1907); Israel Bettan, "The Sermons of Azariah Figo," *HUCA,* VII (1930), pp. 457–495; Simonsohn, *op. cit.,* p. 56 (Introduction).

16. For the date of Figo's death see Blau, *op. cit.,* p. 85; the date of Shema'ya di Medina is given as Siwan 13 (June 3) 1648 by Steinschneider, *Cat. Bodl.,* No. 7117, p. 2516f.

17. I am greatly obliged to Erla Broekema, Librarian of the Seminary Ets Haim in Amsterdam, for informing me of the existence of the additional two MSS. of Aboab's treatise and for putting microfilms at my disposal.

18. Information supplied by E. Broekema (July 15 and October 24, 1971). A manuscript of *Nishmat Ḥayyim* written by David Franco Mendes is mentioned by J. S. Da Silva, *Iets over den Amsterdamschen Opperabbijn Isaäc Aboab* (Amsterdam, 1913), p. 12.

19. Viz. 2 Sam. 6:14; 1 Sam. 16:12, 1 Kings 18:37; 1 Kings 3:28.
20. See M. Kayserling, "Isaac Aboab, the First Jewish Author in America," *Publications of the American Jewish Historical Society,* No. 5 (1897), pp. 125–136; idem, *Rabbi Yiṣḥaḳ Aboab Ha-Shelishi,* in *Ha-Goren* (ed. S. A. Horodetzki), III (1902), pp. 155–174; Arnold Wiznitzer, *Jews in Colonial Brazil* (New York, 1960), index *s. v.* Fonseca; Hermann Wätjen, *Das holländische Kolonialreich in Brasilien* (Haag-Gotha, 1921), p. 237; C. R. Boxer, *The Dutch in Brazil 1624–1654* (Oxford, 1957), pp. 181, 274.
21. A pun on the biblical phrase describing the slavery in Egypt (Dt. 4:20; 1 Kings 8:51; Jer. 11:4). See the Warsaw, 1864 (Israel reprint 1969), edition of *Shaʿar Ha-Shamayim,* p. 23.
22. See Wiznitzer, *op. cit.,* p. 170.
23. He died on Adar II 27, 5453/April 4, 1693 (see De Castro, *op. cit.,* 68). Morteira died on Shebhaṭ 25, 5420/February 9, 1660.
24. Although it was not uncommon in rabbinic circles of the sixteenth and seventeenth centuries to refer to men of 35 or 40 years of age, even when married, as *baḥurim,* as Meir Benayahu, *Sefer Toledot Ha-'Ari* (Jerusalem 1967), p. 176, note 2, has shown by a wealth of material, Aboab personally does not seem to have taken kindly to the description of him as a *ṣaʿir.*
25. Cf. Isa. 8:14.
26. The sermon in question could not have been the one published in his *Gibheʿat Sha'ul* (No. 48, *parashat wa-yelekh,* Warsaw, 1912, p. 295ff.). Although the latter affirms eternal punishment in hell for certain transgressions, it is philosophically structured, not primarily surveying the Talmudic material as did the sermon spoken of in our text.
27. Abraham Aboab had founded the Synagogue "Keter Tora" in Hamburg before moving to Venice, where he died in 1642. His eulogy by Figo is contained in *Binā La-ʿIttim* (No. 77). See Löwenstein, *op. cit.,* p. 674; Apfelbaum, *op. cit., passim.* Abraham Aboab's eldest son Samuel (1610–1694) was first rabbi in Verona. He became rabbi in Venice in 1650 and was the author of the Responsa *Debhar Shemu'el* (Venice, 1702).
28. See Ḥayyim Hillel Ben-Sasson, *Dor Goley Sefarad ʿal ʿaṣmo,* in *Zion,* 26 (1961), pp. 34–43; B. Netanyahu, *The Marranos of Spain from the Late XIVth to the Early XVIth Century according to Contemporary Hebrew Sources* (New York, 1966).
29. See Yosef Hayim Yerushalmi, *From Spanish Court to Italian Ghetto Isaac Cardoso: A Study in Seventeenth-Century Marranism and Jewish Apologetics* (New York and London, 1971), pp. 21–42.
30. This mystically inspired "halakhic" recognition tallies with Yerushalmi's view (*op. cit.,* p. 39f.) that "even before he began to Judaize, every New Christian was a potential Marrano, whom any of a variety of circumstances could transform into an active Marrano."
31. Sanhedrin 44a; see Jacob Katz, *Yisrael af ʿal pi she-ḥaṭa',* in *Tarbiẓ,* 27 (1958), pp. 203–217.
32. See Gebhardt, *op. cit.,* pp. 124f.

33. Gebhardt, *op. cit.*, p. 259 sq.
34. P. 1f.
35. See H. John McLachlan, *Socinianism in Seventeenth-Century England* (Oxford, 1951), p. 23f.
36. See Leo Strauss's characterization of deistic theology in his *Die Religionskritik Spinozas als Grundlage seiner Bibelwissenschaft* (Berlin, 1930), p. 28f.
37. He was professor of medicine in Altdorf and an Aristotelian philosopher. In his youth he had spent a year (1597–98) as a student in Leiden. See J. C. van Slee, *De Geschiedenis van het Socinianisme in de Nederlanden* (Haarlem, 1914), p. 45. It was he who converted Martin Ruar (1589–1657) to Socinianism (cf. Slee, *op. cit.*, p. 201).
38. *Ernesti Sonneri Demonstratio theologica et philosophica quod aeterna impiorum supplicia non arguant Dei justitiam, sed injustitiam,* in: *Fausti & Laetii Socini, item E. Sonneri tractatus aliquot theologici, nunquam antehac in lucem editi . . .* (Eleutheropoli, 1654).
39. For a discussion of this controversy, see Henry E. Allison, *Lessing and the Enlightenment* (Ann Arbor, 1966), pp. 86–93.
40. In his *Defensio Fidei Catholicae de Satisfactione Christi adversus Faustum Socinum Senensem* (Leiden, 1617).
41. See Cecil Roth, *A Life of Menasseh Ben Israel,* pp. 146–148 *et passim.*
42. See Ernst Benz, "Der Mensch und die Sympathie aller Dinge am Ende der Zeiten," *Eranos-Jahrbuch,* XXIV (1955), p. 157ff.
43. See Gershom Scholem, *Einige kabbalistische Handschriften im Britischen Museum* (Jerusalem, 1932), p. 28f.; idem, *Von der mystischen Gestalt der Gottheit* (Zurich, 1962), p. 223.
44. See my *Moses Mendelssohn: A Biographical Study* (The University of Alabama Press, University, Alabama, 1973), index *s. v.* Eternal Punishment. An attempt at reconciling Enlightenment sentiment with the traditional doctrine of hell was made by Mendelssohn's friend Naftali Hirz (Hartwig) Wessely in his *Ma'amar Ḥikkur Din* (Berlin, 1786).

II

MYSTICAL LEADERSHIP AND PERSONALITIES

9.

The *Ẓaddiq* as *Axis Mundi* in Later Judaism

Arthur Green

The history of Judaism as presented to us by the *Wissenschaft des Judentums* of the nineteenth and early twentieth centuries depicted a religious civilization which seemed to have little in common with those societies to which the emerging methodology of the history of religions was first being applied in that same time period. With the exception of certain minor "fringe" phenomena, Judaism comprised a world of sober theology, law, and ethics. The battle with myth had been won once and for all in the biblical period, and thus the comparative method of myth, ritual, and symbol studies could contribute little to an understanding of the main lines in postbiblical Jewish thought. This image of Judaism has now been laid to rest, at least in most scholarly circles if not in popular preaching, by the work of Erwin Goodenough, Gershom Scholem, Jacob Neusner, and many others. The present paper, resting particularly on Scholem's conclusions concerning the ongoing presence of mythical motifs in medieval Judaism, particularly as crystallized in Kabbalah, seeks to examine the holy man traditions in medieval and postmedieval Jewish sources, and to demonstrate the perseverence with which myths of sacred person survived and developed in the literature of later Judaism.

One of the most precious notions of modern Jewish apologetics has been the idea that in Judaism there are no uniquely holy persons. Both prophecy and priesthood had ceased to function in postbiblical Israel. The rabbi, working as scholar, teacher, and legal authority, claimed for

Reprinted by permission of the American Academy of Religion from *JAAR* 45, no. 3 (1977).

himself neither the personal charisma of the prophet nor the sacerdotal role of the priest; every Jew had equal and direct access to God through Torah and prayer. The recent work of Jacob Neusner and his school has done much to rectify this one-sided presentation insofar as the Talmudic rabbi is concerned (Neusner). Outside of the rabbinate, per se, such terms as *zaddiq* and *hasid* were taken by apologists to be embodiments of moral or pious perfection in the language of Jewish authors, but were not to represent what are seen in studies of India, tribal Africa, or Siberia as "holy man" traditions. If all of Israel is holy and chosen, a "kingdom of priests," so the argument would go, there is no need for the holy man in his classic roles as intercessor, as administrator of sacraments, or as source of blessing. Of course any student of the history of religions, particularly in noting the minority status Jews held in the Hellenistic, Iranian, Christian, and Muslim realms, all of them replete with cults of saints and holy men, must have raised his eyebrows at the ability of such a religious society as a whole to remain faithful to so lofty and rarified a position.

Another "sacred cow" of that view of Judaism, reinforced more recently by the Zionist influence on Jewish historiosophy, concerns the relationship of classical Judaism to its notions of sacred space. While Judaism after the destruction and dispersion was forced, so it is claimed, to reduce its dependency upon the Temple Mount and other loci of mythic or cosmological significance, the nexus of relationship between the Jew and the Holy Land was never compromised or weakened either by the full symbolization of sacred space (i.e., Jerusalem becoming the heavenly Jerusalem alone) or by the transference of that sacrality to any other place.

In applying Mircea Eliade's insights around the symbol of *axis mundi* to the holy man traditions of later Judaism, both of these notions will of necessity be challenged. While neither is by any means being called into question here for the first time, some will still be surprised to discover in Jewish mysticism, particularly after the sixteenth century, a highly developed theory of sacred person, standing at the center of the cosmos and having about him a clearly articulated aura of a new Jerusalem. The fact is that postexilic Jews maintained a highly complex and ambivalent attitude toward their traditions of sacred space (cf. Goldenberg). While longing for a return to the Holy Land continued unabated, the dispersed community of necessity had to have within it various means of more ready access to the sacrality which its great shrine had once provided;

Israel wandering through the wilderness of exile was to find that it still had need of a portable Ark of the Covenant. One of the ways in which this was provided was by a transference of *axis mundi* symbolism from a particular place to a particular person: the *zaddiq* or holy man as the center of the world.

It should be noted at the outset that such a transference of sacred space symbolism to that of sacred person takes place in Christianity from the very beginning. When the author of John 2:19–20 has Jesus speak of his own body as the Temple, the stage has been set for the assertion that Christ himself is the *axis mundi* upon which the new edifice of Christianity is to be erected. Sacred person has become the new sacred center. Indeed, if there remains a geographical point which serves as *axis mundi* for classical Christianity, it has moved a very significant few hundred yards from the Temple Mount to the Mount of Calvary. In Islam also, though in rather different form, there exists an association of holy man and *axis mundi*. While the rigors of Muslim orthodoxy and anti-Christian reaction did not allow that the prophet himself be described in such terms, Sufi masters from the eighth century onward speak of the *qotb*, a single holy man who is the "pole," standing at the height of the world's spiritual hierarchy. In later Shiʾite and Ismaʿili conceptions of the Imām and his role in the cosmos the matter is even more clearly articulated.

I

In beginning our examination of this motif in the history of Judaism, we turn first to certain phenomena of popular Hasidism, that eastern European pietistic revival which may be said to have been the last development within classical Judaism before the advent of modernity. Among the disciples of Rabbi Menahem Mendel of Kotzk, one of the great Hasidic masters of nineteenth-century Poland, a song was current which reflects the attitude of a disciple to a visit at the master's court. The chorus of that song runs as follows:

> Keyn Kotzk furt men nisht;
> Keyn Kotzk geyt men.
> Veyl Kotzk iz dokh bimkoim ha-mikdesh,
> Kotzk iz dokh bimkoim ha-mikdesh.
> Keyn Kotzk darf men oyleh regel zeyn.[1]

To Kotzk one doesn't "travel"[2]
To Kotzk one may only walk.
For Kotzk stands in the place of the Temple,
Kotzk is in the Temple's place.
To Kotzk one must walk as does a pilgrim.

The place where the *zaddiq* dwells, be it the miserable Polish town that it is, becomes the new Temple, the place of pilgrimage. A generation or two before Kotzk, we are told that the disciples of Rabbi Nahman of Bratslav, of whom we shall have more to say later, were heard running through the streets of that town shouting: "Rejoice and exult, thou who dwellest in Bratslav!" in an ecstatic outburst following the *zaddiq's* establishment of his "court" in that place (*Avaneha-Barzel* 13). Of course *zahali wa-roni yoshevet Bratslav* is a play on Isa. 12:6, except that Bratslav has replaced the "Zion" of the biblical source. Nahman has come to Bratslav; a new Zion has been proclaimed. The town of Sadegora, the later dwelling-place of Rabbi Israel of Ruzhin, was described as "the place of the Temple" and the verse "They shall make me a sanctuary and I will dwell in their midst" (Exod. 25:8) was applied to it (Nisensohn:93).[3] To provide a more contemporary example, I am told that the Jerusalem meeting-place of the Lubavitch *hasidim* contains within it a scale model of the Lubavitcher *rebbe's* headquarters at 770 Eastern Parkway in Brooklyn! Where, indeed, is the true Jerusalem?

It will be noted that the sources thus far quoted are hardly the theoretical writings of the great Hasidic masters, let alone the classics of Judaism. We shall come to these later. But it is just these epiphenomena of popular religion, so often ignored by traditional Jewish scholarship, that the student of the history of religions is learning to take seriously.

We will also note that the claim made in these reports is in a certain way a conservative one. In all of them it is not the *zaddiq* himself as person who seems to have become the *axis mundi* or new Jerusalem, but rather the place where the *zaddiq* dwells. Our contention is, however, that this can only be the very latest stage of development, one which already assumes the notion of the *zaddiq* himself as sacred center. We should also make it clear that we are not claiming by way of these examples that Jewish mysticism or Hasidism abandoned its awareness of or commitment to Jerusalem as the center of the universe. As Eliade has amply shown us, the peculiar logic of *homo religiosus* has no difficulty in absorbing the notion that the cosmos may have more than one center.

II

This image of the *zaddiq* as one who stands at the center of the cosmos will not come as a complete surprise to anyone familiar with the rabbinic sources in this area. A particularly oftquoted dictum (*Ḥag.* 12b) immediately comes to mind:

> Upon what does the earth stand? . . . R. Eleazar ben Shamuᶜa says:
> Upon a single pillar, and *zaddiq* is its name. Thus scripture says:
> "*Zaddiq* is the foundation of the world." (Prov. 10:25)

In order to understand the later developments in the Kabbalistic/Hasidic tradition, it is indeed to the rabbinic sources, and particularly to their uses of the term *zaddiq*, that we must first turn our attention. Our best guide in this matter is Rudolph Mach, whose monograph on the subject offers both an exhaustive collection and a perceptive analysis of the materials.

The problem in the rabbinic literature is that the term is both very widely and loosely used; there are many cases where it is applied so generally that a specific meaning can hardly be assigned to it. It does seem possible, however, to delineate two general strands in the material. First, *zaddiq* is used in the forensic sense: "righteous" as what our legal nomenclature would term "innocent." The world is divided between *zaddiqim* and *reshaᶜim*, those found righteous and those found wicked by the standards of heavenly judgment. This sort of righteousness is acquired by proper behavior, especially by conquest of the passions. Minimally, one may be a *zaddiq* in this sense simply by belonging to the better half of humanity, or by being more possessed of merits than burdened by sins.

The second usage of the term *zaddiq*, however, is a much more exacting one, and it is that which will prove of interest to us here. This usage takes the *zaddiq* to be a unique individual, a wonderman from birth, heir to the biblical traditions of charismatic prophecy as embodied in Moses and Elijah, and at the same time the rabbinic version of the Hellenistic god-man or quasi-divine hero (Mach: 53ff.)[4] It is in the former sense primarily that Joseph is the archetypical *zaddiq:* his righteousness is acquired through suffering, and passes its greatest test in his conquest of passion when confronting the advances of Potiphar's wife. In the latter sense, it is rather Moses who is the ideal type, recognized from birth as containing the hidden light of creation or as being the bearer of the divine presence in the world.[5]

Both of these uses of the term *zaddiq* have their place in the rabbinic legends on the creation of Adam, and this leads to some confusion. When we are told that God saw both *zaddiqim* and *resha'im* proceeding from Adam's descendants, and that He turned to look only at the deeds of the *zaddiqim* so that the sight of the wicked would not dissuade Him from man's creation, we are seemingly dealing with the former, the forensic use of the word *zaddiq* (*Gen. Rab.* 8:4). When the Aggadah says, however, that God took counsel with the souls of the *zaddiqim* for advice concerning the future of this humanity He was creating, the same Aggadic motif seems to have slipped into the second usage. God would hardly be consulting all those who are to be found more righteous than wicked among Adam's offspring; He is rather seeking out the counsel of those unique individuals scattered through history whose task it will be to sustain the world.

This is indeed the function of the *zaddiq* in that second sense of the term: he is the sustainer of the world. A great number of rabbinic dicta attest to this function in one way or another. Of Hanina ben Dosa, a disciple of Yohanan ben Zakkai and an ideal type of rabbinic folk-piety, we are told: "The entire world is sustained for the sake of Hanina My son." Or, more generally, "The entire world is sustained by the merits of the *zaddiqim*" (*Ber.* 17b). "God saw that the *zaddiqim* were few; He rose up and planted them in each generation" (*Yoma* 38b). "As long as there are *zaddiqim* in the world, there is blessing in the world; when the *zaddiqim* die, blessings vanish" (*Sifre Deut.* 38). It is in this sense also that our original passage is to be taken: the *zaddiq* is the pillar upon whom the world rests in the sense that he is the one through whose merits the world is sustained. The cosmological background of this figure of speech should, however, not be ignored. It may not be in a purely metaphoric sense that the rabbis are speaking here.

There are recorded several discussions among the rabbis as to the number of *zaddiqim* whose presence is required in a given generation to offset the world's wickedness and to allow for its continued existence. The Palestinian sources prefer the numbers thirty and forty-five (Mach:

135f.), both of which are as yet unexplained. It is the Babylonian tradition, quoted in the name of Abaye, that fixes on the number thirty-six, a figure which becomes so important in later Jewish folklore. Both Mach, and Scholem have indicated the source of this number in Egyptian astrological traditions (Mach: 137ff.; Scholem, 1971:251ff.). At the same time, however, there seems to be present among the Palestinian rabbis a notion of singular spiritual leadership in a generation. Both the *tanna* R. Eleazar and the *amora* R. Yohanan proclaim that the world was created, or is sustained, for the sake of a single *zaddiq* (*Yoma* 38b). R. Simeon ben Yohai, who will be of great importance to us a bit later, seems to shock us with his immodesty when he says: "If there are thirty, twenty, ten or five *zaddiqim* in the world, my son and I are among them. If there are two, we are they, and if one, it is I" (*Gen. Rab.* 35:2).

The notion of singular leadership in a generation also exists in rabbinic sources outside the specific *zaddiq*-terminology. God takes care, we are told, not to dim the light of one generation's leader until the sun of the next has begun to shine in the world (*Qidd.* 72b).[6] Both in the generation of Hillel and in the days of Yavneh, it is reported, a heavenly voice was heard by the assembled sages to proclaim: "There is one among you who is fit to receive the holy spirit, except that the generation is not worthy" (*Yerushalmi Sotah* 9, 24b; Büchler: 8f.). This seems to point to a single charismatic leader of Israel, one who may be revealed as such only in a deserving generation. While the term *zaddiq ha-dor* (*the zaddiq* of the generation) does not appear in the old rabbinic sources,[7] it seems clear that such a notion is not entirely foreign to the rabbis' thinking.

III

As we turn our attention from the early rabbinic materials to the speculative universe of thirteenth-century Kabbalah, particularly as manifest in the Zohar, a number of new factors enter to complicate our discussion. Here *zaddiq* has become a conventional term for the ninth of the ten divine emanations *(sefirot):* the same word thus designates an aspect of the divine Self and a particular group of humans. This ninth level of divinity is otherwise commonly referred to as *yesod* ("foundation"), as Joseph, as the phallus of *Adam Qadmon,* or, in better Kabbalistic language, as "the sign of the holy covenant." This complex of associations is hardly accidental. Joseph is the *zaddiq* by virtue of *shemirat ha-berit*, sexual purity in the face of temptation. *Zaddiq* is the foundation of the world based on the verse in Proverbs and on the rabbinic reading we have mentioned, as the reproductive organ is the foundation of the human body. It is this ninth emanation, standing in the central sefirotic column, which serves as the vehicle through which divine life flows into the feminine *malkhut* or *shekhinah*, the last of the *sefirot,* and thence into the corporeal world. One will therefore find in Kabbalistic literature abundant references to *zaddiq* as pillar, as foundation, and so forth, including all the expected phallic associations of such terms. The earthly *zaddiqim* are those who stand in particular relation to that element of divinity, arousing the upper flow by virtue of their deeds below.

There is a single pillar that reaches from earth to heaven and *zaddiq* is its name. It is named for the *zaddiqim*. When there are *zaddiqim* in the world, it is strengthened; when there are not, it becomes weak. It bears the entire world, as Scripture says: "*zaddiq* is the foundation of the world" (Prov. 10:25). If it is weakened, the world cannot exist. For that reason, the world is sustained even by the presence of a single *zaddiq* within it. (*Bahir,* ed. Margaliot 102)

It is probably because of this association of the human *zaddiq* with the *zaddiq* figure in God that the early Kabbalists of Provence and Gerona tended to employ the term *zaddiq* as the embodiment of their pietistic ideal, rather than *ḥasid,* the term more usual to other medieval sources (Tishby, 1961: 659, 667).[8] The Kabbalists do not, however, perhaps disappointingly to readers of Norman O. Brown, draw out into words the implicit notion that the earthly *zaddiq* is to be seen as the phallus of the human community. The frequent associations of *zaddiq* with pillar, foundation, etc., which we could easily be tempted to seize upon in our search for *axis mundi,* refer almost always to God as *zaddiq.* Our primary interest here is in his human counterpart, of whom the Zohar but rarely says: "He who knows these secrets and serves with wholeness, cleaving to his Lord . . . draws blessing into the world. Such a man is called *zaddiq,* the pillar of the cosmos (Zohar 1:43a).

We should also call attention to the belief of the Zohar and of nearly all Kabbalists in metempsychosis. When such authors speak of one *zaddiq* standing in the place of another, they may often (though not always) be claiming that the latter-day leader is none other than his predecessor reincarnate.

The central figure of the mystical dialogues which comprise the large part of the Zohar is R. Simeon ben Yohai, that same Simeon ben Yohai who had proclaimed the possibility that he be the single leader of his generation back in second-century Palestine, here recreated in the imagination of a thirteenth-century Spanish Kabbalist. Now that briefly recorded claim has been expanded into a much fuller narrative, in which God himself is forced to recognize R. Simeon's unique status.

"Abraham will surely be" (Gen. 18:18); YiHYeH (= will be) has a numerical equivalent of thirty.

One day Rabbi Simeon went out and saw that the world was completely dark, that its light was hidden. Said Rabbi Eleazar to him: Come, let us see what it is that the Lord desires. They went and found an angel in the form of a great mountain with thirty lashes of fire issuing from its mouth.

"What are you planning to do?" Rabbi Simeon asked the angel.

"I seek to destroy the world, for there are not thirty *zaddiqim* in this generation. Thus the Holy One, blessed be He, said concerning Abraham: "He will surely be," meaning that Abraham was equivalent to thirty."

Said Rabbi Simeon: "I beg of you, go before the Holy One and tell Him that I, the son of Yohai, am to be found in the world."

The angel went to God and said: "Master of the World, surely that which ben Yohai has said is known to You."

God answered: "Go and destroy the world. Pay no heed to ben Yohai."

When the angel returned to earth, ben Yohai saw him and said: "If you do not leave, I decree that you will not be able to return to heaven, but will be in the place of 'Aza and 'Aza'el [the fallen angels]. When you again come before God, say to Him: 'If there are not thirty righteous ones in the world, let it be twenty, as is written: "I shall not do it for the sake of the twenty" (Gen. 18:31). And if not twenty, then ten, for it says further: "I shall not destroy for the sake of the ten" (ibid. 32), and if there are not ten, let it be two—my son and I—as Scripture says: "The matter *(davar)* will be upheld according to two witnesses" (Deut. 19:15). Now *davar* refers to the world, as Scripture says: "By the word *(davar)* of God the heavens were made" (Ps. 33:6). If there are not two, there is one, and I am he, as it is written: "*Zaddiq* [in the singular] is the foundation of the world." ' "

In that hour a voice went forth from heaven saying: "Blessed is your lot, Rabbi Simeon, for God issues a decree above and you nullify it below! Surely of you it was written: 'He does the will of them that fear Him' (Ps. 145:19)." (Zohar Hadash, *wa-yera*, 33a)

The second-century Rabbi Simeon, according to an old Aggadic source, had also claimed that he, with the help of the prophet Ahijah of Shilo, could sustain Israel until the advent of messiah *(Gen. Rab.* 35:2).[9] Now the author of the Zohar has its central character announce that "through this book Israel will come forth from exile" (Zohar 3:124b). The Zohar abounds with praises of R. Simeon, who is commonly referred to in that work as "the holy lamp." He is described as the new Moses and the new Solomon (Zohar 2:148b–149a). A pillar of cloud hovers over him, as it did over the desert tabernacle when God spoke with Moses. As all the sages of the world once turned to Solomon to reveal his wise secrets, now they turn to R. Simeon. While there are other sages and *zaddiqim* present in the pages of the Zohar, it is completely clear to the author that none of them approaches the singular role of this figure. He is, both in name and function, the single leader of his generation.

Blessed is that generation in which R. Simeon ben Yohai lives. Blessed is its lot both above and below. Of it Scripture says: "Blessed are you, O land whose king is free" (Eccles. 10:17). What is the meaning of 'free'? He lifts up his head to offer revelations and is not afraid. And what is the meaning of 'your king'? This refers to R. Simeon, master of Torah, master of wisdom.

When R. Abba and the companions saw R. Simeon, they would run after him saying: "They walk behind the Lord; He roars like a lion" (Hos. 11:10). (Zohar 3:79b; cf. also 2:15a)

The association of *zaddiq* of the generation with "king of the land" should already raise our antennae to the possibility of *axis mundi* symbolism here. Certainly there is something of sacral kingship in the air. When R. Simeon is referred to as *qayyema de-ᶜalma,* pillar of the cosmos (Zohar Ḥadash 24a; Tishby, 1957:31), we are yet closer to a notion of holy man as sacred center. But we need not rely upon any passages of dubious intent. The Zohar finally tells us quite explicitly that R. Simeon is to be viewed in light of Israel's ancient traditions of sacred space:

R. Simeon went out to the countryside, and there he ran into R. Abba, R. Hiyya, and R. Yose. When he saw them he said: "This place is in need of the joy of Torah." They spent three days there, and when he was about to depart each of them expounded upon a verse of Scripture.

R. Abba began: " 'The Lord said to Abram after Lot had departed from him ... raise up your eyes and see ... all the land which you see I will give to you and your seed forever.' (Gen. 13:14–15) Was Abraham to inherit all that which he saw and no more? How far can a man see? Three, four, perhaps five miles — and He said 'All the land which you see'? But once Abraham had looked in the four directions, he had seen the entire land. Further, God lifted him up over the Land of Israel and showed him how it was the connecting-point of the four directions, and thus he saw it all. *In the same way, he who sees Rabbi Simeon sees the entire world; he is the joy of those above and below.*"

R. Hiyya began: " 'The land upon which you are lying I will give to you and to your offspring.' (Gen. 28:13) Was it only that place which God promised him, no more than four or five ells? Rather at that time God folded the entire Land of Israel into those four ells, and thus that place included the entire land. If that place included the whole land, how much more clear it is *that Rabbi Simeon, lamp of the world, is equal to the entire world!*" (Zohar 1:155b–156a, based on sources in *Gen. Rab.* 44:12 and *Ḥul.* 91b)

Seeing R. Simeon is parallel to Abraham's vision of the Holy Land; R. Simeon contains the entire world as Jacob's rock at Bethel contained the entire Land of Israel. The *zaddiq* stands at the center of the cosmos, the place where the four directions meet. He is thus the earthly extension of that element within the Deity which is called *zaddiq,* a this-worldly continuation of the Kabbalistic *ʿamuda de-emzaʿita,* the central pillar of the universe. He is in a highly spatial sense the earthly counterpart to the pillar of the sefirotic world.

We should take special note of the Zohar's claim that R. Simeon's generation is unique in having such a leader. While some of the later Kabbalistic sources will claim that such a soul is necessarily present in *every* generation (Zohar 3:273a, R.M.; *Shaʿar ha-Gilgulim* 29b; *Shaʿar ha-Pesuqim, wa-etḥanan,* perhaps based on *Gen. Rab.* 56:7), others seem to agree that the appearance of such a soul is a rare event in human history, and that very few such *zaddiqey ha-dor* exist, each serving to sustain the world for a number of generations that come in his wake. Nathan of Nemirov, the leading disciple of Nahman of Bratslav, claimed in the early nineteenth century that this soul had appeared but five times in Israel's history: it was present in Moses, R. Simeon, Isaac Luria, the great sixteenth-century Kabbalist, Israel Baʿal Shem Tov, the first central figure of Hasidism, and in his own master. It will next appear in the person of the messiah (*Ḥayyey MoHaRaN* II, *gedulat hassagato* 39).

But we are running a bit ahead of ourselves. We have made passing reference earlier to the Zohar's R. Simeon as a figure of Moses *redivivus* (*ʿEmeq ha-Melekh* 4b, 33b).[10] In order to understand the spatial centrality assigned to R. Simeon, we shall first have to turn our attention to the Kabbalistic Moses.

It is now well known through Scholem's monumental interpretations of Lurianic Kabbalah and Sabbatianism that the Kabbalists saw the soul of Adam as containing within it all those souls that were to be born in all future generations (Scholem, 1973:36ff., 302ff.). In this way Kabbalah comes much closer to containing a notion of original sin than most writers on Judaism have been willing to ascribe to the Jewish tradition. A less well-known but perhaps equally significant part of the Kabbalistic myth is the notion that the soul of Moses contained within it the souls of all Israel. Each Jewish soul, according to Luria, is related to one of the six hundred thousand mystical letters of the Torah. Each Israelite has a particular soul-root which is also manifest in a letter of Scripture. The soul of Moses, however, contains *all* of these; it is called the *neshamah kelalit,* the general or all-inclusive soul. It is because Moses' soul contains both the entire Torah and the entire people that he becomes the instrument of revelation. The structural parallel to classical Christianity is obvious here; revelation is being depicted in nearly incarnational terms. Moses receives the Torah as an outward sign that his own soul is the full embodiment of Torah.[11] According to another formulation, Moses is related to Israel as the soul is related to the body; the leader is his people's soul (*Sefer ha-Gilgulim* 63a).[12]

We now understand the centrality of Moses and the Mosaic revelation in the salvific scheme of Kabbalah. The old rabbinic sources had already seen Sinai as the event which redeemed Israel from the curse of Eden (*Shabbat* 146a). If all souls were tainted by the sin of Adam, the Kabbalists now claim, all the souls of Israel are redeemed by their presence in the soul of Moses as he ascends the mountain. Alas, the sin of the Golden Calf interrupts this moment, and Sinai does not become the final redemption. But Israel's access to this great purification continues to be through Moses. Primarily, of course, the way to achieve this access is through Moses' Torah; in this sense Kabbalah remains faithfully rabbinic. (Else it would be precisely that Christian faith garbed in the symbols of Jewish esoterica which some Renaissance humanists indeed hoped it to be!) Nevertheless, the figure of Moses himself remains important here, and the fact that R. Simeon is believed to be Moses' soul reincarnate, an old/new leader who can bring all the souls of Israel to God and compose a book which now *will* effect the final redemption, is what makes him so essential to the mythic structure of the Kabbalah. No wonder that he stands at the center of the world![13]

IV

We now turn to the further development of this motif in eastern European Hasidism, where it was to receive its fullest and most radical treatment. Here a new type of charismatic leader had taken central stage in the Jewish community; claims are made both for his spiritual powers and for his temporal authority which seem to go far beyond anything previously articulated in Jewish sources. Of the rich legacy of holy men and religious leaders from Israel's past, various paradigmatic figures are brought forth to justify the emphasis placed on the centrality of the *rebbe* and his boundless powers. Elements of both sacral kingship and cultic priesthood are drawn out of biblical sources in defense of the Hasidic master. Several dynasties within the movement claimed descent from the House of David; particularly in the traditions of the Ruzhin/ Sadegora dynasty was the motif of kingship treated with great seriousness, including an assumed right to regal life-style (Nisensohn). It is told that R. Abraham Joshua Heschel of Apt, in leading that portion of the Yom Kippur liturgy in which the words of the ancient high priest are recounted, changed the text from the third to the first person ("Thus did I say . . ."), for he recalled that he had filled that office in a prior incarnation (*'Eser Orot* 114). Many a collection of Hasidic homilies, in dealing with the Torah portions of Leviticus, will make a complete transference from priest to *rebbe* in verse after verse, almost as a matter of course.

It is the model of *zaddiq*, however, that is most prevalent in the Hasidic discussions of leadership; by the second generation of the movement this term was well on its way to becoming the universally recognized appellation for a Hasidic master. As popularly conceived, it is through this *zaddiq* that the devotee must turn to God; the *zaddiq*, being at once bound to both heaven and earth,[14] becomes a channel through which others may ascend to God and by means of which blessing comes down into the world (*Degel Maḥaneh Ephraim, be-haʿalotekha* 199b; *Maggid Devaraw le-Yaʿaqov* 64b). As is the way of Hasidic literature, the discussion here draws on the whole of the earlier tradition, but focuses the materials in such a way as to emphasize the values of the new movement. This is most strikingly seen in the following passage from the writings of the Baʿal Shem Tov's successor, the Maggid of Miedzyrzec:

We begin with the Zohar's interpretation of "One generation passes and another comes" (Eccles. 1:4). There is no generation which does not have a *zaddiq* like Moses (Zohar 1:25a; Gen. R. 56:7). This means that Moses included the entire six hundred thousand of the generation. Thus the rabbis said: a woman in Egypt gave birth to six hundred thousand from one womb.[15] This is why "One generation passes and another comes" is said in the singular and not the plural: it refers to the *zaddiq* of the generation. Thus the rabbis say: "Before the sun of Moses set," (Qiddushin 72b), etc., as Scripture tells us that *"zaddiq* is the foundation of the world." Now it is known that *yesod* [the ninth *sefirah*, = *zaddiq]* has the power to ascend and draw the divine abundance forth from above, because it includes all.[16] The same is true of the earthly *zaddiq:* he is the channel who allows the abundance to flow down for his entire generation. Thus the rabbis said: "The whole world is sustained for the sake of Hanina My son." This means that Hanina brought the divine flow forth for all of them, like a pathway through which all can pass; R. Hanina himself became the channel for that flow [a supraliteral reading of *Ber.* 17b]. In the same was he [the *zaddiq]* the ladder of which it is said: "They go up and down on it" (Gen. 28:12). Just as he has the power to cause the downward flow of divine bounty, so can his entire generation rise upward through him. *(Or Torah, noah)*

Every generation has a *zaddiq* like Moses or like R. Hanina ben Dosa; he is the channel of flow in both directions between the upper and lower worlds. Here the *axis mundi* symbolism as regards the *zaddiq* is quite fully developed; he is the all-inclusive central pillar linking heaven and earth. Jacob's ladder, perhaps the oldest and best-known *axis mundi* symbol of Jewish literature, has undergone a far-reaching transformation. The *zaddiq* is no longer the dreaming observer of the angels who go up and down the ladder's rungs, as was the biblical Jacob. Nor is he a participant in the constant movement along the ladder, a reading which is found in various other Hasidic comments on this passage. Here the *zaddiq* himself *is* the ladder; it is through him that others may ascend to God.

It is not clear whether the Maggid believed in a *single zaddiq* who was the pillar of a given generation, or whether he accepted the notion that there might be more than one such figure in the world at a given time. While this passage seems to point to a singular figure, and such a claim was later made concerning the Maggid himself (*'Eser Orot* 24),[17] many other passages in his writings and those of his disciples seem to point in the other direction. Even in such a work as the *No'am Elimelekh,* where the emphasis placed upon the *zaddiq*'s powers and the importance of his role in the devotional life of the devotee seems utterly boundless, the idea of a single *zaddiq ha-dor* is not prominent. In the writings of Shne'ur Zalman of Liadi, founder of the HaBaD/Lubavitch school, the phrase "the spreading forth of Moses in each generation" is quoted (e.g., *Torah Or* 68c), but here as earlier it seems to refer more to the presence of Moses in every Jew, or at least in every *zaddiq*, than it does to a single figure. The same is true in the writings of Menahem Nahum of Chernobyl, yet another disciple of the Maggid and a major theoretician of early Hasidism (*Me'or 'Eynayim, bereshit* 11a). The reality of Hasidic life, which saw many contemporary figures revered as *zaddiqim*, tended to encourage the notion that each *hasid* would have to seek out his own master, the one whose soul-root was closest to his own, that *zaddiq* then becoming for him the center of his own subjective cosmos. It should be noted that even in circles where the legitimacy of many *zaddiqim* was recognized, the followers of a particular master would show no hesitation in ascribing symbols of the sacred center to their own leader. Again, the world can have more than one center. Thus R. Uri of Strelisk, a disciple of Jacob Isaac of Lublin around the turn of the nineteenth century, is supposed to have said: "He who comes here is to imagine that Lublin is the Land of Israel, that the master's court is Jerusalem, his room is the Holy of Holies, and that the *shekhinah* speaks through his mouth" (*Nifle'ot ha-Rabbi* 202).[18] After his master's death, R. Uri himself was regarded as a *zaddiq*, and presumably would have expected his disciples to relate to his court in the same way. Nor would he have wanted the disciples of any other master to treat that *zaddiq* with any less of such "respect."

With regard to the Ba'al Shem Tov himself, however, the situation was somewhat different. There is some reason to believe that the BeSHT, unlike the circle of preachers from whose midst he and the Hasidic movement emerged in the third and fourth decades of the eighteenth century, did believe in a single *zaddiq ha-dor,* and perhaps that he saw himself in this way (Weiss: 85f.). Since we have virtually no access to the BeSHT's life or teachings except as filtered through the writings of adulating disciples and descendants, the truth of his own belief on such a matter is difficult to determine. It is quite clear, however, that long after the Ba'al Shem's death the claim that he had been *zaddiq ha-dor,* in the fullest sense of that term, was widespread among the *hasidim.* Here was the one figure whose memory was most universally revered in Hasidic circles; devotion to the BeSHT and his teaching was taken as a defining characteristic of adherence to the movement. It should not surprise us then, that the editor of *Shivhey ha-BeSHT,* the legendary biography of the master first published in 1815, makes the claim that the

Ba'al Shem Tov's soul was that of Moses and Rabbi Simeon reincarnate (*Shivḥey ha-BeSHT* 8)!

The Ba'al Shem Tov had two grandsons who became important figures in the history of Hasidism. The elder of these two brothers, Moses Hayyim Ephraim of Sudilkov, was the author of *Degel Maḥaneh Ephraim*, a collection of homilies which is an important source for his grandfather's teachings. R. Ephraim, as he is called, does mention the belief that his grandfather possessed the soul of R. Simeon ben Yohai (*Degel, be-shalaḥ* 101a).[19] When it comes to the question of singular versus collective leadership in his own time, however, the author clearly opts for the latter; he speaks rather frequently of the *zaddiqim*, in the plural, of a given generation (*Degel, zaw* 156b, *emor* 181b). Like other writers on the subject, he seems to accept the reality of his times. His younger brother Barukh, however, was of a rather different mind. Barukh of Medzhibozh became embroiled in public controversies with nearly all the *zaddiqim* of his day. While both power politics and differences in religious attitudes contributed to these conflicts, underlying both lay the fact that Barukh considered himself to be the sole legitimate heir to his grandfather's mantle of leadership and, as the reigning *zaddiq* in the BeSHT's town of Medzhibozh, viewed all other claimants as usurpers.

It was only the nephew of both Ephraim and Barukh, however, who took up the notion of singular leadership and gave it a truly central place in his reading of Judaism. We refer to Rabbi Nahman of Bratslav (1772–1810), the problematic and tormented great-grandson of the BeSHT and one of the great religious geniuses of Israel's history.[20] Influenced alike by the rich rabbinic/Kabbalistic legacy in this realm and by his own family's personal claims with regard to it, *zaddiq ha-dor* became a major motif in Nahman's writings; it is in large part through his often unacknowledged influence that the term came to be present in other latter-day Hasidic parlance as well.

Nahman sought to bring about a new revival within Hasidism. He felt that the *ḥasidim* had, in his words, "grown cold" since the time of the Ba'al Shem Tov (*Ḥayyey MoHaRaN, siḥot ha-shayakhim la-sippurim* 19), and that a new spark needed to be kindled. The great enemy of true Hasidism, as far as he was concerned, was popular *zaddiq*ism, in part as personified by his own Uncle Barukh. Nahman sought to elevate and purify the *zaddiq* figure far beyond anything that was known elsewhere in Hasidism. The chief vehicle of this new revival from within was to be the notion of *zaddiq ha-dor,* with Nahman himself as its standard bearer. If there is only one true *zaddiq* at the center of his generation, the misdeeds of lesser figures are of no importance, except insofar as they verify that *zaddiq*'s claim to singular leadership. Though recognized in this role only by a small band of disciples, Nahman maintained that recognition was not at first essential to his role. "There is one," he writes, "who has no apparent authority at all, but nevertheless in a deeply hidden way he rules over his entire generation, even over the *zaddiqim"* (*Liqq.* 56:1).

It was widely whispered in early Bratslav circles that Nahman was a reincarnation of R. Simeon; it has been shown that the figure of R. Simeon as portrayed prominently even in some of Nahman's own teachings is nothing but a thinly veiled reference to the author himself (*Liqq.* 29; *Sippurim Nifla'im* 166; Piekarz: 13ff). He refers to the *zaddiq* of the generation as the Holy of Holies and also as the *even shetiyah,* the mythical rock at the center of the world from which Creation originated and upon which the Temple was built (*Liqq.* 61:7). He is the true source of insight, needed for all proper interpretation of Torah in his time: "Know that there is a soul in the world through which the meaning and interpretation of Torah is revealed. This is a suffering soul, eating bread and salt and drinking measured bits of water, for such is the way of Torah. All interpreters of Torah receive from this soul" (*Liqq.* 20:1). How characteristically Jewish a way to speak of *axis mundi!* The spatial imagery is there, to be sure; as students of Eliade we could ask for nothing better than the sacred rock at the center of the world. But here *zaddiq* as *axis mundi* is also the channel of interpretive power through which Israel has access to the Torah. The primal energy which radiates from the center now manifests itself as literary creativity through the ongoing promulgation of the oral Torah. This soul *is* in effect the oral Torah for its time, the bearer of the ongoing Mosaic revelation.

When Nahman moved his court to the Ukrainian town of Bratslav in 1802, he quoted in his initiatory sermon a passage from the Zohar in which God shows Abraham the way to the Land of Israel. That sermon is shot through with images of the Holy Land, a point which could hardly be lost on its hearers (*Liqq.* 44). Bratslav is here being proclaimed a new center, the residence of the single true *zaddiq.* Now we understand why it was that the disciples ran through the streets shouting cries of exultation as though to the dwellers in Zion. The single *zaddiq*, the portable ark or Holy of Holies, has found a new resting-place. The shouting *hasidim* must have seen in themselves a reflex of the dancing David, exulting as the ark of the Lord was brought into their city and a new cosmic center was proclaimed.

It will come as no surprise to the reader of Eliade to discover that the *zaddiq* in Bratslav is also described as a great tree, of which the disciples are leaves and branches (*Liqq.* 66:1, 176).[21] In one brief passage among the several that employ this metaphor, however, Nahman breaks new ground in the notion of *axis mundi.* He lends to the tree imagery a doubly ironic twist, a twist that thoroughly summarizes this uniquely complex figure's view of this regard. Nathan, the faithful disciple, recalls that his master once said: "You see in me a great and wondrous tree with beautiful branches and roots. But at bottom I lie truly in the earth" (*Hayyey MoHaRaN* II, *gedulat hassagato* 5). In the Hebrew in which it is recorded, the statement has little impact. What does it mean here to "lie in the earth"? Translate the phrase back into the Yiddish in which it was originally spoken, however (published Hasidic texts are most often Hebrew summary translations of oral Yiddish), and its meaning is obvious. "You see in me a great and wondrous tree *... ober fun unten lig ikh take in dʾerd*—at bottom I am rotting in Hell!" The statement is a confession of all Nahman's well-documented torments and inner doubts about himself and his worthiness for the role which he had chosen.

Nahman, however, is more complex than this. Translate the same Hebrew phrase not into Yiddish but into the other language of Jewish mystical piety, Aramaic, and you come up with a precise paraphrase of Dan 4:11–12: *ilana ... be-ram shorshohi be-areʿa shevuqu.* But why should this seemingly obscure verse have a place in Nahman's self-description? The fact is that these words in Daniel follow immediately upon a verse that has major importance in Bratslav. Dan 4:10 contains the phrase *ʿir we-qadish min shemaya nehit,* "a holy angel come down from heaven." This phrase is well known in Bratslav and in Nahman's own writings as an acronym for *SHiMeʿoN* (Simeon), Nahman's mystic alter ego (Nathan's introduction to *Liqq.,* cf. Piekarz: 14f.). Nahman was a master of literary form and was one who had wide experience in disguising and yet revealing himself through many masks. Here, in the double pun, he is at once presenting himself as the great tree, the holy angel on earth, the new Rabbi Simeon, and a miserable sinner who is rotting in Hell. The *zaddiq* has indeed become the *axis mundi*, here in a unique blending of sacral persona and real person; he is the great tree who in an entirely new way unites the three-tiered cosmos in his own person.

NOTES

1. First recorded by Ruth Rubin among her *Yiddish Folksongs*, Prestige International 13019. Her informant for the song was a former resident of Tyszowce (Tishevits), Poland, a town where there were Kotzker *ḥasidim*. Such Yiddish songs, intended in a semihumorous vein, are not unknown among the *ḥasidim*: witness the highly ambiguous *Brider, Brider,* recorded by the Bobover group on CCL 636. It is nevertheless not completely clear that this song was not a *maskil*'s parody of the journey to Kotzk.

2. The phrase "to travel *(furen)* to a *zaddiq*" means "to be the disciple of a master." In Hasidic circles the question *"tsu vemen furt ir"* (lit.: "to whom do you travel") would mean: "To which *zaddiq* do you owe your loyalty?"

3. The description here is interestingly attributed to R. Hayyim of Nowy Sacz (Sandz), an opponent of the Sadegora dynasty.

4. Gershom Scholem, in his two treatments of the term *zaddiq* and its history (Scholem, 1962, 1969) seems to largely ignore the second rabbinic usage of the term. In seeking to make the point that throughout pre-BeSHTian Hasidic literature *ḥasid* is always a more extreme category of description than the relatively normative *zaddiq*, he has selected the rabbinic *zaddiq*-usages only from the former of the two categories here outlined. He is then able to find in Hasidism "a complete turnabout of terminology" (Scholem, 1962:114). Might one not better speak of a second rabbinic usage of the term *zaddiq*, described in some detail by Mach, a usage which is picked up by the early Kabbalah and much emphasized in the Zohar, thence passing on into Hasidism, where the terminology of the Zohar as well as that of the early rabbis becomes essential in the formulation of the new ideal type? Isaiah Tishby has already disagreed with Scholem on his treatment of the term *zaddiq* (cf. 1961: 663ff.).

5. On Joseph's conquest of his passions, cf. *Ruth Rab.* 6:4 and *Pirke Rabbi Eliezer* 39. This aspect of *zaddiq* is discussed by Mach (26ff.). The association between Joseph as *the* prototypical *zaddiq* and this event is only made explicit, however, in Zohar 1:59b and 1:153b–154a. Cf. also the passage from Moses De Leon's responsa quoted by Tishby (1961:664). On Moses as *zaddiq*, cf. *Sotah* 12a, *Exod. Rab.* 1:20, 24.

6. But see also *Tanḥuma, lekh lekhah* 5 which seems to disagree.

7. I have not been able to pinpoint the first usage of *zaddiq ha-dor* as a

technical term. It is not to be found in early rabbinic sources, and was probably born of the medieval exegesis of Gen. 6:9. Parallel terms *(gedol ha-dor, ḥasid sheba-dor)* are early but do not necessarily indicate a belief in singular leadership.

8. Interestingly, Kabbalists did not develop a notion of earthly *ḥasid* parallel to *ḥesed* in the sefirotic world. Such a claim is made for Abraham alone in *Bahir* 191 (132), but is not developed. Of course the whole mythicosexual quality of the energizing of the upper world would have been thrown off balance by such a notion. For an example of the term *zaddiq* specifically referring to a person who has powers above, cf. *Recanati, qedoshim,* 26d (based on the usage in *Moʿed Qatan* 16b), where the term is almost translatable as "sorcerer."

9. This is the most likely source of the notion that Ahijah was the teacher of the Baʿal Shem Tov.

10. In *Shaʿar ha-Gilgulim* 2:8a–10a Luria is seen as such a figure. *Tiqquney Zohar* 69 (ed. Margaliot 111b) claims that Moses will return at the end of days to reveal the meaning of the Zohar! This already seems to assume the identity of Moses and Rabbi Simeon.

11. The Zohar (2:11b and Zohar Ḥadash *yitro* 35a) compares the *tevah* in which the infant Moses floated on the Nile to the *tevah* in which Torah scrolls are kept in the synagogue. (Cf. also *Qaneh* 12a–b; *Shaʿar ha-Pesuqim* 56a, 98a; *Megalleh ʿAmuqot ofan* 113.) This claim is later repeated in *Degel Maḥaneh Ephraim, wa-yiqra* 148.

12. This is the proper Sefer *ha-Gilgulim;* the work to which we have referred earlier is a version of *Shaʿar ha-Gilgulim,* misnamed *Sefer* by the Przemysl publisher. Though these formulations are original in Kabbalistic thinking, they hark back to that strand of old rabbinic tradition which saw Moses in nearly divine terms, a tendency largely eliminated in medieval Judaism outside of Kabbalah. On the rabbinic material, cf. Meeks. While the parallels to Christianity and even more directly to Samaritanism are noteworthy, the development here is not necessarily influenced by non-Jewish sources.

13. Certain Kabbalists believe that Moses is present in every generation. The idea is first expressed in the later portions of the Zohar literature. Cf. Zohar 3:216b and 273a (both *Raʿaya Mehemna*) and *Tiqquney Zohar* 69 (112a, 114a); Tishby (1961:688). When spelled out, however, these sources seem to refer more to the presence of Moses in *every* Jewish soul than to the existence of an individual Moses-figure in each generation.

14. Hasidic authors tirelessly quote with regard to the *zaddiq* a passage in Zohar 1:31a, *de-aḥid bi-shemaya we-areʿa* ("who holds fast to heaven and earth"). The reference in that source, however, is to *zaddiq* as an aspect of God, not to the earthly *zaddiq*. On the human *zaddiq,* cf. Zohar 1:43a and 2:15a.

15. The Zohar is quoting *Cant. Rab.* 1:15:3. The Midrashic context makes it clear that R. Judah ha-Nasi is merely making a startling assertion to awaken a sleepy audience; he goes on to explain that Moses is *as important as* the

entire generation. The Kabbalists read his assertion literally to support their assertion that the soul of Moses contained all the others.

16. *Yesod,* often referred to by the name *kol* ("all"), includes the flow of all eight upper *sefirot.*

17. The statement is in the name of Israel of Ruzhin, the Maggid's great-grandson. Of course in such a statement the Ruzhiner was making a similar claim for himself as the Maggid's heir.

18. Quoted in Heschel (291). Cf. also *Or ha-Nifla'ot* 22b for a lengthy comparison of the death of a *zaddiq* with the destruction of the Temple. Some of this of course is the eulogist's hyperbole, but the choice is interesting. It is also told with regard to the BeSHT that one of his disciples, R. Wolf Kutzis, sought to undertake a pilgrimage to the Holy Land. When he went to a ritual bath to prepare for his journey, he was told in a vision that the ark and the tablets of the law were to be found, respectively, right there in Medzhibozh and in the Ba'al Shem's heart. Recorded at Lubavitch in the 1940s. I have not found this tale in any printed collection, though Wolf Kutzis' intended journey is the object of another legend in *Oheley Zaddiq* 8a.

19. He quotes this in the name of R. Lipa of Khmelnik, and seemingly with a certain hesitation.

20. Cf. my biography of R. Nahman, University of Alabama Press, 1978.

21. The tree image for master and disciple is already found in Vital's *Sha'ar ha-Gilgulim* 1b.

WORKS CONSULTED

A. Traditional Hebrew Sources

Avaneha-Barzel	Abraham Hazan. Jerusalem, 1961.
Bahir	Ed., R. Margaliot. Jerusalem, 1951.
Degel Mahaneh Ephraim	Moses Hayyim Ephraim of Sudilkov. Jerusalem, 1963.
'Emeq ha-Melekh	Naftali Bachrach. Amsterdam, 1648.
'Eser Orot	Israel Berger. Israel, 1973.
Gilgulim (Sefer ha-Gilgulim)	Hayyim Vital. Vilna, 1886.

Ḥayyey MoHaRaN	Nathan of Nemirov. New York, 1965.
Liqqutey MoHaRaN (Liqq.)	Nahman of Bratslav. Jerusalem, 1969.
Maggid Devaraw le-Yaʿaqov	Dov Baer of Miedzyrzec. Jerusalem, 1962.
Megalleh ʿAmuqot	Nathan Spira of Cracow. Lvov, 1858.
Meʾor ʿEynayim	Menahem Nahum of Chernobyl. Jerusalem. 1966.
Nifleʾot ha-Rabbi	Moses Walden. Piotrkow, 1912 (?).
Noʿam Elimelekh	Elimelekh of Lezajsk. Warsaw, 1908.
Or ha-Niflaʾot	Moses Walden. Piotrkow, 1913.
Or Torah	Dov Baer of Miedzyrzec. Jerusalem, 1968.
Qaneh (Peliʾah)	Anonymous. Korzec, 1784.
Recanati ʿal ha-Torah	Menahem Recanati Lvov, 1880.
Shaʿar ha-Gilgulim	Hayyim Vital. Przemysl, 1875.
Shaʿar ha-Pesuqim	Hayyim Vital. Jerusalem, 1868.
Shivḥey ha-BeSHT	Dov Baer of Linitz. Berlin, 1922.
Sippurim Niflaʾim	Samuel Horowitz. Jerusalem, 1961.
Tiqquney Zohar	Ed., R. Margaliot. Jerusalem, 1948.
Torah Or	Shneʾur Zalman of Liadi. New York, 1954.

B. Modern Works

Brown, Norman O.
  1966   *Love's Body*. New York: Random House.

Büchler, Adolf
  1922   *Types of Palestinean-Jewish Piety*. London: Jews' College.

Dresner, Samuel
  1960   *The Zaddik*. London: Abelard-Schumann.

Eliade, Mircea
  1954   *The Myth of the Eternal Return*. New York: Bollingen.

  1959   *The Sacred and the Profane*. New York: Harcourt, Brace, and
            World.

  1963   *Patterns in Comparative Religion*. New York: Meridian.

Goldenberg, Robert
  1975   "The Broken Axis." Unpublished paper delivered to the Ameri-
            can Academy of Religion, Chicago (October).

Heschel, Abraham Joshua
  1973   *Kotzk: In Gerangel far Emesdikeyt*. Tel' Aviv: Ha-Menorah.

Mach, Rudolph
  1957   *Der Zaddik in Talmud und Midrasch*. Leiden: Brill.

Meeks, Wayne
  1968   "Moses as God and King," *Religion in Antiquity*. Jacob Neusner,
            ed. Leiden: Brill, 354–71.

Neusner, Jacob
  1969–70 "The Phenomenon of the Rabbi in Late Antiquity." *Numen*
            16,1–20; 17,1–18.

Nisensohn, S.
  1937   *Dos Malkhusdige Khsides*. Warsaw: Khsides.

Piekarz, Mendel
  1972   *Ḥasidut Braslav*. Jerusalem: Mossad Bialik.

Scholem, Gershom
  1962   *Von der mystischen Gestalt der Gottheit*. Zürich: Rhein.

  1969   "Three Types of Jewish Piety." *Eranos Jahrbuch* 38, 331–47.

  1971   *The Messianic Idea in Judaism*. New York: Schocken.

  1973   *Sabbatai Sevi: The Mystical Messiah*. Princeton: Bollingen.

Tishby, Isaiah

    1957   *Mishnat ha-Zohar*, Vol. 1. Jerusalem: Mossad Bialik.

    1961   *Mishnat ha-Zohar*, Vol. 2. Jerusalem: Mossad Bialik.

Weiss, Joseph

    1951   "Reshit Zemiḥatah shel ha-Derekh ha-Ḥasidit." *Zion* 16, 46–105.

10.

The Art of Metoposcopy: A Study in Isaac Luria's Charismatic Knowledge

Lawrence Fine

Among the most important roles which Isaac Luria (1534–1572), the preeminent kabbalist of sixteenth-century Safed, played in the lives of his disciples was that of physician of the soul. Before they could practice rituals which were intended to enable them to bind their souls to the divine realm, and to "repair" that realm in accordance with the teachings of Lurianic mythology, his disciples had first to mend their *own* souls, to cleanse and purify them of all imperfection.[1] No individual whose own soul had failed to achieve a certain level of perfection could hope to engage successfully in the intricate and elaborate contemplative rituals—such as the *Yiḥudim*[2]—which Luria devised. A person had to undergo a period during which he cultivated certain spiritual and moral traits and atoned for whatever sins he might have committed. Luria, in fact, provided his followers with highly detailed rituals of atonement by which they were to mend their souls. These penitential acts were known as *tikkunei avonot* ("amends of sin") whose purpose, in the words of Ḥayyim Vital's son Shmuel, was to "mend his soul" and "cleanse him from the filth of the disease of his sins."[3] Ḥayyim Vital (1542–1620), Luria's chief disciple, himself introduces the *tikkunei avonot* with a discussion of the relationship between one's soul and sin.[4] The following passage provides a lucid account of the Lurianic theory of sin and the effectiveness of genuine repentance:

Reprinted by permission of the Association for Jewish Studies from *AJS Review* 11, no. 1 (1986).

Man is created from matter and from form, which consists of soul [nefesh], spirit [ruaḥ], and super-soul [neshamah], the divine portion from above, as it is said: "and [God] breathed into his nostrils the breath [nishmat] of life" [Gen. 2:7]. And his body is dark matter from the side of the "shell," luring and preventing man from [achieving] perfection of his soul [in order] to cut it [i.e., his soul] off from the Tree of Life. . . . and so "there is not a righteous man upon the earth that doeth good and sinneth not" [Eccles. 7:20]. It is known that sin is a blemish, stain, and rust in the soul, and that it is the sickness of the pure soul. When it [is immersed] in filth and stain, it is unable to perceive and achieve the true perfection, which is [attainment of] the mysteries of the Torah. . . . And the transgression becomes a barrier separating the soul from her Creator, preventing her from perceiving and comprehending holy and pure supernal matters, as it is said: "The law of the Lord is perfect, restoring the soul" [Ps. 19:8]. . . .

When the soul is pure and unblemished, then the supernal holy matters take shape in her, and when she dwells in rust and stain everything becomes bitter-sweet [i.e., evil appears as good]. [This is] similar to the sick person who, when he is ill, abhors the good things and loves things which aggravate his illness. The doctor, in order to restore his health, gives him spices, including gall, by which his nature will return to what it originally was, and his health as before. So, too, the sick soul, to remove the sickness from her, must receive the bitterness of medicine and "return" in [the form of] mortification and fasts, sackcloth, ashes, and stripes, ritual immersions, and purifications from filth and the stains of sin. [This is] in order to be able to attain and comprehend supernal matters, which are the mysteries of the world.[5]

Only the weapons of ascetic piety are potent enough to cleanse the soul of the filth that clings to it. Luria himself, proclaims Vital, is the diagnostician and healer of diseased souls! Luria's powers stem from the spirit of prophecy which he possessed, meriting him divine light and esoteric knowledge with which to teach his followers. But Luria only revealed his knowledge to those disciples who were completely pure and worthy. To this end he prescribed for each of his students personalized penitential deeds to meet their specific needs.

He would not reveal any of the mysteries of this holy knowledge to one in whose soul he perceived, with the aid of the Holy Spirit, a blemish—until he gave him penitential acts to straighten out all he did crookedly. And like the expert doctor who prescribes for each sick person the proper medicine to cure this illness, so too [Isaac Luria], may he rest in peace, used to recognize the sin, tell him where he had incurred a blemish, and prescribe for him the penitential act needed for this transgression in order to cleanse his soul, so that he could receive the divine light, as it is written: "O Jerusalem, wash thy heart from wickedness, that thou mayest be saved" [Jer. 4:14].[6]

Isaac Luria did what any good physician would do; he carefully diagnosed the specific maladies which his "patient" had and prescribed the appropriate cure. Among the several diagnostic techniques which Luria had at his disposal, according to Ḥayyim Vital and others, the most important appears to have been his capacity to discern and interpret the meaning of Hebrew letters visible upon an individual's forehead, a variation on the medieval art known as metoposcopy.

Metoposcopy was one of the wide array of divinatory or mantic arts practiced especially in the Middle Ages and the Renaissance, along with similar arts such as chiromancy (palmistry) and physiognomy (form and shape of various other physical features, particularly facial features). As with these other "sciences," metoposcopy was employed for purposes of judging an individual's character and personality, and in many cases, for predicting one's future. As Jewish sources themselves attest, a variation of this art was known at least as early as late antiquity, but it flourished in the Middle Ages and most especially in the Renaissance. In the sixteenth and seventeenth centuries the publication of metoposcopic works proliferated. Like chiromancy, metoposcopy was primarily concerned with the significance of lines, in this case, on the forehead, and was typically associated with astrological notions.[7]

The purpose of the present study is to examine the theory and practice of metoposcopy according to Lurianic teachings, and, more broadly, to explore the ways in which Luria's disciples regarded this type of knowledge on their master's part.

I

In the various lists detailing Isaac Luria's extraordinary abilities with which our sources provide us, one of the standard items is his skill at metoposcopy.

Concerning his attainments, it is impossible for one to relate them [even] in general terms, no less in detail. However, these are the wondrous and true things which I witnessed with my own eyes: He knew how to make a future soul appear before him, as well as the soul of a living or deceased person, from among the early as well as later sages. He could inquire of them whatever he wished concerning knowledge of the future and secret mysteries of the Torah. The prophet Elijah, may his memory be a blessing, would also appear to him and teach him. He could also recognize the letters on the forehead and [was adept at] the science of physiognomy, as well as at [recognizing] the lights that are upon the skin and body of an individual. [He was also skilled at recognizing] the lights in the hair, the chirping of birds, and the language of trees and plants. [He understood] even the speech of inanimate things, as Scripture says: "For the stone shall cry out of the wall [and the beam out of the timber shall answer it]" [Hab. 2:11]. [He knew] the language of the burning candle and the flaming coal; he was able to see the angels who announce all the proclamations [from on high], as is well known, and to converse with them. His knowledge was expert concerning all the plants and the genuine remedies [which they provided]. There are many other such things which cannot even be related. Those who hear of them will not believe them when told. I have recorded that which my eyes have seen in all truth.[8]

The theoretical basis for the recognition of letters upon the forehead (ḥokhmat ha-parzuf) has to do with a set of kabbalistic beliefs concerning the relationship between language and creation as a whole. These beliefs go back, in part, to the first systematic attempt at speculative thought in Hebrew, the *Sefer Yezirah,* probably written sometime between the third and sixth centuries.[9] According to the opening chapter of this brief and highly enigmatic book, God brought all of creation into existence "by means of thirty-two wondrous paths of wisdom." These thirty-two paths comprise "ten *sefirot beli mah,*" the ten fundamental numbers, and the twenty-two letters of the Hebrew alphabet. The bulk of the book's speculative efforts concern the function and role of these letters in the process of cosmogony. Everything that exists came into being through combinations of the alphabet's letters, particularly by means of two hundred and thirty-one "gates," combinations of the letters into sets of two in which every letter of the alphabet is joined to every other. All existence is invested with these different combinations of letters and is nourished by their power.

When, centuries later, medieval kabbalists appropriated the ideas of the *Sefer Yezirah,* this linguistically founded world was understood as an expression of divine self-disclosure or emanation. According to this conception, the Hebrew letters and their combinations are not merely *instruments* by which the Creator wrought creation, but forms assumed by the divine itself. That is, not only can the revelation of deity be described in terms of the ten *sefirot,* the most familiar and typical symbolic system of the kabbalists, but it can be imagined as well as the ever unfolding *word* of God which expresses itself in a virtually infinite variety of combinations and gradations. In this symbolism the Torah is understood to comprise a vast network of "names," each of which signifies a particular concentration of divine power or energy. As such these "names" possess a plenitude of meaning not exhausted by conventional human language.

Nowhere is the divine/linguistic constitution of all creation more evident than in the case of human beings themselves. According to Ḥayyim Vital, the twenty-two letters of the alphabet are present in *each* of the three aspects of the human soul, in ascending hierarchical order, *nefesh, ruaḥ,* and *neshamah.*[10] Each is constructed, so to speak, on the basis of the letters of the Hebrew alphabet. The character and quality of each set of letters are somewhat different in accordance with the different levels of the soul's tripartite division. The letters present in the *nefesh* are small, those of the *ruaḥ* are medium in size, and those of the *neshamah* are largest of all. These three dimensions of soul clothe one another, as it were, with the body's skin constituting the outer covering of all. In the case of a wicked individual, the lights/letters of the soul remain covered and concealed by the skin. But when a person perfects himself by practicing the commandments and studying the Torah, he gradually purifies the various parts of soul, thus enabling the power and light of the letters within each part to come to the surface. The letters are unveiled and manifest themselves in a way which is visible to the skilled eye. The appearance of the letters on the skin allows one who can recognize them and determine their meaning virtually to see the divine part of the human personality, the soul itself. One "sees" the soul in the sense that the letters are a relatively material expression of that which is otherwise immaterial. In the case of one who has sufficiently mended all three grades of soul, the entire alphabet belonging to *each* grade will appear, at one time or another, on the body's skin, most especially upon the forehead.[11]

According to Vital, the forehead discloses the soul's letters best of all, due, in part, to the fact that the letters of the alphabet as a whole correspond to the *sefirah Binah,* which, in turn, is symbolized by the forehead.[12] The particular letters which appear on a person's forehead depend upon the commandments which that individual performs properly. For there is a letter to correspond to each and every precept (although we are informed about only a few of the details of this correspondence). Thus, the person who performs all the commandments on a regular basis, and in whom there is no sin, will bear all the letters upon his forehead. Certain letters, however, will appear more brightly than at other times under various conditions. When one performs particular *mizvot*, the appropriate letters shine especially brightly on that same day. Sometimes a certain word—such as the word *hayyim* (signaling that a person can expect to continue in life)—will appear briefly and then disappear. One skilled in this art, then, must be careful to gaze at the right time upon an individual's forehead. An exception is the deed of charity *(zedakah)*, whose letters remain shining brightly upon one's forehead for an entire week. This is demonstrated by the scriptural text: "And his righteousness *[zidkato]* endureth forever" (Ps. 111:3).

The *level* of soul which one has achieved is also discernible on the basis of the size of the letters which appear. Thus, if a person has only perfected the level of *nefesh*, the letters will be small, and so on. If an individual manifests only one set of letters, having attained only the level of *nefesh,* and more than one of a particular letter is required to spell out a word on his forehead, the letter will initially appear brightly in one place in the word, and reappear a second or third time as needed.

The letters of the alphabet also possess a sefirotic correspondence. That is, it is possible to identify different letters with each of the ten *sefirot*. By virtue of this one can ascertain the sefirotic root of a person's soul, for the appropriate letters will appear more frequently than the others.[13]

The recitation of the one hundred *berakhot* (blessings) required daily of every individual also induces the manifestation of letters.[14] For just as the 613 *mizvot* as a whole have their corresponding letters, so too do the *berakhot* that one recites, such as in the course of daily prayer. The lights of the letters which appear on the skin as a result of reciting *berakhot* are special insofar as there is light *surrounding* each letter; this surrounding light is more luminescent than that of the letter itself. If one sees that the opposite is the case, that the light of the letter is more intense than the surrounding light, it signals that the blessing was not performed properly. Moreover, if one fails to perform certain *berakhot* altogether, their corresponding letters do not appear at all. If a *berakhah* is recited with a mistake, then the letter will appear but will be incomplete or imperfectly formed. And if it is performed correctly, but without appropriate contemplative intention, the letter will be present, but will be dark and unillumined.

If the appearance of letters signifies virtuous behavior, then their absence indicates sinfulness, be it a sin of commission or omission. One who is responsible for some transgression will be lacking in the corresponding letters, which will thereby fail to display themselves on his forehead. Indeed, someone upon whose forehead *no* letters are discernible can expect to meet his death within thirty days unless he performs acts of great restitution and repentance.[15]

There are other indications of the presence of sinfulness, or that something tragic has befallen the individual involved. Sometimes a particular letter will appear broken in the middle. In the case of the letter *bet,* for example, this indicates that one's son has died. At other times letters may appear upside down or lying on their side. There is one letter, for example, which, if it appears abnormally, indicates that a man has had intercourse with his wife in an improper manner. In this connection, Vital relates an interesting incident. The wife of a certain individual had demanded of him that he engage in intercourse, something which he didn't want to do, since it happened to be a weekday rather than Sabbath, the preferred time for marital love. Luria informed Vital that he had recognized the letter *gimel* on the man's forehead, but that it appeared upside down. The *gimel,* Luria told Vital, symbolizes the *sefirah Yesod,* the *sefirah* associated with male procreative vitality, human and divine. Insofar as the man involved did not intend to stimulate *Yesod* by having sex at what he considered to be an improper time, the *gimel* appeared in this unusual manner. Luria indicated that such an act should not be considered a transgression, despite the fact that it occurred on a weekday. Were it a sin the letter would have been turned upside down, but would not have shone brightly as it did. In general, when a letter manifests itself upside down, it signifies that the realm of the feminine is involved. For this reason, the letters on the forehead of a male whose soul-ancestry *(gilgul)* derives from the feminine side of the divine structure will consistently appear upside down.[16]

If a person experiences a nocturnal emission *(tumat keri),* says Luria, the evidence of his impurity will appear on his forehead the following day. If he seeks to cleanse himself of this impurity through ritual immersion in water, then the evidence will remain during the day but will be only mildly visible. However, if he does not undergo ritual immersion, the sin will be discernible until he does so.

The transgressions of a person who, by virtue of other deeds he has carried out, merits the "extra" soul which people can acquire on the

Sabbath, will not be visible upon the forehead during the course of the Sabbath itself. This is due to the fact that the powers of evil have no potency on the Sabbath. The very presence of the additional Sabbath soul can be determined by gazing upon the forehead. For as soon as one performs the ritual immersion required as preparation for the Sabbath, the extra Sabbath soul manifests itself, the evidence for which is found upon his forehead.

Interestingly, we learn that scholars of the Torah experience a special kind of dispensation. If a person is a great scholar of Torah, and particularly if he is a student of Kabbalah *(ḥokhmat ha-emet)*, his study has the effect of covering over the sins for which he is responsible, providing that they are minor transgressions. In such instances, one's sins are not visible upon the forehead.[17] If, however, they are significant sins, then they will be discernible, scholarly merit notwithstanding.

In this connection, Ḥayyim Vital indicated that there were limitations to his master's abilities to diagnose the status of the soul on the basis of metoposcopy. At times he had to resort to more direct communication with an individual's soul.

He possessed another kind of skill; he could call forth the *nefesh, ru'aḥ,* or *neshamah* of an individual, and speak with it [directly]. He would inquire of it and ask it questions, and it would answer whatever it was he desired to know, even including matters of detail. He told me that there are some things which he is unable to discern when he gazes upon the letters of the forehead, due to their being too subtle and concealed. However, when he inquires and searches out a person's soul [directly], then he is able to learn things with great accuracy and clarity.[18]

While the forehead was the most common place for the materialization of the soul's letters, they could appear on any part of the body. "Know that in each and every organ of a person's body, there are letters engraved, informing us about that individual's actions. But the primary place is the forehead, as indicated earlier."[19] In addition, other parts of the body have special features which are instructive with respect to one's conduct and character, especially the eyes, fingernails, and all types of bodily hair. In the case of hair, for example, color, length, type of hair, and the way that it lies, all are clues to a person's status, although we are provided no details about this.

II

There are a substantial number of anecdotal reports by Vital and other Safed scholars about Isaac Luria's practice of the art of metoposcopy. Such evidence clearly suggests that Luria actually engaged in this activity, and that it was not merely a matter for theoretical discussion. Moses Galante, for example, writes that he had personally seen sages who had the ability to practice the art of "determining [the letters on] the countenance."[20] Similarly, Elijah de Vidas, author of the influential treatise on kabbalistic piety, *Reshit Hokhmah*, writes:

. . . our sages taught: "On seeing the sages of Israel one should say, 'Blessed be He who hath imparted of His wisdom to them that fear Him' " [B. T. *Berakhot* 58a]. In Safed, located in the upper Galilee, there have already appeared sages for whom it was appropriate to recite this blessing. They were capable of practicing the art of physiognomy [*hokhmat ha-parzuf*] and were able to inform a man concerning all that he had done—whether it was good or evil. To be sure, these individuals did not merit this wonderful wisdom (which is akin to possessing the Holy Spirit) except on account of their virtuous deeds and saintly behavior.[21]

There can be little doubt that both Galante and de Vidas had in mind Isaac Luria, although it is interesting to note that each of them implies that there may have been others with this skill. Eleazar Azikri preserves a story bearing upon Luria's knowledge of metoposcopy in his *Sefer Haredim*.[22] Azikri reports that Luria once gazed upon the face of a certain sage and told him that "the transgression of cruelty toward animals is inscribed upon your countenance." The distressed man returned home to discover that his wife had failed to feed their turkeys and had left them to wander in the street. After making sure that his wife took corrective action to care properly for the animals he came again before Luria. Without knowing what had taken place, Luria informed him, upon looking into his face, that the transgression had been expiated. The sage then proceeded to tell Luria what had transpired. Vital reports an incident in which Luria gazed upon the forehead of a certain sage and informed him that in his entire life this man had never recited a certain prayer correctly.[23]

Elsewhere, we learn in more general terms that Luria "used to recognize, upon the forehead of a man, the virtuous deeds and the sins which he had committed or had contemplated committing. He knew the gravity of the injury brought about by each transgression, where [on high] the harm had its impact, and the nature of the harm. He [also] knew the restitution that was required [for its repair], in terms of fasts, contemplation, and the recitation of scriptural verses. He would provide each and every individual with the means of atonement in accordance with the sin he had committed."[24]

Our sources also indicate that Luria utilized his skill for a purpose other than determining a person's moral status, although even here the soul's perfection was at issue. In *Sha'ar ha-Gilgulim* Vital writes that every single evening his master would gaze upon the face of each of his disciples. He would see a scriptural verse shining upon the forehead; the visualized verse was one that pertained to that particular student's soul, in accordance with the Lurianic notion that every soul possesses interpretations of Scripture that are unique to it. Luria would then partially explain the esoteric meaning of the verse, in terms of the significance that it held for that individual's spiritual condition. The disciple was then instructed to concentrate upon the explanation he had been given, and to recite the verse before going to sleep. He did this so that when his soul ascended to the upper realm during sleep, he might gain full knowledge of the verse's meaning. In such a way the individual's soul would increase in purity, and ascend to still higher levels in the divine realm, where it would enjoy the revelation of additional mysteries of the Torah.[25]

Elsewhere Vital describes this activity in a somewhat different way. Luria would gaze upon the forehead of each student after sunset, and determine what *kind* of text his soul would study that night when it ascended on high, be it some rabbinic work such as the Mishnah, or an esoteric one such as the Zohar. Here too he instructed the disciple to recite this text before falling asleep.[26]

Vital also preserves several anecdotes in which he himself was involved. On one occasion, he writes, Luria identified the letters *alef, bet,* and *gimel* on his forehead. This demonstrated, according to Luria, that Vital needed to show compassion toward his father.[27] In a different version of this tradition we learn that the letters *alef* and *bet,* spelling out the word *av* ("father"), were written in normal fashion, while the *gimel* was upside down.[28]

In *Sefer ha-Ḥezyonot,* Vital's dream diary, he describes an incident according to which Luria is reported, on a Sabbath eve, to have seen on

Vital's forehead the words, "Prepare a throne for Hezekiah, king of Judah."[29] This revealed that he was invested with the soul of King Hezekiah as his "extra" Sabbath soul, says Vital. Sometime during that Sabbath day Vital became angry while in his house, by reason of which Hezekiah's soul departed. The following week Vital repented for having been angry, whereupon, on the next Sabbath eve, Luria recognized the spirits of both Hezekiah and Rabbi Akiva upon Vital's forehead. Again, however, Vital experienced anger, causing these spirits to leave him. After Vital had wept and repented once again for the sin of anger, Luria informed him that the spirit of Ben Azzai had invested itself in him, despite the fact that Ben Azzai and Vital did not share the same soul-ancestry. Ben Azzai was, however, Akiva's son-in-law.

In this story, then, Luria is reported to have been able to determine the coming and going of Vital's visiting souls by gazing on his forehead. It is interesting to observe that in this series of incidents Luria is not said to have determined the deeds for which Vital was responsible, but the effect those deeds had upon his spiritual state.

In another entry in his diary, Vital reports a story with a similar theme.[30] His teacher is able to explain the meaning of a dream that Vital had by reference to the name of Rami bar Ḥami, which Luria had seen on Vital's forehead the evening before. The conclusion Luria reached was that Vital was invested with the soul of this Babylonian amoraic sage. In *Sha'ar ha-Miẓvot* Vital preserves yet another story, according to which he spoke the name of Samael (i.e., Satan) while conversing with someone at night. The following morning Luria looked at his face and told him that he had violated the prohibition against uttering the names of other gods. Writes Vital, "he strictly warned me that under no circumstances, neither during the day nor the night, should I utter Samael's name." To do otherwise can have injurious consequences, causing one to fall prey to sin or to be punished.[31]

The common feature in these incidents is Isaac Luria's role in bringing to Vital's attention a sin he had committed, either by explicitly informing him of what he had done wrong or, as in the case of the Hezekiah story, by determining whether the souls with which he had been invested had deserted him. These reports, along with the ones described earlier, make it clear that Luria did not use this technique for purposes of predicting the future; nowhere are we told that Luria had prophetic knowledge of what was to come. Rather, he employed the art of metoposcopy in order to determine the status of a person's spiritual condition on the basis of his actions.

While we cannot know whether the incidents reported here occurred as described, what these stories do tell us is that Luria's practice of this art was sufficiently commonplace for it to be mentioned as a matter of fact. In Vital's case the motivation in narrating these incidents was not to impress the reader with Luria's skill as much as to inform him about Vital himself. The reader could be expected to be familiar with the remarkable wisdom and knowledge which Isaac Luria exhibited.

III

The accounts by Ḥayyim Vital and others concerning Isaac Luria's practice of metoposcopy prompt important questions having to do with the character of Luria's knowledge and the source of his authority. While the present study cannot treat these complex issues in the detail they deserve, even a general discussion of such questions will enable us to place the phenomenon of metoposcopy within a broader Lurianic context.

Vital's discussion of the various esoteric skills Luria possessed, and the types of knowledge he exhibited, as seen earlier,[32] suggests the way in which Luria's followers regarded these abilities. They are, in Vital's words, "wondrous and true things" which "it is impossible for one to relate." One has to witness them in order to comprehend their extraordinary nature. Their wondrous character had to do, in significant part, with the fact that they demonstrated Luria's masterful ability to communicate with a wide range of heavenly messengers. Thus he could speak with the souls of departed sages, from the distant as well as the more recent past, inquiring of them "knowledge of the future and secret mysteries of the Torah." He could communicate with the angels on high "who announce all the proclamations . . . and converse with them." He was able to comprehend the language of birds, a language which contains mysteries from above. Most significantly, he experienced revelations from a heavenly agent of even greater importance than the rest of these, Elijah the prophet. As Vital reports, "Elijah would constantly reveal himself to him, speaking to him directly, and instruct him in these mysteries."[33] Luria, then, was considered to have easy and ongoing access to the heavenly realm, and to be uniquely adept at holding direct conversations with a wide assortment of ancient prophets, teachers, and angels.

The deep wisdom, knowledge, and skills acquired by these means, moreover, were believed to be largely *unavailable* through conventional methods of attaining knowledge of the Torah, namely, intellectual study. Vital makes this clear in rather explicit terms: "The secrets of the Torah and her mysteries are not revealed to human beings by the power of their intellects, but only by means of divine vitality which flows from on high, through God's messengers and angels, or through Elijah the prophet, may his memory be a blessing." [34]

Vital amplifies this point in the following words: "There is no doubt that these matters [i.e., esoteric knowledge] cannot be apprehended by means of human intellect, but only through Kabbalah, from one individual [directly] to another, directly from Elijah, may his memory be a blessing, or directly from those souls which reveal themselves in each and every generation to those who are qualified to receive them." [35]

In this context, Vital provides us with Luria's views regarding the history of the transmission of kabbalistic knowledge. Kabbalistic mysteries were taught openly and publicly until the death of Rabbi Simeon bar Yoḥai (Rashbi), to whom tradition ascribes the authorship of the Zohar. Quoting the Zohar's own words on this subject, Vital writes that ever since Simeon bar Yoḥai's death "wisdom has departed from this earth" (Zohar 1, 217a). All of those sages who had borne kabbalistic wisdom since that time have done so in great secrecy, each disclosing his knowledge to a single disciple. What is more, even to these select disciples, kabbalistic masters taught in generalizations only, revealing but a portion of their knowledge. In such a fragmented and fragmentary way kabbalistic wisdom was passed from one generation to the next until the time of Moses ben Naḥman (Naḥmanides), the great Spanish rabbi of the thirteenth century. [36] Following a well-known tradition recorded by Menaḥem Recanati (ca. 1228–ca. 1290), Vital informs us that during this time certain sages *were* privileged to merit direct, personal revelations from Elijah the prophet, including Abraham ben David of Posquières (1120–1191), and the latter's son, Isaac the Blind. Isaac, in turn, passed his tradition on to his two disciples, Ezra and Azriel of Gerona. From them kabbalistic tradition passed to the final teacher of genuine Kabbalah, Moses ben Naḥman. [37]

What was Isaac Luria's place in this process of transmission? Luria, according to Vital, represents nothing less than the first and only appearance of authentic kabbalistic knowledge since Naḥmanides. Even more, his knowledge may be compared only to that of Rabbi Simeon bar Yoḥai himself. For this knowledge has "been neither seen nor heard in all the land since the days of Rabbi Simeon bar Yoḥai, may he rest in peace, until now."[38] Despite the aforementioned claim that true Kabbalah had not manifested itself since Naḥmanides, Vital writes that in every generation God displays his compassion by giving Israel extraordinary individuals *(yeḥidei segullah)* "upon whom the Holy Spirit rested, and to whom Elijah, may his memory be a blessing, revealed himself, instructing them in the secrets of Kabbalah." In our generation, God has not withheld a redeemer from Israel, sending us a saintly angel, "the great rabbi, our saintly teacher, our rabbi and master, Isaac Luria Ashkenazi, may his name be for an everlasting blessing, filled like a pomegranate with [knowledge of] Scripture, Mishnah, Talmud, Pilpul, Midrashim, *Ma'aseh Bereshit,* and *Ma'aseh Merkavah.*"[39] All who witness Luria's knowledge and skills, and all who familiarize themselves with his teachings will recognize "that the human mind [by itself] could not attain such deep and wondrous matters without the power of the Holy Spirit, mediated through Elijah, may his memory be a blessing."[40]

Isaac Luria, then, may be said to have been regarded by his circle as an individual possessing knowledge of a charismatic type, that is, as a person to whom direct and exceptional knowledge of the sacred had been vouchsafed. Luria's charisma, his especially close relationship to the sacred, was evidenced not only by his remarkable saintliness, but even more significantly, by his unusual knowledge and esoteric skills, mysteries which are typically beyond the grasp of ordinary human beings.[41] Mastery of the art of metoposcopy, the knowledge of which, it was believed, could only have come from on high, should be understood as one aspect—albeit a most important one—of a type of knowledge which helped establish Luria as a teacher and religious mentor of unique status in Safed.

From an historical point of view, this legitimization by the Lurianic fellowship of the charismatic mode of acquiring religious truth is, in my view, extremely significant. The effort to gain kabbalistic knowledge through such means stands, of course, in marked contrast to traditional rabbinic methods of developing teachings through various types of textual inquiry. While different hermeneutical styles may be brought to bear upon such inquiry, the common factor is the essentially *intellectual* process of studying an existing text for the purpose of clarifying, interpreting, or furthering meaning. For meaning is believed to reside within the texts themselves; one need only apply the appropriate techniques in order to ferret out the intention of the text. This was the case not only for the rabbis of late antiquity; it was true for the medieval philosophers, biblical exegetes of various types, as well as most kabbalists.

In Luria's case appeal was not made to the inherent meaning of existing texts which could be discovered through rational inquiry, but to some heavenly source. Knowledge, as we have seen, was regarded as deriving directly from on high, rather than from an individual's own intellectual power to determine God's will. Whereas the talmudic sages went out of their way to deny the possibility of further prophecy, claiming instead that the privilege of understanding the meaning of Torah was now a more "earthly" one,[42] the Lurianists reasserted the contention that more direct channels of communication were not only possible, but urgently preferable.

As we have already seen, there were earlier kabbalists whom kabbalistic tradition regarded as having gained their knowledge in this way. But it was not until the fifteenth and sixteenth centuries that we encounter the proliferation of this type of activity on a large scale. The revelatory *maggid* of the Turkish kabbalist Joseph Taitaẓak, the heavenly disclosures experienced by Moses Cordovero and Solomon Alkabeẓ during their walks amidst the grave sites of Safed, Joseph Karo's maggidic visitations, and Ḥayyim Vital's technique of communing with the soul of a departed *tanna,* are all vivid examples of the emergence of a new point of view.[43] When Isaac Luria arrived in Safed from Egypt in the year 1570, then, he found himself in cultural surroundings which were highly supportive of men who sought knowledge of Torah from on high, and who were successful in those efforts. Luria was not, however, merely another example of a general tendency. Rather, in Luria we see a rich and full realization of this tendency. Luria stood out in large part because he was perceived as a virtuoso at such activity, as one who was gifted beyond compare. Through the strength of his impressive personality, as well as through the power of his teachings themselves, Luria was well positioned to raise the phenomenon of charismatic experience to a status which it had not known for centuries.[44]

IV

Luria's capacity to diagnose the moral status of his disciples and others through the art of metoposcopy has also to be understood within the specific context of the redemptive process of which he and his circle believed themselves to be a part. The project of redemption, toward which Isaac Luria's mythological teachings were directed in their entirety, required each of his disciples to assume responsibility for the extremely complex task of *tikkun. Tikkun* refers to the elaborate activity of mending the cosmic flaws brought about by the intradivine rupture known as the "breaking of the vessels," as well as by human sin. At its deepest levels this was to be accomplished through the performance of intricate contemplative and theurgic rites, described in such detail in the Lurianic literature. But such rites, as mentioned earlier, could be practiced successfully only by individuals who were thoroughly worthy, that is, by those who had already achieved a degree of *personal tikkun.* Luria's expertise at diagnosing sin and offering precise penitential exercises with which to purify the soul was perceived by his circle as an essential demonstration of Luria's *redemptive* role. Luria was indeed a "redeemer," as Vital tells us, insofar as healing the soul was an indispensable stage in the larger task of messianic redemption, and insofar as he imparted techniques of contemplation to those he deemed worthy to play a further and more advanced role in the process.

For Isaac Luria and his followers believed that theirs was the final, messianic generation, and that the time was ripe for the increased disclosure of heavenly secrets.

. . . for this wisdom was concealed since the days of Rashbi, may he rest in peace, until now, as he [i.e., Rashbi] taught: "Permission is not given to reveal it until the final generation, until the king Messiah comes." Now is the time, for on account of our saintly teacher, our honored master, Rabbi Isaac Luria, may his memory be a blessing, by means of the spirit of prophecy which appeared in him, our eyes have begun to be enlightened with the light of divine wisdom, hidden [until now] from the eyes of all living things.[45]

The connection between Simeon bar Yoḥai and Isaac Luria goes even deeper. Luria regarded himself as Simeon bar Yoḥai *redivivus,* and believed his closest disciples to be reincarnations of Rashbi's comrades.[46] While there is rich and diverse evidence attesting to this, one tradition is of particular relevance to our subject. According to this tradition—

recorded in several places in slightly different versions [47]—Luria and his disciples journeyed to the same place where Rashbi and his fellowship had engaged in a dramatic study session, an event known in the Zohar as the Holy *Idra* ("threshing floor"). According to the Zohar, in the course of this event Rashbi and his disciples revealed recondite mysteries of the Torah.[48] Luria is reported to have sat in the exact spot that Rashbi had occupied, and to have placed each of his disciples in the position of one of Simeon bar Yohai's comrades, revealing to each disciple the comrade with whose soul he was bound through the process of metempsychosis. Luria is also reported to have engaged in a ritual known as *yihud* ("unification") by lying stretched out upon Rashbi's grave, as a result of which Rashbi revealed to Luria "all that he had learned in the academy on high, just as a man speaks with his friend." [49] According to one version of this story, Luria and his disciples also engaged in the study of the *Idra* itself, in the course of which Luria revealed the secret meaning of Simeon bar Yohai's *Idra* teachings.[50] It is clear from this that Isaac Luria and his circle believed that they were reenacting and furthering the redemptive work that had been carried out by Rashbi and his fellowship.

The mythological basis for this tradition lies in an intricate set of Lurianic teachings concerning the transmigration of souls, particularly those of Luria's own inner circle.[51] For present purposes it is sufficient to point out that Luria devised a transmigratory chain which linked Joseph and his brothers, Rabbi Akiva and the other "Ten Martyrs," Rashbi and his comrades, and Luria's fellowship. Each group represented a decisive stage in the process of *tikkun*. Through their efforts to bring about *tikkun* in the supernal realm, the members of these circles occupied critical roles in the redemptive process.[52] Moreover, each group galvanized around a central figure who stood at the center of these efforts. This process had reached a new and critical stage with Isaac Luria and his disciples; for they believed that their actions were capable, at least potentially, of realizing the redemption once and for all.

The Safed kabbalists appear to have thought that the year 1575 would witness the beginning of the messianic age. According to the Lurianists, sin and exile had caused the exile of the inner secrets of the Torah; in the messianic age, however, these mysteries would be revealed once again. The redemption of holiness, which lies at the heart of Lurianic mysticism, extended even to the redemption of the Torah itself.

Whereas now only fragments of the Torah's deep mysteries are available, in the messianic future every Israelite will achieve knowledge of the Torah in its entirety. The special knowledge merited in the unredeemed state by Luria—and to a lesser degree by his disciples and others—was regarded as a *sign* of the coming redemption. But it was far more than a mere signal. For this knowledge, a "knowledge of the future and secret mysteries of the Torah," was also a means through which Isaac Luria could facilitate the task of *tikkun*.

NOTES

1. Major expositions of Lurianic mythology are found in I. Tishby, *Torat ha-Ra ve-ha-Kelippah be-Kabbalat ha-Ari* (Jerusalem, 1960); G. Scholem, *Major Trends in Jewish Mysticism* (New York, 1941), lecture 7; idem, *Sabbatai Sevi* (Princeton, 1973), pt. 1; J. Avivi, *Binyan Ariel* (Jerusalem, 1987); R. Meroz, *Redemption in Lurianic Teaching*, Ph.D. Dissertation (Hebrew), Hebrew University (Jerusalem, 1988). For a general introduction to the religious life of Safed in the sixteenth century, see L. Fine, *Safed Spirituality* (New York, 1984).

2. For a detailed study of the *Yiḥudim*, see L. Fine, "The Contemplative Practice of *Yiḥudim* in Lurianic Kabbalah," in *Jewish Spirituality*, ed. A. Green, vol. 2 (New York, 1987), pp. 64–98.

3. The *tikkunei avonot* are discussed in *Sha'ar Ruaḥ ha-Kodesh* of the *Shemonah She'arim*, pp. 40–64 (see below, n. 4). They are studied in the above-mentioned article.

4. Ḥayyim Vital was responsible for the most detailed versions of Lurianic teachings, among which the *Shemonah She'arim* ("Eight Gates") is the most important. All references to the *Shemonah She'arim* are to the Yehudah Ashlag edition (Tel Aviv, 1962).

5. *Sha'ar Ruaḥ ha-Kodesh* of the *Shemonah She'arim*, p. 39 (hereafter cited as *SRH*).

6. *SRH*, p. 40.

7. For treatments of non-Jewish approaches to metoposcopy, see L. Thorndike, *A History of Magic and Experimental Science* (New York, 1923–58), especially vols. 6–8; K. Seligman, *Magic, Supernaturalism and Religion* (New York, 1948), pp. 256–261; S. Alexandrian, *Histoire de la philosophie occulte* (Paris, 1983), pp. 201–203. Concerning the development of the physiognomic arts in Judaism, see nn. 11–12 below.

8. *SRH*, p. 19. Other versions of this list are found in *Sefer ha-Gilgulim* (Przemysl, 1875), p. 26; *Shivḥei ha-Ari* (Bardejov, 1929), pp. 6–7; *Sefer Toledot ha-Ari*, ed. M. Benayahu (Jerusalem, 1967), p. 156; *Eleh Toledot Yiẓhak*, Benayahu, pp. 248–251.

9. For discussion of the *Sefer Yezirah*, see G. Scholem, *Ursprung und Anfänge der Kabbala* (Berlin, 1962), pp. 20–29; idem, "The Name of God and the Linguistic Theory of the Kabbalah," *Diogenes* 79 (1972): 59–80; idem, *Kabbalah* (New York, 1974), pp. 23–30. See as well the studies by I. Weinstock and N. Aloni in *Temirin*, vol. 1 (Jerusalem, 1972), pp. 9–99. Luria's use of the *Sefer Yezirah* in this connection is explicitly acknowledged, *SRH*, pp. 15–16. For broader discussions of the relationship between language and Kabbalah, see G. Scholem, *On the Kabbalah and Its Symbolism* (New York, 1965), pp. 32–86; idem, the *Diogenes* article mentioned above, as well as its continuation in *Diogenes* 80 (1972): 164–194.

10. *SRH*, p. 16. This idea is already found in the Zohar, in the context of its discussion of physiognomic matters. See, for example, Zohar 2, 73a, where we learn that the mystery of the twenty-two letters is engraved within the *ruaḥ* of an individual, and that these letters can appear on the face.

According to the anthropological views of the Kabbalah, the soul is considered to have three aspects. The *nefesh* is automatically present and active in every individual; the two more elevated levels, however, are *latent*. These manifest themselves only in the case of persons who are spiritually advanced and who have strived to develop themselves through religious activity. Such activity aids in the cultivation of the higher powers of cognition and results in the fullest maturation of the soul. Later kabbalists— including the Lurianists—added two other levels of soul. These are *ḥayyah* and *yeḥidah*, and are considered to represent still higher stages of spiritual attainment, present only in the most select figures. These two aspects of soul do not figure in the Lurianic discussion of metoposcopy.

11. *SRH*, pp. 15–16. The primary Lurianic account of metoposcopy is found in *SRH*, pp. 15–22. The earliest Jewish interest in physiognomy, in general, appears to go back to a Qumran document, published as 4Q 186. According to this text certain physiognomic criteria, such as the size and shape of the thighs, toes, fingers, hair, eyes, beard, teeth, height, and quality of voice, can be examined to ascertain an individual's moral and spiritual status. Such criteria, along with a person's zodiacal sign, were used to determine a person's fitness for membership in the "House of Light," that is, the righteous among Israel. Concerning this, see *Discoveries in the Judean Desert*, vol. 5, *Qumran Cave 4*, ed. J. M. Allegro (Oxford, 1968), pp. 89–91.

Physiognomic considerations play little role in conventional rabbinic materials, but were of great interest to the Merkavah mystics. As in the Qumran text, the Merkavah literature indicates that physiognomic criteria were employed to determine eligibility for admission into the circle of mystics. These criteria have to do with the character of the nose, lips, eyes, eyebrows, eyelashes, and sexual organs, although greatest significance was attached to the lines and letters upon the palm and forehead. These texts already speak, albeit in an unsystematic and exceedingly obscure way, of certain letters which appear on the hand and forehead. The primary text in this connection is *Hakkarat Panim le-Rabbi Yishmael*, which speaks of twelve letters that are visible on the forehead, although it does not specify which letters these are. This chapter and related materials are analyzed in two articles by G. Scholem, "Hakkarat Panim ve-Sidrei Sirṭuṭin," in *Sefer Assaf* (Jerusalem, 1953), pp. 459–495 (see particularly, pp. 481–485), and "Ein Fragment zur Physiognomik und Chiromantik aus der Spatantiken judischen Esoterik," in *Liber Amicorum: Studies in Honor of Professor Dr. C. J. Bleeker* (Leiden, 1969); see also idem, "Chiromancy," in Scholem's *Kabbalah* (Jerusalem, 1974), pp. 317–319; I. Gruenwald, "Ketaim Hadashim mi-Sifrut Hakkarat Panim ve-Sidrei Sirṭuṭin," *Tarbiz* 40 (1971): 301–319; idem, *Apocalyptic and Merkavah Mysticism* (Leiden, 1980), pp. 218–224. The most extensive treatment of physiognomy, chiromancy, and metoposcopy in medieval Jewish literature, prior to the Lurianic texts, is found in the zoharic corpus. Concerning this, see below, n. 12.

12. *SRH*, pp. 15–16. While the Lurianic notions of metoposcopy described here do not appear to have any direct link to the material found in the Merkavah literature (see above, n. 11), they are unmistakably indebted, at least to some degree, to the fairly extensive discussions in the zoharic corpus. The literature of the Zohar treats physiognomic, chiromantic, and metoposcopic issues in several places, including: (1) Zohar 2, 71a–78a (along with the parallel version in *Raza de-Razin*); (2) Zohar 2, 272b–276a; (3) *Zohar Hadash* 35b–37c; and (4) *Tikkunei Zohar*, tikkun 70. These speculations are based, in part, on exegesis of Exodus 18:21.

It is worth noting here certain substantial differences between the Zohar's discussions and the Lurianic one: (1) Whereas the Zohar treats in some detail the *several* subjects of physiognomy, chiromancy, and metoposcopy— discussing the significance of the hair, forehead, eyes, face, lips, lines on the hand, and the ears—Luria was almost exclusively concerned with metoposcopy, that is, the forehead. He takes up other matters in the most passing way. (2) The Zohar's analysis of metoposcopy is mostly concerned with the shape of the forehead and with the lines or creases appearing in it, and far less with letters. In Luria's case, on the other hand, there is no discussion of anything but the letters and words which manifest themselves. (3) Whereas the Zohar's discussion incorporates elements of astrological speculation, the Lurianic account has only the briefest passing reference to this (see *SRH*, p. 16) and is clearly not genuinely concerned with astrology. (4) The Zohar tends to indicate how physical characteristics, such as the shape of the forehead or eyes, signify certain moral and spiritual traits in general ways. Thus, for example, a person is said to be inclined toward anger, impulsiveness, or joyfulness. In our texts, Luria is able to determine the specific sins or righteous acts which a person has performed.

13. *SRH*, p. 17.

14. Ibid., p. 18. According to B. T. *Menaḥot* 43b, R. Yose declares it to be the duty of everyone to recite one hundred blessings daily, whereas *Numbers Rabbah* 18 indicates that King David instituted the one hundred daily blessings.

15. *SRH*, p. 16.
16. Ibid., p. 17.
17. Ibid., p. 22.
18. Ibid., p. 17.
19. Ibid., p. 20. See nn. 11–12 above.
20. *Kohelet Ya'akov* (Safed, 1558), p. 57a.
21. Elijah de Vidas, *Reshit Ḥokhmah* (Venice, 1579), "The Gate of Love," chap. 6. Concerning de Vidas, his relationship to Luria, and *Reshit Ḥokhmah*, see Fine, *Safed Spirituality*, pp. 83ff.
22. *Sefer Ḥaredim* (Venice, 1601), p. 25a.
23. *Peri Ez Ḥayyim* (Jerusalem, 1980), *Sha'ar ha-Amidah*, chap. 19.
24. This report is found in a somewhat legendary account of Luria's activities, *Eleh Toledot Yizḥak*, ed. Benayahu in his *Sefer Toledot ha-Ari*, p. 251.
25. *Sha'ar ha-Gilgulim* of the *Shemonah She'arim*, *hakdamah* 17.
26. *Sha'ar ha-Mizvot, Ve-etḥanan*, p. 87.
27. *SRH*, p. 17.
28. *Sefer Toledot ha-Ari*. Benayahu, p. 190.
29. *Sefer ha-Ḥezyonot*, ed. A. Z. Aeshcoly (Jerusalem, 1954), p. 165. Concerning Vital's soul-ancestry in general, and his relationship to Hezekiah in particular, cf. pp. 143–144, 174, 184, 191, 198.
30. *Sefer ha-Ḥezyonot*, p. 173.
31. *Sha'ar ha-Mizvot, Mishpatim*, p. 36.
32. See above, sec. I.
33. *Sefer ha-Gilgulim*, p. 27. The Lurianic literature is replete with stories and references to Luria's experience of meriting the revelation of Elijah. See, for example, the references to Elijah in *Sefer Toledot ha-Ari*, Benayahu, index to the names of individuals, p. 379. Regarding revelations of Elijah experienced by earlier kabbalists, see G. Scholem, *Reshit ha-Kabbalah* (Jerusalem, 1948), pp. 66–98. Concerning the multifaceted role of Elijah in Jewish literature, see A. Wiener, *The Prophet Elijah in the Development of Judaism* (London, 1978).
34. *Sefer ha-Gilgulim*, p. 25a.
35. Ibid., p. 25b.
36. Ibid., p. 37b.
37. In this connection, see M. Idel's study of Naḥmanides' own view regarding what constitutes genuine and legitimate kabbalistic tradition, "We Have No Kabbalistic Tradition on This," in *Rabbi Moses Naḥmanides (Ramban): Explorations in His Religious and Literary Virtuosity*, ed. I. Twersky (Cambridge, Mass., 1983), pp. 51–73. Concerning the question of divine revelations experienced by the earliest kabbalists of the twelfth and thirteenth centuries, see A. J. Heschel, "Al Ruaḥ ha-Kodesh be-Yemei ha-Beinayim," in *Alexander Marx Jubilee Volume* (New York, 1950), pp. 165–207, especially, pp. 190–193; I. Twersky, *Rabad of Posquières: A Twelfth Century Talmudist* (Cambridge, Mass., 1962), pp. 286–300.
38. *Sefer ha-Gilgulim*, p. 26a. Cf. *Shivḥei ha-Ari*, p. 6.

39. *Sefer ha-Gilgulim*, p. 26a.
40. Ibid., p. 27a. It would be mistaken to conclude from this that Luria did not engage also in conventional textual study, of both exoteric and esoteric texts. Concerning this subject, see, for example, the traditions reported in *Sha'ar ha-Mizvot, Parashat Ve-ethanan; SRH*, pp. 34–46. Some of the relevant texts are translated in Fine, *Safed Spirituality*, pp. 68–70.
41. For a discussion of the notion of religious charisma as it is used here, see Charles F. Keyes, "Charisma: From Social Life to Sacred Biography," in *Charisma and Sacred Biography*, ed. M. Williams, *Journal of the American Academy of Religion Thematic Studies* 48, nos. 3 and 4 (1982): 1–22.
42. See, for example, the often-cited text in the Babylonian Talmud, *Bava Mezia* 59b. On the question of revelation and authority, see G. Scholem, "Religious Authority and Mysticism," in his *On the Kabbalah and Its Symbolism*, pp. 5–31; idem, *The Messianic Idea in Judaism* (New York, 1971), pp. 282–303.
43. Concerning the experiences of Joseph Taitazak, see G. Scholem, "Ha-Maggid shel R. Yosef Taitazak ve-ha-Giluyim ha-Meyuhasim Lo," *Sefunot* 11 (1977): 69–112. On the revelations accorded Cordovero and Alkabez, see R. J. Z. Werblowsky, *Joseph Karo, Lawyer and Mystic* (Oxford, 1962), pp. 51–55, as well as Y. Liebes, *Ha-Mashiah shel ha-Zohar—le-Demuto ha-Meshihit shel R. Shimon bar Yohai* (Jerusalem, 1982), pp. 107–109. On Karo, see Werblowsky, *Joseph Karo*, passim. Vital's technique is studied in L. Fine, "Mishnah as a Vehicle for Mystical Inspiration: A Contemplative Technique Taught by Hayyim Vital," *Revue des études juives* 141 (1982): 183–199. In this connection, see L. Fine, "Maggidic Revelation in the Teachings of Isaac Luria," in *Mystics, Philosophers, and Politicians*, ed. J. Reinharz and D. Swetschinski (Durham, N.C., 1982), pp. 141–157. See also the study by M. Idel, "Iyyunim be-Shitat Ba'al Sefer ha-Meshiv," *Sefunot*, n.s. 2, no. 17 (1983): 185–266, in which he discusses this book's influence upon the development of the kind of revelatory techniques mentioned here. See, as well, the survey of such techniques in Werblowsky, *Joseph Karo*, pp. 38–83.
44. One ought not to underestimate the influence which the *personality* of Isaac Luria exerted upon later mystical developments, particularly Sabbatianism and Hasidism, in significant part through the hagiographical works on Luria, *Shivhei ha-Ari* and *Toledot ha-Ari*. In this connection, see J. Dan, *Ha-Sippur ha-Ivri be-Yemei ha-Beinayim* (Jerusalem, 1974), chap. 11. This is a subject which deserves further investigation.
45. *SRH*, pp. 39–40.
46. This has already been noted and briefly discussed by Y. Liebes in his important study, mentioned in n. 43, *Ha-Mashiah shel ha-Zohar*, pp. 109–110 and passim.
47. See *Shivhei ha-Ari*, p. 17; *Sefer Toledot ha-Ari*, Benayahu, pp. 179–180; *Sefer ha-Hezyonot*, p. 153.
48. The section of the Zohar entitled *Idra Rabba* is in Zohar 3, 287b–296b.

For an English translation of these sections, see R. Rosenberg, *The Anatomy of God* (New York, 1973). The *Idra Rabba* is studied in the monograph by Liebes mentioned in the preceding note. In general, the *Idra Rabba* played an exceedingly important role in Isaac Luria's thinking.

49. *Shivḥei ha-Ari*, p. 17.

50. *Sefer Toledot ha-Ari*, pp. 179–180.

51. The subject of metempsychosis constitutes a major topic in Lurianic teachings, the primary accounts of which are *Sha'ar ha-Gilgulim, Sefer ha-Gilgulim*, and *Sefer ha-Ḥezyonot*, pt. 4. A survey of the history of metempsychosis in kabbalistic literature may be found in G. Scholem, *Pirkei Yesod be-Havanat ha-Kabbalah u-Semaleha* (Jerusalem, 1976), a German version of which is found in idem, *Von der mystischen Gestalt der Gottheit* (Zurich, 1962). A thorough study of the place of metempsychosis in Luria's mythology, and its relationship to his fellowship's self-understanding, is still needed.

52. See, for example, the account in Vital's *Sefer ha-Ḥezyonot*, pp. 210–229; *Sefer ha-Gilgulim* (Vilna, 1886), chap. 35. Cf. Liebes, *Ha-Mashiaḥ shel ha-Zohar*, p. 109, n. 95. Concerning the messianic roles of Luria (and Vital), see D. Tamar, "Ha-Ari ve-ha-Raḥu ke-Mashiaḥ ben Yosef," *Sefunot* 7 (1963): 167–177; Scholem, *Sabbatai Sevi*, pp. 52–58.

III

DEVOTIONAL PRACTICES AND MYSTICAL EXPERIENCE

11.

Prayer and Devotion in the Zohar

Isaiah Tishby

A. "WORSHIP IN THE HEART" BEFORE THE ZOHAR

I

The essential nature of prayer is defined in the Talmud: "What is worship in the heart? It is prayer." [1] This is a suitable point from which to start our explanation of the problems connected with prayer and devotion in rabbinic literature and in the various strands of medieval Jewish philosophy. "Worship in the heart" may be interpreted in two ways. (a) It emphasizes the fact that prayer is a substitute for the sacrificial offerings that ceased when the Temple was destroyed. In this sense it implies that although proper worship cannot be resumed until the Temple is rebuilt, the gap is to some extent filled by "worship in the heart." (b) It makes the point that prayer is superior to sacrificial worship in that prayer is "in the heart," in man's innermost being, and thus does not depend on external physical ritual. These two interpretations are indicative of two different and sometimes contrary tendencies in Judaism: the external ritualistic approach, which emphasizes above all the correct fulfillment of the practical commandments; and the internal spiritualistic approach, which places the highest value on the intellectual and spiritual striving to achieve emotional or rational contact with supernatural elements.

The author of the phrase "worship in the heart" does not reveal his

Reprinted from *The Wisdom of the Zohar* by Isaiah Tishby, by permission of Oxford University Press, Oxford, and the Littman Library of Jewish Civilization, Oxford, 1989.

precise intention, but in other statements both types of interpretation are quite clearly expressed. I have already referred to a number of contradictory views concerning the relative worth of prayer and sacrifice.[2] These differences of attitude find their way indirectly into the rabbinic explanation of how the three statutory prayers originated. One view is that "the patriarchs instituted the prayers." This means that they are historically earlier than both Tabernacle and Temple, and implies that they are of higher intrinsic worth than sacrifice. Another view, however,[3] is that "they were instituted as a parallel to the daily-offerings." This makes the prayers dependent on the sacrifices. In other words they are regarded as of subordinate value during the period of the Temple's existence and as mere substitutes after its destruction.

These contrasting attitudes, the ritualistic and the spiritualistic, are highlighted even more in the doctrines about prayer itself. On the one hand, prayer is treated as part of the intricate web of Jewish law, and it is surrounded with masses of legislative detail. On the other hand, we are constantly warned against regarding prayer as a merely external, ritualistic exercise: for example, "Be careful in your reading of the *Shema* and the *Amidah*, and, when you pray, do not regard your prayer as a fixed mechanical task, but as an appeal to God for mercy and grace."[4] The example of "the early pious ones" who "used to wait an hour before praying in order to concentrate their minds on their Father in heaven"[5] was cited in order to show that the recitation of prayers as required by the law was not enough. The basic requirement was to purify the heart and concentrate the mind, not only during prayer but also before and after it.[6] Descriptions of the rabbis' profound meditation or excitement in prayer also indicate a concern with spirituality.[7]

The standpoint of the rabbis in Talmud and midrash with regard to the problem we are discussing can be seen in the arguments they had concerning the value of "intention" in an area much wider than that of the liturgy.[8] The question of whether "the commandments required intention" or not[9] applied to all the practical precepts in general. But the essential meaning of "intention" *(kavvanah)* in this argument is bound up with the correct fulfillment of the commandments. It means simply the intention to carry out one's religious obligation through an understanding of its import, and it is contrasted with the performance of what appears to be a commandment for non-religious purposes, or at least not for the purpose of fulfilling the commandment; for example, sounding the *shofar* just in order to make music, or eating *mazzah* unwillingly. The insistence on *kavvanah* in this sense does not therefore imply a desire for inner religious spirituality, although if one does not demand this simple kind of *kavvanah*, one adopts an extremely formalistic view, dispensing with the most elementary kind of conscientiousness, and regarding as valid the most perfunctory kind of religious acts. We do find, however, in the Talmud and in midrashim, demands for *kavvanah* of a different kind, requiring spiritual concentration and an internal religious awareness in the performance of the commandments. Sometimes the rabbis valued an action in terms of mental attitude, as in the famous dictum, "It matters not whether you do much or little so long as your heart is directed to heaven." [10] But mental concentration and correct intention were required above all in prayer and in all its attendant practices, and prayer had a particular significance because of this. [11]

II

In the philosophical literature of the Middle Ages we see a change in the evaluation of *kavvanah*, both in general and particularly with reference to prayer. [12] The philosophers from Sa'adia Gaon onward criticized, some gently, others less so, those who presented religion as the fulfillment of the practical commandments according to the literal requirements of the law—and nothing more. For them *kavvanah* was the chief requirement in the performance of the *mizvot*. They differed only in their understanding of what *kavvanah* entailed. Some stressed intellectual comprehension and speculative inquiry; others emphasized humility, self-effacement, and an attempt at spiritual communion through emotional enthusiasm and ecstasy. They all, however, agreed on the prime obligation and importance of inner religious awareness. One can understand, therefore, how insistent the philosophers were on inwardness in prayer, whose statutory verbal formulation was in their view just the outer garb of worship in the heart.

This spiritualist attitude reached its peak of expression in that wonderful philosophico-mystical work of morality, *The Duties of the Heart* (*Hovot ha-Levavot*) by Rabbi Bahya ben Joseph ibn Pakuda. When Bahya explains the main reasons that prompted him to compose this book, he says that he wanted to correct the tendency to deprive Judaism of all inner content, and he states quite forcibly that the performance of the commandments can be truly evaluated only by the measure of spiritual involvement: "Our members cannot perform an act unless our souls have chosen it first"; "the foundation and the pillar of action is the intention of the heart and conscience"; "when intentions are defective, deeds are not acceptable to God, numerous and insistent as they may be." [13] Religious acts are to be valued not for their quantity but for their spiritual quality: "A man's one good deed can outweigh many good deeds performed by himself or another, and the same is true of an evil act. All is according to intention and purpose. The thought of a good deed by a true worshiper and his desire to carry it out, even if he prove unable to do so, may be balanced against many a good deed carried out by others." [14] This means that a pure intention that is not realized may be worth more than a precept that is fulfilled accurately but without any spiritual motivation. Bahya's real originality, which involved almost a reversal of values in Judaism, was that he based religion on a system of spiritual obligations that had no exterior manifestation: the duties of the heart. And he wrote his book in order to explain what they were and how highly they were to be prized. He also insisted, however, on the fulfillment of the practical commandments, the physical obligations: "We have already shown that man is composed of a soul and a body— both are God's graces given to us, one exterior, one interior. Accordingly, we are obliged to obey God both outwardly and inwardly." [15] Nevertheless, Bahya gave the body a very inferior status, regarding it even as something negative and harmful, conferring no benefit or advantage except in its role as servant to the spirit. In the same vein, physical acts rank low in the scale of religious values. The essence is "inward obedience," which "is expressed in the duties of the heart . . . in all the duties performed by faith and conscience without the activity of the external body members. . . . Thus . . . the duties of the members are of no avail to us unless our hearts choose to do them and our souls desire their performance." [16]

In his account of the commandments Bahya assigns to prayer an intermediate position,[17] but in actual fact he regards prayer mainly as a duty of the heart. It is only because the organs of speech have to be used in prayer that he mentions the physical aspect, but his view is that "words are a matter of the tongue, but meaning is a matter of the heart. The words are like the body of the prayer, but the meaning is like its soul. When a man prays only with his tongue, his heart preoccupied with something other than the meaning of the prayer, then his prayer is like a body without a soul, or a shell without contents, for only his body is present; his heart is absent from his prayer." [18] Consequently, one must rid oneself of any extraneous thought that is not relevant to prayer: "Free your body of all its movements and prevent your senses and thoughts from being preoccupied with any of the matters of this world when you are engaged in prayer." [19] This is not absolutely necessary in the performance of merely physical duties, for these are "things in which the doer is not harmed by having his heart occupied with something else." [20]

A crucial distinction between prayer and the physical obligations arises when Baḥya explains *kavvanah* (intention). "When a man undertakes to perform one of the duties of the body ... he must direct his intention to God before he performs it, so that the root of his deed will be obedience to God and the expression of his thanks and gratefulness, his glorification and praise." In other words, intention here primarily means the acknowledgement that the divine commands are about to be fulfilled. With prayer, however, the stress is on the emotional side, the yearning of the soul to submit itself to God. "You must know, O my brother, that the purpose of prayer is the heart's contrition for God's sake and its submission to Him, as well as its glorification of its Creator and the giving of thanks and praise to His name, and the putting of all the heart's hopes in Him." [21]

Baḥya does not shrink from the logical, but daring, conclusion that the liturgy was formulated only in order to assist the majority of worshipers who are not able on their own to summon up the proper religious feelings. When, however, we come to the real meaning of prayer, the words are of little importance: "Prayer is made [up] of words and meaning. The words need the meaning, but the meaning is in no need of words, when it is possible to convey it with the heart. For the meaning is the root of our purpose and the basis of our intention." [22] The spiritual concept of prayer reaches its peak in these statements, once the affirmations of fidelity to tradition are removed.

From certain statements in Maimonides we see that he too did not consider the true value of prayer to reside in the words. They were just the outer form required from the masses who were not sufficiently able to offer pure, spiritual worship. He explains sacrificial legislation as an agreement on God's part to the continuation of an idolatrous form of worship, because the generation of Sinai would not have been able to accept a prohibition of sacrifices. It is in this context that Maimonides

writes: "it would have been contrary to the nature of man, who generally cleaves to that to which he is used; it would in those days have made
the same impression as a prophet would make at present if he called us
to the service of God and told us in His name that we should not pray
to Him, not fast, not seek His help in time of trouble; that we should
serve Him in thought and not by any action."[23] In other words, true
religion could dispense with prayer, fasting, and imploring God for
mercy. All that was really necessary was a spiritual form of worship "in
thought and not by any action." However, since most people were not
ready for this exalted stage, we had to accept the forms of prayer as
divinely ordained. This spiritual attitude is also apparent in the fact that
the belief that God hears prayer and supplication and responds to them
is included among the necessary beliefs, that is, among those beliefs
which are meant to educate and guide the masses, not among the true
beliefs and opinions.[24]

Apart from these remarkable ideas that we can read between the lines
of Maimonides' teachings, his spiritual approach is also expressed quite
clearly and openly. In the simplest and most straightforward formulation
of his views, in his *Mishneh Torah*, he defines and evaluates the purposes
of prayer, and in so doing he squeezes every spiritual drop he can out of
the earlier sources: "Every prayer that is uttered without correct intention *(kavvanah)* is no prayer. And if a man prays without *kavvanah* he
should pray again with *kavvanah*. . . . What is *kavvanah*? One should
empty one's mind of every thought, and regard oneself as if one were
standing in the presence of the *Shekhinah*."[25] In his philosophical work
he is very insistent that one should rid oneself of all preoccupation
with worldly matters, and concentrate solely and exclusively upon God.
Maimonides differs from Bahya's concept of the religious life, including
his view of prayer as "the intellectual worship of God,"[26] that is, the
intellectual ascent of man toward communion with God. In Maimonidean thought the worship of God, through prayer, study, and the fulfillment of the practical precepts prepares the way for philosophical,
speculative contemplation.

III

In the German pietistic movement that was active in the twelfth and
thirteenth centuries, both as a popular ethical force and as a mystical,

theosophical current confined to very restricted circles, prayer and *kavvanah* were treated in two ways.

In the *Sefer Ḥasidim* (Book of the Pious), a collection of the ethical teachings of the German pietists, there is great emphasis on pure and simple devotion, and the value of a religious act is measured by purity of intention and motive. Of course, the book places tremendous importance on the practice itself of the commandments, and it requires precise compliance with every detail of religious observance and tradition. But when it comes to a choice between sincerity of intention and practice, preference is given to the former. There is, for example, the well-known story of the illiterate herdsman who did not know any prayers and was not able to learn them, but who expressed his sincere devotion to God by offering to look after His animals for nothing.[27] The best thing to do, however, was to combine correct practice with absolute sincerity.[28]

When it comes to prayer, one of the principal themes of the *Sefer Ḥasidim*, the importance of sincere intention is stressed again and again,[29] as in the statement that "prayer depends on the heart. If the heart is good, one's prayers are accepted, and one's prayer is pure."[30] Like the *ḥasidim* of old, the German *ḥasidim* sought to wait a while before praying in order to direct their minds properly toward the Holy One, blessed be He.[31] *Kavvanah* was thought to be absolutely essential if prayer was to be valid: "if a man does not pray the first prayer of the *Amidah* right to the end with *kavvanah* he should say the prayer again. . . . And if his concentration is interrupted by a worldly thought he should stop a while and then continue his prayer."[32] "It is forbidden to think of Torah during prayer; how much more of other things. And if a man sees that it is altogether impossible to concentrate on prayer, he should not pray."[33]

In the mystical literature of the German *ḥasidim*, especially in the writings of Rabbi Eleazar of Worms, we can see a new method of understanding prayer and *kavvanah*. The different parts of the liturgy and the individual words themselves have a secret content: references to angels and to other supernatural forces that can be understood only by a complex mystical interpretation. It is no longer sufficient to address oneself to God with a pure heart and with the correct emotions of fear, love, and joy. The Jew who prays has to know the mystical secrets of the Godhead, which according to German hasidic theosophy has three aspects: the hidden, infinite God, who created the universe, and who is both present within it and exalted above it; the concealed *Shekhinah*, who is the internal glory and the sanctity of God; and the manifest *Shekhinah*, who is the external glory of God, and His greatness or sovereignty. This latter, in the accounts of the vision of the Chariot, is depicted as the king or the cherub seated upon the throne.[34] The actual words of prayer are addressed to the figure upon the throne: "The [divine] unity has no end. It is everything. And if it had not imaged itself through the prophets and shown itself to them as a king seated upon the throne they would not have known to whom they should pray."[35] The inner intention *(kavvanah)*, however, is directed toward the concealed *Shekhinah*: "All God-fearers, when they pronounce a benediction, and offer praise and obeisance to God, should direct their minds to His sanctity only, that is, to His glory, which has no form or shape, only voice and speech."[36] Sometimes it seems as if the object of *kavvanah* is meant to be the Godhead itself in both its transcendent and immanent aspects,[37] but the major view is that the hidden Creator is beyond the reach of one who prays.

The reason for this restriction on the object of one's devotion is explained in a statement by a pupil of Rabbi Eleazar of Worms:[38] "One should remember that the Creator is called 'the Cause of causes.' He is beyond the reach of all thought or allusion. . . . Therefore a man should intend to pray in such a manner that his prayer will be received by the Creator through the power of the special cherub, emanated and created from His great fire. . . . Do not ask why it is possible to direct one's prayer to a cherub through whom it will be accepted by the Cause of causes, and not to the Cause of causes Himself. For the Creator enabled Moses, our teacher, to hear his voice, saying (Exodus 23:21), 'Take heed of him (i.e., the angel), and listen to his voice; do not rebel against him; for he will not pardon your transgression; for My name is in him.' This means: Do not change the object of your devotion, but incline your heart toward him when you pray." Since the nature of the Creator is beyond man's comprehension, his prayer cannot be offered to Him directly, but only through an intermediary, the cherub (the *Shekhinah*), who acts as a bridge between man and God. The author of this passage, who thought it necessary to justify the view of the German *ḥasidim*, emphasizes later on that it is forbidden to believe that the cherub "has power and greatness of his own. Everything emanates from His power. But the fact that the cherub is powerless on his own should not prevent one from directing one's prayer to him, 'for My name is in him,' for his name is 'Great Metatron' and he is called 'the lesser *YHVH.*' " Therefore, the "emanated and created" one can take the place of the Emanator and Creator, and receive prayer.

The simple methods of prayer and *kavvanah* advocated by the *Sefer Hasidim*[39] are separated by a considerable distance from the complex theosophical procedures of the German Jewish pietists. The one thing they have in common, however, is their meticulous attachment to the liturgical text. Both the pure and simple *kavvanah* and the theosophical *kavvanah* or understanding are inextricably connected with the actual words of prayer. The well-known tradition transmitted by Rabbi Jacob ben Asher[40]— "The German *hasidim* were in the habit of counting or calculating every word in the prayers, benedictions, and hymns, and they sought a reason in the Torah for the number of words in the prayers"— has its origin in the practices of the mystics, but its respect for the text of the prayers reflects the spirit of popular hasidism as well.[41] This insistence on the correct traditional text, to serve as the basis for *kavvanah,* marks a fundamental difference from the philosophical approach. But, on the other hand, it is identical to the view of the Provençal and Spanish kabbalists, the contemporaries of Rabbi Judah the Pious and Rabbi Eleazar of Worms.

IV

The teachings of the early kabbalists concerning prayer and *kavvanah* have already been expounded in the studies of Gershom Scholem, and I shall do no more than summarize his conclusions and add a little more material.

The first steps were indicated in the *Sefer ha-Bahir,* where liturgical verses and blessings were associated with specific *sefirot.* But the approach was unsystematic, and even the single individual ideas lacked the most important element, namely, the practice of spiritual concentration and of directing the heart and mind toward the *sefirot* when one recites the prayers and blessings. According to Scholem[42] the most original ideas should be attributed to the school of Rabbi Abraham ben David and his son Rabbi Isaac the Blind in southern France. These were later expanded and systematized by the circle of kabbalists in Gerona. They thought that individual verses in the liturgy and even separate words

alluded to the divine *sefirot,* and that consequently when one pronounced the words of a prayer one should consciously concentrate upon
the particular *sefirot* to which they referred, and thus elevate one's
thinking to the divine realm.

Rabbi Abraham ben David and Rabbi Jacob Nazir, who were among
the founders of the doctrine of contemplative meditation, taught that
one's thoughts could be directed even toward "the Cause of causes," to
the hidden God above the *sefirot.* But Rabbi Isaac the Blind and his
disciples maintained that only the *sefirot* could be the direct object of
prayer, and that contact between man and *En-Sof* could be achieved
only through them.[43] In his commentary to the *Sefer Yezirah* Rabbi
Isaac writes:[44] "All the awesome attributes (i.e., the *sefirot*) may be
objects of meditation, for every attribute derives from the attribute that
is above, and they are transmitted to Israel as objects of meditation,
from the attribute that is manifest in the heart as far as *En-Sof.* For the
only way to pray is by means of finite things [by which] a man may be
received and raised in thought as far as *En-Sof.*" In order to be uplifted
in this way, one needs to cleanse one's mind of all alien thoughts and
bodily desires, and immerse oneself in spiritual meditation and in a deep
yearning for communion: "True *kavvanah* [is achieved] when a man
rids his heart of all alien thoughts, which are physical desires . . . and
thinks of abstract and not concrete things, and imagines that he is
standing in the presence of the celestial *Shekhinah.* And his yearning and
desire should cling to the supernal King, and he should annihilate all his
emotions so that he may cling to the supernal light."[45] The length of
time that the pious ones of old waited before, during, and after prayer
enabled them to prepare and use their *kavvanah* properly: "It was in
this way that the early sages used to spend an hour before prayer, so
that they might rid themselves of other thoughts, and prepare their
methods of concentration *(kavvanah),* and the power with which they
practised it; and an hour during prayer so that they might express their
kavvanah in speech; and an hour after prayer, in order to consider how
they might use in terms of actual deeds the power of *kavvanah* that had
been utilised in speech."[46]

The kabbalists did not regard *kavvanah* as a passive meditative experience. The concentration of thought or of soul was seen by them as a
powerful mystical source of creative energy that could have a positive
effect on the *sefirot,* open a channel of influence in the Godhead, and so

bring blessing to both the upper and the lower worlds. This activation of a flow of blessing is the principal aim of the individual *kavvanot,* which are phrased in such a way that they point to the realization stage by stage of this mystical process. I shall quote two passages to illustrate this point. The first example concerns the response "Amen": [47] "He who responds 'Amen' opens a channel from the master *(omen)* to the pupil *(amun),* and thence to those who pronounce the blessing and to those who are blessed from the well of righteousness, even though he is permitted to prolong his thought, which is infinite, only enough to open the source of blessing and to cause it to flow, and to bring it down in proper measure." The second example concerns the *kavvanah* of the word *"barukh"* (blessed) in the morning benedictions, and comes from the beginning of Rabbi Azriel's *Perush ha-Tefillot:* [48] "Barukh is comprised of every power, from the source of life, from life, and from the light of life. It is blessing; it blesses; and is blessed, like the source of a stream *(berekhah)* that is blessed. It is blessed from the source that is called 'barukh.' "

Those who pray with the correct intention share in the flow of divine influence that they precipitate. They receive both spiritual gifts and the satisfaction of physical needs. He who prays with *kavvanah* is rewarded with insight and knowledge, which are impressed upon the soul when it is illumined with divine light: "He who prays should imagine that [God] speaks with him and teaches him and directs him, and he should receive His words with fear and awe and great trembling, and he should remember that everything that [God] teaches man is limitless." [49] There is an important passage that portrays the process of correct meditation in prayer stage by stage as the ascent of the human will toward union with the divine will; and this is similar to its description of *kavvanah* in the mystery of sacrifice. The passage explains that a central feature of this union of wills is the bringing down of influence in order to satisfy the needs of the man who prays: "The lower Will does not achieve completion if it draws near out of self-interest, but only if it draws near and is clothed with the desire to reveal the hidden identity in the concealed mystery. When it draws near in this way the upper Will will draw near to it and give it added strength and desire to perfect everything, even to satisfy its own self in which the upper Will has no part." [50] A magical element is introduced here into mystical *kavvanah.* [51] When the human will ascends it appears to reach a point of self-annihilation by becoming interfused with the divine will. But as it fades into nothingness it becomes stronger by activating the divine will to bestow upon it as much influence as it requires. This process, however, cannot start unless the original intention is directed solely toward the divine world, "to reveal the hidden identity in the concealed mystery," without any thought of seeking personal advantage, for "the lower Will does not achieve completion if it draws near out of self-interest." A similar attitude is implied in the principles of prayer composed by Rabbi Azriel: "Know, my son, that the Eighteen Benedictions contain the needs of the body, and the needs of the soul, and the need of the life of the soul, which is the life of the world to come. . . . Know, my son, that every prayer that does not contain the need of the life of the soul, which is the life of the world to come, is like matter without form, and it is called 'prayer by rote'; the flow of life does not well out thereby from the source. It is like standing water." [52] In my view, "the need of the life of the soul," which is also called "the life of the world to come" concerns mainly the provision of divine influence in order to satisfy the needs of the *sefirot* below *Binah,* which is the source of influence and called "the world to come." [53]

The drawing out of divine influence is connected with the mystery of unification, which, according to the kabbalah, is the most important activity that man can engender within the Godhead. When thought ascends or when the two wills are joined, the gulf between man and God is abolished. But in the mystery of unification the divisions and the differentiated aspects within the Godhead itself are removed. The *sefirot* become inextricably linked to one another; they are all comprised together, and they ascend in this unified state to *En-Sof.* It is this ascent that Rabbi Azriel calls in terms peculiar to himself "the hidden identity in the concealed mystery." [54] This event, which represents the peak of mystical activism in kabbalah, is portrayed as the underlying purpose of reciting prayers and blessings: "This is the great principle of Torah concerning the aim of prayer and blessings: to attune one's thought in faith as if it were attached to the world above, to compose the [divine] name with its letters, and to include thereby the ten *sefirot,* like the flame that is attached to the glowing coal. He should mention [the name] by mouth [only] by substitute expressions, but in his heart he should compose it in its form as it is written." [55] Rabbi Azriel does not mention here the way in which the process of unification is completed by raising the united *sefirot* to *En-Sof.* I shall therefore quote from a different source: [56] "You should know that in the process of unification, when a man mentions the names and many subjects, he should take care to unify everything as far as *En-Sof,* in order to demonstrate that it is the cause of all and that from it comes all and so that no division or severing should appear in the world as a result of his mentioning the names; for just as a tree has many branches all growing from the one central trunk, as you know, and all sprouting from one another, so it is with the matter of unification."

This passage deals with the correct intention *(kavvanah)* one should have in reciting the *Shema,* which is the very root of the "mystery of unification." "Mentioning the names" refers to the first stages of unification when the worshiper arranges, combines, and mingles the *sefirot* in a number of different ways, by mingling, for example, *Hesed* and *Din* with *Rahamim* or by uniting *Tiferet* and *Malkhut.* This last is sometimes portrayed even in early kabbalah as intercourse between male and female.

One account of the mystery of unification stresses the link between prayer and sacrificial worship, the fire on the altar being transferred to the fire of ecstasy in "worship in the heart": "The righteous and the pious and the men who perform great deeds pray on their own and they unify the great name and tend the fire of the altar that is in their hearts. Then, out of pure thought, all the *sefirot* are unified and are linked to one another until they extend to the source of the flame whose height is infinite." [57] This holy unification, which is established by ecstasy and pure thought, involves nondivine worlds and beings as well, from the Throne of Glory down to the world of nature and physical creatures. Therefore correct intention in prayer can achieve the mystic goal of total unity. [58]

The kabbalists of Provence and Spain emphasized the mystical-spiritual character of prayer to a far greater extent than the German *hasidim.* And even though there is some evidence to suggest that they were influenced at certain points by German hasidism, the way in which they transformed prayer into a detailed system of mystical meditation was absolutely original to the early teachers of kabbalah. At the same time, however, despite their extreme spiritualization of prayer, the kabbalists, like the German pietists, were adamant that the traditional texts of the liturgy should be followed. The activation of the inner *kavvanoth* in both heart and mind could not be achieved without the exact recitation of the words in the prayers. The insistence of the kabbalists on the correct verbal forms was motivated by their opposition to certain trends among the philosophers, who in the thirteenth century sought to seek a practical outlet for their spiritual tendencies by belittling prayer and religious observances.

Rabbi Jacob ben Sheshet Gerondi, the fiercest opponent of rationalistic philosophy that the kabbalists produced, waged open warfare against the speculative spiritualization of the liturgy. First of all, he describes the negative attitude of the philosophers toward spoken prayer and prayers of petition: "They say that prayer consists only in recitation in the mind and the heart. This is the basic principle. The speaker has no advantage. It is better that one's will should be acceptable than that one should have words on one's tongue. They consider that to pronounce prayer on the lips is foolish; it is a sin committed by the mouth. He who opens his lips acts stupidly, and every mouth speaks folly. Is there any delight in words? The voice of the fool multiplies words. Can a man gain anything by petitioning God? Will He save him from his evil state? Therefore [they say] prayers of praise are of no benefit, and even less petitions, requests for mercy and healing, which the poor and wretched seek. The sage would not petition for his needs were it not for the stupid community, for he is not able to keep silence." The philosophers described here pursued to their extreme logical conclusion some of the ideas propounded by Rabbenu Baḥya and by Maimonides and his disciples. They regarded verbal prayer, and particularly prayers of petition, as sinful, because they imply a deficiency within God, as if it were necessary to provide God with information and as if He actually heard and responded to the needs of the supplicant. The rabbi who says prayers with the congregation and includes his own petitions with theirs is simply adapting himself to "the stupid community"; "for he is not able to keep silence" and commune with God in thought alone.

Rabbi Jacob ben Sheshet castigates this spiritual approach as a form of heresy and as "throwing off the yoke of the kingdom of heaven," and he requests strict adherence to the traditional liturgy: "Woe to those who requite evil upon themselves! They err in their thoughts and are perverse in their words. They also know no shame. They rely on the sages of the Gentiles, and are enamored of foreign things, and all those who follow them. They do not know or understand. They walk in darkness. They have forsaken the broad highways of the Torah, and tread crooked paths. . . . 'Words that are in the heart' are not words at all, and when [the sages of old] talked of 'worship in the heart' they were being more strict, not more lenient. . . . The early fathers prescribed fixed times for prayer and petition . . . and he who departs from the ordinance of prayer lacks faith in His holy ones and offers no praise to His angels. He will be cut off from his people, and his place will know him no more. . . . He who presumes not to seek God's help will be regarded in an evil light by Him. He will surely requite him. He will not delay showing His hostility, but will requite him to his face. He who exempts himself from statutory prayer, and relies on his intellect and his thoughts, is guilty of great evil and vanity. Woe to those who follow their ways and pay heed to their words, for their support is like that of a reed."[59] In the heat of this polemic the kabbalist belittled more than he should the value of "worship in the heart." Nevertheless, although kabbalah was a strong moving force in the spiritualization of prayer, it undoubtedly also acted as a brake on the tendency to destroy the traditional forms of prayer and substitute spontaneous free meditation.[60]

B. THE ZOHAR'S UNDERSTANDING OF "WORSHIP IN THE HEART"

I

The kabbalistic understanding of prayer and *kavvanah* was transmitted through the schools of the Spanish kabbalists at the end of the thirteenth century. As far as this particular topic was concerned, the author of the Zohar also belonged to the tradition of Rabbi Isaac the Blind and his disciples in Gerona. Traces of their influence can be seen in his general ideas and attitudes. Furthermore, paraphrases of their actual words can be found in the Zohar, whose author drew especially heavily on the writings of Rabbi Azriel. As was his wont, he interpreted their statements quite freely and added fresh nuances using homiletical methods and mythical imagery. He also broadened the whole canvas by including themes and motifs from aggadic and halakhic literature, and by presenting detailed discussions of certain laws and customs.

In this section I shall concentrate on explaining basic ideas and questions of a general nature in the Zohar, and in the following section I shall deal with some of the details of the Zohar's mystical concept of prayer and the *kavvanot*.[61]

In the introduction to the section *The Tabernacle and the Temple* I have already dealt with the strong link in the Zohar between prayer and sacrifice. I tried to show there that the two types of worship were regarded as parallel in both their practice and their influence. And although some passages do suggest that prayer is superior to sacrifice, the author of the Zohar, unlike the author of the *Raya Mehemna* and the *Tikkunei ha-Zohar,* does not exalt prayer at the expense of sacrifice, for he regards the latter also as worship of a very high order. This is not the case, however, when he makes a comparison between prayer and the other practical religious precepts. Here the Zohar stresses the fact that prayer is superior because it is a spiritual form of worship, whereas the other practical commandments are of lesser worth because their fulfillment depends on physical objects and activity. Nevertheless, the Zohar requires strict observance of the latter, and attributes mystical purposes to all the commandments.

In one of the basic passages that deal with the superior standing of prayer, a distinction is made between the practical worship of the outer, visible parts of the body and the spiritual worship of the inner organs. Prayer is the better way to worship God because "it is the innermost form of worship; it is the foundation of everything." It results in "the restoration of the spirit *(ruah),* which is the innermost precious worship of the Holy One, blessed be He. . . . Man's prayer is the worship of the spirit, and it depends on supernal mysteries and men do not know [them]." [62] This passage goes on to say [63] that the liturgy comprises six basic commandments, which have a practical aspect as well: the fear of God, the love of God, the blessing of the divine name, the unification of the divine name, the blessing of the priests, and martyrdom. These six are equal in worth to six hundred, and if you add the thirteen divine attributes of mercy, they amount to 613. In other words, prayer is equal in value to the total complement of the 613 commandments in the Torah.

The particular value of prayer can also be seen in the status that it confers upon the worshiper vis-à-vis God. If a man observes the commandments he becomes God's servant; if he gains a knowledge of God through the secrets of the Torah he gains the status of God's son; but prayer confers upon him the status of both servant and son. Since prayer is by nature an inner mystical experience whose accomplishment, however, is achieved by an external physical act, namely, verbal enunciation, it occupies an intermediate position between mystical perception and practical religious performance, and the worshiper can therefore enjoy two statuses.[64] The author of the Zohar, however, following the kabbalists who preceded him, insisted that strict attention should be paid to the spoken word of prayer. By using the anthropomorphic image of God as primordial man *(Adam Kadmon)*, he explains how the speech and sound of prayer find their way into the ears of the Holy One, blessed be He: "Whatever a man thinks or whatever he meditates in his heart cannot be realized in fact until he enunciates it with his lips. . . . And the word that he enunciates cleaves the air and goes up and flies through the world. And a sound is produced from it.[65] The winged creatures take this sound up to the king, and it enters his ears. . . . Therefore, every prayer and petition that man wishes to lay before the Holy One, blessed be He, must be enunciated in words by the lips, because if he does not enunciate them his prayer is no prayer, and his petition is no petition."[66]

Another passage explains the necessity for enunciation both in prayer and in studying, in a very polemical fashion: "Come and see. If a man says that there is no necessity for actual deeds, or to utter words or make them audible—may his spirit expire! . . . For thought does not accomplish anything, and no sound is produced by it, and it does not ascend. But once [a man] has produced a word from his mouth, that word becomes a sound and it cleaves atmospheres and firmaments, and it goes up and another matter is aroused.[67] . . . And whoever produces a holy word from his mouth, a word of Torah—a sound is made from it that ascends, and the holy ones of the supernal king are aroused and they are crowned near his head, and then there is joy in the upper and in the lower worlds."[68] This polemic is directed against contemporary philosophers, and resembles the accusation that Rabbi Moses de Leon leveled against the philosophers, that they mocked the carrying of the *lulav* and *etrog*, the recitation of blessings, and the wearing of *tefillin*.[69]

But in passages such as this the author of the Zohar, like Rabbi Jacob ben Sheshet in the first half of the thirteenth century, indulges in polemical exaggeration when he says that "thought does not accomplish anything." Other passages, which express his standpoint more accurately, emphasize the superiority of thought and inner feelings.[70] According to Psalm 19:15 there are two modes in prayer: the words of the mouth, and the meditations of the heart, "one for the lower level, and one for the upper level."[71] This means that the actual words of prayer are for *Malkhut* and the inner meditations for *Tiferet*. The superior power of inwardness in prayer, and in all other ways of serving God, is expressed in connection with the consequences of good or evil thoughts in man's sexual life: "All the affairs of the world depend on thought and intention. . . . For, to be sure, will and thought have consequences and perform deeds in whatever area is necessary. Therefore prayer requires the will and intention to direct [one's heart]. And, similarly, with all modes of serving the Holy One, blessed be He, intention and thought perform deeds and have consequences in whatever area is necessary." Here we have the basic principle that correct intention (kavvanah) is the foundation of prayer, and we must now look at the many passages that deal directly with the value and meaning of kavvanah.

The value of kavvanah, usually called re'uta (i.e., will, desire, or sincerity), in the whole range of human activity is repeatedly stressed in the Zohar.[72] The main discussions of kavvanah, however, center on the mystical purpose of prayer. According to one passage, the processes of kavvanah constitute a special inner-mystical order of prayer, side by side with the external words of prayer: "For there is an order [for the eulogies of the Holy One, blessed be He] that exists in words, and there is an order that exists in the will and intention of the heart [when one seeks] to know and meditate, so that one can meditate from one stage to the other as far as En-Sof, for there is the resting place of all intentions and thoughts, and they do not exist in words at all. But just as [En-Sof] is concealed, so all matters relating to him are in concealment."[73] One should prepare oneself for prayer by observing the ritual precepts of donning tallit and tefillin, and one must also enunciate the words, but "happy is the man who knows how to sway and serve his Master with heartfelt sincerity. Woe to the man who tries to sway his Master with a heart that is distant and without sincerity. . . . Even more blameworthy is he if he comes to unify the holy name and does it improperly." Ritual acts and speech have no effect on the upper world and do not draw a man closer to the Holy One, blessed be He, unless they are accompanied by kavvanah.[74]

Even the situation of the soul in the future world is determined by the amount and quality of kavvanah. The soul naturally gains reward for good deeds, but only to a lesser degree, in the earthly Garden of Eden. But the supreme spiritual reward in the celestial Garden of Eden is granted only for purity of kavvanah. "These [garments] result from the good deeds that a man performs in this world when he fulfills the precepts of the Torah. And the soul lives in the Garden of Eden below because of them, and clothes itself in these precious garments. When the soul ascends to the door of the firmament above, other exalted precious garments are prepared for it, and these come from sincerity and the intention of the heart in Torah and in prayer; for when this sincerity ascends to the world above, it serves to adorn the one who adorns himself, and a portion remains for the individual, and garments of light are made from it so that the soul may clothe itself with them when it ascends on high. . . . Garments below in the garden upon earth are from deeds; garments above are from spirit and sincerity and the intention of the heart."[75] This eschatological image of the garments of the soul provides a clear indication of the superiority of spiritual intention over physical deed.[76]

However, in its evaluation of worship without *kavvanah* the Zohar is not at all consistent. It says in connection with the performance of the commandments that, although the best course is to fulfill them with proper *kavvanah*, nevertheless even without *kavvanah* they do bring some benefit to those who perform them. The Holy One, blessed be He, raises them Himself to their place among the *sefirot*, as if they had been performed with *kavvanah*.[77] With prayer also the question is asked: "What should a man do if he wants to pray and his mind is distracted because of his grief so that he cannot offer praise to his Master as he should?" And the answer given is: "Even though he cannot give his full concentration or sincerity, why should he diminish the praise due to his Master? Let him declare the praise of his Master, even though he cannot give it his full attention, and then let him say his prayer."

Nevertheless, in contrast to this sympathetic attitude toward those whose mental or spiritual deficiencies prevent them from praying with proper sincerity and concentration, several passages denigrate and criticize very sharply those who pray without *kavvanah*. "If a man comes to unify the holy name and does not do so sincerely and with concentration, yet appears to promote blessing in the upper and lower worlds, his prayer is rejected and they all proclaim evil against him." "They who think upon his name" are those who concentrate on the mystery of the mystic unification, and "whoever approaches his Master and utters prayers without completing the unification and without concerning himself with his Master's glory and forging bonds as we have said—it were better for him had he not been created."[78] And of the man "who does not know how to unify the holy name, forge the bond of faith, bring blessings to the necessary place, and honor the name of his Creator" it is said "those that despise Me shall be lightly esteemed" (1 Samuel 2:30).[79] It is extremely difficult to reconcile these two different points of view.

As far as the spiritual condition of the worshiper is concerned, mystical *kavvanah* is depicted as a concentration of heart and will, with the addition sometimes of thought or knowledge or spirit, and accompanied by fear and love of God. And, since prayer involves words, concentration may include the mouth and speech.[80] I shall give a detailed example that also mentions certain parallels with the *sefirot* and activity in the upper world: "Happy is the man who knows how to walk in the way of truth. As for anyone who does not know how to declare the praise of his Master, it were better for him had he not been created, because prayer has to come from thought and sincerity (lit., the will of the heart), and from sound, speech, and lips, so that perfection, binding together, and unification may be effected in the world above. . . . Thought produces will; will that proceeds from thought produces an audible sound; and the audible sound ascends to forge links from the bottom to the top, lower halls with the upper regions."[81] According to this account, thought, "the will of the heart," voice, and speech are produced one from the other just like the chain reaction in the emanation of the *sefirot*,[82] and it is because of this parallel between the development of human power in prayer and the hidden divine emanation "that perfection, binding together, and unification may be effected in the world above."

Some passages speak of how all the parts of the human body cooperate in order to promote *kavvanah*. One passage, which deals with the unification which results from reciting the *Shema*, explains how the bodily limbs join together in concentrating on unification and how this prepares the way for bringing together the celestial limbs in the figure of *Adam Kadmon*.[83] According to another passage the involvement of all the limbs in *kavvanah* helps to make man into a tabernacle for the *Shekhinah* to dwell in. "Come and see. When a man applies his will to worship his Master, the will alights first upon the heart, which is the support and foundation of the whole body. Then this good will suffuses all the bodily organs, and the will of all the bodily organs and the will of the heart combine together, and they attract the radiance of the *Shekhinah* to dwell with them, and that man becomes a portion of the Holy

One, blessed be He." [84] It is possible that in his presentation of *kavvanah* as a religious phenomenon that involves the human body *in toto,* the author of the Zohar has in mind a type of religious ecstasy that is accompanied by movements of the different parts of the body to help the soul to reach the peak of its mystical ascent.

The concentration of the powers of the soul, with or without the involvement of the physical parts of the body, was not seen by the Zohar as passive introverted contemplation, or as the communion of man with God within the depths of his soul, preparatory to the soul's receiving divine illumination. It was rather a preparation for a daring journey to distant parts, for the ascent of the *kavvanah* or the soul to the heights of the Godhead. The traveler has to pass many places on the way, through the cosmos, the abodes of the angels, and the celestial halls, as I shall explain below, but the ultimate goal is the world of the *sefirot,* the area where the soul originated and the scene of its theurgic activity.

The Zohar describes the soul's ascent to the world of the *sefirot* in various ways. In this world there are different stages and boundaries. Several passages [85] stress the fact that the *kavvanah*'s first object is the *Shekhinah,* the lowest *sefirah,* which is called "gate" or "door" to indicate its role as the entrance to the divine domain. From other passages it would appear that the worshiper is to concentrate first on *Ḥesed* and *Gevurah,* [86] but here the author of the Zohar was simply following his source material and did not bother to mention that the *Shekhinah* was the first stage. Sometimes he misses out the actual stages in the ascent, and speaks only of the highest *sefirah* as the ultimate goal of meditation. "Come and see. A man should direct his prayer to the realm above, to the supernal depth, from which all blessings and every freedom flow, and from which they emerge in order to sustain all." [87] "The supernal depth" is *Binah,* the source from which influence flows down upon the *sefirot.*

The highest stage that can be reached by *kavvanah* directly is mentioned in the *Idra Rabba:* [88] "When Rav Hamnuna Sava wanted to pray he used to say: I shall pray to the Master of the nose; I shall beg mercy of the Master of the nose." From the preceding and the following lines it is clear that "the Master of the nose" is a reference to *Keter,* the first *sefirah.* However, Rav Hamnuna's idea seems to have been cited as an example of great audacity, which few others could imitate. There are, to be sure, a number of references to contemplation of, or ascent to "the mystery of *En-Sof*" or "as far as *En-Sof,*"[89] but the implication is always an ascent by way of the *sefirot* and not direct contact. We seem to come across an example of *kavvanah* being directed without any intermediary toward *En-Sof* in the following passage: "Every man who desires to petition the king should direct his thought and his will to the root of all roots, in order to draw blessings from the depth of the well, so that it may pour out blessings from the well-spring of all." "The root of all roots" is sometimes used in kabbalistic literature as a designation of *En-Sof,*[90] but the author of the Zohar uses it here possibly to refer to one of the upper *sefirot, Keter* or *Hokhmah;*[91] anyway, he does not speak of meditating directly upon "the root of all roots," but only of the desire to draw influence from it.

II

The term *"tikkun"* (repair, restoration, amendment) occurs very frequently in the Zohar, and thenceforward it developed into a central concept in the history of kabbalah. It signifies both the positive function that man fulfills generally when he serves God, and also the purpose of prayer in particular. One passage describes the act of prayer as a process involving four different grades of *tikkun:* "The first *tikkun* is the restoration of oneself, self-perfection; the second *tikkun* is the restoration of this world; the third *tikkun* is the restoration of the world above throughout all the hosts of heaven; the fourth *tikkun* is the restoration of the holy name through the mystery of the holy chariots, and the mystery of all the worlds above and below with the proper kind of restoration."[92] This is to say that the worshiper, the physical world, the world of the angels, and the sefirotic system, which is symbolised by the tetragrammaton *YHVH*, can all be restored by human prayer. The *tikkun* of the worshiper is accomplished by his purifying himself of earthly desires,[93] by fulfilling religious precepts before praying,[94] and through the sanctification of prayer and *kavvanah*. The *tikkun* of this world is accomplished by the recital of the Halleluyah Psalms and the prayer "Blessed be He who spake," which stimulate the forces of nature and all created beings to praise and glorify God, and which also sustain the created world with blessings. The intermediate world and the angels are "restored" by the recital of the prayer "Creator of ministering spirits." The *tikkun* of the sefirotic system is accomplished by the recital of the central core of Jewish prayer, namely, the *Shema* and the *Amidah*.

The "restoration" of the lower and the upper worlds is realized when the prayer that is directed toward them reaches its goal. The ascent of prayer and its arrival at the scene of its activity are depicted in many passages as a long and difficult journey, very similar to the ascent of the soul at night. The way it moves through both the physical and the spiritual cosmos, through the lower and the upper firmaments, is described in short, generalized phrases, and also in some detail. Here are a few very common general accounts: "Man's prayer splits atmospheres, splits firmaments, opens doors, and ascends aloft" [95] "Every single word of prayer that a man utters through his mouth ascends aloft and splits firmaments, and enters the place that it enters" [96] "All the words that a man utters through his mouth in that prayer ascend aloft, and split atmospheres and firmaments, until they reach the place that they reach, and they form themselves into a crown upon the king's head, and a crown is made from them." [97] The recurrence of the word "split" implies the existence of obstacles that prayer encounters and has to overcome. The angels of destruction, agents of *sitra aḥra*, lie in wait for prayers on the pathways they take in their ascent, and if there is some blemish in them they are liable to be snapped up by the powers of uncleanness.[98] Prayers that are unblemished ascend from one stage to the next through firmaments and halls, assisted by holy angels whose function and activity are described at length with all kinds of mythical imagery. A leading role in the receipt and raising of the prayers to greater heights is played by Metatron, and he is portrayed fulfilling this function in all sections of the Zohar.[99] The firmaments and halls become unified and ascend together because of the power of the prayers that pass through them, and even the angels that assist the prayers to ascend are themselves helped by them and are raised higher. The Zohar, following traditional rabbinic statements,[100] affirms that the angels are, as it were, Israel's companions, and that they listen for their prayers, because they are not allowed to begin to utter song or sanctification until they can hear the voices of Israel below.[101] Therefore the prayers of Israel help to "restore" and to raise the angels aloft.[102] In the *Raya Mehemna*[103] and the *Tikkunei ha-Zohar*,[104] prayer is likened to Jacob's ladder: [105] it links the lower and the upper worlds and companies of angels ascend and descend on it.

All these ascents and *tikkunim* are no more than preparations for the most sublime *tikkun* of all, the *tikkun* of the Godhead in the mystery of unification *(yiḥud)*, which involves areas and powers from the nondivine world as well, and which indeed enables them to achieve their own *tikkun.* Sometimes this unification of the *sefirot* is discussed in a very generalized and rather vague way as a conjunction of different levels, or as a unifying ascent from one level to another, from *Malkhut* to *Keter.*[106] In all sections of the Zohar, however, apart from the *Midrash ha-Ne'elam,* the central image in accounts of the unification that is effected by the *kavvanot* of prayer is that of the *tikkun* of the *Shekhinah* through the mystery of intercourse. Long passages and complete sections, dealing mainly with the mystical interpretation of prayer and its *kavvanot,* describe in great detail the preparations necessary for intercourse, the act itself, and its consequences.[107] I shall deal with these matters below in section c when I discuss the *kavvanot* of the *Shema* and the *Amidah.* Here I shall confine myself to giving just the outlines, with the help of examples.

The *Shekhinah* in exile, separated from her "husband," benefits from the worshiper's concentration *(kavvanah)* on unification, even if the amount of influence released thereby is not sufficient to raise her from her abject state. She receives help and comfort in her exile by the tempering of Judgment *(Din)* with Mercy *(Rahamim).*[108] According to a passage in the *Tikkunei ha-Zohar,*[109] Israel should turn in its prayers and its petitions toward the *Shekhinah* in exile, because it is through her and because of her merit that the Holy One, blessed be He, will respond to Israel, since He sheds light around her in order to protect her from *sitra ahra.* The main purpose of prayer is to bring the *Shekhinah* out of her solitude in exile and to return her to her place and her status in the divine realm, in order to demonstrate that she is not divorced from her husband.[110]

The *Raya Mehemna* and the *Tikkunei ha-Zohar* speak a great deal about the stimulation of the *Shekhinah* and the way in which she is raised up, but there is little stress on the mystery of unification. Through the prayers and the recital of the *Shema* the *Shekhinah* is given new life, as it were, in the presence of the Holy One, blessed be He.[111] When the prayers are pronounced properly she is raised up and shines like the rainbow in her full array of colors, but if the prayers are unfit she is held back and darkened, as if she were enwrapped "in a garment of black cloud." She is brought by means of prayer as an offering to the Holy One, blessed be He, and "when she ascends, she ascends like a dove, and when she descends, she descends like an eagle, for she is the consort who is not afraid of any bird in the world."[112]

In most passages, however, in the main body of the Zohar and in the other sections, the mystery of intercourse is depicted with striking imagery. The sequence of *kavvanot,* either in a single prayer or during the course of a number of prayers, is presented as a kind of mytho-dramatic scenario portraying the celebration of the divine union. He who wishes to direct his prayer aright must imagine and experience the event at every stage and in all its details, from the adornment of the bride and her entry, accompanied by her maidens, under the marriage canopy to her seclusion with the bridegroom and their love-making. Concentration on the mystery of intercourse begins with trying to summon together all the powers of the *Shekhinah,*[113] and arousing her desire for intercourse: "He who wishes to unify the exalted, holy name, must unify from the side of *zot* (i.e., "this," the *Shekhinah*) . . . so that the two may be united, the Righteous One and Righteousness (i.e., *Yesod* and *Malkhut*) in a single union"; "the only way in which the desire and yearning of the Assembly of Israel (i.e., the *Shekhinah*) for the Holy One, blessed be He, reach fulfillment is through the souls of the righteous, for they stimulate the flow of the lower waters toward the upper, and at that moment the fulfillment of desire and yearning [is accomplished] through one union, which bears fruit."[114] When the *Shekhinah* has been aroused and is full of yearning, this activates and brings together the *sefirot* from Ḥesed to *Yesod,* which represent the body and limbs of the male, or, using another image, Jacob and the other patriarchs.[115] Once the bride and groom have secluded themselves and are prepared for sexual union, intercourse takes place. The worshiper during his concentration must ensure that nothing comes between the two lovers during divine intercourse: "At that time, when she is divested of her garments, she is united with her husband, flesh to flesh . . . for thus should the male be united with the female—flesh to flesh—and this too is the closeness of the union in the world above; nothing must come between. . . . This is why the sages taught[116] that when a man prays and unites the Holy One, blessed be He, with His *Shekhinah,* nothing should come between him and the wall which is next to him,[117] so that there should be no separation or division between the Holy One, blessed be He, and His *Shekhinah.* The mystery of this matter may be seen in 'And they were both naked, the man and his wife' (Genesis 2: 25)—'naked,' flesh to flesh without any garment whatsoever. And it is written concerning that moment when the Holy One, blessed be He, and His *Shekhinah* are together without any garment whatsoever 'Your Teacher shall not hide Himself any more, but your eyes shall see your Teacher' (Isaiah 30: 20)."[118] The *kavvanot* of prayer in the Zohar are full of daring, powerful, erotic images such as these.

When the act of intercourse is complete, the power of the united forces, comprising the *sefirot* from *Ḥesed* to *Malkhut*, illumines the upper *sefirot*, and the whole system ascends to *En-Sof*.[119] The hosts of heaven are included in this act of union.[120] The lower firmaments are united with the upper, inner firmaments, and the whole cosmos, both physical and spiritual, is elevated as far as *En-Sof*.[121] This represents the summit of unification and restoration: perfect and harmonious unity between the upper and lower worlds within the hidden, divine source. "Here (i.e., through the recital of the *Shema*)[122] the wife is united with her husband, and once they have become united with one another in a single union they then need to unify the limbs and to join the two Tabernacles[123] together throughout all the limbs with a willing heart, so as to ascend and cleave to *En-Sof*, in order to unify everything there, so that both upper and lower worlds should be of the same purpose . . . that all the limbs might be brought together to the same place from which they sprang, the inner hall,[124] and all things be restored to their place, to their origin, foundation, and root, to the place that is the root of the covenant.[125] . . . 'One'—to unify everything from there upward as one, to raise the will to bind everything in a single bond, to raise the will in fear and love higher and higher as far as *En-Sof*. And let not the will depart from all the levels or limbs, but let it ascend with them all to make them cleave to one another, so that all shall be one bond with *En-Sof*. . . . 'One'—the mystery of upper and lower and the four corners of the world is to unify upper and lower, as it has been explained, and the four corners of the world. These are the mystery of the upper Chariot,[126] so that all may be comprised together in a single bond, in a single unification, as far as *En-Sof*."[127] This passage with its insistent and passionate repetition of images of unification in all their variety shows how powerful is the mystic drive to overcome and destroy all the divisions and differences in the world, so that in the end the whole of existence is united within the depths of God.

The special importance and particular sanctity of prayer can also be seen in its relationship with *sitra aḥra*. As I have already explained in the introduction to the section *The Tabernacle and the Temple*, the Zohar's view is that in the process of sacrificial worship one has to set aside a portion for *sitra ahra* in order to mollify him and prevent him from doing harm. Therefore even some of the sacrifices that were actually offered on the altar were meant for him. We find that the Zohar adopts a similar attitude with regard to other practical religious precepts, including commandments and customs connected with prayers and blessings, for example, setting aside for *sitra ahra* the threads of hair on the *tefillin*,[128] or the water used for washing the hands before grace after meals.[129] However, the author of the Zohar does not go so far as to give the power of evil a share in the prayers or blessings themselves.[130] Nevertheless, he does not altogether ignore the existence of "the other side," either in connection with the separate prayers or in connection with *kavvanah*. He points out that one must beware of the harm that he can cause and of the baleful influence that he can exert, particularly during the evening prayer which, according to one view,[131] was not made obligatory because *sitra ahra* rules at night. And even the invitation to recite the grace after meals, and the cup of wine that is drunk therewith, are portrayed as means to keep *sitra ahra* at a distance and to destroy his power.[132] *Sitra ahra*, however, can receive none of the prayers themselves, except for those which are in some way invalid.[133]

III

The *tikkunim* (restorations) during the process of unification open the supernal source of influence and cause it to flow down from one level to the next. This flow of influence begins by spreading bliss and satisfaction throughout the sefirotic system, and then by means of the *Shekhinah* it reaches all areas of existence including the most insignificant creatures in the physical world. Many passages, especially those dealing with the *kavvanot* of blessings, maintain that the sole aim is to bring down this stream of influence, and they do not mention any other purpose at all.[134] There are two main images in the Zohar for the descent of this influence: one is the stream of water flowing out from the depths of the supernal fountain, and the other is the blessing of life emanating from the source of life. Both these images originate from the *kavvanot* (purposes) of prayer propounded by the school of Rabbi Isaac the Blind.

One passage clearly states that the influence originates in the intercourse between *Hokhmah* and *Binah,* and we can apply this idea to the elucidation of other and more obscure passages. "Come and see. Every desire and every effort of will by which man seeks to cause blessings to pour down from the upper to the lower world and so unify the holy name should strive, by praying to the Holy One, blessed be He, with true intention and sincerity, to draw from the deep river, as it is written 'From the depths I call You, O Lord' (Psalm 130: 1); for there is to be found the depth of all, in the supernal depths, which are the supernal beginning where father and mother are in union."[135] The unification of the name, which is connected here with the drawing down of influence, completes the act of unification from the upper to the lower worlds. It is quite clear from the fact that "father" and "mother" are mentioned that "the depth of all" is *Binah,* the mother of the lower *sefirot,* who nourishes and feeds her children. This concept occurs in a number of passages,[136] all of which interpret "From the depths I call You, O Lord" in the above manner: I call You, O Lord, with the mystical intention of drawing the flow of influence down from the divine depths, that is, from *Ḥokhmah* and *Binah.*[137] In one passage about the prayer of the penitent sinner, the verse is explained in terms of "the depth of the well," which is the "profoundest of depths,"[138] but even there the reference is clearly to *Binah,* which is the level for repentance in the sefirotic world.

Descriptions of life and the source of life occur in an important passage concerning the *kavvanot* of the benedictions. "In the benedictions with which man blesses the Holy One, blessed be He, his purpose is to draw out life from the source of life for the holy name of the Holy One, blessed be He, and to cause some of the supernal oil to pour over it . . . and these blessings are drawn out by man, through [his] words, from the supernal source, and all the levels and sources are blessed, and they become full so that they can empty [the blessings] upon all the worlds, and all are blessed together."[139] The source of life, the supernal source, is identified in what follows with the supernal throne, and although from some expressions in this passage "the source of life" could possibly be explained as a reference to *Ḥokhmah,* other expressions and the content in general make one believe that *Binah* is meant.[140] In other words, the supernal source is the same as the supernal depth that I have already discussed. The supernal life and the supernal oil signify the influence that emanates from *Binah* and, since she receives it through her intercourse with *Ḥokhmah,* we can say that it is the influence from *Ḥokhmah,* and even from *Keter.*

The drawing down of influence from the source of life is also mentioned in connection with the Eighteen Benedictions of the *Amidah* prayer. "The seventh hall, 'Lord, open my lips,' is a profound mystery, [to be said] in a whisper without a sound. Here the intention is to raise the will from the lower to the upper realm as far as *En-Sof*, and to bind the seventh with the seventh from the lower to the upper, and, subsequently, from the upper to the lower, in order to draw down blessings through all the worlds from the source of life, which is the supernal seventh hall, with devout intention and the eyes closed. . . . This supernal seventh hall, which is the source of life, is the first blessing, and this is the first hall, the beginning of all, from the upper to the lower." [141] Here, apparently, "the source of life" is located in the area of the halls below the *sefirot*, but the term is also connected with the supernal seventh hall, which in my view is the *sefirah Binah*, as the conclusion of the passage indicates: "This is the first hall, the beginning of all, from the upper to the lower." It is possible that the lower seventh hall, which it is the prayer's intention to bind to the supernal seventh hall, is also within the area of the *sefirot*, and signifies the *Shekhinah*, linked to *Binah*, the supernal *Shekhinah*.[142]

He who recites prayers participates himself in a number of different ways in the divine influence. Some remarks apparently imply that he who unifies the divine name in prayer is rewarded with a perception of mysteries through the illumination of the soul. "They extend to him a thread of love . . . the light of the wisdom of holy knowledge settles upon him." "Through these mysteries a man may cleave to his Master, in order to gain knowledge of the perfection of wisdom in the supernal mystery, when he worships his Master in prayer with sincere devotion and intention." [143] These statements, however, are not sufficiently clear, and one cannot be absolutely certain that they concern the acquisition of a specific mystical insight through the ascent of *kavvanah*, like the "nourishment" in the school of Rabbi Isaac the Blind.

We get much more precise information about the way that concentration in prayer influences the *Shekhinah*'s descent into the world. There is a general statement to the effect that the different parts of the liturgy have been so arranged as to bring the *Shekhinah* down into the world.[144] A poetic account describes the *Shekhinah* as a bird who nestles with her brethren, the six lower *sefirot*, beneath the wings of her mother, *Binah*. The people of Israel can attract her toward them by the subdued tones of their prayers. "Although she is beneath her mother's wings she raises her head and pays heed to the whispering of the voice. She flies to them, emerging from beneath the mother's wings. When Israel have taken her, they keep hold of her, whispering to her and binding her so that she should not fly away. . . . While she is bound in their hands they whisper and she chirps with them, flying aloft and then descending." [145] By this ruse Israel succeed not only in capturing the holy bird, the *Shekhinah*, and keeping her with them, but also in bringing down the other *sefirot*, who come to reside with Israel because they are attracted by the chirping of the *Shekhinah* and the whispered prayers.

According to another passage, reciting the Eighteen Benedictions in subdued tones is intended to retain one's hold on the *Shekhinah* and the Holy One, blessed be He, to prevent them from severing their links with the worshiper completely as they ascend toward *En-Sof*. "If this glory tries to depart, Israel below take hold of it and restrain it, not permitting it to move away from them. That is why the prayer is said in a whisper, like someone speaking in secret with the king: while he is closeted with him, [the king] will not leave him."

These passages describe how the *Shekhinah* is brought down to the people of Israel, or to the world, and kept there. But elsewhere we read of the *Shekhinah* settling upon an individual worshiper. Those who pray with the correct intention and devotion of both mind and body cause the radiance of the *Shekhinah* to descend upon them,[146] and as for the man who unifies the divine name in the proper manner by reciting the *Shema*—"the *Shekhinah* comes and settles upon his head and blesses him with an abundance of blessings." [147] In a piece of daring erotic imagery, causing the *Shekhinah* to descend upon the worshipers is described as marrying the divine wife with the consent of her husband.[148]

The man who prays with correct mystical intention derives blessing also in terms of provision for his physical needs. The author of the Zohar sees no harm at all in petitioning explicitly for one's own needs. Indeed, when dealing with the Eighteen Benedictions, he states that before asking for the satisfaction of one's own wants one should praise and glorify the Holy One, blessed be He,[149] and he expresses himself in a very concrete way: "One should not ask for one's own sustenance before praying to and sustaining one's Master. The king eats first, and then his servants eat afterward." [150] However, he gives a warning that a man should not attempt to discover whether his petition has been granted or not, for even the requests of the righteous are sometimes rejected.[151] But even in conditional passages such as these the Holy One, blessed be He, is said to respond to the prayers that the righteous offer on their own behalf.

Other passages actually stress the obligation to pray for one's own needs, because it is forbidden to rely either on one's own merits or on miracles.[152] Even the man who is well provided for should pray daily for food, because when a righteous man prays for his own personal needs he stimulates a flow of divine influence that also satisfies the needs of the upper world.[153] One passage[154] enumerates nine different ways of directing one's own personal petitions. The source of one's principal needs—children, life, and food—is attributed to *Binah*, the origin of the influence that benefits the divine powers, and this *sefirah* is called "the holy planet"[155]—a designation based on a nonliteral interpretation of a sentence in the Talmud.[156] Yet another passage[157] gives an even higher source for food: "What does *razon* mean?[158] It means the will that originates from *Atika Kadisha* (i.e., *Keter*). The will derives from it to provide food for all." So we find that in this way the Zohar sees an interconnection between the needs of the divine world and the needs of the lower worlds, the needs of the whole and of the part, the needs of the soul and of the body. They all receive influence from the hidden supernal source, and all areas of existence are united thereby in the mystery of total unification.

C. THE MYSTICAL SIGNIFICANCE OF THE STATUTORY PRAYERS

I

In explaining the basic principles of prayer and *kavvanah* in the preceding section I also touched on a number of specific details, but this subject occupies so much space in the Zohar that one must, to do it justice, deal with some other specific mystical connotations of prayer and *kavvanah*. While dealing with these particular points I shall be able to throw light also on kindred matters in other areas.[159]

At the very beginning I should like to restate a central concept that I have already emphasized several times but have not yet even mentioned in the context of prayer and *kavvanah*—the concept of correspondence. Particular prayers or particular methods of prayer are considered by the

Zohar to be images or symbols of divine *sefirot,* and sometimes it is this correspondent relationship that gives a mystical-kabbalistic flavor to ordinary everyday matters even outside the realm of kabbalistic teaching. The correspondence does not necessarily determine the object of *kavvanah.* For example, a prayer may represent a particular *sefirah,* but in reciting the prayer the worshiper need not concentrate specifically on that *sefirah,* or on that *sefirah* alone. However, the principle of correspondence is extremely important in the teaching of correct intention in prayer, and even more so in the understanding of the mystical meaning of prayer. Let us see how this principle is applied to the three statutory prayers and to communal prayer in the synagogue.

The rabbinic statement[160] that the Morning, Afternoon, and Evening Prayers were instituted by the patriarchs is interpreted in the Zohar in accordance with accepted kabbalistic symbolism, which sees Abraham, Isaac, and Jacob as representatives of *Hesed, Gevurah,* and *Tiferet.*[161] This interpretation fits in to some extent with the mystical significance of the times of the three prayers, but it does not really suit the Evening Prayer, because *Tiferet,* symbolized by Jacob, is associated with daylight, while night, the time for the Evening Prayer, is the province of *Malkhut,* the *Shekhinah.* Therefore, the institution of the Evening Prayer by Jacob is explained as if in this case *Tiferet* were acting on behalf of his spouse, the *Shekhinah.* "Come and see. Isaac certainly instituted the Afternoon Prayer. Just as Abraham instituted the Morning Prayer to match the level with which he was associated, so Isaac instituted the Afternoon Prayer to match the level with which he was associated. . . . Jacob instituted the Evening Prayer, for he certainly supports her (i.e., night, the *Shekhinah*) and provides all her needs . . . for she has no light of her own at all."[162]

When the sun rises in the morning the light rays of *Hesed* (Love) begin to spread. Therefore the Morning Prayer provides an opportunity to convey this stream of light to the *Shekhinah* and stimulate the power of *Hesed,* the right arm, to embrace her. In the Afternoon Prayer, however, which is recited while the sun is in decline, one must mollify the power of Judgment, which begins to rule as the evening shadows thicken, and also to repulse the *sefirah Gevurah,* the left arm, which unites with *Hesed* in embracing the *Shekhinah.*[163] The intended purpose of the Afternoon Prayer is fraught with danger because the worshiper has to combat "the accusers that are in the world and the furious spirits of Judgment that are assembled at such a time." Therefore "a man must concentrate his mind in all his prayers, and in this prayer more than any, because Judgment is abroad in the world."

The Sabbath Afternoon Prayer is different, because this is "the acceptable time,"[164] the proper time for softening Judgment, and for the joy of intercourse in the divine world, "for in very truth the Afternoon Prayer on the Sabbath is not like the weekday one. In the afternoon on weekdays Judgment is suspended over the world, and it is not an 'acceptable time.' But on the Sabbath, when all anger lapses, and everything is united together, even though Judgment is aroused, it is an occasion for softening [Judgment]. . . . Judgment is softened at that time, and joy pervades all."[165] In the *Idra Rabba* and the *Idra Zuta* the difference between weekday and Sabbath is given an anthropomorphic interpretation. On weekdays God rules in the angry shape of *Ze'ir Anpin* (the Short Countenance), who directs the world with judgment, and who in the afternoons at the height of his power reveals his brow in order to punish sinners. But on the Sabbath God acts in his radiant form of *Atika Kadisha*, who is all Love and Mercy, and when he reveals his brow in the afternoon it is to sweep away sin and to subdue the fury of Judgment. "This brow is called *'razon'* (will, or favor), and when this will is revealed the highest will appears throughout all worlds, and all the prayers uttered below are accepted, and the countenance of *Ze'ir Anpin* is illumined, and everything is bathed in Mercy, and all judgments are concealed and subdued. On the Sabbath, at the time of the Afternoon Prayer, which is the hour when all the judgments are aroused, this brow is revealed and all the judgments are subdued, and Mercy appears throughout all worlds, and for this reason there is no Judgment on the Sabbath, neither in the world above nor in the world below."[166]

When we come to the Evening Prayer, which is associated with the *Shekhinah*, we find that the author of the Zohar concerns himself with the mystical significance of the fact that according to Jewish law this prayer is not obligatory but optional.[167] He tries to explain this in two different ways. There is one passage[168] that contains both interpretations. The first is that the *Shekhinah* receives light as a result of the daytime prayers, which are directed toward the male forces that bestow their influence upon her. But at night she is, until midnight, bathed in darkness, and prayer has no power to provide her with any additional light. The second interpretation is that, since the purpose of prayer is to bring *Tiferet* and *Malkhut* closer together and finally to unite them, and since this purpose is achieved by the prayers during the day, there is no obligation to do more, "for since the woman has been placed between the two arms, and has been united with the body, no more is necessary. This is why we must stimulate the two arms [in the Morning and Afternoon Prayers] so that she may be placed between them." The first interpretation, which stresses the *Shekhinah*'s separation from her husband at nighttime, in contrast to the second, which assumes that their union is continuous, is also expressed in other ways. At nighttime the *Shekhinah* is preoccupied with providing nourishment for the forces of the lower world, and so it is not the right time for prayers to be recited in order that she should receive influence from above. Furthermore, *sitra aḥra* rules at night and any influence brought down then might reach his agents and give them added power.[169]

The author of the *Tikkunei ha-Zohar* and the *Raya Mehemna* also provides his own version of these two solutions, highlighting the difference between them. According to the first, the reason why the Evening Prayer is not obligatory is that the *Shekhinah* is separated from the other *sefirot* in exile, which is symbolized by the darkness of night, "for she is on her own without her husband, and because she is without her husband she is poor and wretched."[170] According to the other solution, however, the meaning of the law is that, although the *Shekhinah* is immersed with Israel in the exile of the husks, the link between her and *Tiferet* remains unbroken, "and she remains in her husband's domain."[171]

The author of the Zohar stresses the great importance of prayer in the synagogue and interprets it in a mystical fashion. He specifically emphasizes the obligation of praying with a quorum of ten (the *minyan*). Every synagogue is a kind of Temple or sanctuary, and the *Shekhinah* dwells there,[172] and there is, to match it, a synagogue in the upper world; consequently, prayers must be recited in a building with windows, on the pattern of the upper world.[173] The worshiper should purify himself at home by cleansing the body and donning *tallit* and *tefillin* before going to the synagogue.[174] He should try to unite himself in spirit with the patriarchs who instituted the prayers.[175] As he enters the synagogue he should concentrate particularly on *Ḥesed* and *Gevurah*, symbolized by Abraham and Isaac, who are the gateways to the upper *sefirot*.[176] If a man prays in the synagogue with great awe and sanctity he is proclaimed in the upper world to be "a servant of the Lord."[177] But as for the man who profanes the holiness of the place by indulging in secular conversation—"woe to him who manifests separation, woe to him who diminishes faith, woe to him who has no share in the God of Israel, who displays that there is no God, that He is not present there, and that he does not fear Him, but treats the restoration of the upper world with disrespect."[178]

The quorum of ten represents the ten camps of angels and the ten *sefirot*. The members of the *minyan* restore the heavenly powers with their prayers,[179] and they build up and perfect, as it were, the parts of the body of the divine *Adam Kadmon*. The honor of the *Shekhinah*, who arrives at the synagogue first and waits for the worshipers to come, demands that the first ten should arrive together at a fixed time for prayer. But the man who enters first to announce the imminent arrival of his companions, and who can spend time alone with the *Shekhinah*, achieves the distinction of rising to the level of the supernal Righteous One, *Yesod*, and is united with the *Shekhinah* in the mystery of inter-course.[180]

Congregational prayer is more important than the prayer of the individual, "for it ascends with many hues, and comprises many facets, and because it comprises many hues it becomes a crown and is placed on the head of the righteous one who lives forever. But the prayer of the individual is not included and is of only one hue, and therefore the prayer of the individual is not as likely to be accepted as the prayer of the congregation."[181] Congregational prayer is like a wreath of multicolored flowers, whereas the prayer of the individual is like a solitary bloom, or like a bunch of flowers that are all of the same kind and that cannot be made into a crown. The prayers of individuals are examined as they ascend and if they are unfit or impure, or if those who utter them are blemished because of sin, they do not gain admittance to the abode of prayers. This is not the case, however, with the prayers of a congregation, for "there may be many that are uttered by the unworthy, but they all come before the Holy One, blessed be He, and He does not take heed of their sins . . . even though they may not all have been uttered with the correct intention and devotion."[182] Therefore "wherever a man recites his prayers, he should join in with the community, in the totality of the community."[183]

The way in which the Zohar provides a kabbalistic justification for the preeminence of the statutory prayers and congregational worship is typical of Jewish mysticism. It is true, of course, that the mystics of other faiths also by and large retained their allegiance to the official and traditional modes of worship, but much more tenuously, and in the case of prayer the most important thing for them was the free, spontaneous, intimate dialogue between the individual soul and God.[184] The kabbalists, as we have seen, also stressed inner spirituality, but at the same time they reinforced very strongly the traditional values and the communal nature of Judaism, and tried to instill mystic individual *kavvanah* into the established congregational liturgy.

The last topic that I wish to discuss in this section on the details of the mystical meaning of prayer is the relative value of lowering and raising the voice. Jewish law states that the Eighteen Benedictions should be recited quietly, and the rabbis went out of their way to denounce those who raised their voice in prayer.[185] The Zohar gives a mystical turn to these traditional precepts, and states in its kabbalistic explanation that "whoever recites his prayer before his Master should not allow his voice to be heard while he is praying. Whoever allows his voice to be heard while he is praying—his prayer is not heard."[186] The reason given in this passage is that prayer belongs to the level of *Malkhut,* which stands for the voice that is not heard, in contrast to *Tiferet,* which is the voice that is heard. Another passage[187] states that the angels who receive the prayers, "those who have ears," pay heed only to those "who recite their prayers in a low voice, with inner concentration, so that their prayer cannot be heard by another."[188] But here the prohibition of praying aloud is given a completely opposite explanation: "Prayer belongs to the supernal world, and whatever belongs to the supernal world does not have to be heard." This means that since the *kavvanah* of prayer is directed toward *Binah,* who is called "the supernal world," it is necessarily above the level of the voice that is heard. A third explanation links the duty of praying in subdued tones with the mystery of intercourse, which is instigated by the recital of the Eighteen Benedictions, for "then all is quiet above and below because of the kisses of desire."[189] Behind these different explanations lies the fear that if one raised one's voice one might disrupt the union that the soul achieves with the divine powers through inner devotion and concentration.

However, it is better to raise the voice than to lower it when one is pleading for help at a time of distress,[190] and prayer accompanied by tears is better even than a simple plea: "A cry is better than [ordinary] prayer, because a man cries to his Master with heartfelt sincerity . . . but tears come from the heart and with the will of the whole body." [191] On the basis of the rabbinic statement that "the gates of weeping are never closed," [192] the Zohar exalts the value and the potential influence of pouring out one's thoughts in tears. [193] The highest value of all is placed on the tearful outcry uttered without any words whatsoever: "A plea necessarily entails prayer. . . . A cry [means] that one cries but says nothing . . . therefore, a cry is more to be valued than all the others, for a cry comes from the heart. . . . He who prays and weeps and cries so much that there is no feeling left in his lips—that is perfect prayer, prayer in the heart, and it never returns empty". So we see once again that even without mentioning any specifically mystical aims the Zohar upholds the traditional idea of prayer as "worship in the heart."

II

In discussing the purposes *(kavvanot)* of specific prayers, I should like to concentrate on the Eighteen Benedictions, the Sanctification *(Kedushah),* prostration, and the recital of the *Shema.*

The prayers that precede the Eighteen Benedictions—apart from the *Shema,* which constitutes an important section in its own right—are regarded as preparatory in a mystical sense to the *Amidah.* [194] As the worshiper approaches the Eighteen Benedictions, the mystical purpose of which is to aid the process of intercourse in the upper world, he must concern himself with preparing the bride, the *Shekhinah,* for her progress to the marriage canopy. Here is one of the accounts that deal with the various stages in this preparation. "He who is in awe of his Master and concentrates his mind and his will in prayer helps in the restoration of the upper world. . . . At first, through the hymns and praises that the celestial angels recite in the world above, and through the order of praises that Israel recite below, [the *Shekhinah*] adorns herself and beautifies herself with her finery, as a wife adorns herself for her husband. And then through the order of prayer—the prayers that are recited while one is seated—her handmaidens are beautified and her company [of angels], and they are all adorned with her. After everything has been prepared, and they are all ready, they come to [the prayer] 'True and firm.' . . . [195] Then everything is in a state of readiness, both she and her maidens, until they come to [the prayer 'Rock of Israel . . . O Lord,] who hast redeemed Israel.' [196] Then everyone must stand erect, because when we come to [the prayer] 'True and firm . . .,' and everything is prepared, her maidens bear her aloft, and she raises herself to the supernal king." [197]

Intercourse begins as the benediction concerning redemption leads into the *Amidah*, because this symbolizes the union of male and female. "When we reach 'who hast redeemed Israel' and then begin the *Amidah* . . . the righteous one is stimulated to achieve union in the necessary place, with love, affection, joy, and pleasure, and all the limbs are joined together in a single desire, the upper worlds with the lower, and all the luminaries shine resplendently, and they all stand in a single union, through this righteous one who is called 'good' . . . and this one unites all in a single union." [198]

This account would seem to imply that at the very beginning of the recital of the Eighteen Benedictions actual intercourse takes place by means of *Yesod*, the male sexual organ, the supernal "righteous one." But the passage states immediately afterward that the first stage of union consists only of the mystery of kissing, and that it is only at the end of the *Amidah*, at the prayer beginning "He who makes peace," [199] "that the river (i.e., *Yesod*) that flows out of Eden has intercourse."

Other passages explain that the first three benedictions are directed toward *Ḥesed, Gevurah,* and *Tiferet,* the two arms and the body, which are involved in embracing and kissing; that the last three benedictions are aimed at *Neẓaḥ, Hod,* and *Yesod,* the two legs and the penis, which complete the act of intercourse, and that between these two processes, which unify the divine powers, the time is right for the worshiper to petition for his own needs through the intermediate benedictions. "As soon as we reach [the prayer that ends] 'who hast redeemed Israel,' the holy supernal king moves with his retinue to receive her. And we must stand in awe and trembling before the supernal king, because at that time he stretches out his right arm *(Ḥesed)* toward her, and then his left arm *(Gevurah)*, which he places beneath her head. And then they embrace each other with a kiss. These are the first three [benedictions], and one must exert one's mind and will to concentrate on all the correct purposes of the *Amidah*—one's mouth, mind, and will, all together. Once the supernal king and his consort are united in joy through these kisses, whoever has a request to make should make it, for this is the hour of [divine] goodwill. When the worshiper has put his request to the king and his consort, he should devote himself in mind and will to the three others,[200] in order to stimulate secret joy, because through these three she is blessed with another form of embrace. One should then prepare oneself to part from them and leave them in the hidden joy of these three."[201] With the same system in mind the Zohar also assigns specific aims to the individual words of the three first and last benedictions.[202]

In the *Tikkunei ha-Zohar* a place for personal petition is found among the first and the last three benedictions as well. "In the first three a man should arrange the praises he says like a servant who sets out his praise before his master, for these three write down all the merits. The last three seal them, and therefore a man must conduct himself then like a servant who receives his reward from his master, and departs; for the receptacle is present there, the seal of truth, the holy *Malkhuth*. In the intervening [benedictions] he must make his petition, for the *vav* is present there, one in charge of writing and one in charge of sealing, the upper *vav* and the lower *vav*, comprising twelve parts.[203] The first three are the head and the two arms. The last three are the body and the two legs."[204] In matching the benedictions to the *sefirot*, the author shows definite originality, especially in seeing the twelve intermediate benedictions as being directed toward *Tiferet* and *Yesod*, symbolized by the upper *vav* and the lower *vav*. It would seem also that he differs from the author of the Zohar in interpreting the aims of the first and last three benedictions. With regard to the first three he has, in addition to the two arms, the head, which usually signifies the upper *sefirot*. And in connection with the last three he mentions the body, which as a rule signifies *Tiferet*. It is possible, however, that the aims of the benedictions are identical in both interpretations, and that we simply have a variation in the meaning of the anthropomorphic symbols: in other words, the head is meant to signify *Tiferet* and the body *Yesod*. This possibility is strengthened by the purpose he assigns to the intermediate benedictions, where *Tiferet* is described as being "in charge of writing," that is, as one of the "writing" *sefirot* in the first three benedictions, and *Yesod* as "in charge of sealing," that is, one of the "sealing" *sefirot* in the last three benedictions. The satisfaction of the worshiper's needs occurs in the last three because when they are recited the *Shekhinah*, the "receptacle," receives a flow of influence through the mystery of intercourse.

Another version of the aims *(kavvanot)* of the Eighteen Benedictions, which also maintains that petitions for private needs can be included in all of them, is particularly interesting because it shows how the author of the *Tikkunei ha-Zohar* used the writings of earlier kabbalists. The author turns to Moses, "the faithful shepherd" *(raya mehemna)*, and asks him to help the other "prophets" or "masters of prophecy," [205] who knock at the portals of the *Shekhinah*'s palace and offer their petitions as they recite the Eighteen Benedictions: "[In] the first three benedictions of the *Amidah* they put their requests concerning the soul so that through them they might come into the presence of the Cause of causes, where the life of the soul exists; the intermediate benedictions are intended for petitions that concern the needs of the body; [in] the last three benedictions they receive a reply from the king to all their requests." [206] One can see from the nature of the objects of prayer and also from the terms used in this passage that it was influenced by the teachings of Rabbi Azriel of Gerona: "Know, my son, that the Eighteen Benedictions contain the needs of the body, and the needs of the soul, and the need of the life of the soul, which is the life of the world to come"; "although one should not make a request concerning needs of the body in the first three benedictions, one should petition about the life of the soul, for life is derived from it." [207]

The Sanctification *(Kedushah)* [208] is recited three times in the morning liturgy: before the *Amidah,* during the repetition aloud of the *Amidah,* and in the prayer "A redeemer shall come to Zion" after the *Amidah.* [209] On the first two occasions Israel and the angels offer their praises together, the first *Kedushah* being addressed to the *Shekhinah,* and the second to the *sefirot* above her, and they are therefore in Hebrew, the language of the angels. The third, however, the *Kedushah de-sidra,* is an additional one for every individual Jew to recite, and so it is in Aramaic, and excludes the angels. [210] In one passage we find the idea that once the angels have opened the gates to Israel's prayers through the *Kedushot* that they recite together and that contain praises addressed to the angels themselves, Israel play a trick on them and offer an additional *Kedushah* that the angels cannot understand. "We must take great care with this *Kedushah* and conceal it among ourselves, so that we may be sanctified through it from beginning to end, more than the *Kedushot* that the celestial angels recite with us. . . . They allow us in love to enter the gates above because we praise them in our prayers, and because of this we can take an additional *Kedushah* and enter the celestial gates. You might think that this is deceitful, but it is not so, for the celestial angels are more holy than we are, and they receive greater sanctity, and if we did not attract and receive these *Kedushot* we could not possibly be their companions, and the glory of the Holy One, blessed be He, would not be perfected above and below at one and the same time. We therefore strive to be partners with them, and then the glory of the Holy One, blessed be He, can be exalted above and below at one and the same time."[211] The angels are in fact deceived, but it is a sacred kind of deception that does no harm, because it is practiced solely in order to put Israel on the same level of holiness as the angels.

The opening words of the *Kedushah*, "Holy, holy, holy," represent the three worlds from which the prayer arises,[212] and also stand for the *sefirot Hesed, Gevurah,* and *Tiferet,*[213] to which the prayer ascends and which it serves to unite. One passage mentions a rather complex object for this prayer, comprising the whole sefirotic system, from *Hokhmah* which is called *"Kodesh,"* through *Tiferet,* called *"Kadosh,"* to *Malkhut,* called *"Kedushah."* At the same time, the simple object, namely *Hesed, Gevurah,* and *Tiferet,* is depicted as if it were confined only to kabbalists of limited ability. "If a man concentrates on the three levels of the patriarchs in unison, in order to unify them through the *Kedushah,* even if he cannot concentrate at a higher level it is good enough". The differentiation of the *kavvanot* in this way reflects the place of the Zohar in the development of kabbalistic thinking about them. Taking *Hesed, Gevurah,* and *Tiferet* as the object of the *Kedushah* is quoted by the Gerona school in the name of Rabbi Isaac the Blind,[214] while the *kavvanah* of *Hokhmah, Tiferet,* and *Malkhut* is a development and crystallization of the *kavvanot* of the *Kedushah* by Rabbi Azriel of Gerona.[215]

The mystical purpose of prostration after the Morning *Amidah*[216] is expressed in different and contrary ways in the Zohar. Common to them all, however, is a connection between the act of prostration and the completion of the act of intercourse at the end of the *Amidah*. One passage[217] contains two different ideas: "What is the reason [for prostration]? Because that particular time is the hour for intercourse, and every man should conduct himself with modesty in the presence of his Master and cover his face out of shame, and also include his own soul in the intercourse of souls, for the abode then contains souls and spirits from the world above and the world below."[218] The first part of this extract explains prostration as a sign of modesty in the presence of the divine powers who are engaged in intercourse. But according to the last part, the worshiper who prostrates himself actually intends by his act to have his soul included among those that are formed within the *Shekhinah* through the mystery of intercourse. This second idea involves the renewal of the soul, a kind of rebirth, by making it participate in the insemination of new souls. It is explained at greater length in another passage:[219] "When [the *Shekhinah*] receives souls and spirits, then is the time to commit one's own soul with those that she receives, for that is the moment for the bond of life. . . . For if at the time she receives souls and spirits through the pleasure of a single union, a man devotes his own heart and will to this and offers his own soul in union and if it is accepted at that time with the desire of the souls, spirits, and breaths[220] that she receives, then that man will be bound up in the bond of life both in this world and the next." The soul that immerses itself in the life-flow of souls that is aroused within the *Shekhinah* will become part of her, "the bond of life," while it is still in the physical world. That is to say, the renewal of life that the soul gains will be the kind of eternal life that is experienced in the world to come. "Committing one's soul" is here used in the sense of seeking personal union with the *Shekhinah*. And the phrase is likewise used in other contexts. After the flow of influence has descended, through the recital of the *Amidah*, to the *sefirot* as far as the *Shekhinah*, it extends farther down to the creatures (*Hayyot*) of the Chariot and to the other lower powers, and "then man, the image who comprises all images,[221] falls and prostrates himself, and commits his body and his spirit to the man above who stands above those images,[222] and who comprises all images, so that [the worshiper] may stimulate him to act on his behalf."[223] The supernal "man" who is above the creatures of the Chariot is the *Shekhinah,* and by committing himself to her when the influence is flowing from her, the worshiper is able to make her presence rest upon him.

There are a number of passages that depict prostration as a committal of the spirit in the sense of a symbolic death, and this idea is explained in various ways. A conservative view is that the worshiper commits his soul to the *Shekhinah* in order to fulfill the commandment to sacrifice one's life to sanctify the divine name.[224] A more extreme view sees prostration as a sign that the worshiper is ready to die at the hands of the *Shekhinah,* who is depicted as the Tree of Death. Since the bond between the worshiper and *Tiferet,* the Tree of Life, has been broken, and since *Tiferet* had been united with the *Shekhinah* and had, thanks to the efficacy of the Eighteen Benedictions, afforded her protection, the worshiper must now express in symbolic fashion his subordination and subservience to the Tree of Death, in order to save himself from actual death. "When he has finished the *Amidah* a man must give the impression that he has departed from the world, for he has left the Tree of Life, and entered the realm of the Tree of Death, who returns his surety (i.e., his soul) to him. . . . The mystery of the matter is that there are some sins for which no atonement can be made until a man departs from the world. . . . And he does indeed give himself up to death, and commits his soul to this place, not simply as a surety as at night-time, but like someone who has actually departed from the world."[225] There can be no doubt that here the power of death is granted to the *Shekhinah.* The soul is deposited with her at night, and she either punishes it or forgives it for its sins.

Another passage, however, explains it in a way that can be interpreted quite differently. "Since during this prayer a man commits himself to death, he should concentrate his attention upon, and try to please, the side where death may be found, just like an ape in the mountains and the desert places: it pretends to be dead, and appears dead, at the approach of an animal of which it is afraid. The animal comes up to it, intending to kill it or at least to bite it, but when it sees the ape on the ground as if it were dead it thinks that it really is dead, and goes away, and has no evil designs upon it." [226] Both the beginning and the end of this passage speak of committing one's soul to the *Shekhinah* for the sanctification of the divine name and in order to atone for sin, but the little parable in the middle introduces a new note. It entails deceiving the power of death, who is portrayed as a beast of prey, by simulating death itself. This ruse seems to be aimed at *sitra aḥra,* who lies in wait for man and tries to kill him.[227]

The various mystical purposes of the recital of the *Shema*[228] occupy a very large place in the Zohar, and I can deal here only with a few specific points. The unification aspect is paramount and is brought out in a number of different ways. Certain phrases in the *Shema* were thought to allude to the Ten Commandments. "These verses, therefore, constitute a great principle of the Torah. Happy is the man who completes its recital twice every day, since then the holy name is sanctified by his mouth, as it should be."[229] The twenty-five letters in the first verse of the *Shema* plus the twenty-four letters in the second stand for the forty-nine gates of *Binah*. Consequently, whoever combines them properly by concentrating on celestial unification "is considered by the Holy One, blessed be He, to have implemented the whole Torah, which has forty-nine aspects."[230] He who concentrates on unification while reciting the first verse for the sake of sanctifying the divine name "is thought actually to have surrendered his soul for the sanctification of the name."[231] As the worshiper says each word of the *Shema*, he brings down holiness on one of the 248 parts of his body.[232]

The *Shema*, like the Eighteen Benedictions, is also credited by the Zohar with efficacy in influencing the mystical process of intercourse, but in this case the unification of the *sefirot* is concentrated on one or two verses, and each separate word and even individual letters are given specific mystical aims. The six words of the first verse represent the six upper "extremities," the male forces from *Ḥesed* to *Yesod*, while the six words of the second verse represent the six lower "extremities," the angels of the *Shekhinah*, who are regarded as her handmaids. The purpose in reciting the first verse therefore is to gather together the various male powers and inflame them with desire for the *Shekhinah*, while the second verse is recited in order to arouse the *Shekhinah*, to collect her retinue together with her, and to bring her to the marriage canopy. During the exile, when *sitra aḥra* is at the height of his powers and is able to seize the *Shekhinah* and interrupt the process of intercourse, the second verse is recited in subdued tones, and the unification implicit in the last word[233] is concealed "so that an alien should not be involved in that joy . . . but in the time to come, when that side departs from her and is banished from the world, the word 'one' will really be pronounced . . . openly, audibly, not in a whisper, and not in secret."[234]

There is also an allusion to the mystery of intercourse in that the letter *ayin* of the word *shema* and the letter *dalet* of the word *eḥad* are both written large. The letter *ayin* represents the seventy names of the Holy One, blessed be He, which are a manifestation of the seven *sefirot* from *Ḥesed* to *Malkhut*. The letter *dalet* represents the *Shekhinah*; therefore one should prolong the pronunciation of this letter in the traditional manner in order to unite her with the male forces: "With this unification one should bind 'fear' (*yir'ah* i.e., the *Shekhinah*), because one should prolong the letter *dalet* of *eḥad,* for the *dalet* of *eḥad* is large. This is the significance of the verse 'And let the dry land appear' (Genesis I:9). The *dalet* that is 'the dry land' should appear and be bound in this unification." [235]

The recital of the *Shema* is also given a much more far-reaching significance. According to this, one's aim should be to link the united male and female with *Ḥokhmah* and *Binah,* and then to cause the whole system of the *sefirot* to ascend and become joined to *En-Sof.* The attainment of this purpose is " 'One'—to unify everything from there upward as one, and to raise the will to bind everything in a single bond, to raise the will in fear and love higher and higher as far as *En-Sof;* and let not the will depart from all the levels or the limbs, [236] but let it ascend with them all in order to make them cleave to one another, so that all shall be one bond with *En-Sof.* " [237]

We also find in the Zohar that the *kavvanot* in the recital of the *Shema* may be directed mystically to the unification of the three divine names contained in the first verse: *YHVH, Elohenu, YHVH.* [238] These names are explained in many different ways and are represented by various symbols. One passage mentions the unification of the names as if it were a most recondite mystery, and declines to give an explanation: " 'Hear, O Israel'—at this moment the wife is united with her husband and everything is comprised into a single unity, and this is the 'Hear, O Israel' of unification. After this it unifies three powers, 'The Lord, our God, the Lord is One'—so that all may be one. . . . And this is the mystery of unification through three powers, as the holy luminary has explained and discussed it in several places, and we have no right to discuss it further." [239] Rabbi Jose, in whose name this passage is transmitted, mentions the explanation of this mystery at other points in the Zohar, but the explanations vary and are sometimes contradictory. The author of the Zohar himself says that "several ways of unification have been discussed and they are all true. Let a man follow the way he wishes." [240] And he also transmits in the name of Rabbi Simeon ben Yohai the view that "the unification may be arranged in four ways." [241] However, an examination of the many passages scattered throughout the Zohar reveals only three methods of unifying the divine names, [242] but even these are not always clear.

The first method is to treat the names as if they referred to *Ḥesed, Gevurah,* and *Tiferet;* expressed on one occasion [243] through the color symbolism of white, red, and yellow, and on another[244] through the symbols of fire, water, and spirit. According to this method the purpose in unifying the names is to prepare for the act of intercourse by bringing together and uniting the three *sefirot,* which may be seen as the body and the two arms of the male.

The second method, which is the most commonly referred to and explained, includes the *sefirot Ḥokhmah* and *Binah* in the unification of names. In a few passages the three names are thought to represent *Ḥokhmah, Binah,* and *Tiferet* through the letter symbolism of Y, H, and V, or through the symbols of the head called "father" (i.e., *Ḥokhmah*), of "the valley of streams" *(Binah),* and of "the trunk of the tree" *(Tiferet).*[245] Other passages match the three names with the four sections written in the *tefillin,* which correspond to *Ḥokhmah, Binah, Ḥesed,* and *Gevurah.* When one recites the *Shema,* however, one thinks of *Ḥesed* and *Gevurah* as being combined together in *Tiferet,* and so there are three divine names and not four. "In the *tefillin* of the head there are four sections, each one on its own, but here there are three names. . . . The first *YHVH* is the supernal point, the beginning of all (i.e., *Ḥokhmah*); *Elohenu* is the mystery of the world to come *(Binah);* the last *YHVH* comprises both right and left (*Ḥesed* and *Gevurah*) together in one unit."[246] According to this method also, in both its formulations, the unification of divine names is regarded as a preparation for intercourse, but here the gathering together of the male powers involves as well the two upper *sefirot,* which represent the head, the home of the brain, which was thought to be the source of semen.

In the third method the three names stand for *Ḥokhmah, Tiferet,* and *Malkhut:* "One at the top, the place of the beginning, whence paths extend to all sides;[247] one in the middle, the mystery where Moses included himself among Abraham and Isaac; one is the measure of King David;[248] there is a single method of restoration for them all."[249] In the light of this passage it would seem that the account of the unification of names as a joining together of head, trunk, and path *(shevil)*[250] also alludes to the unification of *Ḥokhmah, Tiferet,* and *Malkhut.* The meaning is that when the worshiper recites the divine names in the *Shema,* he should concentrate on unifying the whole structure of the *sefirot* together, after the mystic act of intercourse. The author of the Zohar came to no final conclusion about this subject. Sometimes[251] he prefers the first method, the unification of *Ḥesed, Gevurah,* and *Tiferet;* at others[252] he favors the second, the matching of the names with the sections in the *tefillin*.

In the descriptions of the way in which the divine names are united by the recital of the *Shema*, prominence is given in a number of passages to the basic unity of these three names. Let me give two clear examples. "Here are three names. How can they be one? Even though we say 'one' [in the *Shema*] how can they be one? It is through a vision of the holy spirit that [the mystery of their unity] becomes known, and they [appear] in the vision of the closed eye, so that it is known that these three are 'one' . . . three hues, but they are one." [253] The paradoxical mystery of three being one is revealed and explained to the kabbalist in a mystical-ecstatic experience. Another passage [254] presents the mystery of the trinity of names as a riddle: "They are two and one is joined to them and then they are three, and when they become three they are one." The solution is: "The two are the names in the *Shema*, namely *YHVH*, *YHVH*. *Elohenu* is joined to them, and it is the seal of the signet, truth. And when they are joined together they are one in a single unification."

Trinitarian formulations such as these provided ammunition for Christian "kabbalists" who endeavored to show that the Zohar displayed Christian tendencies. [255] The Zohar's presentation of the mystery of the trinity, however, is quite different from the Christian one, because in the former the all-embracing unification, which completes and perfects the mystery of the Godhead, involves the unification of the ten *sefirot* with *En-Sof*. There is no denying the possibility, nonetheless, that despite his firm anti-Christian attitude the author of the Zohar might have been influenced in his formulation of the mystery of the Godhead by the theology of the rival faith.

At all events, the complex teaching of kabbalah on mystical unification, which was a major element in the liturgical processes of kabbalistic religious life, ran counter to the basic and simple faith in the divine unity preached by traditional Judaism. Not for nothing did the more conservative rabbis of the thirteenth and fourteenth centuries fulminate against the new ideas of the kabbalists, saying that by directing their prayers toward different divine powers they were guilty of a kind of idolatry, and were more culpable than even the Christians. Here, for example, is a passage from Rabbi Abraham Abulafia: "The kabbalists intended to unify the divine name and so avoid belief in a trinity, but they made a division into ten. Just as the Gentiles say that there are three and that the three are one, some kabbalists believe and proclaim that God is the ten *sefirot,* and that the ten are one." [256]

There is no clear reaction in the main body of the Zohar to these accusations concerning the kabbalistic purposes of prayer. But the author of *Tikkunei ha-Zohar* states the main charge of the opponents of kabbalah, and then replies to it. "The question arises: Why pray to the Holy One, blessed be He, at various different levels? Sometimes we pray to Him through a certain *sefirah* and a certain attribute; sometimes prayer is [directed] to the right (i.e., to *Ḥesed*) . . . sometimes to the left *(Gevurah)* . . . sometimes to the central pillar *(Tiferet),* sometimes to the righteous one *(Yesod);* each prayer to a certain level. But, of course, YHVH is in every *sefirah,* and prayer is the *Shekhinah.* When the world needs mercy she ascends on the right, and when the world needs to be judged she ascends on the left, but always near *YHVH,* since He is everywhere." [257] This means, according to this particular kabbalist's doctrine concerning the nature of God, that the emanated powers are no more than agents of *En-Sof,* the Emanator, and that consequently prayers offered to the *sefirot* by means of the *Shekhinah* are really directed toward the one and only God, the Emanator who has the name of the divine essence YHVH, and who dwells within the *sefirot* and activates them. However, the author of the Zohar himself, who saw the *sefirot* as a revelation of the essence of God, can solve the problem only by resorting to the mystery of unity in plurality: "He is they, and they are He, like a flame attached to a burning coal, and there is no division there." [258] Prayers that are directed toward the different separate *sefirot* are directed at the same time to the one indivisible God.

NOTES

1. B.T. *Ta'anit* 2a. Cf. *Sifre Devarim,* sec. 41; B.T. *Megillah* 20a.
2. See also H. Z. Reines, "Ha-Mikdash u-Vet ha-Knesset," *Sinai* (Year 22) 44:213–24.
3. Both views are in B.T. *Berakhot* 26b.
4. Mishnah *Avot* 2: 13. Cf. also Mishnah *Berakhot* 4: 4.
5. B.T. *Berakhot* 30b (Mishnah).
6. See B.T. *Berakhot* 32b.
7. See ibid., 28b–34b.
8. See H. G. Enelow, "Kawwana: the Struggle for Inwardness in Judaism,"

Studies in Jewish Literature issued in honor of Professor Kaufmann Kohler (Berlin, 1913), pp. 82–88.

9. See B.T. *Berakhot* 13a–13b; B.T. *Eruvin* 95b–96a; B.T. *Pesaḥim* 114b; B.T. *Rosh ha-Shanah* 28a–29a.

10. B.T. *Berakhot* 5b, 17a, and elsewhere.

11. See L. Löw, *Gesammelte Schriften* (1898), 4:268–69, 278–79; Montefiore and Loewe, *A Rabbinic Anthology* (London, 1938), pp. 272–75, 342–50.

12. In what follows I deal only with the views of Baḥya ibn Pakuda and Maimonides. Enelow, op. cit., pp. 88–97, deals also with Sa'adia Gaon and Judah Halevi.

13. *The Book of Direction to the Duties of the Heart*, trans. Menahem Mansoor (London, 1973), pp. 89, 91, 97.

14. Ibid., p. 99.

15. Ibid., p. 89.

16. Ibid.

17. See ibid., p. 365.

18. Ibid.

19. Ibid., p. 367.

20. Ibid., p. 364.

21. Ibid., pp. 367, 366.

22. Ibid., p. 366. See also G. Vajda, *L'Amour de Dieu dans la théologie juive du moyen âge* (Paris, 1957). I have grave doubts as to whether Vajda is justified in saying that there is not much originality in Baḥya's views here when they are compared with traditional rabbinic statements.

23. *The Guide for the Perplexed*, vol. 3, chap. 32 (trans. Friedlander). See C. Neuburger, *Das Wesen des Gesetzes in der Philosophie des Maimonides* (Danzig, 1933), pp. 56–58.

24. See *Guide for the Perplexed*, vol. 3, chap. 28; and J. Becker, *Mishnato ha-Philosophit shel ha-Rambam* (Tel-Aviv, 1956), pp. 74–79.

25. *Mishneh Torah, Hilkhot Tefillah*, 4: 15–16.

26. See *Guide for the Perplexed*, vol. 3, chap. 51.

27. *Sefer Ḥasidim*, ed. Wistinetzki (Berlin, 1891–93), nos. 5–6.

28. See ibid., nos. 1050, 1118, 1941–42.

29. See Enelow, "Kawwana," pp. 97–99.

30. No. 1590.

31. No. 451. However, the rabbinic statement about "the ḥasidim of old" was interpreted more widely as if it demanded a period of silence "before every benediction," to induce proper concentration. See also nos. 456, 1605. However, according to no. 427, the raising of the voice could also assist concentration.

32. No. 441.

33. No. 445. See also no. 1590, based on B.T. *Berakhot* 30b. On the subject of alien thoughts during prayer see also nos. 440, 1065, and 1974.

34. See G. Scholem, *Major Trends in Jewish Mysticism* (New York, 1941), pp. 110–18.

35. Rabbi Eleazar of Worms, *Sode Razaya,* ed. J. Kamelhar (Bilgoraj, 1936), p. 32.
36. *Sha'arei ha-Sod ve-ha-Yihud ve-ha-Emunah,* ed. A. Jellinek, in *Kokhevei Yizhak,* no. 27 (1867), p. 13. Both these quotations are cited by Scholem, *Major Trends,* p. 116. See also his article "Der Begriff der Kawwana in der alten Kabbala," *MGWJ* (1934), pp. 494–96.
37. See Scholem, *Major Trends,* p. 110.
38. This passage is quoted from MS Adler 1161, fol. 65b in Scholem, *Reshit ha-Kabbalah* (Jerusalem, 1948), p. 78, n. I. Whoever wrote it had been influenced by kabbalistic ideas.
39. Sometimes, e.g., in nos. 1585 and 1588, there are allusions to mystical *kavvanah* in the *Sefer Hasidim* as well. See Enelow, "Kawwana," pp. 99–100.
40. *Tur, Orah Hayyim,* sec. 113. See G. Scholem, *Major Trends,* pp. 100–103. [The translation is taken from Scholem.]
41. See *Sefer Hasidim,* nos. 11 and 1575.
42. *Reshit ha-Kabbalah,* pp. 93–98.
43. See G. Scholem, "Te'udah Hadashah le-Toledot Reshit ha-Kabbalah," *Sefer Bialik* (1934), pp. 148–50; *Reshit ha-Kabbalah,* pp. 72–73, 96–97. In Rabbi Jacob ben Sheshet's *Meshiv Devarim Nekhohim,* chap. 20 (Oxford MS 1585, fol. 56b–57a), it says: "The beginning of every eulogy and blessing that man pronounces before the Holy One, blessed be He, is ascent as far as *En-Sof,* and after this he draws out blessing through emanation, and pronounces the blessing." This at first sight seems to indicate that one should direct one's thoughts straight to *En-Sof,* and draw influence down from there to the *sefirot.* But it goes on to say that "the source of blessing is the ascent to *En-Sof* . . . which thought cannot grasp . . . and the beginning of the ascent is *Hokhmah,* which receives from that which thought cannot grasp," and this would seem to imply that one's meditation ascends to *Keter.* The author, however, may not be too precise in his use of terminology, and perhaps he really meant to say that the limit for meditation was *Hokhmah,* "the beginning of the ascent," as would appear from his summary of the matter (fol. 58a): "When a man starts to bless the Holy One, blessed be He, he should raise his thought to the furthest limit of that which he can weigh or measure, and then pronounce the blessing." *Keter,* "which thought cannot grasp," can certainly not be weighed or measured by the human mind. See also *Perush ha-Aggadot le-Rabbi Azriel,* ed. I. Tishby (Jerusalem, 1945), p. 39, n. 16.
44. Quoted by G. Scholem, *Der Begriff der Kawwana,* p. 497, n. 2. See also *Reshit ha-Kabbalah,* pp. 113–15.
45. G. Scholem, *Der Begriff der Kawwana,* p. 506, n. 5, from *Sefer Or Zarua* by Rabbi David, the son of Judah the Pious.
46. Ibid., p. 512; *Reshit ha-Kabbalah,* p. 144. From *Sha'ar ha-Kavvanah,* probably written by Rabbi Azriel of Gerona.
47. Quoted in *Perush ha-Aggadot le-Rabbi Azriel,* p. 23, n. 2.

48. Quoted by Scholem, *Der Begriff der Kawwana,* p. 501, n. 3.
49. *Perush ha-Aggadot le-Rabbi Azriel,* p. 39. Mystical perception in this state of exaltation in prayer is called "nourishment" in the writings of Rabbi Isaac the Blind. See G. Scholem, *Der Begriff der Kawwana,* pp. 496–501; *Reshit ha-Kabbalah,* p. 117.
50. Scholem, *Der Begriff der Kawwana,* p. 512. The quotation is from *Sha'ar ha-Kavvanah.*
51. See ibid., pp. 508–11.
52. G. Scholem, "Seridim Ḥadashim mi-Kitvei Rabbi Azriel mi-Gerona," *Sefer Gulak ve-Klein* (Jerusalem, 1942), pp. 214–15. In the passage quoted there (n. 12) from Rabbi Azriel's commentary to the liturgy it is explained that "the need of the life of the soul" takes precedence in prayer over "the needs of the body," and this is consistent with my understanding above of the passage from the *Sha'ar ha-Kavvanah.* But another principle there (no. 10) contradicts this: "Seek mercy, my son, for the needs of the body, and after that for the needs of the soul, and after that for the life of the world to come." I am not able to resolve this contradiction.
53. This interpretation differs in one important respect from that of Scholem, "Seridim Ḥadashim," n. 12.
54. On the meaning of *hashva'ah* (identity) see Scholem, *Reshit ha-Kabbalah,* p. 139.
55. *Perush ha-Aggadot le-Rabbi Azriel,* p. 16.
56. Scholem, "Seridim Hadashim," p. 222 *(Sod Keriat Shema le-Rabbi Ezra).*
57. Scholem, *Der Begriff der Kawwana,* p. 506, n. 1.
58. See Scholem, *Reshit ha-Kabbalah,* pp. 118–22, 139–41; idem, "Tradition und Neuschöpfung im Ritus der Kabbalisten," *Eranos-Jahrbuch,* 19 (1951): 133–36.
59. Jacob ben Sheshet, *Sha'ar ha-Shamayim* in *Ozar Neḥmad* 3: 164–65. He also gives a mystical explanation of why it is essential "to enunciate each individual word" (ibid., pp. 158–59).
60. See Scholem, *Reshit ha-Kabbalah,* pp. 134–36.
61. Enelow, "Kawwana," pp. 100–105, deals very generally with the mystical intentions of prayer in kabbalah, and particularly in the Zohar.
62. Zohar II, 201a.
63. Ibid., 202b.
64. The fact that the author of the Zohar gave prayer this intermediate position may indicate that he was influenced by Rabbenu Baḥya, who considered prayer to be an obligation midway between the duties of the heart and the duties of the physical members.
65. The sound, or voice, is formed in the world above, because prayer in the world below is said silently.
66. Zohar III, 294a–294b *(Idra Zuta).*
67. This is a reference to profane thought or speech on the Sabbath. Profane speech activates the power of *sitra aḥra,* whereas profane thought does not.

68. Zohar III, 105a. For the influence of human speech on the upper worlds, see also Zohar III, 31a–31b, 112a.
69. See Scholem, *Major Trends in Jewish Mysticism*, p. 397, n. 154.
70. See *Zohar Ḥadash, Ruth*, 80a.
71. Zohar I, 169a.
72. See ibid., 195b; II, 69a, and often.
73. Zohar II, 244b.
74. See Zohar III, 183b.
75. Zohar II, 210a–210b.
76. See Scholem, "Levush ha-Neshamot ve-Ḥaluka de-Rabbanan," *Tarbiz* (1956), pp. 297–306.
77. See Zohar II, 93b.
78. Zohar I, 262a.
79. Zohar III, 285a. See also II, 178a–178b (in the column adjoining the *Sifra di-Ẓeniuta*).
80. See Zohar II, 69b, 200b, 250b.
81. Zohar II, 262b.
82. Thought is *Ḥokhmah;* "the will of the heart" *Binah;* sound *Tiferet;* and speech *Malkhut.*
83. See Zohar III, 263a.
84. Zohar II, 198b.
85. See ibid., 57a; III, 20a, 285a.
86. The entrance between the two cherubim mentioned in Zohar III, 164a, also refers to *Ḥesed* and *Gevurah*. Cf. *Zohar Ḥadash, Ruth*, 87a. And see *Perush ha-Aggadot le-Rabbi Azriel*, p. 17, n. 13; p. 71, n. 7.
87. Zohar I, 229a. On the prayer's ascent to *Binah*, see also II, 153b, 202a.
88. Zohar III, 130b.
89. See Zohar II, 132b, 144a, 213b, 244b, 260b.
90. On the various uses to which this term is put see Scholem, "Ikvotav shel Gabirol ba-Kabbalah," *Me'assef Sofrei Erez Yisrael* (1940), p. 174.
91. In my view Rabbi Azriel of Gerona also used "the root of all roots" as a term for *Keter*. See *Perush ha-Aggadot le-Rabbi Azriel*, p. 82, n. 9; p. 90, n. 9.
92. Zohar II, 215b. See also II, 201b (the *tikkun* of the spirit).
93. See Zohar II, 134b.
94. See Zohar III, 265a.
95. Zohar II, 201a.
96. Zohar III, 55a.
97. Ibid., 260b.
98. See ibid., 243a *(Raya Mehemna); Zohar Ḥadash, Tikkunim*, 108a.
99. See Zohar I, 37b; III, 278a–278b *(Raya Mehemna); Zohar Ḥadash, Bereshit*, 10b *(Midrash ha-Ne'elam); Tikkunei ha-Zohar*, preface, 2a.
100. See B.T. *Ḥullin* 91b; *Shir ha-Shirim Rabbah*, 8: 15.
101. See Zohar I, 40a, 90a *(Sitrei Torah);* II, 18b, and elsewhere.
102. See Zohar II, 164b.

103. See Zohar I, 266b *(hashmatot);* III, 243a, 306b *(tosafot).*
104. *Tikkun* 45, 83a.
105. This simile was apparently taken from the mystical approach to prayer of the German *ḥasidim.* See Scholem, *Major Trends,* p. 100.
106. See *Zohar Ḥadash, Terumah,* 41a–42a.
107. See Zohar I, 41a–45b; II, 131b–132b, 200a–201a, 260b–262a.
108. The tempering (lit., sweetening) of Judgment is depicted as one of the most important objects of *kavvanah,* particularly during the grace after meals. See I, 250a–250b; II, 157b, 162a, 168b–169a.
109. *Tikkun* 6, 21b–22a.
110. See Zohar II, 216b.
111. See III, 255a *(Raya Mehemna).*
112. See also *Tikkunei ha-Zohar, Tikkun* 18, 32b–37b; *Zohar Ḥadash, Tikkunim,* 97a, 108b–109a.
113. See Zohar II, 128b, 133b, 200b.
114. Zohar I, 244a.
115. See Zohar I, 148a.
116. See B.T. *Berakhot* 5b.
117. [Lit., "his *Shekhinah.*" There is a play here on the word *shakhen,* which means "near to, adjoining."]
118. *Tikkunei ha-Zohar, Tikkun* 58, 92a.
119. See Zohar II, 259b.
120. See Zohar III, 263a *(Raya Mehemna?).*
121. Zohar II, 213b.
122. [Whose opening line is "Hear, O Israel, the Lord is our God, the Lord is One."]
123. *Binah* and *Malkhut.*
124. *Binah,* the source of the lower *sefirot,* the "limbs."
125. *Ḥokhmah.*
126. *Ḥesed, Gevurah, Tiferet,* and *Malkhut.* The meaning here, however, seems to signify the inclusion of the actual corners of the globe, the physical cosmos, in the mystery of unification. See Scholem, *Reshit ha-Kabbalah,* pp. 113–14, 120–22.
127. Zohar II, 216a–216b.
128. See Zohar II, 237b.
129. Ibid., 154b, 169a.
130. The statement in the Zohar (II, 173a) that "Israel below are unable to unite themselves with their Master until they have repulsed 'the other side' and given him a portion with which he can occupy himself" seems to refer, according to the commentators, to the evacuation of the body before prayer.
131. See Zohar II, 130a.
132. See Zohar III, 186b, 191b.
133. See Zohar I, 23b; II, 248b, 250a.
134. Here is a list of the principal passages in the Zohar that deal with the way

in which divine influence can be brought down by concentrated intention *(kavvanah)* in the recital of prayers and blessings, especially the grace after meals: I, 207b–208a, 243b–244a, 250a; II, 87b, 168a–168b, 218a–218b; III, 190b.

135. Zohar III, 26a.

136. See ibid., 265b.

137. See Scholem, *Major Trends,* p. 33.

138. See Zohar I, 229a; III, 285a–285b.

139. Zohar III, 270b–271a *(Raya Mehemna?).*

140. Cf. *Zohar Ḥadash, Ruth,* 87d.

141. Zohar II, 260b–261a.

142. In Zohar II, 238a it says that they who unify the holy name through concentration in prayer raise the *Shekhinah* to intercourse with *Tiferet,* and thereby receive blessings from the source of life. The most detailed account of the source of life occurs in III, 34a: "Rabbi Hiyya began by quoting 'For with You is the source of life. In Your light shall we see light' (Psalm 36: 10). 'For with You is the source of life'—this is the supernal oil that flows unceasingly and that exists within the most supernal *Hokh-mah.* This is the meaning of 'With You'—it exists with You and is never separated from You through [Your] love of all. 'Source of life' because it is the source and fountain of life, producing life for the supernal tree, and kindling lights. The tree is therefore called 'Tree of Life,' the tree that is planted and has taken root because of the source of life." Clearly, "the source of life" here is *Binah,* which gives life to *Tiferet,* the Tree of Life. However, *Binah* itself is called "the supernal oil," which is unusual. Maybe the symbol of oil is intended only for the word "life," that is, for the influence that derives from the source of life. The passage continues (III, 34b) and explains the words "source of life" in the scriptural verse in terms of *Tiferet* and *Yesod,* but only because of their connection with *Binah.* And I think this is the way we should understand II, 157a where *Yesod* is said to be "the spirit of the source of life." The phrase refers to *Binah* also in I, 127b, II, 91b *(Raya Mehemna?)* and 135b. We can therefore see that the term "source of life" in the Zohar had originally a consistent meaning. See Scholem, "Ikvotav shel Gabirol ba-Kabbalah," pp. 165–66. Scholem believes that the author of the Zohar used the term to indicate both *Binah* and *Yesod.*

143. Zohar II, 213b.

144. Zohar II, 245a.

145. Zohar III, 254a–254b.

146. See Zohar II, 198b.

147. Zohar II, 161a.

148. Ibid., 134b–135b.

149. See Zohar I, 169a; II, 261a.

150. Zohar III, 226a.

151. See Zohar I, 202a; II, 15a.

152. See Zohar I, 167b–168a.

153. See ibid., 199b; II, 62a–62b.

154. Zohar II, 178a (in the margins of the *Sifra di-Zeniuta*). It would appear to be a later addition.

155. See Zohar II, 252b; III, 79b; and elsewhere. See the notes in *Nizozei Zohar*.

156. B.T. *Mo'ed Katan* 28a: "Life, children and food do not depend on merit but on the stars." The Zohar interprets the word *mazzal* (planet, star) as if it were derived from the verb *nazal* (to flow) and applies the term to *Binah*.

157. Zohar II, 62a.

158. In Psalm 145: 16, which in this context must be translated "You open Your hand and *razon* (lit., will, desire) satisfies every living creature."

159. Because of shortage of space I have to pass over complete topics, such as the mystical purpose of the benedictions, especially the grace after meals, and the Sabbath and Festival prayers. In this and other introductions I can deal with them only incidentally.

160. B.T. *Berakhot* 26b.

161. These three prayers, when recited on the Sabbath, are on a different plane, representing the three upper Sabbaths, namely, *Binah, Yesod,* and *Malkhut.* See Zohar I, 5b; II, 95a *(Raya Mehemna?)*.

162. Zohar I, 132b.

163. See ibid., I, 132b–133a, 178a; II, 21a–21b (which belongs to the *Midrash ha-Ne'elam*), 129b–131a. *Zohar Hadash, Bereshit,* 18a *(Midrash ha-Ne'elam)* gives an aggadic explanation of the times of the prayers, so as to match the singing of the angels.

164. [*Et razon,* lit., "the time of (the divine) will, or favor."]

165. Zohar II, 156a.

166. Zohar III, 288b. See also III, 129a, 136b, 293a.

167. See B.T. *Berakhot* 27b; B.T. *Yoma* 87b.

168. Zohar I, 132b–133a.

169. See Zohar II, 130a, 162b.

170. Zohar I, 23b (this belongs to the *Tikkunei ha-Zohar*). See also *Tikkunei ha-Zohar, Tikkun* 5, 20a–20b; *Zohar Hadash, Tikkunim* 108b.

171. Zohar III, 242a *(Raya Mehemna)*.

172. See also Zohar II, 201b.

173. See ibid., 250b, 251a.

174. See Zohar III, 120b, 260a, 265a.

175. See Zohar I, 11a; III, 8b.

176. See Zohar III, 8b; 164a.

177. See ibid., 196a.

178. Zohar II, 131b; see also II, 205b.

179. See Zohar II, 164b.

180. See ibid., 131a–131b.

181. Zohar I, 167b.

182. Ibid., 234a. See also II, 245b.

183. Zohar I, 160b. See also II, 246a.
184. See F. Heiler, *Das Gebet* (Munich, 1920), pp. 284–321; E. Underhill, *Mysticism* (London, 1942), pp. 306–27.
185. See B.T. *Berakhot* 24b, 31a; B.T. *Sotah* 32b.
186. A man who has an unpleasant voice, that is, a voice that is displeasing to the congregation, should not pray aloud even during songs and prayers of praise (Zohar I, 249b). One should, however, study aloud (Zohar III, 39a–39b).
187. Zohar II, 202a. See the commentary *Mikdash Melekh* to this passage and to I, 209b.
188. See Zohar III, 230b *(Raya Mehemna)*.
189. Zohar II, 128b. See also *Tikkunei ha-Zohar*, Tikkun 10, 25a.
190. See Zohar I, 132a–132b; III, 138a–138b *(Idra Rabba)*.
191. *Zohar Hadash, Ruth*, 80a.
192. B.T. *Baba Mezia* 59a.
193. See Zohar I, 132b; II, 245b; *Tikkunei ha-Zohar*, Tikkun 11, 26b.
194. [*Amidah*, lit., "standing," is another name for the Eighteen Benedictions. See *The Authorised Daily Prayer Book*, trans. S. Singer (London, 1962), pp. 46–56. This work will be referred to in the notes as P.B.]
195. [P.B., p. 44.]
196. [P.B., p. 46.]
197. Zohar II, 200b. See also 131a–132b; *Zohar Hadash, Terumah*, 69b–70a.
198. Zohar II, 128b.
199. [P.B., p. 56.]
200. To *Nezah, Hod*, and *Yesod*, the object of the last three benedictions.
201. Zohar II, 200a.
202. See ibid., 260b–262a; *Zohar Hadash, Terumah*, 42a.
203. [The letter *vav* has the numerical equivalent of six.]
204. *Tikkunei ha-Zohar*, Tikkun 10, 26a. See also Zohar III, 223a *(Raya Mehemna)*.
205. It would appear from the context that "prophecy" is regarded here as a level attained by kabbalists who pray with mystical aims. See A. Jellinek, *Ginzei Hokhmat ha-Kabbalah* (Leipzig, 1853), p. 16 *(Iggeret shel R. Avraham Abulafia)*.
206. *Tikkunei ha-Zohar*, Tikkun 18, 32b.
207. G. Scholem, "Seridim Hadashim mi-Kitvei R. Azriel mi-Gerona," p. 214, and also ibid., n. 12.
208. ["Holy, holy, holy is the Lord of hosts," etc.]
209. [P.B., pp. 40, 47, and 76 respectively.]
210. See Zohar II, 132b–133a. On the joint recitation of the first two *Kedushot* by Israel and the angels, see also I, 231a–231b; II, 217a; 247b; III, 190b.
211. Zohar II, 129a–129b.
212. See Zohar III, 190b.
213. See Zohar II, 52a.
214. " '*Kadosh* (holy)' for *Hesed*, '*Kadosh*' for *Din*, '*Kadosh*' for *Rahamim*.

This is the significance of the [musical sign] *tevir* on the second *kadosh*, because it implies breaking [Aramaic *tevir*]. This is what I have heard in the name of the pious Rabbi Isaac, son of Rabbi Abraham" (Jacob ben Sheshet Gerondi, *Meshiv Devarim Nekhoḥim*, chap. 17, Oxford MS 1585, fol. 51a). The same opinion is quoted in the name of Rabbi Isaac the Blind in Rabbi Meir ibn Sahula's commentary to Nahmanides' commentary to the Pentateuch (*Ve-zot ha-berakhah*, 34d).

215. See Scholem, "Seridim," pp. 219–22. In the *Sefer ha-Bahir* (Vilna), sec. 48, fol. 13b, there is already a more all-embracing *kavvanah:* " 'Kadosh'— *Keter Elyon;* 'Kadosh'—the root of the tree (i.e., *Binah* or *Tiferet*); 'Kadosh'—specially attached to them all (apparently referring to *Malkhut*)." See Scholem, *Das Buch Bahir* (Leipzig, 1923), pp. 96–97. Rabbi Jacob ben Sheshet offers as his own explanation (op. cit., chap. 17, fol. 50b) a more exalted *kavvanah* for the *Kedushah:* " 'Kadosh' for *En-Sof;* 'Kadosh' for Ḥokhmah; 'Kadosh' for the world of the letters (i.e., *Binah*)."

216. [During the *Taḥanun*, P.B., pp. 65ff.]

217. Zohar II, 129a.

218. This passage describes the *Shekhinah* as the *idra* (chamber), the abode of the *sefirot* and of celestial influence.

219. Zohar II, 200b.

220. *Nefashot, ruḥot, neshamot.*

221. See I. Tishby, *The Wisdom of the Zohar*, pp. 295–98, 677–79.

222. I.e., upon the creatures of the Chariot.

223. Zohar III, 241b.

224. See Zohar II, 202b. Death is not explicitly mentioned here, however.

225. See also Zohar III, 176b.

226. *Zohar Ḥadash, Terumah,* 42a.

227. It was apparently from a combination of these passages that the idea developed in Lurianic kabbalah that prostration was a kind of leap of the soul into the domain of the husks, the domain of death, in order to raise sparks of holiness from there. See Tishby, *Torat ha-Ra ve-ha-Kelipah be-Kabbalat ha-Ari* (Tel Aviv, 1942), pp. 128–30.

228. [P.B., pp. 41–42.]

229. Zohar III, 268a.

230. Ibid., 264b. See the comments in Margaliot's *Niẓoẓei Zohar*.

231. Zohar III, 195b.

232. See *Zohar Ḥadash, Aḥarei*, 48a *(Midrash ha-Ne'elam)*.

233. *Va-ed*, the last word of the second verse is identified through an interchange of letters with *eḥad* ("one"), the last word of the first verse.

234. On the processes of unification and intercourse, see also Zohar I, 12a, 18a–18b, 148a; II, 161b–162a; III, 263a–263b *(Raya Mehemna)*.

235. Zohar I, 12a. See also II, 160b; III, 236b, 258a *(Raya Mehemna)*, 263a. The letters *ayin* and *dalet* are also explained in these passages in the sense of *edut* (testimony), which the Holy One, blessed be He, or the *Shekhinah* gives concerning those who recite the *Shema*, namely, that they have taken

upon themselves "the yoke of the kingdom of heaven" [a phrase signifying that they have proclaimed the unity of God by reciting the *Shema*].

236. Even when one is concentrating on *En-Sof* attention must still be paid to the *sefirot*.

237. Zohar II, 216b. This *kavvanah* is cited as "the unification practiced by Rav Hamnuna Sava, who learned it from his father, and his father learned it from his teacher, and it goes back as far as Elijah." This chain of transmission sounds like a paraphrase of the tradition concerning the kabbalah of Rabbi Isaac the Blind. See Tishby, "Ha-Mekubbalim Rabbi Ezra ve-Rabbi Azriel u-Mekomam be-Ḥug Gerona," *Zion* 9 (1944): 180, 183–84; Scholem, *Reshit ha-Kabbalah*, pp. 95–96. I have not, however, found this actual *kavvanah* ascribed to Rabbi Isaac the Blind, and it would appear to be original to the author of the Zohar.

238. ["The Lord, our God, the Lord (is one)."]

239. Zohar II, 160b.

240. Ibid., 43b.

241. Ibid., 162a.

242. Perhaps the two versions of the second method, described below, should be thought of as two different methods.

243. Zohar I, 18b.

244. Zohar II, 43b. Apparently, the obscure version in III, 162a, also alludes to this method.

245. See Zohar III, 263a. The obscure reference in I, 15b: "*YHVH Elohenu YHVH*—these are the three levels that represent this supernal mystery", may also allude to *Ḥokhmah, Binah,* and *Tiferet.* "The supernal mystery" referred to is the mystery of *ehyeh asher ehyeh* ("I am that I am"), which is interpreted in terms of these three *sefirot.*

246. Zohar II, 162a. See also III, 236b *(Raya Mehemna),* 263a.

247. The thirty-two paths of *Ḥokhmah.*

248. *Tiferet* is symbolized by Moses, and is joined together with *Ḥesed* and *Gevurah,* which represent Abraham and Isaac. David is a symbol of the *Shekhinah.*

249. *Zohar Ḥadash, Va-etḥanan,* 56d.

250. See Zohar III, 203b–204a. According to the commentaries to the Zohar that I have consulted the reference is to *Ḥokhmah, Binah,* and *Tiferet,* but the explanation is forced, and certainly does not match the version of the passage in the *Zohar Ḥadash.*

251. Zohar II, 43b.

252. Ibid., 162a.

253. Ibid., 43b.

254. Zohar III, 162a.

255. The views in the Zohar that I have discussed make it easier to understand how the apostate Paulus de Heredia could fabricate a Christian "Zoharic" extract dealing with the mystery of unification through the recital of the *Shema.* It is quoted by Scholem in "Zur Geschichte der Anfänge der

christlichen Kabbala," in *Essays presented to Leo Baeck* (London, 1954), p. 183.

256. A. Jellinek, *Ginzei Hokhmat ha-Kabbalah,* p. 19. See also, n. 6, the quotation from Rabbi Isaac ben Sheshet, "I have heard a philosopher denigrating the kabbalists, saying that the Christians believe in three in one, but the kabbalists believe in ten in one."

257. *Zohar Hadash, Tikkunim,* 80b.

258. Zohar III, 70a.

12.

Kabbalistic Rituals of Sabbath Preparation

Elliot K. Ginsburg

At noon the *qelippah* [evil "shell"] separates from the Holy; in the later afternoon, during ritual immersion, the holy light of Shabbat pours forth.
—Isaiah Horowitz, *Shenei Luḥot ha-Berit:*
"Massekhet Shabbat" (early seventeenth century)

This late source articulates a notion whose roots lie in the classical tradition: the incremental arrival of Shabbat. For the devotee does not enter into the Sabbath at once, but progressively, building up to the moment of full-Shabbat like water heating up to the boiling. Through the mime of ritual the Kabbalist successively strips away the layers of *ḥol* (weekday) and aligns himself with the dramatic changes unfolding in the pneumatic world. Moreover, he comes to anticipate the Sabbath-order as he prepares for it. There is a sense that Sabbath's arrival is inevitable, and this prospect fills him with joy.

In a sense, the preparatory phase of Shabbat stands "betwixt and between" modalities, belonging fully to neither the fading world of *ḥol* nor to the world of complete-Shabbat which it asymptotically approaches. It is a kind of corridor bridging two discrete realms, a period of profound change.

Kabbalistic ritual almost always dramatizes a sacred event and is part of a larger mythic system or Story. In the Zoharic tradition,[1] the dominant mythic subtext—the underlying drama—of Friday afternoon concerns *Shekhinah* and Her Liberation/Redemption from weekday Exile.

Reprinted from *The Sabbath in the Classical Kabbalah* by Elliot K. Ginsburg, by permission of the State University of New York Press, Albany, 1989.

This process generally unfolds in three stages, depicting first Her separation from Her entanglement in *Siṭra' 'Aḥra'* and the setting of clear boundaries between them; then Her purification; and, finally, Her renewal as She is adorned in bridal raiment and brought to the threshold of the King's Palace. Only after these events have occurred can the divine wedding—Shabbat—take place.

Meanwhile in the earthly realm, a related pre-Sabbath scenario is unfolding. The Jew, *Shekhinah*'s symbol, is ritually aligning himself with the cosmic changes, progressively overcoming his sense of Exile as he prepares for the seventh day. He too must be transformed; before he can enter the blessed state of Shabbat, the stain of the week must be left behind. So as the changes occur on high, the devotee reflects them below in his purified body and clean cloak, in his enlarged soul, in his newly adorned home, even in the way social space is redefined via the *ʿeruv*.[2] Through the preparatory rituals, Sabbath progressively suffuses his world, displacing both the presence and the memory of *ḥol*. His world symbolically purged and regenerated, Shabbat comes to exist both within him and without him: an ambience projected externally, assimilated internally.

There are several striking aspects to the rituals we shall consider in this section. They are physically active—extroverted—rituals with little opportunity for the contemplative inwardness afforded by mystical prayer, for example. They evince a dualistic world-view, starkly contrasting the profane week and the holy Sabbath. It is as if by highlighting the differences between the two realms while overlooking their points of continuity, the Kabbalists wished to heighten the transformative power of Shabbat, to dramatize the profound sense of renewal they felt.

These rituals both symbolize and modulate this transformative process, enabling *Shekhinah* to again become a Bride and the Jew to regain—for a day—his Edenic lustre.[3]

PROJECTING THE SABBATH INTO THE SPATIAL REALM: THE CASE OF ONE'S HOME AND COURTYARD

The transformations of Shabbat are oft depicted in spatial terms: to enter the Sabbath is to enter the Temple, to dwell under the Sukkah of Peace, to leave behind Exile and enter "the Land of Israel." Two preparatory rituals highlight these spatial dimensions of the Sabbath-cosmos, helping to project Shabbat into one's immediate surroundings. They are the acts of cleansing and adorning one's home, and the establishment of a Courtyard-Fusion or *'eruv*.

The Significance of Transforming One's Abode

In the Kabbalistic tradition the Rabbinic custom of making one's home ready for Shabbat (TB Shab. 119b) takes on mythic resonance, directing the adept's attention from his immediate setting to the divine realm and the approaching Sabbath-cosmos. According to the *Zohar* and TZ/RM, as the adept prepares his home, it—like the celestial world it reflects— becomes a Wedding Canopy ready to receive the Bride who is at once Shabbat and *Shekhinah:*

One must prepare a comfortable seat with several cushions and embroidered covers from all that is found in the house, like one who prepares for a bride. For the Sabbath is a Queen and a Bride. (Z 3:272b [RM])

And more tellingly:

Observe the Sabbath throughout the generations *[DoRoTaM].* [Ex. 31:16] . . . The word *DoRoTaM* hints at the notion of dwelling *[DiRoTaM]:* When the Sabbath enters, the dwelling place must be prepared like the chamber of the bridegroom set to receive his bride. . . .[4]

In so doing the Bride is welcomed into the devotee's hearth and home, and the numinous presence of *Shekhinah*/Shabbat felt:

The Holy Bride is ushered into Israel's abode, to be in their midst, as the Sabbath begins. (Z 3:300b–301a)

The early fifteenth-century work, *Sefer ha-Qanah,* builds on this notion, likening the newly ordered home to a nuptial chamber. Each of the major furnishings mentioned in the Talmudic paradigm is taken as a symbol of the divine coupling which is to follow:

"Your table should be set, your bed made-up, and the candles burning" [TB Shab. 119b]: The table alludes to the Community of Israel which is set in the sphere of Compassion *[Tif'eret];* the bed alludes to the Community of Israel who is made-up, adorned for the Groom. . . . The burning candles are the Eastern Candle, an allusion to *Tif'eret* which burns with [i.e., unites with] the Western Candle, the Community of Israel.

The home, in short, becomes a microcosm, a sacred reflection of the divine world.[5] As the devotee arranges his abode, he becomes a kind of bridal attendant, setting the stage for the coming hierogamy. Unlike most Kabbalistic rituals, this act of adornment is focused not so much on that which is happening at this very moment as on that which will happen on high, in a short while. It is anticipatory. As he orders the home, preparing the bed and festive table, the adept directs his thoughts to the Sabbath-cosmos and beckons it into his domestic setting.[6]

In sixteenth century Safed, this preparatory act came to take on more immediate and detailed significance; it will be considered briefly here. While the *Zohar* and *Qanah* focused on the act of adornment, Moses Cordovero and his circle imputed mythic significance to the preliminary act of cleansing the home, as well. Cordovero maintained:

One must sweep out the cobwebs from one's house [on Sabbath eve], symbolizing the mystery of "making one's home ready [for Shabbat] by lighting candles . . . and making up the bed." [TB Shab. 119b][7]

He explained that this act symbolizes the liberation of *Shekhinah* from the *qelippot,* which "according to the Tiqqunim" (i.e., TZ) may be likened to a cobweb. Although the Zoharic sources cited above likened the home to *Shekhinah*'s bridal chamber, here, however, it is implicitly homologized to the Bride Herself. Isaiah Horowitz explicated further:

For in the Kabbalistic literature *Malkhut* is called *Bayit,* the Home, the Wife.[8] She is the "rose among the thorns" [Cant. 2:2]; "around [Her] the evil ones roam." [Ps. 12:9] They are the *qelippot* who wish to prevent *shelom bayit* [conventionally, domestic tranquility or harmony]. They are the spider whose web we must sweep out of the house. This is the inner meaning of the [liturgical] verse "abominations will be removed from the land"[9]—from the supernal Land *[Malkhut].* They should especially be removed for the holy Sabbath, the mystery of *Malkhut.*

Only after *Shekhinah* is purified and separated from the defiling forces of the week, can the sacred marriage take place. This union occurs at the very inception of Shabbat, at candlelighting:

The Sabbath candles intimate this for they correspond to "Remember" and "Keep," as stated in the *Bahir* [182]. The candles represent the union of the supernal lights, as in "I will grant peace *[Yesod]* to the land *[Malkhut]."* [Lev. 26:6] . . . For this reason, the candles are called *shelom bayit* [TB Shab. 23b].

the union of *Shalom—Yesod*—and *Bayit,* the *Shekhinah.*[10] Hence, in this tradition strand, the ordering of the home dramatizes the stages of *Shekhinah*'s transformation: its cleansing dramatizes Her Liberation/

Purification, whereas its adornment intimates Her ultimate reintegration into the divine sphere.

The Establishment of Courtyard-Fusions: 'Eruvei Ḥaẓerot

If cleaning the home serves to project the Sabbath-cosmos into the domestic sphere, several halakhot accomplish much the same in the social sphere. Brief mention should be made of the Kabbalistic re-interpretation of tehum Shabbat: the restricted area in which one is permitted to travel during the seventh day.[11] In the Zohar the physical tehum Shabbat is homologized to the divine Sabbath, or the sefirotic realm, whereas the area beyond is correlated with Sabbath's antipode, Siṭra' 'Aḥra'. Consider, e.g., Zohar 2:64a:

"Let no man go out from his place" (Ex. 16:29) [i.e., outside tehum Shabbat] . . . For this Place is precious and holy, but beyond it lies "other gods" . . .

Kabbalistically, the outer limit of one's "Place" is Shekhinah, the divine limen:

"His Place" refers to the lower Glory [Shekhinah], the mystery of the Diadem of Shabbat."

According to another passage (2:207a), by remaining within his Sabbath-Place, the Jew dramatizes Shekhinah's integration within the sefirotic realm; for on Shabbat Shekhinah has come home: "She does not rest anywhere outside the boundaries assigned to Her."[12]

A second example of symbolically projecting the Sabbath into the social sphere is the preparatory rite of "establishing a courtyard-'eruv." This 'eruv is a Rabbinically instituted device which originally had purely functional significance. Zvi Kaplan (EJ 6:849) explains:

While carrying between private and public domains [Reshut ha-Ya-ḥid and Reshut ha-Rabbim] is forbidden on the Sabbath, the rabbis also forbade carrying between two private domains. For example, if several houses opened into one courtyard [as was generally the case in urban Jewish communities in the Middle Ages], an object could not be removed from one house to another, nor from a house to the courtyard [which was also considered a private domain]. . . . To facilitate such carrying, a loaf of bread (called 'eruv ḥazerot) owned by all the residents is placed in one of the houses [each Friday afternoon], thereby symbolically creating mutual ownership of all the dwellings. The houses and courtyard are thereby "mixed" [me'uravim] into one private domain.

In the STM, TZ, and TY this legal fiction was given a mythic rationale, transposing the halakhah into a cosmic key. Their reading exemplifies what may be called the "hypernomian" aspect of Kabbalistic ritual. That which was functional is shown to be cosmically necessary, rooted in the ontological structure of the universe. Employing a hermeneutic at once hyperliteral and mystical, the three Kabbalists correlated the private domain *(Reshut ha-Yaḥid)* with the "Realm of (Divine) Unity," while the public domain *(Reshut ha-Rabbim)* was taken to denote the "Realm of Multiplicity" and Evil outside the Sabbath Cosmos. Joseph of Hamadan wrote:

Reshut ha-Yaḥid refers to the ten sefirot which are one. His Name is called the Domain of Unity. *Reshut ha-Rabbim* is so named because it contains the mystery of *Perud,* Multiplicity . . . (STM, Meier ed.: 293)

In both the TZ and TY, preparation of the courtyard *ʿeruv* dramatizes the integration of *Shekhinah* into divinity and more generally, the complete sefirotic fusion that takes place on Shabbat. For as the *ʿeruv* is established, the formerly disparate private domains become one unified *Reshut ha-Yaḥid,* symbolizing the restoration of divine harmony. Moreover, the establishment of this *ʿeruv* symbolically demarcates between the two opposing modalities, *Reshut ha-Yaḥid* and *Reshut ha-Rabbim,* redrawing the cosmic boundaries. Hence, one who carries an article outside the private domain, spiritually leaves the realm of Shabbat and enters the domain of *Siṭra' 'Aḥra'.* This profaning act has theurgic valence as well, sullying Shabbat/*Shekhinah,* which according to the TY, is the *ʿeruv* (here, in the sense of boundary marker) par excellence. In Meir ibn Gabbai's words,

The *ʿeruv* is the symbol of the crowned Bride, the locus at which the [sacred and profane] domains meet.[13]

Dwelling at the limen, She remains vulnerable to the encroachment of *Siṭra' 'Aḥra'.* The TZ explains:

Whoever carries from *Reshut ha-Yaḥid* to *Reshut ha-Rabbim* brings *Shekhinah* into "confusion and chaos, darkness and the abyss" (Gen. 1:2),

reversing the order of Creation, polluting the Sacred with the Profane.

Such a person causes Her to be cloaked in the *qelippot* of the four Exiles. (TZ 30 [73a])[14]

According to another passage, TZ 48 (85a), improper carrying may also dis-order higher rungs, including *Tif'eret/Yesod:*

One who removes an article from its Place, taking it outside its domain, is considered as one who uprooted the Tree of Life and placed it in the "Alien Realm" . . . the Realm of Multiplicity . . . the realm of Shabbetai [the saturnine *Siṭra' 'Aḥra'*].

Perhaps the richest symbolization of the courtyard *'eruv* is from TZ 24 (69a):

Just as one needs the protection of the covenant lest one pass under the rule of the Foreign One *[Siṭra' 'Aḥra']*, so one needs the protection of Shabbat lest one leave the Realm of Unity *[Reshut ha-Yaḥid]* and enter the Realm of Multiplicity *[Reshut ha-Rabbim].*

According to Rabbinic definition (TB Shab. 6a), a private domain is an enclosed space not less than four handbreadths square bounded by walls not less than ten handbreadths high. In the TZ's understanding, there is nothing arbitrary about these dimensions. Rather, they have symbolic resonance, pointing to *Shekhinah*'s re-integration into the divine realm:

The Realm of Unity is *Shekhinah;* Her "width is four" [encompassing] the Tetragrammaton, YHWH.[15] "Its height is ten" refers to [the sefirotic totality]. *Reshut ha-Rabbim* is the serpent, the harlot [i.e., Lilith], the poison of the 'Other God' who is Sammael. . . . Her husband is the profanation of the Sabbath *[Malkhut].*

For this reason, whoever carries from *Reshut ha-Yaḥid* unto *Reshut ha-Rabbim* is liable to be stoned [ff. Ex. 31:14]. The *'eruv* delineates the Middle Column and within it, *one may carry from home to home,* between the supernal *Shekhinah [Binah]* and the lower one *[Malkhut].*

Here we see the clearest example of how one's immediate social world may serve as a microcosm, a reflection of the supernal realm.[16]

Too much significance should not be claimed for the actual establishment of the *'eruv,* however; like the Zoharic treatment of adorning the home, it has primarily anticipatory significance, becoming fully functional only when the Sabbath begins. Nonetheless, preparing the *'eruv* directs the devotee's attention to the altered cosmos of Shabbat, while enabling him to project this new order into his immediate environs.

INTERNALIZING SHABBAT: THE BODY AS MICROCOSM

In order to receive the holiness [of Shabbat] that flows into our world, we must prepare and perfect the body, for the body is the throne for the spiritual. . . . Like the house, the body must be restored.

—M. Cordovero, *Tefillah le-Mosheh* 10:2

If the preceding rituals tended to externalize the Sabbath-cosmos, projecting it into the devotee's surroundings, the ensuing series of rites— nail-paring, bathing or ritual immersion, and dressing in fresh clothes— dramatize the progressive internalization of Sabbath-order. The devotee himself now becomes the locus of symbolic activity, his body a microcosm of the changes occurring on high. While the preceding rituals were largely anticipatory in nature, these three are immediately transformative, representing and effecting changes in both the devotee's status and that of divinity. Together they form a kind of ritual triptych whereby the Kabbalist formally leaves behind *ḥol* and existentially enters Shabbat.

Nail-Paring

The first act of bodily preparation that we shall consider is that of nail-paring.[17] This rite—whose origins seemingly lie in Ashkenazic magical concerns—was adopted by certain Kabbalists for expressly mythic reasons. It is a striking illustration of Mary Douglas' remark that "no experience is too lowly to be taken up into ritual and given a lofty meaning."[18] Kabbalistic rationales for nail-trimming "in honor of Shabbat" are all relatively late, appearing first in the *Peli'ah* (36b), and later in the TY and *Shoshan Sodot*.[19] However, a mythic subtext for nail-pairing, in general, had been presented much earlier, in the *Zohar*. Basing himself on a midrashic tradition,[20] Moshe de Leon wrote that the finger- and toenails are the last vestige of humanity's Edenic garb:

The primordial garment that Adam wore in the Garden was composed of those [protective] Chariots called the Backside; they were . . . garments of nail.

Here the *Zohar* is imaging Adam as a microcosm of the divine world. According to several Zohar sources, *Shekhinah* Herself is surrounded by *qelippot* or shells, quasi-angelic entities portrayed in a wide array of images: as Chariots of Light, as a coarse garment or outer shell, as a kind of divine Backside shielding the Face within, or most importantly here, as "nails" covering the divine corpus.[21] The function of these nails is to separate and protect the divine world from defiling forces without. They constitute a kind of buffer zone between the two realms. Moshe de Leon explained that a similar protective garb enfolded Adam prior to the Sin. He was in perfect symbolic alignment with the divine archetype, and so, protected from all evil:

As long as Adam was in the Garden all these Chariots surrounded him and no evil thing could draw near him. However, when he sinned he was divested of that garment and clothed in profane ones. . . . Nothing of that primordial garment remains except for the nails at the tips of the fingers and toes. And these nails contain an alien impurity at their outer edges. (Z 2:208b)

His womblike *qelippah* now broken and diminished, Adam (and all persons after him) became susceptible to pollution; the mundane dirt trapped under the nails becomes a symbol for humanity's post-Edenic diminution, and their vulnerability before the forces of *Siṭra' 'Aḥra'*.[22]

In his TY (46a) Meir ibn Gabbai drew upon this very myth and on Moshe de Leon's subsequent warning that "we should not allow the nails with their impurity to grow" (Z 2:208b) and included nail-paring in the preparatory rites. By implication, this act reverses humanity's post-Edenic (and post-Sabbath) diminution. Through nail-paring the adept ritually purges himself of the stain of the week and divests himself of its demonic forces; he thereby re-sacralizes his vulnerable border. As we shall see, nail-paring serves as a necessary prelude to the most crucial transformation, the reception of the Sabbath-soul, the new "Edenic garb."

On an explicit level, however, Meir ibn Gabbai provided not an Edenic rationale for this rite but one that drew on the homology between Sabbath, *Shekhinah* and the Temple. For the Sabbath, like the *miqdash*, may only be entered in a state of ritual purity:

And since one must not bring an impurity into the Sanctuary, one must pare them on Sabbath eve, so that the Sacred [the Sabbath and kabbalistically, *Shekhinah*] is not profaned on account of this impurity.[23]

Nail-paring seems to function as a rite of boundary-definition, a means of separating the Sacred and the Profane as Sacred Time draws near. It protects the sacred at its most vulnerable point, the margin, and prevents further conflation of the two modalities. Mary Douglas has shed light on this phenomenon:

All margins are dangerous. If they are pulled this way or that the shape of fundamental existence is altered. Any structure of ideas is vulnerable at the margins. We should expect the orifices of the body to symbolize its specially vulnerable points . . . e.g., bodily parings, skin, nails, hair clippings, etc. (*Purity and Danger:* 121)

In a sense, nail-paring protects several margins: occurring at Sabbath's limen, it aims to properly establish the sacred boundaries of Shabbat and of the devotee. By implication, it reflects the securing of proper boundaries in the divine world, as well.

The full protection of sacred boundaries entails not only an act of separation, but proper placement of the profane. Given the dangerous quality afforded the filthy edge of the nails, it is not surprising that their parings must be disposed of with great care. If the act of paring represents the separation of the sacred and demonic realms (the first stage of purification), proper disposal symbolizes the elimination or destruction of the demonic for the duration of Shabbat.[24] Meir ibn Gabbai underscored the importance of proper disposal, building upon a Talmudic teaching on the same theme:

We read in *Mo'ed Qaṭan,* Chapter "These are Permitted to Shave" [18a]: "Three things were said in reference to nails: One who burns them is pious *[ḥasid]*; one who buries them is just *[ẓaddiq]*; and one who throws them away is a villain *[rasha']*."

The reason for this is that nails intimate *Din* [here, *Siṭra' 'Aḥra'*]. One who removes it by burning the parings promotes Peace and Compassion [the beneficent forces of divinity] in the world . . . "One who buries them is just": Even though he did not remove *Din* from the world totally, still he impedes *Din* and quiets it. However, this falls short of the deed of the pious one. "One who throws them away is a villain": for he causes *Din* to flow into the world. (TY 46b)

This is a good example of an apotropaic rite. By following the example of the *ḥasid,* the mystic helps obliterate *Din* for the duration of the Sabbath. Improper disposal of the nails, however, may effect the "decreation of the world," to use Bruce Lincoln's phrase,[25] disrupting the newly harmonious Cosmos.

The complex symbolization of nails has only been touched on here. We shall return to this theme later, in the discussion of *Havdalah.*[26]

Bathing and Ablution

In order to honor the Sabbath one should, as a matter of religious duty, wash his face, hands, and feet with hot water on Friday.
—RaMBaM, *Mishneh Torah* (Shabbat 30:2)

The Rabbinic rite of bathing before the Sabbath is turned into a transformative act par excellence in the Zoharic tradition; indeed, in the TY, it serves as the liminal moment between *ḥol* and existential Shabbat, forming a kind of initiatory rite into the Sabbath-cosmos. In the *Zohar* itself, this act retains a somewhat more modest function. Let us analyze its significance there first. Bathing serves to spiritually purify the devotee, to cleanse him of the polluting stain of the week and to separate him from the influence of its archetype, *Siṭra' 'Aḥra'*, so that he may fully enter into the Sabbath. Read psychologically, this rite absolves (or more literally, dissolves) the guilt accrued over the week, affording the adept spiritual liberation, a new beginning. It should be noted, however, that this theme of expiation reached conscious articulation only later, in the Safed Kabbalah.[27] The *Zohar* itself describes the underlying dynamic of bathing more in metaphysical than in psycho-ethical terms. The polluting aspects of the weekday cosmos are placed in the foreground, thereby heightening the sense of purification:

When the Sabbath arrives, the holy People must wash their bodies from the stain of the week. What is the reason? Because during the week Another Spirit *[Siṭra' 'Aḥra']* sets forth and holds sway over the People. When one needs to get out from under that spirit and enter into the other, holy spirit, he must bathe so that he might receive the supernal holy Spirit. (2:204a)

The act of bathing, in other words, symbolically effects a change in personal status, enabling the devotee to move from one realm—one spiritual ambience—to another. In the most visceral way, a whole environment is stripped off, dissolved. Indeed, Moshe de Leon elsewhere likened this evil realm to a defiling garment:

When the Evil Inclination holds sway over a person, it fashions a garment for him . . . as it is said, "She caught him in a garment." [Gen. 39:12] (Z 1:190b)

But as the Jew bathes, he leaves the enveloping presence of the profane week, "gets out from under that Spirit" and so "enters the other, holy spirit," an intriguingly vague term, evoking both Shabbat and the now imminent realm of divinity. Bathing is a preparatory act, as well, setting the stage for what I have termed the "existential Shabbat," or, the reception of the Sabbath-soul.

The power of the ritual lies in its physical immediacy: in all likelihood, this bath was the sole one for the entire week; in a literal as well as figurative sense, the stain of the week was being removed! The ritual works by integrating a gross physiological or sensory experience with powerful but abstract ideational motifs or myths. Put in Turnerian language[28] it might be said that as the Kabbalist bathes and focuses on the underlying mythos of Shabbat, the ideational and sensory poles of meaning interpenetrate so that the physical aspects of bathing are ennobled—symbolized—and the attendant Kabbalistic myth vitalized, "made real." Physically cleansed and refreshed, the Kabbalist is also spiritually renewed, purified of the pollution of the week.

Later mystics heightened the transformative impact of bathing by suggesting that one not only wash his limbs but actually immerse his entire body in a *miqveh* or body of "living water." This action carries with it a wealth of other associations which, even if not explicitly discussed, provide a kind of backdrop for the rite. Unlike bathing, ablution (Hebrew: *ṭevilah*) is traditionally associated with significant changes in ontological status. In the Rabbinic tradition, e.g., it was utilized by women to mark the formal conclusion of *niddah,* their periods of menstrual "impurity"; by men after the pollution of a seminal emission; by converts as they entered Judaism; and by women about to enter marriage.[29] In fine, *ṭevilah* functioned as a sacred means of transforming the impure into the pure, the uncanny into the orderly— and by implication, for leaving behind a lesser stage of existence and entering a higher one. In analyzing *ṭevilah* in Sabbath-preparation, two broad questions must be asked: first, when did this ritual become part of Sabbath preparation, and second, how might its symbolic significance be interpreted, in light of (a) the mystics' own explanations, (b) certain observable characteristics, and (c) other contextual clues?

Historically, the emphasis on pre-Sabbath ritual immersion is relatively late. The literature from before the fifteenth century contains but two or three passing references to this custom, in exoteric sources of Middle Eastern provenance.[30] The *Zohar* and TZ/RM, e.g., never explicitly mention ablution or *ṭevilah,* instead using the terms *reḥiẓah* and *'asḥa'ah,* both meaning simply to "wash" or "bathe."[31] The first explicit mention of *ṭevilah* in Kabbalistic sources is found in the Byzantine works, the *Qanah* and *Peli'ah* (early fifteenth century). Their author viewed immersion as the most efficacious form of purification:

Let him wash his face, hands, and feet so that the course of the profane week may be lifted from him, as it is said: "From the *sweat* of your brow [reference to the polluting stain of the week] shall you get bread to eat." [Gen. 3:19]. How much more so is this true of one who immerses himself on Sabbath eve. . . . (*Qanah* 65a)

Similarly, the *Peli'ah* (36b) states:

One then washes his face, hands, and legs near evening upon completing his preparations. And if he does so through ablution, nothing could be finer *['ein ke-maʿalatah]!* [32]

The first source to prescribe *ṭevilah* as the sole method of purification is the TY; in this sense it foreshadowed the heightened concern with *ṭevilah* found in the Safed Kabbalah. In Meir ibn Gabḥai's schema, ablution is a ritual of pivotal importance: marking not only the entry into a new ambience, but the internalization of that ambience via reception of the Sabbath-soul. To appreciate the dynamic of the ritual, it is important to recall its performance context: according to the TY, the devotee has already performed the initial act of spiritual separation through nail-paring and has affirmed the redrawn cosmic-boundaries of Shabbat via the *ʿeruv*. The devotee now divests himself of the defiling garb of the week, and in the waning light of the day, immerses himself in the river. Ibn Gabbai's description reveals the influence of the *Zohar*, even as he went beyond it:

During the week Another Spirit holds sway over the world and on Sabbath eve the holy people must cleanse themselves of this [impurity] to enter into the mystery of the Holy Faith [Shabbat/the sefirotic world] . . . they do so by immersing themselves in the river. (TY 46b)

As the devotee emerges, he feels the numinous presence of the Supernal Mother, *Shekhinah,* the womb-like "Shelter of Peace." She spreads Her wings and "crowns [him] with a Sabbath-soul." So begins the existential Shabbat.

In its underlying structure this ritual comes to serve as a kind of rite of passage, with the three distinct phases noted by A. van Gennep and V. Turner: 1) separation, as the devotee strips himself of his ordinary garb. This is followed by 2) a moment of liminality as the naked devotee immerses himself in the river. For an instant, he is structurally invisible, without defining garb, dissolved, as it were, in the enveloping waters. His old status no longer holds, while his new identity is not yet manifest. As he emerges from the water, he enters a new spiritual ambience: Shabbat, the realm of divinity, of *Shekhinah*. With regard to his personal identity, 3) as he is wreathed with his Sabbath-soul, he is re-aggregated or re-structured; the devotee re-enters the social sphere on a higher level of being.[33]

But if *ṭevilah* constitutes a rite of passage—a corridor between two radically distinct worlds and two somewhat less distinct personal identities—it does so in an unusual way. For classically, the term connotes one-time (or at least, infrequent) changes in ontological status of enduring impact. In the case of Shabbat, however, there is a *weekly* act of transformation whose impact begins to wane after Shabbat ends, and which by definition requires weekly renewal. Examination of the Kabbalistic evidence suggests the need to develop a new theoretical category embracing such regularly recurring (and reversible) transformations.

Finally, a hypothesis for further testing. In this section, discussion has centered on nail-paring and *ṭevilah,* two relatively obscure rites that were adopted and mythically recast by Kabbalists (notably by adepts of Byzantine-Turkish provenance)[34] and ultimately popularized due to the efforts of their spiritual heirs, the mystics of Safed.[35] Although these two rituals are employed in multiple settings in the tradition, it is striking that both acts were an integral part of women's rituals of purification upon leaving *niddah*. According to *Zohar* 3:79a, complete purification entails not only *ṭevilah* but also paring one's nails and hair, those extremities especially susceptible to pollution:

The nails and hair grow, and therefore when a woman comes to purify herself she must cut off the hair which grew in the days of her pollution and pare her nails along with the filth that clings to them. For, as we have learned concerning the mystery of pollution, the filth of nails awakens Another Filth *[Siṭra' 'Aḥra'],* and therefore they must be completely hidden away. Whoever does so, awakens *Ḥesed* in the cosmos.

It seems possible that in their desire to develop rituals of purification and regeneration, certain Kabbalists drew on those models long available for women. This may simply be a matter of adapting rituals for similar strategic purposes (i.e., purification and renewal), but one cannot help but wonder whether the identification formed between the mystic and the divine Female was a subliminal factor encouraging such adaptation. For the Zoharic tradition had commonly described *Shekhinah*'s passage into Shabbat in terms of Her purification from *niddah*. Indeed, Meir ibn Gabbai himself did so on at least two occasions in the TY.[36] In this study, however, no classical sources have been found which correlate the myth of *Shekhinah*'s purification from *niddah* with *ṭevilah* and nail-paring on Sabbath eve.[37] So far as is known such associations were first made in the Safed Kabbalah. One later source, the *Shenei Luḥot ha-Berit*, drew upon the obvious menstrual associations in these rites and imaged the devotee himself as "a woman in *niddah*." According to I. Horowitz, on Friday afternoons:

One should investigate his deeds and awaken in repentance, repairing that which is flawed. . . . Thereafter he should cut his nails and immerse himself in water, *like a woman purifying herself after niddah.* ("Massekhet Shabbat")[38]

This general topic merits further investigation.[39]

The Rite of Dressing:
The *Tolaʿat Yaʿaqov's* Account

If immersion is a rite of transformation in the TY, the contiguous act of dressing is one of confirmation, visibly affirming the devotee's new ontological status. The act takes on mythic resonance as well. By putting on clean clothes the devotee is said to represent the changes occurring in the supernal realm. Loosely basing himself on a TZ passage (69 [108b-109a]), Meir ibn Gabbai explained that divinity is garbed in "ten lower crowns during the week." These crowns (issuing from the world below divinity) dim the divine light and serve as a barrier between God and humankind: "But on Shabbat, He is divested of them and dressed in several garments of light," issuing from the divine world itself. Accordingly, Meir ibn Gabbai bade the devotee to don "fresh clothes so as to emulate the Creator," newly adorned in royal vestment. Through dressing "in accord with one's means," the devotee is afforded intimate access to the divine realm: now "he may be seen before the King dressed in accord with the celestial paradigm." (TY 46b)[40]

In this way the Kabbalist adds a distinctively mythic rationale to the Talmudic teaching that "one's Sabbath garments should not be like one's weekday garb." (TB Shab. 113a) The nature of the mystical rereading may be brought into sharper relief when juxtaposed with Moses Maimonides' explanation of the custom (*Mishneh Torah,* "Shabbat" 30:2). Basing himself on Rabbinic sources, Maimonides simply averred that changing one's garb is a way of honoring Shabbat. For him, the act of dressing is primarily of metaphorical significance: one dresses on Shabbat as one does to meet a king:

> The sages of old used to assemble their disciples on Friday night, put on their best clothes, and say: "Come, let us go forth, to meet the Sabbath, the king." Honoring the Sabbath involves putting on clean clothes. . . .

By contrast, the act takes on precise symbolic and cosmic significance in the Zoharic tradition. Putting on new clothes honors not only the Sabbath, but God. More to the point, it becomes an exemplary gesture, whereby the person mirrors the divine archetype and partakes of its splendor.

The Significance of "Dress" in the *Zohar* and *Tiqqunei ha-Zohar/Ra'aya' Meheimna'*

But what does the Kabbalist mean when he speaks of the regarbing of divinity? To more fully grasp this notion and its implications for Sabbath-dress, it is helpful to turn to the *Zohar* and its ancillary sources. Of particular interest is the TZ/RM, which developed the garbing of divinity into a primary mythic motif.

The Zohar and TZ/RM both speak of the cloaking of divinity in an array of worlds, potencies, and attributes, all suggestively symbolized as *levushin,* or garments. This symbolism implicitly rests on a neo-Platonic view of reality; the cosmos is envisioned as a series of concentric spheres, with divinity at its innermost core. Each consecutive sphere constitutes a mediating principle, a *levush* (garment) or *qelippah* (shell) from the perspective of what lies inside, but a body or *moha'* (kernel) from the perspective of what lies outside. Taken as a whole, the manifold spheres between divinity and the terrestrial world are imaged as layers of God's *levush.*[41] In a sense, the entire world is God's garb. This pantheistic notion is aptly described in TZ 22 (65a):

> *Shekhinah* has many garments, from which the Holy One created the divine Throne and the angels, the *hayyot* and the seraphim, heaven and earth and all the creatures therein.

In most cases, however, only certain aspects of the cosmos—e.g., the angelic worlds, and in the more dualistic accounts, Siṭra' 'Aḥra' as well—serve this cloaking function. Full-blown pantheism is thereby deflected. The following passage is exemplary (Z 3: 273a [RM]):

Shekhinah's garments consist of the holy angels from on high and Israel from below.

Alongside this model of cosmic garbing stands a second one, according to which divinity may be garbed by the descent of shefaʿ from on high, or by the ascent of the sacred energy released through performance of the miẓvot below. In contrast to the first model, garbing here serves to adorn divinity with more refined light rather than cloaking it in coarser stuff. Here the implicit cosmological model is not one of concentric spheres, but of a great Chain of Being. The movement is not so much in-out, as up-down. The focal point of this garbing is the lower sefirot, especially the Holy One and Shekhinah, primary recipients of the divine flow. To cite one example from the Qanah:

Know, my son, that the Sabbath garments are the divine blessing [shefaʿ] that She [Shekhinah] receives from the upper sefirot. . . . (65a)

The symbolism of levushin is an apt one for the Kabbalist, because these cosmic entities—be they outer worlds or shefaʿ from on high—serve much the same expressive role that clothing does in the social sphere. Clothing may hide, reveal, frame, adorn, constrain—in short, make a symbolic statement about its wearer's status and personality,[42] so too, the type of clothing divinity is said to put on is always a theological statement. As shall be seen, God's garbing generally serves multiple roles.

Revealment Versus Concealment

The garments may express or reveal the hidden divine personality and its attributes of action. Thus, Shekhinah's harsh weekday garb expresses rigorous divine Justice in the world, the quality of Din. According to one Zoharic account, She garbs Herself in these harsh qelippot during the week—and takes on a rather fierce appearance—so as to direct the world in its current imperfect state. By contrast, on Shabbat, when Ḥesed pervades the cosmos, such external garments—armor of sorts—

are not needed; and so at this hour divinity is arrayed in garments of *Ḥesed,* pure Love, which the *Zohar* terms "the garment of Glory of the Sabbath." (2:204a)

If the garments of divinity may serve to reveal or express aspects of the divine personality, they may also serve as barriers between God and humanity, as masks concealing the divine light.

The multiple garments in which divinity is cloaked are often a way of symbolizing the mystery of the divine-human encounter, of capturing the paradox of mystical experience. For each revealment—each stripping away of a layer—is followed immediately by a concealment, a sense of heightened mystery. There are always deeper layers within.

At other times, these garments seem to protect the adept from the blinding intensity of divine light: there is a sense in which divinity must be cloaked, mediated, to be withstood. As the Zoharic Comrades often recalled: "No man shall see Me and live." (Ex. 33:20) This imagery conveys the dangerous, awesome aspect of religious experience, and the ambivalent reactions of attraction and repulsion that such powerful encounters often elicit.[43]

If the divine garments come to protect or shield the person, they are sometimes understood to protect divinity as well. In several accounts, those *qelippot* nearest *Shekhinah* are understood to protect Her from the harsher aspects of undiluted Evil, the more external *qelippot.*

But if masking may serve a beneficent function, more frequently it is seen as a tragic distancing, the erection of a thick barrier between person and God. Thus, the *qelippot* that protect *Shekhinah* also conceal Her: their function is dual, ambivalent.

Several sources portray this distancing or concealment in a more unequivocally negative light. Consider TZ 69 (109a), where the *qelippot* are seen as the consequence or outgrowth of human sin:

"[There is] an unclean spirit over the Land" [ff. Zech. 13:2], namely those *qelippot* which cause a separation between the Holy One and Israel. This is the hidden meaning of "But your *iniquities* have been a barrier between you and your God." [Isa. 59:2]

This barrier that occludes the divine light is breached through devotional life and temporarily removed on Shabbat, as God takes off the harsh clothes needed for the weekly rule and dons holy garb, luminiscent, gossamer:

On high [i.e., on Shabbat] the Holy One wears *qelippot* as well. But they are cloaks made of many shades of beautiful light.

These are garments of pure *Ḥesed* which transmit, refract the divine light. As they are donned the world is lit up, warmed.

Divestment Versus Adornment as Ideals

According to the TZ/RM even this re-garbing falls short of the ultimate state. Its author envisions the eschaton as a world wherein all the mediating garments will be stripped off, where full revelation, face-to-Face beholding, will be possible. TZ 69 continues:

In the time to come the Holy One will remove these *qelippot* entirely and be disclosed before Israel like the kernel of a nut, as it says: "Then shall your Guide no longer be hidden away, and your eyes shall behold your Guide." [Isa. 30:20]

In that age of complete Shabbat divinity will be fully disclosed to itself, as well:

There will no longer be any barriers between the Holy One and *Shekhinah* and Israel.

The garb of Exile, which separates as it protects, will no longer be needed.

An even more striking account of cosmic divestment may be found in Z 2:116a [RM]. At the present time, due to human sin, both humanity and divinity are garbed in *qelippot;* a double-barrier stands between them:

Whoever is garbed in the *qelippot* of the "terrestrial" body . . . skin, flesh, bones and sinews, is not fully alive. His spirit within is dead. He does not truly see, he does not hear or speak; his limbs have no vitality. . . . Within this body . . . one cannot perceive the angels, much less *Shekhinah* or *a fortiori,* the Holy One above Her. . . . Because of their sins they are garbed in these *qelippot* and because of these *qelippot* Scripture says, "But your iniquities have been a barrier between you and your God." [Isa. 59:2]

In a startling re-reading of Isa. 6:2, God Himself is said to put on the four *qelippot* as a response to human sin:

Because of these *qelippot* the Holy One is covered over with wings, as it says: "With two He covered His face, and with two He covered His legs."

Through the life of miẓvot one can transcend the terrestrial *qelippah*, but a partial barrier remains around divinity. In the time to come, however, divinity will no longer be kept under wraps: the concealing wings will be lifted and God fully revealed:

But in the time to come "your Guide will no longer be hidden under wings and your eyes will truly see your Guide." [Isa. 30:20]

Alongside this ideal of stripping away the barriers, of piercing to the core, is the ideal of adornment, itself an expression of divine-human intimacy and cosmic vitality. Through the life of miẓvot divinity is crowned, the Bride bedecked, the Lovers enrobed in sefirotic light. Accordingly, prayer is oft symbolized as an act of mystical coronation, each word a point of ascending light. The *Zohar* (2:207b), for instance, explains that each of the seventy words of the Sabbath *Qiddush* mounts upward to grace *Malkhut*, "wreathing [Her] with seventy crowns." Speaking more generally, the *Zohar* (3:160b) avers:

When prayer is being offered, all the words that a person utters ascend on high, cleaving their way through ethers and firmaments until they reach their destination. There they are woven into a crown to adorn the King's head.

The coronation from below is said to stimulate a coronation from on high. As Israel adorns the King, the supernal Mother blesses Him from above. Mixing regal and nuptial imagery Moshe de Leon added:

It is the Jubilee's desire to crown the Witness *[Tif'eret]* and shower Him with blessing, to cause the sweet springs *[shefaʿ]* to flow over Him, as it is written, "Go forth, daughters of Zion, and gaze upon King Solomon, upon the crown with which His Mother adorned Him on this his wedding day." [Cant. 3:11]

Even more common is the dual adornment of *Shekhinah*, from above and below, "from all sides" (Z 2:207b).[44] As we have already seen, Sabbath observance helps garb *Shekhinah* in raiment of glory, divesting Her of the profane weekly garb that is said to sully and constrain Her, while decorating Her in bridal garments and regal apparel. Speaking more generally, the TZ/RM's author enthusiastically proclaimed that each consequential act that the Jew undertakes may be understood as a garbing of *Shekhinah*:

She wears garments of light whenever Israel gives forth light through the performance of good deeds. . . . But when Israel does evil, *[Shekhinah]* is garbed in black garments . . . in Lilith; at such time, She says, "Do not gaze upon me for I am swarthy." [Cant. 1:6] (TZ 22 [65a])

Summarizing the Zoharic literature, it might be said that the Kabbalist is the one who knows best how to adorn the Bride, the one who—in his sacred activity—becomes Her *shoshevin* or bridal attendant.[45]

Sabbath-Dress in the *Tiqqunei ha-Zohar/Ra'aya' Meheimna'*

The mythic images presented above are but a small portion of an extensive Zoharic literature, yet even this sampling should alert us to the complex significance garments have for the Kabbalist, and the symbolic resonance that donning fresh garb for Shabbat may have. If the broad array of *levush* imagery creates a web of remote influences that subliminally color the experience of dressing for Shabbat, a more limited cluster of myths form the immediate subtext, those proximate influences which explicitly undergird and give shape to the devotee's experience.[46] These myths dramatize the re-garbing of divinity on Sabbath eve; many are self-consciously correlated with the Kabbalist's own regarbing. Concentrated in the TZ/RM, they symbolize the transformation of divinity and cosmos on Shabbat, much as the marital motif does elsewhere in the tradition.

Although the degree of transformation varies from myth to myth, all entail the removal of the lesser garments of the week and the donning of holier garments for Shabbat. On occasion, this transformation is but a matter of degree, suggesting a harmonistic view of the relations between Sabbath and *ḥol*. During the week, it is said, the Holy One is also dressed in holy raiment; but on Sabbath, He is cloaked in yet holier—more refined and inward—garb:

On Sabbath . . . He is dressed in royal garb, the ten sefirot of *Beri'ah* [the world just below divinity], but on weekdays, He is cloaked with ten bands of angels [i.e., from the third world, *Yeẓirah*] who minister to the ten sefirot in *Beri'ah*. (TZ Intro: 3b)

A similar notion is expressed throughout the *Zohar* itself. Moshe de Leon wrote that *Shekhinah* is garbed in the angelic realm during the week; on Shabbat, however, She is adorned in divine light alone, the effulgence of the sefirotic realm.[47]

But more frequently the TZ/RM depicts a more radical transformation, a fundamental shift in modalities. In this schema divinity is garbed in the *qelippot* of *Siṭra' 'Aḥra'* during the week, only to divest them on Shabbat. In several accounts this weekday garbing is not seen in a wholly negative light: indeed, by 'wearing' Evil divinity maintains control over it, neutralizing its excesses and directing its energy for positive ends. Consider TZ 69 (108b–09a):

As there is a holy kingdom so is there a sinful one. [The author goes on to show how *Siṭra' 'Aḥra'* forms a counter-sefirotic world, opposite divinity]. . . . These are the ten Lower Crowns, which are the *qelippot* for the ten sefirot [of divinity]. The sefirot are the fruit *[moḥa']* within. These *qelippot* form a barrier between Israel and their Father in heaven. The Holy One and *Shekhinah* are cloaked in these *qelippot*, that *Shekhinah* may uphold the dicta, "His Kingdom *[Malkhut]* rules over all" [Ps. 103:19] and "For *'Elohim* is King over all the earth. . . ." [Ps. 47:8],

including the realm of evil. This harsh framing of divinity is not without its loving aspect. The TZ explains that the coarse garb that *Shekhinah* wears while in Her weekly Exile is an expression of Her solidarity with suffering Israel, and ultimately has a protective function:

In Exile . . . She dons [harsh] garments so as to protect Israel, who are themselves garbed in the *qelippot* [surrounded by their enemies] below. Hence, the verse: "In all their troubles [kabbalistically, the *qelippot*], He is troubled." [Ps. 91:15]

In Her divinity, *Shekhinah* is not sullied by donning these garments nor is She subject to them; rather, She uses them "like a woodcutter uses an axe." Nonetheless, on Shabbat, Exile ends and harshness departs from the world. Divinity is thus able to take off these *qelippot*. On Shabbat,

the Holy One wears *qelippot* as well. But they are cloaks made of many shades of beautiful light. [I.e., unlike the ordinary *qelippot* they do not filter out the divine light]. . . . The Holy One is garbed in *qelippot* during the week. But on Shabbat, He is divested of them and arrayed in holy garments.

There is a radical shift in modalities:

Of these ten holy garments, it is said: "the Lord *BaDaD yanḥennu*,"

conventionally read: "alone led him," but here:

wears Ten; no 'alien god' at His side." [Dt. 32:12] For *BaDaD [Beit Dalet Dalet]* in gematria is ten, [ten holy garments] corresponding to the ten *qelippot* worn during the week. When He wears the holy garb, it is said: "*BaDaD*, these other ten, sit outside; they dwell beyond the Camp" [Lev. 13:46],

far from divinity, in the now quiescent realm of Sammael or radical Evil.

There are two texts which provide an explicit mythic commentary to ritual dressing. Both are focused on the liminal sefirah, *Shekhinah*, whose fate may be seen as a cosmic cipher for (or from a critical point of view, as the projection of) the fate of Israel. Again a kind of dualistic model of transformation is employed. First, TZ 24 (69a–b):

Shekhinah is like an orchard in Exile: She is the fruit within. She is called "the nut" [within the shell], as King Solomon stated: "I went down to the nut garden." [Cant. 6:11]. Shekhinah is the kernel within, as it is written: "The glory of the Princess is within . . ." [Ps. 45:14] The outer qelippah [shell] connotes the alien domains which clothe Her. But on Shabbat, the Queen divests Herself of this garb and puts on beautiful raiment.

In accord with the divine paradigm:

Israel below must renew itself each Shabbat, by putting on beautiful raiment, as well.

This symbolic act is given theurgic import, arousing supernal blessing:

This will cause Her to be bound to the [sefirot]—enabling Her to be filled with divine blessing, to be irrigated from on high.

The second text is the most dualistic of all and may be contrasted with the earlier sources. In virtually all of them some positive purpose was served by Shekhinah's donning of the qelippot; moreover, She was in control of them, and impervious to their defiling qualities. In this radical myth, however, Shekhinah is the prisoner of Siṭra' 'Aḥra' and its femi- nine personification, Lilith. They form a kind of straitjacket that both constrains and defiles Her. Indeed, they are likened to "the shells of Death" (cf. Z 3:243b [RM]). Each Sabbath eve, She must be divested of this garb or liberated; then purified; and, finally, adorned in holy rai- ment. This three-fold process provides a mythic subtext for the devotee's actions below: his stripping off of the garment of the week, his bathing, and his re-garbing for Shabbat. The sharply dualistic view articulated by the myth serves to heighten the sense of transformation and renewal conferred by the Sabbath. The TZ passage (48 [85a–b]) reads:

Regarding the Splenetic One [Shabbetai/Lilith] it is written: "Take that which imprisons you [neʿalekha] off of your feet" [Ex. 3:5], the soiled shoe, the fetid drop, "for the ground on which you stand is holy ground," namely Shabbat. Concerning Lilith, Shekhinah says: "I had taken off my robe—was I to don it again? I had bathed my feet—was I to soil them again?" [Cant. 5:3]

As the devotee engages in the three-fold process of purification and renewal, he aligns himself with the transformations on high and becomes Shekhinah's symbol. The TZ adds:

For this reason one must change his clothes [on Sabbath eve] . . . and must add to the holy by taking from the profane.

Mircea Eliade has shed light on this ritual process, whereby the person becomes a cosmic symbol:

By consciously establishing himself in the paradigmatic situation to which he is pre-destined, man cosmicizes himself. . . . He reproduces on the human scale the system of rhythmic influences . . . that characterize and constitute a world, that . . . define any universe. (*The Sacred and the Profane:* 172)

But Sabbath-dress is not without magical valence, as well; indeed, the two modalities of Kabbalistic ritual freely mix here. By dressing in clean, preferrably light-colored clothing (black being the color of Lilith/ Shabbetai),[48] the Jew—like *Shekhinah,* his archetype—escapes from the clutches of Lilith, that "snake-filled pit, which is Israel's Exile." The devotee ascends unto the divine realm, unto Shabbat:

Whoever honors the Sabbath escapes from this pit. Whoever sins, remains ensnared. . . . He who observes the Sabbath ascends unto *Malkhut,* who is the Sabbath. . . .

The aesthetic delight that wearing beautiful clothing confers also has apotropaic value, warding off the doleful presence of Lilith, the antithesis of Shabbat. Based on a complex web of associations drawn from Kabbalah and medieval astrology alike, Lilith is associated with the melancholic planet Saturn (Heb.: *Shabbeta'i*) which, in the Gentile world, was commonly thought to hold sway over the seventh day.[49] Engaging in Sabbath-delight banishes Lilith/Saturday while strengthening *Shekhinah*/Shabbat:

On Saturn's day it behooves Israel to make certain changes: to eat and drink sumptuously, to wear fine raiment, to enjoy themselves . . . to display abundant mirth. When [Saturn/Lilith] realizes there is no resting place for her, she flees. (TY 55a)

And:

On the Sabbath, one must . . . exhibit joy in contrast to the maidservant Lilith, that bitter presence

who according to Z 3:272b [RM], "remains in darkness, wearing black garments like a widow." The devotee must model himself after *Shekhinah.* Accordingly, one must adorn oneself in beautiful clothing. If one does so he is the child of Shabbat, the child of the Queen. But if not, he is the child of Lilith. (ZH "Yitro": 33d–34a, written by TZ's author)[50]

Clothing, in short, reveals one's spiritual parentage, indicating just "who" one is.

Hence, within the context of the Kabbalistic Shabbat, *levush* becomes a deceptively complex symbol of purification and regeneration, both human and divine; dressing becomes yet another means of aligning oneself with the changes on high, a way of expressing "Shabbat."

CONCLUSION

The phases of Sabbath-preparation which have just been examined may be viewed in a slightly different light. In a sense these rituals detail the progressive rapprochement of the Sabbath and Jew, their meeting and interpenetration. As the Jew enters the Sabbath, the Sabbath enters the Jew. This dual process is evoked in the imagery employed on Sabbath eve. The Jew is said to dwell within Shabbat—"under the *Sukkah* of Peace," within the Temple, at the Edenic center—while the Sabbath is said to dwell within the devotee's abode and within the chambers of his soul. Externalized, the Sabbath envelops him; internalized, the Jew becomes its honored host.

Through preparation and joyful anticipation, the devotee's world has been scoured clean, purified, in a sense, reborn. Having divested his home of all polluting influences, then freshly adorning it, the Jew prepares a nuptial chamber for the Bride. Having divested himself of the profane through the acts of nail-paring, disrobing, and ablution, the devotee has become temporarily empty, spiritually ready to receive and be filled with Shabbat.

As the devotee begins the Sabbath prayers, the forces of *Din* are fully vanquished. The "world that is fully Shabbat" has arrived. *Shekhinah* and devotee have now entered the Palace[51] and a different modality holds sway, a different music, heard. The world is protected, quietly joyous; borders secured, the mythic focus shifts from the limen between the sefirotic and lesser worlds to the intradivine pleroma, the Sabbath-cosmos par excellence. As the mythic focus shifts, so does the function of Kabbalistic ritual. Themes of liberation and separation give way to coronation and *hieros gamos*. Those apotropaic rituals that punctuate the week are no longer needed, for in Meir ibn Gabbai's words, "the Sabbath protects the cosmos." (TY 48a and 58b) Quite the contrary, such rituals sound a jarringly dissonant note in the Sabbath-music: they are counter-transformative, waking the slumbering forces of *Din*. The Sabbath-observer focuses on the joyous events unfolding in the divine world and knows "rest, quietude and safety." (TY 47b) He completes his prayers and walks home from the synagogue to greet his family and "receive his Guest in joy." As he does so, he feels the numinous presence of angels and the divine Mother:

He is accompanied by angels on either side, with *Shekhinah* arching over all, like a mother [bird] hovering over her fledglings. At that moment, "a thousand arrows may fall at your side and ten thousand at your right hand but it shall not reach you . . . no harm shall befall you." [Ps. 91:7] (ZH, " 'Aḥarei Mot": 48d)

The vulnerability of Exile has given way to security; tension to a certain ease. Sabbath peace reigns. In a profound sense, the Jew has come "home."

In this fashion do the Zoharic Kabbalists describe the entry into Shabbat.[52]

NOTES

Abbreviations

RM   *Raaya Meheimna*
TY   Meir ibn Gabbai's *Tolaat Yaaqov*
TZ   *Tiqqunei Zohar*
TZH   *Tiqqunei Zohar Hadash*
Z   *Zohar*
ZH   *Zohar Hadash*

1. I shall deal mainly with Zoharic sources in this chapter: the *Zohar* itself (including the ZH), the TZ/RM, and the TY. I shall also refer to the *Qanah* with some frequency and will occasionally bring in other sources for purposes of clarification.
2. *ʿEruv* marks off boundaries beyond which one may not go on the Sabbath.
3. The rituals considered here are drawn both from *minhag* (custom) and from the miẓvot proper. In the Zoharic tradition both are equally efficacious, as Jacob Katz has pointed out in his pioneering study, *Halakhah ve-Qabbalah* (Jerusalem, 1984). See esp. pp. 34–51 ("Hakhraʿot ha-Zohar bi-Dvar Halakhah").

4. In Ex. 31:16, the word *DoRoTaM* is written *ketiv ḥaser,* with the vocallic *Waw* missing. In the *Zohar* this unusual spelling becomes the occasion for a mystical midrash. Moshe de Leon has reread the extended verse to mean: "The Children of Israel shall keep the Sabbath, preparing their dwelling places for the [divine] Sabbath *[la-ʿasot ʾet ha-Shabbat le-dirotam]."*

5. The home as microcosm is a recurring motif in many religious traditions. See Mircea Eliade, *The Sacred and the Profane:* 45–47 and esp. 172–79 ("Body-House-Cosmos").

6. *Peliʾah* 36b stresses the mental refocusing that accompanies these domestic preparations: "In whatever one does, he should think of the Sabbath's honor, for thinking and recitation are akin," having transformative powers!

7. Quoted in his disciple E. de Vidas' *Tozeʾot Ḥayyim* sec. 90; replicated (and explicated) in I. Horowitz, *Shenei Luḥot ha-Berit,* "Massekhet Shabbat." Also cf. the versions preserved in M. Cordovero's own *Tefillah le-Mosheh,* Gate 10:2 and *ʿOr Yaqar,* Part 8:13.

8. Ff. TB Yomaʾ 13a and Shabbat 118b, et al. The former reads: "His house— that means his wife!"

9. From the *ʿAleinu* Prayer.

10. *Shenei Luḥot ha-Berit:* Ibid. On candlelighting as the mystical *shelom bayit* or sefirotic coupling, see the many examples provided in my discussion of *hieros gamos,* Chap. 1.

11. The Rabbis interpreted the Biblical injunction "Let no man go out of *his place* on the seventh day" (Ex. 16:29) to mean that a person should not travel long distances—i.e., more than 2,000 cubits—outside his town or "place of residence." Cf. TB ʿEruv. 51a. For elaboration on this law, see MT, "Shabbat": Chap. 27; Ṭur OḤ 398; and the synopsis in EJ 6:849 ("Eruv").

12. For a more complex example of this homology, see *Zohar* 2:63b–64a, where the Sabbath-Place variously connotes the physical *teḥum Shabbat;* a stage of mystical awareness; and the sefirotic realm from *Binah* to *Malkhut.*

    Also see the somewhat different connotation of *teḥum Shabbat* in Z 1:5a. On the one hand, the *teḥum Shabbat* delimits and restricts, establishing firm boundaries between permitted and forbidden, sacred and profane. However, it also expands the notion of one's place by allowing one to travel "2,000 cubits *beyond* the town limits." Z 1:5a emphasizes this expansive sense of the *teḥum* and so too, the increased holiness of Shabbat. Discoursing on the mystery of the sefirotic Sabbaths, the *Zohar* begins:

    " ʾEt Shabbetotai" (Lev. 19:30): The particle *ʾet* is added to *include* [within the divine Sabbath] the *teḥum Shabbat* which extends an additional 2,000 ʿcubits' in all directions.

    The divine Sabbath is thereby enlarged, coursing beyond "Her Place" *(Shekhinah)* into the realm below.

    For more on the mystical symbolization of *teḥum Shabbat,* see Z 2:207a; *Rimmon* (MS Brit. Museum) 98a–b; TZ Intro (12a) and 21 (55b); and TZḤ 103a.

13. TY 46b. For the entire TY passage see *Sod ha-Shabbat:* Section 4.
14. Also Cf. TZ 21(60a).
15. Kabbalistically, the entire sefirotic world.
16. For another mystical interpretation of the Sabbath domains, see OK to Shab. 2a. Its author, Todros Abulafia, associated the various domains not only with rungs in the supernal world but with stages of mystical cognition.

    For a fascinating interpretation of the *ʿeruv* used to symbolically unify an entire town, see Joseph ben Shalom Ashkenazi, *Perush le-Farashat Bere'shit:* 192. Here it is Diadem/*Malkhut* that is *Reshut ha-Rabbim:*

    > Know that Diadem receives energy from all the sefirot. Hence, She is called *[Reshut] ha-Rabbim,* [here meaning] the "Realm of Plenty."

    By means of the supernal *ʿeruv*—the integration of sefirotic domains on Shabbat—"carrying" from *Reshut ha-Yaḥid* unto *Reshut ha-Rabbim* is made possible: i.e., *shefaʿ* flows from the upper sefirot unto *Malkhut.* The full text reads:

    > " 'And God blessed the seventh day' [Gen. 2:2]: He blessed it *behoẓa'ah* [conventionally, by providing for additional expenditure, but here: by carrying]." (Gen. R 11:3) for [normally] it is forbidden to carry *[le-hoẓi']* from *Reshut ha-Yaḥid* to *Reshut ha-Rabbim.* Know that Diadem receives energy from all the sefirot. Hence, She is called *Reshut ha-Rabbim,* the Realm of Plenty. [Carrying from] *Reshut ha-Yaḥid* [to another domain] is one of the categories [of prohibited labor]. Therefore, our Rabbis of blessed memory established *ʿeruvin, the fusion of the rungs and their union on Shabbat* [emph. mine]. Were not the rungs unified, one could not carry from *Reshut ha-Yaḥid* to *Reshut ha-Rabbim* or vice versa.

    From the standpoint of the devotee, the humanly constructed *ʿeruvin* are here purely symbolic, a means of reflecting the divine harmony of Shabbat.

17. This is the first act of bodily preparation in the TY. Curiously, I have found no Zoharic sources which incorporate the well-known custom of fasting on Friday afternoon—"so as to eat with heightened appetite on Friday night." (On this practice, see TJ Taʿan. 2:12, s.v. "R. Abin"; TB Pes. 99b–100a and ʿEruvin 40b; Isaac b. Moshe of Vienna's *'Or Zaruʿa* "ʿErev Shabbat" sec. 21; and Tur OH 249.) By contrast, the custom of preparatory fasting was of concern to some Byzantine Kabbalists. The *Pel'iah* (36b), e.g., considers it part of a mystical "rite of passage":

    > On Sabbath eve, one should not eat from *Minḥah* onward, so that he may enter the Sabbath with appetite *[ta'avah/*desire] for the groom neither eats nor drinks [on the day of the Wedding] but enters the Bride's home [i.e., Shabbat] with appetite."

    By fasting, the adept separates himself from his profane weekday status and prepares to become a groom unto Shabbat/*Shekhinah!* (For further comment, see Appendix I below.)

    Shoshan Sodot (77b) appends a sefirotic rationale to the traditional reason for fasting. Although the Sabbath day is under the sway of the divine

Sabbath *(Yesod)*, Friday is correlated with *Hod*, a rung on the Left with close ties to *Din*. Hence, on Friday:

> It is the custom of *ḥasidim* to fast all day.... The reason is that *Zaddiq*, the Foundation of the World, [holds sway on] Shabbat, while the eve of the Sabbath [belongs to] *Hod*, a "day" of *Din*/Judgment. Therefore, one is not to provide the soul with [gustatory] delights, but should starve it; this enables one to come to the King's table with great appetite [i.e., increasing *ʿOneg Shabbat*] ...

The subsequent popularity of fasting on Friday—for Kabbalistic reasons— owes much to the Safed Renaissance. For one influential example, see *Re'shit Ḥokhmah*, "Gate of Holiness" 7:98, where E. de Vidas gives fasting a mystico-ethical coloration.

18. *Purity and Danger* (London, 1966): 114
19. Zohar 2:208b does counsel one to pare the nails daily, but makes no special provisions for entering Shabbat:

> Therefore a person must not let his fingernails of impurity grow, for as they grow so does the impurity of that Camp *[Siṭra' 'Aḥra']*. One should attend to them daily and cut them. ...

Non-Kabbalistic enjoinders to trim the nails before Shabbat are fairly numerous, however. Although the evolution of this rite is still inadequately understood, a fuller sense of its early history would allow a better assessment of its Kabbalistic recasting. According to the mid-sixteenth Kabbalist Naftali Hirz Treves, preparatory nail-paring was practiced among Ḥasidei 'Ashkenaz. He attributed the following parable to the Roqeaḥ:

> Once a rabbi died and appeared before his disciple in a dream. He had a stain on his forehead. The disciple asked why this happened. He replied: Because I was not careful to refrain from talking during the benediction of *meʿein shevaʿ* [on Friday evening] and when the Ḥazzan recited *Qiddush*, nor *was I careful to trim my nails on Sabbath eve*. [emph. added] Thus far, the words of [the Roqeaḥ].
>
> Moreover, *Sefer ha-Gan* [early thirteenth century, only fragments extant] enjoins not trimming them on Thursday for they will have already grown by Shabbat. Thus far, the words of the Roqeaḥ. (*Siddur Mal'ah ha-'Arez Deʿah:* "Maʿariv le-Shabbat," s.v. "Va-Yekhullu")

Although I suspect that these are genuine early thirteenth century Ḥasidic teachings, I have been unable to locate them in extant sources. The earliest established sources to incorporate nail-pairing into Sabbath preparation are the Provençal halakhic anthologies *Kol Bo* (section 35) and *'Orḥot Ḥayyim* ("ʿErev Shabbat," sec. 12). Both of these sources, dating from the turn of the fourteenth century, recast the dream parable related above. A brief mention of nail-paring is also found in the early fourteenth century *Sefer ha-Minhagim* from the school of Meir b. Baruch of Rothenburg:

> On [Friday afternoon] one should not eat from *Minḥah* onwards. He should be scrupulous concerning wine for *Qiddush* and in paring one's nails, sharpening his knife, etc. (Elfenbein ed., p. 7)

The Spanish work *Sefer Abudraham,* ca. 1340, holds that one may pare one's nails "in honor of Shabbat from Wednesday on" (pp. 368–69) whereas the *Shevilei 'Emunah* (1360) is the first source to call it a miẓvah. This Spanish source betrays certain magical concerns (similar to those found in Abudraham):

It is a miẓvah to pare one's nails on Sabbath eve, beginning with the third finger on the left and concluding with the thumb; with the right hand begin with the thumb and conclude with the third finger. Do not alter this order and do not pare two that are adjacent to each other because this causes forgetfulness. . . . (Warsaw 1887 ed., p. 157a)

Only in *Sefer ha-Peli'ah* (ca. 1410) does one find an explicit Kabbalistic rationale for trimming the nails in preparation for Shabbat. See n. below for details.

20. Cf. Gen. R 20:12; *Targum Yerushalmi* [Pseudo-Jon.] to Gen. 3:7 and 3:21; and PRE 14. For discussion see *Sod ha-Shabbat* n. 51.

21. E.g., the sefirotic world is commonly likened to the ten fingers and the grades immediately below, to the nails. For further discussion of these and other related images, see the analysis of the Havdalah blessing over the fire in chap. 4.

22. Cf. the similar notion expressed in *Peli'ah* 36b:

See and understand what our Rabbis of blessed memory said. Adam was created without any *Din* for he was entirely nail. When he sinned, *Din* entered into him.

23. See *Sod ha-Shabbat:* Section 3 for a complete rendering.

24. In the popular imagination, demons were thought to reside in the nail-parings. See Z 2:208b and 3:79a, et al. Also see the Talmudic source (MQ 18a) quoted in the ensuing TY text.

25. See his article "The Treatment of Hair and Fingernails Among the Indo-Europeans," in *History of Religions* 16:351–62 (1977). The quoted phrase is found on p. 360.

26. The TY's interpretation of nail-paring had an important effect on later observance. It was quoted in such influential sources as the *Shenei Luḥot ha-Berit* ("Massekhet Shabbat"); *Be'er Heiṭev* to Sh.A OḤ 260; *Maṭṭeh Mosheh* 4:211; and the more recent *Ṭaʿamei ha-Minhagim ve-'Oẓar ha-Dinim* of Sperling (sec. 254–55).

   The TY's multi-layered rationale for nail-paring and disposal may be compared with the more monochromatic *ṭeʿamim* found in *Sefer ha-Peli'ah* and *Shoshan Sodot*. The *Peli'ah* focuses primarily on the magical-apotropaic aspects of the *paring* and its beneficial effects on the devotee:

[On Sabbath-eve] one should pare his nails for "every addition is deemed equal to a loss" [TB Ḥullin 58b, Bekh. 40a], affecting the [neighboring] limb too. The force of impurity derives nourishment from *Pardes* [the sefirotic world]. Therefore, remove from yourself that which causes injury to the People. . . . (fol. 36b)

The Talmudic reference is to a basic law of *kashrut:* the abnormal addition of a limb or organ causes the animal to be treated as though both the normal and the abnormal limb were missing, rendering the creature unfit for consumption. Kabbalistically, the 'abnormal' growth of the dirty nails sullies the Sabbath-cosmos, causing *Siṭra' 'Aḥra'* to be nourished instead of the terrestrial world. The addition of dirt under the nails, in other words, represents a loss for us. Conversely, to pare the nails is to starve or eliminate Evil for the duration of Shabbat, enabling us to receive blessing from on high.

    Shoshan Sodot (78b), by contrast, stresses the theurgic or intra-divine consequences of nail-paring: it symbolizes and effects "the removal of the external *qelippot,* the Ten Bands of Impurity that adhere to *Malkhut.*"

27. Cf. e.g., *Re'shit Ḥokhmah* ("Sha῾ar ha-Qedushah": Chap. 2) and esp. the *Shenei Luḥot ha-Berit* cited on p. 414 above.
28. See V. Turner's *Forest of Symbols* (Ithaca, 1967): Chap. 1 (esp. 28ff.) and *Dreams, Fields and Metaphors* (Ithaca, 1974): 55–57.
29. It had previously been associated with the entry into sacred space, as well— prescribed, e.g., for *kohanim* about to perform their priestly service and for pilgrims about to enter the Temple Mount. A Geonic tradition also associated it with the entry into *Yom Kippur,* the most solemn of days. See n. below for further discussion.
30. On the evolution of this custom, see n. 34 below.
31. The only conceivable allusion to *ṭevilah* is in Z 2:136b: "When Rav Hamnuna Sava used to come out of the river on Friday afternoon he would rest a little on the bank . . ." Although Safed Kabbalists interpreted Rav Hamnuna's act as *ṭevilah* (cf. *Toẓe'ot Ḥayyim* sec. 91 and *'Or Yaqar* vol. 9:64), they may well be reading contemporary practice back into the *Zohar.* The Zohar source contains no explicit evidence that anything more than *reḥiẓah* is taking place.
32. For another reference to ablution in the *Peli'ah,* see the vignette on fol. 7d, which begins: "One time I went to immerse myself *l[i-ṭhol]* in the water; it was Sabbath eve, and as I went out from the water. . . ."
33. One of the richest discussions of aquatic symbolism may be found in the writings of Mircea Eliade. (See *The Sacred and the Profane:* 129–36 and *Patterns in Comparative Religion:* 188–215.) Although his theories cannot be applied wholesale to the material at hand, I have been informed by several of his insights regarding immersion and emersion. His claims regarding death-birth symbolism seem less applicable here.

    On the three stages in rites of passage, see A. van Gennep, *The Rites of Passage* (Chicago, 1960), esp. pp. 10–11 and 21; and V. Turner, *The Forest of Symbols:* 93ff.
34. On the evolution of the custom of nail-paring, see n. 19 above. The historical development of *ṭevilah* in preparation for Shabbat is not yet sufficiently understood. It seems that it was sporadically practiced in certain Middle Eastern locales long before its appearance in the *Qanah* and *Peli'ah.* The

first mention of pre-Sabbath ablution is in 2 *Maccabees* 12:38. It is told that upon returning to the town of Adullam on Sabbath eve, Judah and his men "purified themselves as was their custom and celebrated the Sabbath." It is not certain, however, whether this ablution was for the "honor of Shabbat," as suggested by G. Alon and H. Albeck (see, e.g., the former's *Meḥqarim be-Toledot Yisra'el* [Tel Aviv, 1957] 1:156–57) or a means of purifying the soldiers from the blood on their hands prior to their entering the town (ff. Num. 31:19). This latter reading, which was first suggested by Ralph Marcus (*Law in the Apocrypha* [New York, 1927]: 80), seems more likely in my estimation. For further discussion, see L. Schiffman, *The Halakhah at Qumran:* 107.

A second piece of evidence is preserved in the responsa of the mid-eighth century Gaon of Sura, R. Yehudai (in B. Lewin, *'Oẓar ha-Ge'onim*, "Rosh ha-Shanah" [Jerusalem, 1928], *teshuvah* 14). R. Yehudai was asked whether "one needs to recite the blessing over *ṭevilah* on Sabbath eve, the eve of festivals [cf. *Sifra'* "Shemini" 4:9 and TB RH 16b] and the eve of Yom Kippur." Despite the fact that he responded in the negative—noting that one was not *obligated* to perform these ablutions—the *she'elah* demonstrates that pre-Sabbath immersion was practiced in at least some circles in Babylonia.

A third attestation is found in the *'Eshkol ha-Kofer* (sec. 150) of Judah Hadassi, the twelfth century Karaite sage from Constantinople. He noted that on the eve of Shabbat one "should bathe and sanctify himself in purity *[le-hitqaddesh be-ṭaharah*—apparently, through ablution] in order to pray to his Maker." As Zvi Ankori has noted, Hadassi's work was not original but anthological, reflecting current beliefs and practices of Byzantine Jews. Unfortunately, no other references to pre-Sabbath ablution are found in the Byzantine literature of that period. As a result, it is unclear whether the *Qanah* and *Peli'ah*'s emphasis on *ṭevilah* was an outgrowth (and kabbalization) of an enduring Byzantine practice or a renovation—for mystical reasons—of a custom that had fallen into desuetude.

A final point. The Byzantine-Turkish Kabbalistic emphasis on pre-Sabbath ablution may conceivably be related to a broader phenomenon: the new stress on ritual purification that began with Hai Gaon's renewal of *ṭevilah* for men who had nocturnal emissions *(ba'alei qeri)*. This eventuated in a growing tendency in certain High Medieval communities to do ablution before the performance of highly significant miẓvot, e.g., before blowing the shofar; before reciting the priestly benediction and performing *nesi'at kappayim* (the priestly lifting of hands); before leading the prayers; and most commonly of all, before entering Yom Kippur, the "Sabbath of Sabbaths." Still, direct historical linkage is hard to establish; indeed, with the exception of the last example, these ritual ablutions were limited to the Ashkenazic setting (where references to pre-Sabbath *ṭevilah* have not been found). So the question of influence remains moot.

On the requirement of ablution before *nesi'at kappayim* and before leading prayers, see Y. Zimmer's recent article "Mo'adei Nesi'at Kappayim," *Sinai* 100 (1987): 452–70. On the more widely disseminated custom of performing *tevilah* on Yom Kippur eve, see the aforementioned responsum of Yehudai Gaon; *hilkhot Yom ha-Kippurim* in *Siddur Rav 'Amram, Siddur Rav Sa'adiah Ga'on, Siddur RaSHI, Sefer ha-Manhig*, and the *Kol Bo;* Jacob of Marveges' *She'elot u-Teshuvot min ha-Shamayim* (sec. 83), *Sefer ha-Minhagot* in S. Assaf, *Sifran shel Ri'shonim:* 151, and Ṭur OḤ 606. Of special Kabbalistic interest is Z 3:100b and 3:214b. This entire issue requires further investigation.

35. The possible connection between the ritual adaptations of Byzantine-Turkish provenance and the full-blown ritual creativity of Safed Kabbalah needs to be investigated. Many of the Safed adepts had previously spent time in the Turkish-Balkan setting, where they were exposed to a wide array of *minhagim*, not to mention the *Qanah, Peliah*, and TY.

36. See, e.g., TY 43b and 49b; and *Sod ha-Shabbat:* Section 12.

37. Perhaps the closest parallel is Z 3:100b which correlates the adept's ablution on the eve of Yom Kippur with *Shekhinah's* ritual purification prior to Her marriage and union with the Holy One. See n. 34 above for further discussion. Another intriguing source is de Leon's *Sodot*, MS Schocken fol. 91a, wherein the newly liberated *Shekhinah* ritually immerses Herself on *Sabbath eve* in preparation for Her union with "Joseph the Ẓaddiq" *(Yesod):*

> On the sixth day . . . as He is aroused *[be-hit'oreruto]*, the Bride immerses Herself *[tovelet]* in the water which "flows from Lebanon [a cipher for the upper sefirotic world]." [Cant. 4:15]

There is, however, no mention of a parallel *tevilah* on part of the adept here.

38. For similar imagery, see Ḥayyim of Chernovitz, *Sidduro shel Shabbat* (reprint, Jerusalem, 1960): Root 1, Branch 3, Section 5.

39. It should be noted that ritual ablution was given added layers of meaning by various Safed Kabbalists in the sixteenth century. To cite but two examples: Moshe ibn Makhir, the *ro'sh yeshivah* of the neighboring town of 'Ein Zeiton, recorded many of the new Sabbath rituals developed in the Safed milieu. In his *Sefer Seder ha-Yom* (41b), he wrote that:

> The pietists of old used to go down to the river to immerse themselves. Afterwards they went out to greet the Bride and received their Sabbath-soul in purity and holiness.

This seems straightforward enough, but then he adds a surprising and somewhat cryptic remark:

> They used to immerse themselves with their wives in order to direct their hearts to one Place.

This passage portrays ablution as a mystery rite, apparently symbolizing the union of the supernal Bride and Groom. This rite also has magical significance for the adept and his wife. One plausible reading: The joint ritual purification transforms and elevates them as a couple, enabling them to "direct their hearts to one Place"—to have singularly elevated thoughts during marital union—so that they may draw a high soul into conception.

Another striking description of ablution is found in the *Kanfei Yonah* (3:45). Here the act of *ṭevilah* self-consciously assumes three distinct stages: (1) separation from weekday status; (2) alignment with the divine transformations, and (3) re-integration into a higher ontological order. According to its author there are three separate immersions. The first is to remove the polluting presence of sins and the spirit of *ḥol:*

One should immerse oneself on Sabbath eve, either before *Minḥah* or thereafter, at any event, after noon. . . . When in the water, he should bow towards the West [kabbalistically, *Shekhinah*] and recite for the first dip, "I hereby immerse myself stripped of the garments of the profane week."

As he immerses himself a second time, he focuses on the transformations occurring in the supernal world and aligns himself with it:

He should enter a second time, saying, "I hereby immerse myself in order to receive the luminescence of Shabbat, Remember *[Tif'eret]* and Keep *[Shekhinah]* in union."

As he concentrates on various divine Names,

Clouds of Glory encompass the person in the water.

Only at this juncture may he receive his additional soul:

Thereafter, he immerses himself a third time, saying: "I hereby immerse myself in order to receive a Sabbath-soul." When he emerges, let him walk backwards *like one departing from the Temple.*

Through the later popularization of the Safed Kabbalah, *ṭevilah* became a standard feature of Sabbath-preparation in many communities. For recent examples see A. Sperling's *Ṭaʿamei ha-Miẓvot:* 119ff.; M. Zborowski and E. Herzog, *Life Is With People* (New York, 1952): 41; and B-Z Muẓapi (ed.), *ʿOlamo shel Ẓaddiq* (Jerusalem, 1985/86): 145–46. Also see EJ 11:1534 ("Miqveh").

40. On the royal nature of Sabbath-garments, also see J. Giqatilia, *Sodot,* section 10, "Garments":

To wear garments that are appropriate for royalty, holy vestment. For it is fitting that one who stands in the king's palace should wear royal garments. For this reason, our Sages of blessed memory said: "The clothing that one wore when cooking a dish for one's master [here, connoting the profane week] should not be worn when offering him a cup of wine [i.e., on Shabbat]." [TB Yoma' 23b] The mystery is "You shall make holy vestments [to wear in the Sanctuary]" [Ex. 28:2], truly.

The symbolism developed in *Shoshan Sodot* should also be noted. The custom of washing one's clothing on Thursday is given Kabbalistic meaning:

Thursday corresponds to the rung of *Ḥesed,* which removes all impurity. Hence, it is proper to cleanse one's garments on this day, in order to be purely attired when greeting the King and Queen. (77b)

Later (fol. 78a), R. Moshe ben Jacob noted that the change of clothes parallels *Shekhinah*'s re-garbing:

The reason for washing the body and donning new clothes: During the week *Malkhut* functions [in the lower world] through the aspects of *Din*, strict Judgment, and *Raḥamim*, Compassion: they are Her garments [cf. Z 2:204a and *Qanah* 65a]. . . . But on Shabbat *Malkhut* wears Sabbath-finery, royal vestment, pure Compassion. To emulate this paradigm, it is proper to remove one's weekday garments, which suggest *Din*, and don Sabbath vestment, which intimates Compassion.

41. This structure is sometimes extended to the divine world as well. That is, the lower (or more outward) sefirot serve as the garment to the potencies above (or within). See Z 3:283a (RM): *"Shekhinah* is the cloak covering all Three *[Ḥesed, Gevurah, Tif'eret]."*

    The image of divinity cloaked in layered garments appears in older Greek, Iranian, and Jewish sources, as well. See R. Eisler, *Weltenmantel und Himmelszelt* (Munich, 1910); R. C. Zaehner, *Zurvan: A Zoroastrian Dilemma* (Oxford, 1955); A. Altmann, "A Note on the Rabbinic Doctrine of Creation" in his *Studies in Religious Philosophy and Mysticism:* 128–39; and G. Scholem, *Jewish Gnosticism:* 57–62. The older imagery lacks the pantheistic sweep found in much of the Kabbalistic imagery, however. See the ensuing TZ text for illustration.

42. See T. Polhemus' anthropological study, *Fashion and Anti-Fashion* (London, 1978).

43. On the often ambivalent responses to the sacred, see Mircea Eliade, *Patterns in Comparative Religion:* 14, 17–18, 417–20, and 460. On Zoharic use of Ex. 33:20, see Z 1:98a, 211b, 226a and 3:147a. On the awesome "Face of God," also see ZḤ 22c–23a (MN). This motif was well-developed (indeed, more frequently and powerfully expressed) in earlier Jewish Mysticism. Cf. G. Scholem, *Jewish Gnosticism:* Chap. 8 and the numinous hymn from *Heikhalot Rabbati,* reprinted in T. Carmi, *Penguin Book of Hebrew Verse* (New York, 1981): 196–97.

44. Cf., e.g., Z 1:2a:

When the males of Israel perform the miẓvot of the Three Festivals [adorning Her from below], Her Mother lends the Daughter Her garments and decorates Her with Her own adornments.

45. Perhaps the most striking example of the mystical adorning of the Bride is the *Zohar's Tiqqun Leil Shavuʿot.* See 1:8a and 3:98a–b; also see Moshe de Leon's *Sodot,* MS Schocken 14 fol. 86a–b. For discussion, see G. Scholem, OKS: 138 and Y. Wilhelm, "Sidrei Tiqqunim" in ʿAlei ʿAyin (Jerusalem, 1948–52): 125–30.

46. On the distinction between remote and proximate influences in mystical experience, see Robert Ellwood, *Mysticism and Religion* (Englewood Cliffs, NJ, 1980): 70.

47. Cf. Z 2:204a.

48. On wearing light and gaily colored garments on Shabbat, see ZḤ "Yitro"

34a and 37a (TZ?). (The injunction to wear white garments is a later insertion, introduced into the 1663 Venice ed. of ZH [fol. 59b]). On Lilith and her spiritual children wearing black, see Ibid. 37a and Z 3:272b (RM). For broader discussion, see Sod ha-Shabbat nn. 380–82.

49. See R. Klibansky, F. Saxl, and E. Panofsky, *Saturn and Melancholy* (London, 1964) for discussion. For Jewish parallels see *Sod ha-Shabbat*, nn. 378–79 and R. Kiener, "The Status of Astrology in the Early Kabbalah," *Meḥqerei Yerushalayim be-Maḥshevet Yisra'el* 6:3–4 (1987): 28, English section.

50. There is a highly complex historical backdrop for this symbolization of Lilith/Shabbetai which I hope to address in a future article. For some initial thoughts, see my dissertation "The Sabbath in the Classical Kabbalah" (Ph.D. thesis, University of Pennsylvania, 1984), pp. 531–38. A condensed version may be found in my comments to *Sod ha-Shabbat*, nn. 378–83.

51. On *Shekhinah* entering the Palace as Sabbath begins, see Z 2:135a–b ("Raza' de-Shabbat").

52. It should be noted that there are a few Byzantine sources that hold a somewhat different view of the Sabbath mythos and its underlying rhythms. Perhaps the most prominent example is *Sefer ha-Qanah*. Its author, a highly creative adept, had strong dualist tendencies which he here extended into Sabbath proper. That is, he prolonged the anti-demonic rituals of "separation" far beyond the halakhic boundary of candlelighting, well into the Sabbath day. (Curiously, these 'radical' views are not evident in the same author's *Peli'ah*. They are, however, intermittently evident in the anthology *Shoshan Sodot* [completed 1498], where uncited teachings from the *Qanah* appear.) It is worthwhile noting the broad outlines of the *Qanah*'s distinctive vision.

The preparatory rituals mentioned in the text are few in number and concerned primarily with the time just prior to Shabbat. The first ritual mentioned is that of changing garments:

> And how does one honor the Sabbath? With special garments not worn during the week. Know, my son, that the Sabbath garments are the divine blessing [shefaᶜ] that She [Shekhinah] receives from the upper sefirot. For during the week She receives both *Din* and Compassion, and acts through them. But on Shabbat all the shefaᶜ is of Compassion. So one is bidden to change his clothes . . . in accord with this [transformation on high].

One thereby exemplifies the flow of divine blessing into the world. In contrast to the other sources (including the *Peli'ah*), bathing *follows* the act of dressing. The text reads:

> After he has changed, let him wash his face, hands and feet so that the path of the profane week may be lifted from him. . . . (65a)

This is a glimpse of a trait that courses through *mizvat Shabbat* in the *Qanah:* that is, the beneficent Sabbath-cosmos must repeatedly be re-won, for it is not stable or secure. Despite the devotee's and *Shekhinah*'s transformation on Sabbath eve, *Din* is a force to be reckoned with throughout the day. Whereas the *Zohar* depicts *Din* as a kind of slumbering demon that is best left alone and forgotten, the *Qanah* devotes a good deal of energy to actively warding it off. For example, the act of candlelighting must be done so as to confuse the demonic powers:

It would be proper to light two candles corresponding to the East *[Tiferet]* and West *[Malkhut]*. . . . However, one should light three, for Satan and the demonic powers do not see threes and they will not cause any harm. (65b)

The Friday night *Qiddush* has a dual function: it is both an antidemonic ritual and the occasion for the divine marriage. The author explained:

Through reciting the *Qiddush* on Friday night, one sanctifies (or betroths) the [Queen] unto the King and banishes the profane ways.

Drawing on the sefirotic association of wine with *Gevurah*, he avers:

One makes a blessing over the wine to appease [and hence neutralize] *Din*. . . .

The ultimate purpose of the final *Qiddush* blessing—*Qiddush ha-Yom*—is to bring divine blessing down from *Ḥokhmah* unto *Malkhut;* but to do that the demonic realm must first be "attacked":

We then say that Shabbat is "first among the holy convocations" meaning that Shabbat alludes to *Binah,* called the Great Sabbath, the first of the [active sefirot]. Therefore, we say "in commemoration of the Exodus from Egypt," because *Binah* lets *Tiferet* ride on the Arms *[Ḥesed* and *Gevurah]* and makes war with Egypt *[Sitra' 'Aḥra']* and brings us [the Community of Israel/*Malkhut*] from slavery to freedom.

For those who did not prepare for Shabbat beforehand, the *Qiddush* serves as the rite of separation, a kind of *Havdalah.* Paraphrasing a halakhic discussion to TB Pes. 99b–100a (cf. Tos. ad loc.), the *Qanah* notes:

If one were eating a meal on Friday afternoon and Shabbat drew near, one should stop the meal, recite the weekday Grace after the meal, and thereafter, *recite the Qiddush and separate the Profane from the Holy.*

The first two sacramental meals, which are occasions for *hieros gamos* in the Zoharic tradition take on anti-demonic valences in the *Qanah.* The first meal, corresponding to *Shekhinah,* facilitates Her liberation from the realm of harsh *Din,* while ushering Her into the Realm of Compassion. Evidently, *Shekhinah*'s status in the divine realm is not secure until well into Friday evening. The second meal, corresponding to *Tif'eret,* has even stronger anti-demonic overtones, alluding to *Tif'eret*'s "war against Sammael" which will come to a head in the future.

Only the third Meal, parallel to *Keter,* is devoid of apotropaic significance. For this Meal points to the "supernal Source . . . a rung without *Din.*" Finally, on Saturday afternoon, complete Shabbat is attained, and "All is Compassion." The author explained the rabbinic custom of using only one *ḥallah* for the third meal in mystical terms. During the first two meals two *ḥallot* are required since the divine world is not yet integrated: by holding two *ḥallot* together, *qeruv* [union] is promoted. However, at *Seuʿdah Shelishit* only one loaf is required for "all is in union" already: that which was two is now one! (66a–b)

For parallels in the *Shoshan Sodot,* see fol. 76b (on *Qiddush*); 76b–77a (on the sacramental meals); 78a (on dressing); and 78a–b (on candle-lighting). Also noteworthy is the apotropaic significance accorded the *berak-hah meʿein shevaʿ* on Friday night (79a). Through proper recitation, the supernal entities unite "so that [finally!] the Opposing Forces are snuffed out and gone." Nonetheless, this anthological work is hardly systematic or univocal in its symbolism; it also incorporates views that are akin to those found in Gerona and Zoharic sources.

13.

Mystical Techniques

Moshe Idel

I. NOMIAN AND ANOMIAN MYSTICAL TECHNIQUES

Like mystics of other faiths, Kabbalists used certain techniques in order
to induce paranormal states of consciousness. But despite the great
importance of these practices, their history and description have received
only scant attention in the modern study of Jewish mysticism.[1] The very
existence of elaborate systems of mystical practices constitutes significant evidence for the reliability of the confessions of Jewish mystics. The
fact that those Kabbalists who related their mystical experiences are
the same Kabbalists who described mystical techniques enhances their
credibility as to the practical use of the techniques and the experiential
nature of their mystical life.[2]

Unlike unitive terminology, which is heavily influenced by external
sources, the descriptions of mystical techniques combine ancient and
presumably authentically Jewish elements with practices that were absorbed from alien sources. One can distinguish between two main types
of Kabbalistic techniques, which I will designate nomian and anomian.
Nomian refers to the internalized halakhic practices that were performed
by the Kabbalists with "intention" or *kavvanah,* one of the important
goals of which was *devekut.* Thus, *nomian* stands for the spiritualization
of the halakhic *dromenon,* which is thereby transformed into a mystical
technique. *Anomian* refers to those forms of mystical activity that did
not involve halakhic practice. I should like to stress from the outset that

anomian is far from synonymous with alien practices. Although some anomian techniques may indeed have stemmed from non-Jewish sources, others were practiced by ancient Jewish mystics but did not become a part of the halakhic way of life. It was precisely the anomian practices that, during the later stages of development of Jewish mysticism, became the most esoteric part of Kabbalistic techniques. Before I enter into detailed discussion, it should be remarked that part of the material to follow stems from anonymous treatises or from literary genres such as hagiographical and pseudepigraphic works. I decided to include such material when there was sufficient reason to suppose that, even if it did not reflect the actual practices of the persons to whom it was attributed, the details provided in these texts can nevertheless be useful for a better understanding of certain techniques. Actual or spuriously attributed practices may have been imitated by the mystics.

I shall present below four main mystical techniques. The first two— weeping and the ascent of the soul—exemplify the continuity of Jewish mysticism throughout the centuries, notwithstanding the changes in theological conceptions that occurred; the last two—combination of letters and visualization of colors—are representative of the more intensive types of techniques characteristic of the medieval period. I deliberately ignored a long series of other devices for attaining paranormal states of consciousness, such as oneiric techniques,[3] isolation,[4] or mental concentration,[5] which I have described elsewhere. Of the four techniques dealt with here, the first two are analyzed extensively, whereas the third and fourth ones are, for various reasons, only generally surveyed.[6]

II. WEEPING AS MYSTICAL PRACTICE

I shall begin my description of the techniques by focusing on a practice— unnoticed before—that can be traced back through all the major stages of Jewish mysticism over a period of more than two millennia. I refer to the recommendation of the use of weeping as a means for attaining revelations—mostly of a visual character—and/or a disclosure of secrets.[7] Before introducing the relevant material, I will review the role played by weeping in Judaism. Within the nomian framework, weeping was incumbent for a limited time within the period of mourning for either a member of one's family or an outstanding sage. It is obvious from the halakhic regulations that, although weeping was obligatory during the period of mourning, it was not viewed as appropriate common behavior. Weeping was likewise recommended in connection with mourning for the Destruction of the Temple, either as part of the rite of *Tikkun Ḥazzot* or as an integral component of the observance of the Ninth of *Av*. The shedding of tears on the latter occasion was indeed highly appreciated, God himself being portrayed as weeping for the Destruction of the Temple.[8] In addition to these instances of bewailing a personal or national loss, weeping was seen as part of the process of repentance.

All these occurrences of weeping were past-oriented, being directed toward an event or events that had already taken place. The future-oriented uses of weeping were more limited; repentance and weeping could contribute to the coming of the Messiah, and groups of mourners were established to hasten this event. According to another version, weeping was part of the effort toward repentance that aimed at safeguarding the Jews from the dreadful events anticipated in the period immediately preceding the arrival of the Messiah. These past- and future-oriented types of weeping were connected with value concepts that were themselves an integral part of the midrashic-talmudic view of life and history. Although participation in these future-oriented practices was not seen as obligatory, they were intended to achieve goals of national importance.

I shall discuss here two present-oriented uses of weeping elaborated upon in Jewish mystical texts. The first was mystical weeping: that is, the effort to receive visions and information about secrets as the direct result of self-induced weeping.[9] The second type, the theurgical one, was intended to induce "weeping" above—internal processes within the Divine triggered by the shedding of human tears. This present-oriented theurgic activity will be analyzed in the chapter on Kabbalistic theurgy, but the main differences between these two kinds of present-oriented weeping ought to be noted here. The latter activity was essentially a theurgic reinterpretation of the nomian recommendations to weep; the focus of this technique was the supernal processes, the Kabbalist being the instrument and not the goal of this activity. Mystical weeping, by contrast, posited as the ultimate goal of weeping the acquisition of paranormal consciousness by the Kabbalist. Although it can be viewed as a spiritual interpretation of nomian practices, it can just as easily be defined as an anomian activity, as nowhere was disclosure of secrets, or even study of esoteric topics, let alone visions of God, part of the midrashic-talmudic conception of things. Moreover, the occurrence of the earliest evidence for this practice in pre-talmudic or midrashic texts is an important proof of its independence from classical halakhic regulations. On the other hand, there are only scanty references to this perception of weeping in classical rabbinic sources, an issue to which I shall return at the conclusion of this discussion.

The earliest evidence for mystical weeping is found in the apocalyptic literature. One version of II Enoch states that this patriarch was "weeping and grieving with [my] eyes. When I lay down on my bed, I fell asleep; and two huge men appeared to me." [10] An interesting parallel occurs in IV Ezra; the angel who has previously revealed some secrets to the prophet ends his speech by saying, "and if you pray again, and weep as you do now, and fast for seven days, you shall hear yet greater things than these." [11] Later, Ezra indicates, "I fasted seven days, mourning and weeping, as Ariel the angel has commanded me," and he received a second vision. [12] The third one is also preceded by a similar process: "I wept again and fasted seven days as before." [13] Similar statements occur in the Apocalypse of Baruch. Baruch and Jeremiah had repeated the same practice: "we rent our garments and wept and mourned and fasted for seven days, and it happened after seven days that the Word of God came to me." [14] A common feature of "apocalyptic" weeping was a state of desolation, associated with the Destruction of the Temple or other signs of religious decline; the feeling of despair was expressed in weeping, followed by comforting revelations.

The connection between weeping and paranormal perceptions taking place in dreams is also evident in a midrashic story: [15]

One of the students of R. Simeon bar Yoḥai had forgotten what he learned. In tears he went to the cemetery. Because of his great weeping, he [R. Simeon] came to him in a dream and told him: "When you wail, throw three bundles,[16] and I shall come." The student went to a dream interpreter and told him what had happened. The latter said to him: "Repeat your chapter [that is, whatever you learn] three times, and it will come back to you." The student did so and so indeed it happened.

The correlation between weeping and visiting a grave seems to point to a practice intended to induce a vision. This was, to be sure, part of a larger context in which graveyards were sites where one might receive a vision.[17] Falling asleep weeping, which is mentioned here, also seems part of the sequence: visiting a cemetery—weeping—falling asleep weeping—revelatory dream. As we shall see later, this sequence, with the exception of the use of graves, repeats itself in R. Ḥayyim Vital's experience. It is evident that this story was preserved in the Midrash because it was focused upon obtaining a remedy—the mnemonic technique of repetition—for the forgetting of the Torah. Again, the connection between weeping and improving one's knowledge of Torah will recur.

Against this background, I shall analyze a passage from *Midrash Hallel,* a late Midrash, elaborating upon a theme[18] that had already been discussed in the earlier *'Avot de-Rabbi Nathan:*[19]

"Who turned the rock into a pool of water, the flint into a fountain[20] of water."[21] We have taught that R. 'Akiva and ben 'Azzai were as arid as this rock, but because they were anguished for the sake of the study of Torah, God opened for them an opening to [understand] the Torah, to those matters which the School of Shammai and the School of Hillel were unable to understand. . . . and matters which were closed to the world were interpreted by R. 'Akiva, as it is said: "He binds the floods that they trickle not; and the thing that is hidden, he brings forth to light."[22] This demonstrates that R. 'Akiva's eye[23] had seen the *Merkavah,* in the same manner that Ezekiel the prophet had seen it; thus it said: "Who turned the rock into a pool of water."

The metamorphosis from a rock into a fountain of water is a metaphor for R. 'Akiva's transformation from an ignoramus into the source of both halakhic and esoteric knowledge—a metamorphosis that was the result of his anguish, accompanied by weeping. Job 28:11 contains the Hebrew word *bekhi* ("weeping"), usually translated here as "trickle." The anonymous interpreter evidently understood the verse as indicating that through "weeping" God caused the hidden things to surface;[24] decisive proof for the role of weeping in bringing about R. 'Akiva's new status is the emphatic mention of his "eye." The entire passage may be interpreted on two levels: weeping transformed R. 'Akiva from a rock into a fountain; his eye, which caused it, received a vision of the divine chariot. Following the two verses in the Book of Job, we may summarize the subjects hinted at in *Midrash Hallel;* suffering and weeping open the way to (1) revelation, that is, vision: "his eye sees every precious thing," or the vision of the *Merkavah;* and (2) understanding of esoteric matters: "he brings forth the things which are hidden."[25] These two effects of suffering and weeping occur in some

Kabbalistic texts that will be analyzed below. It ought to be emphasized that the combination of vision and of the secrets of the Torah indicates that these secrets are more than unknown information hidden from the eyes of preceding generations; I assume that their understanding has some transformative value for "R. 'Akiva," who is presented here as a "fountain," presumably of the teachings of the Torah.

Before proceeding with our discussion, however, it would be worthwhile to analyze briefly the combination of weeping with placing one's head between one's knees. This posture is mentioned in connection with Elijah on Mount Carmel, probably as part of his prayer; [26] it recurs in the Talmud as part of R. Ḥanina ben Dosa's prayer for the life of R. Yoḥanan ben Zakkai's son.[27] In yet another passage, the Talmud mentions R. Eleazar ben Dordia's attempt to repent, in which he places his head between his knees and weeps.[28] The outcome of R. Eleazar's sorrow and weeping is death, envisaged by a talmudic authority as the acquisition in a moment of the bliss of the world to come.[29] This story cannot in itself serve as decisive evidence for the technical status of weeping; however, its association with the posture of Elijah is highly suggestive, as in both the Heikhalot literature and in a later description of its practices [30] the mystical vision of the supernal palaces is attained by using Elijah's posture.[31] As we have already seen, R. 'Akiva attained his vision of the *Merkavah* through means of weeping. Nowhere in the texts related to the Heikhalot literature, however, are these two practices combined.

The single exception of which I am aware, probably conveying a certain casual affinity between a pattern of acts and a revelatory experience, states as follows:

R. Ishmael said: I devoted myself to the pursuit of wisdom and the calculation of the holidays and moments and of the [eschatological] dates and times and periods [of times], and I turned my face to the Supreme Holy One through prayer and supplications, fasting and weeping. And I said: "God, Lord of Ẓevaot, Lord of Israel, until when shall we be neglected." [32]

R. Ishmael's prayer had an overt messianic goal: to know the date of the redemption, that is, to receive a revelation whereby he might receive occult information thereof. It seems that the more "mathematical" methods for achieving knowledge of the secret date of the end of the suffering of Israel either were inappropriate or had to be attained by a mystical technique, which included weeping, together with other types of ascetic practices.

Nevertheless, we may assume that such a combined practice existed in ancient Jewish mysticism, and not only on the evidence of the talmudic story about R. Eleazar. The *Zohar* describes R. Simeon bar Yoḥai as both practicing Elijah's posture and weeping in connection with a mystical experience.[33] The mystic asked who could disclose to him the secrets of the Torah and then "wept and placed his head between his knees and kissed the dust." His friends encouraged him, saying, "be happy in the happiness of your Lord." He then wrote down all he had heard that night and learned it without forgetting anything. R. Simeon remained in this posture the entire night and in the morning lifted his eyes and saw a vision of light representing the Temple. Thus, for R. Simeon, as for R. 'Akiva in *Midrash Hallel,* weeping is connected both with the disclosure of secrets of the Torah and with a vision; although the *Merkavah* is not identical with the Temple, the similarity between *Midrash Hallel* and the *Zohar* passage is striking.[34] Can we perhaps infer from this that the author of the *Zohar* had available to him a source in which weeping and Elijah's posture were already combined in the talmudic text?

An important instance in which weeping was part of a larger pattern culminating in a mystical experience is found in a thirteenth-century Judeo-Arabic treatise, *Perakim be-Haẓlaḥah,* spuriously attributed to Maimonides. The Oriental author describes the act of prayer in these words:

The one praying shall turn to God, blessed be he, standing on his feet and delighting in his heart and lips[!]. His hands shall be stretched and his vocal organs shall murmur and speak [while] the other limbs tremble and shake; he shall not cease singing sweet melodies, humbling himself, imploring, bowing and prostrating himself [and] weeping, since he is in the presence of the Great and Majestic King, and [then] he will experience an ecstatic experience and stupefaction, insofar as he will find his soul in the world of the intellects.[35]

No doubt the anonymous author presents here an intentional device for an ideal prayer ending in a mystical experience.

The weeping technique is powerfully expounded by R. Abraham ha-Levi Berukhim, one of Isaac Luria's disciples. In one of his programs for attaining "wisdom," after specifying "silence" as the first condition, he names the second condition: in all your prayers, and in every hour of study, in a place which one finds difficult, in which you cannot understand and comprehend the propaedeutic sciences or some secret, stir yourself to bitter weeping until your eyes shed tears, and the more you can weep—do so. And increase your weeping, as the gates of tears were not closed and the supernal gates will be opened to you.[36]

It is obvious that, for Luria and Berukhim, weeping is an aid to overcoming intellectual difficulties and receiving secrets.[37] It is plausible to interpret the final sentence as referring to a revelatory experience, in which the supernal gates are opened. This text is recommended for a practical purpose; it appears that R. Abraham Berukhim indeed had the opportunity to apply this recommendation, as it is reported that Luria had revealed to him that he would die unless he prayed before the Wailing Wall and saw the *Shekhinah*. It is then reported: [38]

When that pious man heard the words of Isaac Luria, he isolated himself for three days and nights in a fast, and [clothed himself] in a sack, and nightly wept. Afterward he went before the Wailing Wall and prayed there and wept a mighty weeping. Suddenly he raised his eyes and saw on the Wailing Wall the image of a woman, from behind,[39] in clothes which it is better not to describe, that we have mercy on the divine glory. When he had seen her, he immediately fell on his face and cried and wept and said:[40] "Zion,[41] Zion, woe to me that I have seen you in such a plight." And he was bitterly complaining and weeping and beating his face and plucking his beard and the hair of his head, until he fainted and lay down and fell asleep on his face. Then he saw in a dream the image of a woman who came and put her hands on his face and wiped the tears of his eyes. . . . and when Isaac Luria saw him, he said: "I see that you have deserved to see the face of the *Shekhinah*."

It is clear that the two visions of the woman—that is, of the *Shekhinah*—are the result of R. Abraham's bitter weeping: the former a waking vision of the back of the *Shekhinah*, the latter a vision of her face, which occurs only in a dream. The first one provokes anxiety; the second, comfort.

Akin to the story of R. Abraham Berukhim is the autobiographical confession of his friend, R. Ḥayyim Vital: [42]

In 1566, on the Sabbath eve, the eighth of *Tevet*, I said *Kiddush* and sat down to eat; and my eyes were shedding tears, and I was sighing and grieving since . . . I was bound by witchcraft[43] . . . and I likewise wept for [my] neglect of the study of Torah during the last two years. . . . and because of my worry I did not eat at all, and I lay on my bed on my face, weeping, and I fell asleep out of much weeping, and I dreamed a wondrous dream.

As in the ancient apocalyptic texts and in R. Abraham Berukhim's story, Vital seems to have combined here weeping, sorrow, and—to a certain extent—even fasting. The last is indeed curious, as the entire incident took place on the eve of the Sabbath, a time when the consumption of a ritual meal is incumbent upon all Jews. The content of the dream that followed is intricate, and this is not the place to deal with it. It is sufficient to note that Vital had a highly elaborate revelation, paralleled by revelations already found in other Kabbalistic works: it is reported as a revelation rather than as a dream.[44] What is certainly novel in Vital's relating of the revelatory dream is his vision of a beautiful woman whom he thought to be his mother, who in the dream asked him:[45] " 'Why are you weeping, Ḥayyim, my son? I have heard your tears and I have come to help you.'... and I called to the woman: 'Mother,[46] Mother, help me, so that I[47] may see the Lord sitting upon a throne, the[48] Ancient of Days, his beard white as snow, infinitely splendid.' "

The references to biblical prophetic visions, found only in Safrin's quotation, are extremely relevant to our discussion. In the first stage, Vital apparently wept in order to receive an answer to two problems that were troubling him: his sexual impotence and his interruption of the study of the Torah. In the revelatory dream, he saw himself as weeping in order to obtain a vision of God. Vital's request to see God, formulated in prophetic verses, reminds one of the end of the passage in *Midrash Hallel*, in which R. 'Akiva's vision of the *Merkavah* is compared to that of Ezekiel.

Also relevant to our subject is Nathan of Gaza's description of his own vision. After a complacent description of his religious perfection, the Sabbatian prophet indicates:[49]

When I attained the age of twenty, I began to study the *Zohar* and some of the Lurianic writings. [According to the Talmud], he who wishes to purify himself receives the aid of heaven; thus, he sent to me some of his holy angels and blessed spirits, who revealed to me many of the mysteries of the Torah. In the same year, my force having been stimulated by the visions of the angels and the blessed souls, I was undergoing a prolonged fast during the week before the feast of Purim. Having locked myself in a separate room in holiness and purity, and reciting the penitential prayers of the morning service with many tears, the spirit came over me, my hair stood on end and my knees shook, and I beheld the *Merkavah*.[50] And I saw visions of God all day long and all night, and I was vouchsafed true prophecy like any other prophet, as the voice spoke to me, beginning with the words "Thus speaks the Lord." . . . The angel that revealed himself to me in a waking vision was also a true one, and he revealed to me awesome mysteries.

The vision of the *Merkavah*, quite unusual in the medieval period, is depicted here as following a protracted fast that culminated in the shedding of tears. Interestingly, Nathan was vouchsafed not only a visual experience but also "awesome mysteries." Thus, the two topics mentioned in the early Middle Ages *Midrash Hallel* recur in the experience of the seventeenth-century Kabbalist. Again, as in the midrashic source, the vision of the *Merkavah* is apparently related to the "awesome mysteries"—the latter concerning Sabbatai Ṣevi's messianism, Nathan having envisioned Ṣevi's image engraved on the *Merkavah*.[51]

Mystical weeping also seems to have been cultivated in certain Ḥasidic circles. Before discussing in detail the evidence for this practice, I shall cite a highly interesting dream of R. Joseph Falk, the cantor of the Besht: [52]

In his dream he saw an image of an altar to which the dead man ascended, and he saw him put his head between his knees and begin to cry the *Seliḥah:* "Answer us, O god, answer us. Answer us, our father," and so on throughout the alphabet. After that he said: "Answer us, O God of our fathers, answer us. Answer us, O God of Abraham, answer us. Answer us, O revered of Isaac, answer us. Answer us, O mighty one of Jacob, answer us. Answer us, O compassionate one, answer us. Answer us, O king of the chariots, answer us." Then he ascended to heaven.

This technique of entreaty—Elijah's posture and crying—seems to reflect the older motif of weeping while sitting in Elijah's posture. R. Israel Ba'al Shem Tov interpreted it as an attempt to ascend to a higher level by the recitation of the "answer us" formula. Therefore, according to the earliest Ḥasidim, crying and, I assume also tears, seem already to have been part of a mystical technique.

A younger contemporary of Ba'al Shem Tov, R. Elijah, the gaon of Vilna, also presumably cultivated the device of weeping. His main disciple, R. Ḥayyim of Volozhin, reported to R. Elijah's grandson that his grandfather had several times been very pained and had fasted and avoided sleeping for one or two days and wept copiously because God had withheld from him a certain secret of the Torah.[53] But, he continued, when the secret was revealed to R. Elijah, his face became joyful and his eyes lighted up. R. Ḥayyim's report points to a certain pattern of

behavior intended to attain knowledge of hidden secrets of the Law. The
fact that it was used several times points to the apparently technical
nature of the pattern. We can see that in early Ḥasidism and in the
practice of their opponents, the *Mitnaggedim,* weeping was employed as
a component of mystical technique.

An interesting example of the relationship between weeping and revelation is reported by R. Isaac Yehudah Yehiel Safrin, in his *Megillat
Setarim* and *Netiv Mizvotekha,* in which he relates an experience of his
own.[54] I shall present here a combined version of this mystical confession, based on the author's account in these two books:

> In 1845, on the twenty-first day of the 'Omer, I was in the town of Dukla.[55] I
> arrived there late at night, and it was dark and there was no one to take me
> home, except for a tanner who came and took me into his house. I wanted to
> pray *Ma'ariv* and to count the 'Omer, but I was unable to do it there, so I went
> to the Beit Midrash alone, and there I prayed until midnight had passed. And I
> understood from this situation the plight of the *Shekhinah* in exile,[56] and her
> suffering when she is standing in the market of tanners.[57] And I wept many
> times before the Lord of the world, out of the depth of my heart, for the
> suffering of the *Shekhinah.* And through my suffering and weeping, I fainted and
> I fell asleep for a while, and I saw a vision of light,[58] splendor and great
> brightness, in the image of a young woman[59] adorned with twenty-four orna-
> ments.[60] . . . And she said: "Be strong, my son," and so on. And I was suffering
> that I could not see but the vision of her back[61] and I was not worthy to receive
> her face. And I was told that [this was because] I am alive, and it is written, "for
> no man shall see me, and live."[62]

The vision of the feminine apparition possessing maternal features—
she calls R. Isaac "my son"—is characteristic of the Kabbalistic image
of weeping, and is shared by the visions of R. Abraham Berukhim and
R. Ḥayyim Vital. R. Levi Isaac of Berdichev must also have experienced
such a vision. In *Netiv Mizvotekha,* prior to the passage cited above,
after quoting R. Ḥayyim Vital's account from *Sefer ha-Ḥezyonot,* R.
Isaac wrote:

> "And it happened to the holy R. Levi Isaac, that on the evening of *Shavu'ot* he
> achieved the vision of the *Shekhinah* in the image of . . . and she said to him:
> 'My son, Levi Isaac, be strong, for many troubles will befall you, but be strong,
> my son, for I shall be with you.' "[63]

R. Levi Isaac therefore also experienced a vision of *Shekhinah,* who
appeared to him as a young woman, although R. Isaac Safrin censored
this word, just as he did when he related his own vision shortly thereaf-

ter. Moreover, the time when the well-known master of Ḥasidism attained this vision is also significant for two reasons; the eve of *Shavu'ot*
is close in time to the period when Safrin experienced his own vision, on
the twenty-first day of the *'Omer;* in addition, the night of *Shavu'ot* was
the precise time when two noted Kabbalists received their revelation of
Shekhinah. I refer to the vigil of R. Joseph Karo and R. Solomon ha-Levi
Alkabeẓ.[64] Therefore, R. Levi Isaac attempted to imitate the experience
of his Kabbalist predecessors. Safrin, however, does not even hint at the
experience of these two sixteenth-century figures, although it is impossible to assume that he was unaware of it, as it was printed in the
famous *Sheney Luḥot ha-Berit.*[65] His failure to mention it is all the more
inexplicable since he alludes to the less well-known cases of R. Abraham
Berukhim and R. Ḥayyim Vital. But the answer to the quandary is
simple and highly relevant to the understanding of Safrin's view. In the
heading to the discussions we quoted above, he writes, "The revelation
of the *Shekhinah* [happens] by means of and following the suffering that
one is caused to suffer, by means of which he feels the suffering of the
Shekhinah, and the fact that this revelation has a form and an image is
on account of his being corporeal."[66] This title postulates a visual
revelation of the *Shekhinah* as a female image resulting from suffering—
two elements that are absent in the vigil of Karo and Alkabeẓ. In their
session, the *Shekhinah* was audible through the lips of Karo, but invisible. Safrin and the examples he adduces deal exclusively with the visible
revelations of the *Shekhinah.* Furthermore, in the *Shavu'ot* vigil the
technique used by the Kabbalists entailed study of various passages
excerpted from Jewish classical sources. If participation in and affliction
for the fate of the *Shekhinah* occurred, these were the result of the
revelation, not its cause. In the cases of Abraham Berukhim, Ḥayyim
Vital, Levi Isaac, and Safrin, weeping preceded the appearance of the
Shekhinah. In other words, Safrin viewed self-induced suffering culminating in weeping as a technique for contemplating the image of the
Shekhinah.[67] He seems to have striven for the vision of the face of the
Shekhinah, a quest similar to Vital's desire, but he was prevented from
doing so because of his human condition.[68]

The activation of the eye ends in a visual experience. In the case of
Karo and Alkabeẓ, the organ activated was the lips; indeed, the *Shekhinah* spoke from the throat of Karo. The correlation between the technique and the nature of the revelation is striking; Safrin regarded weep-

ing as a trigger for the mystical experience. We can propose an even
more elaborate explanation: his presence at night in a small town was
a premeditated device intended to induce a state of deep melancholy
culminating in weeping. His journey to Dukla can be seen as part of a
self-imposed exile, a *Galut* imitating the self-exile of the *Shekhinah;*
the reward for this "participation mystique" was the revelation of the
Shekhinah.[69] As it took place during the period between Passover and
Shavu'ot, we can suppose that the journey was a preparatory exercise in
suffering and weeping whose goal was the revelation on the eve of
Shavu'ot; the *Shekhinah,* however, made its appearance sooner than expected.

According to another passage from Safrin, penitential prayer performed with weeping and a broken heart may bring about the appearance of divine light and a "second birth." [70] But the most important case
in which weeping is used in order to induce an experience of the *Shekhinah* is absent from Safrin's collection of examples in *Netiv Mizvotekha.*
I refer to the custom of R. Ẓevi Hirsch of Zhidachov, R. Isaac Safrin's
main teacher in Kabbalah matters; in his commentary on the *Zohar,*
Safrin relates an event pertinent to our discussion: [71]

It was his [R. Ẓevi Hirsch's] custom regarding the matter of holiness to pray in
order to bring upon himself a state of suffering, uneasiness and affliction on
every eve of Sabbath. This was done in order to efface himself completely before
the Sabbath, so as to be able to receive his light,[72] blessed be he, during the
prayer and the meal of the Sabbath [eve] with a pure, holy, and clear heart. This
was his custom regarding the matter of holiness, owing to his constant fear lest
arrogant and alien thoughts would enter his heart. Once, on the feast of
Shavu'ot, hundreds of people crowded around him. Before the [morning] prayer,
with the [first] light of dawn, I entered one of his rooms, but he did not see me,
for he was pacing about the room to and fro, weeping and causing heaven and
earth to weep with him before God.[73] And it is impossible to write it down. And
he humbled himself before God with a mighty weeping, supplicating that he not
be rejected from the light of his face.[74] . . . then I was overcome by a great
trembling, because of the awe of the *Shekhinah,* and I opened the door and
ran away.

According to this report of R. Isaac Safrin, R. Ẓevi Hirsch's self-
afflictions were a means of preparing himself to receive the divine light
on the Sabbath eve, as well as on at least some feasts; weeping, however,
is related only in connection with the *Shavu'ot* account. Moreover,
Safrin witnessed an overwhelming feeling of the presence of the divine

countenance, seemingly induced by the self-abasement and weeping of his uncle. Although an experience of the *Shekhinah* is not directly mentioned, the fact that Safrin attests such an experience is clear evidence that R. Zevi Hirsch himself intended to induce such an experience; that the occasion of this event is *Shavu'ot* is evidence, too, that the master from Zhidachov is continuing an already existing tradition concerning the possibility of experiencing the presence of the *Shekhinah* on *Shavu'ot*. I have already mentioned the major predecessors—Karo, Alkabez, and Levi Isaac of Beridichev—but here we learn for the first time of the occurrence of weeping as part of an actual practice. Safrin's vision of the *Shekhinah* can now be seen in the context of a broader mystical endeavor, cultivated in Hasidic circles, to attain experiences of the *Shekhinah,* and we can well assume that this was a continuation of earlier Kabbalistic practices.

I shall now turn to the relationship between weeping and secrets. At the end of Safrin's *Commentary* to the first volume of the *Zohar,* he confesses: [75]

By much weeping, like a well, and suffering I became worthy to be transformed into "a flowing stream, a fountain of wisdom;" [76] no secret was revealed to me, nor a wondrous apprehension, but afterward I became like dust and wept before the Creator of the universe like a spring, lest I should be rejected from the light of his face, and for the sake of gaining apprehensions out of the source of wisdom, and I became as a flowing well, weeping.

This voluminous commentary on the *Zohar,* one of the most comprehensive of its kind, was composed, according to the author's confession, with the help of revelations triggered by, among other things, weeping.

As late as the second half of the nineteenth century, the old mystical technique of weeping was still being practiced in order to attain the same goals alluded to in *Midrash Hallel:* visual revelation and disclosure of secrets. Following in the footsteps of his father, R. Eliezer Zevi Safrin confesses in the introduction of his own commentary on the *Zohar* that when he was mature,[77]

I once woke in [the middle] of the night and wept greatly with a broken heart before God, for the exile of the *Shekhinah* and of the community of Israel, the holy ones who are suffering . . . and I woke up after the middle of the night on the second day as well, and I wept even more than the previous day for the same things. And before daybreak I went to sleep for half an hour, so that my mind would be calm and tranquil for the [morning] prayer. And during my sleep I saw in a dream that I was standing in the Land of Israel.[78] . . . and it is possible that because of this dream which I was worthy to see, that Old Holy Man[79] gave me the strength to interpret the holy book of the *Zohar*.

Before concluding our discussion of this mystical practice, some general observations on the nature of the material above are in order.

1. In all the cases analyzed, the practice of weeping was attributed to, or practiced by, figures who were part of the Jewish elite; in other words, it was nowhere recommended that weeping be popularly used as a means of inducing the vision of the *Shekhinah*. It was intended for, and indeed practiced by, the very few who were interested in experiencing such a vision.

2. The passages quoted above are excerpted from texts that did not belong to the mainstreams of talmudic-midrashic literature. The absence of halakhic treatment of mystical weeping is no mere matter of chance; rabbinic thought proposed alternative means to attain the goals of mystical weeping. According to one dictum, the study of the Torah for its own sake is rewarded by the disclosure of its secrets to the student;[80] a midrashic statement recommends the study of the Torah in the Land of Israel for whoever wishes to contemplate the *Shekhinah*.[81] Thus, the nomian way of receiving secrets or visions of the *Shekhinah* did not include weeping but provided an avenue not only for the elite but for all Jews.[82]

3. Again, the aforementioned revelations were described as attained in a state of desolation and mourning for the sake of the *Shekhinah* and participation in her suffering because of an incapacity to learn Torah. A talmudic-midrashic view concerning the indwelling of the *Shekhinah*, however, affirms that "the *Shekhinah* does not dwell [on one] either through sadness, or laziness, or frivolity of mind, but through the joy of performing a commandment."[83] Thus, there is an overt contradiction between the talmudic requirements and the mystical weeping triggered by an initial state of desolation.

These remarks heighten the anomian character of the weeping technique; whatever it promises can be attained as well within the framework of classical halakhic activities, such as the study of Torah or the performance of commandments. As the earliest evidence of the existence of this technique is ancient, it seems to me that the practice must have been suppressed in rabbinic sources for a long period but was revived upon the emergence of Kabbalah, which was interested in attaining mystical experiences far beyond the "normal mysticism" inherent in the rabbinic system. A closer inspection of the ancient materials in the above discussions seems to deny the likelihood that the medieval practices were propagated through the perusal of ancient literary evidence alone. It is hardly reasonable to assume that *Midrash Hallel,* for example, is the source of the later practices. Therefore, assuming that there are no crucial texts that have escaped my examination of the pertinent literature, we can presume the oral transmission of this ancient mystical technique, probably among the elite.

I should like to note that early Christian ascetic traditions may have been influenced[84] by ancient Jewish traditions concerning the mystical possibilities inherent in weeping and, directly or indirectly, Sufi asceticism as well.[85] These kinds of ascetic practices have been presented in unrestrained ways, as neither Christianity nor Islam was interested in obliterating extreme types of asceticism. This proposal is, for the time being, a hypothesis, as no significant research has been conducted in this direction. But the very fact that such an ascetic practice existed in ancient Jewish texts, as well as later on, may foster a novel approach to this issue.[86]

Finally, a brief remark on the psychological mechanism triggering these experiences: weeping is never described as a discrete practice; it is always part of a more elaborate sequence of ascetic exercises—fasting, mourning, self-induced suffering—and is commonly their last step. In some instances, the mystic is actually exhausted by the time he begins weeping; a state of falling asleep or sometimes previous fainting gives concrete evidence of this exhaustion.

On the other hand, the hyperactivation of the ocular system represents a concentration on one mode of perception at the very moment when all other doors of perception are progressively being repressed. This new balance of stimuli prepares the way for paranormal states of consciousness focused upon visual experiences. In such cases, the ideas or concepts upon which one has focused his intellectual and emotional activity tend to reveal themselves through the hyperexcited medium. From a more strictly psychological point of view, the visions that follow a painful and sorrowful state of mind can be related to what Marganita Laski designated as "desolation ecstasies."[87]

III. ASCENT OF THE SOUL

The next type of mystical technique I wish to present is the ascent of the soul in order to perceive the supermundane entities—the *Merkavah,* the seat of glory, the angelic company, or God himself—as well as to receive sublime secrets. The following presentation will exclude discussion of bodily journeys to heaven, on the one hand, and the mental ascent from the material to the spiritual, on the other.[88] My focus will be, rather, on the celestial ascent of the soul, in which the body is left below, commonly in a cataleptic situation or during the night's sleep, in order to undergo a paranormal experience and return to the body thereafter.[89]

This device is part of a more complex technique, including reciting divine names, chanting hymns, fasting, and assuming special bodily postures. These components, as well as the act of ascent, have nothing to do with halakhic prescriptions and may therefore be classified as an anomian type of mystical technique.

The ascent of the soul has been repeatedly discussed by scholars of ancient religions; the long sequence of studies dedicated to this topic renders superfluous any further presentation of the basic facts concerning this matter.[90] I should like to dwell, however, upon the recent discussions of Morton Smith, who has emphasized the importance of the ascent experience for a better understanding of certain passages concerning Jesus himself in early Christian literature.[91] According to this scholar, "We can fairly conclude that one or more techniques for ascent into heaven were being used in Palestine in Jesus' day, and that Jesus himself may well have used one." [92] As Smith indicates, Paul attributed an ascent to Jesus,[93] saying that he was caught up to the third heaven "whether in the body or out of the body." [94] Therefore, the conception of the soul ascending to Paradise—"out of the body"—for the sake of an ineffable experience, even before death, was current among Jews of the first century.[95] This obviously represents a concept different from the more widespread belief in the possibility of bodily ascent to heaven, which seems to have prevailed much earlier. This mystical perception of celestial ascent is a remarkable parallel to the frequent ascent of the soul to heaven in order "to draw life" for her body during the night.[96]

According to some discussions in Heikhalot literature, it is obvious that, alongside what was seemingly conceived as bodily ascent, the ancient Jewish mystics also practiced ascent of the soul. In *Heikhalot*

Rabbati, R. Neḥuniya ben ha-Kaneh is described as sitting in the Temple, apparently in Elijah's posture, while contemplating the divine chariot and the wondrous glory.[97] As it is evident that R. Neḥuniya was in the world and at the same time also contemplating on high, it must be assumed that it was his soul that ascended above. The same conclusion applies to the passage that immediately follows the discussion on R. Neḥuniya's recall by his students. There, the "descenders to the chariot" were requested to employ worthy amanuenses, whose role was to record the revelations of the mystics. Thus, those who did not ascend (or descend) to the *Merkavah* heard what was revealed to those who did, from the latter's mouths.[98] I presume that the mystics, whose bodies remained in this world while their souls wandered in the higher realms, functioned as transmitters of supernal secrets through the collection of their speeches by their amanuenses.[99]

Related to this perception of the *Merkavah* experience is the report of R. Hai Gaon, who elaborated on our topic in a singular way. In one of his responsa, he indicates: [100]

Many scholars thought that one who is distinguished by many qualities described in the books, when he seeks to behold the *Merkavah* and the palaces of the angels on high, he must follow a certain procedure. He must fast a number of days and place his head between his knees and whisper[101] many hymns and songs whose texts are known from tradition. Then he perceives within himself and in the chambers[102] [of his heart] as if he saw the seven palaces with his own eyes, and it is as though he entered one palace after another and saw what is there. And there are two *mishnayot* which the *tannaim* taught[103] regarding this topic, called the *Greater Heikhalot* and the *Lesser Heikhalot,* and this matter is well known and widespread. Regarding these contemplations, the *tanna* taught: "Four entered Pardes"—those palaces were alluded to by the term *Pardes,* and they were designated by this name. . . . For God . . . shows to the righteous, in their interior, the visions of his palaces and the position of his angels.

The contemplation of the *Merkavah* is here compared to the entrance into *Pardes,* both of which activities are, according to R. Hai Gaon, allegories for the inner experience attained by the mystics.[104] I believe that the mystical flight of the soul to the *Merkavah* has here been interpreted allegorically; the supernal palaces can be gazed at and contemplated not by referring to an external event but by concentrating upon one's own "chambers." The scene of revelation is thus no longer the supermundane hierarchy of palaces, but the human consciousness.

According to a younger contemporary of R. Hai Gaon, R. Nathan of Rome, the gaon's intention was that the ancient mystics[105] "do not ascend on high, but that they see and envision in the chambers of their heart like a man who sees and envisions something clearly with his eyes, and they hear and tell and speak by means of a seeing eye,[106] by the divine spirit." Therefore, the earliest interpretation of R. Hai's view emphasizes inner vision rather than mystical ascent. This type of mystical epistemology is congruent with Hai's view concerning the revelation of the glory of God to the prophets through the "understanding of the heart"—'ovanta' de-libba'. Therefore, far from expounding a mystical ascent of the soul, the gaon offers a radical reinterpretation of ancient Jewish mysticism. In the vein of more rationalistic approaches, he effaces the ecstatic or shamanic aspects of the Heikhalot experiences in favor of their psychological interpretation. Although I imagine that this recasting of an earlier religious mentality was motivated by R. Hai's adherence to rationalist thinking,[107] I cannot ignore the possibility that his psychological perception may bear some affinities to much earlier views of the Merkavah.[108] But even if such early understandings of Merkavah mysticism indeed existed, they were seemingly marginal in comparison to the bodily and spiritual ascent cultivated by the Heikhalot mystics. This kind of rationalization consistently reveals a reserved attitude toward the object of interpretation;[109] therefore, R. Hai Gaon seems to have been reacting against a relatively common practice, as we may infer from his remark "and this is a widespread and well-known matter." Even the opening statement of the quotation, although formulated in the past tense, bears evidence of the recognition of the technique by "many scholars."[110] On the ground of R. Hai's passage we can therefore conclude that the use of Elijah's posture in order to attain paranormal states of consciousness perceived as visions of the Merkavah was still on the agenda of Jewish mystics, notwithstanding R. Hai Gaon's attempt to attenuate some of its "uncanny" facets.[111]

The main heirs of Heikhalot mysticism were the Ashkenazic Ḥasidic masters of the twelfth and thirteenth centuries, who preserved the ancient texts, probably redacted parts of them, and, I assume, also continued the practice of their mystical techniques. Some of the figures related to Franco-Ashkenazic Jewish culture were regarded as "prophets"[112] or as having various types of intercourse with the higher worlds.[113] I should like to give here two significant examples of the acknowledgment of the existence of an ascent of the soul. It is reported of R. Mikhael the Angel, a middle-thirteenth century French figure, that

> [he] asked questions, and his soul ascended to heaven in order to seek [answers to] his doubts. He shut himself in a room for three days and ordered that it not be opened. But the men of his house peered between the gates[!], and they saw that his body was flung down like a stone. And so he laid for three days, shut in and motionless on his bed like a dead man. After three days he came to life and rose to his feet, and from thence on he was called R. Mikhael the Angel.[114]

Thus, the ascent heavenward was a technique to solve problems. The nature of the questions is not specified in this passage, but on the basis of the range of questions asked of heavenly instances, they may include both halakhic and theological issues. Even more interesting is the report regarding R. Mikhael's compatriot and older contemporary, R. 'Ezra of Moncontour. R. Moses Botarel mentions a tradition received from his father, R. Isaac, asserting: "The soul of the prophet from the city of Moncontour ascended to heaven and heard the living creatures singing before God a certain song;[115] and when he awoke he remembered this song and told his experience as it was, and they wrote down the song."[116]

This particular technique of composing verses is not, however, unique. The prominent early medieval *paytan* R. Eleazar ha-Kallir is described as having ascended to heaven and asked the Archangel Michael the manner in which the angels sing and how their songs are composed. Afterward he descended and composed a poem according to the same alphabetical order.[117] Interestingly, R. Eleazar ascended to heaven by the use of the divine name, an ascent technique attributed by Rashi to the four who entered *Pardes*[118]—no doubt an affinity expressing an attempt to include this famous poet among the *Merkavah* mystics. This also seems to be the tendency of another report concerning this poet; R. Zedakiah ben Abraham [119] states in the name of his father, who heard it from his masters, the Ashkenazic sages, that while R. Eleazar was composing his well-known poem, *The Fourfold Living Creatures,* "fire surrounded him." [120] This phrase has an obvious connection with the mystical study of sacred texts or discussions of *Merkavah* topics, particularly in the *Merkavah* tradition.[121] Again, in a third description of R. Eleazar, likewise of Ashkenazic origin, he is referred to as "the angel of God," [122] an epithet reminiscent of R. Mikhael mentioned above. Thus, R. 'Ezra of Moncontour's study in the celestial academy via the ascent of his soul, and his transmission of a poem he heard there, find close parallels in the tradition regarding a much earlier person, portrayed with the help of motifs connected with the *Merkavah* traditions.

The ascent of the soul gained a certain impetus from the Safedian Kabbalah onward. Its main hero, R. Isaac Luria, is reported as one

whose soul ascended nightly to the heavens, and whom the attending angels came to accompany to the celestial academy. They asked him: "To what academy do you wish to go?" Sometimes he said that he wished to visit the academy of R. Simeon bar Yoḥai, or the academy of R. 'Akiva or that of R. Eliezer the Great or those of other *tannaim* and *amoraim,* or of the prophets. And to whichever of those academies he wished to go, the angels would take him. The next day, he would disclose to the sages what he received in that academy.[123]

This quote reveals one of two ways by means of which the mystic may acquire supernal secrets of the Kabbalah: he may either ascend to study Torah together with ancient figures, as above, or else be taught by Elijah or others who descend in order to reveal Kabbalistic secrets, as we read in other texts concerning Luria.[124]

The frequency of heavenly ascent is indeed remarkable: every night Luria visited one of the celestial academies and thereafter transmitted the teachings to his students. This perception of Luria is no doubt closely connected to the huge amount of Kabbalistic material he communicated that produced the extensive Lurianic literature. Nor is the description of the celestial academies as the mystical source of this esoteric lore any novelty in Kabbalah. According to R. Shem Tov ibn Gaon, the mystic who sees divine visions is like one who dreams with eyes shut; once he opens his eyes, he forgets those visions and prefers death to life, as the ideal is[125] "to ascend from the lower academy to the supernal academy and to subsist from the splendor of the *Shekhinah*[126] and not worry about his sons or the members of his family, because of his great cleaving."

Significantly, immediately prior to this passage, R. Shem Tov mentions the need to fathom intellectually the secrets of the *Merkavah* and the structures of the Creation. The result is not only beatific or divine visions but also an impressive explosion of literary creativity, consisting in "copying" the contents revealed in his mind as if from a book.[127] The affinity of this description to Luria's own creativity is startling; we must remember that R. Shem Tov's work quoted above was partially composed in Safed, where he lived during his last years.

Such perceptions of the celestial academy as a source of mystical revelations recur in the visions of Solomon Molkho, at least one of which appears shortly after a reference to dream revelations.[128] Although these texts make no explicit mention of the ascent of the soul, I assume, from the fact that these were events connected to dreams, that we can infer in Molkho as well the existence of a visionary technique perceived as a spiritual ascent to a higher academy. Thus, Luria's portrayal as a mystic adept in these celestial universes is not an invention of Kabbalistic thought.

We find several discussions of spiritual ascent in the writings of Luria's main disciple, R. Ḥayyim Vital. In his mystical diary, he reported a dream of one of his acquaintances, R. Isaac Alatif, concerning himself, which Vital described as follows: [129]

Once I fainted deeply for an hour, and a huge number of old men and many women came to watch me, and the house was completely full of them, and they all were worried for me. Afterwards the swoon passed and I opened my eyes and said, "Know that just now my soul ascended to the seat of glory, and they sent my soul back to this world in order to preach before you and lead you in the way of repentance[130] and in matters of charity."

Although the dream itself concerns Vital, one cannot infer from it his own stand regarding this technique. Nevertheless, we can assume that the ascent to the seat of glory has a certain mystical implication, perhaps an effort to contemplate God, such as Vital attempted according to one of his dreams.[131] The cataleptic state here reminds one of the earlier description of R. Mikhael the Angel.

R. Israel Ba'al Shem Tov was well known for his practice of soul ascent. In the famous epistle to his brother-in-law, he relates: [132]

On *Rosh ha-Shanah* of the year 5507 [1746], I performed an incantation for the ascent of the soul, known to you. And in that vision I saw wondrous things, which I had never seen until then from the day that I became spiritually aware. And it is impossible to relate and to tell what I saw and learned in that ascent hither, even in private. But when I returned to the lower Paradise, I saw the souls of living and of dead persons, both of those with whom I was acquainted and of those with whom I was not acquainted . . . numberless, in a to-and-fro movement, ascending from one world to the other through the column[133] known to adepts in esoteric matters. . . . And I asked my teacher and master[134] that he come with me, and it is a great danger to go and ascend to the supernal worlds, whence I had never ascended since I acquired awareness, and these were mighty ascents. So I ascended degree after degree, until I entered the palace of the Messiah.

Thus, in 1746, R. Israel was already familiar with the practice of ascending heavenward. In order to attain this experience, which surpassed all his previous ascents, he made use of a device known also to his brother-in-law, R. Gershon of Kutow. The mystical nature of the revelations received by R. Israel is obvious, concerning as they did the eschatological meaning of the dissemination of his mystical teachings.[135] One of the anticipated results of the spread of Ḥasidic lore would be, the Messiah told R. Israel, that all Jews would become able to "perform yiḥudim and ascensions" as he did.[136] This inclusion of the ascent as a common ideal is highly significant; until then a privilege for a small elite, it was included in the Ḥasidic program to be diffused to a larger public.[137]

Another known ascent is that of 1750, introduced by the phrase "and on Rosh ha-Shanah 1750 I performed an ascent of soul, as is known."[138] From this epistle it seems obvious that the practice of spiritual ascent was a common experience for the founder of Ḥasidism. Indeed, he is described as disclosing to one of his followers that each night, when he ascended above, he was preceded by R. Ḥayyim ben 'Atar, his older contemporary and a paragon of Eastern Jewish mysticism. According to R. Israel, ben 'Atar was more rapid in his ascent, although he considered himself superior to the Moroccan sage.[139]

As we have seen above, in his own opinion at least two of R. Israel's contemporaries either practiced this mystical technique or—as in the case of R. Gershon—were aware of its details. Moreover, this list can easily be expanded to include at least one leading figure of R. Israel's entourage. R. Yeḥiel Mikhael of Zloczow, a student of the Besht and of the Great Maggid, was portrayed by R. Abraham Joshua Heschel of Apt as sleeping for only two reasons, one of them being his wish to ascend to heaven.[140] In the generations immediately following the death of the Besht, the importance of such spiritual ascents of the soul was manifestly attenuated. In lieu of this mystical technique, commonly connected with the state of sleep or of dreaming, the major students of the Great Maggid preferred mystical activities performed in a waking state.

During the mid-nineteenth century, however, there was a revival of interest in spiritual ascent. In some of R. Isaac Yehudah Yeḥiel Safrin's writings, R. Israel's ascents are mentioned and elaborated upon far more than in Ḥasidic writings of the preceding hundred years. R. Israel is portrayed as attaining spiritual perfections, and he mentions, inter alia, "the ascents of the soul and ascents to *Pardes*" and "the apprehensions of R. 'Akiva and his companions."[141] The affinity between ascent of the soul and ascent to the *Merkavah* or to *Pardes* is self-evident. We can easily perceive the connection between the two also in Safrin's *Heikal ha-Berakhah,* in which the journey of the four who entered *Pardes* is described as a celestial ascent, taking place after one had stripped himself of corporeality and uncleanness.[142] In contrast to the ancient discussion of the *Pardes* journey in which the ascent seems to have taken place *in corpore,* for Safrin it is a spiritual experience. Moreover, according to this Ḥasidic master, even Moses' ascent to receive the Torah was an ascent of the soul. In his commentary on the *Zohar,* he interprets Moses' abstention from eating and drinking for forty days in a way reminiscent of the description of R. Mikhael the Angel. The body of Moses, he states:[143]

was thrown in the cloud with but little vitality,[144] as it is for all those who practice ascents of the soul, such as our master R. Israel the Besht, and others like him. [But] their body is thrown down like a stone for only a short hour or two, no more; however, Moses' body was thrown down for forty days and [the vitality] returned to it after forty days, and he was [again] alive.

Moses was thus the incomparable master of ascent of the soul, as he sustained his mystical experience for an uncommonly long period and nevertheless returned to life.[145] Thus, even the receiving of the Torah is seen as accomplished by the help of this mystical technique. No wonder that R. Isaac Safrin himself practiced it. In his mystical diary, he confessed:[146]

I performed a *yiḥud* and linked myself with the soul of our divine master, Isaac Luria. And from this union I was overcome by sleep, and I saw several souls until I was overwhelmed by awe and fear and trembling, as was my custom. And from this it seemed that I shall rise to greatness.[147] And I ascended further and I saw R. [Abraham] Joshua Heschel . . . and I awakened.

This experience was doubtless closely related to that of R. Israel Ba'al Shem Tov. It is rare, however, for a later mystic to confess that he seemingly employed this technique in order to communicate with the souls of the dead. In any event, as late as 1845,[148] this ancient practice remained viable enough to be used.

Even a superficial examination of the above material will yield the impression that nearly all of the medieval authors mentioned above in connection with heavenly journeys were of Franco-Ashkenazic extraction. I know of no Sephardic mystic involved in this type of mystical technique: Vital's report might have been the result of Luria's influence, while R. Ḥayyim ben 'Atar's practice of this technique, as attested by the Besht, is uncorroborated by authentic evidence from his writings or other independent testimonies.[149] It is difficult to determine if this is a mere coincidence or whether this sequence of Ashkenazic authors who reported on ascent of the soul can be described as a continuous tradition. I tend to accept the second possibility, notwithstanding the serious gap between the evidence for the twelfth and thirteenth centuries and Luria. Interestingly, the extant material concerning the technique of weeping would seem to suggest a pattern similar to that of the ascent technique. In that case, the only exception seems to be in my proposed understanding of the *Zohar* passage; otherwise, we find only persons who were Ashkenazic by origin or under obvious Ashkenazic influence, such as Berukhim or Vital. This conclusion holds true also in the case of a practice of oneiric divination: the majority of earliest European evidences for the usages of *She'elat Ḥalom* are of Ashkenazic origin. As we shall see in the following section, Abraham Abulafia's mystical technique also derives from Ashkenazic sources. We may therefore infer that the Ashkenazic provinces were an important source of older esoteric traditions—in our case, mystical techniques[150]—which were at times accepted and adopted by Spanish Kabbalah, whereas others remained the patrimony of Ashkenazic culture alone. This conclusion holds true not only for the movement of these techniques from the Rhineland to Provence and Spain but also for the transmission of important segments of Kabbalah in general, a point to be elaborated elsewhere.

IV. COMBINATION OF LETTERS OF THE DIVINE NAME

Ongoing recitations of letters and divine names are well-known techniques for the attainment of paranormal states of consciousness; they are used alike by Christian,[151] Muslim,[152] Hindu,[153] and Japanese[154] mystics. Most, if not all, of these techniques seem to operate upon the consciousness of the mystic by enabling him to focus his attention upon a short phrase or sentence—"There is no God but Allah," "Jesus Christ," "*Namou Amida Boutso*"—or even a few letters, as in the

Hindu *Aum*. This relatively simple device is comparable to fixing one's vision upon a point;[155] the mystic must escape the impact of external factors, and in this respect his activity is similar to that of someone undergoing sensory deprivation.

Ancient Jewish sources, primarily those of Heikhalot literature, present a technique closely parallel to those found in non-Jewish forms of mysticism.[156] These affinities become evident when one compares some of the details shared by the Jewish and non-Jewish techniques. In another type of Jewish technique, however, the psychological result is different, given the discrepancy between this technique and its parallels on one important issue—namely, the use by Jewish mystics of a complex and intricate system of letters to be pronounced or meditated upon. Instead of the simple formulas of non-Jewish techniques, the Jewish texts evince elaborate combinations of letters with hundreds of components. Moreover, as we shall see, according to Jewish practice the mystic had not only to pronounce them according to strict, fixed patterns but had also actively to construct these combinations as part of the mystical practice. The effect of combinatory techniques was the result both of the process of their utterance and of the hyperactivation of the mind required to produce the contents that were pronounced. These monotonous repetitions of well-known phrases or divine names thus achieved not a calmness or stillness of the mind but rather a high excitation of the mental processes, triggered by the unceasing need to combine letters, their vocalizations, and various bodily acts—movements of the head or hands or respiratory devices.[157] Although superficially similar to a variety of mystical techniques based upon language, the Kabbalistic practice possessed an idiosyncratic psychological mechanism, only rarely occurring in such techniques. I shall briefly discuss here some sources concerning the pronunciation or repetition of divine names—a practice paralleled in non-Jewish techniques; I shall then discuss the medieval use of combinations of letters, which differs significantly from the more ancient technique.

It is a striking fact that a detailed and systematic technique of letter combination forming the divine name appears for the first time in a work of R. Eleazar of Worms and, under his influence, among Spanish Kabbalists. More than in the other examples of mystical techniques attested by Franco-German sources prior to their appearance in Spanish Kabbalah, in this case there are reliable indications that the repercussions of this technique in Spain were directly connected to the Ashke-nazic culture.[158] Abraham Abulafia explicitly mentions R. Eleazar's works as books he had studied; thus, the transition can easily be proven.[159] The other two Kabbalists of the late thirteenth and fourteenth centuries acquainted with combination techniques—R. Joseph ben Sha-lom Ashkenazi and R. David ben Yehudah he-Ḥasid—were either Ash-kenazic by origin (the former) or had visited Germany (the latter).[160] We can reasonably conclude, then, that the mystical techniques surveyed below passed from Germany to Spain. According to the historical evi-dence, this movement took place only from the middle of the thirteenth century, thereby excluding Provençal and most Catalan theosophical Kabbalah from its influence. Thus, in contrast to the Ashkenazic influ-ence on the emergence of the Kabbalah in those centers with regard to theosophical issues, this mystical technique was cultivated in Spanish circles relatively late. The delay can be understood in terms of the topic's esoteric nature, a feature that seems to be corroborated by the fact that, even centuries after R. Eleazar of Worms had recorded some details of this technique, they remained in manuscript, as did the mystical hand-books of Abulafia and his disciples.[161]

Several indications of recitations of names—either angelic or divine—are extant in Heikhalot literature.[162] These recitations, as we have seen above, were still practiced during the Gaonic period.[163] There is conclu-sive evidence that the pronunciation of mystical names was known and cultivated in Germany, at least during the lifetime of R. Eleazar of Worms. The anonymous author of *Sefer ha-Ḥayyim*[164] indicates: "He pronounces the holy names or names of the angels in order to be shown [whatever] he wishes, or to inform him of a hidden matter, and then the Holy Spirit reveals itself to him, and his flesh . . . trembles . . . because of the strength of the Holy Spirit."[165]

The fiery attack by R. Moshe of Taku, written shortly after the *floruit* of R. Eleazar, is highly instructive. He speaks of persons "void of understanding" and "heretics who pose as[166] prophets and are accus-tomed to pronouncing the holy names; and sometimes, they direct [their heart] when they read them [pronounce the names] and their soul is terrified. . . . But when the power of the pronounced name leaves him, he returns to his initial state of confused reason."

These statements provide appropriate background to understand R. Eleazar's statement that neither the divine names nor their vocalizations ought to be written down, lest those "devoid of understanding" use them.[167] R. Eleazar's fears can easily be understood in light of the criticism of a more conservative figure such as Taku; significantly, both use the same phrase, *haserey da'at*, in order to describe those who make use of the divine names. R. Eleazar, however, confesses that[168] "some future things and spirits were revealed to us by means of the [divine?] attributes[169] through the pronunciations of the depths of the names[170] in order to know the spirit of the wisdoms."

The use of the phrase "revealed to us" clearly shows that this refers to a practical technique, not a repetition of no longer active formulas;[171] therefore, the three above-mentioned statements, like the analogous evidence in the preceding section concerning the ascent of soul, are conclusive proof of the experiential use of the pronunciation of divine names. The names cited by R. Eleazar shortly before the above text are mystical names already occurring in Jewish texts related to Heikhalot literature, such as *Adiriron, Bihriron,* and so on.[172] Moreover, the assertion of this Ashkenazic Hasidic master that each of the forty-two letters of the divine name is a divine name in itself obviously reflects an ancient Jewish conception.[173] It is therefore reasonable to assume that R. Eleazar preserved ancient mystical material and techniques that had been passed down to Spanish Kabbalists via the intermediacy of Ashkenazic masters, the most important of whom, Abraham Abulafia, elaborated upon the received traditions in a relatively detailed fashion.[174] Abulafia also explicitly refers to Heikhalot literature as an important source of his use of divine names.[175] Before entering into a brief presentation of Abulafia, however, I should like to discuss the influence on two important Kabbalists who flourished in Spain of a peculiar pattern of combination of divine letters occurring in R. Eleazar. In his *Sefer ha-Shem,*[176] R. Eleazar discusses the combination of the letters of the Tetragrammaton with each of the letters of the alphabet.[177] Moreover, these combinations are in turn combined with their vocalizations by two of the six vowels.

R. Eleazar explains the combinations of these letters only on the cosmological and theological levels, with no reference to their possible use as a mystical technique. However, the fact that not only letters but also vowels are included in this table points to a praxis of pronunciation. Against the background of the earlier evidence concerning R. Eleazar's revelation using divine names, and the fact that he perceived their vocalization as connected with the use of these names, we can infer that, notwithstanding his silence, the author conceived these combinations as a mystical practice. This assumption is corroborated by a description of the creation of a *golem* (the vivification of a humanlike form made out of clay) by R. Eleazar, in which he wrote that we must pronounce all the letters of the alphabet over every limb of the *golem,* combined with one of the letters of the Tetragrammaton and vocalized according to the six vowels mentioned above.[178] Thus, despite the author's silence, the table found in *Sefer ha-Shem* was meant to be pronounced as part of a magical praxis for the creation of a *golem* by a certain incantation of combinations of letters. According to Scholem, this technique can culminate in ecstasy.[179] This assumption seems to be corroborated by R. Eleazar's confession that he received a revelation by means of the divine names.

R. Eleazar's letter combinations were copied by R. David ben Yehudah he-Ḥasid, who presumably learned them during his visit in Regensburg.[180] He, however, considered the thirty-six combinations and vocalizations to be paralleled by the thirty-six movements of the *lulav,* an issue I was unable to locate in Ashkenazic texts. R. David's contemporary, R. Joseph Ashkenazi, an important source for some of his Kabbalistic ideas, elaborated upon R. Eleazar's table in his *Commentary on Genesis Rabbah*[181] and in an unidentified discussion of the creation of a *golem.*[182] These two Kabbalists do not, strictly speaking, belong to the ecstatic Kabbalah; however, both of them were interested in combinatory techniques, as indicated in their works. R. Joseph quoted Abraham Abulafia's *Commentary on Sefer Yeẓirah* and, as we shall see in the next section, preserved an important text on ecstasy and visualization of the divine names;[183] R. David apparently received revelations of Elijah.[184] Although I cannot conclusively describe these Kabbalists as following the mystical technique of R. Eleazar, the supposition that they were more than mere repositories of the Ashkenazic master's views seems a reasonable one.

There is little room for doubt as to the use of R. Eleazar's technique of combination for mystical purposes by his older contemporary, R. Abraham Abulafia. In his mystical handbook, *'Or ha-Sekhel,* one finds a similar table, albeit in slightly changed form: instead of six basic vowels, Abulafia prefers only five; thus, his tables consist of twenty-five basic combinations of letters and vowels.[185] As in R. Eleazar, Abulafia's table is no more than a sample for the recitation of the combinations of all twenty-two letters, combined with the four letters of the Tetragrammaton. According to this table, the pronunciation of the divine name involves many sublime matters, and whoever does not take care when performing it endangers himself. For this reason, asserts Abulafia, the ancient masters concealed it. But the time has now come to reveal it, since, as he says, the messianic eon has begun.[186] Abulafia's assessment is indeed interesting: he argues that he merely reveals a hidden technique that has been in existence for a long time. This assertion strengthens the earlier assumption that R. Eleazar's table was intended to serve mystical, and not only magical, purposes.

Abulafia was more than a Kabbalist who disclosed esoteric techniques; his 'Or he-Sekhel was an attempt to integrate this technique into a speculative system including a philosophy of language and a definition of the ultimate goal of the technique—the attainment of unio mystica.[187] Thus, he succeeded in imposing an elaborate mystical technique on a larger public, as convincingly indicated by the relatively large number of manuscripts of 'Or ha-Sekhel.[188] In early sixteenth-century Jerusalem, R. Yehudah Albotini composed a mystical handbook, Sullam ha-'Aliyah, based upon Abulafia's techniques, including among other things the tables found in 'Or ha-Sekhel.[189] Moreover, Abulafia's tables, accompanied by some of his explanations, were quoted in one of the classics of Kabbalistic literature, Cordovero's Pardes Rimmonim.[190] Significantly, this Safedian Kabbalist begins his extensive discussion of pronunciation of the divine name with Abulafia's system,[191] afterward mentioning that of R. Eleazar of Worms, copied from a secondary source.[192] As we learn from the testimony of R. Mordecai Dato, a disciple of Cordovero, his master, influenced by Abulafia's works beyond their quotation, practiced Abulafian techniques and taught them to his students.[193] Furthermore, he regarded Abulafia's technique as a "Kabbalistic tradition transmitted orally, or the words of a Maggid [celestial messenger]."[194] It is no wonder, then, that he considered Abulafia's type of Kabbalah as superior even to that of the Zohar.[195] Cordovero, however, not only contributed to the dissemination of Abulafia's tables, as he did with those of R. Eleazar; quoting Abulafia's explanations, he also propagated the view that the union of the human and divine minds was to be achieved through this technique,[196] which, as Abulafia put it, "draws down the supernal force in order to cause it to be united with you."[197] This Hermetical understanding of Abulafia's

technique[198] had an important influence on the Hasidic perception of
devekut as attained by causing divine spiritual force to descend upon the
mystic.[199] Strangely, the old Ashkenazic mystical technique had to travel
throughout Spain and Italy, as well as Safed, before it eventually returned to Ashkenazic mysticism.

I have surveyed the history of one combinatory technique. A few
others, connected with the recitation of the alphabet according to the
permutations of letters given in *Sefer Yeẓirah,* were used both by R.
Eleazar of Worms and by Abulafia.[200] The latter presented several elaborate techniques in his other handbooks: *Sefer Ḥayye ha-'Olam ha-Ba,*
Sefer ha-Ḥeshek and *Sefer 'Imrei Shefer.* This willingness to propose
more than one technique as a suitable path for attaining a mystical
experience is decisive proof that Abulafia transcended the magical perception shared by the mystics that there was one and only one way to
attain the supreme experience. Although his various techniques shared
some elements in common, such as the need for isolation, breathing
exercises, bodily movements, and the wearing of clean garments, they
differed in many basic details. Abulafia also cultivated the pronunciation
of letters of the divine names inscribed variously in different kinds of
circles, a technique having nothing to do with the table technique mentioned above. These circles consisted of permutations of some of the
biblical and later divine names according to different combinatory techniques; the use of circles is also conspicuous in *Ḥayye ha-'Olam ha-Ba,*
which was aptly designated *The Book of Circles.*[201] No wonder, then,
that one of the most elaborate visions reported by Abulafia is that of a
circle, a Kabbalistic mandala including both cosmic and psychological
structures.[202] Interestingly, the vision of circles recurs in the works of
other ecstatic Kabbalists, who used Abulafian or similar techniques of
combinations of letters, such as R. Isaac of Acre, R. Shem Tov ibn Gaon,
and R. Elnathan ben Moses Kalkis.[203]

In *'Or ha-Sekhel* Abulafia emphasizes, more than does R. Eleazar in
his works, that his tables, as well as his circles, are methods for facilitat-
ing all possible combinations of the letters of the divine names. These
letters are sometimes permutated without adding other letters; at other
times—as in the table—the entire alphabet is used in order to pronounce the letters of divine names. Although the pronunciation of the
Tetragrammaton was conceived as a transgression of both biblical and
rabbinic interdictions, there was no attack on Abulafia's technique on

this ground in the Kabbalistic material with which I am acquainted. Although it is a conspicuously anomian technique, the recitation of letters as described by Abulafia managed to escape the fierce criticism to which his prophetic and messianic activities were subjected.

We can summarize this short survey of one of Abulafia's techniques by stating that the incorporation of R. Eleazar's method of combination of letters into the Spanish Kabbalah fertilized it by allowing for the construction of a more elaborate technical path intended to attain mystical goals such as revelations and union with supernal beings. This technique remained the patrimony of a few, albeit important, Kabbalists, contributing to the emergence of extreme types of mystical experiences.

V. VISUALIZATION OF COLORS AND KABBALISTIC PRAYER

The final type of mystical technique to be surveyed here is a nomian one relating to a particular understanding of the Kabbalistic meaning of *kavvanah*—that is, that intention which, according to the Talmud, should accompany the performance of the commandments. In Provence and Catalonia, the Kabbalists had already emphasized the mystical significance of such intention; it was no doubt connected to the theosophical system of Sefirot, toward which the Kabbalist was to direct his thought throughout prayer.[204] The basic assumption of earlier Kabbalah, which remained unchanged for centuries, was that the words of prayer were symbols of the supernal divine potencies and hence could serve either as starting points for the contemplation of higher entities or as ways of influencing them, or as both together.

According to this understanding, *kavvanah* effects an elevation of human thought from the words of prayer to the sefirotic realm, apparently achieved without any intermediary mental operation or external factor. The intrinsic affinity of language to its sources in the divine realm enables human thought to ascend to the Sefirot and to act upon them.[205] Externally, the Kabbalist is supposed to recite the standard prayer text; the mystical *kavvanah* is an additional activity, in no way intended to change the halakhic regulations of prayer.[206] Mystical *kavvanah* can therefore be defined as a nomian technique, using as it does the common prayers as a vehicle for accomplishing mystical and theurgical aims.

But this presentation of mystical prayer fails to answer certain basic questions concerning the psychological processes enabling the shift from language to Sefirot. Is concentration on the symbolic connotations of a given word the only mental operation that ensures the mystical elevation of thought? How does the linguistic medium, corporeal in both its written and its oral forms, enable human thought or soul to penetrate utterly spiritual dimensions of reality? Can *kavvanah* be regarded as an attempt to interiorize the supernal pattern of Sefirot in some unknown way in order to cleave to and be capable of influencing it?[207] No answers to these and similar questions regarding the psychological aspects of *kavvanah* have been proposed, since they were evidently never asked by academic research. I cannot propose an answer or even a range of alternative answers, as the material involving the technical part of *kavvanah* is very scanty. No descriptions of the stages of *kavvanah* are extant, nor are confessions concerning the inner changes in one's consciousness provided by early Kabbalists. I suppose that we can view this technique as involving an extensive process of deautomatization, every word being pronounced not as part of an automatically performed prayer but in a meticulous way.[208] The Kabbalist would direct his attention toward both the precise pronunciation of the sounds and their symbolic significance.

I should like to elaborate here upon a far more complex technique that was part of Kabbalistic prayer—namely, the enactment of *kavvanah* through the visualization of colors as part of traditional prayer. What follows is a sampling of some significant texts treating these issues out of several score that I have identified, almost all in manuscripts, and that I hope will be printed and analyzed in detail elsewhere. Let me start with a brief historical survey of the emergence of the technique.[209] Early Kabbalistic discussion of prayer never mentioned the visualization of colors in general nor in connection with prayer in particular.[210] With the exception of a single text attributed (in my opinion spuriously)[211] to an eary Kabbalist—R. 'Azriel of Gerona[212]—even the question of the experience of light or lights in prayer is absent in texts composed in the first three quarters of the thirteenth century.[213] The earliest texts explicitly referring to this technique are those connected to the name of R. David ben Yehudah he-Hasid, a Spanish Kabbalist of the late thirteenth and early fourteenth centuries.[214]

R. David[215] said: We are not allowed to visualize the ten Sefirot, except in accordance with the *rashey perakim* which reach you, such as *Magen David* to *Hesed* and *Honen ha-Da'at*[216] to *Tiferet*. Therefore, you should always visualize that color which is [attributed to the Sefirah according to] the *rashey perakim*, that color being the *ḥashmal* of the Sefirah, the *ḥashmal* being the covering[217] [or dress] of that very Sefirah around [it]. Afterward you shall draw [downward] by your visualization the efflux from "the depth of the river" to the worlds down to us—and this is the true [way], received [in an esoteric manner] by oral tradition.

According to R. David, any attempt to visualize the Sefirot themselves is forbidden; instead, we must visualize their colors. For this reason, the focus of human activity during Kabbalistic prayer was not upon the sefirotic domain but rather upon the realm of colors produced by the creative imagination of the Kabbalists. These imaginary colors, being the "covering" of the Sefirot, formed a lower ontological level open to human contemplation and manipulation. The exact relationship between the fact that the colors were humanly created and their ontic status as surrounding the Sefirot is not altogether clear; it may have related to the world of lights emanating from the Sefirot according to the theosophy of the anonymous author of *Tikkuney Zohar* and *Ra'ya Meheimna*.[218] The peculiar correspondences between the Sefirot and their parallels in the imaginative world of colors appear in a highly esoteric tradition that was transmitted orally, and even then only in an abbreviated form or in notes—*rashey perakim*. The aim of this type of prayer was obviously theurgic; by means of the process of visualization, the Kabbalist drew the efflux from the supernal realm to the world under it and finally into our world. We can therefore surmise that the process of visualization enabled the ascent of the Kabbalist's imaginative faculty to a higher ontological level, and only afterward could he attract the divine efflux downward.[219]

Before proceeding to the description of this technique of prayer, I should like to discuss briefly two texts that seem to me to be highly significant for understanding the mystical nature of visualization of colors. From the conceptual point of view, the closest Kabbalistic system of thought to this appears in the writings of R. Joseph ben Shalom Ashkenazi, also called R. Joseph ha-'Arokh, a late-thirteenth-century Kabbalist who emigrated from Germany to Barcelona.[220] The affinities are unmistakable, some already having been noted by Scholem.[221] This Kabbalist affirmed: [222]

The philosophers have already written on the issue of prophecy, saying that it is not improbable that there will be a person to whom matters will appear in his imaginative faculty, comparable to that which appears to the imaginative faculty in a dream. All this [could take place] while someone is awake, and all his senses are obliterated, as the letters of the divine name [stand] in front of his eyes,[223] in the gathered colors.[224] Sometimes, he will hear a voice,[225] a wind, a speech, a thunder, and a noise with all the organs of his hearing sense, and he will see with his imaginative faculty with all the organs of sight, and he will smell with all the organs of smell, and he will taste with all the organs of taste, and he will touch with all the organs of touch, and he will walk and levitate.[226] All this while the holy letters are in front of his eyes, and its colors are covering[227] it; this is the sleep[228] of prophecy.

The problems posed by this text are numerous and complex. From our perspective, it is important only to stress the occurrence of colors in close connection with the divine name and the fact that an altered state of consciousness is induced by the appearance of these colored letters. Although it is not obvious from a first reading of the passage, it seems plausible to surmise that the letters and their colors emerge as the result of the activation of the imagination—that is, that their appearance is the result of an effort of visualization. The difference between the occurrence of the Sefirot in R. David and of the divine name in R. Joseph is obvious, although not as significant. For the Kabbalist, the divine name and its letters are among the most common symbols of the ten Sefirot; moreover—and this is a decisive proof of the affinity between these two Kabbalists on the issue of colors—R. Joseph repeatedly refers to the symbolism of color for Sefirot in his writings, far more than did any of the preceding Kabbalists.[229] Highly interesting is his description of the contemplation of the "prophet" or "unifier" *(meyaḥed)*, who looks to the "holy lights" that, however, appear and disappear intermittently. According to this passage, the colors are by-products of the increasing inner movement of the Sefirot and therefore are constantly changing.[230] They seem to be entities "standing" in front of the prophet's eyes in a relatively steady manner. The psychological state described is very close to one of anesthesia, allowing for the arousal of the faculty—imagination—which can now mold the sense perceptions by their activation from within; for the Kabbalist—who bases himself on philosophers—this state is tantamount to prophecy. For the time being, we can conclude that, in the view of R. Joseph Ashkenazi, the visualization of letters and colors is a technique for achieving the prophetic state.

Let us turn now to another Kabbalist, otherwise unknown, who indicates that[231] "when you vocalize *Devarekha*,[232] you shall visualize[233] in your thought, the letter of the Tetragrammaton before your eyes, in a circle [or sphere] with a color red as the fire, and your thought is performing many things." This passage constitutes solid evidence that the Kabbalists practiced visualization of the Tetragrammaton in colors. Hence, our understanding of R. Joseph Ashkenazi's first text quoted above is corroborated by this additional source. R. Tanḥum describes a circle, including a visualized Tetragrammaton, vocalized with the vowels of the word *Devarekha* and the color "red as the fire." This circle, or at least a similar one to that described by Tanḥum, is evidently extant in a manuscript.[234] As I have shown elsewhere, just before and after this circle, this manuscript includes Kabbalistic material stemming from the writings of R. Joseph Ashkenazi and R. David ben Yehudah he-Ḥasid.[235] The circle consists of a diagram containing ten concentric circles, each one representing a Sefirah whose name is inscribed on it and beside which is the name of the color corresponding to the Sefirah and a vocalized Tetragrammaton. Thus, next to the Sefirah *Gevurah* we read the phrase "red as the fire" and a vocalization of the Tetragrammaton identical with that of *Devarekha*. We can therefore assume that the list of colors and the vocalization of the Tetragrammaton in the concentric circles constitute detailed instructions for visualizing the Tetragrammaton in various colors corresponding to the Sefirot. We can furthermore assume that this list is at least some part of the "notes" mentioned by R. David when he wrote, "you shall always visualize according to that color which is [attributed to] the Sefirah [according to] the *rashey perakim*.

On the basis of this material, as well as of other material there is not room for here, I consider the existence of traditions dealing with visualization of colors, as well as their actual practice, an established fact. But before returning to the subject of mystical prayer, I should like to discuss the significance of the circle. In the Kabbalistic material accompanying this figure, there are no instructions regarding either the role it may fulfill or the meaning of the various details inscribed within the circles. The way in which R. Tanḥum refers to the circle, however, opens the possibility that we can envision not only the details as instructions for visualization but also the circle itself as part of this process. R. Tanḥum states, "You shall visualize the letter of the Tetragrammaton before your eyes in a circle in your thought," and so on. I see no reasonable argument against interpreting his words as a recommendation for visualizing the divine name along with the color and the circle. If this understanding is correct, then the circle can be regarded as a Kabbalistic mandala incorporating the colors corresponding to the ten divine powers, the Sefirot, and their names. Interestingly, this diagram draws a distinction between the first Sefirah, *Keter,* and the other nine, designated as *Ze'ir 'Anpin*—the lower divine configuration according to zoharic symbolism. The latter is an obvious anthropomorphic symbol, which in the *Zohar* refers to the second and lower divine head, that consisting of the Sefirah of *Tiferet* alone or of the Sefirot between *Ḥokh- mah* and *Yesod,* whereas in the works of R. David it includes ten Sefirot or, as in the diagram, nine.[236] In other contexts of R. David's thought, this configuration is manifestly anthropomorphic; the fact that the con- cept appearing in the diagram differs from that of the *Zohar* does not obliterate its anthropomorphic character. If the understanding proposed above is correct, then the process of visualization includes not only divine names, colors, and a circle or circles but also an anthropomorphic configuration symbolizing an aspect of the divine realm. The outer circle is the well-known list of thirty-two mystical paths by means of which the world was created, and the second circle contains the names of all the realms of reality—for example, stones, planets, spheres, angels, and various kinds of living creatures, such as fish, animals, and man. It is obvious that the compiler wished to express the idea of the macrocosmos that stands beside the divine macranthropos.

The phenomenological affinity between this diagram and the Hindu mandala is interesting. The two practices share the process of visualiza- tion and of imaginary representation of divine forces and colors; in both cases the circle also has a macrocosmic aspect.[237] There are also clear differences, however: the Kabbalistic diagram is graphically different from those forms of mandala that I could see, their details are conspicu- ously unrelated, and the construction of a mandala is accompanied by a special liturgy, whereas I would suppose that the visualization of the Kabbalistic diagram accompanies Jewish ritualistic prayer. These differ- ences notwithstanding, one cannot underrate the possibility that Hindu traditions infiltrated into Kabbalah, perhaps via the intermediacy of Sufi material. As I hope to show elsewhere, R. David lived for a time in Acre, a fact that may be a clue to the penetration of an alien mystical technique into a Jewish milieu.

Let us return now to colors and prayer; the previous assumption that the diagram contained the "notes" mentioned in R. David's text can be substantiated by the comparison of the details about Sefirot and colors with a short anonymous commentary on the prayer *Shema' Yisrael.* This highly interesting document is based upon the visualization of the divine names included in this prayer in various colors, most of which correspond to the list of colors and Sefirot in the diagram. Since the similarity between the colors and Sefirot in the diagram and the commentary is astonishing, including the peculiar ways used for denoting the colors, the conclusion that the diagram list was intended to supply instructions for visualization of divine names in prayer is inescapable. I shall give here only one sentence to exemplify this conclusion: "Don't pronounce the word *Israel* until one visualizes the divine name, which is *YHWH,* with its vowels and its color, and one visualizes it as if the last letter of the [divine] name, namely *H,* surrounds the entire world, from above and below."[238]

We learn that the visualization of the letters and colors is accompanied by the vision of the letters as circles that bear explicit macrocosmic overtones. The vision of the letters as circles is probably not identical with the diagram; this difference notwithstanding, this is incontrovertible evidence that, during prayer, not only were colors visualized but also circles. Our previous understanding of the diagram as a mandala is thus partially confirmed by the anonymous commentary on the *Shema' Yisrael.* Moreover, the pronunciation of the first Tetragrammaton in this prayer ought to be directed[239] "to *Binah* in the color of green, like the color of the rainbow, the entire [divine] name." Compare this to the diagram in which the third Sefirah corresponds to the color "green as the rainbow."[240] Finally, the following passage from a Kabbalistic responsum[241] dealing with prayer illuminates the purpose of visualization as perceived by the Kabbalists themselves:[242]

When you shall think upon something which points to the *Keter* and pronounce it with your mouth, you shall direct [your thought] to and visualize the name *YHWH* between your eyes with this vocalization, which is the *Kammaz* under all the consonants, its visualization being white as snow.[243] And he will direct [your thought] so that the letters will move and fly in the air, and the whole secret is hinted at in the verse, "I have set the divine name always before me."[244]

According to this passage, the visualized colored letters are meant to ascend.[245] Thus, human imagination is ontologically creative, its products being able to ascend to the supernal *Merkavah.* This peculiar ascent may elucidate the allusion of R. Tanḥum that, by the means of visualized divine names, "your thought is performing many things"; this performance is accomplished by drawing the influx downward into the lower worlds and finally into our world, as stated at the end of R. David's passage.

The two different results of visualization of colored divine names can be summarized as follows: according to R. Joseph Ashkenazi, it induces a paranormal state of consciousness, and hence this technique can be appropriately regarded as a mystical practice. The second result is a theurgic one: if my reconstruction of the process of causing the letters to ascend and enabling the descent of the divine influx is correct according to this Kabbalistic school, then imagination is fraught with theurgic powers.

This Kabbalistic technique has passed unnoticed by modern scholarship. One of the major reasons for this is the fact that none of the texts dealing with the details of visualization is extant; they are available only in manuscripts that are, at the present time, generally ignored by scholars. This situation is not a matter of mere chance but rather a result of the technique's highly esoteric nature. A few statements will demonstrate this esotericism.

Underneath the diagram, we read: "All these allusions must be transmitted orally"—a wording virtually identical with that found at the end of R. David's passage quoted earlier.[246] Even more impressive are the statements of the anonymous author of the Kabbalistic responsum; I shall quote here only a part of his elaborations on the esoteric nature of the visualization: [247] "Know that this is a Kabbalistic tradition which was handed down to you, and we are writing it down, [but] it is forbidden to disclose it or to pass it down to everyone, but [only] to 'those who fear the divine name and take heed of his name,' [248] blessed be he, 'who tremble at his word.' "[249]

Owing to this atmosphere of mystery, the details of the technique of visualization remained hidden in fragments of various manuscripts; nevertheless, it was hardly neglected by the Kabbalists. My brief exposition of some of its texts, which represent only the initial stage of its crystallization, can be complemented by a longer historical survey, which is not possible here. I shall refer now only to some milestones of its evolution.

As I have attempted to show elsewhere, R. David ben Yehudah he-

Hasid's extensive commentary on prayer, *'Or Zaru'a,* was composed as an exoteric Kabbalistic commentary, esoterically alluding to the performance of prayer with the help of visualization technique.[250] On the ground of several fragments elaborating on prayer and visualization, I conjecture that its practice was cultivated in the Kabbalistic school of R. David ben Yehudah he-Hasid, which is characterized by the transmission of additional esoteric issues.[251] This technique was well known to the generation of Kabbalists who were exiled from the Iberian Peninsula and came to Jerusalem and Safed, as we learn from the existence of a handbook for visualization known in these cities.[252] R. Moses Cordovero was well acquainted with this technique, as we learn from his *Pardes Rimmonim:*

> It is good and fitting if he wishes to visualize these *havvayot* [that is, the different vocalizations of the Tetragrammaton] according to their color, as then his prayer will be very effective, on the condition that his [mystical] intention is that there is no other possible way to represent the activity of a certain attribute [but] the certain [corresponding] color. And as the colors in the gate of colors are many, we shall not discuss here the colors. But when he is interested to direct [his prayer], behold that gate which is before [the eyes] of the disciple.[253]

The effectiveness of visualized colors is here, for the first time, hinted at in a Kabbalistic treatise that was intended to be studied by a larger public; the details, however, were not delivered. The last major Kabbalistic figure to mention the technique of visualization is R. Hayyim Vital. In the unprinted part of his *Sha'arey Kedushah,* he gives a text, which was partly discussed above, ending with the ascent of thought to the highest firmament, the *'Aravot,* where[254] "he shall visualize that above the firmament of *'Aravot* there is a very great white curtain, upon which the Tetragrammaton is inscribed in [color] white as snow,[255] in Assyrian writing in a certain color." I cannot explain how one can visualize white letters on a white curtain, nor why a "certain color" is mentioned in addition to the white one. Whatever the explanation, it is clear from this that Vital was interested in color visualization, as is evident also from the fact that he twice copied the aforementioned passage of R. Joseph Ashkenazi.[256]

At this point, it would be pertinent to compare the technique of visualization with that of letter combination. In both, the letters of the divine names are crucial; the letters visualized, however, are always those of the Tetragrammaton, which maintain their regular order—a significant difference from the continuous changes in the positions of the letters in Abulafia's technique. The fluctuating element in the visualization technique is that of the vowels, which change together with the colors, according to most of the passages referring to visualization. Moreover, the visualizer is not supposed to write down the divine names nor to pronounce them, as Abulafia would recommend. Visualization is a process to be accomplished in addition to regular prayer and concomitant with it, whereas Abulafia's practices are independent of the Jewish rites.

Notwithstanding its novelty in the field of Kabbalah, then, the mystical interpretation of *kavvanah* became a sacrosanct technique that was absent from the early Kabbalah insofar as we know. Although the early Kabbalists discussed the problem of *kavvanah* in principle, nowhere did they propose a detailed sequence for the enactment of mystical prayer. The fact that an alien technique, and this is presently my evaluation of the origin of color visualization, was adopted by Kabbalists only demonstrates the readiness, at the end of the thirteenth century, to expand Kabbalah in various ways. It was exactly at this period that we can also detect other influences of Sufic views among the Kabbalists, as is attested by the appearance of the concepts of "world of imagination"[257] and "equanimity."[258]

Let me now summarize the above discussion. In all known periods of the development of this mystical tradition, Jewish mystics were in possession of, and apparently practiced, a wide variety of mystical techniques. Some of these bore obvious magical color, whereas in a few this aspect was overcome; all of them included a deep involvement of the mystic, who was expected to invest considerable effort in order to attain his religious goal. The understanding of Jewish mysticism must, therefore, take into consideration the practical and experiential facets of this phenomenon to a far greater extent than has been done up to now. The integration of the analyses of those mystical techniques that produced the experiential aspects of Jewish mysticism in the academic study of Kabbalah will presumably reinforce the more extreme interpretation of Jewish mysticism proposed above. It can also contribute to a more balanced view of Jewish mysticism as not only a system of theosophical symbolism, abstract speculations, and "moderate" "communion" but as a full-fledged mystical phenomenon including a variety of speculations, experiences, and techniques.

NOTES

1. Exceptions are Werblowsky's important discussion in *Karo*, pp. 38–83, and Lawrence Fine, "Maggidic Revelation in the Teachings of Isaac Luria," in *Mystics, Philosophers and Politicians: Essays in Jewish Intellectual History in Honor of Alexander Altmann*, ed. J. Reinharz and D. Swetschinski (Durham, N.C., 1982), pp. 141–152; Fine, "Recitation of *Mishnah* as a Vehicle for Mystical Inspiration: A Contemplative Technique Taught by Hayyim Vital," *REJ* 116 (1982): 183–199; Louis Jacobs, *On Ecstasy: A Tract by Dobh Baer of Lubavitch* (New York, 1963).

2. Among these figures we may include Abraham Abulafia, Isaac of Acre, Cordovero, Luria, and Vital, as well as some Hasidic masters.

3. See Idel, "Inquiries," pp. 201–226.

4. I hope to discuss this practice in a separate study.

5. Idel, *"Hitbodedut* as Concentration."

6. For letter combinations, see Idel, *The Mystical Experience in Abraham Abulafia*, Chap. 1.

7. An elaborate study of this mystical technique is in progress.

8. See Peter Kuhn, *Gottes Trauer und Klage in der rabbinischen Überlieferung* (Leiden, 1981); Melvin Glatt, "God the Mourner—Israel's Companion in Tragedy," *Judaism* 28 (1979): 79–80.

9. I do not refer to any instances of weeping as the result of ecstatic experiences, as these are not part of specific technique; on this type of weeping, see Schatz-Uffenheimer, *Quietistic Elements*, pp. 42–43; Z. Gries, "Hasidic Conduct (Hanhagot) Literature as an Expression of Ethics" (in Hebrew) (Ph.D. diss., Hebrew University, 1979), pp. 165–167.

10. Version A, in the translation of F. I. Anderson, in J. H. Charlesworth, ed., *The Old Testament Pseudepigrapha* (New York, 1983), p. 107. In the parallel version, J, ibid., p. 106, Enoch is reported to have wept in the dream preceding the revelation.

11. Translation of B. M. Metzger, in ibid., p. 532.

12. Ibid.

13. Ibid., p. 535.

14. Translation of A. F. J. Klijn, in ibid., p. 623.

15. *Ecclesiastes Rabbah* 10:10.

16. According to S. Lowy, "The Motivation of Fasting in Talmudic Literature," *JJS* 9 (1958): 34, R. Simeon appeared in a dream to his former disciple.

17. On the opposition to visiting cemeteries for occult purposes, see ibid., pp. 33–34.

18. On this Midrash, see Samuel T. Lachs, "Midrash Hallel and Merkabah Mysticism," *Gratez College Anniversary Volume* (Philadelphia, 1971), pp. 193–203, esp. p. 199.

19. Cf. Jellinek, *BHM*, V, p. 97. An interrelation between *za'ar* and secrets is also implied in a Merkavah text; see Scholem, *Jewish Gnosticism*, p. 113.

20. On the ancient Jewish view of wells of wisdom, see David Flusser and Shmuel Safrai, "The Essene Doctrine of Hypostasis and R. Meir," *Immanuel* 14 (1982): 45–57. In our text, the mythical well became the human being himself; the whole problem will be the subject of a future study.

21. Psalms 114:8.

22. Job 28:11. The same verse is quoted in a similar context in *'Avot de-R. Nathan,* Version A, Chap. 6. See Urbach, "The Traditions about Merkavah Mysticism," p. 11, and compare to his *The Halakhah: Its Sources and Evolution* (in Hebrew) (Givataim, 1984), p. 186.

23. Compare Job 28:10: "and his eye sees every precious thing."

24. Compare R. Joshua Falk's commentary, *Binyan Yehoshu'a,* on *'Avot de-R. Nathan,* Chap. 6.

25. Although the vision of the *Merkavah* and the disclosure of secrets can certainly be regarded as two separate topics, there does seem to be a close affinity between them. Urbach has noted the similarity between two passages—one appearing in *Midrash Shir ha-Shirim,* ed. Grünhut (Jerusalem, 1897), p. 8.—and one in R. Moshe ibn Tibbon's *Commentary on Shir ha-Shirim* (Lyck, 1874), fol. 9a, cited as a quotation from *Genesis Rabbah.* Cf. E. E. Urbach, "Sermons of Our Sages, the Commentary of Origen to Song of Songs and the Jewish-Christian Polemics" (in Hebrew), *Tarbiz* 30 (1961): 150 n. 7. Thus, the parallelism between "the hidden things" and "the chambers of the *Merkavah*" seems to be significant. On the secrets of Torah and the *Merkavah* in early Kabbalah, see Idel, "Maimonides and Kabbalah," sec. II. Compare also Urbach's treatment of *'Avot de-R. Nathan,* the passage referred to in n. 22 above.

26. I Kings 18:42.

27. *Berakhot* 34b.

28. *'Avodah Zarah* 17a. On the repentance and cathartic function of weeping in Orthodox Christian asceticism, see Ignace Briantchaninov, *Introduction à la tradition ascétique de l'Eglise d'Orient* (Saint-Vincent-sur-Jabron, 1978), esp. pp. 270–276; and also n. 84 below.

29. The acquisition of the world to come in a moment is mentioned in relation to R. Ḥanina ben Teradyon, a hero of ancient Jewish mysticism, *'Avodah Zarah* 18a.

30. *Heikhalot Zutarti,* Schäfer, *Synopse,* no. 424, and the responsum of R. Hai Gaon in *'Oẓar ha-Geonim,* vol. 4 on *Ḥagigah* (Jerusalem, 1931), pp. 13–15, and sec. II below.

31. See Scholem, *Major Trends,* p. 49.

32. MS New York, JTS 1786, fol. 26a. This text is the opening of an eschatological treatise entitled "'Aggadat R. Ishmael," printed in Yehudah Even Shemuel's *Midreshey 'Aggadah* (Jerusalem and Tel Aviv, 1954), p. 148. However, the printed version, which includes some better readings of the above quotation, does not mention the weeping motif.

33. *Zohar* III: 166b. The affinity between weeping and the disclosure of secrets of the Torah reappears several times in the *Zohar,* always in connection

with R. Simeon; see *Zohar* I: 1b, 7b, 11a, 113a; II: 9a, and so on. Compare R. Menaḥem Recanati's *Commentary on the Pentateuch,* fol. 37d, in which he indicates that R. Simeon's weeping is the result of the ecstatic disclosure of secrets, and not a "technical" weeping. However, this understanding is a reading of the Geronese view of ecstasy into the *Zohar.* Compare Chap. III, above.

34. It is noteworthy that, although Ezekiel's prophecies open with a vision of the *Merkavah,* they conclude with a vision of the Temple. See also the sixteenth-century practice of Elijah's posture in order to attain vision of supernal lights; cf. R. Joseph ibn Sayah's *'Even ha-Shoham* adduced in Scholem, *CCCH,* p. 90. This practice was also used by the Sufis. See Ernst Bannerth, "Dhikr et Khalwa d'après ibn 'Ata' Allah," *Institut Dominicain d'Etudes Orientales du Caire, Mélanges* 12 (1974): 69.

35. *De Beatitudine: Capita Duo R. Mosi ben Maimon Adscripta,* ed. H. S. Davidowitz and D. H. Baneth (Jerusalem, 1939), p. 7. There are several discrepancies between the Arabic original and the Hebrew translation, although these are inconsequential for our subject. On music and ecstatic experience, see Idel, "Music and Prophetic Kabbalah," p. 156 n. 27. The term translated here as "ecstatic experience" also has the connotation of "drowning" or "being overwhelmed"; cf. above, Chap. IV, n. 68. On the question of the author of this treatise, see Idel, "Prophetic Kabbalah and the Land of Israel," p. 108 n. 18. Prayer and weeping are indeed also related in medieval texts (cf., for example, *Sefer Ḥasidim,* ed. Jehudah Wistinetzki [Frankfurt, 1924], par. XI, p. 9; par. 415, p. 123; and R. Eleazar of Worms, *Sefer ha-Rokeaḥ* [Jerusalem, 1960], p 30; references provided by Professor I. Marcus). The mystical impact of this act, however, is not easily perceptible in these texts.

36. MS Oxford 1706, fol. 494b. Compare to *Hanhagot ha-'Ari;* cf. Benayahu, *Sefer Toldot ha-'Ari,* p. 319. See also R. Jacob Ẓemah's *Nagid u-Meẓaveh* (Lemberg, 1863), fol. 22a (quoted in the name of Vital's *Collectanaea*). On ascent of the soul in Luria, see below, near n. 123. Compare also R. Isaac Safrin's *Zohar Ḥai,* vol III, fol. 130a, on Luria. On R. Abraham Berukhim and his *hanhagot,* see Fine, *Safed Spirituality,* pp. 47–53.

37. Cf. G. Scholem, *The Dreams of the Sabbatean R. Mordecai Ashkenazi* (in Hebrew) (Jerusalem, 1938), p. 17.

38. *Shivehey ha-'Ari;* cf. Benayahu, *Sefer Toldot ha-'Ari,* pp. 231–232. See also Safrin, *Netiv Mizvotekha,* pp. 86–87.

39. See below, Safrin's vision of the back of the *Shekhinah.*

40. Cf. *Pesikta Rabbati,* ed. Friedmann (Vienna, 1880), fol. 130b; *Yalkut Shim'oni,* Jeremy, no. 293.

41. The version in *Yalkut Shim'oni* here is "Woe to me for your sake, Mother Zion." Compare below Vital's dream, where the phrase "Mother, Mother" occurs in a similar context.

42. *Sefer ha-Ḥezyonot,* ed. A. Z. Aeshcoli (Jerusalem, 1954), p. 42.

43. Tying is a well-known device connected to causing sexual impotence in the

bridegroom, as is clear from our context. See Saul Lieberman, *Greek and Hellenism in Jewish Palestine* (in Hebrew) (Jerusalem, 1962), p. 83 and n. 124.

44. See Aeshcoli's footnote, ibid., p. 43 n. 67.

45. I have here translated a combined version of this segment of the vision, based both upon Aeshcoli's edition, p. 44, and, especially, upon a quotation from *Sefer ha-Hezyonot* found in R. Isaac Yehudah Yehiel Safrin of Komarno, *Netiv Mizvotekha*, p. 87.

46. See above, n. 41.

47. Isa. 6:1.

48. Dan. 7:9.

49. Scholem, *Sabbatai Sevi*, pp. 204–205. Compare this passage to the passages cited above from the apocalyptic literature, where the apparitions of angels precede the fast and weepings—which they apparently prescribe—and are then followed by the main vision or revelation.

50. Another vision of the *Merkavah* is reported later on. See Scholem, *Sabbatai Sevi*, p. 206.

51. Ibid.

52. D. Ben-Amos and J. R. Mintz, eds., *In Praise of the Ba'al Shem Tov* (Bloomington, Ind., and London, 1972), pp. 53–54.

53. See the preface of R. Elijah's grandson to his commentary to *Sifra' de-Zeni'uta* (Vilna, 1891).

54. Ed. Naftali ben Menahem, Jerusalem, 1944, p. 19. This editor has already noted the affinity between the passage in *Megillat Setarim* and the one in *Netiv Mizvotekha* (p. 19 n. 53), but was misled by Safrin's practice of using the third-person form in some of his books even when relating his own experiences. Hence, ben Menahem understood that in the latter work the passage is cited in connection with R. Levi Isaac of Berdichev, who is mentioned shortly before this. However, there is no sound reason to accept this supposition. In *Megillat Setarim*, the author uses the first-person form throughout the account. A number of late nineteenth-century collections of Hasidic hagiography gave our story in the name of R. Levi Isaac of Berdichev, apparently being misled by the peculiar form by which it was referred to in *Netiv Mizvotekha;* see Buber, *Tales of the Hasidim, Early Masters*, p. 204.

55. P. 87. In this version, the author uses the third-person form; I have changed this for the first person in those instances that are missing in the *Megillat Setarim* version. In *Netiv Mizvotekha*, the date given is the twentieth.

56. See on this concept Norman Cohen, "Shekhinta Ba-Galuta: A Midrashic Response to Destruction and Persecution," *Journal for the Study of Judaism* 13 (1982): 147–159.

57. This phrase, as well as the context, stems from the *Zohar* III: 115b.

58. The vision of a shining young woman is also hinted at in Safrin's version of *Sefer ha-Hezyonot*, cited above. On the "virgin of light" as a denotation for the *Shekhinah*, see also M. Idel, "The Attitude to Christianity in *Sefer ha-*

Meshiv" (in Hebrew), *Zion* 46 (1981): 89–90, and in R. Asher Lemlein's vision, on which see Ephraim Kupfer, "The Visions of R. Asher ben R. Meir Lemlein Reutlingen" (in Hebrew), *Kovez 'al-Yad* 8 (18) (Jerusalem, 1976), 402–403; compare p. 398, where a woman dressed in dark clothes is the object of his vision.

59. The young woman is mentioned only in *Megillat Setarim*, where the author uses the first-person form; in *Netiv Mizvotekha*, he wrote: "etc."

60. On these ornaments, see Liebes, "The Messiah of the *Zohar*," p. 214 n. 33.

61. Compare R. Abraham Berukhim's vision above.

62. Exod. 33:20.

63. *Netiv Mizvotekha*, p. 87. Compare the view of repentance and weeping in R. Elimelekh of Lyzhansk's *No'am 'Elimelekh* (Jerusalem, 1960), fol. 29b.

64. See Werblowsky, *Karo*, pp. 109–111. Compare also the experience of Nathan of Gaza discussed by Scholem, *Sabbatai Ṣevi*, pp. 217–218. On the ecstatic nature of *Shavu'ot*, see Liebes, "The Messiah of the *Zohar*," pp. 208–215.

65. *Netiv Mizvotekha*, pp. 18–21.

66. Ibid., p. 86.

67. Compare the relevant account of R. Isaac Safrin on the occasion of the visit to his master, R. Abraham Joshua Heschel of Apt: "Once I was in his presence and he was speaking with a widow and I understood that his words to her were of profound wisdom, concerning the exile of the Shekhinah, who was like a widow, and I began to weep and he wept too" (*Zohar Hai* II: 395a). A slightly different version was related by Safrin's cousin, R. Isaac Eisik of Zhidachov, which was briefly analyzed by Erich Neumann, "Mystical Man," in *The Mystic Vision*, ed. J. Campbell (Princeton, N.J., 1982), p. 411. We may easily see how the very mention of the exile of the *Shekhinah* was sufficient to trigger weeping.

68. It is important to note that for Safrin, the experience of *Shekhinah* without ornaments is higher than that which includes the *Shekhinah* in its ornaments. Compare the parable of the maiden in *Zohar* II, 99a.

69. The need to participate in the exile of the *Shekhinah* was already formulated in the *Zohar* and in Safedian Kabbalah. See Berakhah Zack, "The Galut of Israel and the Galut of the Shekhinah in R. Moshe Cordovero's book *'Or Yakar*" (in Hebrew), *Jerusalem Studies in Jewish Thought* 1, no. 4 (1982): 176–178. However, the weeping and the visible revelation of the *Shekhinah* seem to be absent there. Safrin highly appreciated this practice, as we learn from *Nozer Ḥesed*, p. 65.

70. *Heikhal ha-Berakhah* I, fol. 219c. Interestingly, at the end of the first introduction to his *'Ozar Ḥayyim* and *Heikhal ha-Berakhah* R. Isaac Safrin confesses that, after a hard period, God made him a new creature. Therefore we can assume that the first quotation may reflect a personal mystical transformation, associated with weeping.

On weeping and self-abasement at midnight, see the account of the seer of Lublin, a disciple of R. Jacob Isaac ha-Levi Horowitz, regarding his master, quoted by Safrin in *Heikhal ha-Berakhah* II, fol. 276c, d. It is plausible that the custom of weeping came to Safrin via the intermediary of his uncle, R. Zevi Hirsch of Zhidachov, a student of the visionary of Lublin. On the latter's weeping, see also *'Eser Meorot* in *Sefarim Kedoshim mi-kol Talmidei ha-Besht* (Brooklyn, N.Y., 1981), vol. 2, fol. 45a, 52a.

71. *Zohar Ḥai* II, 426ab.

72. See n. 70 above on the relationship between divine light and weeping in Safrin's work, and below in the quotation from *Zohar Ḥai* II, 455d.

73. Compare Moses' weeping request for heaven and earth to pray for him, in order that he escape death. Cf., for example, *The Sermon on Moses' Death* in Eisenstein, *'Oẓar ha-Midrashim*, p. 380. The same phrase recurs in Safrin's description of his own supplication, in *Zohar Ḥai* II, fol. 456a.

74. Compare below the quotation from *Zohar Ḥai* II, 455d.

75. *Zohar Ḥai* II, 455d.

76. Prov. 18:4. The numerical value of this part of the verse is 629, corresponding to the year 1869, the time when Safrin completed the composition of the first part of *Zohar Ḥai*.

77. *Damesek 'Eli'ezer* (Przemyslani, 1902), vol. 1, fol. 5b–6a (Preface).

78. The content of the dream was analyzed by R. Isaac Safrin, whose son asked him to interpret its meaning.

79. Namely R. Ibba, one of the heroes of the *Zohar*.

80. *'Avot* 6:1. Interestingly, these secrets were regarded as *Ma'aseh Bereshit*, *Ma'aseh Merkavah*, and *Sefer Yeẓirah*. See *Maḥzor Vitri*, ed. S. Horwitz (Jerusalem, 1963), p. 555; and also Idel, "The Concept of Torah," p. 36 n. 38. Compare Safrin's statement (*Megillat Setarim*, p. 14) that, by the means of studying Talmud, one attains an experience of "great light" connected with the indwelling of the *Shekhinah*.

81. *Midrash Tehilim* on Psalms 105:1; Idel, "The Concept of Torah," pp. 36–37 n. 39.

82. See n. 80 above, where Safrin, who used the mystical anomian technique, asserted that he also received a mystical experience by means of a nomian technique. As we know, the statement of *'Avot* 6:1 was the motto of mystical study of Torah in Ḥasidism.

83. *Shabbat* 30a.

84. See mainly the issue of "the gift of tears"; cf. Jean Leclercq, *The Love of Learning and the Desire for God* (New York, 1982), pp. 58–59 and n. 28 above, and some material referred to by Margaret Smith, *The Way of the Mystics* (New York, 1978); see also George A. Maloney, *Inward Stillness* (Denville, N.J., 1975), pp. 105–120.

85. See Smith, *The Way of the Mystics*, pp. 155–157, especially p. 157; "O brethren, will ye not weep in desire for God? Shall he who weeps in longing for his Lord be denied the Vision of Him?" A Sufic group of ascetics was called *bakka'un*—weepers; see ibid., p. 155; Annemarie Schimmel, *Mystical Dimensions of Islam* (Chapel Hill, N.C., 1978), p. 31; and n. 84 above.

86. Compare my discussion in Chap. VI on the preservation of ancient Jewish views in Gnostic texts and their revitalization in medieval Kabbalah.

87. *Ecstasy* (New York, 1968), pp. 168–170.
88. Therefore, types of mental ascent such as those of Bonaventura in Christian mysticism or the ascent of mystical intention—*kavvanah*—in Jewish mysticism are outside the framework of this discussion. These types of ascent were mainly a spiritual journey of one of the faculties of the soul, commonly the rational one, and rarely of the imagination. The Neoplatonic introvertive journey of the soul to the divine inherent in her is also different from the category we are dealing with. On the influence of the latter view in Jewish mysticism, see Idel, "Types of Redemptive Activity," pp. 256–257 n. 20. On the continuity of the practice of "ascent of the soul" from the Heikhalot tradition through R. Israel Ba'al Shem Tov, see also the forthcoming study of Tali Loewenthal, *Communicating the Infinite: The Emergence of the Habad School.*
89. The eschatological ascent of the soul at the time of death is thus excluded from this discussion. On this issue, see Alexander Altmann, "The Ladder of Ascension," in *Studies in Mysticism and Religion Presented to Gershom G. Scholem* (Jerusalem, 1967), pp. 1–29.
90. I shall mention here only two recent studies dealing with ascent of the soul: Allan Segal, "Heavenly Ascent in Hellenic Judaism, Early Christianity, and Their Environment," *Aufstieg und Niedergang der romischen Welt*, II, Principat, vol. 23, 2 (Berlin, 1980), pp. 1333–1394, especially pp. 1388–1394 which contain a selected bibliography; Ioan Petru Culianu, *Psychanodia, I—A Survey of the Evidence concerning the Ascension of the Soul and Its Relevance* (Leiden, 1983). See also the references in n. 91 below.
91. Morton Smith, "Ascent to the Heavens and the Beginnings of Christianity," *Eranosjahrbuch* 50 (1981): 403–429; Smith, *Clement of Alexandria and a Secret Gospel of Mark* (Cambridge, Mass., 1973), pp. 237–249; Smith, *Jesus the Magician* (New York, 1981), pp. 124–125.
92. "Ascent," p. 415.
93. Ibid., pp. 426–428.
94. II Cor. 12:3. On this text, see Peter Schäfer's recent article, "New Testament and Hekhalot Literature: The Journey into Heaven in Paul and in Merkavah Mysticism," *JJS* 35 (1984): 19–35. Schäfer did not consider Smith's, or his predecessors', reading of Paul's statements as possibly related to Jesus himself.
95. See Scholem, *Jewish Gnosticism*, p. 18; and Itamar Gruenwald, "Knowledge and Vision," *Israel Oriental Studies* 3 (1973): 106, who points out the occurrence of the phrase in *Odes of Solomon* 35:7.
96. *Genesis Rabbah* 14:9, pp. 133–134. The nightly ascent of the soul is in no way eschatological, nor does it point to a mystical experience.
97. "Heikhalot Rabbati," Chap. XX, in Wertheimer, *Batey Midrashot* 1:97–99, Schäfer, *Synopse*, no. 225–228. On this passage, see Lawrence H. Shiffman, "The Recall of Rabbi Nehuniah ben Ha-Qanah from Ecstasy in *Heikhalot Rabbati*," *AJSreview* 1 (1976): 269–281; Saul Lieberman in Gruenwald, *Apocalyptic and Merkavah Mysticism* (Leiden, 1980), Appendix, pp. 241ff.

98. *Heikhalot Rabbati,* ibid.

99. See also a peculiar version of the discussion concerning mystical study of *Ma'aseh Merkavah,* preserved in R. 'Azriel's *Commentary on the Talmudic Aggadot,* p. 40, where ben 'Azzai is approached by R. 'Akiva, who says to him: "I heard that you sit down and study, and flames surround you. I said [to myself], 'You have descended to the chambers of the Chariot.' " The standard version of this statement in *Leviticus Rabbah* 16:4 and *Song of Songs Rabbah* on paragraph I, 10 (p. 42) states that "perhaps you deal with the chambers of the Chariot." This discrepancy is crucial; the first version assumes that, while ben 'Azzai has descended (that is, ascended) to the supernal world, the fire surrounded his body here below; according to the second version, the very study of this esoteric subject was sufficient to cause the appearance of the fire. Scholem, *CCCH,* p. 197 n. 4, notices this difference between the versions and infers that the occurrence of the "descending" motif is later; although this may indeed be the case, it cannot be ascertained. If R. 'Aziel's version indeed reflects an older concept, it constitutes an interesting parallel to R. Nehuniya's description in *Heikhalot Rabbati.* Significantly, R. 'Azriel interprets this text as referring to the ascent of human thought to the higher Sefirot and its cleaving there.

100. *'Ozar ha-Geonim,* ed. Levin, on Ḥagigah (Jerusalem, 1932), *Teshuvot,* pp. 14–15. I have partially followed the translation of the first half of the quotation given in Scholem, *Major Trends,* p. 49.

101. That is, the posture of Elijah: see above, sec. III.

102. Scholem's rendering of this as "the interiors and the chambers" (*Major Trends,* p. 49) implies that the phrase refers to external entities, presumably parts of the palaces. However, this understanding seems rather difficult; the form *ba-penimi uva-ḥedri* suggests the subject of the verb, *maniaḥ rosho,* thereby referring to the mystic himself. See also Cohen, *The Shi'ur Qomah: Liturgy and Theurgy,* p. 5, who more adequately translates: "he gazes within himself." However, his general interpretation (pp. 5–6) is erroneous: R. Hai did not imply "a mystic communion with God," nor does his passage "have the ring of truth, as well as the support of the gaon's unimpeachable authority." See my view below that this passage is a reinterpretation—or misinterpretation—of the practices of the Heikhalot mystics. The spiritual understanding of Hai's view of the ancient mystics was first proposed by Adolph Jellinek, *Beiträge zur Geschichte der Kabbala* (Leipzig, 1852), Zweites Heft, pp. 15–16 n. 22, where he affirms that R. Hai was influenced by Sufi mysticism. Our passage has recently been discussed by David Y. Halperin, "A New Edition of the Heikhalot Literature," *Journal of the American Oriental Society* 104, no. 3 (1984): 544, 547, 550–551. However, on p. 544, he translates our phrase, "He thus peers into the inner rooms and chambers," without referring to the possessive form of these nouns; thus Halperin's opinion is that R. Hai's passage reflects a heavenly ascension. See also Halperin, *The Merkabah in Rabbinic Literature* (New Haven, Conn., 1980), pp. 3, 89, 177.

103. Or, "two *mishnayot* taught by the tannaim."

104. See Scholem's view, *Major Trends*, pp. 49–50, in which he claims that R. Hai Gaon is describing a "mystical ascent." Halperin, "A New Edition," pp. 544, 551, accepts Scholem's understanding of this passage, although he disagrees with his assumption that the passage reflects a view occurring in *Heikhalot Zutarti;* he denies the presence of reference to a celestial journey in this treatise and argues that R. Hai misunderstood the earlier source. It is my opinion that the gaon misinterpreted the ancient experiences by transforming an ecstatic experience into an introvertive one.

105. *'Arukh ha-Shalem*, ed. A. Kohut, 1:14, sub voce: *'avney shayish ṭahor.*

106. *'eyn ha-sukkah;* compare *Leviticus Rabbah* I.

107. See Urbach, *'Arugat ha-Bosem*, 1:198 n. 2, 199–200. See also on p. 202 the phrase *ha-sekhel libam*, "the intellect of their heart"; see also David Halperin, "Origen, Ezekiel's Merkavah, and the Ascension of Moses," *Church History* 50 (1981): 263, 273–274. The occurrence of the phrases "cordis oculis" in Origen or *binat levavkhem* in Hebrew texts may evidence a psychologistic interpretation of the vision of the *Merkavah* in ancient Jewish sources; see also Halperin, *Merkabah*, pp. 174–175.

108. See Scholem, *Major Trends*, p. 29, where he refers to Macarius the Egyptian, who in the fourth century interpreted the vision of Ezekiel as the vision of "the secret of the soul." See also n. 107 above.

109. See, for example, R. Hai Gaon's assertion that the mystic may attain visions of palaces and angels, intentionally ignoring the vision of God. For his father's reaction to the book *Shi'ur Komah*, see *'Oẓar ha-Geonim*, ed. B. Levin, *Ḥagigah teshuvot*, pp. 11–12. R. Sherira refuses to endorse an anthropomorphic conception of Godhead.

110. See also R. Hai's reservations concerning mystical and magical practices connected with the divine names: Levin, ibid., pp. 16–24; and Colette Sirat, *Les théories des visions surnaturelles dans la pensée juive du Moyen Age* (Leiden, 1862), pp. 33–35.

111. See especially his view (R. Hai, ibid., p. 15) that inner visions are miraculous events granted by God to the righteous. This attitude is an obvious attempt to discredit the efficacy of the mystical techniques.

112. See Scholem, *Les Origines de la Kabbale*, p. 254. Strangely, he regarded the techniques of Heikhalot literature as degenerating into "mere literature" (see *Major Trends*, p. 51), a curious view in light of reports of the ascents of souls throughout the nineteenth century, as we shall see below.

113. Ibid, pp. 254–255.

114. See R. Abraham of Torrutiel's supplements to *Sefer ha-Kabbalah* of R. Abraham ben David, reprinted in *Two Chronicles from the Generation of the Spanish Exile* (in Hebrew), introduction by A. David (Jerusalem, 1979), p. 28.

115. See Gershom Scholem, "On the Prophecy of R. Ezra of Moncontour" (in Hebrew), *Tarbiẓ* 2 (1931): 244.

116. This poem, consisting of three verses, was printed by Naftali Fried, *Tarbiz* 2 (1931): 514 (in Hebrew).

117. See R. Naftali Zevi Hirsch Treves's *Commentary on the Siddur* (Thiengen, 1560), fol. 40, Ib.

118. On *Ḥagigah* 15b.

119. *Shibboley ha-Leket*, ed. Samuel K. Mirsky (New York, 1966), vol. 1, paragraph 28, p. 46, and *Maḥzor Vitri*, ed. S. Hurwitz (Nuremberg, 1923), p. 364. Compare also to *Shibboley ha-Leket*, p. 176.

120. Printed in Daniel Goldschmidt's *Maḥzor to Rosh ha-Shanah* (Jerusalem, 1970), p. 216. The content of this poem is, significantly, closely related to Ezekiel's vision.

121. See Urbach, "The Traditions about Merkavah Mysticism," pp. 4–10.

122. R. Moshe of Taku's *Ketav Tammim*, in *'Oẓar Neḥmad* IV (1863), p. 85.

123. Benayahu, *Sefer Toldot ha-'Ari*, p. 155. Compare also above, n. 36, where the spiritual ascent is attained by intentional weeping.

124. Ibid., pp. 154–155.

125. *Baddei ha-'Aron*, MS Paris, BN 840, fol. 45a.

126. In a prior sentence, R. Shem Tov speaks about the cleaving to "a pure and clean splendor": ibid., fol. 45a.

127. Ibid, fol. 45a, 45b–46a; see Idel, "*Hitbodedut* as Concentration," par. VI. See also n. 77, where I noted the similarity of this inner perception of the *Merkavah* to R. Hai's interpretation discussed above.

128. See Idel, "Shelomo Molkho as Magician," pp. 204–205, especially n. 78 there. See also below, Chap. IX, sec. II (3), for my discussion of the pneumatic interpreter.

129. *Sefer ha-Ḥezyonot*, p. 112. On the "purely imaginative ascent" of the soul to its root in Vital's *Sha'arey Kedushah*, see Werblowsky, *Karo*, pp. 69–75.

130. We may assume a certain link between the entire situation here and the midrashic dictum that the greatness of repentance is that it reaches the seat of glory. See *Pesikta Rabbati* and Victor Aptowitzer, "Untersuchungen zur Gaonäischen Literatur," *HUCA* 8–9 (1931): 397.

131. See above, sec. I, for the quotation from *Sefer ha-Ḥezyonot*, pp. 42ff. For another interesting discussion of the ascent of the soul, see ibid., pp. 47–49; the precise meaning, however, is elusive.

132. See *Shiveḥey ha-Besht*, ed. J. Mondshine, pp. 235–236, Koretz version.

133. The column linking the lower Paradise to other levels of reality is well known from earlier Kabbalistic sources; see, for example, *Seder Gan 'Eden* in Eisenstein, *'Oẓar ha-Midrashim*, pp. 85–86. The motif of the pillar climbed by shaman or dead souls recurs in various traditions. According to a legend, the last subject discussed by the Besht was the pillar of the souls, see Buber, *Tales of the Ḥasidim: Early Masters*, p. 84.

134. Apparently Aḥijah the Shilonite; on this prophet as a mystical mentor, see Liebes, "The Messiah of the *Zohar*," p. 113 n. 114.

135. On this question, see Scholem, *Explications and Implications*, pp. 309–310; Liebes, "The Messiah of the *Zohar*," pp. 113–114.

136. *Shivehey ha-Besht*, ed. Mondshine, p. 235; see also R. Isaac Safrin's *Zohar Hai* III, fol. 76b.

137. Interestingly enough, ecstatic practices in which the soul leaves the body for several hours during which oracular dreams are experienced were known in Moldavian Carpats: see Mircea Eliade, *Zalmoxis: The Vanishing God* (Chicago and London, 1970), pp. 191–194.

138. Ibid., p. 237.

139. See the texts collected by Mondshine, *Shivehey ha-Besht*, p. 251 and n. 45.

140. See *Mayyim Rabbim* (Brooklyn, N.Y., 1979), p. 140. Compare also the contemporary descriptions of R. Elijah of Vilna in R. Hayyim of Volozhin's preface to R. Elijah's commentary to *Sifra' de-Zeni'uta* (Vilna, 1891), where the master is portrayed as a recipient of a secret by means of the ascent of the soul, although he did not appreciate this pattern as a very high one.

141. *Nozer Hesed*, p. 131.

142. See *Heikhal ha-Berakhah*, vol. I, fol. 31a.

143. *Zohar Hai* III, fol. 129d.

144. Cf. Exod. 24:18. Compare the Lurianic view of Moses' ascent adduced by Scholem, *Sabbatai Sevi*, p. 53.

145. See Philo's allegorization of Moses as the soul ascending to heaven; cf. Segal (n. 1 above), p. 1358.

146. *Megillat Setarim*, pp. 15–16.

147. Compare another dream of R. Isaac Safrin, *Megillat Setarim*, p. 23, where he learned from a certain event that he would "rise to greatness, satisfaction and joy."

148. This is the date of this experience.

149. On the relationship between ben 'Atar and Hasidism, see Dan Manor, "Rabbi Haim ben 'Atar in Hasidic Writings" (in Hebrew), *Pe'amim* 20 (1984): 88–110. Manor mentions neither the Besht's epistle referred to above nor the question of soul ascent in ben 'Atar.

150. See M. Idel, "On the Metamorphosis of an Ancient Technique of Prophetic Vision in the Middle Ages" (in Hebrew), *Sinai* 86 (1980): 1–7.

151. Irenée Hausherr, "La Méthode d'oraison hesychaste," *Orientalia Christiana* 9 (1927): 68–69.

152. G. C. Anawati and L. Gardet, *Mystique musulmane: Aspects et tendances, expériences et techniques* (Paris, 1976), pp. 187–234.

153. See, for example, Mircea Eliade, *Yoga: Immortality and Freedom* (Princeton, N.J., 1971), pp. 200ff., esp. pp. 216–219, where the similarities between the Sufic "dhikr" and parallel Hindu phenomena are noted.

154. D. T. Suzuki, *Essais sur le Bouddhisme Zen* (Paris, 1943), 2:141–151, and passim.

155. See, for example, Eliade, *Yoga*, pp. 47–52.

156. See Anawati and Gardet, *Mystique musulmane*, pp. 189–190.

157. For a detailed description of these components of Kabbalistic mystical techniques, see Idel, *The Mystical Experience in Abraham Abulafia*, Chap. I.

158. On the influence of Ashkenazic theology on Spanish Kabbalah, see Joseph Dan, "The Vicissitudes of the Esotericism of the German Ḥasidim" (in Hebrew), in *Studies in Mysticism and Religion Presented to Gershom G. Scholem* (Jerusalem, 1967), pp. 91–99. Dan, however, does not discuss the influence of R. Eleazar's mystical technique.

159. See, for example, "Ve-Zot li-Yihudah," in Jellinek, *Auswahl*, p. 25.

160. See Matt, *The Book of the Mirrors*, p. 1.

161. See the quotation from R. Eleazar's *Sefer ha-Ḥokhmah* in n. 167 below.

162. See Idel, *The Mystical Experience in Abraham Abulafia*, Chap. I.

163. See Sec. II above.

164. On this treatise, see Dan, *The Esoteric Theology*, pp. 143ff.

165. MS Cambridge, Add. 643, fol. 19a; MS Oxford 1574, fol 34b; MS Vatican 431, fol. 39a.

166. *'Oẓar Neḥmad* III (1860), p. 84. See also Scholem, *Major Trends*, pp. 102–103.

167. *Sefer ha-Ḥokhmah* MS Oxford 1812, fol. 55b. On this treatise, see Joseph Dan, "The Ashkenazi Ḥasidic *Gates of Wisdom*," in *Hommage à Georges Vajda*, ed. G. Nahon and C. Tonati (Louvain, 1980), pp. 183–189; Dan, *The Esoteric Theology*, pp. 44–57.

168. *Ibid*, fol. 55b.

169. *Middot*; the significance is uncertain.

170. The phrase *"Omquei ha-Shemot"* is reminiscent of certain phrases occurring in Abraham Abulafia's works as referring to the highest Kabbalistic path. See Idel, "Maimonides and Kabbalah," nn. 83, 84, 93, 99, and Gikatilla's phrase, n. 105.

171. Compare also R. Eleazar's description of the transmission of the Tetragrammaton to a disciple, which seems to reflect not only an ancient practice but also an extant praxis. Cf. Dan, *The Esoteric Theology*, pp. 74–76; Dan's assertion (p. 75) that the ceremony of transmission of the name has only theological, not magical, overtones must apparently be modified in the direction of more experiential implications of the knowledge gained by the reception of the name.

172. See Idel, "The World of Angels in Human Shape," pp. 1–15.

173. On this issue, see Idel, "The Concept of the Torah," p. 28.

174. See Idel, "The World of Angels in Human Shape," p. 13 n. 52, and Idel, *The Mystical Experience in Abraham Abulafia*, Chap. I; there I deal as well with passages from R. Isaac ibn Latif and R. Moses of Burgos.

175. See, for example, *'Oẓar 'Eden Ganuz*, MS Oxford 1580, fol. 149b, where he mentions the "Chapters of Heikhalot," "The Book of Bahir," and "The Alphabet of R. 'Akiva."

176. MS München 43, fol. 219a. This is a short section from the larger *Sefer ha-Shem*, entitled *'Eser Havvayot*, circulating in some manuscripts. This table was copied from this compendium by R. Yehudah Ḥayyat in his commentary on *Ma'arekhet ha-'Elohut*, fol. 197b, and subsequently in R. Moses Cordovero's *Pardes Rimmonim*, fol. 97c–d. The latter knew of two versions of this table; on the second of these, see n. 192 below.

177. The vowels clearly occur in order to facilitate the pronunciation of the consonants; however, I assume that the mystical and magical feature of the vowels, known from ancient Hellenistic magic, may also have been known in Jewish circles. On vowel mysticism in Abulafia's circle, see also R. J. Zwi Werblowsky, "Kabbalistische Buchstabenmystik und der Traum," *Zeitschrift für Religions und Geistesgeschichte* 8 (1956): 164–169.

178. *Commentary on Sefer Yezirah* (Premizlany, 1883), fol. 15d. On the penetration of this text into Renaissance literature and praxis, see M. Idel, "Hermeticism and Judaism," par. V.

179. Scholem, *On the Kabbalah,* p. 187.

180. See Matt, *The Book of the Mirrors,* p. 95; *'Or Zaru'a,* MS British Library 771, fol. 92b. It was copied from the latter text by R. Moses Cordovero in *Pardes Rimmonim,* fol 98a. R. Menaḥem Recanati was also acquainted with this peculiar theory of thirty-six combinations of letters and vowels, although he did not copy the table; see his *Commentary on the Pentateuch,* fol. 49b. Nevertheless, the commentator on this text, R. Mordecai Jaffe, obviously perceived the original source of Recanati and gives the detailed combinations.

181. See Moshe Hallamish, ed., *Kabbalistic Commentary of Rabbi Joseph ben Shalom Ashkenazi on Genesis Rabbah* (Jerusalem, 1984), p. 256. Here, as in his unidentified text (see n. 182 below), the recitation of the combinations are related to the creation of the golem.

182. MS Sasson 290, pp. 198–200; this text will be printed and analyzed elsewhere. The identification is provisional, as this text is also close to R. David ben Yehudah he-Ḥasid's thought.

183. Ibid., p 199.

184. Idel, "Kabbalistic Material," p. 198.

185. For further details, see Idel, *The Mystical Experience in Abraham Abulafia,* Chap. I.

186. *'Or ha-Sekhel,* MS Vatican 233, fol. 97b, MS Fulda 4, fol. 32b.

187. See Idel, "Abraham Abulafia and *Unio Mystica.*"

188. Idel, *Abraham Abulafia,* pp. 54–55 n. 161.

189. See Gershom Scholem, "Chapters from *Sefer Sullam ha-'Aliyah* of R. Yehudah Albotini" (in Hebrew), *Kiryat Sefer* 22 (1945): 168; David Blumenthal, *Understanding Jewish Mysticism* (New York, 1982), 2:65–66.

190. *Pardes Rimmonim,* fol. 97a–b.

191. Cordovero does not mention Abulafia's name because, at the time he composed *Pardes Rimmonim,* he mistook this for a work of Gikatilla, *Sha'ar ha-Nikkud.* However, in another, later work, he refers correctly to both author and book.

192. See n. 176 above.

193. See M. Idel, "Some Remarks on R. Abraham Abulafia and R. Moses Cordovero" (in Hebrew), *Da'at* 15 (1985): 117–120.

194. *Pardes Rimmonim,* fol. 97b.

195. See Idel, "Some Remarks," p. 120.

196. *Pardes Rimmonim,* fol 97a.
197. Ibid, fol. 97b.:
198. See Chap. III above.
199. For more on this development, see Idel, "Perceptions of Kabbalah" and Chap. VII below.
200. The use of the combinatory techniques of *Sefer Yezirah* for mystical purposes is a highly interesting issue, which cannot be presented here. For the time being, see Nicolas Sed, "Le *Sefer Ha-Razim* et la méthode de 'combinaison des lettres,' " *REJ* 130 (1971): 295–303.
201. See Idel, "Egidio da Viterbo and R. Abraham Abulafia's Books" (in Hebrew), *Italia* 2, nos. 1–2 (1981): 48.
202. See Idel, *The Mystical Experience in Abraham Abulafia,* Chap. III.
203. Cf. ibid.
204. See on this topic Gershom Scholem, "The Concept of Kavvanah in the Early Kabbalah," in *Studies in Jewish Thought,* ed. Alfred Jospe (Detroit, 1981), pp. 162–180.
205. See Scholem, *Les Origines de la Kabbale,* pp. 316–319, 437–446.
206. See Gottlieb, *Studies,* pp. 38–55.
207. See above, Chap. III, on the possibility that a certain Geronese text implies interiorization of the ten Sefirot and their unification.
208. See on this issue Arthur J. Deikman, "Deautomatization and the Mystic Experience," in *Altered States of Consciousness,* ed. C. Tart (New York, 1972), pp. 25–46.
209. Some of the historical details concerning this issue were dealt with in Idel, "Kabbalistic Prayer and Colours."
210. On the problem of color in Jewish mysticism, see Gershom Scholem, "Colours and Their Symbolism in Jewish Tradition and Mysticism," *Diogenes* 108 (1979): 84–111; 109 (1980): 64–77. Scholem, despite his lengthy discussions on color, never refers to their visualization within the context of Kabbalistic prayer!
211. I hope to deal with this attribution in a separate study, in which Kabbalistic commentaries on this small treatise will be printed.
212. See Scholem, "The Concept of Kavvanah," pp. 171–174.
213. The treatise attributed to R. 'Azriel deals exclusively with lights connected to prayer, not with colors; later Kabbalists have nevertheless interpreted these lights as colors.
214. MS Cambridge, Add. 505, fol. 8a.
215. The identification of this R. David with R. David ben Yehudah he-Ḥasid has been proven in Idel, "Kabbalistic Prayers and Colours."
216. The Hebrew phrases stem from the *Amidah* prayer, and constitute strong evidence that visualization is connected with prayer. The sequel of our citation mentions *kavvanah* in prayer.
217. *Ḥashmal* and *Malbush* are numerically equivalent: 378.
218. See Idel, "The World of Angels in Human Shape," p. 58 n. 217, and R. Joseph Ashkenazi's *Commentary to Sefer Yezirah,* fol. 27a, and so on.

219. For more on these processes, see Chap. VIII below.
220. On this Kabbalist, see Moshe Hallamish's preface to *Kabbalistic Commentary*, pp. 11–27; Georges Vajda, "Un Chapitre de l'histoire du conflit entre la Kabbale et la philosophie: La Polémique anti-intellectualiste de Joseph ben Shalom Ashkenazi de Catalogne," *Archives d'histoire doctrinale et littéraire du moyen age* 23 (1956): 45–144.
221. See Gershom Scholem, "The Real Author of the *Commentary on Sefer Yezirah* Attributed to R. Abraham ben David and His Works" (in Hebrew), *Kiryat Sefer* 4 (1927–28): 294–295.
222. Hallamish, *Kabbalistic Commentary*, p. 223.
223. This seems to suggest the technique of contemplating the letters of the divine name—a practice to be analyzed in detail elsewhere—connected to Psalms 16:8. See also n. 244 below.
224. The Hebrew phrase is the biblical *"Marot ha-Zovot";* however, it can be demonstrated that *Marot* is understood here as color, a common medieval meaning of this term.
225. Cf. *Sefer Yezirah* I, 9.
226. *"Vayifrach"*—literally, "he will fly."
227. *"Melubashim bo";* compare R. David's text, previously quoted, where the colors surround the Sefirot; here, they cover the letters of the divine name.
228. *Genesis Rabbah* 17:5, p. 156.
229. See R. Joseph Ashkenazi's *Commentary on Sefer Yezirah*, fol. 9d, 18b, 30b, and so on.
230. Ibid, fol. 27a. Compare also Chap. VI, n. 230.
231. MS Paris Rabbinic Seminary, 108, fol. 95a.
232. The vocalization of the word *"Devarekha"* in Psalms 119:89 was sometimes seen as one of the ways in which the Tetragrammaton was pronounced; see, for example, an early Kabbalistic fragment preserved in MS Oxford 2240, fol. 248b.
233. The verb *"tsayer"* which occurs here is the same verb as in R. David's aforecited text.
234. MS Milano-Ambrosiana 62, fol. 4a. This circle should be compared with R. Joseph Ashkenazi's circles and the accompanying discussions in his *Commentary on Sefer Yezirah*, fol. 18ab, which I hope to do elsewhere.
235. Idel, "Kabbalistic Material," pp. 193–197.
236. See M. Idel, "Again on R. David ben Yehudah he-Ḥasid and R. Isaac Luria" (in Hebrew), *Da'at* 7 (1981): 69–71. The conception of *Ze'ir 'Anpin* as an entity encompassing the Sefirot from Ḥokhmah downward was one embraced by R. Moses Cordovero.
237. For these characteristics of the mandala, see Giuseppe Tucci, *The Theory and Practice of the Mandala* (London, 1961), p. vii.
238. MS New York, JTS 2430, fol. 81a.
239. Ibid.
240. The identical phrase occurs several times in other texts on visualization in prayer, always as a symbol for the third Sefirah.

241. On the Kabbalistic responsa, from which I am quoting the responsum on prayer, see Gershom Scholem, "The Responsa Attributed to R. Joseph Gikatilla," in *Jacob Freimann Festschrift* (Berlin, 1937), pp. 163–170. Strangely, Scholem decided not to publish the responsum on prayer, although all the other responsa, which were certainly less interesting than this, were printed there. Although Scholem indicated he intended to print it elsewhere, it is not even mentioned in his monograph on colors (n. 210 above). I intend to print this responsum from manuscripts in my research on color mysticism.

242. MS New York, JTS 255, fol. 60a.

243. In the diagram, the color of Keter is described as "white as snow"! See also below, in the text quoted from R. Ḥayyim Vital's *Sha'arey Kedushah*, n. 253.

244. Psalms 16:8; see n. 223 above.

245. See also MS New York, JTS 255, fol. 59b.

246. MS Milano-Ambrosiana, 62, fol 4.

247. MS New York, JTS 255, fol. 60a.

248. Mal. 3:16.

249. Isa. 66:2.

250. Idel, "Kabbalistic Prayer and Colours."

251. See Idel, "Kabbalistic Material," pp. 169, 201–206.

252. This manuscript handbook will be published and analyzed in my forthcoming monograph on colors.

253. Gate XXXII, Chap. 2.

254. MS British Library, Margoliouth 749, fol. 16a.

255. See n. 243 above.

256. MS British Library, 749, fol. 14b, 18a.

257. See Idel, "The World of Imagination and R. Nathan's *Collectanaea*," pp. 165–167.

258. See Idel, "*Hitbodedut* as Concentration," pp. 46–50.

14.

Circumcision, Vision of God, and Textual Interpretation: From Midrashic Trope to Mystical Symbol

Elliot R. Wolfson

The use of sexual imagery to depict religious experience is well attested in the history of religions. It should come as no surprise, therefore, to find that the seeing of God, or a Godlike presence, is described in religious texts especially by means of language derived from human sexuality. Such formulation, of course, is not strange to any of the major religious traditions in the Occident or Orient. It is often the case, moreover, that especially the mystics of particular cultures express themselves precisely in this modality. To experience God involves a state of ecstatic union akin to the union of male and female partners in sexual embrace.

   This paper will be a study of one particular motif related to this larger issue in the phenomenology of religious experience. We will examine an idea developed in the *Zohar*, the main sourcebook of thirteenth century Spanish Jewish mysticism,[1] concerning the correlation between two apparently unrelated phenomena: circumcision and the ability to see the *Shekhinah*, the divine Presence. The causal nexus between these two phenomena is suggested by earlier Rabbinic passages but is given an elaborate treatment in the theosophic system of the *Zohar*. As we shall see, implicit in the Zoharic discussion is the notion that mystical experi-

Reprinted from *History of Religions* 27, no. 2 (1987), by permission of the University of Chicago Press, Chicago, 1987. Copyright © 1987 by The University of Chicago.

ence involves a type of sexual union between the initiate and the divine. Beholding the face of the *Shekhinah* becomes in the *Zohar* an actual embrace or penetration of the mystic into the divine feminine. Given the normative halakhic sexual mores, it follows that only one who is circumcised can have such a visionary experience.[2] Circumcision is thus an act of opening that not only ushers the circumcised into the covenantal community of God but also places the individual into an immediate—visual—relationship to the divine.

The phenomenological reciprocity between the opening of circumcision and visionary experience of God functions in the *Zohar* as a model for divine-human relations in another way, though in this case as well the sexual implications are evident. It is stated explicitly that only one who is circumcised is permitted to study the Torah.[3] The underlying notion here, as I shall show, is the congruity between textual interpretation and circumcision. Yet, one may well ask, what is it in the nature of hermeneutics that allows the author of the *Zohar* (assumed to be Moses ben Shem Tob de León, c. 1240–1305)[4] to link it specifically with circumcision? Or, to invert the question, what in the nature of circumcision leads the author of the *Zohar* to limit textual study of the Torah to one who is circumcised? Although a complete answer to this will not be forthcoming until the latter stages of this analysis, I will outline in a preliminary fashion the elements that serve as the basis for this conception.

Circumcision is not simply an incision of the male sex organ[5] but is an inscription, a notation, a marking.[6] This marking, in turn, is the semiological seal, as it were, that represents the divine imprint on the human body.[7] The physical opening, therefore, is the seal that, in its symbolic valence, corresponds to an ontological opening within God. Hence, circumcision provides the author of the *Zohar* with a typology of writing/reading[8] that is at the same time a typology of mystical experience understood in a sexual vein. The opening of circumcision, in the final analysis, is transformed in the *Zohar* into a symbol for the task of exegesis. The appropriateness of this symbolization lies in the fact that the relation of the visionary to the *Shekhinah* engendered by the opening of the flesh is precisely the relationship of the critic or exegete to the text engendered by the semiological seal. This relationship is simultaneously interpretative and visionary. Through exegesis, that which was concealed, hidden, closed—in a word, esoteric—becomes opened, disclosed, manifest—in a word, exoteric. The uncovering of the phallus is conceptually and structurally parallel to the disclosure of the text. The significance of this dynamic for understanding the literary genesis of the *Zohar* should not be ignored.[9] In the closing section of the paper I shall have more to say about this matter.

I

The nexus between circumcision and the appearance of God is, to my knowledge, first enunciated in the following comment in one of the earliest midrashic compilations,[10] *Genesis Rabbah,* on the verse, "The Lord appeared to him [Abraham]" (Gen. 18:1):

It is written, "This, after my skin will have been peeled off; but I would behold God from my flesh" (Job 19:26). Abraham said, After I circumcised myself many converts came to cleave to this sign. "But I would behold God from my flesh," for had I not done this [i.e., performed the act of circumcision], on what account would the Holy One, blessed be He, have appeared to me? [As it is written] "The Lord appeared to him etc." [11]

The anonymous author of this passage, an astute reader of the biblical text, has noted that the theophany to Abraham at the terebinths of Mamre is preceded in Scripture by the account of Abraham's and Ishmael's being circumcised.[12] The conjunction of these two episodes has forged in the mind of the midrashist a more than casual connection between the act of circumcision and the appearance of God. In disregard of other biblical contexts to the contrary [13] (e.g., Gen. 17:1), the author of this comment wishes to state that it is in virtue of the rite of circumcision that God manifests himself to Abraham. "Had I not been circumcised," wonders Abraham, "on what account would God have appeared to me?" That is to say, by means of what deed would he have merited the epiphany of God? The intent of this passage, then, must be seen in light of an idea emphasized time and again in rabbinic literature: without works there is no reward, or, to invert Paul's locution, one is justified by acts alone.[14] Here, as in many other rabbinic sources, it is particularly the act of circumcision that merits a special favor on the part of God.[15] This interpretation is supported by a similar exegesis of the passage from Job: the first clause refers to the act of circumcision, peeling off the skin (i.e., the foreskin), and the second to the vision of God that follows therefrom. "But I would behold God from my flesh," that is, from the flesh of the phallus,[16] the organ of circumcision.

It seems reasonable to suggest, therefore, that this is the import of the midrashic statement: by virtue of the merit of circumcision God appeared to Abraham. The divine manifestation demands some prior deed, a *miṣwah*, which creates a link between man and God. The rite of circumcision, after all, is the mark of the covenant between God and the (male) children of Israel.[17] Through circumcision, then, one merits to stand in the presence of God, or, to put it differently, the appearance of God is itself the reward for the prior act of fulfilling the divine decree.[18]

Yet, there is an additional element alluded to in the above passage from *Genesis Rabbah*. The midrashist asserts that after Abraham was circumcised many converts "came to cleave to this sign,"[19] that is, many desired to convert to the Jewish faith by undergoing the rite of circumcision. We know from other aggadic sources that Abraham and Sarah were viewed as the first proselytizers for God.[20] It may be suggested, however, that in the present context one can find in the portrayal of Abraham as one who encourages conversion through his circumcision a polemic against the dominant claims of Christianity (following Pauline doctrine) that religious conversion is a matter of faith, not works, and that for newcomers into the covenantal community of God (i.e., the Church) circumcision of the flesh was not a necessary initiation rite.[21] Our *midrash* emphasizes, to the contrary, that it was precisely Abraham's own circumcision that induced more converts into the faith of Judaism. In opposition to the claims of Christianity, the rabbis maintained that the rite of circumcision was not only still viable as a religious duty but was also the central feature of a proper conversion process.[22] The emphasis on Abraham's circumcision and its drawing forth a horde of potential converts to cleave to that sign can only be seen as a tacit rejection of the Christian position that circumcision of the flesh had been replaced by circumcision of the spirit (enacted in baptism).

That this explanation is indeed plausible is supported by the continuation of this passage in *Genesis Rabbah*, which doubtless was intended by the redactor(s) to drive the point home with ever greater clarity:

1. R. Isaac[23] began/opened [his discourse]: "Make for me an altar of earth etc." (Exod. 20:21). R. Isaac said: If I [i.e., God] appear to the one who builds an altar for my name's sake and bless him, how much

more so with respect to Abraham who has circumcised himself for my name's sake. [It is thus written] "And the Lord appeared to him etc."

2. R. Levi began/opened [his discourse]: "An ox and a ram for an offering etc. [for today the Lord will appear to you]" (Lev. 9:4). He said: If I [God] appear to the one who sacrifices an ox or ram for my name's sake, how much more so to Abraham who has circumcised himself for my name's sake." And the Lord appeared to him etc."

The comments attributed to R. Isaac and R. Levi, both third-century Palestinian Amoraim,[24] underscore the intrinsic connection between the meritorious deed of circumcision and the appearance of God. For both, circumcision is to be understood as an act of sacrifice.[25] If one who builds an altar or sacrifices animals merits the approach (and blessing) of the divine, how much more so Abraham, whose act of circumcision is likened to an act of self-sacrifice.

The nexus of ideas is reiterated in a twelfth-century midrashic compilation, *Numbers Rabbah,* but with a strikingly new twist. In addition to viewing circumcision as the deed by means of which one merits the reward of seeing god, this midrashic pericope affirms an even deeper correlation between circumcision and the visual revelation of God based on the physical purity of the visionary. In this case the matter is not merely deontological but, rather, ontological. That is, circumcision effects a change in the very substance of the individual—and not only in his ethico-religious stature—which prepares him for the visionary experience. I will cite the passage in full, ostensibly an interpretation of Song of Songs 3:11, "O Maidens of Zion, go forth, And gaze upon King Solomon, wearing the crown that his mother gave him on his wedding day, on his day of bliss." Commenting particularly on the first part of the verse, the anonymous midrashist writes:

It is speaking about the time when the Presence *[Shekhinah]* rested in the Tabernacle *[mishkan].* "Go forth and gaze," as it is said, "And all the people saw and shouted, and fell on their faces" (Lev. 9:24). "The daughters of Zion," those [males] who were distinguished *[ha-meṣuyanim]* by circumcision, for if they were uncircumcised, they would not have been able to look upon the Presence. Rather, they would have fallen as Abraham fell, as it is said, "Abram fell on his face, and God spoke to him" (Gen. 17:3).[26] Similarly with respect to Balaam, "[Words of him who hears God's speech, who beholds visions of the Almighty], prostrate, but with eyes unveiled" (Num. 24:4). And thus it says,

"Moses said, This is the thing [zeh ha-davar] which the Lord has commanded that you do, that the Glory of the Lord may appear to you" (Lev. 9:6). What was "this thing"? He told them about [the rite of] circumcision, as it is written, "This is the reason [literally, 'this is the thing,' zeh ha-davar] why Joshua performed circumcision" (Josh. 5:4). "Which God commanded Abraham to do." This[27] may be compared to a shopkeeper who has a friend who is a priest. He had some unclean thing in his house, and he wanted to bring him [the priest] into the house. The priest said to him: If you want me to go into your house, listen to me and remove that unclean thing from your house. When the shopkeeper knew that there was no unclean thing there, he went and brought the priest into his house. Similarly [with respect to] the Holy One, blessed be He, when He wanted to appear to Abraham, His beloved, the foreskin was hanging from him. When he circumcised himself, immediately [God] was revealed, as it says, "On that very day Abraham was circumcised" (Gen. 17:26), and afterward "The Lord appeared to him" (ibid. 18:1). Therefore Moses said to them. God commanded Abraham, your father, to perform [the act of] circumcision when He wished to appear to him. So in your case, whoever is uncircumcised, let him go out and circumcise himself, "that the Glory of the Lord may appear to you" (Lev. 9:6). Thus Solomon said, "O Maidens of Zion, go forth. And gaze upon King Solomon" (Song of Songs 3:11), the King who desires those who are perfect, as it is written, "Walk before Me and be blameless" (Gen. 17:1), for the foreskin is a blemish on the body.[28]

The author of this *midrash*, in a remarkable reversal of the literal sense of the text, interprets the "daughters of Zion" as referring to those [males] marked or "distinguished" (*meṣuyanim*, an obvious play on the word *ṣiyyon*) by circumcision.[29] Clearly, daughters cannot be so distinguished; thus the midrashic reading effectively effaces the literal sense. More significantly, the midrashist forges an unambiguous connection between the capability of beholding the Presence or Glory of God and circumcision: he who is uncircumcised will fall on his face—as Abraham himself did prior to his circumcision—in the presence of God's manifestation. The alleged reason for this is given by the *midrash* itself: the foreskin is a blemish that acts as a barrier separating the individual and God.[30]

In contrast to the earlier midrashic texts that we examined, there is here an essential link between the act of circumcision and the visionary experience of the divine. Circumcision is not simply one good deed among many in consequence of which the person merits a vision of God. It is precisely and exclusively by means of circumcision that one can see God, for this act removes that potential barrier—symbolized by the cutting of the foreskin[31]—separating human and divine. Circumcision is the vestibule or portal through which one must pass if one is to have a visionary experience of God. The opening of circumcision results in an opening up to God, a receptivity, which enables one to stand in God's presence and to behold the Glory.

II

All that is implied in the midrashic passage from *Numbers Rabbah* is made explicit in the *Zohar,* where it is embellished by an intricate theosophic structure. It is quite clear that in the *Zohar* the nexus between circumcision and the vision of God is reaffirmed and given new layers of meaning. The treatment of this midrashic theme in the *Zohar* must be seen in light of a central category in the kabbalistic (especially Zoharic) conception of religious perfection: man's relation to God, particularly the *Shekhinah,* the feminine hypostasis of God and the last of the divine emanations *(sefirot),* is viewed in a decidedly sexual manner. One who is uncircumcised cannot see God (or the *Shekhinah*), for seeing involves some sort of intimate contact, touching, immediacy, and only one who is circumcised can have such an experience.

The issue of openness/closedness is connected particularly in the *Zohar* with the problem of circumcision and visionary experience. Commenting on Gen. 18:1, "And the Lord appeared to him [Abraham]," R. Abba said: "Before Abraham was circumcised he was closed *['atim].* When he was circumcised all was revealed and the Presence rested upon him in its completeness."[32] The closure of Abraham, or, more specifically, Abraham's phallus, has an objective correlate: an obscured vision of the divine. That is, before his circumcision Abraham was closed, and hence God was not fully revealed to him. The act of circumcision, on the other hand, is an opening, a removal of closure, which corresponds objectively to a disclosure of God. The relationship of God to a particular man is dependent upon the physical condition of the latter: if closed (uncircumcised), then the vision is obscured; if opened (circumcised), then the vision is complete. It is highly significant that comprehension is here linked especially to the phallus: when Abraham was uncircumcised, and therefore closed, he lacked comprehension of the divine; when he was circumcised, and therefore opened, all was revealed to him. As Moses Cordovero (1522–70) expressed it in his commentary to this passage in the *Zohar:* "Closure brings about the removal of comprehension." [33] (Subsequently, I shall return to the connection between the openness of the phallus and the possibility of comprehension, specifically understood as a hermeneutical mode.)

Even before his circumcision Abraham merited some vision of the divine realm. This is implied in the above passage: "When he was circumcised *all* was revealed to him etc." That is, prior to the circumcision there was, at best, a partial vision of God. This is spelled out in another Zoharic passage, attributed to R. Eleazar, which interprets Gen. 18:1, "And the Lord appeared to him," as referring to a time "after Abraham was circumcised. For before Abraham was circumcised [God] did not speak to him except through the lower gradation, and the upper gradations did not stand over that gradation." [34] In yet another passage the author of the *Zohar* clarifies the difference between Abraham's visionary (prophetic) experience before and after circumcision in more detail:

"The word of the Lord came to Abram in a vision *[ba-maḥazeh]*" (Gen. 15:1). What is [the meaning of] "in a vision"? This is the vision [or mirror, Aramaic: *ḥeizu*], the gradation in which all images *[deyuqnin]* are seen *[ithazyan]*. R. Shimeon said: Before Abraham was circumcised, one gradation spoke with him. And which one was it? It was the "vision" *[maḥazeh]*. . . . When he was circumcised all the gradations rested on this gradation and then it spoke with him. . . . Before he was circumcised those gradations did not rest upon him to speak [to him]. [35]

The divine gradation referred to as the "vision" is the last of the *sefirot,* the *Shekhinah,* so named because this gradation is a prism that reflects all the upper colors or forms. Prior to his circumcision, therefore, God spoke to Abraham through the intermediary of the *Shekhinah.* Indeed, even after the circumcision God continued to speak with Abraham through the *Shekhinah;* however, in the latter case the vision was complete, since all the upper gradations rested upon or stood over the *Shekhinah* in the moment of revelation. While Abraham was uncircumcised his visionary experience was restricted to the lowest emanation. In a subsequent passage de León returns to this distinction in an effort to clarify further the theophanic transformation undergone by Abraham:

Come and see: before Abraham was circumcised [God] spoke to him exclusively from within the vision *[maḥazeh]*, as it is written, "The word of the Lord came to Abram in a vision etc." (Gen. 15:1). "In a vision," (i.e.) by means of that vision *[ḥeizu]*, the gradation in which all the forms are seen . . . and that vision is the secret of the covenant *[raza di-berit]*. If you say it is called *maḥazeh* because it is the vision, (i.e.) the gradation in which all the forms are seen, did you also not say at the outset that before Abraham was circumcised no one spoke to him but that gradation when no other gradation rested upon it? Yet, you now say that [the expression] "in a vision" *[ba-maḥazeh]* refers to that vision [or mirror] in which [are seen] the other gradations! Before Abraham was circumcised it is written, "And the Lord spoke to Abram in a vision" (Gen. 15:1). Indeed, that gradation is the vision of all the supernal gradations, and it is fixed in the appearance of the supernal gradations. And even though at that time Abraham was not circumcised, that gradation was in the appearance of the supernal gradations, and She existed in all those [upper] colors . . . for She is the vision of all the upper colors that are over Her. And thus in that appearance She stood with Abraham and spoke to him, even though he was not circumcised. When he was circumcised, what is written? "And the Lord appeared to Abram." . . . Thus before Abraham was circumcised that gradation [spoke] to him. When he was circumcised immediately [it says], "The Lord appeared to Abram etc." All the [other] gradations appeared on that gradation, and the latter spoke to him in completeness. And Abraham was bound from gradation to gradation and entered the holy covenant which appeared in its completeness.[36]

One senses the tension in the mind of the author of the *Zohar*, struggling to clarify the difference in vision accorded to Abraham before and after his circumcision. The biblical term used in connection with God's appearance to Abraham (before the circumcision) is *maḥazeh*, vision, which is understood kabbalistically to be a symbol for *Shekhinah*, the prism in which all the forms are reflected. Yet the *Zohar* makes the claim that before his circumcision Abraham did not converse with the *Shekhinah* in Her fullness, that is, as reflecting all the upper lights. This apparent tension has led various commentaries on the *Zohar* to offer several responses,[37] none of which, in my view, is sufficient. What is clear is that de León is trying to uphold a qualitative distinction in the nature of the vision that Abraham had before and after his circumcision. There is, on the one hand, something about the act of circumcision that effects a change in the individual resulting in a change in his visionary status. On the other hand, as a result of the circumcision there is a change in the nature of the divine itself, particularly the relation of the last gradation to those above Her. In the latter respect, it may be said that circumcision includes a theurgical dimension.

In the above passage the nexus between circumcision and theophany is reaffirmed by the introduction of another key concept: the identifica-

504   ELLIOT R. WOLFSON

tion of the vision, or *Shekhinah*, as the "secret of the covenant," *raza di-berit*.[38] This should not be construed as an arbitrary or unintentional remark. The biblical term *maḥazeh*, a symbol for the *Shekhinah*, is at the same time the "secret of the covenant." Hence, vision equals Presence equals secret of the covenant; by the principle of transitivity, then, vision equals secret of the covenant. One would therefore not expect this higher gradation to commune with Abraham prior to his circumcision. The symbolic network thus established calls for interpretation.

We may begin to interpret this symbolism by reference to another standard Zoharic notion concerning the twofold nature of the *berit*. According to the *Zohar*, the covenant in its totality comprises two aspects, masculine and feminine, the ninth and tenth *sefirot*, *Yesod* ("Foundation") and *Malkhut* ("Kingship") or *Shekhinah*.[39] The "vision" [*maḥazeh*], spoken of as the *raza di-berit*, "secret of the covenant," corresponds to only one of these aspects, the *Shekhinah*. Prior to Abraham's circumcision he could not possibly have merited a complete theophany, but only a partial one related exclusively to the feminine hypostasis of God: the "secret of the covenant," the "vision," the "lowest gradation." After the circumcision, however, Abraham experienced the masculine and feminine aspects of God, for by means of circumcision one enters into both gradations.[40] Only by appropriating the two dimensions could Abraham experience the full theophanic image:

Come and see: before one is circumcised one is not united to the name of the Holy One, blessed be He; when one is circumcised one enters the name and is united to it.[41] And, if you say that Abraham was united to it before he was circumcised, indeed he was, but not as it is fitting, for out of the supernal love that the Holy One, blessed be He, had for Abraham, He drew him near. Afterward He commanded him to circumcise himself and gave him the covenant, the bond of all the upper gradations. The covenant: the bond to tie everything together, to contain one in the other; the covenant: the bond in which everything is tied. Therefore, before Abraham was circumcised [God] spoke with him only by means of the "vision." [42]

Abraham's bondedness to the sefirotic realm prior to his circumcision was not "proper" or adequate, for it was only out of God's love for him that he was drawn close to the divine. By means of circumcision, however, one properly merits union with the divine; the phallus is the place of the covenant or the knot in which all the upper grades are united. Whereas before the circumcision Abraham was addressed by the "vision," that is, by the *Shekhinah,* after the circumcision he was himself bound to the covenant that binds together the upper forces in the lower grade, that is, the *sefirah* of *Yesod* as united with the *Shekhinah.* In effect, the claim of the *Zohar* is that only one (in this case Abraham) who is circumcised can be united with the *Shekhinah* in Her state of fullness and thereby cleave to the upper realm of the *sefirot.*[43]

However, the circumcision of Abraham also has a theurgical dimension, for it effects a change in the nature of the divine: just as in the fulfillment of circumcision one joins the masculine and feminine potencies in oneself, so too one brings about such a unification above. The *Zohar* exegetically connects this mystery to Gen. 18:1 as well:

Come and see: Before Abraham was circumcised nothing but the [lowest] gradation was upon him, as we have said. After he was circumcised, what is written? "And the Lord appeared to him" (Gen. 18:1). To whom? It is not written. "And the Lord appeared to Abram," for if [God] appeared to Abraham, what more praise is there now than in the beginning, before he was circumcised? For it is written, "And the Lord appeared to Abram" (Gen. 17:1) [i.e., before the circumcision]. This is rather a hidden secret. "And the Lord appeared to him," i.e., to that gradation that spoke with him [Abraham], which did not take place before he was circumcised. For now [after the circumcision] the Voice [sc. *Tif'eret,* "Beauty," the sixth emanation, the central pillar in the divine edifice] was revealed and united with the Speech *[Shekhinah]* when the latter spoke to Abraham. "And he sat in the opening of the tent." "And he" [the verse] does not reveal who. The [Torah] here revealed wisdom, for all the gradations [the *sefirot]* rested upon that lower gradation *[Shekhinah]* after Abraham was circumcised.[44]

The secret of the verse alludes to the fact that Abraham's circumcision initiated a change in the *Shekhinah* in relation to the other *sefirot.* Before Abraham's circumcision, only the *Shekhinah* conversed with him; after his circumcision She was united with Her masculine consort, *Tif'eret,* and the latter was revealed to Abraham through the *Shekhinah.* This is the mystical meaning of Gen. 18:1, "And the Lord," *Tif'eret,* the masculine potency or the attribute of mercy, "appeared to him," that is, to that gradation that spoke to Abraham, the feminine *Shekhinah* or the attribute of judgment. The post-circumcision theophany involved the unification of the Voice *(qol)* and Speech *(dibbur),*[45] the masculine and feminine. At that time, therefore, all the upper grades rested upon the lowest one.

In another context the *Zohar* expresses Abraham's transformation in

slightly different terms but in a way that further elucidates the conceptual link between visionary experience and circumcision. "Come and
see: when Abraham was circumcised he emerged from the foreskin and
entered the holy covenant and was crowned in the holy crown, and
entered the foundation upon which the world stands." [46] By circumcising
himself Abraham thus departed from the realm of the demonic powers
(symbolized by the foreskin) and entered the holy realm.[47] Entrance into
the latter comprises two elements: the first gradation is referred to
alternatively as the "holy covenant" or the "holy crown," that is, the
feminine *Shekhinah,* and the second as "the foundation upon which the
world stands," that is, the masculine *Yesod.* The possibility of seeing
God is now understood as being dependent upon a transference from
the demonic to the sefirotic worlds. Before his circumcision Abraham
could not fully apprehend God because his body was still encased in the
demonic shell, the foreskin covering the phallus.

Like the midrashist in *Numbers Rabbah,* the author of the *Zohar*
here conceives of circumcision as a removal of the impure obstacle
(though in the case of the latter this has become a symbol for a satanic
force) that separates man from God and prevents a complete visionary
relationship. Moreover, circumcision is an opening up of the human
body: "R. Yose said, Why is it written. 'And the Lord will pass over the
door *[ha-petaḥ]*' (Exod. 12:23)? . . . 'Over the door,' over that very
opening *[ha-petaḥ mamash],* that is, the opening of the body *[petaḥ ha-
guf].* And what is the opening of the body? That refers to [the place of]
circumcision." [48] The physiological opening, in turn, structurally parallels the opening in the sefirotic realm, the last gradation, *Shekhinah,*[49]
through which one enters into relationship with God. This, according to
the *Zohar,* is the theosophic significance of the scriptural claim that
Abraham—after his circumcision—was "sitting at the opening of the
tent *[petaḥ ha-'ohel]*" (Gen. 18:1), that is, the *Shekhinah,* "the place
which is called covenant, the secret of faith." [50] Circumcision is thus
an opening up of the phallus that eventuates in the opening up—the
disclosure—of the divine. "Come and see: before Abraham was circumcised he was closed and concealed *['aṭim ve-satim]* from every side.
When he was circumcised he was opened with respect to everything and
was not closed or concealed as before. This is the mystery, as we have
taught, 'And he [Abraham] was sitting at the opening of the tent' (Gen.
18:1), for the *yod* was revealed." [51]

To appreciate fully the import of this passage one must bear in mind that the letter *yod*, already in classical midrashic sources,[52] was conceived of as the letter or mark of circumcision imprinted, as it were, on the phallus. In Zoharic terms, the letter *yod*, the seal of circumcision, the *'ot berit*, corresponds to the *sefirah* of Yesod.[53] By disclosing the *yod* on one's body, the corona of the phallus, the *yod* in the upper realm is likewise disclosed. The result of this process is alluded to in the end of Gen. 18:1, "And he [Abraham] was sitting at the opening of the tent." Two meanings are implied here: Abraham below sat at the tent's entrance, which itself reflects the condition of openness he found himself in on account of the circumcision performed on his body. Theosophically, Abraham symbolizes the *sefirah* of Ḥesed (Love) and the opening of the tent, *Shekhinah*. When the *yod* (*Yesod*) is revealed, then *Ḥesed* is united with the *Shekhinah*, and the forces of judgment are ameliorated.[54]

III

The Zoharic reworking of the midrashic motif can now be fully outlined. By means of circumcision one is opened up in such a way that God may be revealed; the physical opening engenders a space in which the theophany occurs. Indeed, only one who is circumcised can withstand the manifestation of God. In the *Zohar*, however, circumcision is not only a prerequisite for the vision of God, but the place of circumcision, the phallus, is itself the locus of such a vision: one sees God from the circumcised flesh or, put differently, from the semiological seal of the covenant imprinted on that flesh. In one passage de León interprets the same verse from Job, "This, after my skin will have been peeled off; but I would behold God from my flesh" (19:26), which was interpreted in an altogether different way in the section from *Genesis Rabbah*,[55] which I discussed at the outset:

He began another discourse and said, "But I would behold God from my flesh" (Job 19:26). Why [is it written] "from my flesh"? It should be rather "from myself"! It is, literally, "from my flesh." What is that [flesh]? As it is written, "The holy flesh will be removed from you" (Jer. 11:15), and it is written, "And my covenant will be in your flesh" (Gen. 17:13). It has been taught: he who is marked with the holy seal of that sign [of circumcision] sees the Holy One, blessed be He, from that very sign itself.[56]

The flesh whence one beholds God, according to the verse from Job, refers to the flesh of circumcision, the seal of the covenant. One is said to see the Holy One from the sign of the covenant inscribed in one's flesh, the letter *yod*. As we have seen, in the case of the *Zohar* the letter *yod* is not understood simply as a sign of the covenant between God and Israel but is the very sign of the Holy One himself. The double function of the word *'ot* in Hebrew holds the key to unlocking the meaning of the kabbalistic doctrine: *'ot* is both a sign and a letter. One sees God from the sign on one's body, but that sign is nothing other than the letter *yod*. Here we meet a convergence of anthropomorphic and letter symbolism: the physical organ in its essential character is interchangeable with the letter, and the letter with the physical organ. The rite of circumcision thus ushers the individual into a semiological—as well as ontological— relationship with God: the seal of the covenant itself is the divine letter (or sign) inscribed on the flesh. This is the mystical sense of the Jobian claim that from the flesh—that is, from the phallus or place of the covenant—one beholds God.

The dynamic of circumcision, which I have discussed above—the play of closure/openness—informs us about the nature of mystical her- meneutics as well: that which is hidden must be brought to light, and the medium of disclosure is the seal of the covenant. In various ways the author of the *Zohar* establishes a structural affinity between the act of disclosing esoteric truths and that of sexual ejaculation, or in other words between the phallus and the mouth, the covenant of the foreskin and the covenant of the tongue.[57] Thus, for example, the *Zohar* inter- prets Eccles. 5:5, "Don't let your mouth cause your flesh to sin," as referring either to sins of a sexual nature[58] or to the sin of disclosing esoteric truths that one has not received from one's teacher.[59] The impropriety of illicit sexual behavior is parallel to the impropriety of revealing hidden truths that one has not properly received.[60] Indeed, in one place de León interprets the prohibition against idolatry in Exod. 20:4 as the sin of "lying in the name of God."[61] Yet there are two explanations offered for this: one who lies in God's name is either one who reveals secrets of Torah (for Torah equals name of God)[62] or one who has sexual relations with a non-Jew (for phallus equals the name).[63] As Yehuda Liebes has pointed out, the common denominator here can only be that both sorts of sin involve the phallus.[64] Liebes has further shown that, according to the *Zohar*, the mystic exegete below is the symbolic correlate of the *sefirah* of *Yesod* (the phallus) above. When the time is ripe, the exegete, the *Ṣaddiq* in the world, discloses what has been concealed. "It has been taught: In the days of R. Shimeon people would say to one another, 'Open your mouth and illuminate your words' (BT *Berakhot* 22a). After R. Shimeon died, they would say, 'Don't let your mouth cause your flesh to sin.' "[65]

The relation of the phallus and disclosure/concealment of mystical truth is made even clearer in the following remark:

R. Shimeon opened [his exposition] and said, "A base fellow reveals secrets, but a trustworthy soul conceals the matter" (Prov. 11:13). . . . Concerning him who is not settled in his spirit and who is not faithful, the word that he hears goes inside him like that which revolves in water[66] until it is cast outside. Why? Because his spirit is not a firm spirit *[ruḥa de-qiyyuma]*. But he whose spirit is a firm one, concerning him it is written, "A trustworthy soul conceals the matter." "A trustworthy soul" *[ve-ne'eman ruaḥ]*, one's whose spirit is faithful *[qiyyuma de-ruḥa]*, as [it is written], "I will fix him as a peg *[yated]* in a firm place" (Isa. 22:23). The matter is dependent on the secret *[he-raza talya milta]*. It is written, "Don't let your mouth cause your flesh to sin." The world only exists through the secret.[67]

The one who keeps the secret is the "trustworthy soul," *ne'eman ruaḥ*, which is rendered by the *Zohar*: *qiyyuma de-ruḥa*.[68] There can be no doubt that this is a reference to the *Ṣaddiq*, the symbolic correlate below to *Yesod*, whose status as a righteous person is particularly related to the phallus.[69] Such a person is here called *qiyyuma de-ruḥa*, which may be translated "the pillar of the spirit,"[70] for he is one who sustains the spirit, holds it in its place. The word *qiyyuma* functions in the *Zohar*, *inter alia*, as a phallic symbol[71] and may have that shade of meaning in this context as well. The faithfulness or steadfastness of one's spirit is therefore a condition especially connected to the phallus. This interpretation is further substantiated by the proof-text from Isaiah wherein the word *yated*, peg, also must be seen as functioning as a phallic symbol. This symbolism, moreover, enables us to decipher the remark that the "matter is dependent on the secret," that is, on the phallus or its symbolic correlate, the *sefirah* of *Yesod*, which is appropriately called secret for it is the divine gradation that is hidden and concealed from the eye.[72] Hence, R. Shimeon admonishes his comrades, "Don't let your mouth cause your flesh to sin," for the world exists only through the secret, sustained by means of that foundation or pillar *(Yesod)* which must be concealed. Just as the proper disclosure of esoteric truth is bound up with the flesh, with the phallus or the *sefirah* of *Yesod*,[73] so too an improper disclosure is a sin bound up with this limb.

Textual interpretation, as circumcision, involves the dynamic of clo-
sure/openness: as the one who is circumcised stands in relation to the
Shekhinah, so the exegete—through interpretation—enters into an intimate relation with *Shekhinah.* The duplicity of the text as that which
simultaneously conceals and reveals—indeed conceals as that which
reveals and reveals as that which conceals—is a thoroughly appropriate
metaphor to convey the erotic quality of hermeneutical stance.[74] Inasmuch as there is this structural affinity between the interpretative task
and the phallus,[75] the exegete must be circumcised, for penetration into
the text is itself an act of sexual unification. This dynamic doubtless
underlies the Zoharic prohibition of Torah study for the uncircumcised:

R. Abba said: Praiseworthy is the portion of Israel, for the Holy One, blessed be
He, desired them more than all the idolatrous nations. And on account of His
love for them He gave them His laws of truth, planted the Tree of Life in their
midst, and placed His *Shekhinah* amongst them. Why? For Israel are marked by
the holy sign *[reshima qadisha]* on their flesh, and it is known that they are His,
from those who belong to His palace.[76] Therefore, all those who are not marked
with the holy sign on their flesh do not belong to Him; it is known that they all
derive from the side of impurity.[77] It is therefore forbidden to join with them
and to converse with them concerning words [or matters] of the Holy One,
blessed be He. It is also forbidden to instruct them in words of Torah, for the
entire Torah is the name of the Holy One, blessed be He,[78] and each letter of the
Torah is bound to the Holy Name. It is forbidden to instruct the person who is
not marked by the holy sign on his flesh in the words of Torah. How much more
so to be engaged *[le-'ishtaddela]* in it![79]

One who is uncircumcised cannot study Torah, for the Torah is the
name of God, and study thereof involves unification with the name.
Only one who is circumcised can be united with the name, and hence
only such a person can study Torah. The final remark, that it is forbidden to be engaged in the study of Torah with one who is uncircumcised,
serves to emphasize that the esoteric dimension of the tradition cannot
be divulged to anyone who does not have the holy sign inscribed on his
flesh. The aspect of hiddenness or secrecy is indicative of the very essence
of the *sefirah* which corresponds to the phallus.[80] Indeed, the word *sod,*
secret or mystery, is attributed specifically to the divine gradation of
Yesod. Secrets of Torah, therefore, cannot be transmitted to one who is
uncircumcised:

R. Abba opened [his exposition] and said: "The secret of the Lord is with those
who fear Him [to them He makes known His covenant]" (Ps. 25:14). "The

secret of the Lord is with those who fear Him": the Holy One, blessed be He, has not given the upper secret of the Torah except to those who fear sin. To those who do fear sin the upper secret of Torah is disclosed. And what is the upper secret of the Torah? I would say, it is the sign of the holy covenant [*'ot qayama qadisha*], which is called the secret of the Lord, the holy covenant.[81]

The secret of the Lord given to those who fear sin is the holy covenant of God, the *berit qodesh,* that is, the *sefirah* that corresponds to the phallus, *Yesod.* The secrecy and concealment of this particular emanation is emphasized by de León in his Hebrew theosophic writings as well. Thus, for example, in *Sefer ha-Rimmon* he writes that *Yesod* is "called secret, *sod,* for its matter is secrecy, a hidden mystery of the Creator."[82] The process of circumcision, the removal of the foreskin and the uncovering of the corona, is a disclosure of the secret. In the disclosure of the phallus, through the double act of circumcision, the union of the masculine and feminine aspects of God is assured. "When the holy sign [*Yesod*] is uncovered it overflows and the bride [*Shekhinah*] . . . then stands in completeness and her portion is illuminated."[83] Circumcision, therefore, is here viewed as a necessary precondition for studying Torah—exoteric and esoteric—just as in other contexts it is depicted as a necessary precondition for visionary experience or prophetic theophany. He who is closed—uncircumcised—cannot open the text just as he cannot behold the divine Presence. The relationship of exegete to text is like that of the visionary to the *Shekhinah.* Indeed, it may be said that, according to the *Zohar,* insofar as the Torah is the corporeal form of the divine, textual study itself is a mode of visionary experience.[84]

The opening of circumcision is thus not only the opening through which one may see God, but it the opening through which one may study the holy text, the Torah. The particular relation between the covenant of circumcision and the activity of Torah study is further brought to light in the following passage:

R. Jose asked R. Shimeon: It is taught that words [such as] *ve-'aggidah, va-yagged,* and *va-yaggidu,* all [point to] the secret of wisdom [*raza de-ḥokhmata*]. Why does this word [the root *ngd*] allude to the secret of wisdom? He [R. Shimeon] said to him [R. Jose]: Because [in] this word the *gimmel* and *dalet* are found without any separation [between them]. And this is the secret of wisdom, a word that comes in completeness in the secret of the letters. Thus it is when they [the letters] are in wisdom, but *dalet* without *gimmel* is not completion, and so *gimmel* without *dalet,* for the one is bound to the other without separation.

And the one who separates them causes death for himself; and this secret [the separation of *gimmel* and *dalet*] is the [cause and result of the] sin of Adam. Therefore this word *[ngd]* is the secret of wisdom. And even though at times there is a *yod* between the *gimmel* and *dalet,* there is not separation [in that case], for all is one bond.[85]

The word *higgid,* to tell or speak, alludes to the secret of wisdom, for in the root of this word, the letters *gimmel* and *dalet* are contiguous. Symbolically, the *gimmel* corresponds to *Yesod* and the *dalet* to *Shekhinah,* for *Yesod* is that which "bestows upon" *(gomel)* the *Shekhinah* who is the "poor one" *(dal).*[86] The secret of wisdom, therefore, involves the unification of the ninth and tenth *sefirot, Yesod* (masculine) and *Shekhinah* (feminine). It is this (sexual) unification, moreover, that constitutes the nature of telling, speaking, in a word, discourse. Speech *(ngd)* is thus understood by the same structural dynamic that characterizes the play of divine sexuality and the dual nature of circumcision. By means of circumcision the *gimmel* is uncovered and consequently pours forth to the *dalet.* The *yod* that is between them is the sign of the covenant (corona) that acts as a bridge uniting masculine and feminine. Indeed, the three consonants, *gimmel, yod, dalet,* spell the word *gid,* which in rabbinic literature[87] is sometimes used as a euphemism for the phallus. This, no doubt, is the underlying meaning of the concluding statement that, "even though at times there is a *yod* between the *gimmel* and *dalet,* there is no separation, for all is one bond." It is from the union of *gimmel* and *dalet, Yesod* and *Shekhinah,* that discourse *(aggadah)* proceeds, and the secret is disclosed.

I can now sum up the various steps that have been taken along the way in this analysis. Already in rabbinic *midrash* a clear nexus is established between circumcision and the visualization of God, or a Godlike appearance. In the earlier midrashic passage it seems that this nexus is focused on a deontological conception well known from many rabbinic sources: through the doing of good deeds, that is, through fulfilling God's commandments, one is rewarded. In this particular case the good deed is circumcision and the reward the epiphany of God. In a later midrashic context the nexus is reasserted, this time however based on the ontological criterion that only one whose sexual organ is circumcised can stand in the presence of God's glory. This is because it is necessary for one to remove the unholy foreskin before one can withstand the manifestation of God. The author of the *Zohar* further develops this mesh of ideas in the framework of his theosophical conception. Visualization of God, as study of the Torah, involves the unification of man with the feminine potency of the divine; therefore, only one who is circumcised can be said to either see God or study the Torah. Moreover, just as the act of circumcision itself comprises two elements that correspond to the masculine and feminine dimensions of God, so too an act of seeing God—prophetically or textually—comprises these very elements. The opening of circumcision is an opening of the flesh that is, at the same time, an opening within the divine. When the foreskin is removed and the phallus uncovered, then the corresponding limb above, the divine phallus or *Yesod,* likewise is uncovered. In this uncovering the secret of God is disclosed. The hermeneutical process is a structural reenactment of circumcision, involving as it does the movement from closure to openness.[88] The opening of the flesh eventuates in the opening of God, which is reexperienced as the opening of the text.

In conclusion, it may be said that the writing of the *Zohar* itself, a disclosure of hidden layers of meaning, may be understood in light of the various structures that we have sought to uncover. The particular relation established between the phallus *(Yesod)* and secret *(sod)* lends further support to the view that the very process of textual interpretation undertaken by the author of the *Zohar* was understood in terms of this dynamic of closure/openness. The bringing forth of that which was hidden—which is, after all, the raison d'être of this classic of Jewish mysticism—can only be comprehended in light of this dynamic. Yet, as we have seen, the transition from closure to openness is itself characteristic of divine revelation. It can be assumed, therefore, that the writing of this text proceeded from some such experience of divine immediacy—in a word, exposure to God. Students of Jewish mysticism are apt to lose sight of the deeply experiential character of this work. While it is true that the *Zohar* is nominally and structurally a *midrash,* that is, a commentary on Scripture, I have tried to show that in this text the hermeneutical mode is inseparably wedded to the visionary. This paper has provided one vantage point through which this merging of epistemic modes can be understood. Both visualization of God and the hermeneutical task are predicated upon a physiological opening that corresponds to an ontological opening within the divine. Disclosure of what has been concealed—through the opening of the flesh—is the basic structure common to visionary experience and mystical hermeneutics.

NOTES

1. The most comprehensive treatment of the *Zohar* in English remains G. Scholem, *Major Trends in Jewish Mysticism,* 3d ed. (New York: Schocken Books, 1961), chaps. 5 and 6. See also D. Matt, *Zohar, the Book of Enlightenment* (New York: Paulist Press, 1983), pp. 3–39; I. Tishby, *The Wisdom of the Zohar,* trans. by D. Goldstein (Oxford, 1989), pp. 1–126.

2. Conversely, according to the *Zohar,* the Jew who has sexual relations with a non-Jew is guilty of idolatry, i.e., worshiping other gods, which, in Zoharic theosophy, means the forces of impurity. Compare *Zohar Ḥadash* 21a *(Midrash ha-Ne'elam* on Noah); *Zohar* I, 131b; II, 3b, 87b; III, 84a, 142a *(Idra Rabba).* On the connection between idolatry and adultery in earlier rabbinic sources, cf. S. Schechter, *Aspects of Rabbinic Theology* (New York: Schocken Books, 1961), p. 250. In the preparation of this study the following editions have been used: *Sefer ha-Zohar,* ed. R. Margaliot, 3 vols. (Jerusalem: Mosad ha-Rav Kook, 1984); *Zohar Ḥadash,* ed. R. Margaliot (Jerusalem: Mosad ha-Rav Kook, 1978); *Tiqqunei Zohar,* ed R. Margaliot (Jerusalem: Mosad ha-Rav Kook, 1978).

3. Compare *Zohar* III, 72b, 73a, and, ibid., 91b: "The holy Name, which is the Torah, is not made known to one who is not circumcised and who has not entered (the) covenant"; see also *Zohar* I, 236b, where it is said that Simeon and Levi circumcised the inhabitants of Shechem in order to teach them the secrets of Torah. Mention should be made of the fact that the restriction of Torah-study to a Jew is talmudic in origin; see the statement of R. Yohanan in the Babylonian Talmud (BT) *Sanhedrin* 59a, and that of R. Ami, a disciple of R. Yohanan, in *Ḥagigah* 13a. As far as I know, however, the rabbinic restriction is in no way connected with the issue of circumcision. More poignant, perhaps, is the remark of the Roman satirist, Juvenal (60–130 C.E.), in his *Saturae,* 14, lines 96, 104, cited and translated in Menahem Stern, *Greek and Latin Authors on Jews and Judaism* (Jerusalem: Israel Academy of Sciences and Humanities, 1980). 2:102, 3, concerning Moses' refusal to disclose the truths of Torah to any but the circumcised. The similarity between the view of Juvenal and that of the *Zohar* was already noted by Y. Liebes. "The Messiah of the Zohar," in *The Messianic Idea in Jewish Thought: A Study Conference in Honour of the Eightieth Birthday of Gershom Scholem* (Jerusalem: Israel Academy of Sciences and Humanities, 1982), p. 140, n. 205 (in Hebrew).

4. See references given in n. 1 above. To those may be added the discussion in Elliot R. Wolfson, *The Book of the Pomegranate: Moses de Leon's Sefer ha-Rimmon* (Atlanta: Scholars Press, 1988), pp. 3–9 (English section).

5. The biblical injunction for circumcision (see Gen. 17:10–14, Lev. 12:3, cf. Exod. 12:48), and the normative practice derived therefrom, is clearly and unambiguously directed to the male child. There is documentary evidence in the writings of Strabo of Amaseia (first century B.C.E.-first century C.E.) that

some Jews practiced not only circumcision on male children but excision on female children as well. See M. Stern, *Greek and Latin Authors on Jews and Judaism* (Jerusalem: Israel Academy of Sciences and Humanities, 1976), 1:300, 315. Compare, however, L. H. Schiffman, *Who Was a Jew? Rabbinic and Halakhic Perspectives on the Jewish-Christian Schism* (Hoboken, N.J.: Ktav, 1985), p. 84, n. 35.

6. This is based in part on the fact that circumcision is referred to in the Bible (see Gen. 17:11) as an *'ot*, i.e., a sign. The rabbis thus spoke of a "letter" (a secondary meaning of the word *'ot*) which served as the "seal" of the covenant of circumcision, namely, the letter *yod*. Compare *Tanḥuma* (Jerusalem: Lewin-Epstein, 1964), *Ṣav*, 14, *Shemini*, 8, and see n. 53 below.

7. On the "seal" as a designation for circumcision, see G. W. E. Nickelsburg, "Stories of Biblical and Early Post-biblical Times," in *Jewish Writings of the Second Temple Period*, ed. M. E. Stone (Philadelphia: Fortress Press, 1984), p. 73, and references in n. 218.

8. Compare Jacques Derrida, "Shibboleth," in *Midrash and Literature*, ed. G. Hartman and S. Budick (New Haven, Conn.: Yale University Press, 1986), pp. 307–47.

9. Compare Liebes, pp. 138–46.

10. Compare Jacob Neusner, *Midrash in Context* (Philadelphia: Fortress Press, 1984), p. 83.

11. *Genesis Rabbah*, ed. Theodor-Albeck (Jerusalem: Wahrmann, 1965), 48:1 (p. 479), and 48:9 (p. 485). Compare Philo, *Quaestiones et Solutiones in Genesin* (Loeb Classical Library) 3.49, who writes that circumcision is the sign of election for "Israel, that is seeing God." It is difficult to ascertain if Philo had in mind some midrashic tradition akin to what we have found in the Palestinian *Genesis Rabbah*. On the Philonic etymology of Israel as "one who sees God," cf. P. Borgen, *Bread from Heaven* (Leiden: E. J. Brill, 1965), pp. 115–18 (and other references given there, p. 115, n. 3); G. Delling, "The 'One Who Sees God' in Philo," in *Nourished with Peace: Studies in Hellenistic Judaism in Memory of Samuel Sandmel*, ed. F. Greenspahn, E. Hilgert, and B. Mack (Chico, Calif.: Scholars Press, 1984), pp. 27–49. For Philo's views on circumcision, see R. Hecht, "The Exegetical Contexts of Philo's Interpretation of Circumcision," in Greenspahn, Hilgert, and Mack, eds., pp. 51–79.

12. The whole problematic is presumably eliminated by the form-critical method of exegesis, which ascribes different authorship to the two literary strata: Gen. 17:23–27 is a Priestly document that supposedly follows Gen. 17:1–14, which is P's instruction for circumcision, whereas Gen. 18:1–6 is a narrative complex derived from J (ending in Gen. 19:38). See Gerhard von Rad, *Genesis* (Philadelphia: Westminster Press, 1972), pp. 202–4. Yet, one could argue that the crucial question is not that of disparate textual units but, rather, the literary whole achieved by a process of redaction. From this latter perspective, the conjunction of these passages raises the hermeneutical problem addressed by the ancient Jewish exegetes.

13. This is in keeping with what James Kugel has called the "verse-cen-

teredness" of *midrash*; see his "Two Interpretations of Midrash," in Hartman and Budick, eds. (n. 8 above), pp. 94–95.

14. A classic study of this rabbinic conception is A. Marmorstein, *The Doctrine
of Merits in Old Rabbinical Literature* (New York: Ktav, 1968).

15. See ibid., s.v. "circumcision"; and cf. J. Neusner, *Genesis Rabbah: The
Judaic Commentary to the Book of Genesis* (Atlanta: Scholars Press, 1985),
2: 178–79.

16. The foreskin is referred to several times in the Bible itself as the "flesh of the
foreskin"; see Gen. 17:11, 14, 23, 24–25; Lev. 12:3.

17. For a discussion on circumcision as the taxonomy for Judaism in antiquity,
see Jonathan Smith, "Fences and Neighbors," in *Approaches to Ancient
Judaism*, ed. W. S. Green (Chico, Calif.: Scholars Press, 1980), 2:9–15;
Schiffman (n. 5 above), pp. 23–24.

18. Compare *Bereshit Rabbati*, ed. C. Albeck (Jerusalem: Wahrmann, 1940), p.
79. See also the commentary of Naḥmanides on Gen. 18:1 (ed. H. Chavel
[Jerusalem: Mosad ha-Rav Kook, 1960], 1:106–7): "The disclosure of the
Shekhinah . . . is a reward for a precept that has already been fulfilled."
According to another line of interpretation, the nexus between Abraham's
circumcision in Genesis 17 and the theophany at the beginning of chap. 18
is meant to teach us about the virtue of visiting the sick, for God himself in
this case serves as the role model insofar as He comes to visit Abraham
immediately after the circumcision. See, e.g., BT *Baba Meṣi'a* 86b, *Soṭah*
14a; *Genesis Rabbah* 8:13 (p. 67).

19. See the comment of D. Freedman in *Midrash Rabbah* (London: Soncino
Press, 1939), 1:406, n. 4: "Deriving *nikkefu* from *hikkif* [the expression
used in Job 19:26], to surround, i.e., proselytes flocked, surrounding him,
as it were."

20. See, e.g., *Targum Pseudo-Jonathan* on Gen. 12:5 (ed. E. G. Clarke with
collaboration by W. E. Aufrecht, J. C. Hurd, and F. Spitzer [New York:
Ktav, 1984], p. 13); *Targum Onkelos ad loc. (The Bible in Aramaic*, ed.
Alexander Sperber [Leiden: E. J. Brill, 1959]. 1:17); *The Fragment-Targums
of the Pentateuch*, ed. Michael L. Klein (Rome: Pontifical Institute, 1980),
1:49, 132, 2:11; *Genesis Rabbah* 39:14 (pp. 378–79). For other aggadic
sources, see L. Ginzberg, *The Legends of the Jews* (Philadelphia: Jewish
Publication Society, 1913), 1:195, 217; M. Kasher, *Torah Shelemah* (New
York: American Biblical Encyclopedia Society, 1949), 3:555, n. 95.

21. Compare Rom. 2:5–29, 4:9–12; 1 Cor. 7:18: Eph. 2:8–13; Gal. 5:2–6;
Col. 2:11; Phil. 3:3. On baptism, or the circumcision of the spirit, as a
substitute for circumcision of the flesh, see Col. 2:12–13; Gal. 6:13–14;
Origen, *Contra Celsum*, 5:48 (ed. H. Chadwick [Cambridge: Cambridge
University Press, 1953], p. 302); P. Borgen, "Paul Preaches Circumcision
and Pleases Men," in *Paul and Paulinism: Essays in Honour of C. K.
Barrett*, ed. M. D. Hooker and S. G. Wilson (London: SPCK, 1982), pp.
37–46. It should be noted that some church fathers had trouble explaining
the abolishment of circumcision in light of the fact that Jesus himself was

circumcised; see Epiphanius, *Adversus Haereses Panarium* 28.5.2 (cited in M. Werner, *The Formation of Christian Dogma* [Boston: Beacon Press, 1965], p. 90). There is ample Patristic evidence, moreover, that certain Jewish-Christian sects, such as the Ebionites and Nazoraeans, still practiced circumcision and kept the Sabbath; cf. A. F. J. Klijn and G. J. Reinink, *Patristic Evidence for Jewish-Christian Sects* (Leiden: E. J. Brill, 1973), pp. 20, 23–24, 29, 35, 37, 39, 42, 44, 51.

22. See Schiffman (n. 5 above), pp. 23–25; Ginzberg, 5:263–69, n. 318.

23. Compare *Tanhuma*, ed. Solomon Buber (New York: Sefer, 1946), *Vayera* 4; "R. Isaac Nafha." The same reading is found in *Tanhuma, Vayera* 2; *Aggadat Bereshit, 19.*

24. Compare *Genesis Rabbah* 63:13 (p. 698), where it is reported that R. Levi transmitted the following opinion in the name of R. Hama bar Hanina: Esau's rejection of his birthright was tied to his hatred of the blood of circumcision. In this context it is clear that Esau functions as a symbol for the Christian church; see Idrit Aminoff, "The Figures of Esau and the Kingdom of Edom in Palestinian Midrashic-Talmudic Literature in the Tannaitic and Amoraic Periods" (Ph.D. diss., Melbourne University, 1981), pp. 131–33. On this midrashic typology, see also Ginzberg, 5:272, n. 19; G. Cohen, "Esau as a Symbol in Early Medieval Thought," in *Jewish Medieval and Renaissance Studies,* ed. A. Altmann (Cambridge, Mass.: Harvard University Press, 1967), pp. 27–30, and references given on p. 27, n. 31. Compare also *Genesis Rabbah* 65:9 (pp. 726–27), where R. Levi and R. Isaac are involved in anti-Christian polemics as well; see Aminoff, p. 136, n. 18, and pp. 217–20. On R. Isaac and R. Levi, as well as other third-century aggadists, as defenders of Judaism against the attacks of the Church found in the Syriac Didascalia, see A. Marmorstein, "Judaism and Christianity in the Middle of the Third Century," *Hebrew Union College Annual* 10 (1935): 236, nn. 75–76, 243, nn. 111–12.

25. On the connection between circumcision and sacrifices, see G. Vermes, "Circumcision and Exodus IV 24–26," in *Scripture and Tradition in Judaism* (Leiden: E. J. Brill, 1983), pp. 178–92. Some scholars have even suggested that infantile circumcision in ancient Israel on the eighth day must be seen as a replacement for child sacrifice (see Exod. 22:29, Lev. 22:27); cf. W. Eichrodt, *Theology of the Old Testament* (Philadelphia: Westminster Press, 1961), 1:138, n. 3.

26. This interpretation can be traced to earlier sources; cf. *Targum Pseudo-Jonathan* on Gen. 17:3 (ed. E. G. Clarke et al., p. 17); *Genesis Rabbah* 46:6 (pp. 463–64), 47:3 (pp. 472–73); *Tanhuma, Lekh Lekha* 20 (p. 23); *Pirqei de-R. Eliezer* (New York: Om, 1946), chap. 29.

27. The same analogy or parable appears in the lost *Midrash Avkhir* as cited in the midrashic anthology, *Yalqut Shim'oni* (Jerusalem, 1960), vol. 1, sec. 82.

28. *Numbers Rabbah* (Tel Aviv: Moriah, 1960), 12:10; see Marc Saperstein, *Decoding the Rabbis* (Cambridge, Mass.: Harvard University Press, 1980), pp. 97–102.

29. Such an interpretation is found in an earlier midrashic source which doubt-less served as the basis for this passage; cf. *Shir ha-Shirim Rabbah* (Tel Aviv: Moriah, 1960), on Song of Songs 3:11. The connection of this verse to circumcision was probably also suggested to the midrashist by the words "wearing a crown," the latter being a reference to the corona of the phallus disclosed by the act of circumcision (see n. 53 below).

30. The equation of uncleanliness or impurity with uncircumcision is biblical in origin; cf. Isa. 52:1 and Ezek. 44:7. In rabbinic literature one of the names of the evil inclination is "uncircumcised" or the "foreskin"; cf. Schechter (n. 2 above), p. 243.

31. On the cutting of the foreskin as a symbol for the excision of sensual desires in the writings of Philo, see Hecht (n. 11 above), pp. 51–79. The connection between circumcision and the weakening of sexual desire was affirmed as well by medieval Jewish philosophers; see, e.g., Judah ha-Levi, *Sefer ha-Kuzari*, ed. Y. Even Shmuel (Tel Aviv: Dvir, 1972), 1:115; Maimonides, *Guide of the Perplexed*, ed. S. Pines (Chicago: University of Chicago Press, 1963), 3:49.

32. *Zohar* I, 98b. The nexus of circumcision and cleaving to the *Shekhinah* is alluded to as well in the Zoharic claim that before entering the land of Israel (a symbol for *Shekhinah*) Joshua had to circumcise the people; see I, 93b.

33. Moses Cordovero, *Zohar 'im Perush 'Or Yaqar* (Jerusalem: Or Yaqar, 1970), 5:4.

34. *Zohar* I, 97b.

35. Ibid., 88b–89a.

36. Ibid., 91 a–b.

37. See, e.g., Shimeon Lavi, *Ketem Paz* (Jerusalem: Ahabat Shalom, 1981), 1:224: "Before Abraham was circumcised his prophecy was in that lower vision, the image of an image. However, after he was circumcised his prophecy was in the higher vision, as it says, 'And the Lord appeared to Abram.' " The "lower vision" is identified by Lavi as the realm of celestial palaces below the world of emanation, whereas the "higher vision" is the *Shekhinah*, the last emanation which reflects all the upper ones, In addition to difficulties that one may have fitting this interpretation into the text, Lavi contradicts himself, for prior to this passage he wrote: "All the prophecies of the prophets were from the palaces which are below the hidden emana-tion, below *'Ateret* [i.e., *Shekhinah*] except for Moses . . . [whose prophecy] was in *'Ateret* itself." An alternative explanation is offered by Moses Cor-dovero in his commentary *'Or Yaqar* (Jerusalem: 'Or Yaqar, 1967), 4:181. According to him, the change in the visionary status of *Shekhinah* had nothing to do with the divine potency itself but, rather, with the level of comprehension of Abraham. Cordovero's explanation undermines the theurgical dimension of circumcision stressed by the author of the *Zohar* himself, esp. in I, 97a.

38. Compare Moses de León, *Sheqel ha-Qodesh*, ed. A. W. Greenup (London, 1911), p. 67: "And contemplate that the secret of the covenant (*sod ha-*

berit, a translation of the Zoharic *raza di-berit*) is universal faith *(derekh kelal 'emunah)*. And when the foreskin is removed from the phallus—this is the secret of faith. Yet the removal of the foreskin to enter into the secret of the faith [is not complete] until one pulls down [the membrane] and the corona is revealed. When one reaches the corona one enters into the mystery of the way of faith and is bound to faith." See below, nn. 44 and 53.

39. See *Zohar* I, 32a, 47b, 69a, 71b, 72b, 117a: III, 14a, 115b; G. Scholem, "Colours and Their Symbolism in Jewish Tradition and Mysticism," *Diogenes* 109 (1980): 69.

40. Compare *Zohar* I, 96b, 98b *(Sitrei Torah);* III, 14a. Kabbalists explained the androgynous nature of circumcision in terms of the two procedures required in the circumcision ritual by rabbinic law (cf. BT *Shabbat* 173b): *milah* (incision of the foreskin) and *peri'ah* (uncovering of the corona), which correspond symbolically to the two divine emanations, *Yesod* and *Shekhinah*. Compare, e.g., *Zohar* I, 13a, 32a–b; II, 40a, 60b, 125b; III, 91b, 163a.

41. On the connection between the divine name and circumcision, cf. *Zohar* I, 95a, 96b; II, 3b, 32a, 87b; III, 91a; *Tiqqunei Zohar*, secs. 24 (70a), 22(65b), 61 (94b). The correlation between circumcision and the Tetragrammaton is made in a host of thirteenth-century texts, the development of which I have treated in my study "Circumcision and the Divine Name: A Study in the Transmission of Esoteric Doctrine," *Jewish Quarterly Review* 78(1987): 77–112.

42. *Zohar* I, 89a.

43. Compare ibid., II, 61a, 86a, 216a; III, 73a–b.

44. Ibid., I, 98a. The connection between circumcision, visionary experience, and theurgy is brought out clearly in the following comment of de León in his *Sefer ha-Mishqal*, ed. J. Wijnhoven (Ph.D. diss., Brandeis University, 1964), p. 133: "The foreskin is the shell standing on the outside and the phallus is the core on the inside. . . . This is the secret of the proper matter when a person enters the secret of faith. Concerning this secret it says, 'All your males shall appear before the Lord your God' (Deut. 16:16). For one must cleave [to God] and show that place [the phallus] in its Source, the branch in its Root, to unite everything in the bond of the secret of His unity, with one bond and in one secret, so that 'the Lord will be one and His name will be one' (Zech. 14:9)."

45. Compare *Zohar* I, 36a, 145b; II, 25b.

46. *Zohar* I, 91b. On Abraham's flirtation with the demonic in the *Zohar*, see E. Wolfson, "Left Contained in the Right: A Study in Zoharic Hermeneutics," *Association for Jewish Studies Review* II, no. I (1986): 34, n. 34.

47. Compare *Zohar* I, 103b (and the parallel in de León's *Sefer ha-Mishqal.* pp. 131–32): "Come and see: before Abraham was circumcised his seed was not holy for it emerged from the foreskin and clove to the foreskin below. After he was circumcised the seed emerged from holiness and clove to the holiness above." On the separating of the foreskin from the phallus as an

enactment of the separation between the holy and demonic, cf. *Zohar* I, 13a, 95a–b; II, 255b; III, 72b–73a; (see Wolfson, "Mystical Rationalization of the Commandments in *Sefer ha-Rimmon*," *Hebrew Union College Annual* 59 (1988): 247; *Sheqel ha-Qodesh*, p. 67 (cited above, n. 38); *Tiqqunei ha-Zohar, Haqdamah* (11a), sec. 37 (78a); J. Wijnhoven, "The Zohar and the Proselyte," in *Texts and Responses: Studies Presented to Nahum N. Glatzer on the Occasion of His Seventieth Birthday*, ed. M. Fishbane and P. Flohr (Leiden: E. J. Brill, 1975), pp. 124–25.

48. *Zohar* II, 36a.

49. On the *Shekhinah* as "the opening," *ha-petaḥ*, or "the gate," *ha-sha'ar*, cf. *Zohar* I, 7b, 11b, 37a, 47b, 54b, 97b, 103a–b; II, 36a, 158a, 237b, III, 14a, 71b, 256.

50. Ibid., I, 97b *(Sitrei Torah)* also 103a–b (trans. Matt [n. 1 above], pp. 65–68).

51. *Zohar* II, 36a.

52. See n. 6 above.

53. Compare *Zohar* I, 13a, 56a, 95a; II, 36a; III, 142a *(Idra Rabba)*, 215b, 220a; Wolfson, *The Book of the Pomegranate*, p. 240 (Hebrew section); *Sheqel ha-Qodesh*, p. 63. In some Zoharic contexts the letter *yod* refers to the *Shekhinah*, which is said to correspond to the corona of the phallus. (The later symbolism is based on the fact that the word for the corona, *'aṭarah*, literally crown, is a technical name for *Shekhinah*.) Compare *Zohar* I, 93b, 255a *(Ra'aya Meheimna)*; II, 258a *(Ra'aya Meheimna)*; III, 256a *(Ra'aya Meheimna)*, 257a *(Ra'aya Meheimna)*, 263a; *Tiqqunei Zohar*, secs. 13 (29a), 18 (31b), 19 (39b), 21 (62b), 30 (73b), 47 (85a), 70 (120a).

54. Compare *Zohar* III, 142a *(Idra Rabba):* "Everything is dependent upon the opening of the phallus which is called *yod*. And when the *yod* is revealed, the opening of the phallus, the upper *Ḥesed* [Mercy] is revealed . . . and this [gradation] is not called *Ḥesed* until the *yod* is revealed . . . Come and see: Abraham was not called complete with respect to this *Ḥesed* until the *yod* of the phallus was revealed. And when it was revealed, he was called complete, as it is written, 'Walk before Me and be complete.' "

55. The connection of this Zoharic passage to that of *Genesis Rabbah* was already noted by Lavi (n. 37 above), see n. 29, fol. 230b.

56. *Zohar* I, 94a.

57. The correspondence between a "covenant of the foreskin" and a "covenant of the tongue" was first articulated in the Jewish mystical and cosmological text, *Sefer Yeṣirah*, 1:3 (concerning this text, see Scholem, *Major Trends in Jewish Mysticism* [n. 1 above], pp. 75–78). See the reading established by I. Gruenwald, "A Preliminary Critical Edition of *Sefer Yezira*," *Israel Oriental Studies* 1 (1971): 141, and the English rendering, "Some Critical Notes on the First Part of *Sefer Yezira*," *Revue des études juives* 132 (1973): 486: "Ten *sefirot belimah;* ten corresponding to the number of the ten fingers, five against five, and the covenant of the oneness is constituted in the center [as expressed] in the circumcision of the tongue and the mouth and in the circumcision of the foreskin." Compare further *Sefer Yeṣirah* 6:4, where it

is said that God made a covenant with Abraham "between the ten toes of
his feet and it is the covenant of circumcision" and a covenant "between the
ten fingers of his hands which is the tongue." Some scholars assume that the
covenant of the tongue or the mouth refers to a vow of secrecy, mentioned
explicitly in *Sefer Yeṣirah* 1:8, not to disclose mystical truths in public; see
Gruenwald, "Some Critical Notes," pp. 487, 490–91; see n. 79 below.

58. Compare *Zohar* I, 8a.

59. Ibid., II, 87a; cf. *Zohar* III, 79a, 105b, 106b, 128a *(Idra Rabba)*. In III,
159a the verse is used to support the view that one must not inquire about
certain things that are hidden from finite minds and are known only by
God. The last usage may reflect the fact that this verse is applied to the
apostate Elisha ben Abuya in the famous rabbinic legend of the "four who
entered Pardes"; see BT *Ḥagigah* 15b and parallels. The emphasis on the
need to keep truths hidden and the impropriety of revealing a truth that has
not been received directly from a teacher stands in marked contrast to the
general impression that one gets from reading de León's writings, wherein
the mystical imagination seems to have had an almost unbounded reign
over disclosing esoteric matters. On this "innovative" approach of de León,
in contrast to the more "conservative" approach of other mystics, such as
Naḥmanides, see M. Idel, "We Have No Kabbalistic Tradition on This," in
Rabbi Naḥmanides: Explorations in His Religious and Literary Virtuosity,
ed. I. Twersky (Cambridge, Mass.: Harvard University Press, 1983), pp.
51–73. In his discussion of de León, Idel did not take into account these
Zoharic passages, which emphasize secrecy and the esoteric quality of mystical truths; see, in contrast, Liebes (n. 3 above), esp. pp. 138–51. Compare
also the passage from de León's *Mishkan ha-Edut*, cited by Scholem in
Major Trends, pp. 201–2, and my extended analysis of the same passage
(with a fresh translation) in Elliot R. Wolfson, *"Sefer ha-Rimmon:* Critical
Edition and Introductory Study" (Ph.D. diss., Brandeis University, 1986),
1:18–27.

60. It is impossible to make sense out of this unless one assumes that there is
some basic kinship between the phallus and the mouth and that emission
through one is like that of the other. Such a relation was in fact exploited
by the kabbalists; cf., e.g., Gikatilla, *Ginnat Egoz* (Hanau, 1614), 25b:
"Just as a person has the covenant of the mouth between the ten fingers of
his hands, so you will find he has the covenant of the foreskin between the
ten toes [literally, fingers] of his feet. . . . Contemplate that *peh* [i.e., mouth]
corresponds [numerically] to *milah* [circumcision]." Gikatilla thus interprets
the famous passage from *Sefer Yeṣira* (see n. 57 above) in light of a numerical equivalence between the word for mouth, *peh*, and the word for circumcision, *milah*, insofar as both equal eighty-five. See the theosophic reworking
of this numerical equivalence in *Tiqqunei Zohar*, sec. 18(32b): "The Oral
Law *[Torah she-be'al peh]* is where the lower *Shekhinah* is. She is called
mouth *[peh]* from the side of the *Ṣaddiq [Yesod]*, for the numerical value of
peh equals that of *milah.*"

61. *Zohar* II, 87a–b.

62. Compare Scholem, *On the Kabbalah and Its Symbolism* (New York: Schocken Books, 1978), pp. 37–44 (and references to the *Zohar* given on p. 39, n. 3).

63. Compare *Zohar* II, 87b, and n. 41 above. On sexual relations between Jew and non-Jew in the period of the *Zohar*, see Y. Baer, *A History of Jews in Christian Spain* (Philadelphia: Jewish Publication Society, 1978), 1:246 ff.

64. Liebes (n. 3 above), p. 136.

65. *Zohar* III, 79a, 105b. Compare *Zohar Ḥadash, Tiqqunim,* 94b: "The one who reveals secrets of Torah [to the wicked] causes the spring to be removed from the *Ṣaddiq,* who is the foundation of whom it is said 'The secret of the Lord is with those who fear him' (Ps. 25:14), and from the *Shekhinah,* as it is written, 'The waters of the sea fail, and the river dries up and is parched' (Job 14:11). At that time the righteous *(Ṣaddiqim)* below are impoverished from everything, impoverished from secrets of Torah and impoverished in the body. Whoever reveals secrets to the righteous causes the *Ṣaddiq* to shine with secrets of Torah."

66. Aramaic: *ḥizra be-mayya.* Compare BT *Baba Meṣia* 60b: *mayya de-ḥizra* (see M. Jastrow, *A Dictionary of the Targumin, the Talmud Babli and Yerushalmi, and the Midrashic Literature* [New York: Pardes, 1950], s.v. *ḥizra*).

67. *Zohar* III, 128a *(Idra Rabba).*

68. Compare Y. Liebes, *Sections of the Zohar Lexicon* (Jerusalem: Hebrew University, 1976), p. 377, n. 88, and p. 381, n. 96 (in Hebrew).

69. It is one of de León's innovations to define the righteous person, the *ṣaddiq,* solely in terms of sexual propriety. Compare *Zohar* I, 59b; Wolfson, *The Book of the Pomegranate,* pp. 228–29 (Hebrew Section); *Sheqel ha-Qodesh,* p. 62; *Sefer ha-Mishqal,* p. 74.

70. On the meaning of *qiyyuma* in the *Zohar* as pillar, see Liebes, *Sections of the Zohar Lexicon,* p. 360, n. 20, and "The Messiah of the Zohar" (n. 3 above), p. 138, n. 202.

71. See Liebes, *Sections of the Zohar Lexicon,* p. 358, n. 13, p. 361, nn. 23–24, pp. 371–73, n. 68.

72. The theosophic connection between the word "secret," the Aramaic *raza,* which is a translation of the Hebrew *sod,* and circumcision is based ultimately on Ps. 25:14, "The *secret [sod]* of the Lord is with those who fear Him, and to them He makes *His covenant [berito]* known." Compare *Zohar* I, 2b, 236b; III, 43b *(Piqqudin);* Wolfson, *The Book of the Pomegranate,* pp. 227–28 (Hebrew section); *Sheqel ha-Qodesh,* pp. 60–61. See Liebes, "The Messiah of the Zohar," pp. 138 ff. Finally, it should be mentioned that already in classical midrashic sources, e.g., *Genesis Rabbah* 49:2 (pp. 488–89), Ps. 25:14 is interpreted to mean that circumcision is the "mystery" of God given to Abraham.

73. In this regard it is of interest to note that in one of his Hebrew theosophic works, *Sefer ha-Nefesh ha-Ḥakhamah* (Basle, 1608), sec. 12, de León refers to the proliferation of kabbalistic lore as the flowing or spreading forth of

the "spring of mystery," *ma'ayan ha-sod*. The text is cited by Scholem, *Major Trends in Jewish Mysticism* (n. 1 above), p. 396, n. 150, and an English translation appears on p. 201. In the critical edition of the same work, *Sefer ha-Mishqal* (see n. 44 above), the established reading is *me-'inyan ha-sod ha-zeh*, "from the matter of this secret," rather than *ma'ayan ha-sod ha-zeh*, "the spring of this mystery." Compare Scholem, *Major Trends in Jewish Mysticism*, p. 201, who interprets this passage as a "veiled reference" to the dissemination of the *Zohar;* and see my criticism in *"Sefer ha-Rimmon:* Critical Edition and Introductory Study." 1:15–17. In any event, the "spring" is an obvious phallic symbol, which would thus be an appropriate symbol for *Yesod*. It follows, therefore, that even in this passage, if we accept the reading of the *editio princeps,* de León, perhaps unwittingly, links the disclosure of esoteric truth with a phallic symbol, namely, the pouring forth of the fountain or spring.

74. Compare the famous parable of the Princess (the Torah) and her lover (the mystic exegete) in *Zohar* II, 99a–b, where the hermeneutical relationship is depicted in terms of an erotic game of hide-and-seek. On the erotic quality of reading as a dialectic of concealment and disclosure, see R. Barthes. *The Pleasure of the Text,* trans. Richard Miller (New York: Hill & Wang, 1975), pp. 9–10, 14. See also the curious expression of Moses de León in his *Mishkan ha-'Edut, likhtov u-lignoz,* "to write and to conceal." The expression has been discussed by Scholem, *Major Trends in Jewish Mysticism*, pp. 201–2, and cf. my extended criticism in *"Sefer ha-Rimmon:* Critical Edition and Introductory Study," 1:18–27.

75. See Liebes, "The Messiah of the Zohar" (n. 3 above), pp. 138–45.

76. Compare the parable in *Zohar* I, 245b, and its parallel in Wolfson, *"Sefer ha-Rimmon:* Critical Edition and Introductory Study," 2:304:16–22 (see also 1:113–14, 119).

77. The ontological distinction between Jew and non-Jew, the soul of the former deriving from the right, holy side, and that of the latter from the left, demonic side, is one of the basic assumptions of de León's anthropology. Compare *Zohar Ḥadash,* 78d (*Midrash ha-Ne'elam* on Ruth); *Zohar* I, 20b, 131a, 220a; II, 86a; Wolfson, "Mystical Rationalization," pp. 242–44; idem, *The Book of the Pomegranate,* pp. 211–12 (Hebrew Section).

78. See n. 62 above.

79. *Zohar* III, 72b–73a. Compare Gikatilla, *Sha'arei 'Orah,* ed. Ben-Shlomo (Jerusalem: Mosad Bialik, 1978), 1:114–16: "The covenant of *Binah* [Understanding, the third emanation] is the covenant of the mouth, the covenant of the tongue, the covenant of the lips. . . . And the covenant of the living God *[Yesod,* the ninth emanation] is called the covenant of peace . . . the covenant of Sabbath, the covenant of the rainbow . . . the covenant of circumcision. The covenant of *Adonai [Shekhinah,* the tenth emanation] corresponds to the covenant of the Torah. . . . And this is the secret: The covenant of the tongue and the covenant of the foreskin. . . . If Israel had not received the covenant of the flesh [circumcision] they would never have

524 ELLIOT R. WOLFSON

merited the Torah which is the covenant of the tongue. . . . Therefore the Torah is only given to one who has received the covenant of the flesh, and from the covenant of the flesh one enters into the covenant of the tongue, which is the reading of the Torah." Gikatilla's remarks are a theosophic exposition of *Sefer Yeṣirah*, 1:3; see nn. 57, 60 above.

80. See n. 72 above.

81. *Zohar* I, 236b.

82. Wolfson, *The Book of the Pomegranate*, p. 228 (Hebrew section). And cf. *Sheqel ha-Qodesh*, p. 61.

83. Wolfson, *The Book of the Pomegranate*, p. 229 (Hebrew section).

84. I have treated this topic at length in "The Hermeneutics of Visionary Experience: Revelation and Interpretation in the Zohar," *Religion* 18 (1988): 311–45. Compare *Zohar* I, 9a, 94b; II, 163b: Liebes, "The Messiah of the Zohar" (n. 3 above), pp. 98–99, 130–32. The idea that the *Shekhinah* is connected to those engaged in the study of the Torah is a motif found in earlier aggadic sources: see BT *Berakhot* 6a; *Mishnah Avot* 3:6; *Midrash Tehilim* on Ps. 105:1, ed. S. Buber (Jerusalem, 1965), p. 448; *Deuteronomy Rabbah* (Tel Aviv: Moriah, 1960), 7:2; *Zohar* I, 72a, 92b, 115b; II, 200a.

85. *Zohar* I, 234b.

86. The letter symbolism is derived from BT *Shabbat* 104b; see *Zohar* I, 3a, 244b; Wolfson, *The Book of the Pomegranate*, p. 229, n. 5 (Hebrew section).

87. See, e.g., BT *Yevamot* 8b.

88. It is of interest to consider *Zohar* I, 93a, wherein the discussion on the mystical significance of circumcision culminates with an actual visionary experience. After the comrades complete their discussion on circumcision, the man in whose house the discussion ensued says to them: "The completion of what you have said tonight will take place tomorrow. He said to them: Tomorrow you will see the face of the 'master of circumcision' [i.e., the prophet Elijah] . . . for he will come to circumcise my son. . . . R. Abba said: This is a request to [fulfill] a commandment and we shall sit in order to see the face of the *Shekhinah.*" In other contexts in the *Zohar* the seeing of the *Shekhinah* is connected particularly with the study of Torah in accord with kabbalistic principles; see n. 84 above.

15.

Woman As High Priest: A Kabbalistic Prayer in Yiddish for Lighting Sabbath Candles

Chava Weissler

WOMEN AND KABBALAH

The absence of women from Jewish mystical movements presents an enduring puzzle for the historian of religions. How is it that women have played such important roles in Christian and Islamic mysticism, yet so negligible a part in Jewish mysticism.[1] The problem is both social and theological. In sociological terms, women and members of other relatively powerless groups are often participants in ecstatic and mystical movements. Sociologists of religion have speculated that temporal powerlessness has led women to seek spiritual power.[2] Yet the social organization of Jewish mystical circles seems to have made no room for women. A mysticism of the learned, kabbalah requires a knowledge of languages and texts that simply was not made available to most women.[3] Indeed, only a small number of men acquired such knowledge. Most kabbalists were members of an esoteric elite that excluded both men and women. However, the Lurianic revival, Sabbatian messianism, and Hasidism all possessed more of a mass character. Did they also provide opportunities for women to participate, or allow women to assume religious leadership?[4]

Theologically, too, kabbalah presented obstacles to the full participation of women. Within the kabbalistic system, "male" generally signifies

Reprinted from *Jewish History* 5, no. 1 (1991) by permission of *Jewish History* and the University of Haifa Press.

and symbolizes the spiritual and the holy, while "female" descends into the material and the demonic. If women indeed are so intimately connected with physicality *(gashmiut)*, it would seem inconceivable for them to engage in asceticism and strive for spiritual elevation. Furthermore, while kabbalistic theosophical teaching paid great attention to the female aspects of the Godhead, especially the Shekhinah, these were depicted in their relationship to the male mystic, for it was his task to arouse the Shekhinah to unite with her consort *Tiferet*. Could there be a place for women in this symbolic universe?

In eighteenth-century eastern Europe, Lurianic piety, underground Sabbatianism, Frankism, and Hasidism all met in a struggle for the hearts and minds of Jewish men. Did they appeal to women as well? Hasidism is a particularly interesting case. Some scholars have argued that Hasidism was decisively different from earlier mystical movements, and that it gave women greater scope as participants, even leaders. However, as Ada Rapoport-Albert has shown, Hasidic teachings had no special concern for women.[5] Hasidic teachers produced no works for a female audience, nor did they concern themselves with the education or spiritual development of women. Indeed, their attitude to women was similar to pre-Hasidic rabbinic and kabbalistic views. What is more, women were never a part of the institutionalized leadership of Hasidism. The women who are depicted in oral tradition as charismatic figures— usually mothers, sisters, or wives of *zaddiqim*—produced no body of Hasidic writings, nor did they have an enduring following. Even Hannah Rachel Verbermakher (b. ca. 1815), known as the Maid of Ludmir, who tried to act as a Hasidic master, in the end must be seen as a failed *zaddiq,* a deviant who could not play her chosen part.

Several decades before Hannah Rachel's birth, during the formative years of Hasidism, women from Volhynia and Galicia were credited with the authorship of texts in Yiddish, some of which incorporated kabbalistic symbols and other material derived from kabbalistic sources.[6] Do such texts contradict the generally accepted view that women played no part in kabbalah? Are they evidence that Hasidism did in fact provide women with greater spiritual outlets than before? Or do they support the view that Hasidism was of little consequence to women? An even more basic question is, What were the sources these women used? Where did they get their kabbalistic material? The answer suggests that it was the Lurianic revival, not Hasidism, that provided women access to kabbalistic materials in Yiddish translation, thus allowing them to participate in kabbalistic currents of thought.

Because very few women knew Hebrew, and even fewer mastered Aramaic, the classic works of kabbalah were closed to all but the most exceptional women. However, kabbalistic material was available in Yiddish, a language some women learned to read. While a detailed study of kabbalistic literature in Yiddish has yet to be made,[7] a cursory review shows that kabbalistic material began to be incorporated into various genres of popular religious literature in Yiddish by the mid-seventeenth century. Compendia of material from the Zohar and other kabbalistic sources were also published in the late seventeenth and early eighteenth centuries. Examples are the anthology of material from a number of kabbalistic sources, *Sefer Ma'asei Adonai* (vol. 1, Frankfurt am Main, 1691; vol. 2, Fürth, 1694), collected and paraphrased by Simon Akiva Baer b. Joseph; the same author's tales of the patriarchs from the Zohar, *Abbir Ya'aqov* (Sulzbach, 1700); and the Yiddish paraphrase of the Zohar, *Nahalat Zevi*, by Zevi Hirsh Hotsh (Amsterdam, 1711). These books were available to Ashkenazic women who could read Yiddish. We therefore may ask two important questions. First, to what degree did these Yiddish versions expunge or transform technical theosophical and theurgic concepts? Second, to what extent did women utilize these adaptations as sources for their own writings? This article addresses aspects of both these questions.[8]

The second, and perhaps more serious, obstacle to women's kabbalistic activity was theological: the nature of the masculine and the feminine in the kabbalistic system, and the system's view of the feminine as the physical rather than the spiritual. Here, two observations are pertinent. First, while scholarly mystics may have dismissed—for both mystical and practical reasons—the possibility that women *could* strive for spiritual perfection, we must ask whether other segments of the Jewish population—for example, women and non-learned men—had a different view of the matter. In other words, the problem should be considered from the "bottom up" as well as from the "top down." Second, it is instructive to take a comparative glance at Christianity. Medieval Christianity also identified women with physicality and men with spirituality. As Carolyn Walker Bynum has shown, there was a solution to the difficulty this posed for medieval Christian female mystics. In Christianity, the human aspect of Jesus Christ's dual nature was just as important as the divine. Women could identify with the humanity of Jesus, thus giving their very association with physicality a spiritual meaning.[9]

With this in mind, we ask whether the symbolic system of the *sefirot* presented similar possibilities to women. Could women, as contemporary Jewish feminists sometimes argue, identify with the feminine *sefirot*, *Malkhut* (Shekhinah) or *Binah?* Conversely, could they have a special devotion to the masculine *sefirot, Tiferet* or *Yesod,* parallel to the male kabbalists' devotion to *Malkhut?* Either possibility would require reinterpretation of the symbol system of the *sefirot,* but the evidence suggests that insofar as women made use of kabbalistic symbolism, they did not significantly transform its gender representations.

TKHINES: SUPPLICATORY PRAYERS IN YIDDISH

As a way into some of the issues concerning women, kabbalah, and Hasidism, this article examines a portion of one text, which contains a kabbalistic prayer in Yiddish for lighting the Sabbath candles. The text, *Thkine Imrei Shifre,* attributed to a woman named Shifre bas Yosef, was published in eastern Europe, probably in the late eighteenth century. *Tkhines* are a genre of supplicatory prayers in Yiddish, of which women were the primary, although not the exclusive, audience. Women sometimes also wrote *tkhines*.[10] The *tkhine* literature can be roughly grouped into two categories, which I call, in somewhat imprecise shorthand, western European and eastern European.[11]

The western European material, which was published in such cities as Amsterdam, Sulzbach, Fürth, and Prague in the seventeenth and eighteenth centuries (and later reprinted in eastern Europe), consists of encyclopedic, usually anonymous,[12] anthologies of *tkhines* for a wide variety of occasions: the days of the week, fast days, the Sabbath and festivals, the Days of Awe, cemetery visits, pregnancy and childbirth, and the women's *mitzvot*. A standard collection, entitled *Seder tkhines u-va-koshes,* evolved, and was frequently reprinted.[13] It contains about 130 *tkhines,* which range in length from a single paragraph to several pages. A large portion of the material derives from similar voluntary or supplemental devotions in Hebrew that are rooted in Lurianic kabbalah—in particular, *Sha'arei Ziyyon* by Nathan Nata Hannover, and *Sha'ar ha-shamayim,* by Isaiah Horowitz.[14] Yet these *tkhines* contain little overtly kabbalistic material.[15] On the other hand, they cannot be understood if one does not know that there is such a thing as mystical intention in prayer and *mitzvot*. These *tkhines* contain a model of women as distanced participants in the mystical system. One *tkhine* from *Seder tkhines u-vakoshes* acknowledges that "we do not have the power to engage in the mystical intentions and combinations of the holy names ... in all of the prayers," but nonetheless petitions God: "May my prayers rise before you to make a crown on your holy head together with the prayers of those Jews who do know how to engage in mystical contemplation and to combine all the intentions and combinations of the names." [16]

Some of the eastern European *tkhines* contain much more explicitly kabbalistic material. The eastern European works differ from the western European ones in other ways as well. In general, they are much shorter, containing *tkhines* on only a few subjects, such as the Sabbath, the penitential season from the beginning of the month of Elul through Yom Kippur, the women's *mitzvot,* and Rosh Hodesh. In addition, they often include author statements, which attribute the work—in sometimes complicated ways—to a female author. This is not the place for a thorough exploration of the vexing question of the veracity of these statements. Suffice it to say that despite the views of some earlier scholars that all *tkhines* were written by indigent male yeshiva students or by *maskilim,* there is evidence that some, though not all, of these women existed.[17] The eastern European material that has been preserved stems from the late eighteenth up through the nineteenth and twentieth centuries; here, I deal only with eighteenth-century texts.[18]

The eastern European *tkhines* make varied use of kabbalistic material. Some texts, such as the *Shloyshe she'orim,* attributed to the legendary Sore bas Tovim,[19] use kabbalistic sources in much the same way as the western European texts. In its paraphrases of material from *Sefer Hemdat yamim,*[20] *Shloyshe she'orim* summarizes or glosses over technical kabbalistic matters, sometimes to the point of rendering the text extremely difficult to follow. The *Tkhine imohes,* by Sore Rivke Rokhl Leye bas Yukl Horowitz (b. ca. 1715), is also interesting in its use of kabbalistic sources.[21] It contains three sections: a Hebrew introduction, an Aramaic *piyyut,* and a Yiddish paraphrase of the *piyyut.* The Hebrew introduction includes a kabbalistic *derashah* showing the importance of women's prayer, the *piyyut* refers to *imana shekhinta* and other *sefirot,* and the Yiddish paraphrase contains not a trace of kabbalistic material. Although Leye, as the author was known, read kabbalistic literature and was able to make use of kabbalistic symbols and concepts, she knew that her audience was not familiar with kabbalistic terminology and concepts. In the Yiddish portion of the text, she transformed the kabbalistic concept of prayer for the sake of the Shekhinah into something women who were not mystics could grasp—tearful prayer for redemption.

TKHINE IMREI SHIFRE

In contrast to the two *tkhines* mentioned above, *Tkhine Imrei Shifre*[22] contains a great deal of explicitly kabbalistic material in *Yiddish*, most or all of which is derived from the Zohar, through an intermediate source in Yiddish.[23] *Imrei Shifre* consists of four sections: a long *tkhine* on the themes of exile, repentance, and redemption; a *tkhine* to be recited every day; a *tkhine* for the Sabbath, which contains the material to be considered here; and *tokhakhas musar le-shabes* "moral reproof for the Sabbath," which consists almost entirely of translations of portions of the Zohar into Yiddish.

The author attribution found in this text may be substantially correct. Whether real or fictitious, it is an interesting portrait of a *tkhine* author. The title page reads:

Tkhine Imrei Shifre

This *tkhine* was made by the prominent, learned, wealthy woman [*ha-ishah ha-hashuvah hahakhmanit ha-gevirah*], Mistress Shifre, daughter of the late marvelous [*ha-mufla'*] and learned rabbi, our teacher Rabbi Joseph, of blessed memory; the wife of the learned and pious rabbi [*ha-rabbani ha-muflag ba-torah uva-hasidut*], the acute Rabbi Ephraim Segal, *dayyan* in the holy community of Poznan.

Unlike other *tkhines, Imrei Shifre* contains something resembling a rabbinic approbation *(haskamah)*. On the verso of the title page is the following:

Introduction [*Haqdamah*]

Inasmuch as the important, learned woman, wife of the Torah scholar and rabbi, the great luminary in Torah and piety, *dayyan mezuyyan* of the holy community of Brody, our teacher Rabbi Ephraim Segal, as I say that I knew her and was acquainted with her in the past, and now, even more, that all her deeds are for the sake of heaven; and now, her excellent plan is to travel to the Holy Land with her husband;[24] therefore, several rabbis and sages agree [maskimim] that she should publish this tkhine. One ought not to cause her any financial loss. And she has approbations and bans [haskamot ve-haramot] from the eminent scholars of the land, except that the page is too short to hold [all the names].

This is followed by half a page of blank space. Either there were no haskamot, or "the eminent scholars of the land" did not wish to have their names used in a Yiddish pamphlet for women.[25] In any case, although there remains some doubt about the author's historicity, for convenience I refer to the author, whom I assume was a woman, as Shifre.

Like most eastern European tkhines published before 1835, Imrei Shifre does not mention a publisher or a place or date of publication. Fortunately, however, it does contain an internal date. "We have tarried in this dark exile," laments Shifre, "for more than 1,700 years." This places the text sometime after 1770[26] which means that it was written during the formative years of Hasidism.

Like other tkhine authors, whether historically identifiable or not, Shifre is described as a member of the elite. She is wealthy, wise, and belongs to a rabbinical family. I have not yet found any direct historical evidence about the author, and there are certain inconsistencies in the statements on the title page and introduction, particularly in reference to her husband. On the title page he is said to be from Poznan; the introduction says he is from Brody. Another edition of the tkhine gives his location only as Brody.[27]

Whether these statements are accurate or merely fabrications of the publisher, what is the significance of associating this tkhine with certain localities? Poznan was the residence of Shabbetai Sheftel ben Isaiah Horowitz (1590?–1660?; appointed rabbi of Poznan in 1643). Shabbetai Sheftel's Hebrew tehinnot, adapted into Yiddish and entitled Ayn sheyne kestlikhe tkhine, were frequently reprinted. On the title page, he is always referred to as Rabbi Sheftel of Poznan. Perhaps the publisher of Imrei Shifre wished to associate it with an earlier best seller.

More interesting is the association of Imrei Shifre with Brody. This Galician city was in the heartland of eighteenth-century religious ferment among eastern European Jews. Bans were published in Brody against the Frankists in 1752 and against the Hasidim in 1772, just around the time

Imrei Shifre was composed. In addition, for much of the eighteenth century, members of the *kloyz,* mystical pietists of the older Lurianic school, were active in Brody. While some of these mystics were involved in early Hasidic circles, or were sympathetic to Hasidism, others were hostile, and the *kloyz* as a whole supported the 1772 ban.

Imrei Shifre is not the only *tkhine* associated with Brody. The impeccably historical Sore Rivke Rokhl Leye Horowitz, author of *Tkhine imohes,* was the daughter of Yukl Horowitz, who was for some years the rabbi of Brody and seems to have been a member of the *kloyz.* In general, as noted above, the region of Galicia and Volhynia is rich in attributions of *tkhine* authors.

However, it is difficult to assess the significance of the association. It is likely that the composition and publication of numerous *tkhines* in this region at this time had to do with religious ferment in the air. Further study is needed to determine whether any of these texts were Hasidic, anti-Hasidic, or even Sabbatian. *Imrei Shifre* does not seem to contain any specifically Hasidic teachings. It does make reference to the problem of "strange thoughts" during prayer. Although the idea of "strange thoughts" was developed in Hasidic teachings, it had a long history before the rise of Hasidism, and is discussed in various popular Yiddish ethical works.[28] Indeed, it is likely that these pre-Hasidic ethical works were the sources for *Imrei Shifre,* rather than any of the new Hasidic teachings.[29] The *tkhine* breathes the spirit of these works, with their emphasis on repentance, judgment, and punishment of the soul after death. The author of *Imrei Shifre* drew on one such Yiddish work, *Nahalat Zevi,* and probably knew others as well. Thus, the kabbalistic material found in this *tkhine* is best seen as influenced by the Lurianic revival, which led to the publication of mystical morality literature, rather than by Hasidism and its putative opportunities for women. That Brody was a center of pre-Hasidic Lurianic mystical piety further supports this hypothesis.

Tkhine Imrei Shifre is an extremely interesting text. It goes further than any *tkhine* I have seen in attributing explicit kabbalistic significance to women's religious performance. Furthermore, the text argues for the importance of women's Sabbath observance, and seems to assume the importance of women's prayer. The author is conversant with and has borrowed from several earlier *tkhine* texts, including *Seder tkhines u-vakoshes* and *Tkhine imohes* by Leye Horowitz.[30] This places Shifre within the literary tradition of the *tkhines*. This is important, for Shifre takes a common non-kabbalistic motif from *tkhines* for lighting Sabbath candles and gives it a kabbalistic interpretation.

Since the text contains a great deal of material derived from the Zohar, it assumes and makes use of a number of standard kabbalistic images and ideas: the Shelter of Peace for the tenth *sefirah*, the Shekhinah; the candelabrum *(menorah)* as a symbol of the seven lower *sefirot*; the idea that Jews receive a special additional soul on the Sabbath; and the belief that the human and divine worlds are interrelated as microcosm and macrocosm, and that human devotion in prayer and in performing the commandments brings about love and unity among the *sefirot*, and restores, if only momentarily, the Shekhinah from her exile.

Shifre begins her "new *tkhine* for the Sabbath" with a general statement about God's grandeur and power, and the significance of the Sabbath as sanctifying the memory of the creation. She then stresses the importance of women's observance of the Sabbath: "And women must be as scrupulous about the Sabbath as men." She mentions that women are obligated to recite *qiddush*. She then moves on to the significance of candle lighting.[31]

The commandment of **Sabbath candles** was given to the women of the **holy people** that they might kindle lights. The sages said that because Eve extinguished the light of the world and made the cosmos dark by her sin, [women] must kindle lights **for the Sabbath.** But this is the reason for it: Because **the Shelter of Peace** [the Shekhinah] rests on us during the Sabbath, on the [Sabbath-]souls, it is therefore proper for us to do below, in this form, as is done above [within the Godhead], to kindle the lights. Therefore, because the two souls shine on the Sabbath, they [women] must light two candles. As it is written in the verse, **"When you raise** [*be-ha 'alotekha*, here usually understood to mean "when you kindle"] **the lamps, let the seven lamps shine against the face of** [*el mul penei*] **the candelabrum."**[32] [It seems that the verse] should have used a term for kindling rather than one for raising up; but by his kindling **below** the verse *means* raising up: "And the lights which are against the candelabrum, may the seven lights—the candelabrum—shine."[33] He raised the **arousal to the Upper World** [*hit'orerut le-ma 'lah*]. All this was set out **below,** corresponding to the **Tabernacle above** [*mishkan shel ma 'lah*]. Therefore the verse says that the **heavenly candelabrum** corresponds to the **earthly candelabrum.** When the priest below lit the **seven lamps,** he therewith caused the **seven lamps above** to shine. Therefore, by kindling the lamps for the holy Sabbath, we awaken great **arousal** in the Upper World. And when the woman kindles the lights, it is fitting for her to kindle [them] with joy and with **wholeheartedness,** because it is in honor of the Shekhinah and in honor of the Sabbath and in honor of the extra [Sabbath-]soul. Thus she will be privileged to have holy children who will be the light of the world in the Torah[34] and in fear [of God], and who will increase **peace in the world.** And by this means she gives her husband long life; therefore, it is appropriate for women to take great care concerning this.[35]

The text then continues, at some length, with other matters.

Shifre's argument is rather complex. She counters the view of the sages that lighting the Sabbath candles is a religious duty that was assigned to women in atonement for Eve's sin[36] by explaining it as an expression of women's spiritual power and significance. And because the tenth *sefirah,* the Shekhinah, rests on the people of Israel on the Sabbath and bestows the additional Sabbath-souls on them, women must kindle two Sabbath lights.

The earthly act of lighting candles corresponds to the kindling of lights in the realm of the divine, which is a symbol for the union and harmony of the *sefirot* that occurs on the Sabbath.[37] To develop this idea, Shifre uses the pericope Numbers 8:2, which is a description of the candelabrum in the (earthly) Tabernacle. She postulates a correspondence between an upper and a lower candelabrum, based on the reference in Numbers to seven lamps facing or corresponding to the candelabrum. The lower candelabrum was in the earthly Tabernacle, while the upper candelabrum is a symbol of the seven lower *sefirot,* whose divine light illumines the Shekhinah, the heavenly Tabernacle. Lighting the lower candelabrum, an act performed by the High Priest, causes great arousal to love in the upper spheres; in classical kabbalistic terms, the act of the High Priest contributes to the *hieros gamos* of the male and female aspects of God. Helping this union to occur is the sacred and mystical heart of kabbalistic performance of ritual. In her most daring move, Shifre likens the act of the woman to that of the High Priest: By lighting their weekly Sabbath candles, women arouse the *sefirot* to love. This act should be undertaken with joy, because it is in honor of the Shekhinah, of the Sabbath, and of the Sabbath-souls.

THE SOURCES OF THE PASSAGE

The full significance of Shifre's *tkhine* can be assessed only if it is compared to its sources. Much of this passage is a relatively close paraphrase of Zohar I 48b:

The Sabbath light was given to the women of the holy people to kindle, and the Company have said that she extinguished the light of the light of the world, and darkened it, etc., and this is a good explanation [ve-shafir]. But the secret meaning of the matter is that this Shelter of Peace is the Lady of the Cosmos, and the souls that are called Supernal Candles rest in her. Thus, the woman must light the candles, for the Lady adheres to her and acts [through her]. [Or: Thus, the woman must light the candles, for she is in the place of the Lady, who adheres to her when she performs the act: Ve-'al da matronita ba 'ya le-adlaqa de-ha be-dukhtaha itahadat ve-'avdat 'uvda.] And the woman must light the Sabbath candles with joy of the heart and good will, for it is a supernal honor for her, and of great merit for her, so that she will be worthy to have holy sons who will be the light of the world in the Torah and in fear [of God], and who will increase peace in the world. And she gives her husband long life. Therefore, she must take care in [the act of kindling the lights].

Note that the motif of the High Priest lighting the candelabrum, as it appears in the *tkhine*, is interpolated into the middle of this passage. In addition, there is no passage in the Zohar that corresponds precisely to the *tkhine*'s description of the High Priest.[38] There are two possible explanations for this lack of a source passage in the Zohar for the motif of the High Priest. Either Shifre used an intermediate source, which does contain this passage, or she added material of her own composition. Both of these turn out to be correct.

Shifre's immediate source was Hotsh's *Nahalat Zevi*.[39] She made creative use of the material she found there. First, although written in Yiddish, the book was addressed to non-scholarly men, not to women.[40] Nonetheless, Shifre appropriated it as a source and put it to her own use. Second, Shifre combined two separate passages from *Nahalat Zevi*. By doing so, she conveys a new understanding of the significance of women's candle-lighting.

The first passage Shifre uses is Hotsh's paraphrase of Zohar I 48b:

And the commandment of the **Sabbath candle** was given to the women of **the holy people**, that they might kindle the lights. The sages gave a reason [for this]: Because Eve extinguished the light of the world, and made the cosmos dark by her sin, therefore, they [women] should kindle lights **for the Sabbath.** But the secret meaning of it is this: Because the **Shelter of Peace** rests on us on the Sabbath, and [on] the [Sabbath-]souls, therefore, it is proper for women **below** to act as in the form **above**—to kindle the lights. And because the two souls of human beings shine on the Sabbath, therefore she must kindle two lights. And when the woman kindles the lights, it is fitting for her to kindle them **with joy and with wholeheartedness,** because it is in honor of the Shekhinah. And thus she will be privileged to have holy children who will be the light of the world in Torah and in fear [of God] and who will increase **peace in the world**. And by this means she also gives her husband long life; therefore, it is proper for the women to take great care concerning this.[41]

The wording in this passage is very close, although not identical, to that of Shifre's *tkhine*. However, the High Priest is missing.

The High Priest appears in another part of *Nahalat Zevi*, in a passage that begins by translating Zohar III 149a, an interpretation of Numbers 8:2, and continues on into a section interpolated, and apparently written, by Hotsh himself. Shifre uses *only* this interpolation:

Therefore the text uses the term *beha'alotekha* [raising] here, when it would seem it should have used the term for kindling, not for raising. But by kindling the candelabrum below, he [the High Priest] raised the **arousal to the Upper World**. Everything below is set out in correspondence with the **Tabernacle above**. Therefore [the verse] says: **against the face of the candelabrum**. The candelabrum **above** corresponds to the candelabrum **below**. When the Priest below has kindled [the candelabrum], then **"the seven lamps shine"**; by this means he has kindled **the seven lamps above**.[42]

Although the wording here does not correspond as precisely to Shifre's text, this clearly is her source.

In comparing Shifre's text with the Zohar and *Nahalat Zevi*, several interesting differences emerge. First, Shifre rejects rather more definitively than does her source the view that women are commanded to light candles to compensate for Eve's sin. She gives the view of "the sages" *(hakhamim)* and then says, "But *this* is the reason for it" *(Ober di zakh iz der tam der fun)*. *Nahalat Zevi* describes the second view as the "secret" explanation, thus implying that the first reason given is legitimate as midrashic exegesis *(derash)*.[43] Unlike *Nahalat Zevi*, Shifre does not accept an interpretation that describes women's religious activity as punitive.

THE MOTIF OF THE HIGH PRIEST IN THE *TKHINES* FOR CANDLE-LIGHTING

Even more interesting is the interpolation of the motif of the priest lighting the candelabrum in the Tabernacle. *Nahalat Zevi* (and the Zohar) do not associate the High Priest with the Sabbath candles; why does Shifre? The answer lies in the literary tradition of *tkhines* for lighting

Sabbath candles. Let me give two brief examples. The first is from a *tkhine* that appeared in a collection entitled *Tkhines,* published in Amsterdam in 1648 and reprinted in *Seder tkhines u-vakoshes,* which first appeared around 1750. Other passages in *Tkhine Imrei Shifre* also seem to have been influenced by this work.

Lord of the World, I have done all my work in the six days, and will now rest, as you have commanded, and will kindle two lights, according to the requirements of our holy Torah, as interpreted by our sages, to honor You and the holy Sabbath. . . . And may the lights be, in your eyes, like the lights that the priest kindled in the Temple, and let our light not be extinguished, and let your light shine upon us.[44]

The second example is from a later eastern European *tkhine,* the *Shloyshe she'orim,* attributed to Sore bas Tovim. It is perhaps the most popular collection of *tkhines* ever published.

Lord of the World, may my [observance of the] commandment of kindling the lights be accepted as the act of the high priest when he kindled the lights in the dear Temple was accepted. **"Your word is a lamp to my feet and a light to my path"** (Psalm 119:105). This means: Your speech is a light to my feet; may the feet of my children walk on God's path. May my kindling of the lights be accepted, so that my children's eyes may be enlightened in the dear Torah. I also pray over the candles that my [observance of the] commandment may be accepted by the dear God, be blessed, like the light [that] burned from olive oil in the Temple and was not extinguished.[45]

Although both these passages enhance the significance of the woman's act by comparing it to that of the High Priest, neither contains a trace of a kabbalistic interpretation of either act. Whatever the origin of this comparison,[46] Shifre endows it with a very different meaning by setting the motif of the High Priest in the context of the passage in which a correspondence is established between the woman lighting Sabbath candles below and the Shekhinah, who rests upon the Sabbath-souls, above. As far as I know, this motif does not appear in other *tkhines.* Thus, from the point of view of *Nahalat Zevi* and the Zohar, Shifre's innovation is to introduce the High Priest into the discussion of the Shekhinah and the Sabbath candles; from the point of view of the literary tradition of the *tkhines,* it is her addition of material about the Shekhinah and the Sabbath-souls to the motif of the High Priest.

Both Shifre's *tkhine* and *Nahalat Zevi* soften the boldest assertion of the Zohar: "Thus, the woman must light the candles, for the Lady [*matronita*, the Shekhinah] adheres to her and acts [through her]. And the woman must light the Sabbath candles with joy of the heart and good will, for it is a supernal honor for her." While *Nahalat Zevi* makes a comparison between the woman and the Shekhinah,[47] it stops short of carrying it through. Thus, in the two Yiddish works, as opposed to the Zohar, the woman honors, but does not embody, the Shekhinah: "And when the woman kindles the lights, it is fitting for her to kindle [them] with joy and with wholeheartedness, because it is in honor of the Shekhinah and in honor of the Sabbath and in honor of the extra [Sabbath] soul."

In diminishing the significance of the woman's act, Shifre follows *Nahalat Zevi*, which, like other popularizations and adaptations of kabbalistic texts in Yiddish, often blunts the edge of the most daring material. Yet, whereas *Nahalat Zevi's* adaptation of the Zohar means that the woman is no longer seen as acting theurgically, Shifre's combination of the two passages transforms the lighting of Sabbath candles back into a fully kabbalistic act.

In *Nahalat Zevi*, the acts of the High Priest are understood to have cosmic significance. By kindling the earthly candelabrum, the High Priest raises the lights to the heavenly candelabrum and arouses the *sefirot* to love and union. Thus, when in the *tkhine* the woman acts as the High Priest, her deed also has full mystical significance and theurgic efficacy. In the words of the *tkhine*, "Therefore, by kindling the lamps for the holy Sabbath, we awaken great arousal [*hit'orerut*] in the Upper World." This sentence is Shifre's own. It is not in either passage in *Nahalat Zevi*.

CONCLUSION

In its adaptation and transformation of material from *Nahalat Zevi*, *Tkhine Imrei Shifre* is evidence for a limited sort of participation by women in kabbalistic thinking. Whether or not this was the intention of their authors, the Yiddish adaptations of kabbalistic materials that sprang from the Lurianic revival made some kabbalistic symbols and concepts available to women. It may be that the religious ferment surrounding the rise of the Sabbatian, Frankist, and Hasidic movements stimulated women to use these materials to construct their own religious understanding. Even so, Shifre's text is exceptional among *tkhines* for its explicitly kabbalistic interpretation of women's religious activity.

The theological question is how women understood their place in the kabbalistic symbol system and whether they adapted the materials available to them to create a distinctive religious language. *Tkhine Imrei Shifre* transforms the symbol system, but not in a fully coherent way. It rejects the association of women with sin that is inherent in the idea that lighting Sabbath candles is a punishment, yet stops short of fully identifying women with the female aspect of the divine. The woman lighting candles does not act in concert with or as an echo of the Shekhinah, as the text of the Zohar suggests she should. Rather, she takes the active role of the male High Priest, who arouses the upper spheres through his act. The High Priest represents the kabbalistic worshiper, who approaches the world of the Godhead through his relationship to the lowest and mediating (and female) *sefirah,* the Shekhinah. Thus, for a woman to become a full-fledged kabbalistic actor, she must become, symbolically, male.[48] This text, at least, has not achieved a transformation of the kabbalistic system that allows a woman *as woman* to be a kabbalist.

Perhaps Shifre did not grasp the fine points of sefirotic symbolism and did not realize what an ambiguous image she was creating. She was, after all, working within a textual tradition that already contained a comparison between the woman and the High Priest. In addition, until it is ascertained that Shifre bas Yosef or some other woman was the actual author of this text, it cannot be certain that the adaptation was indeed made by a woman.

Despite these unsolved problems, this text does contradict, in a small way, the view that kabbalah was made exclusively "for men and by men."[49] Even if this passage was authored by a man, *someone* thought that women could perform at least one *mitzvah* the way men are supposed to perform all *mitzvot.* Furthermore, this view of the significance of *likht-bentshn*—candle-lighting, a quintessentially womanly act—is found in a *tkhine,* a text specifically aimed at a female audience, making it particularly available to women. The women who *read* this text, who recited it as they performed the gender-specific *mitzvah* of kindling the Sabbath lights, could have thought of this act as having cosmic ramifications.

NOTES

Conversations with Ada Rapoport-Albert stimulated my thinking about the central issue addressed in this article. Elliot Wolfson generously and graciously assisted me in tracking down Zoharic parallels to the *tkhine*. I also profited from the comments of Shaul Stampfer and Moshe Idel. I am grateful to all of them.

I owe a debt of thanks to the Jewish National and University Library, Jerusalem, and to the Library of the Jewish Theological Seminary of America. Without the support of the National Endowment for the Humanities, whose Fellowship for Independent Study and Research (1985) enabled me to spend a semester in Jerusalem, and the Harvard Divinity School, where I spent a year as a research associate in 1986–87, this article could never have been written.

An earlier version of this article was delivered at a session on Kabbalah and Ritual at the Annual Meeting of the American Academy of Religion, December 1987.

1. The lack of female mystics is noted by Gershom Scholem as a distinguishing characteristic of kabbalah; see his *Major Trends in Jewish Mysticism* (New York, 1956), 37.
2. See I. M. Lewis, *Ecstatic Religion* (Harmondsworth, 1971). In their study of medieval Christian saints (*Saints and Society* [Chicago, 1982], 228), Donald Weinstein and Rudolph Bell speculate that "the social powerlessness of women helps to explain the frequency of supernatural activity in their lives." I believe the matter is more complicated. For a detailed examination of the reasons for and meanings of the related phenomenon of female asceticism in medieval Christianity, see Carolyn Walker Bynum, *Holy Feast and Holy Fast* (Berkeley, 1987). For a fascinating discussion of women's involvement in communing with spirits of a rather different kind, see Alex Owen, *The Darkened Room: Women, Power, and Spiritualism in Late Victorian England* (London, 1989).
3. As Scholem points out (*Major Trends*, 37), this is not an absolute obstacle to women's mystical activity. Few Christian or Muslim women were learned, yet this did not prevent them from strongly influencing Christian and Muslim mystical movements.
4. While women seem not to have played a significant role in the leadership of the Sabbatian movement, Eva Frank, Jacob Frank's daughter, was a leader of the Frankist movement. Frankist theology also gave a significant place to the feminine aspect of God. See Bernard D. Weinryb, *The Jews of Poland* (Philadelphia, 1976), 236–61. On women in Hasidism, see Ada Rapoport-Albert, "On Women in Hasidism, S. A. Horodecky and the Maid of Ludmir Tradition," in *Jewish History: Essays in Honour of Chimen Abramsky*, ed. Steven J. Zipperstein and Ada Rapoport-Albert (London, 1988), 495–525. Rapoport-Albert approaches the question of the position of women in Hasidism mainly from the perspective of elite Hasidic literature. As I suggest below, it is also important to take popular literature into account.

5. Rapoport-Albert, "On Women in Hasidism."

6. I have seen Yiddish *tkhines* attributed to women from Dubno, Kremenets, Klewan, and Oleksiniec in Volhynia; Belz, Brody, Bolechow, and Stanislav in Galicia; and Satanov in Podolia. Other areas are also represented, but more sparsely: Lublin, Mohilev, and Krasnik, for example. This is by no means an exhaustive sample; however, even the *tkhines* published in Vilna in the second half of the nineteenth century, when they contain author attributions, generally note that these authors are from Galicia and Volhynia. Only a small number of *tkhines* contain material of kabbalistic derivation.

7. What is needed is a full-scale analysis of which kabbalistic texts were translated, how they were adapted in translation, and what kinds of Yiddish texts they appeared in. Israel Zinberg, *A History of Jewish Literature* (New York, 1975), vol. 7, *Old Yiddish Literature,* 345–52, briefly discusses kabbalistic *musar* literature; Zev Gries discusses kabbalistic *hanhagot (regimen vitae)* in Yiddish in " 'Itsuv sifrut ha-hanhagot ha-'ivrit be-mifneh ha-me'ah ha-shesh-'esreh uva-me'ah ha-sheva'-'esreh u-mashma'uto ha-historit," *Tarbiz* 56 (1987): 527–81, esp. 531–32 and 578–79.

8. For a discussion of a case in which a *tkhine* uses material from *Sefer Ma 'asei Adonai* see Chava Weissler, "Women in Paradise," *Tikkun,* vol. 2, no. 2 (1987): 43–46, 117–20.

9. Carolyn Walker Bynum, " '. . . And Woman His Humanity' : Female Imagery in the Religious Writing of the Later Middle Ages," in *Gender and Religion,* ed. C. W. Bynum, S. Harrell, and P. Richman (Boston, 1986), 257–88; see also the more general discussion of the different uses women and men make of the symbolism of Christianity in Bynum's *Holy Feast and Holy Fast,* chap. 10.

10. The work *tkhine* derives from the Hebrew *tehinnah* (pl. *tehinnot*) "supplication." For an introduction to the *tkhine* literature, see Chava Weissler, "The Traditional Piety of Ashkenazic Women," in *Jewish Spirituality from the Sixteenth-Century Revival to the Present,* ed. Arthur Green (New York, 1987), 245–75; and idem, "Traditional Yiddish Literature: A Source for the Study of Women's Religious Lives," The Jacob Pat Memorial Lecture, February 26, 1987, Harvard University Library (Cambridge, Mass., 1988). For an overview of the methodological problems involved in using *tkhines* and other genres of Yiddish popular religious literature for studying the religious lives of women, see Chava Weissler, "The Religion of Traditional Ashkenazic Women: Some Methodological Issues," *AJS Review* 12 (1987): 73–94.

11. Because these frequently reprinted texts were often published without mentioning a place or date of publication, first editions are difficult to identify. Thus, these terms refer to the place of publication of early editions. The residence of the author or editor is impossible to determine for the many anonymous texts.

12. The one exception I know of is *Seder tkhines,* by Matityahu Sobotki, first

published in Prague in 1718 and reprinted in Fürth in 1780. It formed the basis of a collection entitled *Preger tkhine* (Prague *Tkhine*), which was reprinted numerous times in eastern Europe. These later editions do not contain author statements.

As it is in many other ways, Prague seems to be midway between East and West with regard to *tkhines* as well. Several texts resembling eastern European *tkhines,* short pamphlets with individual female authors, also appeared in Prague. Among these are a *tkhine* to be recited every day, by Rachel bat Mordecai Sofer of Pintshov (end of seventeenth or beginning of eighteenth century), and a *tkhine* for the penitential season, by Bella Horowitz (ca. 1705).

13. I am not certain of the date of the first edition of this collection. Friedburg, *Bet 'eqed sefarim,* p. 1098, no. *tav* 1251, mentions a Fürth, 1755, edition; I have used the next one he cites, Fürth, 1762, which is in the collection of the Jewish Theological Seminary library. This work combines material from at least four earlier collections of *tkhines.*

14. See Solomon Freehof, "Devotional Literature in the Vernacular," *CCAR Yearbook* 33 (1923): 375–474.

15. Weissler, "Traditional Piety," 249–52.

16. *Seder tkhines u-vakoshes* (Fürth, 1762), no. 3. This *tkhine* is an adaptation of a Hebrew prayer intended for men who were not learned in kabbalah. It was composed by Leib Pohavitser and appears in his *Sefer Darkhei Hakhamim* (Frankfort an der Oder, 1683), part 2, *Solet belulah, hilkhot tefillah,* 19c.

17. There is good reason to be suspicious of some attributions, especially in texts from the second half of the nineteenth century, when *maskilim* wrote large numbers of pseudepigraphical *tkhines.* On the controversy about *tkhine* authorship, see Shmuel Niger, "Di yidishe literatur un di lezerin," reprinted in his *Bleter geshikhte fun der yidisher literatur* (New York, 1959), 35–107, esp. 82–85 and 88–94; Zinberg, *Old Yiddish Literature,* 251–53. For a different, older, view, see the *Jewish Encyclopedia* (1904), s.v. "Devotional Literature," esp. 551.

18. A few isolated *tkhines,* printed in other works, have come down to us from the sixteenth and seventeenth centuries. Chone Shmeruk, *Sifrut yidish be-polin* (Jerusalem, 1981), 61–65, 82–83 (#10), 114 (#62), is undoubtedly correct in stating that a much larger number of eastern European *tkhines* were already in existence by the sixteenth century; however, they have not been preserved.

19. On Sore bas Tovim (Sarah bat Mordecai, or bat Isaac, of Satanov), see Zinberg, *Old Yiddish Literature,* 253–56. Zinberg thinks she lived in the early eighteenth century. I have not found any early dated editions of the *Shloyshe she'orim,* nor any independent historical verification of Sore's existence. However, it is likely that she was a historical person. On aspects of the *Shloyshe she'orim,* see Weissler, "Women in Paradise," and idem, "Traditional Piety," 253–56 and 262–67.

20. Part of the *tkhine* for Rosh Hodesh in the *Shloyshe she'orim* is a paraphrase of *Sefer Hemdat yamim,* 4 vols. (Jerusalem, 1969/70; photo offset of Constantinople, 1734/35), vol. 2, *Rosh Hodesh,* 12b–13b *(Enqat Asir).* On the history of this anonymous work, see Isaiah Tishby, "Le-heqer ha-meqorot shel sefer *Hemdat yamim"* and "Meqorot me-reshit ha-me'ah ha-shemonah-'asar besefer *Hemdat yamim,"* both reprinted in his *Netivei emunah u-minut* (Jerusalem, 1982), 108–42, 143–68. As Tishby and other scholars have shown, *Hemdat yamim* is a Sabbatian work, although it was not always recognized as such. As a rule, Sore bas Tovim relied on Yiddish instead of Hebrew sources. If she was consistent, she got the material from *Hemdat yamim* from a Yiddish adaptation, paraphrase, or excerpt, rather than from the original Hebrew text. The implications of the incorporation of Sabbatian material into the *tkhine* require further investigation. The material Sore incorporated is vividly messianic; in my view, this powerful passage contributed a great deal to the popularity of the *Shloyshe she'orim.* Is it merely coincidence that Sore is said to be from Satanov, which seems to have had an active crypto-Sabbatian circle during the eighteenth century? See *Encyclopaedia Judaica* (1972), s.v. "Shabbetai Zevi," esp. col. 1251.

21. See Haim Liberman, "'Tehinnah imahot' u-'tehinnat sheloshah she 'arim,' " in his *Ohel Rahel* (New York, 1979/80), 432–54, esp. 432–33 and 437–38, and the references there. For additional discussion of this text and its use of kabbalistic material, see Weissler, *Voices of the Matriarchs* (Boston, forthcoming), chap. 4.

22. *Tkhine Imrei Shifre* (n.p., n.d.; eastern Europe after 1770?). The edition I use is in the *tkhine* pamphlet collection of the Jewish National and University Library, call no. R41 A460, vol. 6, no 8. I compared it with a different edition, also published without a date or place of publication, in the uncatalogued *tkhine* pamphlet collection of the Jewish Theological Seminary Library. The differences between the two editions are many but small. The title of the *tkhine* could be a play on the common book title *Imrei shefer.*

23. Following its source, this *tkhine* omits references to the *sefirot* in some of its adaptations of Zoharic texts.

24. During this period, groups of both Hasidim and Mitnagdim immigrated to Palestine. Perhaps Shifre and her husband belonged to one of these groups; or maybe the publisher wished to associate this *tkhine* with the holy luster of such a move.

25. There is no blank space in the Jewish Theological Seminary edition.

26. The first section of the text, a *tkhine* on the bitterness of the exile and the need for repentance, may reflect the difficult conditions of war-torn Poland in 1768–72.

27. In both editions, Shifre's husband's name is followed by an inconsistent string of abbreviations: n"y " 'h p"h. The first one stands for *nero ya'ir,* implying he is alive; the second for *'alav ha-shalom,* implying he is dead.

   I examined the following sources in an unsuccessful search for some reference to Shifre's husband: Dov Evron, ed., *Pinqas ha-kesherim shel qehillat Pozna* (Jerusalem, 1966); Meir Wunder, *Me'orei Galizyah* (Jerusalem, 1978–86); *Pinqas ha-qehillot, Polin*, vol. 2: *Galizyah ha-mizrahit* (Jerusalem, 1980); Raphael Halprin, *Atlas ez ha-hayyim*, vol. 7 (Tel Aviv? 1981); N. M. Gelber, "Aus Dem 'Pinax des alten Judenfriedhofes in Brody' (1699–1831)," *Jahrbuch der Jüdisch-Literarischen Gesellschaft* (Frankfurt am Main, 1920), 119–41.

This lack of documentation does not necessarily mean that the author statement on the *tkhine* is fictitious. There were apparently many undocumented rabbis in Brody (Meir Wunder, personal communication conveyed by Shaul Stampfer). In addition, if, as is likely, this *tkhine* was published in the vicinity of Brody, its audience would have known whether or not there was a *dayyan* named Ephraim Segal, which would have limited the publisher's flights of fancy.

28. In *tkhine khadoshe le-khol yom* Shifre writes: "And I pray you, dear Father, help me [resist] Satan, so that I may have no strange thought. Satan and his accusers hinder my prayer; I cannot overcome him. I pray you, dear God, help me to overcome him." See M. Piekarz, *Bi-yeme zemihat ha-hasidut* (Jerusalem, 1978), chap. 6, in which discussions of the problem of "strange thoughts" during prayer are quoted from several Yiddish ethical works. These are Zevi Hirsh Koidanover, *Qav ha-yashar*, chap. 8; Isaac ben Eliakum, *Lev Tov, hilkhot bet ha-keneset*, 8; Yehiel Mikhl Epstein, *Derekh ha-yashar la-'olam ha-ba'*. Any (or all) of these could have been Shifre's source.

Shifre also uses the term *shefa' 'elyonah* [sic]: "The supernal abundance has removed itself from us; the sages go around without a livelihood." Again, this does not seem to be a specifically Hasidic usage of the term *shefa'*.

29. If the author of this *tkhine* were influenced by Hasidic teachings, it would have been by word of mouth or via a manuscript. The earliest published Hasidic work, *Toledot Yaaqov Yosef*, by Jacob Joseph of Polonnoye, first appeared in 1780.

30. The penultimate paragraph of the *tkhine khadoshe le-khol yom* is similar to part of *Seder tkhines u-vakoshes*, no. 57. A passage in the middle of the third page of the *tkhine khadoshe le-shabes* resembles *Seder tkhines u-vakoshes*, no. 49. Parts of a passage on the third page of the *tokhakhas musar le-shabes* resemble parts of Leye's *Tkhine imohes*. These similarities are not close enough to be certain that Shifre has indeed used the earlier works; there may be other sources. However, it seems that she was influenced by the literary tradition of the *tkhines* for lighting Sabbath candles.

31. Boldface type indicates those words that appear in Hebrew in the text. It might be a more exact equivalent to quote them in Latin, for they were in the "high" language, of which women knew phrases but did not fully understand. (Of course, many words of Hebrew origin were also fully incorporated into Yiddish.) Verses or phrases are often quoted in Hebrew in *tkhines*, followed by their translation or paraphrase in Yiddish.

32. Numbers 8:2. The verse begins: "The Lord spoke to Moses, saying: Speak

to Aaron and say to him . . ." The context is the instruction of Aaron (and, by implication, the later High Priests) in how to light the candelabrum in the Tabernacle (later, in the Temple). The verse is difficult to understand. It speaks of "raising" when it means "kindling," and it is not clear what is meant by the lamps shining "against the face of" the candelabrum. (The new Jewish Publication Society version translates the rest of the verse: "When you mount the lamps, let the seven lamps throw their light forward toward the front of the lampstand.") These textual difficulties are used by the *tkhine* (and its sources) in the interpretation of the verse.

33. This is the Yiddish paraphrase of the biblical verse, slightly garbled and out of place; it usually follows the verse, but here has become entangled in the interpretation. In the text of Shifre's Yiddish source, below, in which this sentence does not include the verse paraphrase, it is much clearer: "By his kindling the candelabrum below, he raised the arousal to the Upper World."

34. See B. Shabbat 23b.

35. *Tkhine Imrei Shifre*, [6a–6b].

36. This view is found in the midrash, Genesis Rabba, end of 17; Tanhuma, the beginning of Noah and near the end of Mezora. These passages give similar justifications for the other two "women's commandments"—separating a portion of dough for the priestly tithe *(hallah)* and observing menstrual avoidances and post-menstrual purification *(niddah)*.

37. On the meaning of the Sabbath and its rituals in the kabbalah, see Elliot K. Ginsburg, *The Sabbath in the Classical Kabbalah* (Albany, NY, 1989).

38. There are a number of passages in the Zohar that contain similar themes concerning the High Priest, but none that correspond to the precise wording of the *tkhine*. Thematic parallels for this motif in the Zohar include correspondence between an earthly priest and tabernacle, and a heavenly priest and tabernacle (Zohar I 217a, II 159a, III 134b, 132b [Idra Rabba], 147a); the High Priest kindles the supernal lights (III 34b); and interpretations of the term *be-ha'alotekha* (III 149a: "Come and see, at the time when the priest intended to kindle the lights below, and he would offer incense at that time, then the upper lights would shine"; and see the pages following).

39. The paraphrase was an expansion of a work begun by Hotsh's grandfather, Aviezer Zelig. Hotsh may have been a crypto-Sabbatian. See the (contradictory) statements on this in two articles by Gershom Scholem in the *Encyclopaedia Judaica* (1972), s.v. "Chotsh, Zevi Hirsh ben Jerahmeel"; and s.v. "Shabbetai Zevi," esp. col. 1248.

40. Chava Weissler, " 'For Women and for Men who are Like Women': The Construction of Gender in Yiddish Devotional Literature," *Journal of Feminist Studies in Religion* 5 (2) (Fall 1989): 7–24. Nonetheless, *Nahalat Zevi* appears to have been popular reading material for women.

   In its intended audience, *Nahalat Zevi* is unlike the two other adaptations of kabbalistic material mentioned earlier in the article. The two compendia by Simon Akiva Baer b. Joseph were addressed to both women and men. In fact, *Abbir Ya 'aqov* has a rather sweet little preface which recommends that husband and wife read the book together after they arise from their Sabbath nap.

41. Zevi Hirsh Hotsh, *Nahalat Zevi* (Amsterdam, 1711), Bereshit, col. 5b, also numbered col. 130.

42. Hotsh, *Nahalat Zevi, Bemidbar,* p. 8a, also numbered col. 281 (near the beginning of *Be-ha'alotekha*).

43. The Zohar attributes the first view to its own sages *(ve-ukmuha hevraya)*. It accepts this as a good explanation *(ve-shafir),* then goes on to discuss, in addition, the secret mystical reason for women to have been assigned this commandment.

44. *Seder Tkhines u-vakoshes* (Fürth, 1762), no. 47.

45. Sore bas Tovim [?], *Shloyshe she'orim* (n.p., n.d.; eastern Europe, late eighteenth century?), [3b–4a].

46. I am still looking in midrashic literature for the motif in the form it takes in the *tkhines;* namely, an implicit or explicit comparison of the woman lighting candles with the High Priest lighting the candelabrum. *Yalqut Shim'oni* on Numbers 8:1 (beginning of *Beha'alotekha*) makes a connection between the candelabrum in the Tabernacle and the Sabbath lights. It further makes the point that although the sacrifices cease after the destruction of the Temple, the kindling of Sabbath lights (taken as symbolic of or related to the priestly blessing) continues throughout the ages.

47. *Nahalat Zevi:* "It is proper for the women below to act as in the form above, to kindle the lights." *Imrei Shifre:* "It is therefore proper for us to do below, in this form, as it is done above, to kindle the lights."

48. For a more theoretical discussion of this issue, see Weissler, " 'For Women and for Men Who are Like Women.' "

49. Scholem, *Major Trends,* 37.

Index

About the Editor

Lawrence Fine is Irene Kaplan Leiwant Professor of Jewish Studies at Mount Holyoke College. He taught for many years at Indiana University, and served as the Padnos Visiting Professor of Judaic Studies at the University of Michigan. He is the author of *Safed Spirituality* (New York, 1984), and has written numerous essays on the history of Jewish mysticism.